Economics of the Environment

Selected Readings

FIFTH EDITION

Economics of the Environment

Selected Readings

FIFTH EDITION

Edited by

Robert N. Stavins

HARVARD UNIVERSITY

W. W. Norton & Company

New York   London

For Daniel and Julia

W. W. Norton & Company has been independent since its founding in 1923, when William Warder Norton and Mary D. Herter Norton first published lectures delivered at the People's Institute, the adult education division of New York City's Cooper Union. The Nortons soon expanded their program beyond the Institute, publishing books by celebrated academics from America and abroad. By mid-century, the two major pillars of Norton's publishing program—trade books and college texts—were firmly established. In the 1950s, the Norton family transferred control of the company to its employees, and today —with a staff of four hundred and a comparable number of trade, college, and professional titles published each year—W. W. Norton & Company stands as the largest and oldest publishing house owned wholly by its employees.

The text of this book is composed in New Aster.
with the display set in Frutiger and Europa Arabesque.
Composition by TSI Graphics, Inc.
Manufacturing by the Maple-Vail Book Group, Binghamton, NY.
Book design by Joan Greenfield.
Project editor: Dexter Gasque.
Production manager: Ben Reynolds.

Library of Congress Cataloging-in-Publication Data

Economics of the environment : selected readings / edited by
    Robert N. Stavins.—5th ed. p. cm.
  Includes bibliographical references.
  ISBN 0-393-92701-6

  1. Pollution—Economic aspects. 2. Environmental policy—Costs.
  I. Stavins, R. N. (Robert N.), 1948–

HC79.P55D65   2005
363.7—dc22   2005040524

W. W. Norton & Company, Inc., 500 Fifth Avenue,
New York, N.Y. 10110–0017
www.wwnorton.com

W. W. Norton & Company Ltd., Castle House, 75/76 Wells Street,
London W1T 3QT

1 2 3 4 5 6 7 8 9 0

Contents

Introduction

Almost five years have passed since the previous (fourth) edition of this volume was published, and it is now more than three decades since the first edition appeared, edited by Robert and Nancy Dorfman. Over the years, the area of environmental economics has evolved from a relatively obscure application of welfare economics to a legitimate field in its own right, combining elements from public finance, industrial organization, microeconomic theory, and many other areas of economics. The number of articles on the environment appearing in mainstream economics periodicals has continued to increase, and more economics journals than ever are now dedicated exclusively to environmental and resource topics.

There has also been a proliferation of environmental economics textbooks. Many of these are excellent, but none can be expected to provide direct access to timely and original contributions by the field's leading scholars. As nearly all teachers of environmental economics recognize, it is valuable to supplement the structure and rigor of a text with original readings from the literature. This volume assembles a set of thirty-two key readings that instructors will find to be particularly valuable as a complement to their chosen text and their lectures. Of course, a single volume can contain no more than a sampling of outstanding articles from a diverse field, but the scope of this volume is comprehensive, the list of authors is a veritable "who's who" of environmental economics, and the articles are timely, with more than 90 percent published since 1990, and a third since 2000.

Some courses and textbooks in environmental economics include both the core material of the economics of pollution control and the economics of natural resource management. But the growth of the field has been so great that it is now reasonable to consider these as two different fields of study—environmental economics and natural resource economics, respectively. Although there is inevitably some overlap between the two strands of literature, most research falls clearly within one area or the other. With the few important exceptions noted later, this volume focuses on environmental economics, that is, the economics of pollution control.

To make these readings accessible to students at all levels, a central criterion used in the selection process is that articles should be not only technically sound, original, and well written but also essentially nontechnical in their presentation. Hence, there is virtually no use of formal mathematics in the articles that make up this volume. This should not be confused with a lack of rigor, however, for these articles meet the highest standards of economic scholarship.

Part I of the volume provides an overview of the field and a review of its foundations. One recent article is combined with two of the classics of the field. Don Fullerton and I start things off with a brief essay about how economists actually think about the environment. This is followed by Garrett Hardin's frequently cited article on the tragedy of the commons and Ronald Coase's classic treatment of social costs and bargaining.

Part II examines the costs of environmental protection. This might seem to be an area without controversy or current analytical interest, but that is certainly not the case. We begin with a survey article by Adam Jaffe and his colleagues that reviews the empirical evidence on the relationship between environmental regulation and so-called competitiveness. A revisionist view is provided by Michael Porter and Claas van der Linde, who suggest that the conventional approach to thinking about the costs of environmental protection is fundamentally flawed. Karen Palmer, Wallace Oates, and Paul Portney provide a careful response.

In Part III, the focus turns to the other side of the analytic ledger—the benefits of environmental protection. This is an area that has been even more contentious, both in the policy world and among scholars. Here, the challenging question is how environmental amenities can be valued in economic terms for analytical purposes. We feature a provocative debate on the stated-preference method known as *contingent valuation*. Paul Portney outlines the structure and importance of the debate, Michael Hanemann makes the affirmative case, and Peter Diamond and Jerry Hausman provide the critique. In a recently published analysis, Richard Carson and his coauthors look back at the large-scale contingent valuation study conducted after the Exxon Valdez oil spill to assess the environmental harm caused by the release of 11 million gallons of crude oil into Alaska's Prince William Sound. In the final article in Part III, we turn from ecological concerns to human health. Kip Viscusi examines the much misunderstood concept of the value of a statistical life, reviewing its theoretical foundation, associated empirical methods for estimation, and uses in various legal contexts.

Two principal policy questions need to be addressed in the environmental realm: How much environmental protection is desirable and how should that degree of environmental protection be achieved? The first of these questions is addressed in Part IV and the second in Part V. In Part IV, the criterion of economic efficiency and the analytical tool of benefit-cost analysis are considered as ways of judging the goals of environmental policy. In an introductory essay, Kenneth Arrow and his coauthors ask whether there is a role for benefit-cost analysis to play in environmental, health, and safety regulation. Then Lawrence Goulder and I focus on an ingredient of benefit-cost analysis that noneconomists seem to find particularly confusing, or even troubling, intertemporal discounting. Part IV concludes with Steven Kelman's ethically based critique, followed by a set or responses.

Part V examines the policy instruments—the means—that can be employed to achieve environmental targets or goals. This is an area where economists have made their greatest inroads of influence in the policy world, with tremendous changes having taken place over the past fifteen years in the reception given by politicians and policy makers to so-called market-based or economic-incentive instruments for environmental protection. Tom Tietenberg provides an introduction to these innovative approaches, including both taxes and tradeable permit systems. Lawrence Goulder focuses attention on an important development in this literature, the performance and cost of alternative policy instruments in the presence of existing, distortionary taxes. I examine lessons that can be learned from the innovative SO_2 allowance trading program, set up by the Clean Air Act Amendments of 1990. Finally, Michael Sandel provides a critique of these systems, with responses offered by Eric Maskin, Steven Shavell, and others.

The next three parts of the book treat particularly important environmental policy problem areas. Part VI deals with the burgeoning area of study of the relationship of international trade, economic growth, and environmental quality. Jeffrey Frankel draws on diverse sources of empirical evidence to examine whether globalization is good or bad for the environment. Susmita Dasgupta and her coauthors focus on the relationship between national income and environmental quality characterized by the so-called environmental Kuznets curve, and Scott Barrett uses the lens of economic analysis to investigate how transnational public goods can be provided by international agreements.

Part VII is dedicated to investigations of economic dimensions of global climate change, which may in the long term prove to be the most significant environmental problem that has arisen, in terms of both its potential damages and the costs of addressing it. William Nordhaus provides an outline of economic dimensions of the problem. Thomas Schelling investigates the distributional implications of addressing global warming; Henry Jacoby, Ronald Prinn, and Richard Schmalensee examine fundamental issues associated with the Kyoto Protocol, the international policy established in 1997 to deal with this global environmental threat; and Warwick McKibbin and Peter Wilcoxen provide their vision of the way forward.

Part VIII examines another relatively new area of exploration in environmental economics, ecological values and the broader concept of sustainability. Robert Solow begins with an insightful treatment of an economic perspective of sustainability. Turning to ecological issues, Gardner Brown and Jason Shogren provide a broad, economic assessment of the Endangered Species Act; and Andrew Metrick and Martin Weitzman describe their statistical analysis of why such federal policies have been aimed at preserving and protecting some species but not others.

The final section of the book, Part IX, departs from the normative concerns of much of the volume to examine interesting and important questions of political economy. An economic perspective can provide useful insights on questions that might at first seem to be fundamentally political. Nathaniel Keohane, Richard Revesz, and I utilize an economic framework to ask why our political system has produced the particular set of environmental policy instruments it has. Myrick Freeman reflects on the benefits U.S. environmental policies have brought about since the time of the first Earth Day in 1970. Following this, Robert Hahn, Sheila Olmstead, and I focus on the period of the 1990s, assessing environmental regulation during the Clinton years from an economic perspective. Last, Robert Hahn addresses the question that many of the articles in this volume raise: What has been the real impact on actual environmental policy of the rise of economics in the policy world?

Perhaps even more than most other areas of economic scholarship, environmental economics is a rapidly evolving field. Not only do new theoretical models and improved empirical methods appear on a regular basis, but entire new areas of investigation open up when the natural sciences indicate new concerns or the policy world turns to new issues. For this reason, this volume of collected essays will continue to be a work in progress. I therefore owe a great debt of gratitude to the teachers and students of previous editions who have sent their comments and suggestions for revisions. Thanks are also due to Jennifer Shultis for valuable assistance. Looking to the future, I invite all users of this edition, whether teachers, students, or practitioners, to send me or the publisher any thoughts or suggestions for the next edition.

Robert Stavins
Cambridge, Massachusetts

I

Overview and Principles

1   *How Economists See the Environment**

Don Fullerton

Robert N. Stavins

Don Fullerton is Addison Baker Duncan Centennial Professor of Economics, Department of Economics, University of Texas at Austin, and Research Associate at the National Bureau of Economic Research; and Robert N. Stavins is Albert Pratt Professor of Business and Government, John F. Kennedy School of Government, Harvard University, and University Fellow at Resources for the Future.

On a topic such as the environment, communication among those from different disciplines in the natural and social sciences is both important and difficult. Economists themselves may have contributed to some misunderstandings about how they think about the environment, perhaps through enthusiasm for market solutions, perhaps by neglecting to make explicit all the necessary qualifications, and perhaps simply by the use of jargon.

There are several prevalent myths about how economists think about the environment. By examining them here, we hope to explain how economists really do think about the natural environment.

Myth of the Universal Market

The first myth is that economists believe that the market solves all problems. The "first theorem of welfare economics," as taught to generations of economics students, is that private markets are perfectly efficient on their own, with no interference from government, provided certain conditions are met.

This theorem, easily proved, is exceptionally powerful, because it means that no one needs to tell producers of goods and services what to sell to which consumers. Instead, self-interested producers and consumers meet in the market-place, engage in trade, and thereby achieve the greatest good for the

"How Economists See the Environment," by Don Fullerton and Robert Stavins, from *Nature* 395: 6701. Reprinted from *Nature* copyright © 1998 by Macmillan Magazines Ltd.

*The authors are grateful for suggestions from Robert Frosch, Robert Hahn, Gilbert Metcalf, Richard Revesz, and Thomas Schelling.

greatest number, as if "guided by an invisible hand."[1] This maximum general welfare is what economists mean by the "efficiency" of competitive markets. Economists in business schools are particularly fond of identifying markets where the necessary conditions are met, such as the stock market, where many buyers and sellers operate with good information and low transaction costs to trade well-defined commodities with enforced rights of ownership.

Other economists, especially those in public policy schools, have a different approach to this theorem. By clarifying the conditions under which markets are efficient, the theorem also identifies the conditions under which they are not. Private markets are perfectly efficient only if there are no public goods, no externalities, no monopoly buyers or sellers, no increasing returns to scale, no information problems, no transaction costs, no taxes, no common property and no other "distortions" between the costs paid by buyers and the benefits received by sellers. Those conditions are obviously very restrictive, and they are usually not all satisfied simultaneously in the real world.

When a market thus fails, this same theorem offers guidance. For any particular market, it asks whether the number of sellers is sufficiently small to warrant antitrust action, whether the returns to scale are great enough to justify tolerating a single producer in a regulated market, or whether the benefits from the good are public in a way that might justify outright gov-

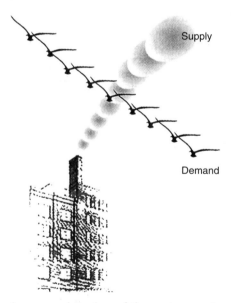

An economist's view of the environment.

---

[1]Smith, A. *An Inquiry into the Nature and Causes of the Wealth of Nations* (Whitestone, Dublin, 1776).

ernment provision of it. A public good, like the light from a lighthouse, benefits additional users at no cost to society.

Environmental economists are interested in pollution and other externalities, where some consequences of producing or consuming a good or service are external to the market (not considered by producers or consumers). With a negative externality, such as environmental pollution, the total social cost of production may exceed the value to consumers. If the market is left to itself, too many pollution-generating products are made.

Similarly, natural-resource economists are interested in common property, or open-access resources, where anyone can extract or harvest the resource freely and no one recognizes the full cost of using the resource. Extractors consider only their own direct and immediate costs, not the costs to others of increased scarcity ("user cost" or "scarcity rent"). The result is that the resource is depleted too quickly.

So, the market by itself demonstrably does not solve all problems. Indeed, in the environmental domain, perfectly functioning markets are the exception rather than the rule. Governments can try to correct these market failures, for example by restricting pollutant emissions or limiting access to open-access resources, which can improve welfare and lead to greater efficiency.

Myth of Market Solutions

A second common myth is that economists always recommend a market solution to a market problem. Economists tend to search for instruments of public policy that can fix one market essentially by introducing another, allowing each to operate efficiently on its own. If pollution imposes large external costs, for example, the government can establish a market for rights to emit a limited amount of that pollutant. Such a market for tradable emission permits will work if there are many buyers and sellers, all are well informed, and the other conditions of the "first theorem" are met. In this case, the government's role is to enforce the rights and responsibilities of permit ownership, so that each unit of emissions is matched by the ownership of one emission permit. Then the market for the output will also work, as the producer has to pay a price for each permit that reflects the social cost of the associated pollution. Equivalently, producers can be required to pay a tax on their emissions that reflects the external social cost. Either way, the result in theory will be the efficient amount of pollution abatement, undertaken at minimum aggregate abatement cost.

This tradable-permit approach has much to recommend it, and can be just the right solution in some cases, but it is still a "market." Therefore the outcome will be efficient only if certain conditions are met. But these conditions are not always met.[2] Could the sale of permits be mo-

---

[2]Hahn, R. W. & Hester, G. L. *Ecol. Law Q.* 16, 361–406 (1989).

nopolized by a small number of buyers or sellers? Do problems arise from inadequate information or significant transaction costs? Will the government find it too costly to measure emissions? If the answer to any such question is yes, the permit market may work less than optimally. The environmental goal may still be met, but at more than minimum cost.

As an example, to reduce acid rain in the United States, amendments to the Clean Air Act of 1990 require electricity generators to hold a permit for each tonne of SO_2 they emit. A robust market for the permits has emerged, in which well-defined prices are broadly known to many potential buyers and sellers. Through continuous emissions monitoring, the government can track SO_2 emissions from each plant. Equally important, penalties are significantly greater than incremental abatement costs and hence are sufficient to ensure compliance. Overall, this market works; acid rain deposition is being reduced by 50 per cent in a cost-effective manner.[3]

A permit market achieves this efficiency through trades because any company that has high abatement costs can buy permits from another that has low costs, so reducing the total cost of abating pollution. These trades also switch the source of the pollution from one company to another, which is unimportant when any emissions equally affect the whole trading area. This "perfect mixing" assumption is certainly valid for global problems such as greenhouse gases or the effect of chlorofluorocarbons on the stratospheric ozone layer. It may also work reasonably well for a regional problem such as acid rain, because acid deposition in downwind states of New England is about equally affected by SO_2 emissions that were traded among upwind sources in Ohio, Indiana or Illinois. But it does not work perfectly, as acid rain in New England may increase if a plant there sells permits to a plant in the mid-west.

At the other extreme, many environmental problems might not be addressed appropriately by tradable-permit systems or other market-based policy instruments.[4] One example is a hazardous air pollutant such as benzene that does not mix in the airshed and so can cause localized "hotspots." Because a company can buy permits and increase local emissions, permit trading does not ensure that each location will meet a specific standard. Moreover, the damages caused by local concentrations may increase nonlinearly. If so, then even a permit system that reduces total emissions might allow trades that move those emissions to a high-impact location and thus increase total damages.

The bottom line is that no specific policy instrument, or even set of policy instruments, is a panacea. Market instruments do not always provide the best solutions, and sometimes not even satisfactory solutions.

---

[3]Schmalensee, R. *et al. J. Econ. Perspect.* 12 No. 3 (Summer 1998).
[4]Hahn, R. W. & Stavins, R. N. *Am. Econ. Rev.* 82, 464–468 (1992).

Myth of Market Prices

The next myth is that, when non-market solutions are considered, economists still use only market prices to evaluate them. No matter what policy instrument is chosen, the environmental goal of that policy must be identified. For example, should vehicle emissions be reduced by 10, 20 or 50 per cent? Economists frequently try to identify the most efficient degree of control that provides the greatest net benefit. This means, of course, that both benefits and costs need to be evaluated. True enough, economists typically favour using market prices, whenever possible, to carry out such evaluations, because these prices reveal how members of society actually value the scarce amenities and resources under consideration.

Economists are wary of asking people how much they value something, as respondents may not provide honest assessments of their own valuations. Instead, actions may reveal their preferences, as when individuals pay more for a house in a neighbourhood with cleaner air, all else being equal.[5]

This is not to suggest that economists are concerned only with the financial value of things. Far from it. The financial flows that make up the gross national product represent only a fraction of all economic flows. The scope of economics encompasses the allocation and use of all scarce resources. For example, the economic value of the human-health damages of environmental pollution is greater than the sum of health-care costs and lost wages (or lost productivity), as it includes what lawyers would call "pain and suffering." Economists might use a market price indirectly to measure revealed rather than stated preferences, but the goal is to measure the total value of the loss that individuals incur.

To take another example, the economic value of part of the Amazon rainforest is not limited to its financial value as a repository of future pharmaceutical products or as a location for ecotourism. That "use" value may only be a small part of the properly defined economic valuation. For decades, economists have recognized the importance of "non-use" value of environmental amenities such as wilderness areas or endangered species. The public nature of these goods make it particularly difficult to quantify these values empirically, as we cannot use market prices! The important fact is that benefit–cost analysis of environmental policies, virtually by definition, cannot rely exclusively on market prices.[6]

Economists insist on trying to convert all these disparate values into monetary terms because a common unit of measure is needed to be able to add them up. How else can we combine the benefits of ten extra miles of visibility plus some amount of reduced morbidity, and then compare these total benefits with the total cost of installing scrubbers to clean stack gases at coal-fired power plants? Money, after all, is simply a medium of exchange, a convenient way to add together or compare disparate goods and services.

---

[5]Smith, V. K. & Huang, J.-C. *J. Polit. Econ.* 103, 209–227 (1995).
[6]Arrow, K. *et al. Science* 272, 221–222 (1996).

Myth of Efficiency

The last myth we address here is that these economic analyses are concerned only with efficiency rather than distribution. Many economists do give more attention to measures of aggregate social welfare than to measures of the distribution of the benefits and costs of policies among members of society. The reason is that an improvement in economic efficiency can be determined by a simple and unambiguous criterion—an increase in total net benefits. What constitutes an improvement in distributional equity, on the other hand, is inevitably the subject of considerable dispute. Nevertheless, many economists do analyse distributional issues thoroughly. The more difficult problem, not yet solved in a satisfactory manner, is how to combine efficiency and distributional issues in a unified analysis.

Available data often permit reliable estimates of the impacts of environmental policies on important subgroups of the population.[7] On the other hand, environmental regulations are neither effective nor efficient tools for achieving redistributional goals. The best economic analyses recognize the contributions and limitations of efficiency and distributional measures.

Where Does This Leave Us?

To summarize, economists do not necessarily believe that the market solves all problems. Indeed, many economists, ourselves included, make a living out of analysing market failures such as environmental pollution in which laissez-faire policy leads not to social efficiency, but to inefficiency. When economists identify market problems, their tendency is first to consider the feasibility of market solutions because of their potential cost-effectiveness, but market-based approaches to environmental protection are no panacea. When market or non-market solutions to environmental problems are being assessed, economists do not limit their analysis to financial considerations but use money as a unit of measurement in the absence of a more convenient unit. And although the efficiency criterion is by definition aggregate in nature, economic analysis can reveal much about the distribution of the benefits and costs of environmental policy.

Having identified and sought to dispel four prevalent myths about how economists think about the natural environment, we acknowledge that our profession bears some responsibility for the existence of such misunderstandings. Like their colleagues in other social and natural sciences, academic economists focus their greatest energies on communicating to their peers within their own discipline. Greater effort can certainly be made to improve communication across disciplinary boundaries.

---

[7]Christiansen, G. B. & Tietenberg, T. H. in *Handbook of Natural Resource and Energy Economics* Vol. 1 (eds Kneese, A. V. & Sweeney, J. L.) 345–393 (North-Holland, Amsterdam, 1985).

2   *The Tragedy of the Commons*

Garrett Hardin

Garrett Hardin was Professor Emeritus of Human Ecology at the University of California at Santa Barbara.

At the end of a thoughtful article on the future of nuclear war, J. B. Wiesner and H. F. York concluded that "Both sides in the arms race are . . . confronted by the dilemma of steadily increasing military power and steadily decreasing national security. *It is our considered professional judgment that this dilemma has no technical solution.* If the great powers continue to look for solutions in the area of science and technology only, the result will be to worsen the situation."[1]

I would like to focus your attention not on the subject of the article (national security in a nuclear world) but on the kind of conclusion they reached, namely, that there is no technical solution to the problem. An implicit and almost universal assumption of discussions published in professional and semipopular scientific journals is that the problem under discussion has a technical solution. A technical solution may be defined as one that requires a change only in the techniques of the natural sciences, demanding little or nothing in the way of change in human values or ideas of morality.

In our day (though not in earlier times) technical solutions are always welcome. Because of previous failures in prophecy, it takes courage to assert that a desired technical solution is not possible. Wiesner and York exhibited this courage; publishing in a science journal, they insisted that the solution to the problem was not to be found in the natural sciences. They cautiously qualified their statement with the phrase, "It is our considered professional judgment. . . ." Whether they were right or not is not the concern of the present article. Rather, the concern here is with the important concept of a class of human problems which can be called "no technical solution problems," and more specifically, with the identification and discussion of one of these.

It is easy to show that the class is not a null class. Recall the game of tick-tack-toe. Consider the problem, "How can I win the game of tick-tack-toe?" It is well known that I cannot, if I assume (in keeping with the conventions of game theory) that my opponent understands the game perfectly. Put another way, there is no "technical solution" to the problem. I can win

---

[1]J. B. Wiesner and H. F. York, *Scientific American* 211 (No. 4), 27 (1964).

only by giving a radical meaning to the word "win." I can hit my opponent over the head; or I can falsify the records. Every way in which I "win" involves, in some sense, an abandonment of the game, as we intuitively understand it. (I can also, of course, openly abandon the game—refuse to play it. This is what most adults do.)

The class of "no technical solution problems" has members. My thesis is that the "population problem," as conventionally conceived, is a member of this class. How it is conventionally conceived needs some comment. It is fair to say that most people who anguish over the population problem are trying to find a way to avoid the evils of overpopulation without relinquishing any of the privileges they now enjoy. They think that farming the seas or developing new strains of wheat will solve the problem—technologically. I try to show here that the solution they seek cannot be found. The population problem cannot be solved in a technical way, any more than can the problem of winning the game of tick-tack-toe.

What Shall We Maximize?

Population, as Malthus said, naturally tends to grow "geometrically," or, as we would now say, exponentially. In a finite world this means that the per-capita share of the world's goods must decrease. Is ours a finite world?

A fair defense can be put forward for the view that the world is infinite; or that we do not know that it is not. But, in terms of the practical problems that we must face in the next few generations with the foreseeable technology, it is clear that we will greatly increase human misery if we do not, during the immediate future, assume that the world available to the terrestrial human population is finite. "Space" is no escape.[2]

A finite world can support only a finite population; therefore, population growth must eventually equal zero. (The case of perpetual wide fluctuations above and below zero is a trivial variant that need not be discussed.) When this condition is met, what will be the situation of mankind? Specifically, can Bentham's goal of "the greatest good for the greatest number" be realized?

No—for two reasons, each sufficient by itself. The first is a theoretical one. It is not mathematically possible to maximize for two (or more) variables at the same time. This was clearly stated by von Neumann and Morgenstern,[3] but the principle is implicit in the theory of partial differential equations, dating back at least to D'Alembert (1717–1783).

---

[2] G. Hardin, *Journal of Heredity* 50, 68 (1959), S. von Hoernor, *Science* 137, 18 (1962).

[3] J. von Neumann and O. Morgenstern, *Theory of Games and Economic Behavior* (Princeton University Press, Princeton, N.J., 1947), p. 11.

The second reason springs directly from biological facts. To live, any organism must have a source of energy (for example, food). This energy is utilized for two purposes: mere maintenance and work. For man, maintenance of life requires about 1600 kilocalories a day ("maintenance calories"). Anything that he does over and above merely staying alive will be defined as work, and is supported by "work calories" which he takes in. Work calories are used not only for what we call work in common speech; they are also required for all forms of enjoyment, from swimming and automobile racing to playing music and writing poetry. If our goal is to maximize population it is obvious what we must do: We must make the work calories per person approach as close to zero as possible. No gourmet meals, no vacations, no sports, no music, no literature, no art. . . . I think that everyone will grant, without argument or proof, that maximizing population does not maximize goods. Bentham's goal is impossible.

In reaching this conclusion I have made the usual assumption that it is the acquisition of energy that is the problem. The appearance of atomic energy has led some to question this assumption. However, given an infinite source of energy, population growth still produces an inescapable problem. The problem of the acquisition of energy is replaced by the problem of its dissipation, as J. H. Fremlin has so wittily shown.[4] The arithmetic signs in the analysis are, as it were, reversed; but Bentham's goal is unobtainable.

The optimum population is, then, less than the maximum. The difficulty of defining the optimum is enormous; so far as I know, no one has seriously tackled this problem. Reaching an acceptable and stable solution will surely require more than one generation of hard analytical work—and much persuasion.

We want the maximum good per person; but what is good? To one person it is wilderness, to another it is ski lodges for thousands. To one it is estuaries to nourish ducks for hunters to shoot; to another it is factory land. Comparing one good with another is, we usually say, impossible because goods are incommensurable. Incommensurables cannot be compared.

Theoretically this may be true; but in real life incommensurables *are* commensurable. Only a criterion of judgment and a system of weighting are needed. In nature the criterion is survival. Is it better for a species to be small and hideable, or large and powerful? Natural selection commensurates the incommensurables. The compromise achieved depends on a natural weighting of the values of the variables.

Man must imitate this process. There is no doubt that in fact he already does, but unconsciously. It is when the hidden decisions are made explicit that the arguments begin. The problem for the years ahead is to work out an acceptable theory of weighting. Synergistic effects, nonlinear variation, and difficulties in discounting the future make the intellectual problem difficult, but not (in principle) insoluble.

---

[4]J. H. Fremlin, *New Scientist*, No. 415 (1964), p. 285.

Has any cultural group solved this practical problem at the present time, even on an intuitive level? One simple fact proves that none has: there is no prosperous population in the world today that has, and has had for some time, a growth rate of zero. Any people that has intuitively identified its optimum point will soon reach it, after which its growth rate becomes and remains zero.

Of course, a positive growth rate might be taken as evidence that a population is below its optimum. However, by any reasonable standards, the most rapidly growing populations on earth today are (in general) the most miserable. This association (which need not be invariable) casts doubt on the optimistic assumption that the positive growth rate of a population is evidence that it has yet to reach its optimum.

We can make little progress in working toward optimum population size until we explicitly exorcise the spirit of Adam Smith in the field of practical demography. In economic affairs, *The Wealth of Nations* (1776) popularized the "invisible hand," the idea that an individual who "intends only his own gain," is, as it were, "led by an invisible hand to promote . . . the public interest."[5] Adam Smith did not assert that this was invariably true, and perhaps neither did any of his followers. But he contributed to a dominant tendency of thought that has ever since interfered with positive action based on rational analysis, namely, the tendency to assume that decisions reached individually will, in fact, be the best decisions for an entire society. If this assumption is correct it justifies the continuance of our present policy of *laissez faire* in reproduction. If it is correct we can assume that men will control their individual fecundity so as to produce the optimum population. If the assumption is not correct, we need to reexamine our individual freedoms to see which ones are defensible.

Tragedy of Freedom in a Commons

The rebuttal to the invisible hand in population control is to be found in a scenario first sketched in a little-known pamphlet in 1833 by a mathematical amateur named William Forster Lloyd (1794–1852).[6] We may well call it "the tragedy of the commons," using the word "tragedy" as the philosopher Whitehead used it: "The essence of dramatic tragedy is not unhappiness. It resides in the solemnity of the remorseless working of things." He then goes on to say, "This inevitableness of destiny can only be illustrated in terms of human life by incidents which in fact involve unhappiness. For it is only by them that the futility of escape can be made evident in the drama."[7]

---

[5]A. Smith, *The Wealth of Nations* (Modern Library, New York, 1937), p. 423.

[6]W. F. Lloyd, *Two Lectures on the Checks to Population* (Oxford University Press, Oxford, England, 1833).

[7]A. N. Whitehead, *Science and the Modern World* (Mentor, New York, 1948), p. 17.

The tragedy of the commons develops in this way. Picture a pasture open to all. It is to be expected that each herdsman will try to keep as many cattle as possible on the commons. Such an arrangement may work reasonably satisfactorily for centuries because tribal wars, poaching, and disease keep the numbers of both man and beast well below the carrying capacity of the land. Finally, however, comes the day of reckoning, that is, the day when the long-desired goal of social stability becomes a reality. At this point, the inherent logic of the commons remorselessly generates tragedy.

As a rational being, each herdsman seeks to maximize his gain. Explicitly or implicitly, more or less consciously, he asks, "What is the utility *to me* of adding one more animal to my herd?" This utility has one negative and one positive component.

1. The positive component is a function of the increment of one animal. Since the herdsman receives all the proceeds from the sale of the additional animal, the positive utility is nearly +1.

2. The negative component is a function of the additional overgrazing created by one more animal. Since, however, the effects of overgrazing are shared by all the herdsmen, the negative utility for any particular decision-making herdsman is only a fraction of −1.

Adding together the component partial utilities, the rational herdsman concludes that the only sensible course for him to pursue is to add another animal to his herd. And another. . . . But this is the conclusion reached by each and every rational herdsman sharing a commons. Therein is the tragedy. Each man is locked into a system that compels him to increase his herd without limit—in a world that is limited. Ruin is the destination toward which all men rush, each pursuing his own best interest in a society that believes in the freedom of the commons. Freedom in a commons brings ruin to all.

Some would say that this is a platitude. Would that it were! In a sense, it was learned thousands of years ago, but natural selection favors the forces of psychological denial.[8] The individual benefits as an individual from his ability to deny the truth even though society as a whole, of which he is a part, suffers. Education can counteract the natural tendency to do the wrong thing, but the inexorable succession of generations requires that the basis for this knowledge be constantly refreshed.

A simple incident that occurred a few years ago in Leominster, Massachusetts, shows how perishable the knowledge is. During the Christmas shopping season the parking meters downtown were covered with plastic bags that bore tags reading: "Do not open until after Christmas. Free parking courtesy of the mayor and city council." In other words, facing the prospect of an increased demand for already scarce space, the city fathers reinstituted the system of the commons. (Cynically, we suspect that they gained more votes than they lost by this retrogressive act.)

---

[8]G. Hardin, Ed., *Population, Evolution, and Birth Control* (Freeman, San Francisco, 1964), p. 56.

In an approximate way, the logic of the commons has been understood for a long time, perhaps since the discovery of agriculture or the invention of private property in real estate. But it is understood mostly only in special cases which are not sufficiently generalized. Even at this late date, cattlemen leasing national land on the Western ranges demonstrate no more than an ambivalent understanding, in constantly pressuring federal authorities to increase the head count to the point where overgrazing produces erosion and weed-dominance. Likewise, the oceans of the world continue to suffer from the survival of the philosophy of the commons. Maritime nations still respond automatically to the shibboleth of the "freedom of the seas." Professing to believe in the "inexhaustible resources of the oceans," they bring species after species of fish and whales closer to extinction.[9]

The National Parks present another instance of the working out of the tragedy of the commons. At present, they are open to all, without limit. The parks themselves are limited in extent—there is only one Yosemite Valley—whereas population seems to grow without limit. The values that visitors seek in the parks are steadily eroded. Plainly, we must soon cease to treat the parks as commons or they will be of no value to anyone.

What shall we do? We have several options. We might sell them off as private property. We might keep them as public property, but allocate the right to enter them. The allocation might be on the basis of wealth, by the use of an auction system. It might be on the basis of merit, as defined by some agreed-upon standards. It might be by lottery. Or it might be on a first-come, first-served basis, administered to long queues. These, I think, are all objectionable. But we must choose—or acquiesce in the destruction of the commons that we call our National Parks.

Pollution

In a reverse way, the tragedy of the commons reappears in problems of pollution. Here it is not a question of taking something out of the commons, but of putting something in—sewage, or chemical, radioactive, and heat wastes into water; noxious and dangerous fumes into the air; and distracting and unpleasant advertising signs into the line of slight. The calculations of utility are much the same as before. The rational man finds that his share of the cost of the wastes he discharges into the commons is less than the cost of purifying his wastes before releasing them. Since this is true for everyone, we are locked into a system of "fouling our own nest," so long as we behave only as independent, rational, free-enterprisers.

The tragedy of the commons as a food basket is averted by private property, or something formally like it. But the air and waters surrounding us

---

[9]S. McVay, *Scientific American* 216 (No. 8), 13 (1966).

cannot readily be fenced, and so the tragedy of the commons as a cesspool must be prevented by different means, by coercive laws or taxing devices that make it cheaper for the polluter to treat his pollutants than to discharge them untreated. We have not progressed as far with the solution of this problem as we have with the first. Indeed, our particular concept of private property, which deters us from exhausting the positive resources of the earth, favors pollution. The owner of a factory on the bank of a stream—whose property extends to the middle of the stream—often has difficulty seeing why it is not his natural right to muddy the waters flowing past his door. The law, always behind the times, requires elaborate stitching and fitting to adapt it to this newly perceived aspect of the commons.

The pollution problem is a consequence of population. It did not much matter how a lonely American frontiersman disposed of his waste. "Flowing water purifies itself every ten miles," my grandfather used to say, and the myth was near enough to the truth when he was a boy, for there were not too many people. But as population became denser, the natural chemical and biological recycling processes became overloaded, calling for a redefinition of property rights.

How to Legislate Temperance?

Analysis of the pollution problem as a function of population density uncovers a not generally recognized principle of morality, namely: *the morality of an act is a function of the state of the system at the time it is performed.*[10] Using the commons as a cesspool does not harm the general public under frontier conditions, because there is no public; the same behavior in a metropolis is unbearable. A hundred and fifty years ago a plainsman could kill an American bison, cut out only the tongue for his dinner, and discard the rest of the animal. He was not in any important sense being wasteful. Today, with only a few thousand bison left, we would be appalled at such behavior.

In passing, it is worth noting that the morality of an act cannot be determined from a photograph. One does not know whether a man killing an elephant or setting fire to the grassland is harming others until one knows the total system in which his act appears. "One picture is worth a thousand words," said an ancient Chinese; but it may take ten thousand words to validate it. It is as tempting to ecologists as it is to reformers in general to try to persuade others by way of the photographic shortcut. But the essence of an argument cannot be photographed: it must be presented rationally—in words.

---

[10]J. Fletcher, *Situation Ethics* (Westminster, Philadelphia, 1966).

That morality is system-sensitive escaped the attention of most codi-fiers of ethics in the past. "Thou shalt not . . ." is the form of traditional ethical directives which make no allowance for particular circumstances. The laws of our society follow the pattern of ancient ethics, and therefore are poorly suited to governing a complex, crowded, changeable world. Our epicyclic solution is to augment statutory law with administrative law. Since it is practically impossible to spell out all the conditions under which it is safe to burn trash in the backyard or to run an automobile without smog control, by law we delegate the details to bureaus. The result is adminis-trative law, which is rightly feared for an ancient reason—*Quis custodiet ipsos custodes?*—Who shall watch the watchers themselves? John Adams said that we must have a "government of laws and not men." Bureau ad-ministrators, trying to evaluate the morality of acts in the total system, are singularly liable to corruption, producing a government by men, not laws.

Prohibition is easy to legislate (though not necessarily to enforce); but how do we legislate temperance? Experience indicates that it can be ac-complished best through the mediation of administrative law. We limit pos-sibilities unnecessarily if we suppose that the sentiment of *Quis custodiet* denies us the use of administrative law. We should rather retain the phrase as a perpetual reminder of fearful dangers we cannot avoid. The great chal-lenge facing us now is to invent the corrective feedbacks that are needed to keep custodians honest. We must find ways to legitimate the needed au-thority of both the custodians and the corrective feedbacks.

Freedom to Breed Is Intolerable

The tragedy of the commons is involved in population problems in an-other way. In a world governed solely by the principle of "dog eat dog"— if indeed there ever was such a world—how many children a family had would not be a matter of public concern. Parents who bred too exuber-antly would leave fewer descendants, not more, because they would be unable to care adequately for their children. David Lack and others have found that such a negative feedback demonstrably controls the fecundity of birds.[11] But men are not birds, and have not acted like them for mil-lenniums, at least.

If each human family were dependent only on its own resources; *if* the children of improvident parents starved to death; *if*, thus, overbreeding brought its own "punishment" to the germ line—*then* there would be no public interest in controlling the breeding of families. But our society is deeply committed to the welfare state,[12] and hence is confronted with an-other aspect of the tragedy of the commons.

In a welfare state, how shall we deal with the family, the religion, the race, or the class (or indeed any distinguishable and cohesive group) that

---

[11]D. Lack, *The Natural Regulation of Animal Numbers* (Clarendon Press, Oxford, England, 1954).
[12]H. Girvetz, *From Wealth to Welfare* (Stanford University Press, Stanford, Calif., 1950).

adopts overbreeding as a policy to secure its own aggrandizement?[13] To couple the concept of freedom to breed with the belief that everyone born has an equal right to the commons is to lock the world into a tragic course of action.

Unfortunately this is just the course of action that is being pursued by the United States. In late 1967, some thirty nations agreed to the following: "The Universal Declaration of Human Rights describes the family as the natural and fundamental unit of society. It follows that any choice and decision with regard to the size of the family must irrevocably rest with the family itself, and cannot be made by anyone else."[14]

It is painful to have to deny categorically the validity of this right; denying it, one feels as uncomfortable as a resident of Salem, Massachusetts, who denied the reality of witches in the seventeenth century. At the present time, in liberal quarters, something like a taboo acts to inhibit criticism of the United Nations. There is a feeling that the United Nations is "our last and best hope," that we shouldn't find fault with it; we shouldn't play into the hands of the archconservatives. However, let us not forget what Robert Louis Stevenson said: "The truth that is suppressed by friends is the readiest weapon of the enemy." If we love the truth we must openly deny the validity of the Universal Declaration of Human Rights, even though it is promoted by the United Nations. We should also join with Kingsley Davis[15] in attempting to get Planned Parenthood–World Population to see the error of its ways in embracing the same tragic ideal.

Conscience Is Self-Eliminating

It is a mistake to think that we can control the breeding of mankind in the long run by an appeal to conscience. Charles Galton Darwin made this point when he spoke on the centennial of the publication of his grandfather's great book. The argument is straightforward and Darwinian.

People vary. Confronted with appeals to limit breeding, some people will undoubtedly respond to the plea more than others. Those who have more children will produce a larger fraction of the next generation than those with more susceptible consciences. The differences will be accentuated, generation by generation.

In C. G. Darwin's words: "It may well be that it would take hundreds of generations for the progenitive instinct to develop in this way, but if it should do so, nature would have taken her revenge, and the variety *Homo contracipiens* would become extinct and would be replaced by the variety *Homo progenitivus*."[16]

---

[13]G. Hardin, *Perspectives in Biology and Medicine* 6, 366 (1963).

[14]U Thant, *International Planned Parenthood News*, No. 168 (February 1968), p. 3.

[15]K. Davis, *Science* 158, 730 (1967).

[16]S. Tax, Ed., *Evolution After Darwin* (University of Chicago Press, Chicago, 1960), vol. 2, p. 469.

The argument assumes that conscience or the desire for children (no matter which) is hereditary—but hereditary only in the most general formal sense. The result will be the same whether the attitude is transmitted through germ cells, or exosomatically, to use A. J. Lotka's term. (If one denies the latter possibility as well as the former, then what's the point of education?) The argument has here been stated in the context of the population problem, but it applies equally well to any instance in which society appeals to an individual exploiting a commons to restrains himself for the general good—by means of his conscience. To make such an appeal is to set up a selective system that works toward the elimination of conscience from the race.

Pathogenic Effects of Conscience

The long-term disadvantage of an appeal to conscience should be enough to condemn it; but it has serious short-term disadvantages as well. If we ask a man who is exploiting a commons to desist "in the name of conscience," what are we saying to him? What does he hear?—not only at the moment but also in the wee small hours of the night when, half asleep, he remembers not merely the words we used but also the nonverbal communication cues we gave him unawares? Sooner or later, consciously or subconsciously, he senses that he has received two communications, and that they are contradictory: 1. (intended communication) "If you don't do as we ask, we will openly condemn you for not acting like a responsible citizen"; 2. (the unintended communication) "If you *do* behave as we ask, we will secretly condemn you for a simpleton who can be shamed into standing aside while the rest of us exploit the commons."

Everyman then is caught in what Bateson has called a "double bind." Bateson and his co-workers have made a plausible case for viewing the double bind as an important causative factor in the genesis of schizophrenia.[17] The double bind may not always be so damaging, but it always endangers the mental health of anyone to whom it is applied. "A bad conscience," said Nietzsche, "is a kind of illness."

To conjure up a conscience in others is tempting to anyone who wishes to extend his control beyond the legal limits. Leaders at the highest level succumb to this temptation. Has any president during the past generation failed to call on labor unions to moderate voluntarily their demands for higher wages, or to steel companies to honor voluntary guidelines on prices? I can recall none. The rhetoric used on such occasions is designed to produce feelings of guilt in noncooperators.

---

[17]G. Bateson, D. D. Jackson, J. Haley, J. Weakland, *Behavioral Science* 1, 251 (1956).

For centuries it was assumed without proof that guilt was a valuable, perhaps even an indispensable, ingredient of the civilized life. Now, in this post-Freudian world, we doubt it.

Paul Goodman speaks from the modern point of view when he says: "No good has ever come from feeling guilty, neither intelligence, policy, nor compassion. The guilty do not pay attention to the object but only to themselves, and not even to their own interests, which might make sense, but to their anxieties."[18]

One does not have to be a professional psychiatrist to see the consequences of anxiety. We in the Western world are just emerging from a dreadful two centuries-long Dark Ages of Eros that was sustained partly by prohibition laws, but perhaps more effectively by the anxiety-generating mechanisms of education. Alex Comfort has told the story well in *The Anxiety Makers*;[19] it is not a pretty one.

Since proof is difficult, we may even concede that the results of anxiety may sometimes, from certain points of view, be desirable. The larger question we should ask is whether, as a matter of policy, we should ever encourage the use of a technique the tendency (if not the intention) of which is psychologically pathogenic. We hear much talk these days of responsible parenthood; the coupled words are incorporated into the titles of some organizations devoted to birth control. Some people have proposed massive propaganda campaigns to instill responsibility into the nation's (or the world's) breeders. But what is the meaning of the word conscience? When we use the word responsibility in the absence of substantial sanctions, are we not trying to browbeat a free man in a commons into acting against his own interest? Responsibility is a verbal counterfeit for a substantial quid pro quo. It is an attempt to get something for nothing.

If the word responsibility is to be used at all, I suggest that it be in the sense Charles Frankel uses it.[20] "Responsibility," says this philosopher, "is the product of definite social arrangements." Notice that Frankel calls for social arrangements—not propaganda.

Mutual Coercion Mutually Agreed Upon

The social arrangements that produce responsibility are arrangements that create coercion, of some sort. Consider bank robbing. The man who takes money from a bank acts as if the bank were a commons. How do we prevent such action? Certainly not by trying to control his behavior solely by a verbal appeal to his sense of responsibility. Rather than rely on propaganda we follow Frankel's lead and insist that a bank is not a commons; we seek the definite social arrangements that will keep it from becoming

---

[18]P. Goodman, *New York Review of Books* 10 (8), 22 (23 May 1968).

[19]A. Comfort, *The Anxiety Makers* (Nelson, London, 1967).

[20]C. Frankel, *The Case for Modern Man* (Harper & Row, New York, 1955), p. 203.

a commons. That we thereby infringe on the freedom of would-be robbers we neither deny nor regret.

The morality of bank robbing is particularly easy to understand because we accept complete prohibition of this activity. We are willing to say, "Thou shalt not rob banks," without providing for exceptions. But temperance also can be created by coercion. Taxing is a good coercive device. To keep downtown shoppers temperate in their use of parking space we introduce parking meters for short periods, and traffic fines for longer ones. We need not actually forbid a citizen to park as long as he wants to; we need merely make it increasingly expensive for him to do so. Not prohibition, but carefully biased options are what we offer him. A Madison Avenue man might call this persuasion; I prefer the greater candor of the word coercion.

Coercion is a dirty word to most liberals now, but it need not forever be so. As with the four-letter words, its dirtiness can be cleansed away by exposure to the light, by saying it over and over without apology or embarrassment. To many, the word coercion implies arbitrary decisions of distant and irresponsible bureaucrats; but this is not a necessary part of its meaning. The only kind of coercion I recommend is mutual coercion, mutually agreed upon by the majority of the people affected.

To say that we mutually agree to coercion is not to say that we are required to enjoy it, or even to pretend we enjoy it. Who enjoys taxes? We all grumble about them. But we accept compulsory taxes because we recognize that voluntary taxes would favor the conscienceless. We institute and (grumblingly) support taxes and other coercive devices to escape the horror of the commons.

An alternative to the commons need not be perfectly just to be preferable. With real estate and other material goods, the alternative we have chosen is the institution of private property coupled with legal inheritance. Is this system perfectly just? As a genetically trained biologist I deny that it is. It seems to me that, if there are to be differences in individual inheritance, legal possession should be perfectly correlated with biological inheritance—that those who are biologically more fit to be the custodians of property and power should legally inherit more. But genetic recombination continually makes a mockery of the doctrine of "like father, like son" implicit in our laws of legal inheritance. An idiot can inherit millions, and a trust fund can keep his estate intact. We must admit that our legal system of private property plus inheritance is unjust—but we put up with it because we are not convinced, at the moment, that anyone has invented a better system. The alternative of the commons is too horrifying to contemplate. Injustice is preferable to total ruin.

It is one of the peculiarities of the warfare between reform and the status quo that it is thoughtlessly governed by a double standard. Whenever a reform measure is proposed it is often defeated when its opponents triumphantly discover a flaw in it. As Kingsley Davis has pointed out,[21] wor-

---

[21] See J. D. Roslansky, *Genetics and the Future of Man* (Appleton-Century-Crofts, New York, 1966), p. 177.

shipers of the status quo sometimes imply that no reform is possible without unanimous agreement, an implication contrary to historical fact. As nearly as I can make out, automatic rejection of proposed reforms is based on one of two unconscious assumptions: (1) that the status quo is perfect; or (2) that the choice we face is between reform and no action; if the proposed reform is imperfect, we presumably should take no action at all, while we wait for a perfect proposal.

But we can never do nothing. That which we have done for thousands of years is also action. It also produces evils. Once we are aware that the status quo is action, we can then compare its discoverable advantages and disadvantages with the predicted advantages and disadvantages of the proposed reform, discounting as best we can for our lack of experience. On the basis of such a comparison, we can make a rational decision which will not involve the unworkable assumption that only perfect systems are tolerable.

Recognition of Necessity

Perhaps the simplest summary of this analysis of man's population problems is this: the commons, if justifiable at all, is justifiable only under conditions of low-population density. As the human population has increased, the commons has had to be abandoned in one aspect after another.

First we abandoned the commons in food gathering, enclosing farmland and restricting pastures and hunting and fishing areas. These restrictions are still not complete throughout the world.

Somewhat later we saw that the commons as a place for waste disposal would also have to be abandoned. Restrictions on the disposal of domestic sewage are widely accepted in the Western world; we are still struggling to close the commons to pollution by automobiles, factories, insecticide sprayers, fertilizing operations, and atomic energy installations.

In a still more embryonic state is our recognition of the evils of the commons in matters of pleasure. There is almost no restriction on the propagation of sound waves in the public medium. The shopping public is assaulted with mindless music, without its consent. Our government has paid out billions of dollars to create a supersonic transport which would disturb 50,000 people for every one person whisked from coast to coast 3 hours faster. Advertisers muddy the airwaves of radio and television and pollute the view of travelers. We are a long way from outlawing the commons in matters of pleasure. Is this because our Puritan inheritance makes us view pleasure as something of a sin, and pain (that is, the pollution of advertising) as the sign of virtue?

Every new enclosure of the commons involves the infringement of somebody's personal liberty. Infringements made in the distant past are accepted because no contemporary complains of a loss. It is the newly proposed infringements that we vigorously oppose; cries of "rights" and "freedom" fill the air. But what does "freedom" mean? When men mutually agreed to pass laws against robbing, mankind became more free, not less so. Individuals locked into the logic of the commons are free only to bring on universal ruin; once they see the necessity of mutual coercion, they become free to pursue other goals. I believe it was Hegel who said, "Freedom is the recognition of necessity."

The most important aspect of necessity that we must now recognize is the necessity of abandoning the commons in breeding. No technical solution can rescue us from the misery of overpopulation. Freedom to breed will bring ruin to all. At the moment, to avoid hard decisions many of us are tempted to propagandize for conscience and responsible parenthood. The temptation must be resisted, because an appeal to independently acting consciences selects for the disappearance of all conscience in the long run, and an increase in anxiety in the short.

The only way we can preserve and nurture other and more precious freedoms is by relinquishing the freedom to breed, and that very soon. "Freedom is the recognition of necessity"—and it is the role of education to reveal to all the necessity of abandoning the freedom to breed. Only so can we put an end to this aspect of the tragedy of the commons.

3   *The Problem of Social Cost**

Ronald Coase

Ronald Coase is Clifton R. Musser Professor Emeritus of Economics at the University of Chicago Law School.

I. The Problem to Be Examined

This paper is concerned with those actions of business firms which have harmful effects on others. The standard example is that of a factory the smoke from which has harmful effects on those occupying neighbouring properties. The economic analysis of such a situation has usually proceeded in terms of a divergence between the private and social product of the factory, in which economists have largely followed the treatment of Pigou in *The Economics of Welfare*. The conclusion to which this kind of analysis seems to have led most economists is that it would be desirable to make the owner of the factory liable for the damage caused to those injured by the smoke, or alternatively, to place a tax on the factory owner varying with the amount of smoke produced and equivalent in money terms to the damage it would cause, or finally, to exclude the factory from residential districts (and presumably from other areas in which the emission of smoke would have harmful effects on others). It is my contention that the suggested courses of action are inappropriate, in that they lead to results which are not necessarily, or even usually, desirable.

II. The Reciprocal Nature of the Problem

The traditional approach has tended to obscure the nature of the choice that has to be made. The question is commonly thought of as one in which A inflicts harm on B and what has to be decided is: how should we restrain A? But this is wrong. We are dealing with a problem of a reciprocal nature. To avoid the harm to B would inflict harm on A. The real question that has to be decided is: should A be allowed to harm B or should B be

"The Problem of Social Cost," by Ronald Coase, from *The Journal of Law and Economics* (October 1960). (Several passages devoted to extended discussions of legal decisions have been omitted.) Reprinted by permission.

*This article, although concerned with a technical problem of economic analysis, arose out of the study of the Political Economy of Broadcasting which I am now conducting. The argument of the present article was implicit in a previous article dealing with the problem of allocating radio and television frequencies ("The Federal Communications Commission," 2 *J. Law & Econ.* [1959]) but comments which I have received seemed to suggest that it would be desirable to deal with the question in a more explicit way and without reference to the original problem for the solution of which the analysis was developed.

allowed to harm A? The problem is to avoid the more serious harm. I instanced in my previous article[1] the case of a confectioner the noise and vibrations from whose machinery disturbed a doctor in his work. To avoid harming the doctor would inflict harm on the confectioner. The problem posed by this case was essentially whether it was worthwhile, as a result of restricting the methods of production which could be used by the confectioner, to secure more doctoring at the cost of a reduced supply of confectionery products. Another example is afforded by the problem of straying cattle which destroy crops on neighbouring land. If it is inevitable that some cattle will stray, an increase in the supply of meat can only be obtained at the expense of a decrease in the supply of crops. The nature of the choice is clear: meat or crops. What answer should be given is, of course, not clear unless we know the value of what is obtained as well as the value of what is sacrificed to obtain it. To give another example, Professor George J. Stigler instances the contamination of a stream.[2] If we assume that the harmful effect of the pollution is that it kills the fish, the question to be decided is: is the value of the fish lost greater or less than the value of the product which the contamination of the stream makes possible? It goes almost without saying that this problem has to be looked at in total *and* at the margin.

III. The Pricing System with Liability for Damage

I propose to start my analysis by examining a case in which most economists would presumably agree that the problem would be solved in a completely satisfactory manner: when the damaging business has to pay for all damage caused *and* the pricing system works smoothly (strictly this means that the operation of a pricing system is without cost).

A good example of the problem under discussion is afforded by the case of straying cattle which destroy crops growing on neighbouring land. Let us suppose that a farmer and cattle-raiser are operating on neighbouring properties. Let us further suppose that, without any fencing between the properties, an increase in the size of the cattle-raiser's herd increases the total damage to the farmer's crops. What happens to the marginal damage as the size of the herd increases is another matter. This depends on whether the cattle tend to follow one another or to roam side by side, on whether they tend to be more or less restless as the size of the herd increases and on other similar factors. For my immediate purpose, it is immaterial what assumption is made about marginal damage as the size of the herd increases.

---

[1]Coase, "The Federal Communications Commission," 2 *J. Law & Econ.* 26–27 (1959).
[2]G. J. Stigler, *The Theory of Price*, 105 (1952).

To simplify the argument, I propose to use an arithmetical example. I shall assume that the annual cost of fencing the farmer's property is $9 and the price of the crop is $1 per ton. Also, I assume that the relation between the number of cattle in the herd and the annual crop loss is as follows:

Number in Herd (Steers)	Annual Crop Loss (Tons)	Crop Loss per Additional Steer (Tons)
1	1	1
2	3	2
3	6	3
4	10	4

Given that the cattle-raiser is liable for the damage caused, the additional annual cost imposed on the cattle-raiser if he increased his herd from, say, 2 to 3 steers is $3 and in deciding on the size of the herd, he will take this into account along with his other costs. That is, he will not increase the size of the herd unless the value of the additional meat produced (assuming that the cattle-raiser slaughters the cattle) is greater than the additional costs that this will entail, including the value of the additional crops destroyed. Of course, if, by the employment of dogs, herdsmen, aeroplanes, mobile radio and other means, the amount of damage can be reduced, these means will be adopted when their cost is less than the value of the crop which they prevent being lost. Given that the annual cost of fencing is $9, the cattle-raiser who wished to have a herd with 4 steers or more would pay for fencing to be erected and maintained, assuming that other means of attaining the same end would not do so more cheaply. When the fence is erected, the marginal cost due to the liability for damage becomes zero, except to the extent that an increase in the size of the herd necessitates a stronger and therefore more expensive fence because more steers are liable to lean against it at the same time. But, of course, it may be cheaper for the cattle-raiser not to fence and to pay for the damaged crops, as in my arithmetical example, with 3 or fewer steers.

It might be thought that the fact that the cattle-raiser would pay for all crops damaged would lead the farmer to increase his planting if a cattle-raiser came to occupy the neighbouring property. But this is not so. If the crop was previously sold in conditions of perfect competition, marginal cost was equal to price for the amount of planting undertaken and any expansion would have reduced the profits of the farmer. In the new situation, the existence of crop damage would mean that the farmer would sell less on the open market but his receipts for a given production would remain the same, since the cattle-raiser would pay the market price for any crop damaged. Of course, if cattle-raising commonly involved the destruction of crops, the coming into existence of a cattle-raising industry might raise the price of the crops involved and farmers would then extend their planting. But I wish to confine my attention to the individual farmer.

I have said that the occupation of a neighbouring property by a cattle-raiser would not cause the amount of production, or perhaps more exactly the amount of planting, by the farmer to increase. In fact, if the cattle-raising has any effect, it will be to decrease the amount of planting. The reason for this is that, for any given tract of land, if the value of the crop damaged is so great that the receipts from the sale of the undamaged crop are less than the total costs of cultivating that tract of land, it will be profitable for the farmer and the cattle-raiser to make a bargain whereby that tract of land is left uncultivated. This can be made clear by means of an arithmetical example. Assume initially that the value of the crop obtained from cultivating a given tract of land is $12 and that the cost incurred in cultivating this tract of land is $10, the net gain from cultivating the land being $2. I assume for purposes of simplicity that the farmer owns the land. Now assume that the cattle-raiser starts operations on the neighbouring property and that the value of the crops damaged is $1. In this case $11 is obtained by the farmer from sale on the market and $1 is obtained from the cattle-raiser for damage suffered and the net gain remains $2. Now suppose that the cattle-raiser finds it profitable to increase the size of his herd, even though the amount of damage rises to $3; which means that the value of the additional meat production is greater than the additional costs, including the additional $2 payment for damage. But the total payment for damage is now $3. The net gain to the farmer from cultivating the land is still $2. The cattle-raiser would be better off if the farmer would agree not to cultivate his land for any payment less than $3. The farmer would be agreeable to not cultivating the land for any payment greater than $2. There is clearly room for a mutually satisfactory bargain which would lead to the abandonment of cultivation.[3] But the same argument applies not only to the whole tract cultivated by the farmer but also to any subdivision of it. Suppose, for example, that the cattle have a well-defined route, say, to a brook or to a shady area. In these circumstances, the amount of damage to the crop along the route may well be great and if so, it could

---

[3]The argument in the text has proceeded on the assumption that the alternative to cultivation of the crop is abandonment of cultivation altogether. But this need not be so. There may be crops which are less liable to damage by cattle but which would not be as profitable as the crop grown in the absence of damage. Thus, if the cultivation of a new crop would yield a return to the farmer of $1 instead of $2, and the size of the herd which would cause $3 damage with the old crop would cause $1 damage with the new crop, it would be profitable to the cattle-raiser to pay any sum less than $2 to induce the farmer to change his crop (since this would reduce damage liability from $3 to $1) and it would be profitable for the farmer to do so if the amount received was more than $1 (the reduction in his return caused by switching crops). In fact, there would be room for a mutually satisfactory bargain in all cases in which change of crop would reduce the amount of damage by more than it reduces the value of the crop (excluding damage)—in all cases, that is, in which a change in the crop cultivated would lead to an increase in the value of production.

be that the farmer and the cattle-raiser would find it profitable to make a bargain whereby the farmer would agree not to cultivate this strip of land.

But this raises a further possibility. Suppose that there is such a well-defined route. Suppose further that the value of the crop that would be obtained by cultivating this strip of land is $10 but that the cost of cultivation is $11. In the absence of the cattle-raiser, the land would not be cultivated. However, given the presence of the cattle-raiser, it could well be that if the strip was cultivated, the whole crop would be destroyed by the cattle. In which case, the cattle-raiser would be forced to pay $10 to the farmer. It is true that the farmer would lose $1. But the cattle-raiser would lose $10. Clearly this is a situation which is not likely to last indefinitely since neither party would want this to happen. The aim of the farmer would be to induce the cattle-raiser to make a payment in return for an agreement to leave this land uncultivated. The farmer would not be able to obtain a payment greater than the cost of fencing off this piece of land nor so high as to lead the cattle-raiser to abandon the use of the neighbouring property. What payment would in fact be made would depend on the shrewdness of the farmer and the cattle-raiser as bargainers. But as the payment would not be so high as to cause the cattle-raiser to abandon this location and as it would not vary with the size of the herd, such an agreement would not affect the allocation of resources but would merely alter the distribution of income and wealth as between the cattle-raiser and the farmer.

I think it is clear that if the cattle-raiser is liable for damage caused and the pricing system works smoothly, the reduction in the value of production elsewhere will be taken into account in computing the additional cost involved in increasing the size of the herd. This cost will be weighed against the value of the additional meat production and, given perfect competition in the cattle industry, the allocation of resources in cattle-raising will be optimal. What needs to be emphasized is that the fall in the value of production elsewhere which would be taken into account in the costs of the cattle-raiser may well be less than the damage which the cattle would cause to the crops in the ordinary course of events. This is because it is possible, as a result of market transactions, to discontinue cultivation of the land. This is desirable in all cases in which the damage that the cattle would cause, and for which the cattle-raiser would be willing to pay, exceeds the amount which the farmer would pay for use of the land. In conditions of perfect competition, the amount which the farmer would pay for the use of the land is equal to the difference between the value of the total production when the factors are employed on this land and the value of the additional product yielded in their next best use (which would be what the farmer would have to pay for the factors). If damage exceeds the amount the farmer would pay for the use of the land, the value of the additional product of the factors employed elsewhere would exceed the value of the total product in this use after damage is taken into account. It follows that it would be desirable to abandon cultivation of the land and to release the factors employed for production elsewhere. A procedure which merely provided for payment for damage to the crop caused by the cattle but which did not allow for the possibility of cultivation being discontinued would result in too small an employment of factors of production in cattle-raising and too large an employment of factors in cultivation of the crop. But given the possibility of market transactions, a situation in which damage to crops exceeded the rent of the land would not endure. Whether the cattle-raiser pays the farmer to leave the land uncultivated or himself rents the land by paying the landowner an amount slightly greater than the farmer would pay (if the farmer was himself renting the land), the final result would be the same and would maximise the value of production. Even when the farmer is induced to plant crops which it would not be profitable to cultivate for sale on the market, this will be a purely short-term phenomenon and may be expected to lead to an agreement under which the planting will cease. The cattle-raiser will remain in that location and the marginal cost of meat production will be the same as before, thus having no long-run effect on the allocation of resources.

IV. The Pricing System with No Liability for Damage

I now turn to the case in which, although the pricing system is assumed to work smoothly (that is, costlessly), the damaging business is not liable for any of the damage which it causes. This business does not have to make a payment to those damaged by its actions. I propose to show that the allocation of resources will be the same in this case is it was when the damaging business was liable for damage caused. As I showed in the previous case that the allocation of resources was optimal, it will not be necessary to repeat this part of the argument.

I return to the case of the farmer and the cattle-raiser. The farmer would suffer increased damage to his crop as the size of the herd increased. Suppose that the size of the cattle-raiser's herd is 3 steers (and that this is the size of the herd that would be maintained if crop damage was not taken into account). Then the farmer would be willing to pay up to $3 if the cattle-raiser would reduce his herd to 2 steers, up to $5 if the herd were reduced to 1 steer and would pay up to $6 if cattle-raising was abandoned. The cattle-raiser would therefore receive $3 from the farmer if he kept 2 steers instead of 3. This $3 foregone is therefore part of the cost incurred in keeping the third steer. Whether the $3 is a payment which the cattle-raiser has to make if he adds the third steer to his herd (which it would be if the cattle-raiser was liable to the farmer for damage caused to the crop) or whether it is a sum of money which he would have received if he did not keep a third steer (which it would be if the cattle-raiser was not liable to the farmer for damage caused to the crop) does not affect the final result. In both cases $3 is part of the cost of adding a third steer, to be included along with the other costs. If the increase in the value of production in cattle-raising through increasing the size of the herd from 2 to 3 is greater than the additional costs that have to be incurred (including the $3 damage to crops), the size of the herd will be increased. Otherwise, it will not. The size of the herd will be the same whether the cattle-raiser is liable for damage caused to the crop or not.

It may be argued that the assumed starting point—a herd of 3 steers— was arbitrary. And this is true. But the farmer would not wish to pay to avoid crop damage which the cattle-raiser would not be able to cause. For example, the maximum annual payment which the farmer could be induced to pay could not exceed $9, the annual cost of fencing. And the farmer would only be willing to pay this sum if it did not reduce his earnings to a level that would cause him to abandon cultivation of this particular tract of land. Furthermore, the farmer would only be willing to pay this amount if he believed that, in the absence of any payment by him, the size of the herd maintained by the cattle-raiser would be 4 or more steers. Let us assume that this is the case. Then the farmer would be willing to pay up to $3 if the cattle-raiser would reduce his herd to 3 steers, up to $6 if the herd were reduced to 2 steers, up to $8 if one steer only were kept and up to $9 if cattle-raising were abandoned. It will be noticed that the change in the starting point has not altered the amount which would accrue to the cattle-raiser if he reduced the size of his herd by any given amount. It is still true that the cattle-raiser could receive an additional $3 from the farmer if he agreed to reduce his herd from 3 steers to 2 and that the $3 represents the value of the crop that would be destroyed by adding the third steer to the herd. Although a different belief on the part of the farmer (whether justified or not) about the size of the herd that the cattle-raiser would maintain in the absence of payments from him may affect the total payment he can be induced to pay, it is not true that this different belief would have any effect on the size of the herd that the cattle-raiser will actually keep. This will be the same as it would be if the cattle-raiser had to pay for damage caused by his cattle, since a receipt foregone of a given amount is the equivalent of a payment of the same amount.

It might be thought that it would pay the cattle-raiser to increase his herd above the size that he would wish to maintain once a bargain had been made, in order to induce the farmer to make a larger total payment. And this may be true. It is similar in nature to the action of the farmer (when the cattle-raiser was liable for damage) in cultivating land on which, as a result of an agreement with the cattle-raiser, planting would subsequently be abandoned (including land which would not be cultivated at all in the absence of cattle-raising). But such manoeuvres are preliminaries to an agreement and do not affect the long-run equilibrium position, which is the same whether or not the cattle-raiser is held responsible for the crop damage brought about by his cattle.

It is necessary to know whether the damaging business is liable or not for damage caused since without the establishment of this initial delimitation of rights there can be no market transactions to transfer and recombine them. But the ultimate result (which maximises the value of production) is independent of the legal position if the pricing system is assumed to work without cost.

V. The Problem Illustrated Anew

The harmful effects of the activities of a business can assume a wide variety of forms. An early English case concerned a building which, by obstructing currents of air, hindered the operation of a windmill.[4] A recent case in Florida concerned a building which cast a shadow on the cabana, swimming pool and sunbathing areas of a neighbouring hotel.[5] The problem of straying cattle and the damaging of crops which was the subject of detailed examination in the two preceding sections, although it may have appeared to be rather a special case, is in fact but one example of a problem which arises in many different guises. To clarify the nature of my argument and to demonstrate its general applicability, I propose to illustrate it anew by reference to four actual cases.

Let us first reconsider the case of *Sturges v. Bridgman*[6] which I used as an illustration of the general problem in my article on "The Federal Communications Commission." In this case, a confectioner (in Wigmore Street) used two mortars and pestles in connection with his business (one had been in operation in the same position for more than 60 years and the other for more than 26 years). A doctor than came to occupy neighbouring premises (in Wimpole Street). The confectioner's machinery caused the doctor no harm until, eight years after he had first occupied the premises, he built a consulting room at the end of his garden right against the confectioner's kitchen. It was then found that the noise and vibration caused by the confectioner's machinery made it difficult for the doctor to use his new consulting room. "In particular . . . the noise prevented him from examining his patients by auscultation[7] for diseases of the chest. He also found it impossible to engage with effect in any occupation which required thought and attention." The doctor therefore brought a legal action to force the confectioner to stop using his machinery. The courts had little difficulty in granting the doctor the injunction he sought. "Individual cases of hardship may occur in the strict carrying out of the principle upon which we found our judgment, but the negation of the principle would lead even more to individual hardship, and would at the same time produce a prejudicial effect upon the development of land for residential purposes."

The court's decision established that the doctor had the right to prevent the confectioner from using his machinery. But, of course, it would have been possible to modify the arrangements envisaged in the legal ruling by means of a bargain between the parties. The doctor would have been willing to waive his right and allow the machinery to continue in operation if the confectioner would have paid him a sum of money which was greater than the loss of income which he would suffer from having to move

---

[4]See Gale on *Easements* 237–39 (13th ed. M. Bowles 1959).

[5]See *Fontainebleu Hotel Corp. v. Forty-Five Twenty-Five, Inc.*, 114 So. 2d 357 (1959).

[6]11 Ch. D. 852 (1879).

[7]Auscultation is the act of listening by ear or stethoscope in order to judge by sound the condition of the body.

to a more closely or less convenient location or from having to curtail his activities at this location or, as was suggested as a possibility, from having to build a separate wall which would deaden the noise and vibration. The confectioner would have been willing to do this if the amount he would have to pay the doctor was less than the fall in income he would suffer if he had to change his mode of operation at this location, abandon his operation or move his confectionery business to some other location. The solution of the problem depends essentially on whether the continued use of the machinery adds more to the confectioner's income than it subtracts from the doctor's.[8] But now consider the situation if the confectioner had won the case. The confectioner would then have had the right to continue operating his noise and vibration-generating machinery without having to pay anything to the doctor. The boot would have been on the other foot: the doctor would have had to pay the confectioner to induce him to stop using the machinery. If the doctor's income would have fallen more through continuance of the use of this machinery than it added to the income of the confectioner, there would clearly be room for a bargain whereby the doctor paid the confectioner to stop using the machinery. That is to say, the circumstances in which it would not pay the confectioner to continue to use the machinery and to compensate the doctor for the losses that this would bring (if the doctor had the right to prevent the confectioner's using his machinery) would be those in which it would be in the interest of the doctor to make a payment to the confectioner which would induce him to discontinue the use of the machinery (if the confectioner had the right to operate the machinery). The basic conditions are exactly the same in this case as they were in the example of the cattle which destroyed crops. With costless market transactions, the decision of the courts concerning liability for damage would be without effect on the allocation of resources. It was of course the view of the judges that they were affecting the working of the economic system—and in a desirable direction. Any other decision would have had "a prejudicial effect upon the development of land for residential purposes," an argument which was elaborated by examining the example of a forge operating on a barren moor, which was later developed for residential purposes. The judges' view that they were settling how the land was to be used would be true only in the case in which the costs of carrying out the necessary market transactions exceeded the gain which might be achieved by any rearrangement of rights. And it would be desirable to preserve the areas (Wimpole Street or the moor) for residential or professional use (by giving non-industrial users the right to stop the noise, vibration, smoke, etc., by injunction) only if the value of the additional residential facilities obtained was greater than the value of cakes or iron lost. But of this the judges seem to have been unaware.

---

[8]Note that what is taken into account is the change in income after allowing for alterations in methods of production, location, character of product, etc.

The reasoning employed by the courts in determining legal rights will often seem strange to an economist because many of the factors on which the decision turns are, to an economist, irrelevant. Because of this, situations which are, from an economic point of view, identical will be treated quite differently by the courts. The economic problem in all cases of harmful effects is how to maximise the value of production. In the case of *Bass v. Gregory* fresh air was drawn in through the well which facilitated the production of beer but foul air was expelled through the well which made life in the adjoining houses less pleasant. The economic problem was to decide which to choose: a lower cost of beer and worsened amenities in adjoining houses or a higher cost of beer and improved amenities. In deciding this question, the "doctrine of lost grant" is about as relevant as the colour of the judge's eyes. But it has to be remembered that the immediate question faced by the courts is *not* what shall be done by whom *but* who has the legal right to do what. It is always possible to modify by transactions on the market the initial legal delimitation of rights. And, of course, if such market transactions are costless, such a rearrangement of rights will always take place if it would lead to an increase in the value of production.

VI. The Cost of Market Transactions Taken into Account

The argument has proceeded up to this point on the assumption (explicit in Sections III and IV and tacit in Section V) that there were no costs involved in carrying out market transactions. This is, of course, a very unrealistic assumption. In order to carry out a market transaction it is necessary to discover who it is that one wishes to deal with, to inform people that one wishes to deal and on what terms, to conduct negotiations leading up to a bargain, to draw up the contract, to undertake the inspection needed to make sure that the terms of the contract are being observed and so on. These operations are often extremely costly, sufficiently costly at any rate to prevent many transactions that would be carried out in a world in which the pricing system worked without cost.

In earlier sections, when dealing with the problem of the rearrangement of legal rights through the market, it was argued that such a rearrangement would be made through the market whenever this would lead to an increase in the value of production. But this assumed costless market transactions. Once the costs of carrying out market transactions are taken into account it is clear that such a rearrangement of rights will only be undertaken when the increase in the value of production consequent upon the rearrangement is greater than the costs which would be involved in bringing it about. When it is less, the granting of an injunction (or the knowledge that it would be granted) or the liability to pay damages may result in an activity being discontinued (or may prevent its being started) which would be undertaken if market transactions were costless. In these conditions the initial delimitation of legal rights does have an effect on the efficiency with which the economic system operates. One arrangement of rights may bring about a greater value of production than any other. But unless this is the arrangement of rights established by the legal system, the costs of reaching the same result by altering and combining rights through the market may be so great that this optimal arrangement of rights, and the greater value of production which it would bring, may never be achieved. The part played by economic considerations in the process of delimiting legal rights will be discussed in the next section. In this section, I will take the initial delimitation of rights and the costs of carrying out market transactions as given.

It is clear that an alternative form of economic organisation which could achieve the same result at less cost than would be incurred by using the market would enable the value of production to be raised. As I explained many years ago, the firm represents such an alternative to organising production through market transactions.[9] Within the firm individual bargains between the various cooperating factors of production are eliminated and for a market transaction is substituted an administrative decision. The rearrangement of production then takes place without the need for bargains between the owners of the factors of production. A landowner who has control of a large tract of land may devote his land to various uses taking into account the effect that the interrelations of the various activities will have on the net return of the land, thus rendering unnecessary bargains between those undertaking the various activities. Owners of a large building or of several adjoining properties in a given area may act in much the same way. In effect, using our earlier terminology, the firm would acquire the legal rights of all the parties and the rearrangement of activities would not follow on a rearrangement of rights by contract, but as a result of an administrative decision as to how the rights should be used.

It does not, of course, follow that the administrative costs of organising a transaction through a firm are inevitably less than the costs of the market transactions which are superseded. But where contracts are peculiarly difficult to draw up and an attempt to describe what the parties have agreed to do or not to do (e.g. the amount and kind of a smell or noise that they may make or will not make) would necessitate a lengthy and highly involved document, and, where, as is probable, a long-term contract would be desirable,[10] it would be hardly surprising if the emergence of a firm or the extension of the activities of an existing firm was not the solution adopted on many occasions to deal with the problem of harmful effects. This solution would be adopted whenever the administrative costs of the firm were less than the costs of the market transactions that it supersedes and the gains which would result from the rearrangement of activities greater than the firm's costs of organising them. I do not need to examine

---

[9]See Coase, "The Nature of the Firm," 4 *Economica*, New Series, 386 (1937). Reprinted in *Readings in Price Theory*, 331 (1952).

[10]For reasons explained in my earlier article, see *Readings in Price Theory*, n. 14 at 337.

in great detail the character of this solution since I have explained what is involved in my earlier article.

But the firm is not the only possible answer to this problem. The administrative costs of organising transactions within the firm may also be high, and particularly so when many diverse activities are brought within the control of a single organisation. In the standard case of a smoke nuisance, which may affect a vast number of people engaged in a wide variety of activities, the administrative costs might well be so high as to make any attempt to deal with the problem within the confines of a single firm impossible. An alternative solution is direct government regulation. Instead of instituting a legal system of rights which can be modified by transactions on the market, the government may impose regulations which state what people must or must not do and which have to be obeyed. Thus, the government (by statute or perhaps more likely through an administrative agency) may, to deal with the problem of smoke nuisance, decree that certain methods of production should or should not be used (e.g. that smoke preventing devices should be installed or that coal or oil should not be burned) or may confine certain types of business to certain districts (zoning regulations).

The government is, in a sense, a superfirm (but of a very special kind) since it is able to influence the use of factors of production by administrative decision. But the ordinary firm is subject to checks in its operations because of the competition of other firms, which might administer the same activities at lower cost and also because there is always the alternative of market transactions as against organisation within the firm if the administrative costs become too great. The government is able, if it wishes, to avoid the market altogether, which a firm can never do. The firm has to make market agreements with the owners of the factors of production that it uses. Just as the government can conscript or seize property, so it can decree that factors of production should only be used in such-and-such a way. Such authoritarian methods save a lot of trouble (for those doing the organising). Furthermore, the government has at its disposal the police and the other law enforcement agencies to make sure that its regulations are carried out.

It is clear that the government has powers which might enable it to get some things done at a lower cost than could a private organisation (or at any rate one without special governmental powers). But the governmental administrative machine is not itself costless. It can, in fact, on occasion be extremely costly. Furthermore, there is no reason to suppose that the restrictive and zoning regulations, made by a fallible administration subject to political pressures and operating without any competitive check, will necessarily always be those which increase the efficiency with which the economic system operates. Furthermore, such general regulations which must apply to a wide variety of cases will be enforced in some cases in which they are clearly inappropriate. From these considerations it follows that direct governmental regulation will not necessarily give better results than leaving the problem to be solved by the market or the firm. But equally there is no reason why, on occasion, such governmental administrative regulation should not lead to an improvement in economic efficiency. This would seem particularly likely when, as is normally the case with the smoke nuisance, a large number of people are involved and in which therefore the costs of handling the problem through the market or the firm may be high.

There is, of course, a further alternative which is to do nothing about the problem at all. And given that the costs involved in solving the problem by regulations issued by the governmental administrative machine will often be heavy (particularly if the costs are interpreted to include all the consequences which follow from the government engaging in this kind of activity), it will no doubt be commonly the case that the gain which would come from regulating the actions which give rise to the harmful effects will be less than the costs involved in government regulation.

The discussion of the problem of harmful effects in this section (when the costs of market transactions are taken into account) is extremely inadequate. But at least it has made clear that the problem is one of choosing the appropriate social arrangement for dealing with the harmful effects. All solutions have costs and there is no reason to suppose that government regulation is called for simply because the problem is not well handled by the market or the firm. Satisfactory views on policy can only come from a patient study of how, in practice, the market, firms and governments handle the problem of harmful effects. Economists need to study the work of the broker in bringing parties together, the effectiveness of restrictive covenants, the problems of the large-scale real-estate development company, the operation of government zoning and other regulating activities. It is my belief that economists, and policy-makers generally, have tended to over-estimate the advantages which come from governmental regulation. But this belief, even if justified, does not do more than suggest that government regulation should be curtailed. It does not tell us where the boundary line should be drawn. This, it seems to me, has to come from a detailed investigation of the actual results of handling the problem in different ways. But it would be unfortunate if this investigation were undertaken with the aid of a faulty economic analysis. The aim of this article is to indicate what the economic approach to the problem should be.

VII. The Legal Delimitation of Rights and the Economic Problem

The discussion in Section V not only served to illustrate the argument but also afforded a glimpse at the legal approach to the problem of harmful effects. The cases considered were all English but a similar selection of American cases could easily be made and the character of the reasoning would have been the same. Of course, if market transactions were costless, all that matters (questions of equity apart) is that the rights of the various parties should be well-defined and the results of legal actions easy to forecast. But as we have seen, the situation is quite different when market transactions are so costly as to make it difficult to change the arrangement of rights established by the law. In such cases, the courts directly influence economic activity. It would therefore seem desirable that the courts should understand the economic consequences of their decisions and should, insofar as this is possible without creating too much uncertainty about the legal position itself, take these consequences into account when making their decisions. Even when it is possible to change the legal delimitation of rights through market transactions, it is obviously desirable to reduce the need for such transactions and thus reduce the employment of resources in carrying them out.

A thorough examination of the presuppositions of the courts in trying such cases would be of great interest but I have not been able to attempt it. Nevertheless it is clear from a cursory study that the courts have often recognized the economic implications of their decisions and are aware (as many economists are not) of the reciprocal nature of the problem. Furthermore, from time to time, they take these economic implications into account, along with other factors, in arriving at their decisions. The American writers on this subject refer to the question in a more explicit fashion than do the British. Thus, to quote Prosser on Torts, a person may

> make use of his own property or . . . conduct his own affairs at the expense of some harm to his neighbors. He may operate a factory whose noise and smoke cause some discomfort to others, so long as he keeps within reasonable bounds. It is only when his conduct is unreasonable, *in the light of its utility and the harm which results* [italics added], that it becomes a nuisance. . . . As it was said in an ancient case in regard to candle-making in a town, "Le utility del chose excusera le noisomeness del stink."
>
> The world must have factories, smelters, oil refineries, noisy machinery and blasting, even at the expense of some inconvenience to those in the vicinity and the plaintiff may be required to accept some not unreasonable discomfort for the general good.[11]

The standard British writers do not state as explicitly as this that a comparison between the utility and harm produced is an element in deciding whether a harmful effect should be considered a nuisance. But similar views, if less strongly expressed, are to be found.[12] The doctrine that the harmful effect must be substantial before the court will act is, no doubt, in part a reflection of the fact that there will almost always be some gain to offset the harm. And in the reports of individual cases, it is clear that the judges have had in mind what would be lost as well as what would be gained in deciding whether to grant an injunction or award damages. Thus,

---

[11]See W. L. Prosser, *The Law of Torts* 398–99, 412 (2d ed. 1955). The quotation about the ancient case concerning candle-making is taken from Sir James Fitzjames Stephen, *A General View of the Criminal Law of England* 106 (1890). Sir James Stephen gives no reference. He perhaps had in mind *Rex. v. Ronkett*, included in Seavey, Keeton and Thurston, *Cases on Torts* 604 (1950). A similar view to that expressed by Prosser is to be found in F. V. Harper and F. James, *The Law of Torts* 67–74 (1956); *Restatement, Torts* §§826, 827 and 828.

[12]See Winfield on *Torts* 541–48 (6th ed. T. E. Lewis 1954); Salmond on the *Law of Torts* 181–90 (12th ed. R. F. V. Heuston 1957); H. Street, *The Law of Torts* 221–29 (1959).

in refusing to prevent the destruction of a prospect by a new building, the judge stated:

> I know no general rule of common law, which . . . says, that building so as to stop another's prospect is a nuisance. Was that the case, there could be no great towns; and I must grant injunctions to all the new buildings in this town. . . . [13]

The problem which we face in dealing with actions which have harmful effects is not simply one of restraining those responsible for them. What has to be decided is whether the gain from preventing the harm is greater than the loss which would be suffered elsewhere as a result of stopping the action which produces the harm. In a world in which there are costs of rearranging the rights established by the legal system, the courts, in cases relating to nuisance, are, in effect, making a decision on the economic problem and determining how resources are to be employed. It was argued that the courts are conscious of this and that they often make, although not always in a very explicit fashion, a comparison between what would be gained and what lost by preventing actions which have harmful effects. But the delimitation of rights is also the result of statutory enactments. Here we also find evidence of an appreciation of the reciprocal nature of the problem. While statutory enactments add to the list of nuisances, action is also taken to legalize what would otherwise be nuisances under the common law. The kind of situation which economists are prone to consider as requiring corrective government action is, in fact, often the result of government action. Such action is not necessarily unwise. But there is a real danger that extensive government intervention in the economic system may lead to the protection of those responsible for harmful effects being carried too far.

VIII. Pigou's Treatment in "The Economics of Welfare"

The fountainhead for the modern economic analysis of the problem discussed in this article is Pigou's *Economics of Welfare* and, in particular, that section of Part II which deals with divergences between social and private net products which come about because

> one person A, in the course of rendering some service, for which payment is made, to a second person B, incidentally also renders services or disservices to other persons (not producers of like services), or such a sort that payment cannot

---

[13]*Attorney General v. Doughty*, 2 Ves. Sen. 453, 28 Eng. Rep. 290 (Ch. 1752). Compare in this connection the statement of an American judge, quoted in Prosser, *op. cit. supra* n. 16 at 413 n. 54: "Without smoke, Pittsburgh would have remained a very pretty village," Musmanno, J., in *Versailles Borough v. McKeesport Coal & Coke Co.*, 1935, 83 Pitts. Leg. J. 379, 385.

be exacted from the benefited parties or compensation enforced on behalf of the injured parties.[14]

Pigou tells us that his aim in Part II of *The Economics of Welfare* is

to ascertain how far the free play of self-interest, acting under the existing legal system, tends to distribute the country's resources in the way most favorable to the production of a large national dividend, and how far it is feasible for State action to improve upon 'natural' tendencies.[15]

To judge from the first part of this statement, Pigou's purpose is to discover whether any improvements could be made in the existing arrangements which determine the use of resources. Since Pigou's conclusions is that improvements could be made, one might have expected him to continue by saying that he proposed to set out the changes required to bring them about. Instead, Pigou adds a phrase which contrasts "natural" tendencies with State action, which seems in some sense to equate the present arrangements with "natural" tendencies and to imply that what is required to bring about these improvements is State action (if feasible). That this is more or less Pigou's position is evident from Chapter I of Part II.[16] Pigou starts by referring to "optimistic followers of the classical economists"[17] who have argued that the value of production would be maximised if the government refrained from any interference in the economic system and the economic arrangements were those which came about "naturally." Pigou goes on to say that if self-interest does promote economic welfare, it is because human institutions have been devised to make it so. (This part of Pigou's argument, which he develops with the aid of a quotation from Cannan, seems to me to be essentially correct.) Pigou concludes:

But even in the most advanced States there are failures and imperfections. . . . there are many obstacles that prevent a community's resources from being distributed . . . in the most efficient way. The study of these constitutes our present problem. . . . Its purpose is essentially practical. It seeks to bring into clearer light some of the ways in which it now is, or eventually may become, feasible for governments to control the play of economic forces in such ways as to promote the economic welfare, and through that, the total welfare, of their citizens as a whole.[18]

Pigou's underlying thought would appear to be: Some have argued that no State action is needed. But the system has performed as well as it has be-

---

[14]A. C. Pigou, *The Economics of Welfare* 183 (4th ed. 1932). My references will all be to the fourth edition but the argument and examples examined in this article remained substantially unchanged from the first edition in 1920 to the fourth in 1932. A large part (but not all) of this analysis had appeared previously in *Wealth and Welfare* (1912).

[15]*Id.* at xii.

[16]*Id.* at 127–30.

[17]In *Wealth and Welfare*, Pigou attributes the "optimism" to Adam Smith himself and not to his followers. He there refers to the "highly optimistic theory of Adam Smith that the national dividend, in given circumstances of demand and supply, tends 'naturally' to a maximum" (p. 104).

[18]Pigou, *op. cit. supra* n. 35 at 129–30.

cause of State action. Nonetheless, there are still imperfections. What additional State action is required?

If this is a correct summary of Pigou's position, its inadequacy can be demonstrated by examining the first example he gives of a divergence between private and social products.

> It might happen . . . that costs are thrown upon people not directly concerned, through, say, uncompensated damage done to surrounding woods by sparks from railway engines. All such effects must be included—some of them will be positive, others negative elements—in reckoning up the social net product of the marginal increment of any volume of resources turned into any use or place.[19]

The example used by Pigou refers to a real situation. In Britain, a railway does not normally have to compensate those who suffer damage by fire caused by sparks from an engine. Taken in conjunction with what he says in Chapter 9 of Part II, I take Pigou's policy recommendations to be, first, that there should be State action to correct this "natural" situation and, second, that the railways should be forced to compensate those whose woods are burnt. If this is a correct interpretation of Pigou's position, I would argue that the first recommendation is based on a misapprehension of the facts and that the second is not necessarily desirable.

Let us consider the legal position. Under the heading "Sparks from engines," we find the following in Halsbury's *Laws of England*:

> If railway undertakers use steam engines on their railway without express statutory authority to do so, they are liable, irrespective of any negligence on their part, for fires caused by sparks from engines. Railway undertakers are, however, generally given statutory authority to use steam engines on their railway; accordingly, if an engine is constructed with the precautions which science suggests against fire and is used without negligence, they are not responsible at common law for any damage which may be done by sparks. . . . In the construction of an engine the undertaker is bound to use all the discoveries which science has put within its reach in order to avoid doing harm, provided they are such as it is reasonable to require the company to adopt, having proper regard to the likelihood of the damage and to the cost and convenience of the remedy; but it is not negligence on the part of an undertaker if it refuses to use an apparatus the efficiency of which is open to bona fide doubt.

To this general rule, there is a statutory exception arising from the Railway (Fires) Act, 1905, as amended in 1923. This concerns agricultural land or agricultural crops.

> In such a case the fact that the engine was used under statutory powers does not affect the liability of the company in an action for the damage. . . . These provisions, however, only apply where the claim for damage . . . does not exceed £200 [£100 in the 1905 Act], and where written notice of the occurrence of the fire and the intention to claim has been sent to the company within seven days of the oc-

---

[19]*Id.* at 134.

currence of the damage and particulars of the damage in writing showing the amount of the claim in money not exceeding £200 have been sent to the company within twenty-one days.

Agricultural land does not include moorland or buildings and agricultural crops do not include those led away or stacked.[20] I have not made a close study of the parliamentary history of this statutory exception, but to judge from debates in the House of Commons in 1922 and 1923, this exception was probably designed to help the smallholder.[21]

Let us return to Pigou's example of uncompensated damage to surrounding woods caused by sparks from railway engines. This is presumably intended to show how it is possible "for State action to improve on 'natural' tendencies." If we treat Pigou's example as referring to the position before 1905, or as being an arbitrary example (in that he might just as well have written "surrounding buildings" instead of "surrounding woods"), then it is clear that the reason why compensation was not paid must have been that the railway had statutory authority to run steam engines (which relieved it of liability for fires caused by sparks). That this was the legal position was established in 1860, in a case, oddly enough, which concerned the burning of surrounding woods by a railway,[22] and the law on this point has not been changed (apart from the one exception) by a century of railway legislation, including nationalisation. If we treat Pigou's example of "uncompensated damage done to surrounding woods by sparks from railway engines" literally, and assume that it refers to the period after 1905, then it is clear that the reason why compensation was not paid must have been that the damage was more than £100 (in the first edition of *The Economics of Welfare*) or more than £200 (in later editions) or that the owner of the wood failed to notify the railway in writing within seven days of the fire or did not send particulars of the damage, in writing, within twenty-one days. In the real world, Pigou's example could only exist as a result of a deliberate choice of the legislature. It is not, of course, easy to imagine the construction of a railway in a state of nature. The nearest one can get to this is presumably a railway which uses steam engines "without express statutory authority." However, in this case the railway would be obliged to compensate those whose woods it burnt down. That is to say, compensation would be paid in the absence of Government action. The only circumstances in which compensation would not be paid would be those in which there had been Government action. It is strange that Pigou, who clearly thought it desirable that compensation should be paid, should have chosen this particular example to demonstrate how it is possible "for State action to improve on 'natural' tendencies."

Pigou seems to have had a faulty view of the facts of the situation. But it also seems likely that he was mistaken in his economic analysis. It is not

---

[20]See 31 Halsbury, *Laws of England* 474–75 (3d ed. 1960), Article on Railways and Canals, from which this summary of the legal position, and all quotations, are taken.

[21]See 152 H.C. Deb. 2622–63 (1922); 161 H.C. Deb. 2935–55 (1923).

[22]*Vaughan v. Taff Railway Co.*, 3 H. and N. 743 (Ex. 1858) and 5 H. and N. 679 (Ex. 1860).

necessarily desirable that the railway should be required to compensate those who suffer damage by fires caused by railway engines. I need not show here that, if the railway could make a bargain with everyone having property adjoining the railway line and there were no costs involved in making such bargains, it would not matter whether the railway was liable for damage caused by fires or not. This question has been treated at length in earlier sections. The problem is whether it would be desirable to make the railway liable in conditions in which it is too expensive for such bargains to be made. Pigou clearly thought it was desirable to force the railway to pay compensation and it is easy to see the kind of argument that would have led him to this conclusion. Suppose a railway is considering whether to run an additional train or to increase the speed of an existing train or to install spark-preventing devices on its engines. If the railway were not liable for fire damage, then, when making these decisions, it would not take into account as a cost the increase in damage resulting from the additional train or the faster train or the failure to install spark-preventing devices. This is the source of the divergence between private and social net products. It results in the railway performing acts which will lower the value of total production—and which it would not do if it were liable for the damage. This can be shown by means of an arithmetical example.

Consider a railway, which is *not* liable for damage by fires caused by sparks from its engines, which runs two trains per day on a certain line. Suppose that running one train per day would enable the railway to perform services worth $150 per annum and running two trains a day would enable the railway to perform services worth $250 per annum. Suppose further that the cost of running one train is $50 per annum and two trains $100 per annum. Assuming perfect competition, the cost equals the fall in the value of production elsewhere due to the employment of additional factors of production by the railway. Clearly the railway would find it profitable to run two trains per day. But suppose that running one train per day would destroy by fire crops worth (on an average over the year) $60 and two trains a day would result in the destruction of crops worth $120. In these circumstances running one train per day would raise the value of total production but the running of a second train would reduce the value of total production. The second train would enable additional railway services worth $100 per annum to be performed. But the fall in the value of production elsewhere would be $110 per annum; $50 as a result of the employment of additional factors of production and $60 as a result of the destruction of crops. Since it would be better if the second train were not run and since it would not run if the railway were liable for damage caused to crops, the conclusion that the railway should be made liable for the damage seems irresistible. Undoubtedly it is this kind of reasoning which underlies the Pigovian position.

The conclusion that it would be better if the second train did not run is correct. The conclusion that it is desirable that the railway should be made liable for the damage it causes is wrong. Let us change our assumption concerning the rule of liability. Suppose that the railway is liable for damage from fires caused by sparks from the engine. A farmer on lands adjoining the railway is then in the position that, if his crop is destroyed by fires caused by the railway, he will receive the market price from the railway; but if his crop is not damaged, he will receive the market price by sale. It therefore becomes a matter of indifference to him whether his crop is damaged by fire or not. The position is very different when the railway is *not* liable. Any crop destruction through railway-caused fires would then reduce the receipts of the farmer. He would therefore take out of cultivation any land for which the damage is likely to be greater than the net return of the land (for reasons explained at length in Section III). A change from a regime in which the railway is *not* liable for damage to one in which it *is* liable is likely therefore to lead to an increase in the amount of cultivation on lands adjoining the railway. It will also, of course, lead to an increase in the amount of crop destruction due to railway-caused fires.

Let us return to our arithmetical example. Assume that, with the changed rule of liability, there is a doubling in the amount of crop destruction due to railway-caused fires. With one train per day, crops worth $120 would be destroyed each year and two trains per day would lead to the destruction of crops worth $240. We saw previously that it would not be profitable to run the second train if the railway had to pay $60 per annum as compensation for damage. With damage at $120 per annum the loss from running the second train would be $60 greater. But now let us consider the first train. The value of the transport services furnished by the first train is $150. The cost of running the train is $50. The amount that the railway would have to pay out as compensation for damage is $120. It follows that it would not be profitable to run any trains. With the figures in our example we reach the following result: if the railway is not liable for fire-damage, two trains per day would be run; if the railway is liable for fire-damage, it would cease operations altogether. Does this mean that it is better that there should be no railway? This question can be resolved by considering what would happen to the value of total production if it were decided to exempt the railway from liability for fire-damage, thus bringing it into operation (with two trains per day).

The operation of the railway would enable transport services worth $250 to be performed. It would also mean the employment of factors of production which would reduce the value of production elsewhere by $100. Furthermore it would mean the destruction of crops worth $120. The coming of the railway will also have led to the abandonment of cultivation of some land. Since we know that, had this land been cultivated, the value of the crops destroyed by fire would have been $120, and since it is unlikely that the total crop on this land would have been destroyed, it seems reasonable to suppose that the value of the crop yield on this land would have been higher than this. Assume it would have been $160. But the abandonment of cultivation would have released factors of production for employment elsewhere. All we know is that the amount by which the value of production elsewhere will increase will be less than $160. Suppose that it is $150. Then the gain from operating the railway would be $250 (the value of the transport services) minus $100 (the cost of the factors of production) minus $120 (the value of crops destroyed by fire) minus $160 (the fall in the value of crop production due to the abandonment of cultivation) plus $150 (the value of production elsewhere of the released factors of production). Overall, operating the railway will increase the value of total production by $20. With these figures it is clear that it is better that the railway should not be liable for the damage it causes, thus enabling it to operate profitably. Of course, by altering the figures, it could be shown that there are other cases in which it would be desirable that the railway should be liable for the damage it causes. It is enough for my purpose to show that, from an economic point of view, a situation in which there is "uncompensated damage done to surrounding woods by sparks from railway engines" is not necessarily undesirable. Whether it is desirable or not depends on the particular circumstances.

How is it that the Pigovian analysis seems to give the wrong answer? The reason is that Pigou does not seem to have noticed that his analysis is dealing with an entirely different question. The analysis as such is correct. But it is quite illegitimate for Pigou to draw the particular conclusion he does. The question at issue is not whether it is desirable to run an additional train or a faster train or to install smoke-preventing devices; the question at issue is whether it is desirable to have a system in which the railway has to compensate those who suffer damage from the fires which it causes or one in which the railway does not have to compensate them. When an economist is comparing alternative social arrangements, the proper procedure is to compare the total social product yielded by these different arrangements. The comparison of private and social products is neither here nor there. A simple example will demonstrate this. Imagine a town in which there are traffic lights. A motorist approaches an intersection and stops because the light is red. There are no cars approaching the intersection on the other street. If the motorist ignored the red signal, no accident would occur and the total product would increase because the motorist would arrive earlier at his destination. Why does he not do this? The reason is that if he ignored the light he would be fined. The private product from crossing the street is less than the social product. Should we conclude from this that the total product would be greater if there were no fines for failing to obey traffic signals? The Pigovian analysis shows us that it is possible to conceive of better worlds than the one in which we live. But the problem is to devise practical arrangements which will correct defects in one part of the system without causing more serious harm in other parts.

I have examined in considerable detail one example of a divergence between private and social products and I do not propose to make any further examination of Pigou's analytical system. But the main discussion of the problem considered in this article is to be found in that part of Chapter 9 in Part II which deals with Pigou's second class of divergence and it is of interest to see how Pigou develops his argument. Pigou's own description of this second class of divergence was quoted at the beginning of this section. Pigou distinguishes between the case in which a person renders services for which he receives no payment and the case in which a person renders disservices and compensation is not given to the injured parties. Our main attention has, of course, centered on this second case. It is therefore rather astonishing to find, as was pointed out to me by Professor Francesco Forte, that the problem of the smoking chimney—the "stock instance"[23] or "classroom example"[24] of the second case—is used by Pigou as an example of the first case (services rendered without payment) and is never mentioned, at any rate explicitly, in connection with the second case.[25] Pigou points out that factory owners who devote resources to preventing their chimneys from smoking render services for which they receive no payment. The implication, in the light of Pigou's discussion later in the chapter, is that a factory owner with a smokey chimney should be given a bounty to induce him to install smoke-preventing devices. Most modern economists would suggest that the owner of the factor with the smokey chimney should be taxed. It seems a pity that economists (apart from Professor Forte) do not seem to have noticed this feature of Pigou's treatment since a realisation that the problem could be tackled in either of these two ways would probably have led to an explicit recognition of its reciprocal nature.

In discussing the second case (disservices without compensation to those damaged), Pigou says that they are rendered "when the owner of a site in a residential quarter of a city builds a factory there and so destroys a great part of the amenities of neighbouring sites; or, in a less degree, when he uses his site in such a way as to spoil the lighting of the house opposite; or when he invests resources in erecting buildings in a crowded centre, which by contracting the air-space and the playing room of the neighbourhood, tend to injure the health and efficiency of the families living there."[26] Pigou is, of course, quite right to describe such actions as "uncharged disservices." But he is wrong when he describes these actions as "anti-social."[27] They may or may not be. It is necessary to weigh the harm against the good that will result. Nothing could be more "anti-social" than to oppose any action which causes any harm to anyone.

Indeed, Pigou's treatment of the problems considered in this article is extremely elusive and the discussion of his views raises almost insuperable difficulties of interpretation. Consequently it is impossible to be sure that one has understood what Pigou really meant. Nevertheless, it is difficult to resist the conclusion, extraordinary though this may be in an economist of

---

[23] Sir Dennis Robertson, I *Lectures on Economic Principles* 162 (1957).

[24] E. J. Mishan, "The Meaning of Efficiency in Economics," 189, *The Bankers' Magazine* 482 (June 1960).

[25] Pigou, *op. cit. supra* n. 35 at 184.

[26] *Id.* at 185–86.

[27] *Id.* at 186 n. 1. For similar unqualified statements see Pigou's lecture "Some Aspects of the Housing Problem" in B. S. Rowntree and A. C. Pigou, "Lectures on Housing," in 18 *Manchester Univ. Lectures* (1914).

Pigou's stature, that the main source of this obscurity is that Pigou had not thought his position through.

IX. The Pigovian Tradition

It is strange that a doctrine as faulty as that developed by Pigou should have been so influential, although part of its success has probably been due to the lack of clarity in the exposition. Not being clear, it was never clearly wrong. Curiously enough, this obscurity in the source has not prevented the emergence of a fairly well-defined oral tradition. What economists think they learn from Pigou, and what they tell their students, which I term the Pigovian tradition, is reasonably clear. I propose to show the inadequacy of this Pigovian tradition by demonstrating that both the analysis and the policy conclusions which it supports are incorrect.

I do not propose to justify my view as to the prevailing opinion by co-pious references to the literature. I do this partly because the treatment in the literature is usually so fragmentary, often involving little more than a reference to Pigou plus some explanatory comment, that detailed exami-nation would be inappropriate. But the main reason for this lack of refer-ence is that the doctrine, although based on Pigou, must have been largely the product of an oral tradition. Certainly economists with whom I have discussed these problems have shown a unanimity of opinion which is quite remarkable considering the meagre treatment accorded this subject in the literature. No doubt there are some economists who do not share the usual view but they must represent a small minority of the profession.

The approach to the problems under discussion is through an exami-nation of the value of physical production. The private product is the value of the additional product resulting from a particular activity of a business. The social product equals the private product minus the fall in the value of production elsewhere for which no compensation is paid by the busi-ness. Thus, if 10 units of a factor (and no other factors) are used by a busi-ness to make a certain product with a value of $105; and the owner of this factor is not compensated for their use, which he is unable to prevent; and these 10 units of the factor would yield products in their best alternative use worth $100; then, the social product is $105 minus $100 or $5. If the business now pays for one unit of the factor and its price equals the value of its marginal product, then the social product rises to $15. If two units are paid for, the social product rises to $25 and so on until it reaches $105 when all units of the factor are paid for. It is not difficult to see why econ-omists have so readily accepted this rather odd procedure. The analysis focusses on the individual business decision and since the use of certain resources is not allowed for in costs, receipts are reduced by the same amount. But, of course, this means that the value of the social product has no social significance whatsoever. It seems to me preferable to use the op-portunity cost concept and to approach these problems by comparing the value of the product yielded by factors in alternative uses or by alternative arrangements. The main advantage of a pricing system is that it leads to the employment of factors in places where the value of the product yielded is greatest and does so at less cost than alternative systems (I leave aside that a pricing system also eases the problem of the redistribution of income). But if through some God-given natural harmony factors flowed to the places where the value of the product yielded was greatest without any use of the pricing system and consequently there was no compensation, I would find it a source of surprise rather than a cause for dismay.

The definition of the social product is queer but this does not mean that the conclusions for policy drawn from the analysis are necessarily wrong. However, there are bound to be dangers in an approach which diverts attention from the basic issues and there can be little doubt that it has been responsible for some of the errors in current doctrine. The belief that it is desirable that the business which causes harmful effects should be forced to compensate those who suffer damage (which was exhaustively discussed in section VIII in connection with Pigou's railway sparks example) is undoubtedly the result of not comparing the total product obtainable with alternative social arrangements.

The same fault is to be found in proposals for solving the problem of harmful effects by the use of taxes or bounties. Pigou lays considerable stress on this solution although he is, as usual, lacking in detail and qualified in his support.[28] Modern economists tend to think exclusively in terms of taxes and in a very precise way. The tax should be equal to the damage done and should therefore vary with the amount of the harmful effect. As it is not proposed that the proceeds of the tax should be paid to those suffering the damage, this solution is not the same as that which would force a business to pay compensation to those damaged by its actions, although economists generally do not seem to have noticed this and tend to treat the two solutions as being identical.

Assume that a factory which emits smoke is set up in a district previously free from smoke pollution, causing damage valued at $100 per annum. Assume that the taxation solution is adopted and that the factory-owner is taxed $100 per annum as long as the factory emits the smoke. Assume further that a smoke-preventing device costing $90 per annum to run is available. In these circumstances, the smoke-preventing device would be installed. Damage of $100 would have been avoided at an expenditure of $90 and the factory-owner would be better off by $10 per annum. Yet the position achieved may not be optimal. Suppose that those who suffer the damage could avoid it by moving to other locations or by taking various precautions which would cost them, or be equivalent to a loss in income of, $40 per annum. Then there would be a gain in the value of production of $50 if the factory continued to emit its smoke and those now in the district moved elsewhere or made other adjustments to avoid the damage. If the factory owner is to be made to pay a tax equal to the damage

---

[28]*Id.* 192–4, 381 and *Public Finance* 94–100 (3d ed. 1947).

caused, it would clearly be desirable to institute a double tax system and to make residents of the district pay an amount equal to the additional cost incurred by the factory-owner (or the consumers of his products) in order to avoid the damage. In these conditions, people would not stay in the district or would take other measures to prevent the damage from occurring, when the costs of doing so were less than the costs that would be incurred by the producer to reduce the damage (the producer's object, of course, being not so much to reduce the damage as to reduce the tax payments). A tax system which was confined to a tax on the producer for damage caused would tend to lead to unduly high costs being incurred for the prevention of damage. Of course this could be avoided if it were possible to base the tax, not on the damage caused, but on the fall in the value of production (in its widest sense) resulting from the emission of smoke. But to do so would require a detailed knowledge of individual preferences and I am unable to imagine how the data needed for such a taxation system could be assembled. Indeed, the proposal to solve the smoke pollution and similar problems by the use of taxes bristles with difficulties: the problem of calculation, the difference between average and marginal damage, the interrelations between the damage suffered on different properties, etc. But it is unnecessary to examine these problems here. It is enough for my purpose to show that, even if the tax is exactly adjusted to equal the damage that would be done to neighbouring properties as a result of the emission of each additional puff of smoke, the tax would not necessarily bring about optimal conditions. An increase in the number of people living or of businesses operating in the vicinity of the smoke-emitting factory will increase the amount of harm produced by a given emission of smoke. The tax that would be imposed would therefore increase with an increase in the number of those in the vicinity. This will tend to lead to a decrease in the value of production of the factors employed by the factory, either because a reduction in production due to the tax will result in factors being used elsewhere in ways which are less valuable, or because factors will be diverted to produce means for reducing the amount of smoke emitted. But people deciding to establish themselves in the vicinity of the factory will not take into account this fall in the value of production which results from their presence. This failure to take into account costs imposed on others is comparable to the action of a factory owner in not taking into account the harm resulting from his emission of smoke. Without the tax, there may be too much smoke and too few people in the vicinity of the factory; but with the tax there may be too little smoke and too many people in the vicinity of the factory. There is no reason to suppose that one of these results is necessarily preferable.

I need not devote much space to discussing the similar error involved in the suggestion that smoke-producing factories should, by means of zoning regulations, be removed from the districts in which the smoke causes harmful effects. When the change in the location of the factory results in a reduction in production, this obviously needs to be taken into account and weighed against the harm which would result from the factory remaining in that location. The aim of such regulation should not be to eliminate smoke pollution but rather to secure the optimum amount of smoke pollution, this being the amount which will maximise the values of production.

X. *A Change of Approach*

It is my belief that the failure of economists to reach correct conclusions about the treatment of harmful effects cannot be ascribed simply to a few slips in analysis. It stems from basic defects in the current approach to problems of welfare economics. What is needed is a change of approach.

Analysis in terms of divergencies between private and social products concentrates attention on particular deficiencies in the system and tends to nourish the belief that any measure which will remove the deficiency is necessarily desirable. It diverts attention from those other changes in the system which are inevitably associated with the corrective measure, changes which may well produce more harm than the original deficiency. In the preceding sections of this article, we have seen many examples of this. But it is not necessary to approach the problem in this way. Economists who study problems of the firm habitually use an opportunity cost approach and compare the receipts obtained from a given combination of factors with alternative business arrangements. It would seem desirable to use a similar approach when dealing with questions of economic policy and to compare the total product yielded by alternative social arrangements. In this article, the analysis has been confined, as is usual in this part of economics, to comparisons of the value of production, as measured by the market. But it is, of course, desirable that the choice between different social arrangements for the solution of economic problems should be carried out in broader terms than this and that the total effect of these arrangements in all spheres of life should be taken into account. As Frank H. Knight has so often emphasized, problems of welfare economics must ultimately dissolve into a study of aesthetics and morals.

A second feature of the usual treatment of the problems discussed in this article is that the analysis proceeds in terms of a comparison between a state of laissez faire and some kind of ideal world. This approach inevitably leads to a looseness of thought since the nature of the alternatives being compared is never clear. In a state of laissez faire, is there a monetary, a legal or a political system and if so, what are they? In an ideal world, would there be a monetary, a legal or a political system and if so, what would they be? The answers to all these questions are shrouded in mystery and every man is free to draw whatever conclusions he likes. Actually very little analysis is required to show that an ideal world is better than a state of laissez faire, unless the definitions of a state of laissez faire and an ideal world happen to be the same. But the whole discussion is largely irrelevant for questions of economic policy since whatever we may have in mind as our ideal world, it is clear that we have not yet discovered how to get to it from where we are. A better approach would seem to be to start our analysis with a situation approximating that which actually exists, to examine the effects of a proposed policy change and to attempt to decide whether the new situation would be, in total, better or worse than the original one. In this way, conclusions for policy would have some relevance to the actual situation.

A final reason for the failure to develop a theory adequate to handle the problem of harmful effects stems from a faulty concept of a factor of production. This is usually thought of as a physical entity which the businessman acquires and uses (an acre of land, a ton of fertiliser) instead of as a right to perform certain (physical) actions. We may speak of a person owning land and using it as a factor of production but what the land-owner in fact possesses is the right to carry out a circumscribed list of actions. The rights of a land-owner are not unlimited. It is not even always possible for him to remove the land to another place, for instance, by quarrying it. And although it may be possible for him to exclude some people from using "his" land, this may not be true of others. For example, some people may have the right to cross the land. Furthermore, it may or may not be possible to erect certain types of buildings or to grow certain crops or to use particular drainage systems on the land. This does not come about simply because of Government regulation. It would be equally true under the common law. In fact it would be true under any system of law. A system in which the rights of individuals were unlimited would be one in which there were no rights to acquire.

If factors of production are thought of as rights, it becomes easier to understand that the right to do something which has a harmful effect (such as the creation of smoke, noise, smells, etc.) is also a factor of production. Just as we may use a piece of land in such a way as to prevent someone else from crossing it, or parking his car, or building his house upon it, so we may use it in such a way as to deny him a view or quiet or unpolluted air. The cost of exercising a right (of using a factor of production) is always the loss which is suffered elsewhere in consequence of the exercise of that right—the inability to cross land, to park a car, to build a house, to enjoy a view, to have peace and quiet or to breathe clean air.

It would clearly be desirable if the only actions performed were those in which what was gained was worth more than what was lost. But in choosing between social arrangements within the context of which individual decisions are made, we have to bear in mind that a change in the existing system which will lead to an improvement in some decisions may well lead to a worsening of others. Furthermore we have to take into account the costs involved in operating the various social arrangements (whether it be the working of a market or of a government department), as well as the costs involved in moving to a new system. In devising and choosing between social arrangements we should have regard for the total effect. This, above all, is the change in approach which I am advocating.

II

The Costs of Environmental Protection

4 Environmental Regulation and the Competitiveness of U.S. Manufacturing: What Does the Evidence Tell Us?*

Adam B. Jaffe

Steven R. Peterson

Paul R. Portney

Robert N. Stavins

Adam Jaffe is Dean of Arts & Sciences and Fred C. Hecht Professor in Economics at Brandeis University; Steven Peterson is Managing Director at Lexecon, an FTI Company, Harvard Square, Cambridge; Paul Portney is President and Senior Fellow at Resources for the Future; and Robert Stavins is Albert Pratt Professor of Business and Government, John F. Kennedy School of Government at Harvard University, and University Fellow at Resources for the Future.

1. Introduction

More than two decades ago, the first Earth Day in 1970 marked the beginning of the modern environmental movement. Since that time, the United States has spent more than $1 trillion to prevent or reduce environmental damages created by industrial and commercial activities. During the latter part of this period, the U.S. economy has moved from a position of approximate trade balance on a long-term basis to a position of chronic trade deficit. The coincidence of these two major trends has led many to suspect that environmental regulation may be playing a major causal role in impairing the "competitiveness" of U.S. firms.[1]

"Environmental Regulation and the Competitiveness of U.S. Manufacturing: What Does the Evidence Tell Us?" by Adam B. Jaffe, Steven R. Peterson, Paul R. Portney, and Robert N. Stavins, from *Journal of Economic Literature*, 33:132–163 (March 1995).

*The authors thank Lawrence Goulder, Raymond Kopp, William Nordhaus, Richard Schmalensee, Martin Weitzman, David Wheeler, and participants in seminars at Harvard University and Resources for the Future for helpful comments. Funding for previous work on this subject from the U.S. Department of Commerce is gratefully acknowledged. The authors alone are responsible for any omissions or other errors.

[1]This argument is related but not identical to expressed concerns about the loss of "competitiveness" of the U.S. as a whole. For a trenchant criticism of the notion that countries "compete" in the same ways that individual firms do, see Paul Krugman (1994).

The conventional wisdom is that environmental regulations impose significant costs, slow productivity growth, and thereby hinder the ability of U.S. firms to compete in international markets. This loss of competitiveness is believed to be reflected in declining exports, increasing imports, and a long-term movement of manufacturing capacity from the United States to other countries, particularly in "pollution-intensive" industries.[2]

Under a more recent, revisionist view, environmental regulations are seen not only as benign in their impacts on international competitiveness, but actually as a net *positive* force driving private firms and the economy as a whole to become more competitive in international markets.[3] During the past few years, a heated debate has arisen in the United States revolving around these two views.[4] This paper assembles and assesses the evidence on these hypothetical linkages between environmental regulation and competitiveness.

The terms of the debate and the nature of the problems have not always been clear, but it is possible to sketch the general nature of the concerns. Much of the discussion has revolved around the fear that environmental regulation may reduce net exports in the manufacturing sector, particularly in "pollution-intensive" goods. Such a change in our trade position could have several effects. First, in the short run, a reduction in net exports in manufacturing will exacerbate the overall trade imbalance. Although we are likely to return toward trade balance in the long run, one of the mechanisms through which this happens is a decline in the value of the dollar. This means that imported goods become more expensive, thus reducing the standard of living for many people. Second, if those industries most affected by regulation employ less educated workers, then this portion of the labor force will be particularly hard hit, because those workers may have an especially hard time finding new jobs at comparable wages. Third, a diminishing U.S. share of world capacity in petroleum-refining, steel, autos, and other industries could endanger economic security. Finally, even in the absence of these income distribution or economic security concerns, the rearrangement of production from pollution-intensive to other industries creates a broader set of social costs, at least in the short run. Because the "short run" could last for years or even decades, these transition costs are also a legitimate policy concern.

---

[2]The theoretical argument that ambitious environmental regulations could harm a nation's comparative advantage is well established, but our focus is exclusively on empirical evidence. On the former, see Rudiger Pethig (1975); Horst Siebert (1977); Gary W. Yohe (1979); and Martin C. McGuire (1982).

[3]These ideas, generally associated most with Michael E. Porter (1991), have become widely disseminated among policy makers. For example, a U.S. Environmental Protection Agency (EPA) conference recently concluded that environmental regulations induce "more cost-effective processes that both reduce emissions and the overall cost of doing business . . ." (U.S. Environmental Protection Agency 1992b).

[4]For an overview of the dimensions of this debate, see Richard B. Stewart (1993). Unfortunately, this debate has often been clouded by the very criteria chosen by proponents of alternative views. For example, there has been substantial debate *and* confusion among policy makers about whether environmental regulations create new jobs and whether such "job creation" ought to be considered a regulatory benefit or cost (if either). See Thomas D. Hopkins (1992).

Table 1 U.S. Emissions of Six Major Air Pollutants, 1970–1991[a]

Year	SO_2	NO_x	VOCs	CO	TSPs	Lead
1970	100[b]	100	100	100	100	100
1975	90	107	82	85	58	72
1980	84	124	79	81	48	34
1981	79	113	77	79	45	27
1982	75	107	71	73	40	26
1983	73	104	74	75	41	22
1984	76	106	77	71	43	19
1985	76	102	72	67	41	9
1986	74	99	67	62	38	3
1987	74	100	68	61	39	3
1988	75	104	68	61	42	3
1989	76	102	63	55	40	3
1990	74	102	64	55	39	3
1991	73	99	62	50	39	2

Source: U.S. Environmental Protection Agency (1992a).
[a]The six "criteria air pollutants" listed are: sulfur dioxide (SO_2); nitrogen oxides (NO_x); reactive volatile organic compounds (VOCs); carbon monoxide (CO); total suspended particulates (TSPs); and lead.
[b]Indexed to 1970 emissions, set equal to 100. Note that these are aggregate national emissions, not emissions per capita or emissions per unit of GNP; the latter two statistics would, of course, exhibit greater downward trends.

There are a number of reasons to believe that the link between environmental regulation and competitiveness could be significant. First, environmental regulation has grown significantly in the United States since 1970, and substantial gains have been achieved in reducing pollutant emissions (Table 1).

But according to the U.S. Environmental Protection Agency (EPA), the annual cost of complying with environmental regulation administered by EPA now exceeds $125 billion in the United States, or about 2.1 percent of gross domestic product (GDP).[5] Furthermore, EPA has projected that annual environmental compliance spending may reach $190 billion by the end of this decade. If that happens, the United States will be devoting nearly 2.6 percent of its GDP to environmental compliance by the year 2000.[6]

---

[5]As we discuss later in some detail, these direct compliance costs represent only a share of the overall social costs of environmental regulation. For example, Weitzman (1994) estimates that the total "environmental drag" on the U.S. economy may be two to three times greater than these fractions of GNP dedicated to compliance spending would suggest.

[6]Figures are in constant 1992 dollars (throughout the paper, unless otherwise specified), assuming a 7 percent cost of capital (U.S. Environmental Protection Agency 1990). These estimates include both capital and operating costs. Projections for compliance costs of existing regulations are based on historical extrapolations. Projections for the costs of new and proposed regulations are based on EPA regulatory analyses. EPA actually makes its projections in terms of gross national product (GNP), rather than gross domestic product (GDP), but any difference between the two is small compared to uncertainty over compliance costs.

Table 2 Pollution Abatement and Control Expenditures for Selected OECD Countries as a Percentage of Gross Domestic Product

	1981	1982	1983	1984	1985	1986	1987	1988	1989	1990
United States	1.5	1.5	1.5	1.4	1.4	1.4	1.4	1.3	1.4	1.4
France	0.9	0.9	0.9	0.8	0.9	0.8	1.0	1.0	1.0	1.0
West Germany	1.5	1.5	1.4	1.4	1.5	1.5	1.6	1.6	1.6	1.6
Netherlands	—	1.2	—	—	1.3	1.5	1.5	—	1.5	—
United Kingdom	1.6	—	—	—	1.3	1.3	—	—	—	1.5

Sources: Organization for Economic Cooperation and Development (1990, p. 40), for years 1981–1985; Organization for Economic Cooperation and Development (1993b, p. 11) for years 1986–1990.

It is extremely difficult to compare this compliance cost burden with that borne by competing firms in other countries. Environmental requirements throughout most of the developing world are less stringent than ours, and related compliance costs are hence generally lower. On the other hand, some data suggest that other countries, such as Germany, have regulatory programs that give rise to regulatory costs roughly comparable to those imposed on U.S. firms (Table 2).[7]

Putting aside the potential effect of differences in regulatory stringency, there are other ways in which environmental regulations may affect competitiveness. Holding constant the *stringency* of environmental standards, the *form* these rules take can potentially affect business location. For instance, U.S. environmental regulations often go beyond specifying numerical discharge standards for particular sources or source categories, and mandate, instead, specific control technologies or processes. If other countries tend to avoid such technological mandates and thus allow more flexibility in compliance, manufacturing abroad may be relatively attractive because sources will have the ability to use new, innovative, and low-cost ways to meet discharge standards.

Another difference between U.S. and foreign environmental regulation should also be recognized: namely, the adversarial approach to regulation typically taken in the United States. Regulatory decisions in the United States are time-consuming and characterized by litigation and other legal wrangling. By way of contrast, a more cooperative relationship is said to exist between regulator and regulatee in some other countries, with the United Kingdom offered as the definitive example (David Vogel 1986). Un-

---

[7]It is indicative of the data problems in this area that the OECD numbers in Table 2 differ in both level *and* trend from the EPA numbers cited above and presented in Table 4. It is our view that the data in the latter table more accurately reflect annual expenditures in the United States to comply with federal environmental regulations. It would be helpful if the environmental agencies of other nations made the same effort as the U.S. Environmental Protection Agency to keep track of and regularly report estimated compliance expenditures.

fortunately, data on these aspects of respective costs are essentially unavailable.

In general, the studies that attempt to analyze directly the effects of environmental regulations on trade and competitiveness are limited in number. If one casts a wide enough net, however, by defining competitiveness rather broadly and by searching for indirect as well as direct evidence, it is possible to identify more than one hundred studies potentially capable of shedding some light on the relationship.[8] It is nearly the case, however, that no two of these studies ask the same question or even examine the same problem. This is one of the challenges of trying to assess the competing hypotheses of the environment-competitiveness linkage.

Despite our relatively broad focus with regard to competitiveness, the scope of this review is somewhat limited in another respect. Specifically, we limit our attention here to studies shedding light on the effects of environmental regulation on manufacturing firms. This is not because of an absence of such regulation in natural resource industries such as forestry, agriculture, mining, and commercial fishing. Indeed, the controversy over the Northern Spotted Owl, the Endangered Species Act in general, and the effects of habitat preservation on the location of timber production is among the most visible U.S. environmental issues of recent times. Similarly, regulations pertaining to pesticide use in agriculture, the reclamation of land mined for coal or non-fuel minerals, or the equipment that can be used by commercial fishing fleets can clearly affect the costs faced by (and hence the international competitiveness of) U.S. firms in these industries.

Rather, we concentrate our attention on manufacturing industries for two reasons. First, that is where the research has been done. With a few exceptions, economists have paid little attention to the effects of environmental regulation on competitiveness in the natural resources sector. By way of contrast, there is a substantial and growing literature focused on the manufacturing sector, as suggested above. Second, the political and policy debate has centered around the possible "flight" of manufacturing from the U.S. to other countries with less stringent environmental standards.

To some extent, this distinction is a peculiar one. To be sure, environmental restrictions on pesticide use or habitat destruction cannot induce someone to move a farm or commercial forest to another country. Such natural capital is immobile, even in the long run. But if concern about competitiveness is primarily a "jobs" issue—and, to many, at least, it is—then it is relevant that environmental regulations pertaining to natural resource industries can affect *where* crops are grown, timber is harvested, fish are caught, or minerals are mined. Nevertheless, because the overwhelming share of attention by policy makers and academics has been devoted to the competitiveness of manufacturing, we concentrate our attention there, as well.

---

[8]For a comprehensive review of the literature, see Jaffe et al. (1993). An earlier survey is provided by Judith M. Dean (1992). See, also U.S. Office of Technology Assessment (1992).

The remainder of this paper is organized as follows. Section 2 outlines an analytical framework for identifying the effects of environmental regulation on international trade in manufactured goods, discusses how different notions of competitiveness fit into that framework, and examines the major categories of environmental regulatory costs. In Section 3, we draw on the available evidence to examine the effects of environmental regulations on international trade in manufacturing. In Section 4, we turn to the empirical evidence regarding the linkage between environmental regulation and investment; and in Section 5, we look at links between regulation and more broadly defined economic growth. Finally, in Section 6, we draw some conclusions.

2. Framework for Analyzing Regulation and Competitiveness

2.1 A Theoretically Desirable Indicator of Competitiveness

The standard theory of international trade is based on the notion that trade is driven by comparative advantage—that countries export those goods and services that they make relatively (but not necessarily absolutely) more efficiently than other nations, and import those goods and services they are relatively less efficient at producing. Because of the anticipated international adjustments that occur when relative costs change, we could measure—in theory, at least—the real effects of regulation (or any other policy change, for that matter) on competitiveness by identifying the effect that the policy would have on net exports *holding real wages and exchange rates constant*.[9] We would wish to measure the reduction in net exports "before" any adjustments in the exchange rate (and hence in net exports of other goods) have taken place, because other industries whose net exports increase to balance a fall in exports should not be thought of as having become more competitive if their export increase is brought about solely by a fall in exchange rates. Similarly, we should not construe an increase in exports brought about solely by a fall in real wages as an increase in "competitiveness."

The unfortunate problem with this analytically clean definition of competitiveness is that it is essentially impossible to implement in practice. We simply are not presented with data generated by the hypothetical experiment in which regulations are imposed while everything else is held constant. In principle, one could formulate a structural econometric model in which net exports by industry, wages, and exchange rates are determined jointly as a function of regulatory costs and resource endowments. We have identified no study that has attempted to do so, and it is not clear that

---

[9]This definition is closely related to those suggested by Laura D'Andrea Tyson (1988), and Organization of Economic Cooperation and Development (1993a).

available data would support such an effort.[10] As a result, we are left with indicators of the effects on competitiveness that are not wholly satisfactory because they fail to take account of the complicated adjustment mechanisms that operate when regulations are imposed. Nevertheless, these indicators can be useful to sort through many of the policy debates regarding the environment-competitiveness linkage.

2.2 Alternative Indicators of "Competitiveness"

The indicators of "competitiveness" that are used in the existing literature can be classified into three broad categories.[11] One set of measures has to do with the change in net exports of certain goods, the production of which is heavily regulated, and with comparisons between net exports of these goods and others produced under less regulated conditions. For example, stringent environmental regulation of the steel industry should, all else equal, cause the net exports of steel to fall *relative* to the net exports of goods the production of which is more lightly regulated. Thus, the magnitude and significance of an econometric parameter estimate that captures the effect of regulatory stringency in a regression explaining changes in net exports across industries could be taken as an indicator of the strength of the effects of regulation on competitiveness.

A second potential indicator is the extent to which the locus of *production* of pollution-intensive goods has shifted from countries with stringent regulations toward those with less. After all, the policy concern about competitiveness is that the United States is losing world market share in regulated industries to countries with less stringent regulations. If this is so, then there should be a general decrease in the U.S. share of world production of highly regulated goods and an increase in the world share of production of these goods by countries with relatively light regulation.

Third, if regulation is reducing the attractiveness of the United States as a locus for investment, then there should be a relative increase in investment by U.S. firms overseas in highly regulated industries. Similarly, all else equal, new plants in these industries would be more likely to be located in jurisdictions with lax regulation.

Finally, in addition to research focusing on these aspects of competitiveness, there exists one other set of important analytical approaches that can shed light on the environment-competitiveness debate. These are analyses focused on the more fundamental link between environmental compliance costs, productivity, investment, and the ultimate social costs of regulation. These analyses, including investigations of the productivity effects of regulation as well as general-equilibrium studies of long-term, social costs of regulation, have implications for both the conventional and the revisionist hypotheses concerning environmental regulation and competitiveness.

---

[10]Later we discuss the quantity and quality of available cross-country compliance-cost data.

[11]We henceforth drop the quotation marks around our use of the term "competitiveness" for convenience of presentation.

Because the economic adjustment to regulation is highly complex, and because there are a multiplicity of issues wrapped up in the term "competitiveness," it is not possible to combine estimates of these different aspects of the process into a single, overall quantification of the effects of regulation on competitiveness.[12] The best that can be done is to assess somewhat qualitatively the magnitude of estimated effects, based on multiple indicators. We return to that assessment shortly.

2.3 A Framework for Analysis

These diverse sets of indicators reflect the various routes through which regulation can conceivably affect competitiveness. First, environmental regulations affect a firm's costs of production, both directly through its own expenditures on pollution reduction and indirectly through the higher prices it must pay for certain factors of production that are affected by regulation. Both direct and indirect costs will affect competitiveness, including measures of trade and investment flows.[13]

It is also true that environmental regulations can reduce costs for some firms or industries, by lowering input prices or by increasing the productivity of their inputs. Such "benefits to industry" could take the form, for example, of reduced costs to the food processing industry when its supplies of intake water are less polluted; likewise, workers may become more productive if health-threatening air pollution is reduced (see Bart D. Ostro 1983). Such benefits would have positive effects on U.S. trade and investment through the same mechanisms by which increased costs would have negative effects. Additionally, firms in the environmental services sector typically benefit from stricter regulations affecting their clients and/or potential clients.[14]

In any case, the degree to which domestic regulatory costs (and benefits) affect trade will depend also on the magnitude of the costs (and ben-

---

[12]Having highlighted a theoretically desirable measure and a set of empirically practical means of assessing the link between environmental protection and economic competitiveness, we should also note the multiplicity of *inappropriate* means of examining this link. Indeed, the amount of published, muddled thinking on this subject seems to exceed the norm. Numerous studies have focused exclusively on "jobs created in the environmental services sector" and taken this to be a measure of net positive economic benefits of regulation (apart from any environmental benefits). A recent example of this approach is provided by Roger H. Bezdek (1993), with numerous citations to other such studies. See Hopkins (1992) and Portney (1994) for critiques of this approach.

[13]For the economy as a whole, there is, of course, no distinction between direct and indirect costs. To measure total industry expenditures for pollution compliance, it would be incorrect to add the increased costs of the steel industry resulting from higher steel prices; to do so would result in obvious double-counting. The necessity of tracking indirect costs arises, however, when the analyst wishes to estimate the impact of regulation on a particular industry, or to compare effects on different industries. We postpone discussion of another notion of "indirect costs," including transition costs and reduced investment, which we refer to for semantic clarity as "other social costs" of regulation. See Section 5, below.

[14]There are, of course, additional benefits of environmental regulation that accrue to society at large rather than to industry. We exclude these here, not because they are unimportant, but because they do not bear on the issue of competitiveness.

Table 3 A Taxonomy of Costs of Environmental Regulation

Government Administration of Environmental
   Statutes and Regulations
      Monitoring
      Enforcement
Private Sector Compliance Expenditures
   Capital
   Operating
Other Direct Costs
   Legal and Other Transactional
   Shifted Management Focus
   Disrupted Production
Negative Costs
   Natural Resource Inputs
   Worker Health
   Innovation Stimulation
General Equilibrium Effects
   Product Substitution
   Discouraged Investment
   Retarded Innovation
Transition Costs
   Unemployment
   Obsolete Capital
Social Impacts
   Loss of Middle-Class Jobs
   Economic Security Impacts

efits) that other countries impose on the firms operating within their borders. Likewise, other nations' policies will also affect the investment decisions of their indigenous firms and of foreign firms, as well. Any changes in investment patterns that do occur ultimately affect trade flows as well, and both trade and investment effects interact with exchange rates.

2.4 Measuring the Costs of Environmental Regulation

In Table 3, we provide a taxonomy of the costs of environmental regulation, beginning with the most obvious and moving toward the least direct.[15] First, many policy makers and much of the general public would identify the on-budget costs to government of administering (monitoring and enforcing) environmental laws and regulations as *the* cost of environmental regulation. Most analysts, on the other hand, would identify the capital and operating expenditures associated with regulatory compliance as the fun-

---

[15]For a very useful decomposition and analysis of the full costs of environmental regulation, see Schmalensee, (1994). Conceptually, the cost of an environmental regulation is equal to "the change in consumer and producer surpluses associated with the regulations and with any price and/or income changes that may result" (Maureen L. Cropper and Wallace E. Oates 1992, p. 721).

damental part of the overall costs of regulation, although a substantial share of compliance costs for some federal regulations fall on state and local governments rather than private firms—the best example being the regulation of contaminants in drinking water. Additional direct costs include legal and other transaction costs, the effects of refocused management attention, and the possibility of disrupted production.

Next, one should also consider potential "negative costs" (in other words, nonenvironmental benefits) of environmental regulation, including the productivity impacts of a cleaner environment and the potential innovation-stimulating effects of regulation (linked with the so-called Porter hypothesis, which we discuss later). General equilibrium effects associated with product substitution, discouraged investment,[16] and retarded innovation constitute another important layer of costs, as do the transition costs of real-world economies responding over time to regulatory changes. Finally, there is a set of potential social impacts that is given substantial weight in political forums, including impacts on jobs and economic security.

Within the category of direct compliance costs, expenditures for pollution abatement in the United States have grown steadily over the past two decades, both absolutely and as a percentage of GNP (Table 4), reaching $125 billion (2.1 percent of GNP) by 1990. EPA estimates these costs will reach 2.6 percent of GNP by 2000.[17]

Even estimates of direct, compliance expenditures vary greatly. For example, Gary L. Rutledge and Mary L. Leonard (1992) estimate that pollution abatement costs for 1990 were $94 billion, rather than $125 billion as estimated by EPA.[18]

There are a number of potential problems of interpretation associated with these data. The questionnaire used by the U.S. Department of Commerce (1993) to collect data for its *Pollution Abatement Costs and Expenditures (PACE)* survey asks corporate or government officials how capital expenditures compared to what they would have been in the absence of environmental regulations. This creates two problems. The first involves the determination of an appropriate baseline. Absent any regulation, firms might still engage in some—perhaps a great deal of—pollution control to limit tort liability, stay on good terms with communities in which they are located, maintain a good environmental image, etc. Should such expenditures be included or excluded in the no-regulation baseline?

---

[16]For example, if a firm chooses to close a plant because of a new regulation (rather than installing expensive control equipment), this would be counted as zero cost in typical compliance-cost estimates.

[17]Recall that these estimates capture, at most, only what we have labelled private sector compliance expenditures in Table 4. As is shown in Table 5, business pollution-abatement expenditures represented about 61 percent of total *direct* costs in 1990. The remainder consisted of: personal consumption abatement (11%); government abatement (23%); government regulation and monitoring (2%); and research and development (3%).

[18]The primary difference between the estimates is due to the fact that EPA includes the cost of all solid waste disposal, while Rutledge and M. L. Leonard exclude some of these costs. See, also: Rutledge and Leonard 1993. The EPA data, however, exclude a significant portion of other expenditures mandated at the state and local level.

Table 4 Total Costs of Pollution Control[a] (millions of 1992 dollars)

	1972	1973	1974	1975	1976	1977	1978	1979	1980	1981	1982
Total Air & Radiation	9,915	11,995	12,725	13,942	15,854	18,071	19,993	21,413	22,313	22,992	23,550
Total Water	12,387	14,352	16,795	18,940	21,769	24,234	26,342	28,707	30,925	33,149	34,832
Total Land	10,543	11,120	11,683	12,235	12,984	14,160	14,897	16,223	17,011	17,660	16,502
Total Chemicals	115	179	229	226	436	510	729	1,066	1,111	989	890
Multi-Media	135	174	576	734	911	1,149	1,129	1,107	1,085	869	757
Total Costs	33,094	37,818	42,009	46,043	51,954	58,124	63,089	68,156	72,446	75,658	76,530
Percentage of GNP	0.88	0.96	1.07	1.19	1.28	1.37	1.41	1.49	1.58	1.62	1.68

	1983	1984	1985	1986	1987	1988	1989	1990	1991	1992	2000
Total Air & Radiation	25,970	27,899	31,885	31,782	33,751	34,482	35,326	35,029	36,852	37,763	46,859
Total Water	37,199	39,099	41,418	44,197	46,904	48,104	50,317	52,604	55,114	57,277	72,705
Total Land	17,034	18,711	19,881	21,884	23,860	25,392	28,760	33,177	37,184	41,186	57,673
Total Chemicals	762	856	966	1,027	1,024	1,137	1,531	1,973	2,356	2,662	3,614
Multi-Media	865	821	859	1,147	1,052	1,475	1,853	2,003	2,493	2,486	2,872
Total Costs	81,829	87,388	92,507	100,037	106,590	110,590	117,826	124,787	133,999	141,375	184,842
Percentage of GNP	1.74	1.74	1.78	1.87	1.92	1.91	1.98	2.13	2.24	2.32	2.61

Source: U.S. Environmental Protection Agency (1990, pp. 8-20 to 8-21).
[a]Assuming present implementation annualized at 7 percent.

Table 5 Expenditures for Pollution Abatement and Control by Section[a] (millions of 1992 dollars)

Sector	1981	1982	1983	1984	1985	1986	1987	1988	1989	1990
Personal Consumption Abatement	10,278	10,307	12,119	13,270	14,254	15,349	13,159	14,316	12,278	10,485
Business Abatement	48,969	45,726	46,031	49,825	51,314	52,994	53,846	55,615	57,784	60,122
Government Abatement	16,446	15,912	15,504	16,760	17,684	18,974	20,727	20,559	21,560	23,122
Regulation & Monitoring	2,190	2,068	1,946	1,823	1,647	1,923	1,838	1,988	2,005	1,980
Research & Development	2,626	2,484	3,115	2,998	3,107	3,186	3,204	3,216	3,303	3,303
Total	80,509	76,495	78,713	84,677	87,914	92,425	92,773	95,694	96,928	99,024

Source: Rutledge and Leonard (1992), pp. 35–38.
[a]Excludes expenditures for solid waste collection and disposal; excludes agricultural production except feedlot operations.

Second, when additional capital expenditures are made for end-of-the-pipe abatement equipment, respondents have relatively little difficulty in calculating these expenditures. But when new capital equipment is installed, which has the effect of both reducing emissions and improving the final product or enhancing the efficiency with which it is produced, it is far more difficult to calculate how much of the expenditures are attributable to environmental standards. Furthermore, it is not always clear whether a regulation is an "environmental regulation." The *PACE* data do not include expenditures for worker health and safety (U.S. Department of Commerce 1993, p. A4), but some expenditures for health and safety essentially control the working environment. Determining precisely which regulatory costs should be included in the costs of environmental regulations is ultimately somewhat arbitrary.[19]

The most striking feature of either annual capital or annual total expenditures for pollution abatement is the degree of variation across industries.[20] For all manufacturing industries combined, 7.5 percent of new capital expenditures in 1991 were for pollution control equipment, and gross annual operating costs for pollution control were 0.62 percent of the total value of shipments. For the highest abatement-cost industries, however, the costs of complying with environmental regulations were dramatically higher (Table 6).

In particular, for the chemicals, petroleum, pulp and paper, and primary metals industries, new capital expenditures for pollution abatement

---

[19]For a detailed discussion of environmental compliance cost measurement problems, see U.S. Congressional Budget Office (1985).

[20]Gross annual costs for pollution abatement are equal to the sum of operating costs attributable to pollution abatement and payments to the government for sewage services and solid waste collection and disposal.

Table 6 Pollution Abatement Expenditures for Selected Industries, 1991 (Monetary amounts are in millions of 1992 dollars.)

Industry	Total Capital Expenditures	Pollution Abatement Cap. Exp. (PACE)	PACE as Percentage of Total Cap. Exp.	Total Value of Shipments	Abatement Gross Annual Cost (GAC)	GAC as Percentage of Value of Shipments
All Industries	$101,773	$7,603	7.47%	$2,907,848	$17,888	0.62%
Industries with High Abatement Costs						
Paper and Allied Products	$9,269	$1,269	13.68%	$132,545	$1,682	1.27%
Chemical and Allied Products	$16,471	$2,126	12.91%	$300,770	$4,164	1.38%
Petroleum and Coal Products	$6,066	$1,505	24.81%	$162,642	$2,931	1.80%
Primary Metal Industries	$6,049	$692	11.45%	$136,674	$2,061	1.51%
Industries with Moderate Abatement Costs						
Furniture and Fixtures	$750	$25	3.29%	$41,183	$140	0.34%
Fabricated Metal Products	$4,190	$182	4.35%	$161,614	$867	0.54%
Electric, Electronic Equipment	$8,356	$241	2.88%	$203,596	$857	0.42%
Industries with Low Abatement Costs						
Printing and Publishing	$5,187	$38	0.73%	$161,211	$235	0.15%
Rubber, Misc. Plastics Products	$4,337	$84	1.95%	$103,576	$454	0.44%
Machinery, except Electrical	$7,546	$132	1.75%	$250,512	$591	0.24%

Source: U.S. Department of Commerce (1993), pp. 12–13.

range from 11 to 25 percent of overall capital expenditures, and annual abatement (operating) costs ranged from 1.3 to 1.8 percent of the total value of shipments.

3. Environmental Regulations and International Trade

3.1 Effects of Regulation on Net Exports

Natural resource endowments have been a particularly important determinant of trading patterns (see, for example, Edward E. Leamer 1984). Having recognized this, we note that when a firm pollutes, it is essentially using a natural resource (a clean environment), and when a firm is compelled or otherwise induced to reduce its pollutant emissions, that firm has, in effect, seen its access to an important natural resource reduced. Industries that lose the right to pollute freely may thus lose their comparative advantage, just as the copper industry in developed countries lost its comparative advantage as copper resources dwindled in those regions. The result is a fall in exports.

This suggests an analytical approach to investigating the environmental protection-competitiveness connection. The primary difficulty in implementing this approach, however, is the limited availability of data on environmental regulatory compliance expenditures, particularly for foreign (and especially for developing) countries. Because such comparative data are generally unavailable, we must rely instead on studies that either examine the effect of environmental controls on U.S. net exports (without considering more general trading patterns) or those that examine international trading patterns (but rely on qualitative measures of environmental control costs in different countries).

First, we can ask whether (all else equal) net exports have been systematically lower in U.S. industries subject to relatively stringent environmental regulations. The evidence pertaining to this question is not conclusive (Table 7). Employing a Heckscher-Ohlin model of international trade, Joseph P. Kalt (1988) regressed changes in net exports between the years 1967 and 1977 across 78 industrial categories on changes in environmental compliance costs and other relevant variables, and found a statistically insignificant inverse relationship. On the other hand, when the sample was restricted to manufacturing industries, the predicted negative effect of compliance costs on net exports became significant. It is troubling, however, that the magnitude and significance of the effect was increased even further when the chemical industry was excluded from the sample, because this is an industry with relatively high environmental compliance costs (Table 6).[21]

Gene M. Grossman and Alan B. Krueger (1993) found that pollution abatement costs in industries in the United States have apparently not af-

---

[21]The explanation appears to be the relatively strong net export performance of the chemical industry (at the same time that it was heavily regulated).

Table 7 Effects of Environmental Regulations on Net Exports

Study	Time Period of Analysis	Industrial Scope	Geographic Scope	Results[a]
Grossman and Krueger 1993	1987	Manufacturing	U.S.-Mexico Trade	Insignificant
Kalt 1988	1967–1977	78 industry categories	U.S. Trade	Insignificant
		Manufacturing		Significant
		Manufacturing w/o Chemicals		More Significant
Tobey 1990	1977	Mining, Paper, Chemicals, Steel, Metals	23 Nations	Insignificant

[a]See the text for descriptions of the results of each study.

fected imports from Mexico or activity in the maquiladora sector[22] along the U.S.-Mexico border.[23] Using 1987 data across industry categories and three different measures of economic impacts—total U.S. imports from Mexico, imports under the offshore assembly provisions of the U.S. tariff codes, and the sectoral pattern of maquiladora activity—they examined possible statistical relationships with: industry factor intensities, tariff rates, and the ratio of pollution abatement costs to total value-added in respective U.S. industries. With all three performance measures, they found that "traditional determinants of trade and investment patterns"—in particular, labor intensity—were very significant, but that cross-industry differences in environmental costs were both quantitatively small and statistically insignificant.[24] Given the physical proximity of Mexico, the large volume of trade between the two countries, and the historically significant differences between Mexican and U.S. environmental laws, these findings cast doubt on the hypothesis that environmental regulations have significant adverse effects on net exports.

---

[22]The maquiladora program was established by Mexico in the 1960s to attract foreign investment. Under the program, qualified firms are exempt from national laws that require majority Mexican ownership and prohibit foreign ownership of border and coastline property. Also inputs for production processes can be imported duty-free, as long as 80 percent of the output is re-exported. For further discussion of the maquiladoras sector in the context of the environmental protection–competitiveness debate, see Robert K. Kaufmann, Peter Pauly, and Julie Sweitzer (1993).

[23]As Grossman and Krueger (1993) point out, however, there is evidence from one government survey suggesting that a number of U.S. furniture manufacturers relocated their California factories across the Mexican border as a result of increases in the stringency of California state air pollution standards affecting paints and solvents (U.S. General Accounting Office 1991).

[24]As we discuss later, this result is consistent with something else the data reveal—international differences in environmental costs (as a fraction of total production costs) are trivial compared with apparent differences in labor costs and productivity.

Finally, environmental regulations in other nations are, of course, also important in determining trade patterns, but here the available evidence again indicates that the relative stringency of environmental regulations in different countries has had no effect on net exports (James A. Tobey 1990). Using a qualitative measure of the stringency of national environmental policies (Ingo Walter and J. Ugelow 1979), Tobey applied what is otherwise a straightforward Hecksher-Ohlin framework to test empirically for the sources of international comparative advantage. In an examination of five pollution-intensive industries—mining, paper, chemicals, steel, and metals—Tobey found that environmental stringency was in no case a statistically significant determinant of net exports. The results could theoretically be due to no more than the failure of the ordinal measure of environmental stringency to be correlated with true environmental control costs,[25] but Tobey's results are essentially consistent with those from other, previous analyses that employed direct cost measures (Walter 1982; Charles S. Pearson 1987; and H. Jeffrey Leonard 1988).

3.2 International Trade in Pollution-Intensive Goods

We can also search for evidence on the impact of environmental regulations on international competitiveness by examining temporal shifts in the overall pattern of trade in pollution-intensive goods.[26] Defining such goods as those produced by industries that incur the highest levels of pollution abatement and control expenditures in the United States, shifts in trade flows can be examined to determine whether a growing proportion of these products in world trade originate in developing countries, where regulatory standards are often (but not always) relatively lax (Patrick Low and Alexander Yeats 1992). The results for the period 1965–1988 show that: (i) the share of pollution-intensive products in total world trade fell from 19 to 16 percent; (ii) the share of pollution-intensive products in world trade originating in North America fell from 21 to 14 percent;[27] (iii) the share of pollution-intensive products originating in Southeast Asia rose from 3.4 to 8.4 percent; and (iv) developing countries gained a comparative advantage in pollution-intensive products at a greater rate than developed countries.[28]

---

[25]For example, a nation might have strict regulations but not enforce them.

[26]Unfortunately, a major constraint faced by any such analysis is a lack of sufficient data on environmental costs and regulations in foreign countries to permit a direct link to be established between observed changes in trade flows and differences in environmental regulations across various countries. Not only are data on environmental regulations sparse, but a further difficulty is separating the impact of environmental costs on trade from shifts in natural resource advantages or other factor endowments, such as labor costs.

[27]This result is consistent with a parallel finding by Kalt (1988) that in 1967 U.S. exports were more pollution-intensive than its imports while the opposite was true by 1977.

[28]These results are consistent with the findings of Robert E. B. Lucas, Wheeler, and Hemamala Hettige (1992), who also found evidence that pollution-intensive industries had migrated from the United States to developing countries, in a study of 15,000 plants (from Census Bureau data) for the period, 1986–1987.

These results may be less meaningful than they may seem at first glance. First of all, Low and Yeats found that industrialized countries accounted for the lion's share of the world's exports of pollution-intensive goods from 1965 to 1988, contradicting the notion that pollution-intensive industries have fled to developing countries. Second, to the extent pollution-intensive industries *have* moved from industrialized to industrializing countries, this may be due simply to increased demand within the latter for the products of pollution-intensive industries. Third, natural resource endowments may partly or largely explain the pattern of pollution-intensive exports.[29]

In general, it would be preferable to examine individual nations' production of pollution-intensive goods relative to world production rather than their share of world trade or the proportion of their exports that are pollution intensive. This is because as world demand grows for pollution-intensive goods, production facilities will be built in new locations close to sources of product demand, and trade in these goods may shrink. A declining volume of world trade in such goods would result in a drop in U.S. exports, even if the United States maintained its *share* of such trade. The drop in overall trade could indicate that other countries were developing expertise in making these goods for domestic consumption, and that the U.S. competitive advantage was shrinking.

The evidence that developing countries are more likely to gain a comparative advantage in the production of pollution-intensive goods than in clean ones[30] is consistent with the change in U.S. trading patterns identified by H. David Robison (1988; see also Ralph D'Arge 1974 and Organization for Economic Cooperation and Development 1985). He found that the abatement content of U.S. imports[31] has risen more rapidly than the abatement content of exports as U.S. environmental standards have grown relatively more stringent than those in the rest of the world. However, the U.S.-Canadian trade pattern has not shifted in this way, presumably because of the similarity of Canadian and U.S. environmental standards and costs. While this result suggests that U.S. environmental regulations have had an affect on trading patterns, Robison's model indicates that, relative to domestic consumption, the effects of increased abatement costs of U.S. trade are quite small, even when no mitigating general equilibrium effects are taken into account.

Observed changes in international trading patterns over the past thirty years thus indicate that pollution-intensive industries have migrated, but

---

[29]The data suggest that countries that export a high proportion of pollution-intensive goods may do so because their natural resource base makes them efficient producers of particular pollution-intensive products. Finland exports paper products, while Venezuela and Saudi Arabia export refined petroleum products.

[30]This result is based primarily on an analysis of one industry, iron and steel pipes and tubes (Low and Yeats 1992).

[31]The abatement content of imported goods is the cost of abatement that would be embodied in those goods had they been produced in the United States.

Table 8 Effects of Environmental Regulations on Trade Patterns in Abatement-Intensive Goods

Study	Time Period of Analysis	Industrial Scope	Geographic Scope	Results[a]
Low and Yeats 1992	1965–1988	"Dirty" industries[b]	World Trade	Generally consistent with migration of dirty industries
Robison 1988	1973–1982	78 industry categories	U.S. Trade	Increased U.S. imports of relatively abatement-intensive goods
			Canadian Trade	No change in relative abatement-intensity of trade

[a]See the text for descriptions of the results of each study.
[b]Dirty industries are those incurring the highest level of abatement expenditure in the U.S.

the observed changes are small in the overall context of economic development (Table 8). Furthermore, it is by no means clear that the changes in trade patterns were caused by increasingly strict environmental regulations in developed countries. The observed changes in international trading patterns are consistent with the general process of development in the Third World. As countries develop, manufacturing accounts for a larger portion of their economic activity.

4. Environmental Regulations and Investment

The spatial pattern of economic activity is party a function of resource endowments and the location of markets; but, to some degree, it is also an accident of history. Although firms may locate where production costs are low and market access is good, there are benefits to firms that locate where other firms have previously located (in terms of existing infrastructure, a trained work force, potential suppliers, and potential benefits from specialization).[32] Under this latter view, productivity and competitiveness arise, at least in part, from the existence of a large industrial base; the ability to attract capital is also an important determinant of competitiveness.

In any case, the choice of a new plant location is obviously a complex one. When choosing between domestic and foreign locations, firms con-

---

[32]See Wheeler and Ashoka Mody (1992) for a brief discussion of these issues in the context of the effects of regulation. For a more general discussion of agglomeration effects, see Krugman (1991).

sider the market the plant will serve, the quality of the work force available, the risks associated with exchange rate fluctuations, the political stability of foreign governments, and the available infrastructure, among other factors. Hence, isolating the effect of environmental regulations on the decision will inevitably be difficult. Two sources of evidence can be used to investigate the sensitivity of firms' investment patterns to environmental regulations: changes in direct foreign investment and siting decisions for domestic plants.

4.1 Direct Foreign Investment

Although there has been little focus on the direct effects of environmental regulations on foreign investment decisions,[33] the results from more general studies can be informative. Wheeler and Mody (1992) found that multinational firms appear to base their foreign investment decisions primarily upon such things as labor costs and access to markets, as well as upon the presence of a developed industrial base. On the other hand, corporate tax rates appear to have little or no appreciable effect on these investment decisions. To the extent that environmental regulations impose direct costs similar to those associated with taxes, one could infer that concerns about environmental regulations will be dominated by the same factors that dominate concerns about taxes in these investment decisions.[34]

General trends in direct investment abroad (DIA) can also provide insights into the likely effects of environmental regulations. If environmental regulations cause industrial flight from developed countries, then direct foreign investment by pollution-intensive industries should increase over time, particularly in developing nations. In fact, from 1973 to 1985, overall direct foreign investment by the U.S. chemical and mineral industries *did* increase at a slightly greater rate than that for all manufacturing industries.[35] Over the same period, however, there was an increase in the proportion of DIA made by all manufacturing industries in developing countries, while the proportion of DIA made by the chemicals industry in developing countries actually fell.[36]

---

[33]There is abundant anecdotal evidence in the press and at least one survey of 1,000 North American and Western European corporations regarding their attitudes toward investing in Eastern and Central Europe (Anthony Zamparutti and Jon Klavens 1993).

[34]Wheeler and Mody (1992) included a composite variable in their analysis designed to measure the effects of a variety of risks associated with various countries. One of the ten components of this composite variable reflects the bureaucratic "hassle" associated with doing business in the countries examined. If this variable had been entered separately, the analysis might have shed more light on the nonpecuniary effects of regulation on location decisions.

[35]Direct investment abroad (DIA) made by the chemical and mineral industries as a proportion of DIA by all manufacturing industries increased from 25.7 percent to 26.5 percent between 1973 and 1985 (H. J. Leonard 1988). Of course, this statistic may simply indicate that markets for these products were growing in developing countries.

[36]The proportion of DIA made by mineral processing industries in developing countries increased from 22.8 to 24.4 percent between 1973 and 1985. This shift could have been caused by changes in comparative advantage due to natural resource endowments (Leonard 1988).

Information is also available on the capital expenditures of (majority-owned) foreign affiliates of U.S. firms. The evidence indicates that those affiliates in pollution intensive industries, such as chemicals, did not undertake capital expenditures at a rate greater than manufacturing industries in general. Majority-owned affiliates in pollution-intensive industries in developing countries, however, did increase their capital expenditures at a slightly greater rate than did all manufacturing industries (H. J. Leonard 1988).[37] Overall, the evidence of industrial flight to developing countries is weak, at best.[38]

4.2 Domestic Plant Location

As suggested above, data on required pollution-control expenditures in foreign countries are insufficient to permit plant-level analyses of the effects of environmental regulations on international siting of plants. Nevertheless, such analyses have been conducted for plant location decisions in the United States in an effort to link such decisions to environmental regulatory factors. Despite the fact that new environmental regulations typically will not cause firms to relocate *existing* plants (due to significant relocation costs), firms have more flexibility in making decisions about the siting of new plants. Indeed, some environmental regulations are particularly targeted at new plants—so-called, "new source performance standards."

There appears to be widespread belief that environmental regulations have a significant effect on the siting of new plants in the United States. The public comments and private actions of legislators and lobbyists, for example, certainly indicate that they believe that environmental regulations affect plant location choices. Indeed, there is evidence that the 1970 Clean Air Act and the 1977 Clean Water Act Amendments were designed in part to limit the ability of states to compete for businesses through lax enforcement of environmental standards (Portney 1990). The House Committee Report on the 1970 Clean Air Act amendments claims that "the promulgation of Federal emission standards for new sources . . . will preclude efforts on the part of States to compete with each other in trying to attract

---

[37]A preliminary study by Charles D. Kolstad and Yuqing Xing (1994) has examined the relationship between the laxity of various countries' environmental regulations and the level of investment by the U.S. chemical industry in those nations. The authors used two proxies for the laxity of environmental regulation: emissions of sulphur dioxide (SO_2) per dollar of GDP, and the growth rate of SO_2 emissions. They found that both measures were positively and significantly related to the amount of inbound direct investment by the chemical industry, and they interpreted this as evidence that strict regulation discourages investment. It seems equally likely, however, that these empirical results are due to omitted variables or causality running in the opposite direction, from investment to pollution.

[38]It has been suggested in the popular press that multinational companies install pollution control equipment in their foreign plants for a variety of reasons—including public relations and stockholders demands—even where and when not required by local laws and regulations (see, for example, "The Supply Police," *Newsweek*, Feb. 15, 1993, pp. 48–49). If true, this could help explain why investment patterns have been relatively unaffected by regulatory stringency.

new plants and facilities without assuming adequate control of large scale emissions therefrom" (U.S. Congress 1979). Likewise, environmental standards became a major obstacle to ratification of the North American Free Trade Agreement (NAFTA) in 1993, largely because of concerns that U.S. companies would move to Mexico to take advantage of relatively lax environmental standards there.

The evidence from U.S. studies suggests that these concerns may not be well founded. Timothy J. Bartik (1985) examined business location decisions as influenced by a variety of factors. While he did not take the stringency of states' environmental regulations into account, his findings are helpful in identifying factors that can affect business location decisions. First, Bartik found that both state taxes and public services are important determinants of location choice;[39] second, he found that unionization of a state's labor force has a strongly negative effect on the likelihood that firms will locate new plants within a given state. Third, he found that the existing level of manufacturing activity in a state seems to have a positive effect on the decision to locate a new plant, consistent with other findings in the international context (Low and Yeats 1992).

While these results indicate that firms are sensitive, in general, to cost variations among states when deciding where to locate new facilities, there is little direct evidence of a relationship between stringency of environmental regulations and plant location choices (although the fact that state taxes were significant could be taken to infer that environmental regulations ought to be significant as well).[40] In a more recent analysis that included measures of environmental stringency, Bartik (1988) found that state government air and water pollution control expenditures, average costs of compliance, and allowed particulate emissions all had small[41] and insignificant effects on plant location decisions.[42] In a subsequent analysis, Bartik (1989) detected a significant, negative impact of state-level environmental regulations on the start-up rate of small businesses, but the effect was substantively small.[43] These results are essentially consistent with those of Arik Levinson (1992), who found that large differences in the stringency of environmental regulations among states had no effect on the locations of most new plants; but the locations of new branch plants of large

---

[39]The effect of state taxes was statistically significant, but not particularly large in Bartik's (1985) analysis. A 10 percent increase in the corporate tax rate (from 5 to 5.5%, for example) will cause a 2 to 3 percent decline in the number of new plants.

[40]In any event, the magnitude of the two effects could be dramatically different, because state taxes may impose a burden that is large relative to the monetary-equivalent regulatory burden.

[41]In the case of highly polluting industries, Bartik (1988) could not reject the possibility of a substantively large effect of environmental regulation, although the estimated effect was statistically not significant.

[42]State spending on pollution control is meant to be a proxy for the likelihood that a plant will face inspection. Bartik experimented with a variety of variables and specifications, and the general results were quite robust to these changes.

[43]A change of one standard deviation in the environmental stringency variable—the Conservation Foundation's rating of state environmental laws and regulations (from Christopher Duerksen 1983)—yielded a 0.01 standard deviation change in the state start-up rate of small businesses.

Table 9 Effects of Environmental Regulations on Domestic Plant Location Decisions

Study	Time Period of Analysis	Industrial Scope	Results[a]
Bartik 1988	1972–1978	Manufacturing branch plants of Fortune 500 companies	No significant effects[b]
Bartik 1989	1976–1982	New small businesses in 19 manufacturing industries	Significant but small effects[c]
Friedman, Gerlowski, and Silberman 1992	1977–1988	Foreign multinational corporations	No significant effects[d]
Levinson 1992	1982–1987	U.S. manufacturing	No significant effects[e]
McConnell and Schwab 1990	1973, 1975, 1979, 1982	Motor-vehicle assembly plants (SIC 3711)	Most insignificant effects[f]

[a]See the text for descriptions of the results of each study.
[b]In a previous study, Bartik (1985) found significant impacts of state corporate tax rates, suggesting that differences in the costs of doing business matter.
[c]A one standard deviation change in environmental stringency yielded a 0.01 standard deviation change in the start-up rate of small businesses.
[d]An exception is that when the sample was restricted to new branch plants built by Japanese firms alone, the environmental variable was both negative and significant.
[e]Although the results are insignificant when the entire sample is considered, state-level environmental regulations exhibit significant effects when the sample is restricted to firms in the most pollution-intensive industries (chemicals, plastics, and electronics).
[f]The insignificance of regional differences in environmental regulation held across a substantial number of alternative measures of environmental regulatory stringency. They found significant effects in the case of countries that were exceptionally far out of compliance with air quality standards.

multi-plant companies in pollution-intensive industries were found to be somewhat sensitive to differences in pollution regulations.[44]

In another plant-location study, Virginia D. McConnell and Robert M. Schwab (1990) found no significant effects of regional differences in environmental regulation on the choice of location of automobile industry branch plants.[45] This finding held across a variety of alternative measures of environmental stringency. Finally, Joseph Friedman, Daniel A. Gerlowski, and Jonathan Silberman (1992) analyzed the determinants of new manufacturing branch plant location in the United States by foreign multi-

---

[44]In work in progress, Wayne B. Gray (1993) uses data from six Censuses of Manufacturing between 1963 and 1987 to examine how the births and deaths of plants are related to a set of state characteristics, including: factor prices, population density, unionization, taxes, education, and various measures of environmental regulation, such as enforcement activity by state and federal regulators, pollution abatement costs, and indices of state-level environmental policy stringency. In this preliminary work, Gray finds significant effects for two of his measures of regulatory stringency—air pollution enforcement and state-level laws—but the respective parameters have opposite signs.

[45]An exception was found in the case of counties that were exceptionally far out of compliance with air quality standards.

national corporations. Among the independent variables they used to explain location choice was a measure of regulatory intensity—the ratio of pollution abatement capital expenditures in a state to the gross product in the state originating in manufacturing. When the investment decisions of all foreign companies were considered together, the measure of environmental stringency—while negative—did not exert a statistically significant effect on new plant investment (Table 9).[46]

5. Environmental Regulations and Economic Growth

The evidence reviewed above does not provide much support for the proposition that environmental regulation has significant adverse effects on competitiveness. This can be placed in perspective by scrutinizing what may be more fundamental, though possibly less direct, evidence related to the overall social costs of environmental regulation.[47]

5.1 Productivity Effects

If firms are operating efficiently before environmental regulations are imposed, new regulations will theoretically cause firms to use more resources in the production process. We can posit five ways in which environmental regulations could negatively affect productivity (see Robert H. Haveman and Gregory B. Christiansen 1981; Robert W. Crandall 1981; and U.S. Office of Technology Assessment 1994). First, by definition, the *measured* productivity of the affected industry will fall because measured inputs of capital, labor, and energy are being diverted to the production of an additional output—environmental quality—that is not included in conventional measures of output and hence productivity (Robert Repetto 1990; Robert M. Solow 1992). Second, when and if firms undertake process or management changes in response to environmental regulations, the new practices may be less efficient than old ones (although, as we discuss below, there are those who suggest that this factor operates in the opposite direction, i.e., regulation-induced process and management shake-ups may increase productive efficiency). Third, environmental investments could conceivably

---

[46]When the sample was restricted to new branch plants built by Japanese firms alone, however, the environmental variable was both negative and significant. In other words, ceteris paribus, states with more stringent regulation were less likely to attract new Japanese-owned branch plants in manufacturing.

[47]One way to gain a perspective on this issue is to ask: Are environmental regulations more costly to a society with an open economy or one with a closed economy? On the simplest possible level, the existence of trade *reduces* the social cost of regulation. Rather than invest in pollution control equipment for its pollution-intensive industries, a country might specialize in the production of cleaner goods and stop producing pollution-intensive goods, choosing to import these goods rather than produce them domestically. Essentially, a country open to international trade has available a means of cleaning up its environment that is not available to countries closed to trade.

crowd out other investments by firms.[48] Fourth, many environmental regulations exempt older plants from requirements, in effect mandating higher standards for new plants. This "new-source bias" can be particularly harmful by discouraging investment in new, more efficient facilities. Fifth, requirements that firms use the "best available control technology" for pollution abatement may increase the adoption of these new technologies *at the time* regulations go into effect, but subsequently blunt firms' incentives to develop new pollution control or prevention approaches over time. This is because their emission standard may be tightened each time the firm innovates with a cost-saving approach.

Empirical analyses of these productivity effects have found modest adverse impacts on environmental regulation. A number of studies focused on the 1970s, a period of productivity decline in the United States (Table 10), attempting to determine what portion of the decline in productivity growth rates could be attributed to increased regulatory costs. When the scope of the analysis is most or all manufacturing sectors, the estimates of the fraction of the decline in the total factor productivity growth rate due to environmental regulations range from 8 percent to 16 percent (Edward Denison 1979; Gray 1987; Haveman and Christiansen 1981;[49] and J. R. Norsworthy, Michael J. Harper, and Kent Kunze 1979). Thus, regulation cannot be considered the primary cause of the productivity slowdown. There is, however, substantial variation by industrial sector: 10 percent for the chemical industry; 30 percent for paper producers (Anthony J. Barbera and McConnell 1990); and 44 percent for electric utilities (Frank M. Gallop and Mark J. Roberts 1983).

Gray and Shadbegian (1993) merged plant-level input and output data from the Census and Survey of Manufactures with plant-level data from the PACE surveys. They estimated equations for productivity at the plant level as a function of pollution control expenditures. If the only effect of pollution control expenditures on productivity were that they do not contribute to measured output, then their coefficient in such a regression ought to be minus one, because, holding inputs (including pollution control expenditures) constant, there ought to be $1 less output for every $1 diverted to pollution control. They found, however, that output fell by $3–$4 for every dollar of PACE spending, suggesting extremely large adverse productivity effects. In subsequent work (Gray and Shadbegian 1994), however, the same authors showed that these results were extremely sensitive to econometric specification, and that the large negative effects in the first paper were largely an artifact of measurement error in output.[50] In a spec-

---

[48]The empirical evidence here is mixed. Adam Rose (1983) finds that pollution-control investments reduce other investments by firms, but on less than a one-for-one basis; Gray and Ronald J. Shadbegian (1993) actually found a positive correlation of environmental investments and "productive investments" for some sectors, such as pulp and paper mills.

[49]Haveman and Christiansen (1981) examine the contribution of environmental regulation to the observed decline in labor productivity, not total factor productivity.

[50]The specification in Gray and Shadbegian (1993) is to regress productivity levels (the ratio of value-added to a weighted average of inputs) on the ratio of PACE expenditures to value-added. If value-added is measured with error, this introduces a downward bias in the coefficient on the PACE/Value-added ratio.

Table 10 Effects of Environmental Regulations on Total Factor Productivity Decline[a]

Study	Time Period of Analysis	Industrial Scope	Results[b] Percentage Share Due to Environmental Regulation
Barbera and McConnell 1990	1970–1980	Chemicals; Stone, Clay, and Glass; Iron and Steel	10%–12%
Barbera and McConnell 1990	1970–1980	Paper	30%
Denison 1979	1972–1975	Business sector	16%
Gallop and Roberts 1983	1973–1979	Electric utilities	44%
Gray 1987	1973–1978	240 manufacturing sectors	12%
Haveman and Christainsen 1981	1973–1975	Manufacturing	8%–12%
Norsworthy, Harper, and Kunze 1979	1973–1978	Manufacturing	12%[c]

[a]Based upon Table A-1 in U.S. Office of Technology Assessment 1994.
[b]See the text for descriptions of the results of each study.
[c]Share of labor productivity decline due to environmental regulation.

ification that is robust to the measurement error problem, they found that the coefficient on PACE expenditures fell to about 1.5 in pooled time-series/cross section regressions, and was not significantly greater than one in fixed-effect regressions. Thus, there remains some evidence of a productivity penalty, but it has to be regarded as weak because the pooled regression is likely to be subject to spurious negative correlation between productivity levels and pollution control expenditures.[51]

Any discussion of the productivity impacts of environmental protection efforts should recognize that not all environmental regulations are created equal in terms of their costs or their benefits.[52] So-called market-based or economic-incentive regulations, such as those based on tradeable permits or pollution charges, will tend to be more cost-effective than regulations requiring technological adoption or establishing conventional performance standards. This is because under the market-based regulatory regime, firms are likely to abate up to the point they find it profitable, and firms that find it cheapest to reduce their levels of pollution will clean up the most. With

---

[51]If some plants are generally inefficient relative to others, then it would not be surprising if they had both higher control costs and lower productivity, even if there were no causal relationship between the two.

[52]Stewart (1993) attributes observed differences in the productivity effects of environmental regulations in the U.S., Canada, and Japan (U.S. Congressional Budget Office 1985) to differences in legal and administrative systems, although he notes that the CBO study did not attempt to control for regulatory stringency.

such incentive-based regulatory systems, regulators can thus achieve a given level of pollution control more cheaply than by imposing fixed technological or performance standards on firms (Robert W. Hahn and Stavins 1991). Furthermore, market-based environmental policy instruments provide ongoing incentives for firms to adopt new and better technologies and processes, because under these systems, it always pays to clean up more if a sufficiently cheap way of doing so can be identified and adopted.[53]

5.2 General Equilibrium Effects

To quantify the overall, long-run social costs of regulation (where costs are measured by the compensation required to leave individuals as well off after a regulation as before—ignoring environmental benefits), a general equilibrium perspective is essential, in order to incorporate interindustry interactions and cumulative effects of changes in investment levels. In general, the overall social costs of environmental regulation will exceed direct compliance costs because regulations can cause reductions in output, inhibit investments in productive capital, reduce productivity, and bring about transitional costs (Schmalensee 1994).

Michael Hazilla and Kopp (1990) compared projected costs for compliance with the Clean Air and Clean Water Acts, with and without allowing for general equilibrium adjustments in labor input and investment by industry. They found that the annual social costs allowing for general equilibrium adjustments were smaller than projected pollution control expenditures in early years, but eventually came to exceed greatly the partial equilibrium projection (because of reductions in investment and labor supply).

Dale W. Jorgenson and Peter J. Wilcoxen (1990) used a model with 35 industry sectors (including government enterprises), a representative consumer, and an exogenous current account balance. Each sector's demand for inputs responds to prices according to econometrically estimated demand functions. There is a single malleable capital good, whose quantity is based on past investment and whose service price is determined endogenously. Investment is determined by the consumer's savings, which is given by the solution to a perfect foresight intertemporal optimization of consumption. They model the dynamic effects of operating costs associated with pollution control, pollution control investment, and compliance with motor vehicle emissions standards. They find that over the period 1974–1985, the combined effect of these mandated costs was to reduce the average growth rate of real GNP by about 0.2 percentage points per year, with required investment having the biggest effect and operating costs the smallest.[54] By 1985, the cumulative effect of this reduced growth is that

---

[53]See Jaffe and Stavins, forthcoming. Some types of market-based instruments can raise special problems in the context of international trade, however, if the policy instruments are not harmonized across nations (Harmen Verbruggen 1993).

[54]Because the compliance expenditures are included in GNP, this reduction in growth is a cost over and above the direct costs.

simulated GNP without environmental regulation would be about 1.7 percent more than the actual historical value. This lost output is of roughly the same magnitude as the direct costs of compliance (Table 4).[55]

The results of any simulation model are, of course, somewhat sensitive to the structure and parameter values employed. This can be a particular concern with computable general equilibrium models because of their size and complexity. Nevertheless, the results examined in this section suggest that there are significant dynamic impacts of environmental regulation in the form of costs associated with reduced investment.

5.3 Economic Growth Enhancement

The vast majority of economic analyses of regulation and competitiveness are based upon the assumption that regulations increase production costs. Nevertheless, there have been some recent suggestions in the literature that regulations may actually stimulate growth and competitiveness. This argument—articulated recently by Porter (1991)[56]—has generated a great deal of interest and enthusiasm among some influential policy makers (see, for example, Senator Al Gore 1992).

There are several levels on which the so-called Porter hypothesis may be interpreted. First of all, it can be taken simply to mean that some sectors of private industry, in particular, environmental services, will benefit directly from more stringent environmental regulations *on their customers* (but not on themselves). Thus, the acid-rain reduction provisions of the Clean Air Act amendments of 1990, which call for significant reductions in sulfur dioxide (SO_2) emissions from electric utilities, are unambiguously good news for the manufacturers of flue-gas purification equipment (scrubbers) and producers of low-sulfur coal.

To push this argument slightly further, it would also not be surprising if environmental regulation induced innovation with respect to technologies to achieve compliance. Surely, catalytic converter technology today is superior to what it would have been if auto emissions had never been regulated. Internationally, it has been suggested that German firms possess some competitive advantage in water-pollution control technology and U.S. firms dominate hazardous waste management, because of relatively stricter regulations (Organization for Economic Cooperation and Development 1992; U.S. Environmental Protection Agency 1993). Jean Lanjouw and Mody (1993) looked at patents originating from inventors in different countries, in patent classes deemed to be environmental technologies, and found that increases in environmental compliance costs were related to increases in patenting of such technologies with a one to two year lag. The existence

---

[55]Jorgenson and Wilcoxen (1992) estimate that the 1990 amendments to the Clean Air Act will impose incremental losses in economic growth that are approximately one-fifth as large as the losses they estimated for regulation in place during the 1974–1985 period.

[56]The idea goes back, at least, to Nicholas A. Ashford, C. Ayers, and R.F. Stone (1985). For a recent explication, see Claas van der Linde (1993).

of such "induced innovation" suggests that projections of compliance costs made *before* regulatory implementation may be biased upwards, because they will inevitably take existing technology as given to some extent. On the other hand, this effect does *not* necessarily suggest that measured compliance costs overstate actual costs, because measured costs will reflect technology as it actually evolved.[57]

Second, putting aside the obvious gainers in the environmental services sector, the Porter hypothesis can be taken to imply that, under stricter environmental regulations, *some* regulated firms will benefit competitively, at the expense of *other* regulated firms. If, for example, larger firms find it less costly to comply than smaller firms, then the former might actually benefit from regulation, if higher prices from reduced competition more than offset *their* increased costs. Similarly, the Chrysler Corporation may have benefitted—relative to General Motors and Ford—from the imposition of automobile fuel-efficiency standards[58] in 1975, because its fleet consisted of smaller-sized models. Somewhat related to this, the hypothesis can be thought of as referring dynamically to the reality that environmental regulation can provide some firms with "early mover" advantages by pushing them to produce products that will in the future be in demand in the marketplace.

The proponents of the Porter hypothesis—in public policy circles—have asserted some significantly stronger interpretations, however, namely that the competitiveness of the U.S. as a whole can be enhanced by stricter regulation.[59] It has been suggested that induced innovation can create lasting comparative advantage for U.S. firms, if other countries eventually follow our lead to stricter regulations and there are strong "first-mover" advantages enjoyed by the first firms to enter the markets for control equipment (see, for example, David Gardiner 1994). Even ignoring export possibilities, it has been suggested that environmental regulation can increase domestic efficiency, either by wringing inefficiencies out of the production process as firms struggle to meet new constraints or by spurring innovation in the long term through "outside-of-the-box thinking."[60] The notion is that the imposition of regulations impels firms to reconsider their production processes, and hence to discover innovative approaches to reduce pollution *and* decrease costs or increase output. If this happened widely enough, total social costs of regulation could be no greater than measured compliance costs. Indeed, if the innovation-stimulating effect of regulation were large enough, then regulation would

---

[57]One could argue that measured costs understate the social cost, because they generally do not include the cost of R&D to develop new control technologies. On the other hand, if, as discussed further below, R&D has large positive externalities, then the next mismeasurement is ambiguous.

[58]Energy Policy and Conservation Act of 1975 (89 Stat. 902), amending the Motor Vehicle Information and Cost Savings Act (86 Stat. 947).

[59]Scott Barrett (forthcoming) calls this notion "strategic standard-setting."

[60]Porter (1990) emphasizes that a number of industrial sectors subject to the most stringent domestic environmental regulations have become more competitive internationally: chemicals, plastics, and paints.

offer the possibility of a "free lunch," that is, improvements in environmental quality without any costs.[61]

Economists generally have been unsympathetic to these stronger arguments, because they depend upon firms being systematically ignorant of profitable production improvements or new technologies that regulations bring forth. (For a more detailed explication of economists' skepticism, see Karen L. Palmer and R. David Simpson 1993, and Oates, Palmer, and Portney 1993.) Nevertheless, specific instances of "cheap" or even "free lunches" may occur. For example, Barbera and McConnell (1990) found that lower production costs in the nonferrous metals industry were brought about by new environmental regulations that led to the introduction of new, low-polluting production practices that were also more efficient.[62] One way in which environmental regulation could theoretically have a positive impact on measured productivity at the industry level is by forcing exceptionally inefficient plants to close. To the degree that production is shifted to other domestic plants with higher productivity, the industry's overall productivity could actually increase. One study suggests that this is what happened when environmental regulations in the 1970s unintentionally accelerated the "modernization" of the U.S. steel industry (U.S. Office of Technology Assessment 1980).[63]

Even if firms are systematically ignorant of potential new processes that are both cleaner and more profitable than current methods of production, there is considerable doubt as to whether regulators would know more about these better methods of production than firm managers, or that continually higher regulatory standards would lead firms regularly to discover new clean and profitable technologies.[64] Moreover, one must be careful when claiming that firms are not operating on their production frontiers: if there are managerial costs to investigating new production

---

[61]Note that the suggestion of proponents of the Porter hypothesis is *not* that the benefits of environmental regulation (in terms of reduced health and ecological damages) exceed the costs of environmental protection. This is obviously possible, and it is an empirical issue. Rather, the notion of a "free lunch" is that—putting aside the benefits of environmental protection—the costs of regulatory action can be zero or even negative (a "paid lunch"). For an example of "free lunch" arguments—both theoretical and empirical—in the context of energy efficiency and global climate change, see Robert Ayers (1993).

[62]Two of five industries studied experienced induced savings in conventional capital costs and operating costs as a result of stricter environmental regulations and consequent increases in environmental capital investment. But, even for these two industries, the indirect effects were not sufficient to offset the direct cost increases. In the other three industries studied, environmental regulations caused both direct increases in environmental capital investments *and* increases in conventional capital costs and operating costs.

[63]While the premature scrapping of "obsolete" capital will raise measured industry productivity, this does not mean that it is socially beneficial. Such plants were, presumably, producing output whose value exceeded variable production costs.

[64]The optimal timing of the adoption of a new technology is obviously a complicated issue. Although early adoption can be better than waiting, if technology advances quickly, it may be optimal for firms to wait to invest until even better processes are available. Regulation may cause firms to invest in clean technologies today, but then discourage investment in still cleaner technologies later. See Jaffe and Stavins (1994).

technologies, then firms may be efficient even if they do not realize that new, more efficient processes exist until regulations necessitate their adoption.[65] In other words, there may be many efficiency-enhancing ideas that firms could implement if they invested the resources required to search for them. If firms do successfully search in a particular area for beneficial ideas, it will appear ex post that they were acting suboptimally by not having investigated this area sooner. But with limited resources, the real question is not whether searching produces new ideas, but whether particular searches that are generated by regulation systematically lead to more or better ideas than searches in which firms would otherwise engage.[66]

Finally, one could argue that regulation, by forcing a re-examination of products and processes, will induce an overall increase in the resources devoted to "research," broadly defined. Even if firms were previously choosing the (privately) optimal level of research investment, this inducement could be (socially) desirable, if the social rate of return to research activities is significantly greater than the private return.[67] Jaffe and Palmer (1994) examined the PACE expenditure data, R&D spending data, and patent data, in a panel of industries between 1976 and 1989. They found some evidence that increases in PACE spending were associated with increases in R&D spending, but no evidence that this increased spending produced greater innovation as measured by successful patent applications.

One empirical analysis that is frequently cited in support of the Porter hypothesis is Stephen M. Meyer (1992), which examines whether states with strict environmental laws demonstrate poor economic performance relative to states with more lax standards. Meyer (1992, p. iv) finds that

> at a minimum the pursuit of environmental quality does not hinder economic growth and development. Furthermore, there appears to be a moderate yet consistent positive association between environmentalism and economic growth.

---

[65]As contrary anecdotal evidence, we should recognize that many business people find economists' skepticism about businesses not operating on their frontiers to be, at best, an indication of the naivete of academic economists, and, at worst, a special case of the joke about the economist who fails to pick up a twenty-dollar bill from the sidewalk because he assumes that if it were not counterfeit someone else would surely have taken it.

[66]As noted above, environmental regulations may lower some firms' costs and increase their productivity by cleaning the environment. Some studies find that environmental regulations are productive when one takes into account the cost of the "environmental inputs" into the production process (Repetto 1990). Studies of this type are tangential to the "Porter hypothesis," because such studies focus on situations where the benefits of environmental regulations are not sufficient to make individual firms undertake cleanup, but are substantial enough that industry as a whole may benefit. For example, it is unlikely that any single firm has an incentive to reduce its smokestack emissions solely to improve its own workers' health, but if every firm lowered its emissions, industry might find that, as a result of the change, fewer work days were lost due to illness. See Lester B. Lave and Eugene Seskin (1977); U.S. Environmental Protection Agency (1982); and Douglas W. Dockery et al. (1993).

[67]A priori, private incentives to engage in research could be either too low (because research generates knowledge externalities enjoyed by other firms) or too high (because research creates negative externalities by destroying quasi-rents being earned by other firms). Empirical evidence seems to confirm that social returns exceed private returns (Edwin Mansfield et al. 1977; Jaffe 1986; and Zvi Griliches 1990).

Unfortunately, his statistical analysis sheds very little light on a possible causal relationship between regulation and economic performance.[68] His approach does not control for factors other than the stringency of a state's environmental laws that could affect the state's economic performance. Consequently, it is quite possible that he has merely found a spurious positive correlation between the stringency of a state's environmental standards and its economic performance. His results are consistent with the hypothesis that poor states with no prospect for substantial growth will not enact tough environmental regulations, just as developing countries are less likely than rich countries to enact tough environmental regulations.[69]

Thus, overall, the literature on the "Porter hypothesis" remains one with a high ratio of speculation and anecdote to systematic evidence. While economists have good reason to be skeptical of arguments based on nonoptimizing behavior where the only support is anecdotal, it is also important to recognize that if we wish to persuade others of the validity of our analysis we must go beyond tautological arguments that rest solely on the postulate of profit-maximization. Systematic empirical analysis in this area is only beginning, and it is too soon to tell if it will ultimately provide a clear answer.

6. Conclusions

Overall, there is relatively little evidence to support the hypothesis that environmental regulations have had a large adverse effect on competitiveness, however that elusive term is defined. Although the long-run social costs of environmental regulation may be significant, including adverse effects on productivity, studies attempting to measure the effect of environmental regulation on net exports, overall trade flows, and plant-location decisions have produced estimates that are either small, statistically insignificant, or not robust to tests of model specification.

---

[68]This has not kept a number of authors from describing Meyer's analysis as absolutely conclusive: "Meyer's study does repudiate the hypothesis that environmental regulations reduce economic growth and job creation" (Bezdek 1993, p. 10).

[69]For some environmental problems, such as inadequate sanitation and unsafe drinking water, there is a monotonic and *inverse* relationship between the level of the environmental threat and per capita income (International Bank for Reconstruction and Development 1992). This relationship holds both cross-sectionally (across nations) and for single nations over time. For other environmental problems, the relationship with income level is not monotonic at all, but an inverted U-shaped function in which at low levels of income, pollution increases with per capita income, but then at some point begins to decline with further increases in income. This is true of most forms of air and water pollution (Grossman and Krueger 1994), some types of deforestation, and habitat loss. Pollution increases from the least developed agricultural countries to those beginning to industrialize fully—such as Mexico and the emerging market economies of Eastern Europe and parts of the former Soviet Union. After peaking in such nations, pollution is found to decline in the wealthier, industrialized nations that have both the demand for cleaner air and water and the means to provide it. Finally, for another set of environmental pollutants, including carbon dioxide emissions, there is an *increasing* monotonic relationship between per capita income and emission levels, at least within the realm of experience.

There are a number of reasons why the effects of environmental regulation on competitiveness may be small and difficult to detect. First, the existing data are severely limited in their ability to measure the relative stringency of environmental regulation, making it difficult to use such measures in regression analyses of the effects of regulation on economic performance. Second, for all but the most heavily regulated industries, the cost of complying with federal environmental regulation is a relatively small fraction of total cost of production. According to EPA, that share for U.S. industry as a whole averages about 2 percent, although it is certainly higher for some industries, such as electric utilities, chemical manufacturers, petroleum refiners, and basic metals manufacturers. This being the case, environmental regulatory intensity should not be expected to be a significant determinant of competitiveness in *most* industries. Labor cost differentials, energy and raw materials cost differentials, infrastructure adequacy, and other factors would indeed overwhelm the environmental effect.

Third, although U.S. environmental laws and regulations are generally the most stringent in the world, the difference between U.S. requirements and those in other western industrial democracies is not great, especially for air and water pollution control.[70] Fourth, even where there are substantial differences between environmental requirements in the United States and elsewhere, U.S. firms (and other multi-nationals, as well) are reluctant to build less-than-state-of-the-art plants in foreign countries. If such willingness existed before the accident at the Union Carbide plant in Bhopal, India, it does not now. Thus, even significant differences in regulatory stringency may not be exploited. Fifth and finally, it appears that even in developing countries where environmental standards (and certainly enforcement capabilities) are relatively weak, plants built by indigenous firms typically embody more pollution control—sometimes substantially more— than is required. To the extent this is true, even significant *statutory* differences in pollution control requirements between countries may not result in significant effects on plant location or other manifestations of competitiveness.

Having stated these conclusions, it is important to emphasize several caveats. First, in many of the studies, differences in environmental regulation were measured by environmental control costs as a percentage of value-added, or some other measure that depends critically on accurate measurement of environmental spending. Even for the United States, where data on environmental compliance costs are relatively good, compliance expenditure data are notoriously unreliable. The problem is more pronounced in other OECD countries, whose environmental agencies have not typically tracked environmental costs. Thus, we may have found little relationship between environmental regulations and competitiveness simply because the data are of poor quality.

---

[70]See Kopp, Diane Dewitt, and Portney (1990) for empirical evidence, and Barrett (1992) for a theoretical argument of why governments should *not* be expected to adopt relatively weak pollution standards for competitive reasons.

In an era of increasing reliance on incentive-based and other performance-based environmental regulations, accurate accounting for pollution control will become an even more pronounced problem. This is because pollution control expenditures increasingly are taking the form of process changes and product reformulations, rather than installation of end-of-pipe control equipment. It will be increasingly difficult (perhaps even impossible) to allocate accurately that part of the cost of a new plant that is attributable to environmental control (Hahn and Stavins 1992). Ironically, in ten years we may know less about total annual pollution control costs than we do now, in spite of increased concern about these expenditures and their possible effects on competitiveness.

A second caveat is that only two of the studies we reviewed controlled for differences in "regulatory climate" between jurisdictions. If the delays and litigation surrounding regulation are the greatest impediments to exporting or to new plant location, these effects will not be picked up by studies that look exclusively at source discharge standards or traditional spending for pollution control equipment as measures of regulatory intensity, unless these direct compliance costs are highly correlated with the costs of litigation and delay.

A third factor that tempers our findings is the difficulty of measuring the effectiveness of enforcement efforts. Subtle differences in enforcement strategies are very difficult to measure, but these differences can lead to variations from country to country that *could* influence competitiveness. Finally, it is important to recall that any comprehensive effort to identify the competitiveness effects associated with regulation must look at both the costs *and* benefits of regulation. To the extent that air or water pollution control effects reduce damages, they may reduce costs for some businesses and thus make them more competitive. Similarly, pollution control can reduce labor costs and enhance competitiveness in some locations under certain conditions.

Just as we have found little consistent empirical evidence for the conventional hypothesis regarding environmental regulation and competitiveness, there is also little or no evidence supporting the revisionist hypothesis that environmental regulation stimulates innovation and improved international competitiveness. Given the large direct and indirect costs that regulation imposes, economists' natural skepticism regarding this free regulatory lunch is appropriate, though further research would help to convince others that our conclusions are well grounded in fact.

Overall, the evidence we have reviewed suggests that the truth regarding the relationship between environmental protection and international competitiveness lies in between the two extremes of the current debate. International differences in environmental regulatory stringency pose insufficient threats to U.S. industrial competitiveness to justify substantial cutbacks in domestic environmental regulations. At the same time, such regulation clearly imposes large direct and indirect costs on society, and there is no evidence supporting the enactment of stricter domestic environmental regulations to stimulate economic competitiveness. Instead, policy makers should do what they can to establish environmental priorities and goals that are consistent with the real tradeoffs that are inevitably required by regulatory activities; that is, our environmental goals should be based on careful balancing of benefits and costs. At the same time, policy makers should seek to reduce the magnitude of these costs by identifying and implementing flexible and cost-effective environmental policy instruments, whether they be of the conventional type or of the newer breed of market-based approaches.

References

Ashford, Nicholas A.; Ayers, C. and Stone, R. F. "Using Regulation to Change the Market for Innovation," *Harvard Environ. Law Rev.*, 1985, *9*, pp. 419–66.

Ayres, Robert U. "On Economic Disequilibrium and Free Lunch." Working Paper. Centre for the Management of Environmental Resources, INSEAD, Fontainebleau, France, June 1993.

Barbera, Anthony J. and McConnell, Virginia D. "The Impact of Environmental Regulations on Industry Productivity: Direct and Indirect Effects," *J. Environ. Econ. Manage.*, Jan. 1990, *18*(1), pp. 50–65.

Barrett, Scott. "Strategy and Environment," *Columbia J. World Bus.*, Fall/Winter 1992, *27*, pp. 202–08.

———. "Strategic Environmental Policy and International Trade," *J. Public Econ.*, forthcoming.

Bartik, Timothy J. "Business Location Decisions in the United States: Estimates of the Effects of Unionization, Taxes, and Other Characteristics of States," *J. Bus. Econ. Statist.*, Jan. 1985, *3*(1), pp. 14–22.

———. "The Effects of Environmental Regulation on Business Location in the United States," *Growth Change*, Summer 1988, *19*(3), pp. 22–44.

———. "Small Business Start-ups in the United States: Estimates of the Effects of Characteristics of States," *Southern Econ. J.*, Apr. 1989, *55*(4), pp. 1004–18.

Bezdek, Roger H. "Environment and Economy: What's the Bottom Line?" *Environment*, Sept. 1993, *35*(7), pp. 7–11, 25–32.

Crandall, Robert W. "Pollution Controls and Productivity Growth in Basic Industries," in *Productivity measurement in regulated industries*. Eds.: Thomas G. Cowing and Rodney F. Stevenson. New York: Academic Press, Inc. 1981, pp. 347–68.

Cropper, Maureen L. and Oates, Wallace E. "Environmental Economics: A Survey," *J. Econ. Lit.*, June 1992, *30*(2), pp. 675–740.

D'Arge, Ralph. "International Trade, Domestic Income, and Environmental Controls: Some Empirical Estimates" in *Managing the environment: International economic cooperation for pollution control*. Ed.: Allen Kneese. New York: Praeger, 1974, pp. 289–315.

Dean, Judith M. "Trade and the Environment: A Survey of the Literature," in *International trade and the environment*. Ed.: Patrick Low. Washington, DC: International Bank for Reconstruction and Development/World Bank, 1992.

Denison, Edward F. *Accounting for slower economic growth: The U.S. in the 1970's*. Washington, DC: Brookings Institution, 1979.

Dockery, Douglas W. et al. "An Association Between Air Pollution and Mortality in Six U.S. Cities," *New Eng. J. Medicine*, 1993, *329*, pp. 1753–59.

Duerksen, Christopher. *Environmental regulation of industrial plant siting*. Washington, DC: Conservation Foundation, 1983.

Friedman, Joseph; Gerlowski, Daniel A. and Silberman, Jonathan. "What Attracts Foreign Multinational Corporations? Evidence from Branch Plant Location in the United States," *J. Reg. Sci.*, Nov. 1992, *32*(4), pp. 403–18.

Gallop, Frank M. and Roberts, Mark J. "Environmental Regulations and Productivity Growth: The Case of Fossil-Fueled Electric Power Generation," *J. Polit. Econ.*, 1983, *91*, pp. 654–74.

Gardiner, David. "Does Environmental Policy Conflict with Economic Growth?" *Resources*, Spring 1994, (115), pp. 20–21.

Gore, Senator Al. *Earth in the balance: Ecology and the human spirit*. New York: Houghton Mifflin Company, 1992.

Gray, Wayne B. "The Cost of Regulation: OSHA, EPA, and the Productivity Slowdown," *Amer. Econ. Rev.*, Dec. 1987, 77(5), pp. 998–1006.

———. "Cross-State Differences in Environmental Regulation and the Births and Deaths of Manufacturing Plants," 1993, work in progress.

Gray, Wayne B. and Shadbegian, Ronald J. "Environmental Regulation and Manufacturing Productivity at the Plant Level." Discussion Paper, U.S. Department of Commerce, Center for Economic Studies, Washington, DC, 1993.

———. "Pollution Abatement Costs, Regulation, and Plant-Level Productivity." Forthcoming working paper, National Bureau of Economic Research, Cambridge, MA, July 1994.

Griliches, Zvi. "Patent Statistics as Economic Indicators: A Survey," *J. Econ. Lit.*, Dec. 1990, *28*(4), pp. 1661–1707.

Grossman, Gene M. and Krueger, Alan B. "Environmental Impacts of a North American Freed Trade Agreement," in *The U.S.-Mexico free trade agreement*. Ed.: Peter Garber. Cambridge, MA: MIT Press, 1993, pp. 13–56.

———. "Economic Growth and the Environment." Working Paper No. 4634. Cambridge, MA: National Bureau of Economic Research, 1994.

Hahn, Robert W. and Stavins, Robert N. "Incentive-Based Environmental Regulation: A New Era from an Old Idea," *Ecology Law Quart.*, 1991, *18*, pp. 1–42.

———. "Economic Incentives for Environmental Protection: Integrating Theory and Practice," *Amer. Econ. Rev.*, May 1992, *82*(2), pp. 464–68.

Haveman, Robert H. and Christiansen, Gregory B. "Environmental Regulations and Productivity Growth," in *Environmental regulation and the U.S. economy*. Eds.: Henry M. Peskin, Paul R. Portney, and Allen V. Kneese. Washington, DC: Resources for the Future, 1981, pp. 55–75.

Hazilla, Michael and Kopp, Raymond J. "Social Cost of Environmental Quality Regulations: A General Equilibrium Analysis," *J. Polit. Econ.*, Aug. 1990, *98*(4), pp. 853–73.

Hopkins, Thomas D. "Regulation and Jobs—Sorting out the Consequences." Prepared for the American Petroleum Institute, Washington, DC, Oct. 1992.

International Bank for Reconstruction and Development/the World Bank. *World development report 1992: Development and the environment*. New York: Oxford U. Press, 1992.

Jaffe, Adam B. "Technological Opportunity and Spillovers of R&D: Evidence from Firms' Patents, Profits, and Market Value," *Amer. Econ. Rev.*, Dec. 1986, *76*(5), pp. 984–1001.

Jaffe Adam B. and Palmer, Karen L. "Environmental Regulation and Innovation: A Panel Data Study." Paper prepared for the Western Economic Association Meetings, June 1994.

Jaffe, Adam B. et al. "Environmental Regulations and the Competitiveness of U.S. Industry." Report prepared for the Economics and Statistics Administration, U.S. Department of Commerce. Cambridge, MA: Economics Resource Group, 1993.

Jaffe, Adam B. and Stavins, Robert N. "The Energy Paradox and the Diffusion of Conservation Technology," *Resource Energy Econ.*, May 1994, *16*(2), pp. 91–122.

———. "Dynamic Incentives of Environmental Regulation: The Effects of Alternative Policy Instruments on Technology Diffusion," *J. Environ & Econ. Manage.* July 1995, *29*(1), forthcoming.

Jorgenson, Dale W. and Wilcoxen, Peter J. "Environmental Regulation and U.S. Economic Growth," *Rand J. Econ.*, Summer 1990, *21*(2), pp. 314–40.

———. "Impact of Environmental Legislation on U.S. Economic Growth, Investment, and Capital Costs," in *U.S. environmental policy and economic growth: How do we fare?* Ed.: Donna L. Brodsky. Washington, DC: American Council for Capital Formation, 1992.

Kalt, Joseph P. "The Impact of Domestic Environmental Regulatory Policies on U.S. International Competitiveness," in *International competitiveness*. Eds.: A. Michael Spence and Heather A. Hazard. Cambridge, MA: Harper and Row, Ballinger, 1988, pp. 221–62.

Kaufmann, Robert K.; Pauly, Peter and Sweitzer, Julie. "The Effects of NAFTA on the Environment," *Energy J.*, 1993, *14*(3), pp. 217–40.

Kolstad, Charles D. and Xing, Yuqing. "Do Lax Environmental Regulations Attract Foreign Investment?" Working Paper, Department of Economics and Institute for Environmental Studies, U. of Illinois, Urbana, Illinois, February 1994.

Kopp, Raymond J.; Dewitt, Diane and Portney, Paul R. "International Comparison of Environmental Regulation," in *Environmental policy and the cost of capital.* Washington, DC: American Council for Capital Formation, 1990.

Krugman, Paul. *Geography and trade.* Cambridge, MA: MIT Press, 1991.

———. "Competitiveness: A Dangerous Obsession," *Foreign Affairs*, Mar./Apr. 1994, *73*(2), pp. 28–44.

Lanjouw, Jean and Mody, Ashok. "Stimulating Innovation and the International Diffusion of Environmentally Responsive Technology: The Role of Expenditures and Institutions." Mimeo, World Bank, 1993.

Lave, Lester B. and Seskin, Eugene. *Air pollution and human health.* Washington, DC: John Hopkins U. Press for Resources for the Future, 1977.

Leamer, Edward E. *Sources of international comparative advantage.* Cambridge, MA: MIT Press, 1984.

Leonard, H. Jeffrey. *Pollution and the struggle for the world product.* Cambridge, UK: Cambridge U. Press, 1988.

Levinson, Arik. "Environmental Regulations and Manufacturers' Location Choices: Evidence from the Census of Manufactures." New York: Columbia U., 1992.

van der Linde, Claas. "The Micro-Economic Implications of Environmental Regulation: A Preliminary Framework," in *Environmental policies and industrial competitiveness.* Paris: Organization of Economic Cooperation and Development (OECD), 1993, pp. 69–77.

Low, Patrick and Yeats, Alexander. "Do 'Dirty' Industries Migrate?" in *International trade and the environment.* Washington, DC: The World Bank, 1992.

Lucas, Robert E. B.; Wheeler, David and Hettige, Hemamala. "Economic Development, Environmental Regulation and the International Migration of Toxic Industrial Pollution: 1960–1988," in *International trade and the environment.* Ed.: Patrick Low. Washington, DC: World Bank, 1992, pp. 67–86.

Mansfield, Edwin et al. "Social and Private Rates of Return from Industrial Innovations," *Quart. J. Econ.*, May 1977, *91*(2), pp. 221–40.

McConnell, Virginia D. and Schwab, Robert M. "The Impact of Environmental Regulation on Industry Location Decisions: The Motor Vehicle Industry," *Land Econ.*, Feb. 1990, *66*(1), pp. 67–81.

McGuire, Martin C. "Regulation, Factor Rewards, and International Trade," *J. Public Econ.*, Apr. 1982, *17*(3), pp. 335–54.

Meyer, Stephen M. "Environmentalism and Economic Prosperity: Testing the Environmental Impact Hypothesis." M.I.T. Mimeo, 1992. Cambridge, MA, updated 1993.

Norsworthy, J. R.; Harper, Michael J. and Kunze, Kent. "The Slowdown in Productivity Growth: Analysis of Some Contributing Factors," *Brookings Pap. Econ. Act.*, 1979, 2, pp. 387–421.

Oates, Wallace; Palmer, Karen and Portney, Paul, "Environmental Regulation and International Competitiveness: Thinking About the Porter Hypothesis." Mimeo, 1993.

Organization for Economic Cooperation and Development. *The macro-economic impacts of environmental expenditures*. Paris, France: Organization for Economic Cooperation and Development, 1985.

———. *OECD environment data compendium*. Paris, France: Organization for Economic Cooperation and Development, 1990.

———. *The OECD environment industry: Situation, prospects, and government policies*. Paris, France: Organization of Economic Cooperation and Development, 1992.

———. *Summary report of the workshop on environmental policies and industrial competitiveness, 28–29 January 1993*. Paris, France: Organization of Economic Cooperation and Development, 1993a.

———. *Pollution abatement and control expenditure in OECD countries*. OECD Environment Monograph No. 75. Paris, France: Organization of Economic Cooperation and Development, 1993b.

Ostro, Bart D. "The Effects of Air Pollution on Work Loss and Morbidity," *J. Environ. Econ. Manage.*, Dec. 1983, *10*(4), pp. 371–82.

Palmer, Karen L. and Simpson, R. David. "Environmental Policy as Industrial Policy," *Resources*, Summer 1993, (112), pp. 17–21.

Pearson, Charles S., ed. *Multinational corporations, environment, and the Third World*. Durham, NC: Duke U. Press and World Resources Institute, 1987.

Pethig, Rudiger. "Pollution, Welfare, and Environmental Policy in the Theory of Comparative Advantage," *J. Environ. Econ. Manage.*, 1975, 2, pp. 160–69.

Porter, Michael E. *The competitive advantage of nations*. New York: Free Press, 1990.

———. "America's Green Strategy," *Sci. Amer.*, Apr. 1991, p. 168.

Portney, Paul R. "Economics and the Clean Air Act," *J. Econ. Perspectives*, Fall 1990, *4*(4), pp. 173–81.

———. "Does Environmental Policy Conflict with Economic Growth?" *Resources*, Spring 1994, (115), pp. 21–23.

Repetto, Robert. "Environmental Productivity and Why It Is So Important," *Challenge*, Sept.–Oct. 1990, *33*(5), pp. 33–38.

Robison, H. David. "Industrial Pollution Abatement: The Impact on Balance of Trade," *Can. J. Econ.*, Feb. 1988, *21*(1), pp. 187–99.

Rose, Adam. "Modeling the Macroeconomic Impact of Air Pollution Abatement," *J. Reg. Sci.*, Nov. 1983, *23*(4), pp. 441–59.

Rutledge, Gary L. and Leonard, Mary L. "Pollution Abatement and Control Expenditures, 1972–90," *Surv. Curr. Bus.*, June 1992, *72*(6), pp. 25–41.

————. "Pollution Abatement and Control Expenditures, 1987–91," *Surv. Curr. Bus.*, May 1993, *73*(5), pp. 55–62.

Schmalensee, Richard. "The Costs of Environmental Protection," in *Balancing economic growth and environmental goals.* Ed.: Mary Beth Kotowski. Washington, DC: American Council for Capital Formation Center for Policy Research, 1994, pp. 55–75.

Siebert, Horst. "Environmental Quality and the Gains from Trade," *Kyklos*, 1977, *30*(4), pp. 657–73.

Solow, Robert M. *An almost practical step toward sustainability.* Washington, DC: Resources for the Future, 1992.

Stewart, Richard B. "Environmental Regulation and International Competitiveness," *Yale Law J.*, June 1993, *102*(8), pp. 2039–2106.

Tobey, James A. "The Effects of Domestic Environmental Policies on Patterns of World Trade: An Empirical Test," *Kyklos*, 1990, *43*(2), pp. 191–209.

Tyson, Laura D'Andrea. "Competitiveness: An Analysis of the Problem and a Perspective on Future Policy," in *Global competitiveness: Getting the U.S. back on track.* Ed.: Martin K. Starr. New York: Norton, 1988, pp. 95–120.

U.S. Congress. *Legislative history of the Clean Air Act.* Part 3. Washington, DC: U.S. GPO, 1979.

U.S. Congressional Budget Office. *Environmental regulation and economic efficiency.* Washington, DC: U.S. GPO, 1985.

U.S. Department of Commerce. *Pollution abatement costs and expenditures, 1991.* Economics and Statistics Administration, Bureau of the Census. Washington, DC: U.S. GPO, 1993.

U.S. Environmental Protection Agency. *Air quality criteria for particulate matter and sulfur oxides.* Research Triangle Park, NC: U.S. Environmental Protection Agency, 1982.

————. *Environmental investments: The cost of a clean environment.* Washington, DC: U.S. Environmental Protection Agency, 1990.

————. *National air quality and emissions trends report.* Office of Air Quality Planning and Standards, EPA-450-R-92-001. Research Triangle Park, NC: U.S. Environmental Protection Agency, 1992a.

————. "The Clean Air Marketplace: New Business Opportunities Created by the Clean Air Act Amendments—Summary of Conference Proceedings." Washington, DC, Office of Air and Radiation, July 24, 1992b.

————. *International trade in environmental protection equipment.* Washington, DC: U.S. Environmental Protection Agency, 1993.

U.S. General Accounting Office. *U.S.-Mexico Trade: Some U.S. wood furniture firms relocated from Los Angeles area to Mexico.* Report Number GAO/NSIAD-91-191. Washington, DC: U.S. General Accounting Office, 1991.

U.S. Office of Technology Assessment. *Technology and steel industry competitiveness.* OTA-M-122. Washington, DC: U.S. GPO, 1980.

————. *Trade and the environment: Conflicts and opportunities.* Washington, DC: U.S. GPO, 1992.

————. *Industry, technology, and the environment: Competitive challenges and business opportunities.* OTA-ITE-586. Washington, DC: U.S. GPO, 1994.

Verbruggen, Harmen. "The Trade Effects of Economic Instruments," in *Environmental policies and industrial competitiveness.* Paris: Organization of Economic Cooperation and Development (OECD), 1993, pp. 55–62.

Vogel, David. *National styles of regulation: Environmental policy in Great Britain and the United States.* Ithaca, NY: Cornell U. Press, 1986.

Walter, Ingo. "Environmentally Induced Industrial Relocation to Developing Countries," in *Environment and trade: The relation of international trade and environmental policy.* Eds.: Seymour J. Rubin and Thomas R. Graham. Totowa, NJ: Allanheld, Osmun, 1982, pp. 67–101.

Walter, Ingo and Ugelow, J. "Environmental Policies in Developing Countries," *Ambio*, 1979, *8*, pp. 102–09.

Weitzman, Martin L. "On the 'Environmental' Discount Rate." *J. Environ. Econ. Manage.*, Mar. 1994, *26*(2), pp. 200–09.

Wheeler, David and Mody, Ashoka. "International Investment Location Decisions: The Case of U.S. Firms," *J. Int. Econ.*, Aug. 1992, *33*(1,2), pp. 57–76.

Yohe, Gary W. "The Backward Incidence of Pollution Control—Some Comparative Statics in General Equilibrium," *J. Environ. Econ. Manage.*, Sept. 1979, *6*(3), pp. 187–98.

Zamparutti, Anthony and Jon Klavens. "Environment and Foreign Investment in Central and Eastern Europe: Results from a Survey of Western Corporations," in *Environmental policies and industrial competitiveness.* Paris: Organization of Economic Cooperation and Development (OECD), 1993, pp. 120–27.

5   *Toward a New Conception of the Environment-Competitiveness Relationship**

Michael E. Porter
Claas van der Linde

Michael E. Porter is the Bishop William Lawrence Professor, Harvard Business School; and Claas van der Linde is on the faculty of the International Management Research Institute of St. Gallen University, Switzerland.

The relationship between environmental goals and industrial competitiveness has normally been thought of as involving a tradeoff between social benefits and private costs. The issue was how to balance society's desire for environmental protection with the economic burden on industry. Framed this way, environmental improvement becomes a kind of arm-wrestling match. One side pushes for tougher standards; the other side tries to beat the standards back.

Our central message is that the environmental-competitiveness debate has been framed incorrectly. The notion of an inevitable struggle between ecology and the economy grows out of a static view of environmental regulation, in which technology, products, processes and customer needs are all fixed. In this static world, where firms have already made their cost-minimizing choices, environmental regulation inevitably raises costs and will tend to reduce the market share of domestic companies on global markets.

However, the paradigm defining competitiveness has been shifting, particularly in the last 20 to 30 years, away from this static model. The new paradigm of international competitiveness is a dynamic one, based on innovation. A body of research first published in *The Competitive Advantage of Nations* has begun to address these changes (Porter, 1990). Competitiveness at the industry level arises from superior productivity, either in terms of lower costs than rivals or the ability to offer products with supe-

---

"Toward a New Conception of the Environmental-Competitiveness Issue," by Michael E. Porter and Claas van der Linde, from *Journal of Economic Perspectives*, 9(4):97–118 (Fall 1995).

*The authors are grateful to Alan Auerbach, Ben Bonifant, Daniel C. Esty, Ridgway M. Hall, Jr., Donald B. Marron, Jan Rivkin, Nicolaj Siggelkow, R. David Simpson and Timothy Taylor for extensive valuable editorial suggestions. We are also grateful to Reed Hundt for ongoing discussions that have greatly benefitted our thinking.

rior value that justify a premium price.[1] Detailed case studies of hundreds of industries, based in dozens of countries, reveal that internationally competitive companies are not those with the cheapest inputs or the largest scale, but those with the capacity to improve and innovate continually. (We use the term innovation broadly, to include a product's or service's design, the segments it serves, how it is produced, how it is marketed and how it is supported.) Competitive advantage, then, rests not on static efficiency nor on optimizing within fixed constraints, but on the capacity for innovation and improvement that shift the constraints.

This paradigm of dynamic competitiveness raises an intriguing possibility: in this paper, we will argue that properly designed environmental standards can trigger innovation that may partially or more than fully offset the costs of complying with them. Such "innovation offsets," as we call them, can not only lower the net cost of meeting environmental regulations, but can even lead to absolute advantages over firms in foreign countries not subject to similar regulations. Innovation offsets will be common because reducing pollution is often coincident with improving the productivity with which resources are used. In short, firms can actually benefit from properly crafted environmental regulations that are more stringent (or are imposed earlier) than those faced by their competitors in other countries. By stimulating innovation, strict environmental regulations can actually enhance competitiveness.

There is a legitimate and continuing controversy over the social benefits of specific environmental standards, and there is a huge benefit-cost literature. Some believe that the risks of pollution have been overstated; others fear the reverse. Our focus here is not on the social benefits of environmental regulation, but on the private costs. Our argument is that whatever the level of social benefits, these costs are far higher than they need to be. The policy focus should, then, be on relaxing the tradeoff between competitiveness and the environment rather than accepting it as a given.

The Link from Regulation to Promoting Innovation

It is sometimes argued that companies must, by the very notion of profit seeking, be pursuing all profitable innovations. In the metaphor economists often cite, $10 bills will never be found on the ground because someone would have already picked them up. In this view, if complying with environmental regulation can be profitable, in the sense that a company can more than offset the cost of compliance, then why is such regulation necessary?

---

[1]At the industry level, the meaning of competitiveness is clear. At the level of a state or nation, however, the notion of competitiveness is less clear because no nation or state is, or can be, competitive in everything. The proper definition of competitiveness at the aggregate level is the average *productivity* of industry or the value created per unit of labor and per dollar of capital invested. Productivity depends on both the quality and features of products (which determine their value) and the efficiency with which they are produced.

The possibility that regulation might act as a spur to innovation arises because the world does not fit the Panglossian belief that firms always make optimal choices. This will hold true only in a static optimization framework where information is perfect and profitable opportunities for innovation have already been discovered, so that profit-seeking firms need only choose their approach. Of course, this does not describe reality. Instead, the actual process of dynamic competition is characterized by changing technological opportunities coupled with highly incomplete information, organizational inertia and control problems reflecting the difficulty of aligning individual, group and corporate incentives. Companies have numerous avenues for technological improvement, and limited attention.

Actual experience with energy-saving investments illustrates that in the real world, $10 bills are waiting to be picked up. As one example, consider the "Green Lights" program of the Environmental Protection Agency. Firms volunteering to participate in this program pledge to scrutinize every avenue of electrical energy consumption. In return, they receive advice on efficient lighting, hearing and cooling operations. When the EPA collected data on energy-saving lighting upgrades reported by companies as part of the Green Lights program, it showed that nearly 80 percent of the projects had paybacks of two years or less (DeCanio, 1993). Yet only after companies became part of the program, and benefitted from information and cajoling from the EPA, were these highly profitable projects carried out. This paper will present numerous other examples of where environmental innovation produces net benefits for private companies.[2]

We are currently in a transitional phase of industrial history where companies are still inexperienced in dealing creatively with environmental issues. The environment has not been a principal area of corporate or technological emphasis, and knowledge about environmental impacts is still rudimentary in many firms and industries, elevating uncertainty about innovation benefits. Customers are also unaware of the costs of resource inefficiency in the packaging they discard, the scrap value they forego and the disposal costs they bear. Rather than attempting to innovate in every direction at once, firms in fact make choices based on how they perceive their competitive situation and the world around them. In such a world, regulation can be an important influence on the discretion of innovation, either for better or for worse. Properly crafted environmental regulation can serve at least six purposes.

First, regulation signals companies about likely resource inefficiencies and potential technological improvements. Companies are still inexperienced in measuring their discharges, understanding the full costs of incomplete utilization of resources and toxicity, and conceiving new ap-

---

[2]Of course, there are many nonenvironmental examples of where industry has been extremely slow to pick up available $10 bills by choosing new approaches. For example, total quality management programs only came to the United States and Europe decades after they had been widely diffused in Japan, and only after Japanese firms had devastated U.S. and European competitors in the marketplace. The analogy between searching for product quality and for environmental protection is explored later in this paper.

proaches to minimize discharges or eliminate hazardous substances. Regulation rivets attention on this area of potential innovation.[3]

Second, regulation focused on information gathering can achieve major benefits by raising corporate awareness. For example, Toxics Release Inventories, which are published annually as part of the 1986 Superfund reauthorization, require more than 20,000 manufacturing plants to report their releases of some 320 toxic chemicals. Such information gathering often leads to environmental improvement without mandating pollution reductions, sometimes even at lower costs.

Third, regulation reduces the uncertainty that investments to address the environment will be valuable. Greater certainty encourages investment in any area.

Fourth, regulation creates pressure that motivates innovation and progress. Our broader research on competitiveness highlights the important role of outside pressure in the innovation process, to overcome organizational inertia, foster creative thinking and mitigate agency problems. Economists are used to the argument that pressure for innovation can come from strong competitors, demanding customers or rising prices of raw materials; we are arguing that properly crafted regulation can also provide such pressure.

Fifth, regulation levels the transitional playing field. During the transition period to innovation-based solutions, regulation ensures that one company cannot opportunistically gain position by avoiding environmental investments. Regulations provide a buffer until new technologies become proven and learning effects reduce their costs.

Sixth, regulation is needed in the case of incomplete offsets. We readily admit that innovation cannot always completely offset the cost of compliance, especially in the short term before learning can reduce the cost of innovation-based solutions. In such cases, regulation will be necessary to improve environmental quality.

Stringent regulation can actually produce greater innovation and innovation offsets than lax regulation. Relatively lax regulation can be dealt with incrementally and without innovation, and often with "end-of-pipe" or secondary treatment solutions. More stringent regulation, however, focuses greater company attention on discharges and emissions, and compliance requires more fundamental solutions, like reconfiguring products and processes. While the cost of compliance may rise with stringency, then, the potential for innovation offsets may rise even faster. Thus the *net* cost of compliance can fall with stringency and may even turn into a net benefit.

How Innovation Offsets Occur

Innovation in response to environmental regulation can take two broad forms. The first is that companies simply get smarter about how to deal with pollution once it occurs, including the processing of toxic materials

---

[3]Regulation also raises the likelihood that product and process in general will incorporate environmental improvements.

and emissions, how to reduce the amount of toxic or harmful material generated (or convert it into salable forms) and how to improve secondary treatment. Molten Metal Technology, of Waltham, Massachusetts, for example, has developed a catalytic extraction process to process many types of hazardous waste efficiently and effectively. This sort of innovation reduces the cost of compliance with pollution control, but changes nothing else.

The second form of innovation addresses environmental impacts while simultaneously improving the affected product itself and/or related processes. In some cases, these "innovation offsets" can exceed the costs of compliance. This second sort of innovation is central to our claim that environmental regulation can actually increase industrial competitiveness.

Innovation offsets can be broadly divided into product offsets and process offsets. Product offsets occur when environmental regulation produces not just less pollution, but also creates better-performing or higher-quality products, safer products, lower product costs (perhaps from material substitution or less packaging), products with higher resale or scrap value (because of ease in recycling or disassembly) or lower costs of product disposal for users. Process offsets occur when environmental regulation not only leads to reduced pollution, but also results in higher resource productivity such as higher process yields, less downtime through more careful monitoring and maintenance, materials savings (due to substitution, reuse or recycling of production inputs), better utilization of by-products, lower energy consumption during the production process, reduced material storage and handling costs, conversion of waste into valuable forms, reduced waste disposal costs or safer workplace conditions. These offsets are frequently related, so that achieving one can lead to the realization of several others.

As yet, no broad tabulation exists of innovation offsets. Most of the work done in this area involves case studies, because case studies are the only vehicle currently available to measure compliance costs and both direct and indirect innovation benefits. This journal is not the place for a comprehensive listing of available case studies. However, offering some examples should help the reader to understand how common and plausible such effects are.

Innovation to comply with environmental regulation often improves product performance or quality. In 1990, for instance, Raytheon found itself required (by the Montreal Protocol and the U.S. Clean Air Act) to eliminate ozone-depleting chlorofluorocarbons (CFCs) used for cleaning printed electronic circuit boards after the soldering process. Scientists at Raytheon initially thought that complete elimination of CFCs would be impossible. However, they eventually adopted a new semiaqueous, terpene-based cleaning agent that could be reused. The new method proved to result in an increase in average product quality, which had occasionally been compromised by the old CFC-based cleaning agent, as well as lower operating costs (Raytheon, 1991, 1993). It would not have been adopted in the absence of environmental regulation mandating the phase-out of CFCs. Another example is the move by the Robbins Company (a jewelry company based in Attleboro, Massachusetts) to a closed-loop, zero-discharge system for handling the water used in plating (Berube, Nash, Maxwell and Ehrenfeld, 1992). Robbins was facing closure due to violation of its existing discharge permits. The water produced by purification through filtering and ion exchange in the new closed-loop system was 40 times cleaner than city water and led to higher-quality plating and fewer rejects. The result was enhanced competitiveness.

Environmental regulations may also reduce product costs by showing how to eliminate costly materials, reduce unnecessary packaging or simplify designs. Hitachi responded to a 1991 Japanese recycling law by redesigning products to reduce disassembly time. In the process, the number of parts in a washing machine fell 16 percent, and the number of parts on a vacuum cleaner fell 30 percent. In this way, moves to redesign products for better recyclability can lead to fewer components and thus easier assembly.

Environmental standards can also lead to innovation that reduces disposal costs (or boosts scrap or resale value) for the user. For instance, regulation that requires recyclability of products can lead to designs that allow valuable materials to be recovered more easily after disposal of the product. Either the customer or the manufacturer who takes back used products reaps greater value.

These have all been examples of product offsets, but process offsets are common as well. Process changes to reduce emissions frequently result in increases in product yields. At Ciba-Geigy's dyestuff plant in New Jersey, the need to meet new environmental standards caused the firm to reexamine its wastewater streams. Two changes in its production process—replacing iron with a different chemical conversion agent that did not result in the formation of solid iron sludge and process changes that eliminated the release of potentially toxic product into the wastewater stream—not only boosted yield by 40 percent but also eliminated wastes, resulting in annual cost savings of $740,000 (Dorfman, Muir and Miller, 1992).[4]

Similarly, 3M discovered that in producing adhesives in batches that were transferred to storage tanks, one bad batch could spoil the entire contents of a tank. The result was wasted raw materials and high costs of hazardous waste disposal. 3M developed a new technique to run quality tests more rapidly on new batches. The new technique allowed 3M to reduce hazardous wastes by 10 tons per year at almost no cost, yielding an annual savings of more than $200,000 (Sheridan, 1992).

Solving environmental problems can also yield benefits in terms of reduced downtime. Many chemical production processes at DuPont, for example, require start-up time to stabilize and bring output within specifications, resulting in an initial period during which only scrap and waste is produced. Installing higher-quality monitoring equipment has allowed

---

[4]We should note that this plant was ultimately closed. However, the example described here does illustrate the role of regulatory pressure in process innovation.

DuPont to reduce production interruptions and the associated wasteful production start-ups, thus reducing waste generation as well as downtime (Parkinson, 1990).

Regulation can trigger innovation offsets through substitution of less costly materials or better utilization of materials in the process. For example, 3M faced new regulations that will force many solvent users in paper, plastic and metal coatings to reduce its solvent emissions 90 percent by 1995 (Boroughs and Carpenter, 1991). The company responded by avoiding the use of solvents altogether and developing coating products with safer, water-based solutions. At another 3M plant, a change from a solvent-based to a water-based carrier, used for coating tablets, eliminated 24 tons per year of air emissions. The $60,000 investment saved $180,000 in unneeded pollution control equipment and created annual savings of $15,000 in solvent purchases (Parkinson, 1990). Similarly, when federal and state regulations required that Dow Chemical close certain evaporation ponds used for storing and evaporating wastewater resulting from scrubbing hydrochloric gas with caustic soda, Dow redesigned its production process. By first scrubbing the hydrochloric acid with water and then caustic soda, Dow was able to eliminate the need for evaporation ponds, reduce its use of caustic soda, and capture a portion of the waste stream for reuse as a raw material in other parts of the plant. This process change cost $250,000 to implement. It reduced caustic waste by 6,000 tons per year and hydrochloric acid waste by 80 tons per year, for a savings of $2.4 million per year (Dorfman, Muir and Miller, 1992).

The Robbins Company's jewelry-plating system illustrates similar benefits. In moving to the closed-loop system that purified and recycled water, Robbins saved over $115,000 per year in water, chemicals, disposal costs, and lab fees and reduced water usage from 500,000 gallons per week to 500 gallons per week. The capital cost of the new system, which completely eliminated the waste, was $220,000, compared to about $500,000 for a wastewater treatment facility that would have brought Robbins' discharge into compliance only with current regulations.

At the Tobyhanna Army Depot, for instance, improvements in sandblasting, cleaning, plating and painting operations reduced hazardous waste generation by 82 percent between 1985 and 1992. That reduction saved the depot over $550,000 in disposal costs, and $400,000 in material purchasing and handling costs (PR Newswire, 1993).

Innovation offsets can also be derived by converting waste into more valuable forms. The Robbins Company recovered valuable precious metals in its zero discharge plating system. At Rhone-Poulenc's nylon plant in Chalampe, France, diacids (by-products that had been produced by an adipic acid process) used to be separated and incinerated. Rhone-Poulenc invested Fr 76 million and installed new equipment to recover and sell them as dye and tanning additives or coagulation agents, resulting in annual revenues of about Fr 20.1 million. In the United States, similar by-products from a Monsanto Chemical Company plant in Pensacola, Florida, are sold to utility companies who use them to accelerate sulfur dioxide removal during flue gas desulfurization (Basta and Vagi, 1988).

A few studies of innovation offsets do go beyond individual cases and offer some broader-based data. One of the most extensive studies is by IN-FORM, an environmental research organization. INFORM investigated activities to prevent waste generation—so-called source reduction activities—at 29 chemical plants in California, Ohio and New Jersey (Dorfman, Muir and Miller, 1992). Of the 181 source-reduction activities identified in this study, only one was found to have resulted in a net cost increase. Of the 70 activities for which the study was able to document changes in product yield, 68 reported yield increases; the average yield increase for the 20 initiatives with specific available data was 7 percent. These innovation offsets were achieved with surprisingly low investments and very short payback periods. One-quarter of the 48 initiatives with detailed capital cost information required no capital investment at all; of the 38 initiatives with payback period data, nearly two-thirds were shown to have recouped their initial investments in six months or less. The annual savings per dollar spent on source reduction averaged $3.49 for the 27 activities for which this information could be calculated. The study also investigated the motivating factors behind the plant's source-reduction activities. Significantly, it found that waste disposal costs were the most often cited, followed by environmental regulation.

To build a broader base of studies on innovation offsets to environmental regulation, we have been collaborating with the Management Institute for Environment and Business on a series of international case studies, sponsored by the EPA, of industries and entire sectors significantly affected by environmental regulation. Sectors studied include pulp and paper, paint and coatings, electronics manufacturing, refrigerators, dry cell batteries and printing inks (Bonifant and Ratcliffe, 1994; Bonifant 1994a,b; van der Linde, 1995a,b,c). Some examples from that effort have already been described here.

A solid body of case study evidence, then, demonstrates that innovation offsets to environmental regulation are common.[5] Even with a generally hostile regulatory climate, which is not designed to encourage such innovation, these offsets can sometimes exceed the cost of compliance. We expect that such examples will proliferate as companies and regulators become more sophisticated and shed old mindsets.

Early-Mover Advantage in International Markets

World demand is moving rapidly in the direction of valuing low-pollution and energy-efficient products, not to mention more resource-efficient products with higher resale or scrap value. Many companies are using innovation to command price premiums for "green" products and

---

[5]Of course, a list of case examples, however long, does not prove that companies can always innovate or substitute for careful empirical testing in a large cross-section of industries. Given our current ability to capture the true costs and often multifaceted benefits of regulatory-induced innovation, reliance on the weight of case study evidence is necessary. As we discuss elsewhere, there is no countervailing set of case studies that shows that innovation offsets are unlikely or impossible.

open up new market segments. For example, Germany enacted recycling standards earlier than in most other countries, which gave German firms an early-mover advantage in developing less packaging-intensive products, which have been warmly received in the marketplace. Scandinavian pulp and paper producers have been leaders in introducing new environmentally friendly production processes, and thus Scandinavian pulp and paper equipment suppliers such as Kamyr and Sunds have made major gains internationally in selling innovative bleaching equipment. In the United States, a parallel example is the development by Cummins Engine of low-emissions diesel engines for trucks, buses and other applications in response to U.S. environmental regulations. Its new competence is allowing the firm to gain international market share.

Clearly, this argument only works to the extent that national environmental standards anticipate and are consistent with international trends in environmental protection, rather than break with them. Creating expertise in cleaning up abandoned hazardous waste sites, as the U.S. Superfund law has done, does little to benefit U.S. suppliers if no other country adopts comparable toxic waste cleanup requirements. But when a competitive edge is attained, especially because a company's home market is sophisticated and demanding in a way that pressures the company to further innovation, the economic gains can be lasting.

Answering Defenders of the Traditional Model

Our argument that strict environmental regulation can be fully consistent with competitiveness was originally put forward in a short *Scientific American* essay (Porter, 1991; see also van der Linde, 1993). This essay received far more scrutiny than we expected. It has been warmly received by many, especially in the business community. But it has also had its share of critics, especially among economists (Jaffe, Peterson, Portney and Stavins, 1993, 1994; Oates, Palmer and Portney, 1993; Palmer and Simpson, 1993; Simpson, 1993; Schmalensee, 1993).

One criticism is that while innovation offsets are theoretically possible, they are likely to be rare or small in practice. We disagree. Pollution is the emission or discharge of a (harmful) substance or energy form into the environment. Fundamentally, it is a manifestation of economic waste and involves unnecessary, inefficient or incomplete utilization of resources, or resources not used to generate their highest value. In many cases, emissions are a sign of inefficiency and force a firm to perform non-value-creating activities such as handling, storage and disposal. Within the company itself, the costs of poor resource utilization are most obvious in incomplete material utilization, but are also manifested in poor process control, which generates unnecessary stored material, waste and defects. There are many other hidden costs of resource inefficiencies later in the life cycle of the product. Packaging discarded by distributors or customers, for example, wastes resources and adds costs. Customers bear additional costs when they use polluting products or products that waste energy. Resources are also wasted when customers discard products embodying unused materials or when they bear the costs of product disposal.[6]

As the many examples discussed earlier suggest, the opportunity to reduce cost by diminishing pollution should thus be the rule, not the exception. Highly toxic materials such as heavy metals or solvents are often expensive and hard to handle, and reducing their use makes sense from several points of view. More broadly, efforts to reduce pollution and maximize profits share the same basic principles, including the efficient use of input, substitution of less expensive materials and the minimization of unneeded activities.[7]

A corollary to this observation is that scrap or waste or emissions can carry important information about flaws in product design or the production process. A recent study of process changes in 10 printed circuit board manufacturers, for example, found that 13 of 33 major changes were initiated by pollution control personnel. Of these, 12 resulted in cost reduction, eight in quality improvements and five in extension of production capabilities (King, 1994).

Environmental improvement efforts have traditionally overlooked the systems cost of resource inefficiency. Improvement efforts have focused on *pollution control* through better identification, processing and disposal of discharges or waste, an inherently costly approach. In recent years, more advanced companies and regulators have embraced the concept of *pollution prevention*, sometimes called source reduction, which uses material substitution, closed-loop processes and the like to limit pollution before it occurs.

But although pollution prevention is an important step in the right direction, ultimately companies and regulators must learn to frame environmental improvement in terms of *resource productivity*, or the efficiency and effectiveness with which companies and their customers use resources.[8] Improving resource productivity within companies goes beyond eliminating pollution (and the cost of dealing with it) to lowering true economic cost and raising the true economic value of products. At the level of resource productivity, environmental improvement and competitiveness come together. The imperative for resource productivity rests on the private costs that companies bear because of pollution, not on mitigating pollution's social costs. In addressing these private costs, it highlights the opportunity costs of pollution—wasted resources, wasted efforts and diminished product value to the customer—not its actual costs.

---

[6]At its core, then, pollution is a result of an intermediate state of technology or management methods. Apparent exceptions to the resource productivity thesis often prove the rule by highlighting the role of technology. Paper made with recycled fiber was once greatly inferior, but new de-inking and other technologies have made its quality better and better. Apparent tradeoffs between energy efficiency and emissions rest on incomplete combustion.

[7]Schmalensee (1993) counters that NO_x emissions often result from thermodynamically efficient combustion. But surely this is an anomaly, not the rule, and may represent an intermediate level of efficiency.

[8]One of the pioneering efforts to see environmental improvement this way is Joel Makower's (1993) book, *The E-Factor: The Bottom-Line Approach to Environmentally Responsible Business*.

This view of pollution as unproductive resource utilization suggests a helpful analogy between environmental protection and product quality measured by defects. Companies used to promote quality by conducting careful inspections during the production process, and then by creating a service organization to correct the quality problems that turned up in the field. This approach has proven misguided. Instead, the most cost-effective way to improve quality is to build it into the entire process, which includes design, purchased components, process technology, shipping and handling techniques and so forth. This method dramatically reduces inspection, re-work and the need for a large service organization. (It also leads to the oft-quoted phrase, "quality is free.") Similarly, there is reason to believe that companies can enjoy substantial innovation offsets by improving resource productivity throughout the value chain instead of through dealing with the manifestations of inefficiency like emissions and discharges.

Indeed, corporate total quality management programs have strong po-tential also to reduce pollution and lead to innovation offsets.[9] Dow Chem-ical, for example, has explicitly identified the link between quality im-provement and environmental performance, by using statistical process control to reduce the variance in processes and lower waste (Sheridan, 1992).

A second criticism of our hypothesis is to point to the studies finding high costs of compliance with environmental regulation, as evidence that there is a fixed tradeoff between regulation and competitiveness. But these studies are far from definitive.

Estimates of regulatory compliance costs prior to enactment of a new rule typically exceed the actual costs. In part, this is because such estimates are often self-reported by industries who oppose the rule, which creates a tendency to inflation. A prime example of this type of thinking was a state-ment by Lee Iacocca, then vice president at the Ford Motor Company, dur-ing the debate on the 1970 Clean Air Act. Iacocca warned that compliance with the new regulations would require huge price increases for automo-biles, force U.S. automobile production to a halt after January 1, 1975, and "do irreparable damage to the U.S. economy" (Smith, 1992). The 1970 Clean Air Act was subsequently enacted, and Iacocca's predictions turned out to be wrong. Similar dire predictions were made during the 1990 Clean Air Act debate; industry analysts predicted that burdens on the U.S. industry would exceed $100 billion. Of course, the reality has proven to be far less dramatic. In one study in the pulp and paper sector, actual costs of com-pliance were $4.00 to $5.50 per ton compared to original industry estimates of $16.40 (Bonson, McCubbin and Sprague, 1988).

Early estimates of compliance cost also tend to be exaggerated because they assume no innovation. Early cost estimates for dealing with regula-

---

[9]A case study of pollution prevention in a large multinational firm showed those units with strong total quality management programs in place usually undertake more effective pollution pre-vention efforts than units with less commitment to total quality management. See Rappaport (1992), cited in U.S. Congress, Office of Technology Assessment (1994).

tions concerning emission of volatile compounds released during paint application held everything else constant, assuming only the addition of a hood to capture the fumes from paint lines. Innovation that improved the paint's transfer efficiency subsequently allowed not only the reduction of fumes but also paint usage. Further innovation in waterborne paint formulations without any VOC-releasing solvents made it possible to eliminate the need for capturing and treating the fumes altogether (Bonifant, 1994b). Similarly, early estimates of the costs of complying with a 1991 federal clean air regulation calling for a 98 percent reduction in atmospheric emissions of benzene from tar-storage tanks used by coal tar distillers initially assumed that tar-storage tanks would have to be covered by costly gas blankets. While many distillers opposed the regulations, Pittsburgh-based Aristech Chemical, a major distiller of coal tar, subsequently developed an innovative way to remove benzene from tar in the first processing step, thereby eliminating the need for the gas blanket and resulting in a saving of $3.3 million instead of a cost increase (PR Newswire, 1993).

Prices in the new market for trading allowances to emit SO_2 provide another vivid example. At the time the law was passed, analysts projected that the marginal cost of SO_2 controls (and, therefore, the price of an emission allowance) would be on the order of $300 to $600 (or more) per ton in Phase I and up to $1000 or more in Phase II. Actual Phase I allowance prices have turned out to be in the $170 to $250 range, and recent trades are heading lower, with Phase II estimates only slightly higher (after adjusting for the time value of money). In case after case, the differences between initial predictions and actual outcomes—especially after industry has had time to learn and innovate—are striking.

Econometric studies showing that environmental regulation raises costs and harms competitiveness are subject to bias, because net compliance costs are overestimated by assuming away innovation benefits. Jorgenson and Wilcoxen (1990), for example, explicitly state that they did not attempt to assess public or private benefits. Other often-cited studies that solely focus on costs, leaving out benefits, are Hazilla and Kopp (1990) and Gray (1987). By largely assuming away innovation effects, how could economic studies reach any other conclusion than they do?

Internationally competitive industries seem to be much better able to innovate in response to environmental regulation than industries that were uncompetitive to begin with, but no study measuring the effects of environmental regulation on industry competitiveness has taken initial competitiveness into account. In a study by Kalt (1988), for instance, the sectors where high environmental costs were associated with negative trade performance were ones such as ferrous metal mining, nonferrous mining, chemical and fertilizer manufacturing, primary iron and steel and primary nonferrous metals, industries where the United States suffers from dwindling raw material deposits, very high relative electricity costs, heavily subsidized foreign competitors and other disadvantages that have rendered them uncompetitive quite apart from environmental costs.[10] Other sectors identified by Kalt as having incurred very high environmental costs can actually be interpreted as supporting our hypothesis. Chemicals, plastics and synthetics, fabric, yarn and thread, miscellaneous textiles, leather tanning, paints and allied products, and paperboard containers all had high environmental costs but displayed positive trade performance.

A number of studies have failed to find that stringent environmental regulation hurts industrial competitiveness. Meyer (1992, 1993) tested and refuted the hypothesis that U.S. states with stringent environmental policies experience weak economic growth. Leonard (1988) was unable to demonstrate statistically significant offshore movements by U.S. firms in pollution-intensive industries. Wheeler and Mody (1992) failed to find that environmental regulation affected the foreign investment decisions of U.S. firms. Repetto (1995) found that industries heavily affected by environmental regulations experienced slighter reductions in their share of world exports than did the entire American industry from 1970 to 1990. Using U.S. Bureau of Census Data of more than 200,000 large manufacturing establishments, the study also found that plants with poor environmental records are generally not more profitable than cleaner ones in the same industry, even controlling for their age, size and technology. Jaffe, Peterson, Portney and Stavins (1993) recently surveyed more than 100 studies and concluded there is little evidence to support the view that U.S. environmental regulation had a large adverse effect on competitiveness.

Of course, these studies offer no proof for our hypothesis, either. But it is striking that so many studies find that even the poorly designed environmental laws presently in effect have little adverse effect on competitiveness. After all, traditional approaches to regulation have surely worked to stifle potential innovation offsets and imposed unnecessarily high costs of compliance on industry (as we will discuss in greater detail in the next section). Thus, studies using actual compliance costs to regulation are heavily biased toward finding that such regulation has a substantial cost.[11] In

---

[10]It should be observed that a strong correlation between environmental costs and industry competitiveness does not necessarily indicate causality. Omitting environmental benefits from regulation, and reporting obvious (end-of-pipe) costs but not more difficult to identify or quantify innovation benefits can actually obscure a reverse causal relationship: industries that were uncompetitive in the first place may well be less able to innovate in response to environmental pressures, and thus be prone to end-of-pipe solutions whose costs are easily measured. In contrast, competitive industries capable of addressing environmental problems in innovative ways may report a lower compliance cost.

[11]Gray and Shadbegian (1993), another often-mentioned study, suffers from several of the problems discussed here. The article uses industry-reported compliance costs and does not control for plant technology vintage or the extent of other productivity-enhancing investments at the plant. High compliance costs may well have been borne in old, inefficient plants where firms opted for secondary treatment rather than innovation. Moreover, U.S. producers may well have been disadvantaged in innovating given the nature of the U.S. regulatory process—this seems clearly to have been the case in pulp and paper, one of the industries studied by the Management Institute for Environment and Business (MEB).

no way do such studies measure the potential of well-crafted environmental regulations to stimulate competitiveness.

A third criticism of our thesis is that even if regulation fosters innovation, it will harm competitiveness by crowding out other potentially more productive investments or avenues for innovation. Given incomplete information, the limited attention many companies have devoted to environmental innovations and the inherent linkage between pollution and resource productivity described earlier, it certainly is not obvious that this line of innovation has been so thoroughly explored that the marginal benefits of further investment would be low. The high returns evident in the studies we have cited support this view. Moreover, environmental investments represent only a small percentage of overall investment in all but a very few industries.[12]

A final counterargument, more caricature than criticism, is that we are asserting that any strict environmental regulation will inevitably lead to innovation and competitiveness. Of course, this is not our position. Instead, we believe that if regulations are properly crafted and companies are attuned to the possibilities, then innovation to minimize and even offset the cost of compliance is likely in many circumstances.

Designing Environmental Regulation to Encourage Innovation

If environmental standards are to foster the innovation offsets that arise from new technologies and approaches to production, they should adhere to three principles. First, they must create the maximum opportunity for innovation, leaving the approach to innovation to industry and not the standard-setting agency. Second, regulations should foster continuous improvement, rather than locking in any particular technology. Third, the regulatory process should leave as little room as possible for uncertainty at every stage. Evaluated by these principles, it is clear that U.S. environmental regulations have often been crafted in a way that deters innovative solutions, or even renders them impossible. Environmental laws and regulations need to take three substantial steps: phrasing environmental rules as goals that can be met in flexible ways; encouraging innovation to reach and exceed those goals; and administering the system in a coordinated way.

---

[12]In paints and coatings, for example, environmental investments were 3.3 percent of total capital investment in 1989. According to Department of Commerce (1991) data (self-reported by industry), capital spending for pollution control and abatement outside of the chemical, pulp and paper, petroleum and coal, and primary metal sectors made up just 3.15 percent of total capital spending in 1991.

Clear Goals, Flexible Approaches

Environmental regulation should focus on outcomes, not technologies.[13] Past regulations have often prescribed particular remediation technologies—like catalysts or scrubbers to address air pollution—rather than encouraging innovative approaches. American environmental law emphasized phrases like "best available technology," or "best available control technology." But legislating as if one particular technology is always the "best" almost guarantees that innovation will not occur.

Regulations should encourage product and process changes to better utilize resources and avoid pollution early, rather than mandating end-of-pipe or secondary treatment, which is almost always more costly. For regulators, this poses a question of where to impose regulations in the chain of production from raw materials, equipment, the producer of the end product, to the consumer (Porter, 1985). Regulators must consider the technological capabilities and resources available at each stage, because it affects the likelihood that innovation will occur. With that in mind, the governing principle should be to regulate as late in the production chain as practical, which will normally allow more flexibility for innovation there and in upstream stages.

The EPA should move beyond the single medium (air, water and so on) as the principal way of thinking about the environment, toward total discharges or total impact.[14] It should reorganize around affected industry clusters (including suppliers and related industries) to better understand a cluster's products, technologies and total set of environmental problems. This will foster fundamental rather than piecemeal solutions.[15]

Seeding and Spreading Environmental Innovations

Where possible, regulations should include the use of market incentives, including pollution taxes, deposit-refund schemes and tradable permits.[16] Such approaches often allow considerable flexibility, reinforce resource

---

[13]There will always be instances of extremely hazardous pollution requiring immediate action, where imposing a specific technology by command and control may be the best or only viable solution. However, such methods should be seen as a last resort.

[14]A first step in this direction is the EPA's recent adjustment of the timing of its air rule for the pulp and paper industry so that it will coincide with the rule for water, allowing industry to see the dual impact of the rules and innovate accordingly.

[15]The EPA's regulatory cluster team concept, under which a team from relevant EPA offices approaches particular problems for a broader viewpoint, is a first step in this direction. Note, however, that of the 17 cluster groups formed, only four were organized around specific industries (petroleum refining, oil and gas production, pulp and paper, printing), while the remaining 13 focused on specific chemicals or types of pollution (U.S. Congress, Office of Technology Assessment, 1994).

[16]Pollution taxes can be implemented as effluent charges on the quantity of pollution discharges, as user charges for public treatment facilities, or as product charges based on the potential pollution of a product. In a deposit-refund system, such product charges may be rebated if a product user disposes of it properly (for example, by returning a lead battery for recycling rather than sending it to a landfill). Under a tradable permit system, like that included in the recent Clean Air Act Amendments, a maximum amount of pollution is set, and rights equal to that cap are distributed to firms. Firms must hold enough rights to cover their emissions; firms with excess rights can sell them to firms who are short.

productivity, and also create incentives for ongoing innovation. Mandating outcomes by setting emission levels, while preferable to choosing a particular technology, still fails to provide incentives for continued and ongoing innovation and will tend to freeze a status quo until new regulations appear. In contrast, market incentives can encourage the introduction of technologies that exceed current standards.

The EPA should also promote an increased use of preemptive standards by industry, which appear to be an effective way of dealing with environmental regulation. Preemptive standards, agreed to with EPA oversight to avoid collusion, can be set and met by industry to avoid government standards that might go further or be more restrictive on innovation. They are not only less costly, but allow faster change and leave the initiative for innovation with industry.

The EPA should play a major role in collecting and disseminating information on innovation offsets and their consequences, both here and in other countries. Limited knowledge about opportunities for innovation is a major constraint on company behavior. A good start can be the "clearinghouse" of information on source-reduction approaches that EPA was directed to establish by the Pollution Prevention Act (PPA) of 1990. The Green Lights and Toxics Release Inventories described at the start of this paper are other programs that involve collecting and spreading information. Yet another important initiative is the EPA program to compare emissions rates at different companies, creating methodologies to measure the full internal costs of pollution and ways of exchanging best practices and learning on innovative technologies.

Regulatory approaches can also function by helping create demand pressure for environmental innovation. One example is the prestigious German "Blue Angel" eco-label, introduced by the German government in 1977, which can be displayed only by products meeting very strict environmental criteria. One of the label's biggest success stories has been in oil and gas heating appliances: the energy efficiency of these appliances improved significantly when the label was introduced, and emissions of sulfur dioxide, carbon monoxide and nitrogen oxides were reduced by more than 30 percent.

Another point of leverage on the demand side is to harness the role of government as a demanding buyer of environmental solutions and environmentally friendly products. While there are benefits of government procurement of products such as recycled paper and retreaded tires, the far more leveraged role is in buying specialized environmental equipment and services.[17] One useful change would be to alter the current practice of requiring bidders in competitive bid processes for government projects to only bid with "proven" technologies, a practice sure to hinder innovation.

---

[17]See Marron (1994) for a demonstration of the modest productivity gains likely from government procurement of standard items, although in a static model.

The EPA can employ demonstration projects to stimulate and seed innovative new technologies, working through universities and industry associations. A good example is the project to develop and demonstrate technologies for super-efficient refrigerators, which was conducted by the EPA and researchers in government, academia and the private sector (United States Environmental Protection Agency, 1992). An estimated $1.7 billion was spent in 1992 by the federal government on environmental technology R&D, but only $70 million was directed toward research on pollution prevention (U.S. Congress, Office of Technology Assessment, 1994).

Incentives for innovation must also be built into the regulatory process itself. The current permitting system under Title V of the Clean Air Act Amendments, to choose a negative example, requires firms seeking to change or expand their production process in a way that might impact air quality to revise their permit extensively, *no matter how little the potential effect on air quality may be.* This not only deters innovation, but drains the resources of regulators away from timely action on significant matters. On the positive side, the state of Massachusetts has initiated a program to waive permits in some circumstances, or promise an immediate permit, if a company takes a zero-discharge approach.

A final priority is new forums for settling regulatory issues that minimize litigation. Potential litigation creates enormous uncertainty; actual litigation burns resources. Mandatory arbitration, or rigid arbitration steps before litigation is allowed, would benefit innovation. There is also a need to rethink certain liability issues. While adequate safeguards must be provided against companies that recklessly harm citizens, there is a pressing need for liability standards that more clearly recognize the countervailing health and safety benefits of innovations that lower or eliminate the discharge of harmful pollutants.

Regulatory Coordination

Coordination of environmental regulation can be improved in at least three ways: between industry and regulators, between regulators at different levels and places in government, and between U.S. regulators and their international counterparts.

In setting environmental standards and regulatory processes to encourage innovation, substantive industry participation in setting standards is needed right from the beginning, as is common in many European countries. An appropriate regulatory process is one in which regulations themselves are clear, who must meet them is clear, and industry accepts the regulations and begins innovating to address them, rather than spending years attempting to delay or relax them. In our current system, by the time standards are finally settled and clarified, it is often too late to address them fundamentally, making secondary treatment the only alternative. We need to evolve toward a regulatory regime in which the EPA and other regulators make a commitment that standards will be in place for, say, five years, so that industry is motivated to innovate rather than adopt increment solutions.

Different parts and levels of government must coordinate and organize themselves so that companies are not forced to deal with multiple parties with inconsistent desires and approaches. As a matter of regulatory structure, the EPA's proposed new Innovative Technology Council, being set up to advocate the development of new technology in every field of environmental policy, is a step in the right direction. Another unit in the EPA should be responsible for continued reengineering of the process of regulation to reduce uncertainty and minimize costs. Also, an explicit strategy is needed to coordinate and harmonize federal and state activities.[18]

A final issue of coordination involves the relationship between U.S. environmental regulations and those in other countries. U.S. regulations should be in sync with regulations in other countries and, ideally, be slightly ahead of them. This will minimize possible competitive disadvantages relative to foreign competitors who are not yet subject to the standard, while at the same time maximizing export potential in the pollution control sector. Standards that lead world developments provide domestic firms with opportunities to create valuable early-mover advantages. However, standards should not be too far ahead of, or too different in character from, those that are likely to apply to foreign competitors, for this would lead industry to innovate in the wrong directions.

Critics may note, with some basis, that U.S. regulators may not be able to project better than firms what type of regulations, and resultant demands for environmental products and services, will develop in other nations. However, regulators would seem to possess greater resources and information than firms for understanding the path of regulation in other countries. Moreover, U.S. regulations influence the type and stringency of regulations in other nations, and as such help define demand in other world markets.

Imperatives for Companies

Of course, the regulatory reforms described here also seek to change how companies view environmental issues.[19] Companies must start to recognize the environment as a competitive opportunity—not as an annoying cost or a postponable threat. Yet many companies are ill-prepared to carry out a strategy of environmental innovation that produces sizable compensating offsets.

---

[18]The cluster-based approach to regulation discussed earlier should also help eliminate the practice of sending multiple EPA inspectors to the same plant who do not talk to one another, make conflicting demands and waste time and resources. The potential savings from cluster- and multimedia-oriented permitting and inspection programs appear to be substantial. During a pilot multimedia testing program called the Blackstone Project, the Massachusetts Department of Environmental Protection found that multimedia inspections required 50 percent less time than conventional inspections—which at that time accounted for nearly one-fourth of the department's operating budget (Roy and Dillard, 1990).

[19]For a more detailed perspective on changing company mindsets about competitiveness and environmentalism, see Porter and van der Linde (1995) in the *Harvard Business Review*.

For starters, companies must improve their measurement and assessment methods to detect environmental costs and benefits.[20] Too often, relevant information is simply lacking. Typical is the case of a large producer of organic chemicals that retained a consulting firm to explore opportunities for reducing waste. The client thought it had 40 waste streams, but a careful audit revealed that 497 different waste streams were actually present (Parkinson, 1990). Few companies analyze the true cost of toxicity, waste, discharges and the second-order impacts of waste and discharges on other activities. Fewer still look beyond the out-of-pocket costs of dealing with pollution to investigate the opportunity costs of the wasted resources or foregone productivity. How much money is going up the smokestack? What percentage of inputs are wasted? Many companies do not even track environmental spending carefully, or subject it to evaluation techniques typical for "normal" investments.

Once environmental costs are measured and understood, the next step is to create a presumption for innovation-based solutions. Discharges, scrap and emissions should be analyzed for insights about beneficial product design or process changes. Approaches based on treatment or handling of discharges should be accepted only after being sent back several times for reconsideration. The responsibility for environmental issues should not be delegated to lawyers or outside consultants except in the adversarial regulatory process, or even to internal specialists removed from the line organization, residing in legal, government or environmental affairs departments. Instead, environmental strategies must become a general management issue if the sorts of process and product redesigns needed for true innovation are to even be considered, much less be proposed and implemented.

Conclusion

We have found that economists as a group are resistant to the notion that even well-designed environmental regulations might lead to improved competitiveness. This hesitancy strikes us as somewhat peculiar, given that in other contexts, economists are extremely willing to argue that technological change has overcome predictions of severe, broadly defined environmental costs. A static model (among other flaws) has been behind many dire predictions of economic disaster and human catastrophe: from the predictions of Thomas Malthus that population would inevitably outstrip food

---

[20]Accounting methods that are currently being discussed in this context include "full cost accounting," which attempts to assign all costs to specific products or processes, and "total cost accounting," which goes a step further and attempts both to allocate costs more specifically and to include cost items beyond traditional concerns, such as indirect or hidden costs (like compliance costs, insurance, on-site waste management, operation of pollution control and future liability) and less tangible benefits (like revenue from enhanced company image). See White, Becker and Goldstein (1991), cited in U.S. Congress, Office of Technology Assessment (1994).

supply; to the *Limits of Growth* (Meadows and Meadows, 1972), which predicted the depletion of the world's natural resources; to *The Population Bomb* (Ehrlich, 1968), which predicted that a quarter of the world's population would starve to death between 1973 and 1983. As economists are often eager to point out, these models failed because they did not appreciate the power of innovations in technology to change old assumptions about resource availability and utilization.

Moreover, the static mindset that environmentalism is inevitably costly has created a self-fulfilling gridlock, where both regulators and industry battle over every inch of territory. The process has spawned an industry of litigators and consultants, driving up costs and draining resources away from real solutions. It has been reported that four out of five EPA decisions are currently challenged in court (Clay, 1993, cited in U.S. Congress, Office of Technology Assessment, 1994). A study by the Rand Institute for Civil Justice found that 88 percent of the money paid out between 1986 and 1989 by insurers on Superfund claims went to pay for legal and administrative costs, while only 12 percent were used for actual site cleanups (Acton and Dixon, 1992).

The United States and other countries need an entirely new way of thinking about the relationship between environment and industrial competitiveness—one closer to the reality of modern competition. The focus should be on relaxing the environment-competitiveness tradeoff rather than accepting and, worse yet, steepening it. The orientation should shift from pollution control to resource productivity. We believe that no lasting success can come from policies that promise that environmentalism will triumph over industry, nor from policies that promise that industry will triumph over environmentalism. Instead, success must involve innovation-based solutions that promote both environmentalism and industrial competitiveness.

References

Acton, Jan Paul, and Lloyd S. Dixon, *Superfund and Transaction Costs: The Experiences of Insurers and Very Large Industrial Firms*. Santa Monica: Rand Institute for Civil Justice, 1992.

Amoco Corporation and United States Environmental Protection Agency, "Amoco-U.S. EPA Pollution Prevention Project: Yorktown, Virginia, Project Summary," Chicago and Washington, D.C., 1992.

Basta, Nicholas and David Vagi, "A Casebook of Successful Waste Reduction Projections," *Chemical Engineering*, August 15, 1988, 95:11, 37.

Berube, M., J. Nash, J. Maxwell, and J. Ehrenfeld, "From Pollution Control to Zero Discharge: How the Robbins Company Overcame the Obstacles," *Pollution Prevention Review*, Spring 1992, 2:2, 189–207.

Bonifant, B., "Competitive Implications of Environmental Regulation in the Electronics Manufacturing Industry," Management Institute for Environment and Business, Washington, D.C., 1994a.

Bonifant, B., "Competitive Implications of Environmental Regulation in the Paint and Coatings Industry," Management Institute for Environment and Business, Washington, D.C., 1994b.

Bonifant, B., and I. Ratcliffe, "Competitive Implications of Environmental Regulation in the Pulp and Paper Industry," Management Institute for Environment and Business, Washington, D.C., 1994.

Bonson, N. C., Neil McCubbin, and John B. Sprague, "Kraft Mill Effluents in Ontario." Report prepared for the Technical Advisory Committee, Pulp and Paper Sector of MISA, Ontario Ministry of the Environment, Toronto, Ontario, Canada, March 29, 1988, Section 6, p. 166.

Boroughs, D. L., and B. Carpenter, "Helping the Planet and the Economy," *U.S. News & World Report*, March 25, 1991, *110*:11, 46.

Clay, Don, "New Environmentalist: A Cooperative Strategy," *Forum for Applied Research and Public Policy*, Spring 1993, *8*, 125–28.

DeCanio, Stephen J., "Why Do Profitable Energy-Saving Investment Projects Languish?" Paper presented at the Second International Research Conference of the Greening of Industry Network, Cambridge, Mass., 1993.

Department of Commerce, "Pollution Abatement Costs and Expenditures," Washington, D.C., 1991.

Dorfman, Mark H., Warren R. Muir, and Catherine G. Miller, *Environmental Dividends: Cutting More Chemical Wastes*. New York: INFORM, 1992.

Ehrlich, Paul, *The Population Bomb*. New York: Ballantine Books, 1968.

Freeman, A. Myrick, III, "Methods for Assessing the Benefits of Environmental Programs." In Kneese, A. V., and J. L. Sweeney, eds., *Handbook of Natural Resource and Energy Economics*. Vol. 1. Amsterdam: North-Holland, 1985, pp. 223–70.

Gray, Wayne B., "The Cost of Regulation: OSHA, EPA, and the Productivity Slowdown," *American Economic Review*, 1987, 77:5, 998–1006.

Gray, Wayne B., and Ronald J. Shadbegian, "Environmental Regulation and Productivity at the Plant Level," discussion paper, U.S. Department of Commerce, Center for Economic Studies, Washington, D.C., 1993.

Hartwell, R. V., and L. Bergkamp, "Eco-Labelling in Europe: New Market-Related Environmental Risks?," *BNA International Environment Daily*, Special Report, Oct. 20, 1992.

Hazilla, Michael, and Raymond J. Kopp, "Social Cost of Environmental Quality Regulations: A General Equilibrium Analysis," *Journal of Political Economy*, 1990, *98*:4, 853–73.

Jaffe, Adam B., S. Peterson, Paul Portney, and Robert N. Stavins, "Environmental Regulations and the Competitiveness of U.S. Industry," Economics Resource Group, Cambridge, Mass., 1993.

Jaffe, Adam B., S. Peterson, Paul Portney, and Robert N. Stavins, "Environmental Regulation and International Competitiveness: What Does the Evidence Tell Us," draft, January 13, 1994.

Jorgenson, Dale W., and Peter J. Wilcoxen, "Environmental Regulation and U.S. Economic Growth," *Rand Journal of Economics*, Summer 1990, *21*:2, 314–40.

Kalt, Joseph P., "The Impact of Domestic Environmental Regulatory Policies on U.S. International Competitiveness." In Spence, A. M., and H. Hazard, eds., *International Competitiveness*, Cambridge, Mass: Harper and Row, Ballinger, 1988, pp. 221–62.

King, A., "Improved Manufacturing Resulting from Learning-From-Waste: Causes, Importance, and Enabling Conditions," working paper, Stern School of Business, New York University, 1994.

Leonard, H. Jeffrey, *Pollution and the Struggle for World Product*. Cambridge, U.K.: Cambridge University Press, 1988.

Makower, Joel, *The E-Factor: The Bottom-Line Approach to Environmentally Responsible Business*. New York: Times Books, 1993.

Marron, Donald B., "Buying Green: Government Procurement as an Instrument of Environmental Policy," mimeo, Massachusetts Institute of Technology, 1994.

Massachusetts Department of Environmental Protection, Daniel S. Greenbaum, Commissioner, interview, Boston, August 8, 1993.

Meadows, Donella H., and Dennis L. Meadows, *The Limits of Growth*. New York: New American Library, 1972.

Meyer, Stephen M., *Environmentalism and Economic Prosperity: Testing the Environmental Impact Hypothesis*. Cambridge, Mass.: Massachusetts Institute of Technology, 1992.

Meyer, Stephen M., *Environmentalism and Economic Prosperity: An Update*. Cambridge, Mass.: Massachusetts Institute of Technology, 1993.

National Paint and Coatings Association, *Improving the Superfund: Correcting a National Public Policy Disaster*. Washington, D.C., 1992.

Oates, Wallace, Karen L. Palmer, and Paul Portney, "Environmental Regulation and International Competitiveness: Thinking About the Porter Hypothesis." Resources for the Future Working Paper 94-02, 1993.

Palmer, Karen L., and Ralph David Simpson, "Environmental Policy as Industrial Policy," *Resources*, Summer 1993, *112*, 17–21.

Parkinson, Gerald, "Reducing Wastes Can Be Cost-Effective," *Chemical Engineering*, July 1990, *97*:7, 30.

Porter, Michael E., *Competitive Advantage: Creating and Sustaining Superior Performance*. New York: Free Press, 1985.

Porter, Michael E., *The Competitive Advantage of Nations*. New York: Free Press, 1990.

Porter, Michael E., "America's Green Strategy," *Scientific American*, April 1991, *264*, 168.

Porter, Michael E., and Claas van der Linde, "Green *and* Competitive: Breaking the Stalemate," *Harvard Business Review*, September–October 1995.

PR Newswire, "Winners Announced for Governor's Waste Minimization Awards," January 21, 1993, State and Regional News Section.

Rappaport, Ann, "Development and Transfer of Pollution Prevention Technology Within a Multinational Corporation," dissertation, Department of Civil Engineering. Tufts University, May 1992.

Raytheon Inc., "Alternative Cleaning Technology." Technical Report Phase II. January–October 1991.

Raytheon Inc., J. R. Pasquariello, Vice President Environmental Quality; Kenneth J. Tierney, Director Environmental and Energy Conservation; Frank A. Marino, Senior Corporate Environmental Specialist; interview, Lexington, Mass., April 4, 1993.

Repetto, Robert, "Jobs, Competitiveness, and Environmental Regulation: What Are the Real Issues?," Washington, D.C.: World Resources Institute, 1995.

Roy, M., and L. A. Dillard, "Toxics Use in Massachusetts: The Blackstone Project," *Journal of Air and Waste Management Association*, October 1990, *40*:10, 1368–71.

Schmalensee, Richard, "The Costs of Environmental Regulation." Massachusetts Institute of Technology, Center for Energy and Environmental Policy Research Working Paper 93-015, 1993.

Sheridan, J. H., "Attacking Wastes and Saving Money . . . Some of the Time," *Industry Week*, February 17, 1992, *241*:4, 43.

Simpson, Ralph David, "Taxing Variable Cost: Environmental Regulation as Industrial Policy." Resources for the Future Working Paper ENR93-12, 1993.

Smith, Zachary A, *The Environmental Policy Paradox*. Englewood Cliffs, N.J.: Prentice-Hall, 1992.

United States Environmental Protection Agency, "Multiple Pathways to Super Efficient Refrigerators," Washington, D.C., 1992.

U.S. Congress, Office of Technology Assessment, "Industry, Technology, and the Environment: Competitive Challenges and Business Opportunities," OTA-ITE-586, Washington, D.C., 1994.

van der Linde, Claas, "The Micro-Economic Implications of Environmental Regulation: A Preliminary Framework." In *Environmental Policies and Industrial Competitiveness*. Paris: Organization of Economic Cooperation and Development, 1993, pp. 69–77.

van der Linde, Claas, "Competitive Implications of Environmental Regulation in the Cell Battery Industry," Hochschule St. Gallen, St. Gallen, forthcoming 1995a.

van der Linde, Claas, "Competitive Implications of Environmental Regulation in the Printing Ink Industry," Hochschule St. Gallen, St. Gallen, forthcoming 1995b.

van der Linde, Claas, "Competitive Implications of Environmental Regulation in the Refrigerator Industry," Hochschule St. Gallen, St. Gallen, forthcoming 1995c.

Wheeler, David, and Ashoka Mody, "International Investment Location Decisions: The Case of U.S. Firms," *Journal of International Economics*, August 1992, *33*, 57–76.

White, A. L., M. Becker, and J. Goldstein, "Alternative Approaches to the Financial Evaluation of Industrial Pollution Prevention Investments," prepared for the New Jersey Department of Environmental Protection, Division of Science and Research, November 1991.

6 Tightening Environmental Standards: The Benefit-Cost or the No-Cost Paradigm?*

Karen Palmer

Wallace E. Oates

Paul R. Portney

Karen Palmer is Senior Fellow at Resources for the Future; Wallace Oates is Professor of Economics at the University of Maryland, and Visiting Scholar at Resources for the Future; and Paul Portney is President and Senior Fellow at Resources for the Future.

Michael Porter and Claas van der Linde have written a paper that is interesting and, to us at least, somewhat astonishing. It is a defense of environmental regulation—indeed, an invitation to more stringent regulation—that makes essentially no reference to the *social* benefits of such regulation. This approach contrasts starkly with the methods that economists and other policy analysts have traditionally used when assessing environmental or other regulatory programs.

The traditional approach consists of comparing the beneficial effects of regulation with the costs that must be borne to secure these benefits. For environmental regulation, the social benefits include the reductions in morbidity or premature mortality that can accompany cleaner air, the enhanced recreational opportunities that can result from water-quality improvements, the increased land values that might attend the cleanup of a hazardous waste site, the enhanced vitality of aquatic ecosystems that might follow reductions in agricultural pesticide use or any of the other potentially significant benefits associated with tighter standards. From this benefit-cost approach emerges the standard tradeoff discussed in virtually every economics textbook.

Porter and van der Linde deny the validity of this approach to the analysis of environmental regulation, claiming it to be an artifact of what they see as a "static mindset." In their view, economists have failed to appreciate the capacity of stringent environmental regulations to induce innova-

"Tightening Environmental Standards: The Benefit-Cost or the No-Cost Paradigm?" by Karen Palmer, Wallace E. Oates, and Paul R. Portney, from *Journal of Economic Perspectives*, 9(4):119–132 (Fall 1995).

*We are grateful for helpful comments on earlier drafts to Albert McGartland, Richard Schmalensee and the editors of this journal. We wish to thank the Environmental Protection Agency, the National Science Foundation and the Sloan Foundation for support that made this work possible.

tion, and this failure has led them to a fundamental misrepresentation of the problem of environmental regulation. There is no tradeoff, Porter and van der Linde suggest; instead, environmental protection, properly pursued, often presents a free or even a paid lunch. As they put it, there are lots of $10 bills lying around waiting to be picked up.

We take strong issue with their view. If this were simply a matter of intellectual sparring, it would be inconsequential outside academe. But their view has found a ready audience in some parts of the policymaking community. For example, Vice President Gore (1992, p. 342) writes that "3M, in its Pollution Prevention Pays program, has reported significant profit improvement as a direct result of its increased attention to shutting off all the causes of pollution it could find." If environmental regulations are essentially costless (or even carry a negative cost!), then it is unnecessary to justify and measure with care the presumed social benefits of environmental programs. Stringent environmental measures (of the right kind) are good for business as well as the environment; in the Washington parlance, we have ourselves a "win-win situation." Not surprisingly, this view has also been warmly received by environmentalists and by regulators eager to avoid being seen as imposing unwanted costs on businesses or lower levels of government. At a time of burgeoning interest in Congress in the economic justification for federal regulations, Porter and van der Linde suggest the cost of environmental regulation may be negligible or even nonexistent.

To clarify the points that are in dispute, we should state at the outset that we agree with Porter and van der Linde on a number of matters. First, we share their enthusiasm for a heavier reliance on incentive-based regulation in lieu of command-and-control. Early returns suggest, for example, that tradable permits for sulfur dioxide emissions will reduce the cost of the 1990 acid rain control program by at least 50 percent when measured against the most likely command-and-control alternative (Burtraw, 1995; U.S. General Accounting Office, 1994; Rico, 1995). Second, we agree that early estimates of regulatory compliance costs are likely to be biased upward because of unforeseen technological advances in pollution control or prevention. Third, we accept that providing information, such as in EPA's "Green Lights" program (through which the agency provides technical assistance concerning energy-efficient lighting), may well help disseminate new technologies. Fourth, we acknowledge that regulations have sometimes led to the discovery of cost-saving or quality-improving innovation; in other words, we do *not* believe that firms are ever-vigilantly perched on their efficiency frontiers.

On this last point, however, we do not find Porter and van der Linde at all convincing concerning the pervasiveness of inefficiencies. The major empirical evidence that they advance in support of their position is a series of case studies. With literally hundreds of thousands of firms subject to environmental regulation in the United States alone, it would be hard *not* to find instances where regulation has seemingly worked to a polluting firm's advantage. But collecting cases where this has happened in no way establishes a general presumption in favor of this outcome. It would be an easy matter for us to assemble a matching list where firms have found their costs increased and profits reduced as a result of (even enlightened) environmental regulations, not to mention cases where regulation has pushed firms over the brink into bankruptcy.

What is needed, we believe, is a more systematic approach to the issue. Following a general observation to put things in context, we begin with a model in which increasing the stringency of incentive-based environmental regulations *must* result in reduced profits for the firm. This model is incomplete in various ways, but it provides a useful baseline for the succeeding discussion. From this baseline, we can then explore the sorts of changes in the model that could produce the result that regulation leads to higher profits—the outcome that Porter and van der Linde seem to suggest is the norm. We are then in a better position to assess the evidence and the weight of their case.

Innovation and Environmental Regulation: An Observation

Porter and van der Linde accuse mainstream environmental economics, with its "static mindset," of having neglected innovation. This charge is puzzling. For several decades now, environmental economists have made their case for incentive-based policy instruments (such as effluent charges or tradable emission permits) precisely by emphasizing the incentives that these measures provide for innovation in abatement technology (Kneese and Bower, 1968, p. 139). Virtually every standard textbook in environmental economics makes the point that incentive-based approaches are perhaps more attractive for reasons of dynamic efficiency than for their ability to minimize the costs of attaining environmental standards at any particular point in time. A substantial literature has developed in recent years that explores the effects of various policy instruments on research and development decisions concerning abatement technology, a literature on which we shall draw in this discussion.[1]

What distinguishes the Porter and van der Linde perspective from neo-classical environmental economics is *not* the "static mindset" of the latter. It is two other presumptions. First, they see a private sector that systematically overlooks profitable opportunities for innovation.[2] Second, and equally important, they envision a regulatory authority that is in a position to correct this "market failure."[3] With properly designed measures, regu-

---

[1]The reader interested in exploring this literature might begin with Magat (1978), Downing and White (1986), Malueg (1989), Milliman and Prince (1989), Parry (1992), Biglaiser and Horowitz (1995) and Simpson (1995).

[2]This, incidentally, seems a rather odd and sad commentary on the private sector to be coming from one of the country's eminent business professors and consultants.

[3]This "market failure," incidentally, is quite different in character from the usual public goods argument that private firms underinvest in research and development because they will have difficulty appropriating enough of the social benefits. What Porter and van der Linde have in mind is a failure of private decision makers to respond to *private* profit opportunities.

lators can set in motion innovative activities through which firms can realize these overlooked opportunities. Their vision thus suggests a new role
for regulatory activity in bringing about dynamic efficiency: enlightened
regulators provide the needed incentives for cost-saving and quality-
improving innovations that competition apparently fails to provide. Regulators can, as Porter and van der Linde put it, help firms "to overcome organizational inertia and to foster creative thinking," thereby increasing their
profits.[4] We find this view hard to swallow, and suspect that most regulated firms would share our difficulty.

Environmental Regulation and Competitiveness: A Proposition

Drawing on some of the early literature on innovation in abatement technology, we now present a model in which even incentive-based environmental regulation results in reduced profits for the regulated firm. The
model essentially formalizes the basic point that the addition (or tightening) of constraints on a firm's set of choices cannot be expected to result
in an increased level of profits. Readers uninterested in the analytics may
wish to skip to the next section.

We emphasize that this model is static in character and fails to address
the inherent uncertainty in research and development (R&D) decisions. In
this sense, it is subject to precisely the sort of criticism that Porter and van
der Linde level in their paper. However, for the same reason, it provides a
useful point of entry into the issue. The model is premised on the assumption that the polluting firm maximizes profits and operates in a perfectly
competitive market; the firm takes competitors' outputs and R&D expenditures as given and also takes any regulations as exogenously determined.
Given these assumptions, the model does not allow for any sort of strategic
interaction. The possible effects of relaxing these assumptions and allowing
game-theoretic strategic interactions among firms, or between the polluting
firm and the regulator, will be discussed in the next section of this paper.

Figure 1 depicts the polluting firm's options. The horizontal axis shows
the "abatement level," so that the reduction in pollution increases as one
moves from left to right. The vertical axis is measured in dollars, which
means that one can graph both the firm's cost of various levels of pollution abatement and compare those costs with market-oriented effluent

---

[4]It is unclear whether Porter and van der Linde view this expanded role for regulation as a general proposition, or whether it is limited to environmental regulation. They appear to suggest the latter when they contend that as waste emissions into the environment, "[Pollution] is a manifestation
of economic waste and involves unnecessary, inefficient or incomplete utilization of resources. . . . "
This we also find puzzling. Whether it is efficient to recycle wastes, to discharge them into the environment or to adopt an entirely new technology that employs fewer polluting inputs depends on the
costs (meaning, of course, the full social costs) of the various alternatives.

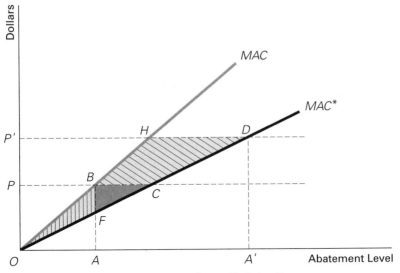

Figure 1 The Incentive to Innovate under an Emission Fee

charges imposed by environmental regulators. The MAC curve (without a star) is the firm's present "marginal abatement cost" function; it indicates the marginal cost incurred by the firm to reduce pollution by an additional unit. The upward slope of the curve implies that the marginal cost of reducing pollution is rising.

Let us now assume that the firm could, if it chooses, reduce its marginal abatement cost function from the curve MAC to MAC*. Notice that with MAC*, a given marginal expenditure has a greater effect on pollution abatement than it would have with MAC. However, to move from MAC to MAC*, the firm must spend money to research and develop new pollution abatement technology. To simplify the problem, we will assume that the R&D expenditure necessary to move from MAC to MAC* is known completely—there is no risk or uncertainty.

This model will presume market-oriented regulators who use effluent charges to encourage pollution abatement. As long as a profit-maximizing firm can abate pollution itself for less than the effluent charge, it will choose to do so. However, after the point where the cost of abating pollution exceeds the effluent charge, the firm will prefer to pay the charge. Let us assume that the firm is initially confronted by an effluent charge of P. It chooses its profit-maximizing level of abatement activity, A, corresponding to the point B, where marginal abatement cost equals the effluent charge.

If the firm has been operating at abatement level A, an implication is that the (annualized) cost of the R&D effort to reduce MAC to MAC* must exceed the gains to the firm. The R&D investment in additional pollution-abatement technology won't pay off; thus outcome B must produce more profits for the firm than does the attainable point C. Figure 1 also depicts the gains to the polluting firm from undertaking the R&D effort, which can be divided into two parts. The source of the first part is that the earlier level of abatement activity becomes cheaper; the amount of gain here is given by the triangle *OFB*. The second part comes from the new technology. The company will choose to abate a greater amount of pollution and thus avoid paying the pollution charge on that additional pollution; the gain here is the triangle *BCF*.

The total gains to the polluting firm from innovation would thus be the area bounded by *OFCB*. Since the firm has not chosen this option, it must be that the cost of the R&D program that would move the firm from MAC to MAC* exceeds the area of the profit that would be gained, *OFCB*.

Now, assume that the environmental authority introduces a new, more stringent market-oriented environmental standard, taking the form of an increase in the effluent fee to *P′*. Without further assumptions, one cannot say whether the firm will respond to the higher effluent charge by sticking with the old technology and ending up at *H* or by investing in the new one and ending up at *D*.[5] But we will prove that both *H* and *D* generate lower profits than *B*. Therefore, it will be unambiguously true in this model that the higher effluent standard reduces profits for the firm.

It is straightforward to show that if the firm sticks with its old technology, the higher effluent charge must reduce its profits. In this case, the firm moves from *B* to *H*, and while this higher level of pollution abatement may be better for society, the firm is unambiguously worse off. It is paying the same amount to abate pollution up to *B* as it was before. Between *B* and *H*, it is paying more to abate pollution than under the previous, lower effluent charge. And above *H*, it is paying the higher effluent charge rather than the previously lower one.[6]

It is only a bit trickier to demonstrate that profits at *D*, where the firm faces a higher effluent charge with the new technology, must be lower than profits at *B*, where the firm chose to face the lower effluent charge with its existing technology. Notice first that along the MAC* frontier, profits at

---

[5]What are some of the factors determining whether the firm chooses to respond to a higher effluent charge by investing in new technology? Overall, of course, the question is whether the cost-savings from the new technology exceed the R&D expenditures. Recent work offers some further insights. Ulph (1994) shows that an increase in an emission tax rate may increase a firm's incentive to engage in environmental R&D, but is likely to decrease its incentive to engage in R&D of a general unit-cost-reducing nature, leading to an ambiguous effect on overall R&D expenditures and on the firm's costs. Simpson (1995) suggests that when R&D is both cost reducing and emission reducing, the incentive effects of an increase in the emissions tax for R&D are lower the more R&D reduces marginal cost and the more competitive are rival firms.

[6]This is an application of a more general principle that for a given technology, profit is decreasing in input prices. In the environmental economics literature, waste emissions are typically treated as an input (along with labor, capital and so on) in the production function. This is reasonable, since attempts to cut back on waste emissions will involve the diversion of other inputs to abatement activities, thereby reducing the availability of these other inputs for the production of goods. Reductions in emissions, in short, result in reduced output. Moreover, given the reasonable assumption of rising marginal abatement costs, it makes sense to assume the usual curvature properties so that we can legitimately construct isoquants in emissions and another input and treat them in the usual way. In this framework, the emissions fee becomes simply the price of an input called "waste emissions."

choice D (given the higher effluent charge) must be lower than profits at point C, given the lower previous effluent charge. As already explained, if technology is constant, the higher effluent charge unambiguously reduces profits. But the basis of this model was that at the lower effluent charge, the firm didn't find it worthwhile to invest in the new technology; that is, profits were lower at C than at B. By transitivity, if profits at B exceed C, and profits at C exceed D, then it must be true that the higher effluent charge reduces profits for the firm, even if it adopts a new technology.

Thus, in this model of innovation in abatement technology, an increase in the stringency of environmental regulations unambiguously makes the polluting firm worse off. Even if the firm can invest and adopt a new, more efficient abatement technology, if that technology wasn't worth investing in before, its benefits won't be enough to raise the company's profits after the environmental standards are raised, either.

This leads us naturally to ask how one might amend the simple model to alter this basic result. We point out that simply making the model dynamic and/or introducing uncertainty will not overturn this result. It is straightforward to show that our basic proposition likewise applies to a firm that maximizes the expected present value of future profits. What elements, then, are missing from this simplified model that could give rise to an *increase* in profits following the imposition of tighter standards?

We can identify two such elements of potential importance. One possibility is strategic behavior, perhaps involving interactions between polluting firms, or between these firms and the regulating agency, or between regulatory agencies in different countries. The second possibility (the one emphasized by Porter and van der Linde) is the existence of opportunities for profitable innovation in the production of the firm's output that for some reason have been overlooked and that would be realized in the wake of new and tougher environmental regulations. The next two sections take up these extensions to the basic model and present some of the relevant empirical evidence.

Strategic Interaction Among Polluters and Regulators

In the basic model, the polluting firm was operating in a competitive environment, taking as given both the behavior of competing firms and the standards set by the regulator. One important line of extension of the analysis is the introduction of strategic interaction among the various participants. There is some recent and ongoing work along these lines. For example, Barrett (1994) has explored a series of models in which regulators and polluting firms behave strategically. He finds that, in the spirit of the Porter-van der Linde thesis, there are indeed cases in which the government can actually improve the international competitive position of domestic exporters by imposing environmental standards upon them. One such case occurs if each firm takes the price of its competitor as fixed and then competes by setting its own profit-maximizing price. If the government sets a strong emission standard—by which Barrett means a standard beyond the point where the marginal benefits of pollution control equal marginal abatement costs—the domestic firm's marginal cost, and therefore its price, will rise. Recognizing that the domestic firm must charge a higher price to comply with the new standard, foreign competitors raise their prices without fear of retaliation. However, an increase in the foreign price raises demand for the output of the domestic firm with a resulting increase in its profits. This result holds when the domestic industry is an oligopoly as well as when it is a monopoly competing in an oligopolistic international market. It *may* also hold under Cournot competition—where each firm takes the quantity produced by its competitors as given and competes by altering the quantity it produces—if the domestic industry is an oligopoly, although this need not be the case.

In general, however, this result is not robust to other changes in the nature of the strategic behavior. For instance, if the domestic firm is a monopolist in its home country and the domestic and foreign firm are Cournot competitors, then the home government can improve the domestic firm's competitive position by reducing its environmental standards below the efficient level. Kennedy (1994) obtains a similar finding in a model with Cournot competition.

In another treatment of the issue, Simpson and Bradford (1996) develop a strategic trade model that explicitly includes R&D expenditures by firms. In this model, firms behave strategically both in setting levels of spending on R&D and in selecting output levels. The government regulates pollution through an emission fee. Simpson and Bradford find that for certain specifications of the cost and demand functions, increasing the emission fee can increase domestic R&D investment, reduce foreign R&D spending and increase domestic welfare (composed of domestic profits plus pollution fee revenues). However, they note that slight variations in the form of the cost function can reverse these results. Ulph (1994) surveys a number of recent papers that explicitly incorporate strategic R&D investment behavior by firms. This body of work indicates that the effect of environmental regulation on R&D is ambiguous and that even in the cases where higher emissions standards lead to higher domestic R&D spending, governments may still be better off selecting a lower-than-social-cost emission tax rate to shift profits from foreign firms to domestic firms.

Overall, this literature suggests that while it is possible to get results like those that Porter and van der Linde suggest are the norm from models that incorporate strategic behavior, such results are special cases. In many instances, these same strategic trade models suggest that the domestic authority should employ *weak* environmental regulations to promote international competitiveness. Moreover, as Barrett (1994) and Simpson and Bradford (1996) suggest, there are typically other sorts of measures that are more effective at improving international competitiveness than strategic environmental regulatory policy. This bottom line does not deny the Porter-van der Linde argument entirely; certain kinds of strategic models can produce outcomes of the type they describe. But it does seem to us that strategic models are unlikely to establish anything close to a general presumption that stringent environmental measures will enhance competitiveness. In addition, such strategic behavior is not what Porter and van der Linde have in mind. We turn to their basic contention now.

Regulation and "Offsets"

Their claim is that technologies exist of which the firm is unaware until prodded into discovering them by stringent environmental regulations. They go on to contend that such regulation will spur firms to innovate and that the newly discovered technologies will generally offset, or more than offset, the costs of pollution abatement or prevention. Our response takes two very different tacks.

First, we spoke with the vice presidents or corporate directors for environmental protection at Dow, 3M, Ciba-Geigy and Monsanto—all firms mentioned by Porter and van der Linde in their discussion of innovation or process offsets. While each manager acknowledged that in certain instances a particular regulatory requirement may have cost less than had been expected, or perhaps even paid for itself, each also said quite emphatically that, on the whole, environmental regulation amounted to a significant *net* cost to his company.

We have little doubt about the general applicability of this conclusion. Fortunately, we need not confine ourselves to speculation and anecdotes about the pervasiveness or the significance of pollution or innovation offsets. There are data available on this matter, and they indicate that such offsets pale in comparison to expenditures for pollution abatement and control.

Each year the Environmental Economics Division of the Commerce Department's Bureau of Economic Analysis (BEA) makes estimates of pollution abatement and control expenditures in the United States. One source for these estimates are Bureau of the Census surveys of manufacturing establishments, state and local governments, electric utilities, petroleum refiners and mining operations. Other information is gathered on federal government expenditures on pollution control, the cost of solid waste disposal, individual spending for motor vehicle pollution control equipment and operating costs and other environmental spending, as well. In 1992, according to BEA, pollution abatement and control expenditures in the United States came to $102 billion (Rutledge and Vogan, 1994, p. 47).

In addition to estimates of environmental spending, BEA also estimates the magnitude of the "offsets" that Porter and van der Linde claim are so pervasive. In fact, the Census Bureau survey of manufacturers (upon which BEA relies for most of its information about offsets) specifically asks respondents to report "cost offsets," which are defined in such a way as seemingly to encompass both the "product" and "process" offsets that

Porter and van der Linde describe (U.S. Commerce Department, 1994).[7] For 1992, BEA estimates that cost offsets for the U.S. amounted to $1.7 billion, less than 2 percent of estimated environmental expenditures. This implies *net* spending for environmental protection in excess of $100 billion in 1992.

Net spending on protecting the environment may be greater than that, however, because there is reason to believe that the BEA estimates of environmental costs are on the low side. According to the Environmental Protection Agency (1990), the total cost associated with federal environmental regulation in the United States in 1992 was $135 billion.[8] EPA's estimates differ from those of BEA for a variety of reasons, some of which are difficult to discern. But some of the difference is due to the fact that EPA counts certain expenditures that BEA ignores (like those associated with measures to improve indoor air quality); because EPA apparently includes some opportunity costs in addition to out-of-pocket expenditures; and because the two agencies use different approaches occasionally even when focusing on the same category of pollution control. Some of the additional costs the EPA includes may give rise to their own offsets, but it is unlikely they will increase in proportion to these added costs. This is especially true where the difference between EPA's estimates and BEA's estimates involve imputed or opportunity costs.

One possible criticism of these estimates of offsets is that certain kinds of offsets in response to more stringent environmental regulation are not easily reportable on the Census Bureau survey form, and hence do not find their way into the Census or BEA estimates. For instance, a manufacturing firm that dropped a product line altogether because it wished to avoid environmental regulations, and entered what instead turned out to be a more profitable product line, would be hard-pressed to report this as an "offset" according to the definition provided in the Census Bureau survey. But even if one doubled or tripled or even quadrupled the estimated offsets that are reported by Census and included in BEA's estimates, the total offsets would be less than $10 billion per year, leaving net annual environmental compliance costs in the range of $100 billion or more.

---

[7]It is worth including one of the examples from the Census Bureau survey to illustrate how closely the survey conforms to the Porter and van der Linde vision of offsets. The survey (U.S. Commerce Department, 1994, p. A-11) contains the following wording: "A manufacturer installs a closed loop recovery system in the production process so as to prevent the dumping of the chemicals into the water system. Since the closed loop recovery system recaptures and reuses the chemicals in the production process, it reduces expenses for chemicals. The pollution abatement portion of the capital expenditure pertaining to the closed loop recovery system is reported in Item 7 [the section of the survey where new capital expenditures are reported]. The operating expenses to maintain the system are reported in Item 3 [the analogous section for operating costs]. The value of recovered chemicals is reported as a cost offset." This example matches perfectly the example of the Robbins Company given by Porter and van der Linde, hence suggesting a close connection between the "offsets" described by Porter and van der Linde and the BEA estimates of offsets based on the Census Bureau survey.

[8]To this must be added the costs of additional control measures introduced by states (like California) that have, in some instances, gone beyond the federal statutes. We know of no estimates of these additional costs, but they may be substantial.

It is impossible to escape the conclusion that the U.S. devotes significant resources, *net of cost savings*, to environmental protection each year. Moreover, we reach this conclusion without making reference to the work of either Jorgenson and Wilcoxen (1990) or Hazilla and Kopp (1990), both of whom showed that the social costs of environmental regulation are *greater* when viewed in a dynamic general equilibrium context than in a static, partial equilibrium setting, because of the manner in which environmental regulations depress "productive" investment and the consequent reduction in the rate of economic growth. Porter and van der Linde deny the validity of this work on the grounds that it fails to factor offsets into account. Since these offsets appear to be quite small—based on both the reports of those who make environmental investments, as well as on hard data—this is hardly a liability of the general equilibrium approach.

One more word about offsets. Suppose that every single dollar a firm spent on pollution control or prevention was matched by a dollar of savings in the form of product or process offsets described by Porter and van der Linde. Would it then be the case that environmental regulation is free? Of course not. The sacrifice would be measured by other opportunities foregone. Firms can and do invest in changing the size and skill mix of their labor force, in their capital base, in the sources and term structure of their financing, their research and development strategies and other things, as well. Each of these investments is expected to do more than return one dollar for each dollar spent—typically firms must project returns that exceed a "hurdle rate" of 20 percent or more before undertaking an investment. Thus, even if environmental compliance produced offsets on a dollar-for-dollar basis—rather than one dollar for every 50 spent, as the data suggest—the foregone return on invested capital would still be a significant cost of regulation.

The International Setting

The original question prompting this debate concerned the impact of environmental regulations on the competitiveness of U.S. industry in the international arena. In a much shorter essay that appeared several years ago in *Scientific American*, Porter (1991) argued that the perverse command-and-control character of most U.S. regulation has seriously handicapped American firms in competitive with foreign rivals. Making the case (with which we enthusiastically agree) for incentive-based policy measures, Porter argued that U.S. firms were losing out to competition from German and Japanese companies, which benefit from more enlightened regulatory regimes.[9]

---

[9]For a more detailed treatment of these particular issues, see our response (Oates et al., 1993) to the Porter (1991) paper.

However, we believe the truth of the matter is rather different. It is not the case that other countries, including Germany or Japan, have made better use of incentive-based approaches than the United States. While other countries appear to have put in place regulatory programs that are less adversarial (and therefore less time consuming) than certain U.S. programs, most environmental regulation in Europe looks every bit as proscriptive as does the U.S. version. In fact, visitors from OECD and developing countries pour through Washington on a regular basis, trying to learn about the sulfur dioxide trading program put in place here five years ago.

Moreover, it is not clear that environmental regulation is harming the competitiveness of U.S. firms. In fact, Porter and van der Linde acknowledge as much, citing Jaffe et al. (1995, p. 157), who conclude in their survey paper that "overall, there is relatively little evidence to support the hypothesis that environmental regulations have had a large adverse effect on competitiveness, however that elusive term is defined."

This finding is important, but it has little to do with innovation offsets. As Jaffe et al. (1995) point out, there are several reasons why the relative stringency of U.S. environmental regulation to date has not been found to have adverse effects on competitiveness. First, for all but the most heavily polluting industries, the cost of complying with federal environmental regulations is a small fraction of total costs, sufficiently small (in most instances) to be swamped by international differentials in labor and material costs, capital costs, swings in exchange rates and so on. Second, although U.S. environmental regulations are arguably the most stringent in the world, the *differentials* between U.S. standards and those of our major industrialized trading partners are not very great, especially for air and water pollution control. Third, U.S. firms (as well as other multinationals) appear inclined to build modern, state-of-the-art facilities abroad, irrespective of the stringency of environmental statutes in the host country. Thus, even a significant difference in environmental standards between, say, the United States and a developing country will mean little to firms not willing to take advantage of lax standards.[10]

This is not to say that cost differentials stemming from international variations in environmental regulations are nonexistent. But as Jaffe et al. (1995, p. 159) conclude, these differentials "pose insufficient threats to U.S. industrial competitiveness to justify substantial cutbacks in domestic environmental regulations." More basically, the case for redesigning environmental programs to make more effective use of market incentives has little to do with international competitiveness; it's a much more straightforward issue of getting environmental value for the expenditures of social resources.

---

[10]The rationale for this behavior appears to be two-fold. First, there is a widespread perception that tighter environmental regulations in the developing countries are inevitable, and that it is less expensive to invest initially in state-of-the-art abatement technology than it will be to retrofit later. Second, the aftermath of certain disasters, notably the Union Carbide catastrophe in Bhopal, India, has made management aware of the dangers inherent in the adoption of less than state-of-the-art control technologies in developing countries.

Conclusion

The underlying message from Porter and van der Linde about environmental regulation is not to worry, because it really won't be all that expensive. But it will. Annual U.S. expenditures for environmental protection, net of any offsets, currently are at least $100 billion, and probably considerably more. From *society's* standpoint, with the benefits of a cleaner environment figures into the balance, every dime of this money may be well spent; the literature is replete with examples of environmental programs that pass a benefit-cost test. But a comparison of the benefits and costs is exactly how one should determine the economic attractiveness of specific programs—not on the false premise of cost-free controls.

argue for cost-benefit on 4/85

References

Barrett, Scott, "Strategic Environmental Policy and International Trade," *Journal of Public Economics*, 1994, *54*:3, 325–38.

Biglaiser, Gary, and John K. Horowitz, "Pollution Regulation and Incentives for Pollution-Control Research," *Journal of Economics and Management Strategy*, Winter 1995, *3*, 663–840.

Burtraw, Dallas, "Efficiency Sans Allowance Traders?: Evaluating the SO2 Emission Trading Program to Date." Resources for the Future Discussion Paper No. 95–30, 1995.

Downing, Paul B., and Lawrence J. White, "Innovation in Pollution Control," *Journal of Environmental Economics and Management*, March 1986, *13*, 18–29.

Gore, Albert, *Earth in the Balance*. Boston: Houghton Mifflin Co., 1992.

Hazilla, Michael, and Raymond Kopp, "Social Cost of Environmental Quality Regulations: A General Equilibrium Analysis," *Journal of Political Economy*, August 1990, *98*, 853–73.

Jaffe, Adam B., Steven R. Peterson, Paul R. Portney, and Robert N. Stavins, "Environmental Regulations and the Competitiveness of U.S. Manufacturing: What Does the Evidence Tell Us?," *Journal of Economic Literature*, March 1995, *33*, 132–63.

Jorgenson, Dale W., and Peter J. Wilcoxen, "Environmental Regulation and U.S. Economic Growth," *Rand Journal of Economics*, Summer 1990, *21*, 314–40.

Kennedy, Peter, "Equilibrium Pollution Taxes in Open Economies with Imperfect Competition," *Journal of Environmental Economics and Management*, July 1994, *27*, 49–63.

Kneese, Allen V., and Blair T. Bower, *Managing Water Quality: Economics, Technology, Institutions*. Baltimore, Md.: Johns Hopkins University Press, 1968.

Magat, Wesley A., "Pollution Control and Technological Advance: A Dynamic Model of the Firm," *Journal of Environmental Economics and Management*, March 1978, *5*, 1–25.

Malueg, David A., "Emission Credit Trading and the Incentive to Adopt New Pollution Abatement Technology," *Journal of Environmental Economics and Management*, January 1989, *16*, 52–7.

Milliman, Scott R., and Raymond Prince, "Firm Incentives to Promote Technological Change in Pollution Control," *Journal of Environmental Economics and Management*, November 1989, *17*, 247–65.

Oates, Wallace E., Karen Palmer, and Paul R. Portney, "Environmental Regulation and International Competitiveness: Thinking About the Porter Hypothesis." Resources for the Future Discussion Paper No. 94–02, 1993.

Parry, Ian, "Environmental R&D and the Choice Between Pigouvian Taxes and Marketable Emissions Permits," unpublished Ph.D. dissertation, University of Chicago, 1992.

Porter, Michael E., "America's Green Strategy," *Scientific American*, April 1991, *264*, 168.

Rico, Renee, "The U.S. Allowance Trading System for Sulfer Dioxide: An Update on Market Experience," *Energy and Resource Economics*, March 1995, *5*:2, 115–29.

Rutledge, Gary L., and Christine R. Vogan, "Pollution Abatement and Control Expenditures, 1972–92," *Survey of Current Business*, May 1994, *74*, 36–49.

Simpson, David, "Environmental Policy, Innovation and Competitive Advantage." Resources for the Future Discussion Paper No. 95–12, 1995.

Simpson, David, and Robert L. Bradford, "Taxing Variable Cost: Environmental Regulation as Industrial Policy," *Journal of Environmental Economics and Management*, forthcoming 1996.

Ulph, Alistair, "Environmental Policy and International Trade: A Survey of Recent Economic Analysis," Milan, Italy: Nota di Lavoro 53:94, Fondazione Eni Enrico Mattei, 1994.

U.S. Department of Commerce (Bureau of the Census), "Pollution Abatement Costs and Expenditures, 1993," Current Industrial Reports; MA200(93)-1, Washington, D.C.: U.S. Government Printing Office, 1994.

U.S. Environmental Protection Agency, *Environmental Investments: The Cost of a Clean Environment.* Washington, D.C.: U.S. Environmental Protection Agency, 1990.

U.S. General Accounting Office, "Allowance Trading Offers an Opportunity to Reduce Emissions at Less Cost," document, GAO/RCED-95–30, 1994.

III

*The Benefits of
Environmental Protection*

7 The Contingent Valuation Debate: Why Economists Should Care*

Paul R. Portney

Paul Portney is President and Senior Fellow at Resources for the Future.

The contingent valuation method involves the use of sample surveys (questionnaires) to elicit the willingness of respondents to pay for (generally) hypothetical projects or programs. The name of the method refers to the fact that the values revealed by respondents are contingent upon the constructed or simulated market presented in the survey. A spirited (and occasionally mean-spirited) battle over such methods is currently being waged, involving competing factions within the federal government, economists and lawyers representing business and environmental groups, and interested academics as well. At issue is a seemingly quite specific question: should environmental regulations currently under development at both the Department of the Interior and the Department of Commerce sanction the use of the contingent valuation method in estimating the damage done by spills of oil, chemicals, or other substances covered by federal law? More generally, the debate raises broad questions about what economists have to say about the values that individuals place on public or private goods.

The two papers that follow this one make cases for and against the use of the contingent valuation method. My aim here is to provide an overview of the technique and the debate surrounding it. I also want to suggest why this debate should matter to economists, both professionally and in their roles as citizens and consumers.

"The Contingency Valuation Debate: Why Economists Should Care," by Paul R. Portney, from *Journal of Economic Perspectives*, 8(4):3–17 (Fall 1994).

*For helpful comments on earlier drafts of this paper, thanks are due Kenneth Arrow, Richard Carson, Ronald Cummings, Peter Diamond, Rick Freeman, Michael Hanemann, Glen Harrison, Barbara Kanninen, Raymond Kopp, Alan Keuger, Edward Leamer, Robert Mitchell, Richard Schmalensee, Howard Schuman, Carl Shapiro, Robert Solow, and especially Kerry Smith and Timothy Taylor. Taylor's many editorial suggestions improved the paper greatly. Any errors are the author's responsibility alone.

The Origins of the Contingent
Valuation Method

As is often the case, it is useful to start with a bit of history.[1]

The first published reference to the contingent valuation method apparently occurred in 1947, when Ciriacy-Wantrup wrote about the benefits of preventing soil erosion (Ciriacy-Wantrup, 1947). He observed that some of these favorable effects (like reduced siltation of streams) were public goods, and suggested that one way to obtain information on the demand for these goods would be to ask individuals directly how much they would be willing to pay for successive increments. However, he never attempted to implement this idea directly.

It wasn't until almost two decades later that the contingent valuation method began to be applied in academic research. In his efforts to determine the value to hunters and wilderness lovers of a particular recreational area, Davis (1963) designed and implemented the first contingent valuation survey that attempted to elicit these values directly.

As a test for the reasonableness of his findings, Davis compared them with an estimate of willingness-to-pay that was based on the "travel cost" approach. The notion here, first suggested by Hotelling in a letter to the National Park Service in 1947, is that the "price" for visiting a park or other recreational area (even one for which entry is free) will vary according to the travel costs of visitors coming from different places (see also Clawson, 1959). Thus, a natural experiment exists where one can measure the quantity of visits to the park demanded by people at a range of prices (that is, coming from different distances) and estimate a demand curve, consumer surplus, and so on. Davis found that the travel cost method of estimating willingness to pay for visits to a recreation area provided a quite similar answer to his contingent valuation survey.

Natural resource and environmental economics then took an enormous jump when John Krutilla published "Conservation Reconsidered," arguably the most influential paper ever written in that subdiscipline (Krutilla, 1967). In less than ten pages, Krutilla identified the importance of the essentially irreversible nature of the development of natural environments, suggested that the divergence between willingness-to-pay and willingness-to-accept compensation for what he called "grand scenic wonders" may be especially large,[2] pointed to the potentially large economic value of preserving genetic variation, and foreshadowed the apparently growing value of outdoor recreation and wilderness preservation relative to what he referred to as "fabricated goods." Most important for our purposes here, Krutilla raised the possibility in this paper of what is now known as "existence value." This is the value that individuals may attach to the mere knowledge that rare and diverse species, unique natural environments, or other "goods" exist, even

---

[1]For a more elegant and detailed history, see Hanemann (1992).
[2]Hanemann (1991) explores this question in a rigorous way.

if these individuals do not contemplate ever making active use of or benefitting in a more direct way from them. Existence value is sometimes referred to as nonuse or passive use value to suggest that the utility derived does not depend on any direct or indirect interaction with the resource or good in question.

Since then, researchers in natural resource and environmental economics (and other branches of economics as well) have made increasing use of contingent valuation techniques to estimate existence values and many other things, as well.[3] For instance, surveys were used to elicit individuals' willingness to pay for such things as a reduction in household soiling and cleaning (Ridker, 1967), the rights to hunt waterfowl (Hammack and Brown, 1974), reduced congestion in wilderness areas (Cicchetti and Smith, 1973), improved visibility in the Southwest (Randall, Ives, and Eastman, 1974), and the value of duck hunting permits (Bishop and Heberlein, 1979), to name but a few. Moreover, contingent valuation methods have been used for the valuation of a large number of non-environmental policies or programs, such as reduced risk of death from heart attack (Acton, 1973), reduced risk of respiratory disease (Krupnick and Cropper, 1992), and improved information about grocery store prices (Devine and Marion, 1979).

But while such studies formed a sort of academic industry, none of them were designed or implemented with litigation in mind. It was not until the late 1980s that contingent valuation studies began to receive the kind of scrutiny routinely devoted to the evidence in high-stakes legal proceedings.

Describing the Methodology

There is no standard approach to the design of a contingent valuation survey. Nevertheless, virtually every application consists of several well-defined elements.[4]

First, a survey must contain a scenario or description of the (hypothetical or real) policy or program the respondent is being asked to value or vote upon. Sticking to environmental issues, this might be a regulatory program that will reduce air pollution concentrations, a land acquisition program to protect wildlife habitats, or a program to reduce the likelihood of oil spills, to name but a few. In some cases, these scenarios are quite detailed, providing information on the expected effects of the program as well as the likely course of events should the program not be adopted. For instance, the scenario might contain an estimate of the reduction in annual

---

[3]For an extraordinary bibliography of papers and studies related to the contingent valuation method, a bibliography that includes 1674 entries, see Carson et al. (1994).

[4]For a thorough description of the contingent valuation method, see Mitchell and Carson (1989).

mortality risk that would be expected to accompany an improvement in air quality; or it might explain the rate at which an endangered species would be expected to recover if it was given additional protection. In other words, the scenario is intended to give the respondent a clear picture of the "good" that the respondent is being asked to value.

Next, the survey must contain a mechanism for eliciting value or a choice from the respondent. These mechanisms can take many forms, including such things as open-ended questions ("What is the maximum amount you would be willing to pay for . . . ?"), bidding games ("Would you pay $5 for this program? Yes? Would you pay $10? What about . . . ?") or referendum formats ("The government is considering doing X. Your annual tax bill would go up by Y if this happens. How would you vote?").

Finally, contingent valuation surveys usually elicit information on the socioeconomic characteristics of the respondents (age, race, sex, income, education, marital status, and so on), as well as information about their environmental attitudes and/or recreational behavior, usually with an eye toward estimating a willingness-to-pay function that includes these characteristics as possible explanatory variables. They may also include follow-up questions to see if the respondent both understood and believed the information in the scenario and took the hypothetical decision-making exercise seriously.

Moving to the Policy Arena

When economists attempt to infer values, we prefer evidence based on actual market behavior, whether directly or indirectly revealed. Thus, a technique like the contingent valuation method—wherein values are inferred from individuals' stated responses to hypothetical situations—could readily be expected to stir lively debate in academic seminars and in the pages of economics journals. But why has the controversy over the contingent valuation method spilled over into the "real world," and why has it become so heated?

The answer lies in two federal laws and one very unfortunate accident. These three things have resulted in government agencies bringing lawsuits against a variety of parties in which the former are attempting to recover large sums of money from the latter for lost existence values (among other types of damages) resulting from damages to natural resources. Many regard the contingent valuation method as being the only technique currently capable of providing monetary estimates of the magnitudes of these losses.

The first law is the Comprehensive Environmental Response, Compensation and Liability Act of 1980, also referred to as CERCLA or, more commonly, as the Superfund law. Its primary purposes were to create a mechanism for identifying sites at which hazardous materials posed a threat to human health or the environment, and to establish procedures through which parties that were deemed responsible for the contamination could be identified and made to pay for the cleanup.

But the Superfund law also contains a sleeper provision: it gave government agencies the right to sue for damages to the natural resources for which they were trustees (including lakes, streams, forests, bays, bayous, marshes, land masses, and so on) resulting from discharges of hazardous substances. The Department of the Interior was subsequently directed to write regulations spelling out what kinds of damages were compensable under this section of Superfund and what kinds of techniques would be admissible for damage estimation. Thus did existence values and the contingent valuation method come to meet the real world.

In 1986, the Department of the Interior (DOI) issued these regulations.[5] Oversimplifying somewhat, the regulations specified that lost nonuse values (largely lost existence values) were recoverable under Superfund only if use values were not measurable, and—in a very qualified way—sanctioned the use of the contingent valuation technique to measure damages. In response to a number of legal challenges, in 1989 a federal court of appeals directed DOI to redraft its regulations, specifically instructing the department to give equal weight to use and nonuse values in damage assessments and to treat the contingent valuation method much more seriously as a valuation technique.[6]

To some extent, however, events overtook the Department of the Interior regulations. In March 1989, the supertanker Exxon Valdez ran aground on Bligh Reef in Prince William Sound, Alaska, spilling 11 million gallons of crude oil into the sea. Although a number of natural resource damage cases had been brought by individual states and the federal government up to that time, none of the incidents precipitating the suits had nearly the visibility and impact of that spill. Among other things, that accident dramatized the potential economic impact of the DOI regulations. Indeed, if in addition to the out-of-pocket losses suffered by fishermen, resort owners, tour guides, recreationists and others directly and indirectly harmed by the accident, Exxon would be forced to pay also for lost nonuse or existence values, the ante would be raised substantially. This possibility focused the attention of Exxon and many other companies on existence values and the contingent valuation method.

The Exxon Valdez spill also caught the attention of Congress. It promptly passed an altogether new law, the Oil Pollution Act of 1990, aimed at reducing the likelihood of future oil spills and providing for damage recovery for any spills that should occur. Under the new law, the Department of Commerce—acting through the National Oceanic and Atmospheric Administration, or NOAA—was directed to write its own regulations governing damage assessment. This became the next battlefield on which to fight about the legitimacy of existence values and the contingent valuation method.

---

[5]See 51 *Federal Register* 27674 (August 1, 1986).
[6]*State of Ohio v. United States Department of Interior*, 880 F. 2d 432 (D.C. Circuit 1989).

The NOAA Panel

The Department of the Interior had worked in relative obscurity when drafting its damage assessment regulations under Superfund. By contrast, NOAA began its parallel task under a spotlight. Environmentalists insisted that the NOAA rules parallel those of Interior, embracing lost existence values as fully compensable damages and identifying the contingent valuation method as the appropriate way to measure them. Not surprisingly, those upon whom these assessments might one day fall—led by the oil companies—pushed hard to exclude existence values and the contingent valuation method from the regulations. Amidst these conflicting pressures, and in recognition of the technical economic nature of the questions at debate, the General Counsel of NOAA, Thomas Campbell, took an unusual step. He asked Nobel laureates Kenneth Arrow and Robert Solow if they would chair a panel of experts to provide advice to NOAA on the following question: is the contingent valuation method capable of providing estimates of lost nonuse or existence values that are reliable enough to be used in natural resource damage assessments?[7]

It is important to note that the panel was *not* asked its opinion on the legitimacy of existence values *per se*. This may have been because the court of appeals had earlier ruled, in the case of the Department of the Interior regulations, that lost existence values were to be treated the same as other economic losses in damage assessments; whatever the reason, the panel was asked to confine its attention solely to the potential reliability of the contingent valuation method.

The NOAA panel met eight times between June and November of 1992. This included an extraordinary all-day hearing in August during which it heard statements from 22 experts, including several of the most prominent names in the economics profession, who either extolled the virtues of the contingent valuation method or condemned it. The panel completed its deliberations in December and, on January 11, 1993, submitted its report to NOAA. The report was published in the *Federal Register* on January 15, 1993.[8]

The NOAA panel may have managed to upset everyone with its report. Those opposed to the use of the contingent valuation method were disappointed by what many took to be the "bottom line" of the panel report. This was the phrase, " . . . the Panel concludes that CV studies [applications of the contingent valuation method] can produce estimates reliable enough to be the starting point of a judicial process of damage assessment, including lost passive-use values." Not surprisingly, this conclusion cheered those government agencies, academic researchers, and others wishing to make continued application of the contingent valuation method in their work.

Nevertheless, the panel reached this conclusion with some reluctance. I believe it fair to say that none of its members would have been comfortable with the use of any of the previous applications of the contingent valuation

---

[7]In addition to Arrow and Solow, the panel included Edward Leamer, Roy Radner, Howard Schuman (a professor of sociology and survey research expert), and myself.

[8]See 58 *Federal Register* 4601 (January 15, 1993).

method as the basis for actual monetary damage awards. (To reiterate, none of these studies was intended for this purpose.) For this reason, the panel established a set of guidelines to which it felt future applications of the contingent valuation method should adhere, if the studies are to produce reliable estimates of lost existence values for the purposes of damage assessment or regulation. Although these guidelines are too numerous to reproduce in their entirety here, seven of the most important are summarized here.

First, applications of the contingent valuation method should rely upon personal interviews rather than telephone surveys where possible, and on the telephone surveys in preference to mail surveys.

Second, applications of the contingent valuation method should elicit willingness to pay to prevent a future incident rather than minimum compensation required for an incident that has already occurred. (Note that the latter would be the theoretically correct measure of damages for an accident that has already taken place.)

Third, applications of the contingent valuation method should utilize the referendum format; that is, the respondents should be asked how they would vote if faced with a program that would produce some kind of environmental benefit in exchange for higher taxes or product prices. The panel reasoned that because individuals are often asked to make such choices in the real world, their answers would be more likely to reflect actual valuations than if confronted with, say, open-ended questions eliciting maximum willingness to pay for the program.

Fourth, applications of the contingent valuation method must begin with a scenario that accurately and understandably describes the expected effects of the program under consideration.

Fifth, applications of the contingent valuation method must contain reminders to respondents that a willingness to pay for the program or policy in question would reduce the amount they would have available to spend on other things.

Sixth, applications of the contingent valuation method must include reminders to respondents of the substitutes for the "commodity" in question. For example, if respondents are being asked how they would vote on a measure to protect a wilderness area, they should be reminded of the other areas that already exist or are being created independent of the one in question.

Seventh, applications of the contingent valuation method should include one or more follow-up questions to ensure that respondents understood the choice they were being asked to make and to discover the reasons for their answer.

These guidelines made a number of proponents of the contingent valuation method quite unhappy. In their view, strict adherence to the panel's guidelines—especially the suggestion that in-person interviews be used to elicit values—would make it very expensive to use the contingent valuation method for damage estimation or regulatory purposes. Moreover, a number of the guidelines seem intended to ensure that applications of the contingent valuation method result in "conservative" estimates of lost existence values—that is, estimates that were more likely to underestimate than to overestimate these values.

The NOAA panel created its long list of requirements because it felt strongly that casual applications of the contingent valuation method should not be used to justify large damage awards, especially in cases where the likelihood of significant lost existence values was quite small. By establishing a series of hurdles for contingent valuation studies to meet, the panel hoped to elevate considerably the quality of future studies and thereby increase the likelihood that these studies would produce estimates that could be relied on for policy purposes.

It should be noted in closing that the NOAA panel report had no special legal standing in NOAA's deliberations. Instead, it was one of literally hundreds of submissions pertaining to the contingent valuation method that NOAA received during the time it was drafting its proposed regulations. Nevertheless, when NOAA published its long-awaited proposed rules on January 7, 1994, it said: "In proposing its standards for the use of CV [contingent valuation] in the damage assessment context, NOAA has relied heavily on the recommendations of the Panel."[9] For instance, the proposed regulations encourage trustees conducting contingent valuation studies to consider using the referendum format, and in-person interviews, as the panel had suggested. In addition, the proposed regulations include a requirement that contingent valuation studies test for the sensitivity of responses to the scope of the damage described in the scenario. The NOAA panel had suggested that if respondents were not willing to pay more to prevent more serious accidents, say, other things being equal, the contingent valuation survey was unlikely to produce reliable results. Interestingly, when the Department of the Interior re-proposed its regulations pertaining to contingent valuation on May 4, 1994, it too included a requirement that contingent valuation studies test for sensitivity to scope.[10] The papers by Diamond and Hausman and also Hanemann in this issue discuss "scope tests" in some detail.

The Importance of the Contingent Valuation Debate

Economists should have a strong interest in the debate surrounding the contingent valuation method. The most obvious reasons have to do with the economic stakes involved; but these are not the only reasons.

Natural Resource Damage Assessments

Currently, the Department of Commerce (acting through NOAA) is involved in approximately 40 lawsuits in which it is seeking to recover damages for

---

[9]See 59 *Federal Register* 1062 (January 7, 1994), p. 1143.
[10]See 59 *Federal Register* 2309 (May 4, 1994).

injury to the natural resources for which it is trustee. The Department of the Interior is involved in roughly another 20 cases. The contingent valuation method. figures into no more than a dozen of these 60 or so cases, though it could prove to be quite influential in those cases.

To illustrate, consider the case of the Exxon Valdez. In late 1991, Exxon settled the natural resource damage suits brought against it by both the federal government and the State of Alaska for $1.15 billion, payable over 11 years. Yet, a state-of-the-art study done for the State in Alaska in the wake of the accident—one using the contingent valuation method to estimate lost existence values nationally—concluded that these losses alone amounted to nearly $3 billion (Carson et al., 1992). Because the case involving the Exxon Valdez was settled out of court, as have all cases involving the contingent valuation method to this point, it is impossible to know whether this study affected the size of the settlement.

It seems highly likely, however, that applications of the contingent valuation method will influence future damage awards or out-of-court settlements. Several of the most heavily regulated industries in the United States are among those affected by either Superfund or the Oil Pollution Act; the chemical and petroleum refining industries are potentially affected by both statutes. This in turn has implications for the amount of deterrence they and others will undertake. If existing state and federal environmental regulations, coupled with the specter of tort liability, already induce something close to the "right" amount of preventive activity by firms in these industries, the possibility of additional liability for lost existence values will push firms beyond the social optimum. On the other hand, if lost existence values are widely accepted as real economic losses that these firms have been ignoring heretofore, the imposition of liability for these losses may move firms closer to the optimum.

These cases alluded to earlier do not provide the only opportunity for damage recovery under Superfund. Currently, there are more than 1,200 sites on EPA's National Priorities List—the list of sites which can be cleaned up using money from the trust fund created for that purpose. Once the appropriate remedy has been selected and implemented at each of these sites, and once liability for the cost of this cleanup has been affixed, the trustees for any damaged resources, such as contaminated groundwater, can bring natural resource damage suits against the responsible parties. In these cases, contingent valuation could be used to estimate possible lost existence values.

New Regulations

Virtually all of the attention that the contingent valuation method has attracted in the policy world has been in the context of natural resource damage assessments under Superfund and the Oil Pollution Act. Nevertheless, I believe that the most significant applications of the contingent valuation method will involve the estimation of the benefits and costs of proposed regulations under Superfund and particularly other environmental laws.

Regulated entities in the United States—private firms, agencies at the federal, state, and local levels, and individuals—currently spend an estimated $130 billion annually to comply with federal environmental regulations alone (EPA, 1990). This is about 2.2 percent of GDP, a larger fraction than is devoted to environmental compliance expenditures anywhere else in the world. Much less is known about the annual compliance expenditures necessitated by other federal regulatory agencies. However, based on a comprehensive review of previous analyses, Hopkins (1992) cautiously estimated that annual compliance expenditures for all federal regulation, environmental and otherwise, were in the vicinity of $400 billion.

Under Executive Order 12044 issued by President Carter, Executive Order 12291 issued by President Reagan, and Executive Order 12866 issued by President Clinton, all federal regulatory agencies must make an effort to quantify as many of the benefits and costs of their proposed actions as possible.[11] This is where applications of the contingent valuation method will likely become important.

Imagine, for example, a proposed regulation that would cost a great deal of money but would provide relatively little in the way of direct benefits in the areas where environmental quality would improve. In such a case, it may be tempting for the regulatory agency to justify its proposed action by alleging that individuals throughout the country derive a psychological benefit (an existence value) from knowing that environmental quality has been improved in the affected areas—even though there will be no environmental improvements in the areas in which they live. A contingent valuation study might be produced to support this assertion, and might make the difference as to whether the proposal passes a benefit-cost test.

There is no reason why existence values should be unique to environmental policy, either. For instance, I might derive utility from knowing that factories are safer as a result of Occupational Safety and Health Administration regulations, that pharmaceuticals carry less risk because of the oversight of the Food and Drug Administration, and that swimming pool slides are safer because of the vigilance of the Consumer Product Safety Commission. All this may be so even though I do not work in a factory, take prescription drugs, or have a swimming pool. In other words, individuals may have existence values for many different "goods," and the inclusion of such values in a regulatory analysis could markedly alter the decision-making calculus.

Which leads me to what I believe has been an important and largely overlooked point in the debate about existence values and the contingent valuation method. To this point, proponents of the technique have envisioned its being used to estimate lost existence values and other *benefits* of

---

[11]Strangely enough, this requirement holds true even when the agency is not allowed to engage in benefit-cost balancing in setting certain kinds of standards. For example, the key sections of many environmental statutes forbid balancing benefits and costs, although such trade-offs are permitted in other parts of these laws and are even required in some other laws (Portney, 1990).

proposed regulatory programs. Thus, the business community tends to oppose such methods because it believes the methods will only be used to support expansive regulation and large damage awards.

But sauce for the goose is surely sauce for the gander. Since costs are the duals of benefits, I see no reason why the contingent valuation method cannot or should not be used for the estimation of regulatory costs as well as benefits.

Consider a hypothetical regulation that would increase costs for a number of petroleum refineries and would force several others to shut down. For the purposes of the required benefit-cost analysis, the EPA would usually count as costs the annual capital cost of the equipment installed by the refineries that would remain in operation, plus any additional annual operating and maintenance costs they would incur. An unusually thorough analysis might occasionally include the (generally temporary) loss of or reduction in income of the workers whose jobs would be lost as a result of the regulation. But typically, the extent of the cost analysis is limited to out-of-pocket expenditures for new pollution control equipment or cleaner fuels.

With contingent valuation available to measure lost existence values, the matter is surely more complicated than this.[12] If I derive some utility from the mere existence of certain natural environments I never intend to see (which I do), might I not also derive some satisfaction from knowing that refineries provide well-paying jobs for hard-working people, even though neither I nor anyone I know will ever have such a job? I believe I do. Thus, any policy change that "destroys" those jobs imposes a cost on me—a cost that, in principle, could be estimated using the contingent valuation method.

Since regulatory programs will always impose costs on someone— taking the form of higher prices, job losses, or reduced shareholder earnings—lost existence values may figure every bit as prominently on the cost side of the analytic ledger as the benefit side. To my knowledge, however, no business organization has commissioned an application of the contingent valuation method to ascertain the empirical significance of these potential additional costs, nor has any academic independently undertaken one.

If the concept of existence value comes to be more broadly interpreted in economics, as I have suggested above that it should, and *if* the contingent valuation method comes to be regarded as a reliable way to measure these values, then applied benefit-cost analysis may be forever changed. It is already difficult to conduct such analyses for government programs that

---

[12]Even without the concern raised by contingent valuation, a number of questions can be raised about the very straightforward cost analysis described here. For example, Hazilla and Kopp (1990) have shown that if one takes a general equilibrium approach to social cost estimation, very different results are obtained when compared to those from a traditional partial equilibrium analysis. This calls into question previous estimates of regulatory compliance costs (see also Jorgenson and Wilcoxen, 1990).

impose hard-to-value, non-pecuniary costs on individuals, that change the distribution of income (either at a point in time or between generations), that affect mortality or morbidity, and that involve the preservation of genetic resources.

Imagine now the difficulty of doing applied benefit-cost analysis when virtually every citizen in the United States is potentially benefitted or injured by virtually every possible program. In principle, at least, it will become extraordinarily difficult to draw bounds around those likely to gain and lose so as to facilitate valuation.

In practice, this problem may be somewhat less daunting. Perhaps it will turn out that existence values apply on the benefit side only in cases of truly unique natural environments like the Grand Canyon, irreplaceable "assets" like the Declaration of Independence, or programs that substantially improve the lives of many beneficiaries. On the other side of the ledger, perhaps only policy changes that inflict massive economic harm on certain groups of people or certain regions will generate losses among those not directly affected by the policy. If so, applied benefit-cost analysis may survive intact, but this empirical question is one that economists ought to be interested in answering.

Putting Theory Into Practice

A final set of reasons for economists to care about the contingent valuation debate have less to do with policy consequences, and more to do with how contingent valuation is affecting economic theory and the practice of empirical economics.

Whatever its shortcomings, the contingent valuation method would appear to be the only method capable of shedding light on potentially important values. Some environmental benefits can be measured in indirect ways. For example, the benefits of air quality improvements can manifest themselves in residential property values; enhanced workplace health and safety may be reflected in wage rates; improvements in recreational opportunities may be revealed in reduced travel costs. But there is simply no behavioral trace through which economists can glean information about lost existence values.

The only likely candidate for such information that I am aware of is voluntary contributions to national or international conservation organizations. But these groups typically provide their contributions with a mixture of public and private goods (an attractive magazine or calendar, for example), which makes it almost impossible to determine how much of one's contribution represents a willingness to pay for the pure preservation of unique natural area or genetic resources. In addition, many contributors to these organizations visit (make *active* use of) the protected areas, thus making it difficult to separate active from passive use values. Finally, the public good nature of the benefits of preservation means that there will be a tendency to underprovide on account of free riding.

According to proponents of the contingent valuation method, asking people directly has the potential to inform about the nature, depth, and economic significance of these values. Economists who hold this position readily admit that direct elicitation of these values will require the skills of other social scientists, including survey research specialists, cognitive psychologists, political scientists, marketing specialists, sociologists, and perhaps even philosophers. In fact, the critical scrutiny directed at the contingent valuation method has led some economists to think more deeply about cognitive processes, rationality, and the nature of preferences for *all* goods, public or private. We may, in other words, come out of this debate with an improved theory of preference and choice.

Another (and related) reason to care about the contingent valuation method debate has to do with the importance of encouraging the development of new analytical techniques. Here the parallels to experimental economics seem to me to be instructive. It was not so long ago that Vernon Smith, Charles Plott and a handful of other economists began to create artificial markets in "laboratory" settings. One purpose was to see whether hypotheses about market equilibration derived from theoretical models were borne out in laboratory settings. Since that time, experimental methods have been used to inform real-word policy-making, including, among other cases, the allocation of airport landing slots by the Civil Aeronautics Board, the auction of T-bills by the Department of Treasury, the sale of air pollution emission allowances by the Environmental Protection Agency, and the design of natural gas contracts by the Federal Energy Regulatory Commission.

Yet despite its increasing acceptance in the economics profession, and its apparent usefulness to decision makers, experimental economics has not had an easy go. Its early critics claimed that the "artificiality" of the laboratory setting rendered meaningless the findings of experimental studies. And it is my impression (but only that) that some journal editors have been reluctant to embrace papers based on experimental studies. To this day, some critics still have grave doubts about its utility.

This seems to me not unlike the state of play regarding the contingent valuation method today. Its detractors have argued that the technique is not only currently unable to provide reliable estimates of lost existence values, but also that it will never be able to do so. On the other hand, at least some proponents of the contingent valuation method appear to believe that even casual applications can produce results reliable enough to be used as the basis for potentially significant damage awards. Both views were rejected by the NOAA panel.

The present struggle is over whether some middle ground exists. There do exist quite careful and thorough applications of the contingent valuation method, with the work of Carson et al. (1992) on the Exxon Valdez oil spill being the best example. I am reluctant to assert that even this study is sufficient to justify monetary penalties. But the estimates from that study are convincing enough to me to suggest that the contingent valuation method should be the object of further research and lively intellectual debate.

Conclusion

Whether the economics profession likes it or not, it seems inevitable to me that contingent valuation methods are going to play a role in public policy formulation. Both regulatory agencies and governmental offices responsible for natural resource damage assessment are making increasing use of it in their work. This has now been reinforced by the Department of the Interior and NOAA–proposed regulations sanctioning the use of the contingent valuation method. Surely, it is better for economists to be involved at all stages of the debate about the contingent valuation method, than to stand by while others dictate the way this tool will be used.

References

Acton, Jan, "Evaluating Public Progress to Save Lives: The Case of Heart Attacks," RAND Research Report R-73-02. Santa Monica: RAND Corporation, 1973.

Bishop, Richard, and Thomas Heberlein, "Measuring Values of Extramarket Goods: Are Indirect Measures Biased?," *American Journal of Agricultural Economics*, December 1979, *61*, 926–30.

Carson, Richard, et al., *A Contingent Valuation Study of Lost Passive Use Values Resulting From the Exxon Valdez Oil Spill*, Report to the Attorney General of the State of Alaska, prepared by Natural Resource Damage Assessment, Inc., La Jolla, California, 1992.

Carson, Richard, et al., *A Bibliography of Contingent Valuation Studies and Papers*. La Jolla, California: Natural Resources Damage Assessment, Inc., 1994.

Cicchetti, Charles J., and V. Kerry Smith, "Congestion, Quality Deterioration, and Optimal Use: Wilderness Recreation in the Spanish Peaks Primitive Area," *Social Science Research*, 1973, *2*, 15–30.

Ciriacy-Wantrup, S. V., "Capital Returns from Soil Conservation Practices," *Journal of Farm Economics*, November 1947, *29*, 1181–96.

Clawson, Marion, "Methods of Measuring the Demand for and Value of Outdoor Recreations," Reprint no. 10, Resources for the Future, Washington, D.C., 1959.

Davis, Robert, *The Value of Outdoor Recreation: An Economic Study of the Maine Woods*, doctoral dissertation in economics, Harvard University, 1963.

Devine, D. Grant, and Bruce Marion, "The Influence of Consumer Price Information on Retail Pricing and Consumer Behavior," *American Journal of Agricultural Economics*, May 1979, *61*, 228–37.

Environmental Protection Agency, *Environmental Investments: The Cost of a Clean Environment*, Report no. EPA-230-12-90-084, 1990.

Hammack, Judd, and Gardner Brown, *Waterfowl and Wetlands: Toward Bioeconomic Analysis*. Baltimore: Johns Hopkins University Press, 1974.

Hanemann, W. Michael, "Willingness to Pay and Willingness to Accept: How Much Can They Differ?," *American Economic Review*, June 1991, *81*, 635–47.

Hanemann, W. Michael, "Preface: Notes on the History of Environmental Valuation in the U.S." In Navrud, Stale, ed., *Pricing the Environment: The European Experience*. London: Oxford University Press, 1992, 9–35.

Hazilla, Michael, and Raymond Kopp, "Social Cost of Environmental Quality Regulations: A General Equilibrium Analysis," *Journal of Political Economy*, August 1990, *98*, 853–73.

Hopkins, Thomas, "The Costs of Federal Regulation," *Journal of Regulation and Social Costs*, March 1992, *2*, 5–31.

Jorgenson, Dale, and Peter Wilcoxen, "Environmental Regulation and U.S. Economic Growth," *RAND Journal of Economics*, Summer 1990, *21*, 314–40.

Krupnick, Alan, and Maureen Cropper, "The Effect of Information on Health Risk Valuation," *Journal of Risk and Uncertainty*, February 1992, *2*, 29–48.

Krutilla, John, "Conservation Reconsidered," *American Economic Review*, September 1967, *356*, 777–86.

Mitchell, Robert, and Richard Carson, *Using Surveys to Value Public Goods: The Contingent Valuation Method.* Washington, D.C.: Resources for the Future, 1989.

Portney, Paul, *Public Policies for Environmental Protection.* Washington, D.C.: Resources for the Future, 1990.

Randall, Alan, Berry Ives, and Clyde Eastman, "Bidding Games for Valuation of Aesthetic Environmental Improvements," *Journal of Environmental Economics and Management*, 1974, *1*, 132–49.

Ridker, Ronald, *The Economic Cost of Air Pollution.* New York: Praeger, 1967.

8 Valuing the Environment through Contingent Valuation*

W. Michael Hanemann

W. Michael Hanemann is Chancellor's Professor of Agricultural and Resource Economics, University of California, Berkeley.

The ability to place a monetary value on the consequences of pollution discharges is a cornerstone of the economic approach to the environment. If this cannot be done, it undercuts the use of economic principles, whether to determine the optimal level of pollution or to implement this via Pigouvian taxes or Coase-style liability rules. Sometimes, the valuation involves a straightforward application of methods for valuing market commodities, as when sparks from a passing train set fire to a wheat field. Often, however, the valuation is more difficult. Outcomes such as reducing the risk of human illness or death, maintaining populations of native fish in an estuary, or protecting visibility at national parks are not themselves goods that are bought and sold in a market. Yet, placing a monetary value on them can be essential for sound policy.

The lack of a market to generate prices for such outcomes is no accident. Markets are often missing in such cases because of the nonexcludable or nonrival nature of the damages: for those affected by it, pollution may be a public good (or bad). The public good nature of the damages from pollution has several consequences. It explains, for example, why the damages are sometimes large—only a few people may want to own a sea otter pelt, say, but many may want this animal protected in the wild. It also explains why market prices are inappropriate measures of value. In the presence of externalities, market transactions do not fully capture preferences. Collective choice is the more relevant paradigm.

This is precisely what Ciriacy-Wantrup (1947) had in mind when he first proposed the contingent valuation method. Individuals should be interviewed and "asked how much money they are willing to pay for successive additional quantities of a collective extra-market good." If the individual values are aggregated, "the result corresponds to a market-demand schedule" (p.

"Valuing the Environment Through Contingent Value," by W. Michael Hanemann, from *Journal of Economic Perspectives*, 8(4):19–43 (Fall 1994).

*I want to thank Richard Carson, Jon Krosnick, Robert Mitchell, Stanley Presser and Kerry Smith for their helpful comments, and Nicholas Flores and Sandra Hoffmann for excellent assistance. I also thank the editors, without whom this paper would be far longer.

1189). Thus, surveys offered a way to trace the demand curve for a public good that could not otherwise be gleaned from market data. Schelling (1968) made a similar point in his paper on valuing health. While the price system is one way to find out what things are worth to people, he wrote, another way is to ask people, whether through surveys or votes. Answering surveys may be hypothetical, but no more than buying unfamiliar or infrequent commodities. "In any case, relying exclusively on market valuations and denying the value of direct enquiry in the determination of government programs would depend on there being for every potential government service, a close substitute available in the market at a comparable price. It would be hard to deduce from first principles that this is bound to be the case" (pp. 143–4).

Schelling's point was not that indirect methods using market transactions have no role, but rather that they cannot always be counted on to provide a complete measure of value. Analysts can often capture some effects of a change in air quality or a change in risk to human health through a hedonic analysis that looks for evidence to property values or wage rates (Rosen, 1974). But people may also value those items in ways not reflected in wages or property values. Similarly with averting expenditures and household production models (Freeman, 1993), which rely on the demand for market commodities that are complements to, or surrogates for, the nonmarket good. If people value that good at least partly for reasons unrelated to their consumption of the complementary private goods, those methods capture just part of people's value—what is called the "use value" component, following Krutilla (1967).[1] They fail to measure the "non-use value" or "existence value" value component, which contingent valuation can capture.

An alternative is to turn to the political system, for example using collective choice models to estimate demands for local public goods (Oates, 1994). However, Cropper (1994) suggests this is unlikely to be useful for the environment because, in the United States, there are few cases where local governments actually set environmental quality. Moreover, as Chase (1968) noted, the method contains an element of circularity: a major reason for the spread of benefit-cost analysis is legislators' desire to obtain information on the public's value for government programs. While it may sometimes be desirable to leave the assessment of value to the legislative process, it is not obvious that this is always so. Measuring liability for damages from pollution is an example. In some cases one wants to ascertain how the public values something, and contingent valuation may be the only way to measure this short of a plebiscite.

Ciriacy-Wantrup (1947) recognized that surveys are not foolproof. The degree of success depends on the skill with which the survey is designed and implemented. But it was time, he felt, that economics took advantage of developments in social psychology and the newly emerging academic field of survey research: "Welfare economics could be put on a more realistic foundation if a closer cooperation between economics

---

[1]For a formal definition, see Hanemann (1994a).

and certain young branches of applied psychology could be established" (p. 1190). This finally occurred in the 1980s, and contingent valuation came of age. Two landmarks were an EPA conference in 1984 that brought together leading practitioners, other economists, and psychologists to assess the state-of-the-art (Cummings et al., 1986), and the publication of what has become the standard reference on contingent valuation, Mitchell and Carson (1989), which puts it in a broader context involving elements from economics, psychology, sociology, political science, and market research.

Contingent valuation is now used around the world (Navrud, 1992; Bateman and Willis, forthcoming), both by government agencies and the World Bank for assessing a variety of investments. A recent bibliography lists 1600 studies and papers from over 40 countries on many topics, including transportation, sanitation, health, the arts and education, as well as the environment (Carson et al., 1994c). Some notable examples are Randall, Ives and Eastman (1974) on air quality in the Four Corners area, the first major non-use value study; Brookshire et al. (1982) on air pollution in Southern California; Carson and Mitchell (1993) on national water quality benefits from the Clean Water Act; Smith and Desvousges (1986) on cleaning up the Monongahela River, Jones-Lee, Hammerton and Phillips (1985) on highway safety; Boyle, Welsh and Bishop (1993) on rafting in the Grand Canyon; Briscoe et al. (1990) on drinking water supply in Brazil; and the study on the *Exxon Valdez* oil spill I helped conduct for the State of Alaska (Carson et al., 1992).

This paper focuses generally on the use of contingent valuation to measure people's values for environmental resources, rather than specifically on natural resource damages. It will describe how researchers go about conducting reliable surveys. It then addresses some common objections to surveys and, lastly, considers the compatibility between contingent valuation and economic theory.

Conducting Reliable Surveys

In all research, details matter. How a contingent valuation survey is conducted is crucial. While there is no panacea, various procedures have been developed in recent years that enhance the credibility of a survey and make it more likely to produce reliable results. These touch all aspects, including sampling, instrument development, formulation of the valuation scenario, questionnaire structure, and data analysis. The main ways of assuring reliability are summarized here.

Suppose one approached people in a shopping mall, made them put their bags down for a moment, and asked them what was the most they would be willing to pay for a sea otter in Alaska or an expanse of wilderness in Montana. This is how the President of American Petroleum Institute and other critics have characterized contingent valuation (DiBona,

1992). The essence of their argument is summarized in titles such as "Ask a Silly Question" and "Pick a Number" (Anon., 1992; Bate, 1994). It does not require any unusual perspicacity to see that this approach is unlikely to produce reliable results. For precisely this reason, it is *not* what good contingent valuation researchers do, and it is *not* what was recommended by the NOAA Panel on Contingent Valuation (Arrow et al., 1993) described in Portney's paper in this issue.

Serious surveys of the general public avoid convenience sampling, such as stopping people in the street; they employ statistically based probability sampling.[2] They also avoid self-administered surveys, such as mail surveys or questionnaires handed out in a mall, because of the lack of control over the interview process. For a major study, the NOAA Panel recommended in-person interviews for their superior reliability. Furthermore, interviews should occur in a setting that permits respondents to reflect and give a considered opinion, such as their home. Unless the study deals with consumer products, shopping malls are a poor choice. Indeed, the only contingent valuation study where people were stopped for a few minutes in a mall was one performed for Exxon (Desvousges et al., 1992).

The crux is how one elicits value. The two key developments have been to confront subjects with a specific and realistic situation rather than an abstraction, and to use a closed-ended question which frames the valuation as voting in a referendum.

A common temptation is to characterize the object of valuation in rather general terms: "What would you pay for environmental safety?" "What would you pay for wilderness?" The problem is that these are abstractions. People's preferences are not measured in the abstract but in terms of specific items. "Paying for wilderness" is meaningless; what is meaningful is paying higher taxes or prices to finance particular actions by somebody to protect a particular wilderness in some particular manner. Therefore, one wants to confront respondents with something concrete. Moreover, one should try to avoid using counterfactuals. "What would you pay not to have had the *Exxon Valdez* oil spill?" is utterly hypothetical because one cannot undo the past. By contrast, "What would you pay for this new program that will limit damage from any future oil spills in Prince William Sound?" offers something that is tangible.

The goal in designing a contingent valuation survey is to formulate it around a specific commodity that captures what one seeks to value, yet is plausible and meaningful. The scenario for providing the commodity may be real; if not, the key is to make it seem real to respondents. They are not actually making a payment during the interview, but they are expressing their intention to pay. The vaguer and less specific the commodity and payment mechanism, the more likely respondents are to treat the valuation as

---

[2]DiBona's scenario actually was the practice in the 1930s when most surveys were "brief encounters" on the street or in stores (Smith, 1987). The 1940s saw the adoption of probability sampling, standardized survey techniques, longer and more complex survey instruments, and in-depth focused interviews (Merton and Kendall, 1946).

symbolic. To make the payment plausible, one needs to specify the details and tie them to provision of the commodity so this cannot occur without payment. There should be a clear sense of commitment; for example, if the program is approved, firms will raise prices, or the government taxes, so there is no avoiding payment once a decision is made.[3]

Until the mid-1980s, most contingent valuation surveys used some version of an open-ended question, like "What is the most you would be willing to pay for . . . ?" Since then, most major contingent valuation studies have used closed-ended questions like "If it cost x, would you be willing to pay this amount?" or "If it cost x, would you vote for this?" Different people are confronted with different dollar amounts. Plotting the proportion of "yes" responses against the dollar amount traces out the cumulative distribution function of willingness-to-pay.[4]

Of course, if people carried utility functions engraved in their brains, the question format would not matter. But they don't, and it does matter. In this country, posted prices are the norm rather than bargaining. In market transactions people usually face discrete choices: here is an item, it costs x, will you take it? Similarly in voting. Moreover, there is abundant evidence that respondents find the open-ended willingness-to-pay question much more difficult to answer than the closed-ended one; for market and nonmarket goods alike, people can generally tell you whether they would pay some particular amount, but they find it much harder to know what is the *most* that they would possibly pay. Indeed, the experience with open-ended willingness-to-pay questions for market goods is that people are more likely to tell you what the good costs than what it is worth to them. In addition to being less realistic and harder to answer, the open-ended format creates incentives which are different from those in the closed-ended format. With the open-ended format, as with an oral auction, there are strategic reasons for stating less than one's full value—a theoretical result strongly supported by experimental evidence. This is not so with a closed-ended format; there, the NOAA Panel held, there is no strategic reason for the respondent to do other than answer truthfully.[5]

For these reasons, the NOAA Panel considered the closed-ended format combined, where possible, with a voting context the most desirable for contingent valuation: "The simplest way to approach the valuation problem," it held, "is to consider a contingent valuation survey as essentially a self-contained referendum in which respondents vote to tax themselves for a particular purpose" (p. 20). This is a rather different conception of contingent valuation from asking silly questions of passers-by.

---

[3]To underscore this, the interviewer may tell respondents that the government uses surveys like this to find out whether taxpayers are willing to pay for new programs it is considering.

[4]The methodology here is to assume a random utility model for individual preferences. This can be estimated using standard techniques for binary choices. Bishop and Heberlein (1979) were the first to use this format; the link with utility theory was developed in Hanemann (1984).

[5]With auctions, it is well documented that formal matters and that oral auctions generate lower prices than posted-price auctions. Why the surprise when the same holds true for open- versus closed-ended payment questions?

In his introduction to this symposium, Portney describes other ways to make a contingent valuation questionnaire more reliable: providing adequate and accurate information; making the survey balanced and impartial; insulating it from any general dislike of big business; reminding respondents of the availability of substitutes, and of their budget constraint; facilitating "don't know" responses; allowing respondents to reconsider at the end of the interview. Several steps can be taken to eliminate any perception of interviewer pressure. At the outset, the interviewer can assure respondents that there are no "right" answers. Before asking the voting question, to legitimate a negative response, the interviewer could say something like: "We have found that some people vote for the program and others vote against. Both have good reasons for voting that way," and then list some reasons for saying "no."[6] Another possibility is if the interviewer does not actually see the respondents' votes, for example by having them write on a ballot placed in a sealed box.

A recent innovation, considered essential by the NOAA Panel, is a "debriefing" section at the end of the survey. This checks respondents' understanding and acceptance of key parts of the contingent valuation scenario. For example, was the damage as bad as described? Did you think the program would work? Did you think you really would have to pay higher taxes if the program went through? This also probes the motives for their answer to the willingness-to-pay question. What was it about the program that made you decide to vote for it? Why did you vote no? Moreover, throughout the survey, all spontaneous remarks by the respondent are recorded verbatim as they occur. After the survey, the interviewer is debriefed and asked about the circumstances of the interview, how attentive the respondent was, whether the respondent seemed to understand the questions and appeared confident in his responses. In this way, one creates a rich portrait of the interview. This information can be exploited in the data analysis. One can monitor for the misunderstandings, measure statistically how they affected respondents' willingness-to-pay, and adjust accordingly. For example, if a subject who voted "yes" appeared to be valuing something different than the survey intended, this case can be dropped or the "yes" converted to a "no."

With any data, different statistical procedures can produce different results. The closed-ended format raises several statistical issues, for example, one might summarize the willingness-to-pay distribution by using its mean, or its median, or another quantile. The mean is extremely sensitive to the right tail of the distribution; that is, to the responses of the higher bidders. For this reason, if the mean is to be used, a nonparametric or bounded influence approach is highly recommended for fitting the willingness-to-pay distribution. The median, by contrast, is usually very robust (Hanemann,

---

[6]For example, the interviewer might note that some people prefer to spend the money on other social or environmental problems instead, or they find the cost is more than they can afford or than the program is worth, or they cannot support the program because it would benefit only one area (Carson et al., 1992).

1984). Another issue is that the choice of dollar bids affects the precision with which the parameters of the willingness-to-pay distribution are estimated; significant improvements can be achieved by using optimal experimental designs (Kanninen, 1993). Statistical techniques can also be used to probe for yea-saying or other response effects, and correct for them if they are present (Hanemann and Kanninen, forthcoming).

While none of these alone is decisive, taken together they are likely to produce a reliable measure of value. Apart from the expense of in-person interviews, they are all eminently feasible.[7] Other essential ingredients are relentless attention to detail and rigorous testing of the instrument, usually in collaboration with survey experts, so that the researcher understands exactly how it works in the field and is sure it communicates what was intended.

It is no coincidence that the handful of studies that Diamond and Hausman select from the contingent valuation literature in their companion paper in this issue violate most of these precepts, as do the Exxon surveys reported in Hausman (1993). None uses in-person interviews. Many are self-administered. Most use open-ended questions. None is cast as voting.[8] Many ask questions with a remarkable lack of detail.[9] Several seem designed to highlight the symbolic aspects of valuation at the expense of substance.[10] The Exxon surveys were designed and fielded in great haste, with little pretesting, just at a time when federal agencies were gearing up for natural resource damage regulations.[11] The only way to justify this is to make the tacit assumption that, if contingent valuation is valid, details of its implementation should not matter. This is fundamentally wrong: measurement results are not invariant with respect to measurement practice in *any* science.

---

[7]Is there an acceptable alternative to in-person surveys? The NOAA Panel felt mail surveys have significant problems rendering them unsuitable. Telephone surveys avoid these problems, but preclude the use of visual aids and need to be short. The most promising alternative is a mail/telephone combination in which an information package is mailed to respondents who are then interviewed by phone (Hanemann, Loomis and Kanninen, 1991). This permits an extensive phone interview which seems to provide many of the benefits of an in-person survey at much lower cost.

[8]Two studies Diamond and Hausman cite as showing a lack of commitment in contingent valuation, Seip and Strand (1992) and Duffield and Patterson (1991), used open-ended questions about payment to an environmental charity. Most of Seip and Strand's subjects who were followed up afterwards said that they had been expressing their willingness-to-pay for environmental problems generally, rather than the particular environmental group. Careful pretesting would have discovered this beforehand.

[9]This is notably a problem in Diamond et al. (1993).

[10]Including Kahneman and Ritov (1993), Kahneman and Knetsch (1992), and Kemp and Maxwell (1993). The last two employs a "top-down" procedure in which respondents are given details of the item only *after* they value it. They are first confronted with something broad, like "preparedness for disasters." After stating their willingness-to-pay for the broad category, they are told what it comprises and asked their willingness-to-pay for *one* of those components. Then, they are told what *this* comprises, and so on. The *change* in the *quantity* of any item is never specified.

[11]Hanemann (1994a,b) critiques these studies.

Objections to Surveys

McCloskey (1985, p. 181) observes that economists generally dislike surveys: "Economists are so impressed by the confusions that might possibly arise from questionnaires that they have turned away from them entirely, and prefer the confusions resulting from external observation." In this section, I discuss four common objections to surveys.

Surveys Are Vulnerable to Response Effects

Small changes in question wording or order sometimes cause significant changes in survey responses (Schuman and Presser, 1981). Since virtually all data used in economics come from surveys (including experiments, which are a form of survey), and all surveys are vulnerable to response effects, it is important to understand why these arise and how they can be controlled. A consensus is beginning to emerge based on insights from psychology and linguistics. Answering survey questions requires some effort, usually for no apparent reward. Respondents must interpret the meaning of the question, search their memory for pertinent information, integrate this into a judgment, and communicate the judgment to the interviewer. Although some are motivated to make the effort, others may become impatient, disinterested, or tired. Instead of searching for an accurate and comprehensive answer, they satisfice, just aiming for some response that will be accepted. Furthermore, interviews are interactions governed by social and linguistic norms that shape assumptions and expectations. Viewing respondents as satisficing agents following norms of conversation has proved helpful in interpreting survey data, explaining response effects, and designing more effective surveys (Groves, 1989; Krosnick, 1991).

Not all response phenomena are equally intractable. Some, such as order effects (for example, bias towards the first item in a list), can be detected and controlled, either by choosing the sequence that produces a conservative result or by randomizing the order of items across interviews.

A second type of effect is where there is a shift in meaning. This is substance, not noise. For example, similar words turn out to mean different things: "allow" is not the same as "not forbid," nor "higher prices" the same as "higher taxes."[12] Or there are framing effects, where subjects respond differently to situations the researcher saw as equivalent. It has been shown through debriefings that the subject perceived the situations as substantively different, because either the researcher induced an unintended change in meaning or context, or the subjects made inferences that went beyond the in-

---

[12]And different words can mean the same thing, as in the movie *Annie Hall* where Woody Allen and Diane Keaton are asked by their psychiatrists how often they have sex. He says: "Hardly ever, maybe three times a week." She says: "Constantly, I'd say three times a week." With consumer expenditure surveys, Miller and Guin (1990) attest that life imitates art.

formation given (Frisch, 1993).[13] In each case, the shift in meaning is a source of error only if the researcher is unaware of it. Through rigorous testing with cognitive techniques, the researcher can come to understand exactly what the instrument means to people, and what they mean in response.[14]

A third phenomenon arises from the inherent difficulty of the task assigned the respondent. In recalling past events or behavior, for example, respondents resort to rounding, telescoping (time compression) and other inferential strategies that yield inaccurate reports of magnitudes and frequencies.[15] Bradburn et al. (1987) emphasize that factual and attitudinal surveys share many similar cognitive processes and errors. There is no easy solution for recall errors. This continues to be a problem for many data used by economists,[16] though not for contingent valuation data since there is no recall.

One cannot avoid the fact that surveys, like all communication, are sensitive to nuance and context and are bound by constraints of human cognition. One tries to detect discrepancies and repair them, but they cannot be entirely ruled out. It is important to keep a sense of proportion. As far as I know, nobody has stopped using data from the Current Population Survey, Consumer Expenditure Survey, Monthly Labor Survey, or Panel Study on Income Dynamics because there are response effects in such surveys. The same should apply to contingent valuation surveys.

The Survey Process Creates the Values

It has been asserted that contingent valuation respondents have no real value for the item, but just make one up during the course of the interview: the process creates the values that it seeks to measure. Debriefings can identify whether subjects were inattentive or unfocused and offered hasty or ill-considered responses, and these can be discarded if desired. But, the issue raised here is more fundamental. Diamond and Hausman feel they

---

[13]When there is incomplete information in a survey, respondents may go ahead and make their own assumptions. Consequently, the researcher loses control over his instrument. Diamond et al. (1993) is a contingent valuation example.

[14]On testing by federal survey agencies, see Tanur (1992). Lack of adequate testing can explain some notable violations of procedural invariance—respondents saw cues or meaning which the researcher didn't intend and failed to detect. An example is the base rate fallacy where "when no specific information was given, prior probabilities are properly utilized; when worthless evidence is given prior probabilities are ignored" (Tversky and Kahneman, 1974). A norm of conservation is to present information one believes relevant. That this was the expectation of subjects could have been detected through debriefings. On violations of conversational norms in base-rate experiments, see Krosnick, Li and Lehman (1990).

[15]Some pronounced telescoping errors are to be found in the Alaska recreation survey conducted by Hausman, Leonard and McFadden (1994).

[16]Juster and Stafford (1991) and Mathiowetz and Duncan (1988) discuss biases in labor supply estimates due to problems with bunching and misreporting in Current Population Survey data. Atkinson and Micklewright (1983) discuss errors in Family Expenditure Survey reports of income and its components. Other inconsistencies between micro- and macro-data sets for the household sector are discussed in Maki and Nishiyama (1993).

know real preferences when they see them, and they do not see them in contingent valuation. Based on the debriefing statements in Schkade and Payne (1993) that show most subjects, faced with an open-ended willingness-to-pay question, think about either what the item could cost or what they have spent on something remotely similar, Diamond and Hausman conclude that these people are just making up their answer rather than evincing "true economic preferences." But, what are "true economic preferences?" If a subject responds thoughtfully to a question about voting to raise taxes for a public good, by what criterion is that not a valid preference?

It is true that economists often assume consumer choice reflects an individual's global evaluation of alternatives, a "top-down" or "stored-rule" decision process. The stored-rule notion traces back to Hobbes and the English empiricists who conceived of cognition in terms of storing and retrieving "slightly faded copies of sensory experiences" (Neisser, 1967). Wilson and Hodges (1992) call this the "filing cabinet" concept of the mind. It long dominated not only economics but also psychology. But it is now being abandoned in the face of accumulating evidence from the neurosciences (Rose, 1992) and elsewhere that all cognition is a constructive process—people construct their memories, their attitudes, and their judgments. The manner of construction varies with the person, the item, and the context. A general principle is that people are cognitive misers: they tend to resolve problems of reasoning and choice in the simplest way possible. This is the emerging consensus not only in survey research, but also in social psychology, political psychology, and market research (Martin and Tesser, 1992; Sniderman, Brody and Tetlock, 1991; Payne, Bettman and Johnson, 1988).

For non-habituated and complex consumer choices, people often make "bottom-up" decisions; that is, they make up a decision rule at the moment they need to use it (Bettman, 1988). Olshavsky and Granbois (1979, p. 98) found that "for many purchases a decision process never exists, not even on first purchase." Bettman and Zins (1977) found that grocery shoppers construct a choice heuristic "on the spot" about 25 percent of the time; bottom-up construction of preferences occurred especially for meat and produce "as might be expected, since consumers cannot really rely on brand name for most choices of this type," less often for beverages and dairy products "where either strong taste preferences may exist or only a limited number of brands are available" (p. 81). This calls to mind a remark by Robert Solow that the debriefings in Schkade and Payne "sound an awful lot like Bob Solow in the grocery store." I suppose critics of contingent valuation would consider that Solow does not have true economic preferences, or that he has true economic preferences when buying milk but not meat.

The real issue is not whether preferences are a construct but whether they are a *stable* construct. While this surely varies with circumstances, the evidence for contingent valuation is quite strong. There is now a number of test-retest studies in the contingent valuation literature, and these show both consistency in value over time and a high correlation at the individual level (Carson et al., 1994b). These levels of consistency are comparable to the most stable social attitudes such as political party identification.

Ordinary People Are Ill-Trained for Valuing the Environment

If, as the NOAA Panel suggests, the goal of a contingent valuation survey is to elicit people's preferences as if they were voting in a referendum, then prior experience or training are irrelevant. These are not a criterion for voting.[17] Nor is their absence an argument against contingent valuation per se. Through direct questioning, one can readily identify which respondents knew of the issue before the interview, or before the oil spill, and determine whether they hold different values from those who did not. How one proceeds in calculating aggregate willingness-to-pay is something that can be decided separately from the survey. Who has standing, and whose values should count, are questions that we as economists have no special competence to judge.

Survey Response Can't Be Verified

There are three ways to validate contingent valuation results: replication, comparison with estimates from other sources, and comparison with actual behavior where this is possible. Replication is useful even on a small scale both to see if results hold up and to check whether the instrument is communicating as intended. This is the single best way for a researcher to determine whether somebody's survey instrument works as claimed.

When contingent valuation measures direct use values, it may be possible to make a comparison with estimates obtained through indirect methods. Knetsch and Davis (1966) conducted the first test, comparing contingent valuation and travel demand estimates (a method described in Portney's paper) of willingness-to-pay for recreation in the Maine woods. The difference was less than 3 percent. There are now over 80 studies, of-

---

[17]Voter ignorance is a constant refrain for Diamond and Hausman. They use it to form a syllogism: voters are ill-informed, contingent valuation is like a referendum, therefore contingent valuation respondents are ill-informed. Both parts are false. Contingent valuation researchers take pains to ensure their samples are representative and their questionnaires intelligible, informative, and impartial, thus avoiding the vagaries of turnout and biased advertising in election campaigns. This is why political scientists are becoming interested in "deliberate polling"—in effect, extended contingent valuation surveys (Fishkin, 1991). Many analysts see a substantial core of rationality in voter behavior. Cronin (1989) finds Magleby's (1984) assessment of voter ignorance in referenda overblown. Fiorina (1981) and McKelvey and Ordeshook (1986) emphasize how campaign protagonists use signals to inform voters. Lupia (1993) analyzes the insurance reform battle in the 1988 California ballot and finds that informational "short cuts" enabled poorly informed voters to act as though they were well informed. What Sniderman (1993) calls "the new look in public opinion research" stresses how ordinary citizens use the information at hand to make sense of politics.

fering several hundred comparisons between contingent valuation and in-direct methods. The results are often fairly close; overall, the contingent valuation estimates are slightly *lower* than the revealed preference estimates and highly correlated with them (Carson et al., 1994a).

The ideal is direct testing of contingent valuation predictions against actual behavior. There are about ten such tests in the literature. Diamond and Hausman mention only five of these. The ones not mentioned yield re-sults quite favorable to contingent valuation.

Bohm (1972) conducted the first test, where subjects in Stockholm were asked their willingness-to-pay to see a new TV program. In five treatments, the program was shown if the group raised 500 Kr, with ac-tual payment based in various ways on stated willingness-to-pay. A sixth treatment asked subjects what was the highest amount they would have given *if* they had been asked to pay an individual admission fee. The mean response was 10.2 Kr (about $2) when the group was asked a hy-pothetical question, versus an overall average of 8.1 Kr when the group actually paid. The difference between contingent valuation and non-contingent valuation means was not statistically significant in four of the five cases.

Bishop and Heberlein (1990) conducted a series of experiments with hunters who had applied for a deer-hunting permit in a favored game pre-serve run by the state of Wisconsin. The most relevant for current practice is an experiment in which they wrote to two groups of hunters offering to sell them a permit at a specified price. In one case, this was a real offer; in the other, it was asked as a hypothetical question. Estimated willingness-to-pay was $31 in the real sale versus $35 in the hypothetical sale, a statistically insignificant difference.

Dickie, Fisher and Gerking (1987) offered boxes of strawberries door-to-door at different prices. One treatment was a real offer—the household could buy any number of boxes at this price. The other asked how many boxes they *would* buy if these were offered at the given price. The result-ing two demand curves were not significantly different. The parameter es-timates were actually more robust over alternative model specifications for the hypothetical than the actual data (Smith, 1994).

Carson, Hanemann and Mitchell (1986) tested the accuracy of voting intentions in a water quality bond election in California in 1985. Closed-ended contingent valuation questions were placed on the Field California Poll a month before the vote, using different figures for the household cost. Adjust for "don't know" responses, the predicted proportion of yes votes at the actual cost was 70–75 percent. The ballot vote in favor was 73 percent.

Cummings, Harrison and Rutström (1993) offered subjects small com-modities at various prices. For one group, it was a real sale. A second group was first asked a hypothetical contingent valuation question—this item is not actually for sale but, if it were, would you buy it now? The experimenter then announced that, after all, she *would* sell the item, but they should feel free to revise their answer. When juicers were the item, 11 percent actu-ally bought them in the real sale; with the second treatment, 41 percent said they would but it if it were on sale, but then only 16 percent did. The 41 percent and 11 percent are significantly different. With calculations, 21 percent would buy in the hypothetical sale, versus 8 percent in the real sale. One wonders whether some respondents interpreted the question as "*if you needed a juicer*, would you buy this one?" Smith (1994) shows that the calculator responses do not generate a downward sloping demand curve for either the actual or hypothetical data. The experimental procedure contained nothing to emphasize commitment or counteract yea-saying in the hypothetical treatment. Cummings and his colleagues have recently added wording like the "reasons to say no" mentioned earlier. In one case, this reduced the hypothetical yes for calculators from 21 percent to 10 percent, not significantly different from the real 8 percent; in another there was no effect (Cummings, 1994).

Other contingent valuation tests have used open-ended payment questions, with predictable difficulties. Boyce et al. (1989) measured willingness-to-pay and willingness-to-accept for a house plant, with mixed results; Neill et al. (1994) measured willingness-to-pay for a map and a picture, with negative results. Both confound the issue by comparing contingent valuation responses to an experimental auction, begging the question of whether auction behavior understates willingness-to-pay. Duffield and Patterson (1991) and Seip and Strand (1992) compare actual and hypothetical contributions to an environmental cause. Diamond and Hausman focus on these studies because they showed a significant difference. But, soliciting an intention to make a charitable donation is a poor test of contingent valuation, because it invites less commitment than soliciting an intention to vote for higher taxes. To make things worse, Seip and Strand used members of the environmental group as the interviewers in their hypothetical treatment, thus increasing pressures for compliance. They compared hypothetical phone responses with responses to an actual mail solicitation. Duffield and Patterson compared hypothetical mail solicitations from the University of Montana with actual mail solicitations from the Nature Conservancy. In both studies, the difference in survey administration introduces a confounding factor which undermines the comparison.[18]

A cleaner test is provided by Sinden (1988) who conducted a series of 17 parallel experiments soliciting actual and hypothetical monetary donations to a fund for assisting soil conservation or controlling eucalypt dieback. In all 17 cases, there was no statistical difference between actual and hypothetical willingness-to-pay.

---

[18]The problem with mail surveys is that people may think the survey is junk mail and throw it out unopened. Duffield and Patterson made no allowance for the difference in sponsor identity on the envelope, which could explain the difference in response rates (Schuman, 1992). Response rates apart, the pattern of contributions was similar in the two treatments. Seip and Strand made no allowance for the fact that phone and mail solicitations generally have different response rates. Infosino (1986) found a sales rate three times higher with telephone than mail in an AT&T marketing effort.

Thus, there is some substantial evidence for the validity of contingent valuation survey responses, although more studies are certainly needed. Many existing studies do not incorporate the refinements in contingent valuation method, described earlier, that emphasize realism and commitment. In this respect, the test by Carson, Hanemann and Mitchell (1986) points in the right direction because it deals directly with expression of voting intentions. The positive results in that study are consistent with other evidence showing that polls in this country reliably indicate public sentiment at the time they are taken, and polls close to an election are generally accurate predictors of the outcome.[19] Kelley and Mirer (1974) found voting intentions correctly predicted the actual vote in four presidential elections for 83 percent of those respondents who voted.[20] Surveys of purchase intentions in market research may not be accurate predictors of subsequent purchase behavior, but surveys of voting intentions are.[21]

Contingent Valuation and Economic Theory

Critics of contingent valuation like Diamond and Hausman, and their coauthors in Hausman (1993), reject contingent valuation as a method of economic valuation because the results of contingent valuation studies are inconsistent with economic theory as they see it. These assertions have become quite widely known. However, careful examination shows that in some cases the claims are not supported by the findings in the contingent valuation literature, and in others they rest on unusual notions about what economic theory does or does not prescribe. I briefly review these issues here, leaving a more detailed treatment to Hanemann (1994a).

Diamond and Hausman, and Milgrom (1993), make a number of statements about what is a permissible argument in a utility function. They ar-

---

[19]Diamond and Hausman seem troubled that voters change their minds during the course of an election campaign. They cite a 1976 electricity rate proposition in Massachusetts where support went from 71 percent in February to 25 percent in the November ballot. They fail to mention the reasons. Magleby (1984, p. 147) identifies opposition spending as the chief cause of such opinion reversals, and that certainly occurred in 1976—opponents outspent supporters more than threefold. In May, the Dukakis administration came out against it, as eventually did businesses, the unions, hospitals, colleges, and major newspapers.

[20]Ajzen and Fishbein (1980) offer some reasons to expect a high level of attitude-behavior correspondence for voting in terms of their theory of reasoned action.

[21]One reason for the difference is timing: unlike elections, people generally control the timing of their market purchases. The result is they may end up buying the commodity, but later than they said (Juster, 1964). This is especially likely for durables, the focus of much literature, since their durability permits delay in replacement. This is consistent with findings that purchase intentions are significantly more accurate for nondurables than durables (Ferber and Piskie, 1965); intentions *not* to purchase durables are highly accurate (Theil and Kosobud, 1968); and predictions of the brand selected when the purchase *does* occur tend to be highly accurate (Ajzen and Fishbein, 1980; Warshaw, 1980).

gue that people should care about outcomes, not about the process whereby these are generated. People should not care whether animals are killed by man or die naturally. They should not care about details of provision or payment for a commodity, only price. Above all, they should value things for purely selfish motives. In their accompanying piece, Diamond and Hausman phrase this argument by saying that respondents should not contemplate "what they think is good for the country," because that reflects "warm glow" rather than "true economic preferences."[22] From this perspective, contingent valuation is unacceptable because it picks up existence values; for those to be allowed in a benefit-cost analysis, Milgrom (1993, p. 431) argues, "it would be necessary for people's individual existence values to reflect only their own personal economic motives and not altruistic motives, or sense of duty, or moral obligation."[23]

This criticism hardly comports with the standard view in economics that decisions about what people value should be left up to them. For example, Kenneth Arrow (1963, p. 17) wrote: "It need not be assumed here that an individual's attitude toward different social states is determined exclusively by the commodity bundles which accrue to his lot under each. The individual may order all social states by whatever standards he deems relevant." Or as Gary Becker (1993, p. 386) writes: "[I]ndividuals maximize welfare *as they conceive it*, whether they be selfish, altruistic, loyal, spiteful, or masochistic." When estimating demand functions for fish prior to Vatican II, no economist ever proposed removing Catholics because they were eating fish out of a sense of duty. Nor, when estimating collective choice models, do we exclude childless couples who vote for school bonds because they lack a personal economic motive.

A more substantive matter is how willingness-to-pay varies with factors that could reasonably be expected to influence it. This has been raised in connection with the embedding effect and the income elasticity of willingness-to-pay. Regarding the latter, Diamond and Hausman assert in this issue that the income effects measured in typical contingent valuation surveys are lower than would be expected if true preferences are measured. McFadden and Leonard (1993, p. 185) make the more specific claim that an income elasticity of willingness-to-pay less than unity constitutes grounds for doubting the validity of the contingent valuation method. There is no basis for either assertion. In the literature on the demand for state and local government services in the United States, the income elasticities

---

[22]"Warm glow" is simply a red herring. I have seen no empirical evidence that people get a warm glow from voting to raise their own taxes, whether in real life or in a contingent valuation study.

[23]Milgrom (1993) also asserts that using contingent valuation to measure altruistic preferences creates double counting. His analysis has three flaws. First, it depends on the particular specification of the utility function, as Johansson (1992) notes; if the argument of the utility function is another's consumption rather than his utility, there is no double counting. Second, it derives its force from the auxiliary assumption that the respondent *does not realize* that the other people for whom he cares will have to pay, too; this is not a problem in a referendum format. Third, in many contingent valuation studies the object of the altruism is often wildlife—sea otters, for example. Since those creatures are *not* surveyed, the issue of double counting is moot.

generally fall in the range 0.3 to 0.6 (Cutler, Elmendorf and Zeckhauser, 1993). With charitable giving by individuals, the income elasticities generally fall in the range of 0.4 to 0.8 (Clotfelter, 1985). The income elasticities in the contingent valuation literature vary with the item being valued, but are generally in the same range (Kriström and Riera, 1994).

The term "embedding effect," introduced by Kahneman and Knetsch (1992), has come to mean several different things. The general notion is captured in the (mis)conception that, with contingent valuation, you get the same willingness-to-pay if you value one lake, two lakes, or ten lakes.[24] This combines three distinct notions. One assertion, which arises when the object of preference is thought to be simply the number of lakes, is that willingness-to-pay varies inadequately with changes in the scale or scope of the item being valued. This is a scope effect. Alternatively, if each lake is seen as a separate argument in the utility function, then the assertion is that a given lake has quite different value if it is first, second or tenth in a set of items to be valued—it gets a high value when the first, but it adds little or nothing to total value when second or tenth. This is a sequencing effect. Thirdly, with either preference structure, the willingness-to-pay for a composite change in a group of public goods may be less than the sum of the willingness-to-pay for the individual changes separately. This is a sub-additivity effect.

The question of how willingness-to-pay varies with the scale or scope of the item being valued in a contingent valuation survey has long been considered, starting with Cicchetti and Smith (1973) who elicited hiker's values for trips in a Montana wilderness area and found that the willingness-to-pay for trips where other hikers were encountered on two nights was 34 percent lower than the willingness-to-pay for trips with no encounters. Many other studies have since reported comparable findings using both internal (within-subject) and external (split-sample) scope tests, including meta-analyses by Walsh, Johnson and McKean (1992) covering over 100 contingent valuation studies of outdoor recreation, and Smith and Osborne (1994) on 10 contingent valuation studies of air quality. Carson (1994) reviews 27 papers with split-sample tests of scope and finds a statistically significant effect of scope on willingness-to-pay in 25 of them.

The two exceptions are Kahneman and Knetsch (1992) and Desvousges et al. (1992). Critics of contingent valuation rely heavily on these two studies when asserting the absence of scope effects in contingent valuation.[25] Some of the problems with these two studies have already been noted, including

---

[24]Though widely believed, this is a myth. It may be traced to Kahneman (1986), which is usually cited as showing that respondents were willing to pay the same amount to clean up fishing lakes in one region of Ontario as in all of Ontario. His data actually show a 50 percent difference. Moreover, the survey involved a brief telephone interview using an open-ended willingness-to-pay question. It provided no detail on how and when the cleanup would occur. Respondents may not have seen cleaning up *all* the lakes as something likely to happen soon.

[25]Also, in their contingent valuation survey, Diamond et al. (1993, pp. 45–46) mention that, using a Kruskal-Wallis test, they found no difference in willingness-to-pay for three wilderness areas ranging in size from 700,000 to 1.3 million acres. If they had run a simple regression of willingness-to-pay on acreage, they would have found a significant scope effect.

their failure to use a closed-ended voting format, the after-the-fact provision of information in Kahneman and Knetsch's "top-down" procedure, and the use of brief shopping mall intercepts by Desvousges et al.[26] The latter elicited people's willingness-to-pay for preventing the deaths of migratory waterfowl. Three separate versions of the questionnaire said that 2,000, 20,000, and 200,000 out of 85 million birds die each year from exposure to waste-oil holding ponds that could be sealed under a new program. Respondents were told that the deaths amounted to *much less than* 1 *percent* of the bird population, to *less than* 1 *percent*, and to *about* 2 *percent*. If respondents focused on the relative impact on the population, it is hard to believe that they would have perceived any real difference among these percentages. The results of the scope test depend crucially on how much one trims the data to remove what are clearly outliers. With a 10 percent trim, one obtains a highly significant scope effect.[27] At any rate, even if one regards these two studies as highly credible evidence that respondents were insensitive to scope, they certainly do not represent the majority finding in the contingent valuation literature regarding the variation of willingness-to-pay with scope.

How much should willingness-to-pay vary with scope? Diamond (1993) asserts that economic theory requires it to increase *more than proportionately* with the number of bird deaths. The variables in his model are the number of birds originally in the population, q_0, the number at risk of dying, q_R, and the number of those that are saved, q_s. Let $q_F \equiv q_0 - q_R + q_s$. Diamond assumes that people should care only about q_F, the ultimate number of birds, not how many were alive initially, at risk, or saved. He also assumes preferences are quasiconcave in q_0. The two assumptions together imply *quasiconvexity* in q_R, which is what makes the elasticity of willingness-to-pay with respect to q_R greater than unity. The conclusion depends critically on the assumption of perfect substitution between q_0, q_s, and $-q_R$. When contingent valuation data disconfirm this, Diamond dismisses the method. Others might be more inclined to believe the data and drop the assumption.[28]

---

[26]Other questions about Kahneman and Knetsch are raised by Harrison (1992) and Smith (1992).

[27]How the survey was administered clearly affected the results. Schkade and Payne (1993) used the same questionnaire as Desvouges et al., but slowed respondents down and made them think about their answer. Their data show a different pattern of willingness-to-pay responses, and a significant relationship between willingness-to-pay and the percentage of birds killed (Haneman, 1994b).

[28]Some, while not sharing Diamond's extreme position on the elasticity of willingness-to-pay, still hold that contingent valuation responses vary inadequately with scale. People's perceptions undoubtedly differ from objective measures of attributes. But this is not just a feature of contingent valuation. In psychophysics, it has been known since the 1880s that there is a general tendency for judgments of magnitude to vary inadequately. Observers standing at a distance overestimate the height of short posts, and underestimate that of tall ones; people reaching quickly for an object overestimate small distances and angles, and underestimate large ones; subjects matching loudness of a tone to a duration overestimate the loudness of short tones, and underestimate the loudness of long ones; people overestimate infrequent causes of death, and underestimate frequent ones; small probabilities are overestimated, large ones underestimated (Poulton, 1989). This "response contraction bias" in judgment or rating is an authentic feature of how people perceive the world, not an artifact of contingent valuation.

With regard to sequencing and sub-additivity effects, these effects are certainly present in contingent valuation responses, but one expects them to occur, and they can be explained in terms of substitution effects and diminishing marginal rates of substitution. When the quality of one lake improves, you value an improvement in a second lake *less* if the lakes are what Madden (1991) calls *R*-substitutes, and *more* if they are *R*-complements. Far from being inconsistent with economic preferences (Diamond et al., 1993, pp. 48–49), sub-additivity is likely to be the norm: while all goods cannot be *R*-complements, Madden shows they *can* all be *R*-substitutes.[29] Similarly, *R*-substitution explains sequence effects: if the lakes are *R*-substitutes, the willingness-to-pay for an improvement in one lake is *lower* when it comes at the end of a sequence of changes in lake improvements than at the beginning while the willingness-to-accept for the change in the lake is *higher* when it comes later in a sequence (Carson, Flores and Hanemann, 1992).[30] It should come as no surprise that the value of one commodity changes when the quantity of another varies: in other words, that willingness-to-pay depends on economic context.[31]

For many economists, the ultimate argument against contingent valuation is that it violates the habitual commitment of the profession to revealed preference. Three points should be noted. First, one must distinguish between private market goods and public goods. Revealed preference is harder to apply to the latter, especially when they are national rather than local public goods (Cropper, 1994). Second, revealed preference is not foolproof, either. It involves an extrapolation from observation of particular choices to general conclusions about preference. One relies on various auxiliary assumptions to rule out factors that might invalidate the extrapolation. Those assumptions are not themselves verifiable if one is restricted to observed behavior. This can sometimes make revealed preference a rel-

---

[29]If the intention of the Diamond et al. (1993) contingent valuation survey was to test the adding-up of willingness-to-pay, it was strangely designed for the purpose. The survey stated that there were 57 federal wilderness areas in the Rocky Mountain states, without identifying them, and said that there now was a proposal to open these to commercial development. In one version, respondents were told that seven unidentified areas had already been earmarked for development, and were asked their willingness-to-pay to protect an eighth area, identified as the Selway Bitterroot Wilderness. In another, respondents were told that eight unnamed areas had been earmarked for development and asked their willingness-to-pay to protect a ninth area, identified as the Washakie Wilderness. In a third version, respondents were told that seven unnamed areas had been earmarked for development and asked their willingness-to-pay to protect two areas identified as Selway and Washakie. In all three cases, respondents were not told the identity or fate of the other 48 or 49 areas. Given that respondents were not indifferent among wilderness areas, as evidenced by the regression mentioned in note 25, I leave it to the reader to decide whether the surveys constitute a sensible basis for testing the adding-up of willingness-to-pay.

[30]In natural resource damages, where willingness-to-accept is the relevant welfare measure, this implies that the usual practice of taking the injured resource as the first item in any possible valuation sequence is a conservative procedure.

[31]The practical implications are that, when one values a program, it be placed in whatever sequence applies under the circumstances, and that one take care when extrapolating results in a benefits transfer exercise because the values might change with the difference in circumstances (Hoehn and Randall, 1989).

atively hypothetical undertaking.[32] Third, there is no reason why observing people's behavior and asking them about behavioral intentions and motives should be mutually exclusive. Fathoming human behavior is never easy; one should utilize every possible source of information.

Above all, one should take a balanced view of the difficulties with each approach. As Sen (1973, p. 258) wrote, "we have been too prone, on the one hand, to overstate the difficulties of introspection and communication and, on the other, to underestimate the problems of studying preferences revealed by observed behavior." In the debate on contingent valuation, critics have shown a tendency to employ simplistic dichotomies. Surveys of attitudes are fallible and subject to the vagaries of context and interpretation; surveys of behavior are unerring. In the market place, people are well informed, deliberate, and rational. Outside it, they are ignorant, confused, and illogical. As consumers, people can be taken seriously; as voters, they cannot. In particular instances, these assertions may be correct. As generalizations, however, they are a caricature.

Conclusions

When cost-benefit analysis started in the United States in the 1930s, economic valuation was generally perceived in terms of market prices. To value something, one ascertained an appropriate market price, adjusted for market imperfections if necessary, and then used this to multiply some quantity. Two things changed this. The first was the recognition, prompted by the "new welfare economics" of the 1940s and especially Hotelling's paper on public utility pricing, that the appropriate welfare criterion is maximization of aggregate consumers' plus producers' surplus. While market prices can safely be used to value marginal changes for market commodities, the impact of nonmarginal changes is measured by the change in areas under demand and supply curves. The second development was Samuelson's theory of public goods and his finding that their valuation must be based on vertical aggregation of individual demand curves.

Together, these developments led to an important paradigm shift—one that contributed directly to the emergence of nonmarket valuation and is

---

[32]Revealed preference estimates are sensitive to the measurement of price, which is often uncertain and precarious for disaggregated commodities (Pratt, Wise and Zeckhauser, 1979; Randall, 1994). The price at which demand falls to zero, needed to estimate consumer's surplus, may lie outside the range of the observed data and be estimated inaccurately (for example, one knows travel cost only for participants, or one believes that participants and nonparticipants have different preferences). This can cause revealed preference to produce a less reliable estimate of use value than contingent valuation (Hanemann, Chapman and Kanninen, 1993). With other variables there may be inadequate variation in the data (for example, attributes are correlated across brands). Hence, revealed preference data alone may yield a less reliable estimate of demand functions than contingent valuation choice data, and one may need to combine both types of data for best results (Adamowicz, Louviere and Williams, 1994).

still evident in the current debate on contingent valuation.[33] This shift changed the focus of valuation away from market prices towards demand and supply functions as the underlying repositories of value. These functions are behavioral relations, and the implication of the paradigm shift was that economics is not just the study of markets, but more generally the study of human preferences and behavior.

The conceptual link to nonmarket valuation is the recognition that, while a demand curve is not observable if there is no market for a commodity, there still exists a latent demand curve that perhaps can be teased out through other means. Indirect methods are one approach to doing this, and contingent valuation is another. In both cases, the details of implementation have a large impact on the quality of the results.

Faced with the assertion that contingent valuation surveys can *never* be a reliable source of information either for benefit-cost analysis or for damage assessment, the NOAA Panel rejected this as unwarranted. Two years later, there is now even more evidence from recent studies and literature analyses to support the Panel's conclusion. However, it would be misleading for me to suggest that contingent valuation surveys can be made to work well in all circumstances. I am sure situations could exist where a contingent valuation researcher might be unable to devise a plausible scenario for the item of interest. Nor would I wish to argue that all contingent valuation surveys are of high quality. The method, though simple in its directness, is in fact difficult to implement without falling into various types of design problems that require effort, skill and imagination to resolve. Each particular study needs to be scrutinized carefully. But the same is true of any empirical study.

While I believe in the feasibility of using contingent valuation to measure people's value for the environment, I do not mean to advocate a narrow benefit-cost analysis for all environmental policy decisions, nor to suggest that everything can or should be quantified. There will be cases where the information is inadequate, the uncertainties too great, or the consequences too profound or too complex to be reduced to a single number. I am well aware of the fallacy of misplaced precision. But this cuts both ways. It also applies to those who suggest that it is better not to measure nonuse values at all than to measure them through contingent valuation. I reply to such critics by quoting Douglass North: "The price you pay for precision is an inability to deal with real-world issues" (*Wall Street Journal*, 7/29/94).

Is expert judgment an alternative to contingent valuation? Experts clearly play the leading role in determining the physical injuries to the environment and in assessing the costs of cleanup and restoration. Assessing what things *are worth* is different. How the experts know the value that the public places on an uninjured environment, without resort to measurement involving some sort of survey, is unclear. When that public valuation is the

---

[33]For an account of the development of nonmarket valuation generally, see Hanemann (1992).

object of measurement, a well-designed contingent valuation survey is one way of consulting the relevant experts—the public itself.

References

Adamowicz, W., J. Louviere, and M. Williams, "Combining Revealed and Stated Preference Methods for Valuing Environmental Amenities," *Journal of Environmental Economics and Management*, 1994, *26*, 271–92.

Ajzen, Icek, and Martin Fishbein, *Understanding Attitudes and Predicting Social Behavior*. New Jersey: Prentice-Hall, Inc., 1980.

Anonymous, " 'Ask a Silly Question . . .' Contingent Valuation of Natural Resource Damages," *Harvard Law Review*, June 1992, *105*, 1981–2000.

Arrow, Kenneth J., *Social Choice and Individual Values*, 2nd ed., New Haven: Yale University Press, 1963.

Arrow, Kenneth et al., *Report of the NOAA Panel on Contingent Valuation*, Washington, D.C.: January 1993, p. 41.

Atkinson, A. B., and J. Micklewright, "On the Reliability of Income Data in the Family Expenditure Survey, 1970–1977," *Journal of the Royal Statistical Society* (A), 1983, *146(1)*, 33–53.

Bate, Roger, "Pick a Number: A Critique of Contingent Valuation Methodology and Its Application in Public Policy." Competitive Enterprise Institute, Environmental Studies Program, Washington, D.C., January 1994.

Bateman, Ian, and Ken Willis (eds.), *Valuing Environmental Preferences: Theory and Practice of the Contingent Valuation Method in the US, EC and Developing Countries*. Oxford, UK: Oxford University Press, forthcoming.

Becker, Gary S., "Nobel Lecture: The Economic Way of Looking at Behavior." *Journal of Political Economy*, June 1993, *101(3)*, 385–409.

Bettman, James R., "Processes of Adaptivity in Decision Making," *Advances in Consumer Research*, 1988, *15*, 1–4.

Bettman, J. R., and M. A. Zins, "Constructive Processes in Consumer Choice," *Journal of Consumer Research*, September 1977, *4*, 75–85.

Bishop, Richard C., and Thomas A. Heberlein, "Measuring Values of Extramarket Goods: Are Indirect Measures Biased?" *American Journal of Agricultural Economics*, December 1979, *61*, 926–30.

Bishop, Richard C., and Thomas A. Heberlein, "The Contingent Valuation Method." In Johnson, Rebecca L., and Gary V. Johnson, eds., *Economic Valuation of Natural Resources: Issues, Theory, and Applications*, Boulder: Westview Press, 1990, 81–104.

Bohm, Peter, "Estimating Demand for Public Goods: An Experiment," *European Economic Review*, 1972, *3*, 111–30.

Boyce, R. R., et al., "Experimental Evidence of Existence Value in Payment and Compensation Contexts." Paper presented at the USDA W-133 Annual Meeting, San Diego, California, February 1989.

Boyle, Kevin J., Michael P. Welsh, and Richard C. Bishop, "The Role of Question Order and Respondent Experience in Contingent-Valuation Studies," *Journal of Environmental Economics and Management*, 1993, *25*, S-80–S-99.

Bradburn, Norman M., Lance J. Rips, and Steven K. Shevell, "Answering Autobiographical Questions: The Impact of Memory and Inference on Surveys," *Science*, April 1987, *236*, 157–61.

Briscoe, John, et al., "Toward Equitable and Sustainable Rural Water Supplies: A Contingent Valuation Study in Brazil," *World Bank Economic Review*, May 1990, 4, 115–34.

Brookshire, David S., Mark A. Thayer, William D. Schulze, and Ralph C. d'Arge, "Valuing Public Goods: A Comparison of Survey and Hedonic Approaches," *American Economic Review*, 1982, 72, 165–77.

Carson, Richard T., "Contingent Valuation Surveys and Tests of Insensitivity to Scope." Paper presented at the International Conference on Determining the Value of Nonmarketed Goods: Economic Psychological, and Policy Relevant Aspects of Contingent Valuation Methods, Bad Hamburg, Germany, July 1994.

Carson, Richard T., and Nicholas E. Flores, "Another Look at 'Does Contingent Valuation Measure Preferences: Experimental Evidence'—How Compelling Is the Evidence?" Economics Department, University of California, San Diego, December 1993.

Carson, R., N. Flores, and W. M. Hanemann, "On the Creation and Destruction of Public Goods: The Matter of Sequencing," working paper 690, Agricultural and Resource Economics, University of California, Berkeley, 1992.

Carson, Richard T., Nicholas E. Flores, Kerry Martin and Jennifer Wright, "Contingent Valuation and Revealed Preference Methodologies: Comparing the Estimates for Quasi-Public Goods," Discussion Paper 94-07, University of California, San Diego, May 1994a.

Carson, Richard T., W. Michael Hanemann, and Robert Cameron Mitchell, "The Use of Simulated Political Markets to Value Public Goods," Economics Department, University of California, San Diego, October 1986.

Carson, Richard T., Kerry Martin, Jennifer Wright," A Note on the Evidence of the Temporal Reliability of Contingent Valuation Estimates," working paper, University of California, San Diego, Economics Department, July 1994b.

Carson, Richard T., and Robert Cameron Mitchell, "The Value of Clean Water: The Public's Willingness to Pay for Boatable, Fishable, and Swimmable Quality Water," *Water Resources Research*, 1993, 29, 2445–54.

Carson, R., et al., *A Contingent Valuation Study of Lost Passive Use Values Resulting from the Exxon Valdez Oil Spill*, Report to the Attorney General of Alaska, Natural Resource Damage Assessment, Inc. La Jolla, CA, November 1992.

Carson, Richard T., et al., *A Bibliography of Contingent Valuation Studies and Papers*, Natural Resource Damage Assessment, Inc., La Jolla, CA, March 1994c.

Chase, S. B., ed., *Problems in Public Expenditure Analysis*, Washington, D.C.: Brookings Institution, 1968.

Cicchetti, Charles J., and V. Kerry Smith, "Congestion, Quality Deterioration, and Optimal Use: Wilderness Recreation in the Spanish Peaks Primitive Area," *Social Science Research*, 1973, 2, 15–30.

Ciriacy-Wantrup, S. V., "Capital Returns from Soil-Conservation Practices," *Journal of Farm Economics*, November 1947, 29, 1188–90.

Clotfelter, Charles T., *Federal Tax Policy and Charitable Giving*. Chicago: The University of Chicago Press, 1985.

Cronin, Thomas E., *Direct Democracy: The Politics of Initiative, Referendum, and Recall*. Cambridge: Harvard University Press, 1989.

Cropper, Maureen L., "Comments on Estimating the Demand for Public Goods: The Collective Choice and Contingent Valuation Approaches." Paper presented at the DOE/EPA Workshop on "Using Contingent Valuation to Measure Non-Market Values," Herndon, VA, May 19–20, 1994.

Cummings, Ronald G., "Relating Stated and Revealed Preferences: Challenges and Opportunities." Paper presented at the DOE/EPA Workshop on "Using Contingent Valuation to Measure Non-Market Values," Herndon, VA, May 19–20, 1994.

Cummings, Ronald G., David S. Brookshire, and William D. Schulze, et al., eds. *Valuing Environmental Goods: An Assessment of the Contingent Valuation Method.* Totowa, New Jersey: Rowman and Allanheld, 1986.

Cummings, Ronald G., Glenn W. Harrison, and E. E. Ruström, "Homegrown Values and Hypothetical Surveys: Is the Dichotomous Choice Approach Incentive Compatible?" Economics Working Paper Series, B-92-12, Division of Research, College of Business Administration, The University of South Carolina, February 1993.

Cutler, David, Douglas W. Elmendorf, and Richard J. Zeckhauser, "Demographic Characteristics and the Public Bundle," National Bureau of Economic Research, Cambridge, NBER Working Paper No. 4283, February 1993.

Desvousges, William H., et al., *Measuring Nonuse Damages Using Contingent Valuation: An Experimental Evaluation of Accuracy.* North Carolina: Research Triangle Institute Monograph, 1992.

Diamond, P. A., "Testing the Internal Consistency of Contingent Valuation Surveys," working paper, MIT, 1993.

Diamond, Peter A., Jerry Hausman, Gregory K. Leonard, and Mike A. Denning, "Does Contingent Valuation Measure Preferences? Experimental Evidence." In Hausman, J. A., ed., *Contingent Valuation: A Critical Assessment.* New York: North-Holland, 1993, 41–89.

DiBona, Charles J., "Assessing Environmental Damage," *Issues in Science and Technology,* Fall 1992, *8,* 50–54.

Dickie, M. A. Fisher, and S. Gerking, "Market Transactions and Hypothetical Demand Data: A Comparative Study," *Journal of American Statistical Association,* March 1987, *82,* 69–75.

Duffield, John W., and David A. Patterson, "Field Testing Existence Values: An Instream Flow Trust Fund for Montana Rivers." Presented at the American Economics Association Annual Meeting, New Orleans, Louisiana, January 4, 1991.

Ferber, Robert, and Robert A. Piskie, "Subjective Probabilities and Buying Intentions," *Review of Economics and Statistics,* August 1965, *47,* 322–25.

Fiorina, Morris P., *Retrospective Voting in American National Elections.* New Haven: Yale University Press, 1981.

Fishkin, J. S., *Democracy and Deliberation: New Directions for Democratic Reform.* New Haven: Yale University Press, 1991.

Freeman, A. Myrick, *The Measurement of Environment and Resource Values: Theory and Method.* Washington, D.C.: Resources for the Future, 1993.

Frisch, Deborah, "Reasons for Framing Effects," *Organizational Behavior and Human Decision Processes,* 1993, *54,* 399–429.

Groves, Robert M., *Survey Errors and Survey Costs.* New York: John Wiley and Sons, 1989.

Hanemann, W. Michael, "Welfare Evaluations in Contingent Valuation Experiments with Discrete Responses," *American Journal of Agricultural Economics,* August 1984, *66,* 332–41.

Hanemann, W. Michael, "Preface: Notes on the History of Environmental Valuation in the USA." In Navrud, Stale, ed., *Pricing the Environment: The European Experience.* Oxford, UK: Oxford University Press, 1992.

Hanemann, W. Michael, "Contingent Valuation and Economics," Working Paper No. 697, Giannini Foundation of Agricultural and Resource Economics, University of California, Berkeley, February 1994a. To appear in Willis, Ken, and John

Corkindale, eds., *Environmental Valuation: Some New Perspectives*, Wallingford, Oxon, UK: CAB International, forthcoming.

Hanemann, W. Michael, "Strictly For the Birds: A Re-examination of the Exxon Tests of Scope in CV," working paper, Giannini Foundation of Agricultural and Resource Economics, University of California, Berkeley, August 1994b.

Hanemann, W. Michael, and B. J. Kanninen, "Statistical Analysis of CV Data." In Bateman, I., and K. Willis, eds. *Valuing Environmental Preferences: Theory and Practice of the Contingent Valuation Method in the US, EC and Developing Countries*. Oxford: Oxford University Press, forthcoming.

Hanemann, W. Michael, David Chapman, and Barbara Kanninen, "Non-Market Valuation Using Contingent Behavior: Model Specification and Consistency Tests." Presented at the American Economic Association Annual Meeting, Anaheim, California, January 6, 1993.

Hanemann, W. M., J. Loomis, and B. Kanninen, "Statistical Efficiency of Double-Bounded Dichotomous Choice Contingent Valuation," *American Journal of Agricultural Economics*, 1991, 73, 1255–63.

Harrison, Glenn W., "Valuing Public Goods with the Contingent Valuation Method: A Critique of Kahneman and Knetsch," *Journal of Environmental Economics and Management*, 1992, 23, 248–57.

Hausman, J. A., ed., *Contingent Valuation: A Critical Assessment*. New York: North-Holland, 1993.

Hausman, J. A., G. K. Leonard, and D. McFadden, "A Utility-Consistent Combined Discrete Choice and Count Data Model: Assessing Recreational Use Losses Due to Natural Resource Damage," paper presented at the National Bureau of Economic Research, Cambridge, Massachusetts, April 15, 1994

Hoehn, J. P., and A. Randall, "Too Many Proposals Pass the Benefit Cost Test," *American Economic Review*, June 1989, 79, 544–51.

Infosino, William J., "Forecasting New Product Sales from Likelihood of Purchase Ratings," *Marketing Science*, Fall 1986, 5, 372–84.

Johansson, Per-Olov, "Altruism in Cost-Benefit Analysis," *Environmental and Resource Economics*, 1992, 2, 605–13.

Jones-Lee, Michael W., M. Hammerton, and P. R. Philips, "The Value of Safety: Results of a National Sample Survey," *Economic Journal*, March 1985, 95, 49–72.

Juster, F. Thomas, *Anticipations and Purchases: An Analysis of Consumer Behavior*. Princeton: Princeton University Press, 1964.

Juster, F. Thomas, and Frank P. Stafford, "The Allocation of Time: Empirical Findings, Behavioral Models, and Problems of Measurement," *Journal of Economic Literature*, 1991, 29, 471–522.

Kahneman, Daniel, "Valuing Environmental Goods: An Assessment of the Contingent Valuation Method: The Review Panel Assessment." In Cummings, R. G., D. S. Brookshire, W. D. Schulze, et al., eds., *Valuing Environmental Goods: An Assessment of the Contingent Valuation Method*. Totowa, New Jersey: Rowman & Allanheld, 1986, 185–94.

Kahneman, Daniel, and Jack L. Knetsch, "Valuing Public Goods: The Purchase of Moral Satisfaction," *Journal of Environmental Economics and Management*, 1992, 22, 57–70.

Kahneman, Daniel, and Ilana Ritov, "Determinants of Stated Willingness to Pay for Public Goods: A Study in the Headline Method," unpublished, Department of Psychology, University of California, Berkeley, 1993.

Kanninen, B. J., "Optimal Experimental Design for Double-Bounded Dichotomous Choice Contingent Valuation," *Land Economics*, May 1993, 69, 128–46.

Kelly, S., and T. W. Mirer, "The Simple Act of Voting," *American Political Science Review*, 1974, *68*, 572–91.

Kemp, Michael A., and Christopher Maxwell, "Exploring a Budget Context for Contingent Valuation Estimates." In Hausman, J. A., ed., *Contingent Valuation: A Critical Assessment.* New York: North-Holland, 1993, 217–69.

Knetsch, J. L., and R. K. Davis, Comparisons of Methods for Recreation Evaluation." In Kneese A. V., and S. C. Smith, eds., *Water Research*, Baltimore: Resources for the Future Inc., Johns Hopkins Press, 1966, 125–42.

Kriström, Bengt, and Pere Riera, "Is the Income Elasticity of Environmental Improvements Less Than One?" Paper presented at the Second Conference on Environmental Economics, Ulvöng, Sweden, June 2–5, 1994.

Krosnick, Jon A., "Response Strategies for Coping with the Cognitive Demands of Attitude Measures in Surveys," *Applied Cognitive Psychology*, 1991, *5*, 213–36.

Krosnick, Jon A., Fan Li, and Darrin R. Lehman, "Conservational Conventions, Order of Information Acquisition, and the Effect of Base Rates and Individuating Information on Social Judgments," *Journal of Personality and Social Psychology*, 1990, *59*, 1140–52.

Krutilla, John V., "Conservation Reconsidered," *American Economic Review*, September 1967, *57*, 777–86.

Lupia, Arthur, "Short Cuts versus Encyclopedias: Information and Voting Behavior in California Insurance Reform Elections," working paper, Department of Political Science, University of California, San Diego, April 1993.

Madden, Paul, "A Generalization of Hicksian q Substitutes and Complements with Application to Demand Rationing," *Econometrica*, September 1991, *59*, 1497–1508.

Magleby, David B., *Direct Legislation, Voting on Ballot Propositions in the United States.* Baltimore and London: The John Hopkins University Press, 1984.

Maki, Atsushi, and Shigeru Nishiyama, "Consistency Between Macro- and Micro-Data Sets in the Japanese Household Sector," *Review of Income and Wealth*, 1993, *39*, 195–207.

Martin, Leonard L., and Abraham Tesser, eds., *The Construction of Social Judgments.* New Jersey: Lawrence Erlbaum Associates, chapter 2, 1992, 37–65.

Mathiowetz, Nancy A., and Greg J. Duncan, "Out of Work, Out of Mind: Response Errors in Retrospective Reports of Unemployment," *Journal of Business & Economic Statistics*, 1988, *6*, 221–29.

McCloskey, Donald, *The Rhetoric of Economics.* Madison: The University of Wisconsin Press, 1985.

McFadden, Daniel, and Gregory K. Leonard, "Issues in the Contingent Valuation of Environmental Goods: Methodologies for Data Collection and Analysis." In Hausman, J. A., ed., *Contingent Valuation: A Critical Assessment.* New York: North-Holland, 1993, 165–215.

McKelvey, Richard D., and Peter C. Ordeshook, "Information, Electoral Equilibria and the Democratic Ideal," *Journal of Politics*, 1986, *48*, 909–37.

Merton, Robert K., and Patricia L. Kendall, "The Focused Interview," *American Journal of Sociology*, 1946, *51*, 541–57.

Milgrom, Paul, "Is Sympathy an Economic Value? Philosophy, Economics, and the Contingent Valuation Method." In Hausman, J. A., ed., *Contingent Valuation: A Critical Assessment.* New York: North-Holland, 1993, 417–41.

Miller, Leslie A., and Theodore Downes-Le Guin, "Reducing Response Error in Consumers' Reports of Medical Expenses: Application of Cognitive Theory to the Consumer Expenditure Interview Survey," *Advances in Consumer Research*, 1990, *17*, 193–206.

Mitchell, Robert Cameron, and Richard T. Carson, *Using Surveys to Value Public Goods: The Contingent Valuation Method*. Washington, D. C.: Resources for the Future, 1989.

Navrud, Ståle, *Pricing the European Environment*. New York: Oxford University Press, 1992.

Neill, Helen R., et al., "Hypothetical Surveys and Real Economic Commitments," *Land Economics*, May 1994, *70*, 145–54.

Neisser, Urlic, *Cognitive Psychology*. Appleton-Century-Crofts, Educational Division, New York: Meredith Corporation, 1967.

Oates, W., "Comments on Estimating the Demand for Public Goods: The Collective Choice and Contingent Valuation Approaches." Paper presented at the DOE/EPA Workshop on Using Contingent Valuation to Measure Non-Market Values, Hemdon, VA, May 19–20, 1994.

Olshavsky, Richard W., and Donald H. Granbois, "Consumer Decision Making—Fact or Fiction?" *Journal of Consumer Research*, September 1979, *6*, 93–100.

Payne, J. W., J. R. Bettman, and E. J. Johnson, "Adaptive Strategy Selection in Decision Making," *Journal of Experimental Psychology Learning, Memory, and Cognition*, 1988, *14*, 534–52.

Poulton, E. C., *Bias in Quantifying Judgments*. Hove, UK: Lawrence Erlbaum Associates, 1989.

Pratt, John W., David A. Wise, and Richard Zeckhauser, "Price Differences in Almost Competitive Markets," *Quarterly Journal of Economics*, May 1979, *93*, 189–212.

Randall, Alan, "A Difficulty with the Travel Cost Method," *Land Economics*, February 1994, *70*, 88–96.

Randall, Alan, Berry C. Ives, and Clyde Eastman, "Bidding Games for Valuation of Aesthetic Environmental Improvements," *Journal of Environmental Economics and Management*, 1974, *1*, 132–49.

Rose, Steven, *The Making of Memory: From Molecules to Mind*. New York: Anchor Books, Doubleday, 1992.

Rosen, S., "Hedonic Prices and Implicit Markets: Product Differentiation in Pure Competition," *Journal of Political Economy*, January–February 1974, *82*, 34–55.

Schelling, Thomas, "The Life You Save May Be Your Own." In Chase, S., ed., *Problems in Public Expenditure Analysis*. Washington, D.C.: Brookings Institution, 1968, 143–44.

Schkade, David A., and John W. Payne, "Where Do the Numbers Come From? How People Respond to Contingent Valuation Questions." In Hausman, J. A., ed., *Contingent Valuation: A Critical Assessment*. New York: North-Holland, 1993, 271–303.

Schuman, H., remarks in transcript of Public Meeting of the National Oceanic and Atmospheric Administration, Contingent Valuation Panel, Washington, D.C.: NOAA, Department of Commerce, August 12, 1992, p. 101.

Schuman, H., and S. Presser, *Questions and Answers in Attitude Surveys*. New York: Academic Press, 1981.

Seip, K., and J. Strand, "Willingness to Pay for Environmental Goods in Norway: A Contingent Valuation Study with Real Payment," *Environmental and Resource Economics*, 1992, *2*, 91–106.

Sen, A. K., "Behavior and the Concept of Preference," *Economica*, August 1973, *40*, 241–59.

Sinden, J. A., "Empirical Tests of Hypothetical Biases in Consumers' Surplus Surveys," *Australian Journal of Agricultural Economics*, 1988, *32*, 98–112.

Smith, Tom W., "The Art of Asking Questions, 1936–1985," *Public Opinion Quarterly*, 1987, *51*, 21–36.

Smith, V. Kerry, "Arbitrary Values, Good Causes, and Premature Verdicts," *Journal of Environmental Economics and Management*, 1992, *22*, 71–89.

Smith, V. Kerry, "Lightning Rods, Dart Boards and Contingent Valuation," *Natural Resources Journal*, forthcoming 1994.

Smith, V. Kerry, and William H. Desvousges, *Measuring Water Quality Benefits*. Boston: Kluwer-Nijhoff Publishing, 1986.

Smith, V. Kerry, and Laura Osborne, "Do Contingent Valuation Estimates Pass a 'Scope' Test?: A Preliminary Meta Analysis." Presented at the American Economics Association Annual Meeting, Boston MA, January 5, 1994.

Sniderman, Paul M., "The New Look in Public Opinion Research." In Finifter, Ada W., ed., *Political Science: The State of the Discipline II*. Washington, D.C.: The American Political Science Association, 1993, 219–45.

Sniderman, Paul M., Richard A. Brody, and Phillip E. Tetlock, *Reasoning and Choice, Explorations in Political Psychology*. Cambridge: Cambridge University Press, 1991.

Tanur, Judith M., ed., *Questions about Questions: Inquiries into the Cognitive Bases of Surveys*. New York: Russell Sage Foundation, 1992.

Theil, Henri, and Richard F. Kosobud, "How Informative Are Consumer Buying Intentions Surveys?" *Review of Economics and Statistics*, February 1968, *50*, 50–59.

Tversky, Amos, and Daniel Kahneman, "Judgment under Uncertainty: Heuristics and Biases," *Science*, 1974, *185*, 124–31.

Walsh, Richard G., Donn M. Johnson, and John R. McKean, "Benefits Transfer of Outdoor Recreation Demand Studies: 1968–1988," *Water Resources Research* 1992, *28*, 707–13.

Warshaw, Paul R., "Predicting Purchase and Other Behaviors from General and Contextually Specific Intentions," *Journal of Marketing Research*, February 1980, *17*, 26–33.

Wilson, Timothy D., and Sara D. Hodges, "Attitudes as Temporary Constructions." In Martin L., and A. Tesser, eds., *The Construction of Social Judgments*. New Jersey: Lawrence Erlbaum Associates, chapter 2, 1992, 37–65.

9 Contingent Valuation: Is Some Number Better than No Number?*

Peter A. Diamond

Jerry A. Hausman

Peter Diamond is Institute Professor, Department of Economics at the Massachusetts Institute of Technology; and Jerry Hausman is John and Jennie S. MacDonald Professor, Department of Economics at the Massachusetts Institute of Technology.

Most economic analyses aim at explaining market transactions. Data on transactions, or potentially collectible data on transactions, are the touchstone for recognizing interesting economic analyses. However loose the connection between a theoretical or empirical analysis and transactions, this connection is the basis of the methodology of judging the credibility and reliability of economic analyses. Generally, individuals do not purchase public goods directly. Lack of data on transactions implies that economists must find other methods to assess surveys asking for valuations of public goods.

To address this problem, we begin with a discussion of the methodology of evaluating contingent valuation surveys. While there is some experimental evidence about small payments for public goods, we work with the assumption that we do not have data on actual transactions for interesting environmental public goods to compare with survey responses of hypothetical willingness-to-pay. This situation creates the need for other standards for evaluating survey responses. Evaluation involves the credibility, bias (also referred to as reliability in the literature), and precision of responses. Credibility refers to whether survey respondents are answering the question the interviewer is trying to ask. If respondents are answering the right question, reliability refers to the size and direction of the biases that may be present in the answers. Precision refers to the variability in responses. Since precision can usually be increased by the simple expedient of increasing the sample size, we will not discuss precision further in this paper. Problems of credibility or of bias are not reduced by increases in

"Contingent Value: Is Some Number Better than No Number?" by Peter A. Diamond and Jerry A. Hausman, from *Journal of Economic Perspectives*, 8(4):45–64 (Fall 1994).

*The authors want to thank Bernard Saffran and four editors for helpful comments.

sample size. Thus credibility and bias must be evaluated when considering the use of such surveys—in benefit-cost analyses, in the determination of damages after a finding of liability, or as general information to affect the legislative process.[1]

We discuss how to judge the content in contingent valuation surveys together with evidence from surveys that have been done. Surveys designed to test for consistency between stated willingness-to-pay and economic theory have found that contingent valuation responses are not consistent with economic theory. The main contingent valuation anomaly that we discuss is called the "embedding effect," and was first analyzed systematically by Kahneman and Knetsch (1992).[2] The embedding effect is the name given to the tendency of willingness-to-pay responses to be highly similar across different surveys, even where theory suggests (and sometimes requires) that the responses be very different.[3] An example of embedding would be a willingness-to-pay to clean up one lake roughly equal to that for cleaning up five lakes, including the one asked about individually. The embedding effect is usually thought to arise from the nonexistence of individual preferences for the public good in question and from the failure of survey respondents, in the hypothetical circumstances of the survey, to consider the effect of their budget constraints. Because of these embedding effects, different surveys can obtain widely variable stated willingness-to-pay amounts for the same public good, with no straightforward way for selecting one particular method as the appropriate one.

In short, we think that the evidence supports the conclusion that to date, contingent valuation surveys do not measure the preferences they attempt to measure. Moreover, we present reasons for thinking that changes in survey methods are not likely to change this conclusion. Viewed alternatively as opinion polls on possible government actions, we think that these surveys do not have much information to contribute to informed policy-making. Thus, we conclude that reliance on contingent valuation surveys in either damage assessments or in government decision making is basically misguided.

---

[1]With two estimates of an economic value, one can analyze directly whether one is a biased estimate of the other. With nonuse value, the lack of an alternative direct estimate of willingness-to-pay makes it relevant to consider credibility directly, as well as the differences between survey results and behavior in other contexts where transactions data are available.

[2]Another failure of contingent valuation surveys to be consistent with economic preferences is that stated willingness-to-pay is usually found to be much less than stated willingness-to-accept. From economic theory, willingness-to-pay differs from willingness-to-accept only by an income effect. Thus, their values should be extremely close in typical contingent valuation circumstances, where the stated willingness-to-pay is a small share of the consumer's overall budget, and willingness-to-pay amounts show a small income elasticity. For further discussion of this problem with contingent valuation surveys and other problems, see Diamond and Hausman (1993) and Milgrom (1993).

[3]The term embedding came from the research approach of "embedding" a particular good in a more inclusive good, and contrasting the stated willingness-to-pay for the good with that obtained by allocating the willingness-to-pay for the more inclusive good among its components (Kahneman, personal communication).

Judging Surveys of Willingness-to-Pay for Public Goods

A number of bases exist for forming judgments about whether particular respondents are answering the right question and whether the response is roughly correct. One widely accepted basis is by reaching the conclusion that a particular response is simply not credible as an answer to the question the interviewer is trying to ask. It is standard practice in the contingent valuation literature to eliminate some responses as being unreasonably large to be the true willingness-to-pay. Thus trimming responses that are more than, say, 5 percent of income for an environmental public good that contains only nonuse value may be criticized for having an arbitrary cutoff, but not for omitting answers that are believed to be credible. Similarly, it is standard practice to eliminate some responses of zero on the basis that these are "protest zeros," that answers to other questions in the survey indicate that individuals do put a positive value on changes in the level of the public good, and thus zero is not a credible answer.

A widely accepted incredibility test indicates that it is not automatic that the response given is an answer to the question that the interviewer wants answered. But we need to go further in considering how to form a judgment on the survey responses; it is not adequate to assume that any response that is not obviously wrong is an accurate response to the question the survey designer had in mind.

A number of additional bases have been used by people arguing that responses are or are not acceptable. The methods we shall discuss include verbal protocol analysis, the patterns of willingness-to-pay responses across individuals, and across surveys.

In considering the relevance of this evidence for the question of whether survey responses are accurate measures of true preferences, it is useful to have in mind some possible alternative hypotheses of how people respond to such surveys, since the responses are not simply random numbers. Several hypotheses have been put forward as alternatives to the hypothesis that the responses are measures of true economic preferences. Individuals may be expressing an attitude toward a public good (or class of public goods), expressed in a dollar scale because they are asked to express it in a dollar scale (Kahneman and Ritov, 1993). Individuals may receive a "warm glow" from expressing support for good causes (Andreoni, 1989).[4] Individuals may be describing what they think is good for the country, in a sort of casual benefit-cost analysis (Diamond and Hausman, 1993). Individuals may be expressing a reaction to actions that have been taken (for example, allowing an oil spill) rather than evaluating the state of a resource.

Under all of these alternative hypotheses, responses are not an attempt by an individual to evaluate his or her own preference for a public good.

---

[4]This approach was developed for actual charitable contributions, not survey responses. Kahneman and Knetsch (1992) call it the purchase of moral satisfaction.

For example, people doing casual benefit-cost analyses may be reflecting how much they think people generally care about the issue. We think that different hypotheses are likely to be appropriate for different people. Thus the question is not whether the hypothesis of an accurate measurement of preferences is the single best hypothesis, but whether the fraction of the population for whom the hypothesis of accuracy is reasonable is sufficiently large to make the survey as a whole useful for policy purposes.

All of these alternatives are based on what individuals are trying to do; there are further questions of standard survey biases (such as interviewer bias, framing bias, hypothetical bias) and whether people have enough information to express a preference with any accuracy, even if they are attempting to express a preference. Insofar as this understanding is faulty, expressed preferences are not an expression of true economic preferences.

Verbal Protocol Analysis

For verbal protocol analysis, individuals are asked to "think aloud" as they respond to a questionnaire, reporting everything that goes through their minds. Everything the subjects say is recorded on audio tapes that are transcribed and coded for the types of considerations being mentioned. Schkade and Payne (1993) have done such an analysis using a contingent valuation survey that asks for willingness-to-pay to protect migratory waterfowl from drowning in uncovered waste water holding ponds from oil and gas operations.

The transcripts show the inherent difficulty in selecting a willingness-to-pay response and the extent to which people refer to elements that ought to be irrelevant to evaluating their own preferences. If people are trying to report a preference, we would expect them to consider inputs into the forming of their preferences, such as how much they care about birds, how important the number of killed birds are relative to the numbers in the species. Conversely, we would not expect them to report a willingness-to-pay just equal to what they think the program will cost. Respondents verbalized many diverse considerations. Perhaps the most common strategy involved first acknowledging that something should be done and then trying to figure out an appropriate amount. About one-fourth of the sample mentioned the idea that if everyone did his part then each household would not have to give all that much. About one-sixth of the sample made comparisons with donations to charities. About one-fifth of the sample said they just made up a number or guessed an answer. Many respondents seemed to wish to signal concern for a larger environmental issue. This pattern may reflect the unfamiliarity of the task the respondents faced.

These findings strongly suggest that people are not easily in touch with underlying preferences about the type of commodity asked about. The findings do not lend support to the hypothesis that responses are an attempt to measure and express personal preferences. To the extent that individuals consider costs to everyone, the analysis supports the hypothesis of casual benefit-cost analysis. To the extent that individuals look to their own charitable contributions for a guide, the analysis is consistent with hypotheses that explain actual contributions, such as the warm glow hypothesis.

Variation in Willingness-to-Pay Across Individuals

If stated willingness-to-pay is a reflection of true preferences, then we would expect certain patterns of answers across different individuals (other things equal). We would expect self-described environmentalists to have larger willinesses-to-pay. We would expect individuals with higher incomes to have larger willingnesses-to-pay. Both results do occur. However, such results do not distinguish among the various hypotheses that were spelled out above since we would expect roughly similar results from any of them. Thus this potential basis for evaluation does not have much bite.[5] We do observe that the income effects that are measured in typical surveys are lower than we would expect if true preferences are measured, lower for example than measured income elasticities for charitable giving.[6]

Variation in Willingness-to-Pay Across Surveys

Another approach to forming a judgment is to compare willingness-to-pay responses to different questions, whether in the same or in different surveys.

Multiple Questions. If a survey question reveals a true valuation, it should not matter whether the question is asked by itself or with other questions, nor if asked with any other questions, what the order of questioning is. However, when Tolley et al. (1983) asked for willingness-to-pay to preserve visibility at the Grand Canyon, the response was five times higher when this was the only question, as compared to its being the third such question. Attempts to claim this result to be consistent with preferences have relied on income effects and substitution effects. Neither of these rationalizations for the anomalous results is compelling, as we explain in a moment.

The importance of question order was also shown in a study by Samples and Hollyer (1990) asking for the values of preserving seals and whales. Some respondents were asked for willingness-to-pay to preserve seals first, followed by a question about whales. Others were asked for willingness-to-pay in the reverse order. Seal value tended to be lower when asked after whale value, while whale value was not affected by the sequence of ques-

---

[5]The importance of the lack of bite of such considerations comes, in part, from the fact that the contingent valuation study of the Exxon Valdez spill that was done for the state of Alaska (Carson et al., 1992) included such analyses, but none of the more powerful split-sample consistency tests that we discuss below.

[6] The empirical finding of low income elasticities is also inconsistent with the typical finding of a large divergence between willingness-to-pay and willingness-to-accept, discussed in footnote 2.

tions.[7] Thus the sum of willingness-to-pay depended on the sequence of the questions asked. The authors offer an explanation (p. 189) "based on debriefing sessions held with the interviewer."

> Apparently, when respondents valued seals first, they used their behavior in this market situation to guide their responses to whale valuation questions. Since whales are generally more popular than seals, respondents were reluctant to behave more benevolently toward seals compared with humpback whales. Consequently, whale values were inflated in the S-W questionnaire version to maintain a relatively higher value for the humpbacks. This behavioral anchoring effect did not exist in the W-S version, where whales were valued first.

To have the value of preserving both seals and whales depend on the sequence in which the questions are asked is not consistent with the hypothesis that stated willingness-to-pay accurately measures preferences. These results can be interpreted in two ways. One interpretation is that contingent valuation studies that ask two questions rather than one are unreliable. The other interpretation is that the warm glow hypothesis is supported, since having expressed support for the environment in the first question permits a sharp fall in the second response. This effect is not present, however, when such a response would seem illogical to the respondent. More generally, one needs to decide whether a given pattern of responses is a result of survey design issues or a result of the underlying bases of response. This distinction is especially important when the pattern of results appears anomalous with or contradictory to the hypothesis that preferences are accurately measured.

Single Questions and the Embedding Effect. Alternatively, one can ask a single willingness-to-pay question each to different samples. For example, assume that one group is asked to evaluate public good X; a second is asked to evaluate Y; and a third is asked to evaluate X and Y. What interpretations could we make if the willingness-to-pay for X and Y (together) is considerably less than the sum of the willingness-to-pay for X and the willingness-to-pay for Y?[8] One interpretation is that we are seeing an income effect at work. That is, having "spent" for X, one has less income left to purchase Y. Given that the stated willingness-to-pay amounts are very small relative to income and that measured income elasticities are very small, the attempted income effect argument does not explain the differences found.

A second interpretation is to assume that individual preferences have a large substitution effect between X and Y. In some settings the assumption on preferences needed to justify the results is implausible. For example, Diamond et al. (1993) asked for willingness-to-pay to prevent logging

---

[7]Samples and Hollyer used dichotomous choice surveys. They estimated that whales were valued at $125 when asked about first, and $142 when second. Seals were valued at $103 when asked about first and $62 when second. When they asked about both (together) in a single question, the estimated values were $131 and $146 in two surveys.

[8]This approach is similar to the work that was initiated by Kahneman (1986) and done recently by Kahneman and Knetsch (1992), Kemp and Maxwell (1993), Desvousges et al. (1993), Diamond et al. (1993), McFadden and Leonard (1993), Loomis, Hoehn and Hanemann (1990).

in one, two, and three particular wilderness areas. Stated willingness-to-pay to preserve two (and three) areas was less than the sum of willingness-to-pay to preserve each of them separately.

At first look, this result appears to be an appropriate substitution effect, since protecting one area results in being less willing to protect another. However, preferences should be defined over wilderness remaining, not over proposals for development that are defeated. If preferences are concave over the amount of wilderness available (or, more generally, if different wilderness areas are substitutes), then willingness-to-pay is larger the smaller the quantity of wilderness remaining. This implies that the willingness-to-pay to preserve two threatened areas should be larger than the sum of willingness-to-pay to preserve each as the lone area threatened with development.[9] Instead, stated willingness-to-pay was roughly the same for preserving one, two or three threatened areas, making the amount for several areas together significantly less than the sum of the amounts for the areas separately. Note that these surveys vary both the number of areas threatened and the number to be preserved. Neither the income effect nor the substitution effect can plausibly explain the embedding effect in this experiment. The hypothesis that this survey is eliciting individual preferences is not consistent with individuals having reasonably behaved preferences. However, from the point of view of the warm glow hypothesis, this pattern makes sense. That is, the warm glow hypothesis is that individuals are primarily reporting an expression of support for the environment, an expression that does not vary much with small changes in the precise environmental change being described.

A similar variation in responses across surveys appears in the study of Desvousges et al. (1993). They described a problem killing 2000, 20,000 and 200,000 birds. The willingness-to-pay to solve this problem was roughly the same in all three cases. Since the number of surviving birds is smaller the larger the problem, concave preferences over surviving birds should have resulted in more than a 100-fold variation in willingness-to-pay across this range.[10] Thus this study shows a contradiction between stated willingness-to-pay and the usual economic assumptions on preferences. Again, the study

---

[9]For derivation of the convexity of willingness-to-pay when preferences are concave and the scenario is varied in this way, see Diamond (1993). That paper also contains a number of other implications of preferences for willingness-to-pay that can be used for internal consistency tests.

[10]Proponents of contingent valuation have made several critiques of this study. One critique is that it was a mall stop survey. But similar results followed when the questionnaire was used for the verbal protocol study cited above, which involved subjects coming to be interviewed. Another criticism is that in addition to the absolute numbers, the survey questions described the number of birds at risk as "much less than 1%" of the population, "less than 1%," and "about 2%." Thus, one can wonder whether respondents were paying attention to the absolute numbers which varied 100-fold or the percentages which varied from "much less than 1%" to "about 2%." Interpreting "much less than" as less than half, about 2% is at least a four-fold increase over less than half of 1%. If some people were paying attention to the percentages and some to the absolute numbers, the range should have been between four-fold and 100-fold. If, as Hanemann suggests, respondents did not perceive any real difference between "much less than 1%" and "about 2%," it is noteworthy that they perceived a large difference between zero and "much less than 1%." Moreover, these percentages were selected by the authors since they were the percentages in three actual oil spills: Arthur Kill, Nestucca, *Exxon Valdez.* This pattern of results is consistent with the responses being dominated by a "warm glow."

is consistent with the hypothesis that the responses are primarily warm glow, and so need not vary noticeably over moderate differences in the resource.

Adding-up Test. One difficulty in the approach described above is that the plausibility of the willingness-to-pay patterns depends on assumptions on the plausible (concave) structure of preferences. Another approach to tests of consistency that does not rely on an assumption of concave preferences is to attempt to measure the same preference in two different ways. This test can be constructed by varying the background scenario as well as varying the commodity to be purchased. For example, assume that one group is asked to evaluate public good X; a second group is told that X will be provided and is asked to evaluate also having Y; and a third is asked to evaluate X and Y (together). Now the willingness-to-pay for X and Y (together) should be the same as the sum of the willingness-to-pay for X and the willingness-to-pay for Y, having been given X (the same up to an income effect that can be measured in the survey and that empirically is small).[11] Thus, Diamond et al. (1993) varied the number of wilderness areas being developed as well as the number that could be protected. In this way the sum of two areas separately evaluated (with different degrees of development) should be the same as the value of preserving two areas (apart from a very small income effect). Again, the results of the survey are inconsistent with the responses being a measure of preferences.[12]

Embedding still infects even very recent work done by experienced contingent valuation analysts who were well aware of the problem. Schulze et al. (1993) asked for willingness-to-pay for partial and complete cleanup of contamination of the Clark Fork National Priorities List sites in Montana. After removing protest zeroes and high responses, the mean stated

---

[11]Willingness-to-pay is a function of the two vectors giving alternative levels of public goods and the level of income. Thus the willingness-to-pay to improve the environment from z to z'' of someone with income I can be written $\text{WTP}(z, z'', I)$. The change from z to z'' can be broken into two pieces, a change from z to z' and a change from z' to z''. From the definition of willingness-to-pay, one has $\text{WTP}(z, z'', I) = \text{WTP}(z, z', I) + \text{WTP}(z', z'', I - \text{WTP}(z, z', I))$.

This adding-up test makes no use of an assumption on the magnitude or sign of income or substitution effects. One could do an adding-up test without the adjustment of income shown in the equation by comparing $\text{WTP}(z, z'', I)$ with $\text{WTP}(z, z', I) + \text{WTP}(z', z'', I)$. This comparison would involve a deviation from exact adding-up because of the income effect. With a willingness-to-pay on the order of $30 and a household income level of $30,000, even an income elasticity of one—higher than the elasticity typically measured in contingent valuation surveys—would lead to a $.03 deviation from exact adding-up. For a formal derivation, see the revised version of Diamond (1993).

[12]In brief response to Hanemann's criticisms of our analysis, we note that he does not address this adding-up test and seems comfortable accepting the idea that the less wilderness preserved, the less people care about any particular area of wilderness. These two tests do not rely on any assumption of different wilderness areas being interchangeable, as indicated by the vector interpretation of z in the previous footnote. In terms of Hanemann's test mentioned in his note 25 of whether willingness-to-pay to protect each of the areas is the same, we note that he did not do the statistical test correctly. Moreover, this reference is an example of Hanemann's trait of ignoring the central criticism while attacking a side issue. In Diamond et al., the focus is on the adding-up test, not a scope test. The adding-up test was clearly rejected.

willingness-to-pay for complete cleanup was $72.46 (standard error of $4.71) while the mean response for a considerably smaller partial cleanup was $72.02 (s.e. $5.10). As part of the survey, respondents were asked whether their responses were just for this cleanup or partly to clean up other sites or basically as a contribution for all environmental or other causes (or other). Only 16.9 percent reported their answers as just for this cleanup; that is, a vast majority of respondents recognized an embedding effect in their own responses. These respondents were asked what percentage of their previous answer was for this cleanup, and the willingness-to-pay responses were adjusted by these percentages. After this adjustment, the mean stated willingness-to-pay for complete cleanup was $40.00 (s.e. $2.62) while the mean response for partial cleanup was $37.15 (s.e. $2.71).

These numbers (and the large fraction of people recognizing that they are embedding) support the hypothesis that the responses are dominated by a warm glow. No reason is offered by the authors for the conclusion that the adjustment they do removes the dominance of warm glow. Neither do they perform an adding-up test such as that described above. This adding-up test could have been done by asking a third sample for willingness-to-pay to extend a "planned" partial cleanup to a complete cleanup. In short, the embedding problem does not appear to be one that contingent valuation practitioners know how to solve.

With a pattern of results that are inconsistent with the usual economic assumptions, two interpretations are always possible: the surveys were defective or the contingent valuation method as currently practiced does not measure with accuracy. One should consider all the surveys that attempt to test for consistency in order to judge which interpretation is likely to be correct. The studies we have described have been criticized as not done well enough to be an adequate test.[13] However, they are the only quantitative tests we are aware of. No comparable comparison tests have been done by proponents of the accuracy of contingent valuation, although the embedding effect has long been recognized.

Differing Payment Vehicles. It is interesting to note what two contingent valuation proponents, Mitchell and Carson (1989), have written about the question that respondents are trying to answer. In discussing the sensitivity of responses to the payment vehicle (the way in which the hypothetical payment is to be collected), they write (pp. 123–24):

> It was earlier assumed that only the nature and amount of the amenity being valued should influence the WTP [willingness-to-pay] amounts; all other scenario components, such as the payment vehicle and method of provision, should be neutral in effect . . . More recently, Arrow (1986), Kahneman (1986), and Randall (1986) have argued against that view, holding that important conditions of a sce-

---

[13]One can ask whether the patterns of thought reflected in the responses to the questions in any particular survey also occur in other survey settings. Cognitive psychology has found a number of such patterns that are robust. We think that the patterns reflected in these surveys are similarly robust.

nario, such as the payment vehicle, should be expected to affect the WTP amounts. In their view, which we accept, respondents in a CV [contingent valuation] study are not valuing levels of provision of an amenity in the abstract; they are valuing a policy which includes the conditions under which the amenity will be provided, and the way the public is likely to be asked to pay for it.

In other words, Mitchell and Carson appear to accept the idea (consistent with the findings about some respondents by Schkade and Payne, 1993) that individuals' responses arise from casual benefit-cost analyses, not solely from an examination of their own preferences over resources. For welfare analysis and damage measurement, benefit-cost studies may be different from preferences. We will return to this issue.

Evaluation of Bias: Calibration

Surveys about behavior often have systematic biases relative to the behavior they ask about. Thus, it is common to "calibrate" the responses—that is, adjust for the biases—as part of using them for predictive purposes. In particular, when using surveys to estimate demand for new products, it is standard practice to use a calibration factor to adjust survey responses in order to produce an estimate of actual demand (Urban, Katz, Hatch, and Silk, 1983). As Mitchell and Carson (1989, p. 178) have written: "Such 'calibration' is common in marketing designed to predict purchases. If a systematic divergence between actual and CV [contingent valuation] survey existed and could be quantified, calibration of CV results could be undertaken."

As some evidence on the need for calibration, comparisons of hypothetical surveys and actual offers often find large and significant differences. These comparisons have been done for private goods (Bishop and Heberlein, 1979; Dickie, Fisher and Gerking, 1987; Neill et al., 1993).[14] Comparisons have also been done for charitable donations (Duffield and Patterson, 1992; Seip and Strand, 1992). These studies find a need to calibrate, with calibration factors involving dividing stated willingness-to-pay by a number ranging from 1.5 to 10.

How this calibration should be extended to the public good context is unclear, since the public good context includes both unfamiliar commodities and unfamiliar transactions. But the lack of study of appropriate calibration factors is not a basis for concluding that the best calibration is one-for-one.[15]

---

[14]On the Dickie, Fisher and Gerking (1987) study, see also the critique by Hausman and Leonard (1992).

[15]In its proposed rules for damage assessment, the National Oceanic and Atmospheric Administration (1994) has proposed a default calibration of dividing by two, in the absence of direct arguments by trustees of natural resources for a different calibration factor.

Welfare Analysis

If an accurate measure of willingness-to-pay for the pure public good of the existence of an environmental amenity were available, the measured willingness-to-pay would belong in benefit-cost analysis, just like a pure public good based on resource use. Similarly, the measure should be included in the incentives government creates (through fines and damage payments) to avoid damaging an environmental amenity. As we know from the pure theory of public goods, we would simply add individual willingness-to-pay across the population.[16] In this section, we consider the welfare implications of using stated willingness-to-pay as if it were an accurate measure of preferences in the case that the responses are generated by the alternative hypotheses given above.

One set of problems arises even if willingness-to-pay is being measured accurately, if measured willingness-to-pay contains an altruism component. That is, individuals may be willing to pay to preserve an environmental amenity because of their concerns for others (who may be users or also nonusers). Consider what happens if society adds up everyone's willingness-to-pay and compares the sum with the cost of some action. As a matter of social welfare evaluation we might conclude that such altruistic externalities are double counting, since a utility benefit shows up in the willingness-to-pay of both the person enjoying the public good and the people who care about that person. For example, consider the income distribution problem in a three-person economy. If two of the people start to care about each other, is this change in preferences a reason for a government to increase the level of incomes allocated to the two of them? Similarly, we can ask if the government should devote more taxes to cleaning up lakes where neighbors are friendly with each other than to lakes where neighbors do not know (or care about) each other.

Moreover, if altruistic externalities are thought to be appropriately included in the analysis, it is necessary to include all such externalities for accurate evaluation. In particular, if people care about each other's utilities, they care about the costs borne by others as well as the benefits received by others. An adjustment for altruism must include external costs as well as external benefits if we are to avoid the possibility of a Pareto worsening from an action based on a calculation that appears to be a Pareto improvement (Milgrom, 1993).

A second general problem arises when stated willingness-to-pay may be a poor guess, even though it may be the best guess individuals have of their true willingness-to-pay. Individuals often face the problem of trying to form judgments about the gains from a purchase in settings where the

---

[16]For the correct use of a benefit-cost calculation, we need to be considering the marginal project for finding the optimum. With many projects under consideration, and a nonoptimal starting point, one does not get the right answer by asking about many projects independently and carrying out all that pass the test (Hoehn and Randall, 1989).

link between the commodity and utility is hard to evaluate. One example is the grade of gasoline to buy, assuming that one wants to minimize cost per mile. In the case of environmental amenities, individuals may have a derived demand based on their beliefs about the relationship between the amenity and variables they really care about. For example, they may care about the survival of a species and not know about the range of natural variation in population size, about the probability of survival as a function of population size, nor about the effect of environmental damage on population size. Such derived preferences may be a poor guide to policy; it may be more informative to have expert evaluation of the consequences of an environmental change than to consult the public directly about environmental damage.

The issues just discussed were based on the hypothesis that stated willingness-to-pay is a measure of an individual preference over an outcome. Under the hypothesis that responses reflect casual benefit-cost evaluations rather than preferences, it would be inappropriate to add any other benefits to those coming from a contingent valuation survey since such benefits are presumably included by the respondents, however imperfectly, in their benefit-cost analyses. But if contingent valuation is just a survey of benefit-cost estimates, rather than preferences, it might be better to have a more careful analysis done by people knowing more about environmental issues and about the principles of benefit-cost analysis. Moreover, if responses are benefit-cost estimates rather than preferences, they do not measure a compensable loss in damage suits.

The embedding effect is supportive of the hypothesis that responses are primarily determined by warm glow. If respondents get pleasure from thinking of themselves as supportive of the environment, the willingness-to-pay for this warm glow is not part of the gain from a *particular* environmental project—unless there are no cheaper ways of generating the warm glow. That is, if an individual wants to see the government do at least one environmental project (or n projects) a year in order to feel "environmentally supportive," the person should support one project, but not any particular project. Moreover, if different samples are asked about different projects, the responses will appear to support many projects, even though the warm glow comes from the desire to support a single project.

An illustration of this view comes from the fact that when individuals are asked simultaneously about many projects, stated willingness-to-pay is far below the sum of stated willingness-to-pay from asking about the projects separately. For example, Kemp and Maxwell (1993) asked one group for willingness-to-pay to minimize the risk of oil spills off the coast of Alaska, and found a mean stated willingness-to-pay of $85 (with a 95 percent confidence interval of ±$44). Then they asked a different sample for willingness-to-pay for a broad group of government programs, followed by asking these people to divide and subdivide their willingness-to-pay among the separate programs. By the time they reached minimizing the risk of oil spills off the coast of Alaska, they found a mean of $0.29 (with a 95 percent confidence interval of ±$0.21).

These findings make little sense if responses are measures of preferences, and considerable sense if the response is primarily a warm glow effect from a desire to express support for protecting the environment. In the latter circumstance, we would expect little warm glow for any single project in a context where respondents are asked about many government projects affecting the environment. Therefore warm glow may need to be purged from stated willingness-to-pay even if (as witnessed by charitable contributions) people really are willing to pay for some warm glow.[17]

A different complication arises if people do not really care about the resource, but care about the activity that might harm a resource. For example, the stated willingness-to-pay to clean up a natural oil seepage might be zero while the stated willingness-to-pay to clean up a man-made oil spill is positive. This outcome is the flip side of the "protest zero," where people state no willingness-to-pay to repair environmental damage that they feel is someone else's responsibility. As noted earlier, it is standard practice to consider this zero not to be an accurate measure of preferences, on the assumption that people care about the resource.

Survey results suggest that many answers are heavily influenced by concern about actions, not resources. For example, Desvousges et al. (1993) find a large stated willingness-to-pay to save small numbers of common birds. The finding seems much more likely to reflect a feeling that it is a shame that people do things that kill birds rather than a preference over the number of birds. Concern over the actions of others is different from concern about the state of the environment. Concern about actions is conventionally part of the basis of punitive damages, but not compensatory damages. That is, deliberately or recklessly destroying the property of others opens one up to liability for compensatory damages for the value of the property destroyed and also punitive damages. On the other hand, the legal system does not compensate people who are upset that others engage in actions such as reading *Lady Chatterley's Lover*. When and how such concerns should affect public policy is a complex issue, one not explored here.

One complication from the perspective of benefit-cost analysis is that preferences over acts (as opposed to states of the world) do not provide the consistency that is necessary for consistent economic policy. For example, if people are willing to pay to offset an act, then proposing and not doing an act appears to generate a welfare gain. For example, consider the warm glow from blocking development of a wilderness area. If one proposes two projects and has one blocked, are people better off (from the warm glow) than if one project is proposed and happens? Does this imply that the gov-

---

[17]In the context of the bird study by Desvousges et al. (1993), Kahneman (personal communication) has proposed to purge the warm glow by extrapolating willingness-to-pay as a function of birds saved back to zero and then subtracting this amount from the estimate of willingness-to-pay at any particular level of birds. This approach involves a curve-fitting extrapolation and the assumption that warm glow is totally insensitive to the magnitude of the problem, an assumption that is probably not completely correct.

ernment would do good by proposing projects that it does not mind seeing blocked? More generally, the relationship of benefit-cost analysis and Pareto optimality has been developed and is understood in a setting where preferences are defined over resources.

We note that under the hypothesis of Kahneman and Ritov (1993), responses to contingent valuation surveys are expressions of attitudes toward public goods that the respondents are required to state in dollar terms. Responses are then not measures of willingness-to-pay and provide no quantitative basis for estimates of environmental damages, although like polls generally, they do alert the government about concerns of the public.

The "Some Number Is Better than No Number" Fallacy

We began this essay by arguing that stated willingness-to-pay from contingent valuation surveys are not measures of nonuse preferences over environmental amenities. We then considered some of the welfare implications of treating the responses as if they were a measure of nonuse preferences when they were generated by different considerations. We concluded that such welfare analysis would not be a guide to good policy. Our conclusion is often challenged by the common Washington fallacy that even if stated willingness-to-pay is inaccurate, it should be used because no alternative estimate exists for public policy purposes. Put more crudely, one hears the argument that "some number is better than no number."[18] This argument leads to the claim that it is better to do benefit-cost studies with stated willingness-to-pay numbers, despite inaccuracy and bias, rather than use zero in the benefit-cost analysis and adjust for this omission somewhere else in the decision-making process.

To evaluate this argument, one needs a model of the determination of government policy.[19] Ideally, one would like to carry out a number of government decisions twice: once using zero in the benefit-cost study, and a second time using stated willingness-to-pay, with associated adjustments of the decision process in recognition of the inclusion or omission of a contingent valuation number. Such a comparison would rec-

---

[18]The history of economic policy awaits an investigation, similar to the famous study of the sociologist R. K. Merton on the history of Newton's "on the shoulders of giants" remark, to trace the lineage of the "some number is better than no number" fallacy.

[19]One can also consider how a social welfare maximizing planner might use the information in contingent valuation surveys. There is useful information if people are expressing preferences that are not otherwise accessible to the planner. However, if the other hypotheses are the correct description of the bases of willingness-to-pay responses, then the planner would not be receiving useful information. Treating the responses as measures of what they do not measure would mislead such a planner.

ognize that much more input goes into government decisions than just the benefit-cost study. That is, the comparison is not between relying on contingent valuation and relying on Congress, but between relying on Congress after doing a contingent valuation study and relying on Congress without doing a contingent valuation study.[20] Thus one is asking whether inclusion of such survey results tends to improve the allocation process, even if the numbers are not reliable estimates of the preferences called for by the theory. Similarly, one can ask whether the combination of fines and damage payments will result in more efficient decisions to avoid accidents with or without a contingent valuation estimate of nonuse value.

Judge Stephen Breyer (1993) has recently reviewed government responses to public perceptions of risk. Since he feels that public perceptions of risk are inaccurate and that Congress is responsive to these public perceptions, Breyer wants to increase the role of administrative expertise in designing public policy to deal with risks. A similar situation seems to exist with respect to contingent valuations of nonuse value. If we conclude that contingent valuation is really an opinion poll on concern about the environment in general, rather than a measure of preferences about specific projects, public policy is likely to do better if the concern is noted but expert opinion is used to evaluate specific projects and to set financial incentives to avoid accidents. One could hope for a more consistent relative treatment of alternative natural resources in this way.

In both economic logic and politics, we expect that using contingent valuation in decision making about the environment would soon be extended to other policy arenas where existence values are equally plausible. We do not expect that policy would be improved by using contingent valuation to affect the levels and patterns of spending for elementary school education, foreign aid, Medicaid, Medicare, AFDC, construction of safer highways, medical research, airline safety, or police and fire services. Yet people have concerns for others in all of these areas that parallel their concern for the environment.

Concern for other people naturally includes concern about their jobs. Thus, in considering rules that limit economic activity to protect the environment, it is as appropriate to include a contingent valuation of existence value for destroyed jobs as the one for protection of the environment. The fact that jobs may be created elsewhere in the economy does not rule out concern about job destruction per se. These possible extensions of the use of contingent valuation increase the importance of considering the "some number is better than no number" fallacy.

---

[20]The results of a contingent valuation survey are not binding. Thus a respondent who was behaving strategically would select a response that reflected his or her belief in how the results of the survey would affect actual outcomes. Thus we do not understand how the NOAA Panel could conclude that with a dichotomous choice question there is no strategic reason for the respondent to do otherwise than answer truthfully.

Referenda

We have heard the argument that if referenda are legitimate, so too is contingent valuation. That is, one can consider a contingent valuation survey to be a forecast of how voters would respond to a binding referendum. This perspective raises the same issues considered above. How should we decide how to interpret the bases of how people vote in referenda? Since different bases imply different appropriate uses of the responses, how should voting responses be used for economic analysis? Moreover, the necessity of calibration remains, since no obvious reason exists for people necessarily to vote the same in binding and nonbinding referenda. And, as in the previous section, we can ask whether we think we get better policies with or without such surveys.

It is interesting to consider issues raised by polls about actual referenda, as well as by the referenda themselves. Sometimes polls are accurate predictors of voting outcomes; sometimes, they are not, even when they are taken close to election day. Sometimes, repeated polls about the same referendum find very large changes in expressed intentions as a referendum campaign proceeds.

Magleby (1984) has analyzed statewide polls in California and Massachusetts for which at least three separate surveys were done. In some cases, the polls show roughly the same margin over time. Magleby calls these "standing opinions" and believes that this stability comes from the deep attachment to their opinions that voters hold on some controversial issues such as the death penalty and the equal rights amendment. In some cases, the polls show significant changes in the margin of preferences, but no change in the side that is ahead. Magleby calls these "uncertain opinions." Examples of such votes involve handgun registration and homosexual teachers. In some cases, significant changes in voting intentions occur as the campaign proceeds, with victory in the actual election going to the side that had at one time been far behind. Magleby calls these outcomes "opinion reversals." For example, in a referendum for flat rate electricity, a February poll showed 71 percent in favor, 17 percent opposed, and 12 percent undecided. The actual vote was 23 percent in favor, 69 percent opposed and 7 percent skipping this question. Other examples of such votes are a state lottery and a tax reduction measure. In his analysis of 36 propositions in California, Magleby found that on 28 percent of the issues, voters held standing opinions, on 19 percent voters had uncertain opinions, and on 53 percent he found opinion reversals. That is, in a majority of cases, early opinion polls were not good predictors of election outcomes. Moreover, they were not even good predictors of later opinion polls, after the campaign had run for some time.

It seems to us that responses to contingent valuation questionnaires for a single environmental issue are likely to be based on little information, since there is limited time for presentation and digestion of information during a contingent valuation survey. This conclusion suggests that the results of such surveys are unlikely to be accurate predictors of informed opinions on the same issues if respondents had more information and further time for reflection, including learning of the opinions of others. Such surveys are therefore unlikely to be a good basis for either informed policy-making or accurate damage assessment.

Even if a contingent valuation survey were a good predictor of an actual referendum, one can also question the use of actual referenda to obtain economic values. Considerable skepticism exists about the extent to which voting on a referendum represents informed decision making (see, for example, Magleby, 1984). In the functioning of a democracy, it may be more important to place some powers directly with the voters, rather than with their elected representatives, than to worry about the quality of decision making by voters.[21] However, incorporating contingent valuation survey responses in benefit-cost analyses or judicial proceedings does not seem to have a special role in enhancing democracy. In the looser context of legislative debate, such opinion polls may have a role to play, although the net value of that role is unclear.

NOAA Panel Evaluation of Contingent Valuation

In light of the controversy and the stakes involved, the National Oceanic and Atmospheric Administration recently appointed a prestigious panel to consider the reliability of contingent valuation studies of nonuse values in damage suits.[22] The panel's Report (NOAA, 1993) begins with criticisms of contingent valuation. In discussing the alleged inconsistency of some results with rational choice, the Report states (p. 4604) that: "some form of internal consistency is the least we would need to feel some confidence that the verbal answers correspond to some reality." The Report also addresses the need for rationality (p. 4604).

> It could be asked whether rationality is indeed needed. Why not take the values found as given? There are two answers. One is that we do not know yet how to reason about values without some assumption of rationality, if indeed it is possible at all. Rationality requirements impose a constraint on the possible values, without which damage judgments would be arbitrary. A second answer is that, as discussed above, it is difficult to find objective counterparts to verify the values obtained in the response to questionnaires.

In discussing "warm glow" effects, the Report recognizes the claim that contingent valuation responses include a warm glow. They write (p. 4605):

---

[21]The allocation of a decision directly to the voters, rather than indirectly through the choice of elected representatives, and the form in which referenda are put to voters are both methods of agenda control. In many settings, design of the agenda has large effects on voting outcomes.

[22]Kenneth Arrow (co-chair), Robert Solow (co-chair), Edward Leamer, Paul Portney, Roy Radner, and Howard Schuman.

"If this is so, CV [contingent valuation] responses should not be taken as reliable estimates of true willingness to pay."

The Report states that the burden of proof of reliability must rest on the survey designers. It states (p. 4609) that a survey would be unreliable if there were "[i]nadequate responsiveness to the scope of the environmental insult," as occurred in the embedding examples we have discussed. Unfortunately, the Panel did not elaborate on how to test for reliability.[23] We interpret the view they express to call for testing of the internal consistency of responses to the same survey instrument with different levels of environmental problem and policy successes. The Report cites no existing study that has passed such internal consistency tests.

The Report presents a set of guidelines which would define an "ideal" contingent valuation survey (and are summarized in Portney's paper in this issue). The Report asserts (p. 4610) that studies meeting such guidelines can produce estimates "reliable enough to be the starting point" of a judicial process of damage assessment. The Report offers no reason for reaching this conclusion, although the finding that surveys that do not meet their guidelines may be biased is not a basis for concluding that surveys that do meet their guidelines are not biased. In particular, they state no reason for reaching the conclusion that following their guidelines implies that responses are not dominated by a "warm glow." The Panel does not explicitly call for testing whether a survey done according to their guidelines is reliable. In particular, they do not mention a need to check the internal consistency of responses. Nor do they explain their conclusion that the inconsistencies between stated willingness-to-pay and economic theory come from survey design issues and would go away if the survey had followed their guidelines.

Conclusion

We believe that contingent valuation is a deeply flawed methodology for measuring nonuse values, one that does not estimate what its proponents claim to be estimating. The absence of direct market parallels affects both the ability to judge the quality of contingent valuation responses and the ability to calibrate responses to have usable numbers. It is precisely the lack of experience both in markets for environmental commodities and in the consequences of such decision that makes contingent valuation questions so hard to answer and the responses so suspect.

We have argued that internal consistency tests (particularly adding-up tests) are required to assess the reliability and validity of such surveys. When these tests have been done, contingent valuation has come up short. Contingent valuation proponents typically claim that the surveys used for these tests were not done well enough. Yet they have not subjected their

---

[23]Nor, we add, do Portney or Hanemann in this symposium.

own surveys to such tests. (We note that Hanemann does not address the question of which split-sample internal consistency tests, if any, he thinks a contingent valuation survey needs to pass.) There is a history of anomalous results in contingent valuation surveys that seems closely tied to the embedding problem. Although this problem has been recognized in the literature for over a decade, it has not been solved. Thus, we conclude that current contingent valuation methods should not be used for damage assessment or for benefit-cost analysis.

It is impossible to conclude definitely that surveys with new methods (or the latest survey that has been done) will not pass internal consistency tests. Yet, we do not see much hope for such success. This skepticism comes from the belief that the internal consistency problems come from an absence of preferences, not a flaw in survey methodology. That is, we do not think that people generally hold views about individual environmental sites (many of which they have never heard of); or that, within the confines of the time available for survey instruments, people will focus successfully on the identification of preferences, to the exclusion of other bases for answering survey questions. This absence of preferences shows up as inconsistency in responses across surveys and implies that the survey responses are not satisfactory bases for policy.

References

Andreoni, James, "Giving with Impure Altruism: Applications to Charity and Ricardian Equivalence," *Journal of Political Economy*, December 1989, *97*, 1447–58.

Bishop, R. C., and T. A. Heberlein, "Measuring Values of Extramarket Goods: Are Indirect Measures Biased?," *American Journal of Agricultural Economics*, December 1979, *61*, 926–30.

Breyer, Stephen, *Breaking the Vicious Circle: Toward Effective Risk Regulation.* Cambridge: Harvard University Press, 1993.

Carson, Richard T., et al., "A Contingent Valuation Study of Lost Passive Use Values Resulting from the Exxon Valdez Oil Spill," A Report to the Attorney General of the State of Alaska, 1992.

Desvousges, W. H., et al., "Measuring Natural Resource Damages with Contingent Valuation: Test of Validity and Reliability. In Hausman, J., ed., *Contingent Valuation: A Critical Assessment.* Amsterdam: North-Holland Press, 1993, 91–164.

Diamond, P. A., "Testing the Internal Consistency of Contingent Valuation Surveys," working paper, MIT, 1993.

Diamond, P. A., and J. A. Hausman, "On Contingent Valuation Measurement of Nonuse Values" In Hausman, J., Ed., *Contingent Valuation: A Critical Assessment.* Amsterdam: North-Holland Press, 1993, 3–38.

Diamond, P. A., J. A. Hausman, G. K. Leonard, and M. A. Denning, "Does Contingent Valuation Measure Preferences? Experimental Evidence." In Hausman, J., ed., *Contingent Valuation: A Critical Assessment.* Amsterdam: North-Holland Press, 1993.

Dickie, Mark, Ann Fisher, and Shelby Gerking, "Market Transactions and Hypothetical Demand Data: A Comparative Study," *Journal of the American Statistical Association*, March 1987, *82*, 69–75.

Duffield, John W., and David A. Patterson, "Field Testing Existence Values: An Instream Flow Trust Fund for Mountain Rivers," mimeo, University of Montana, 1992.

Hausman, J. A., *Contingent Valuation: A Critical Assessment.* Amsterdam: North-Holland Press, 1993.

Hausman, J. A., and G. Leonard, *Contingent Valuation and the Value of Marketed Commodities.* Cambridge: Cambridge Economics, 1982.

Hoehn, John, and Alan Randall, "Too Many Proposals Pass the Benefit Cost Test," *American Economic Review*, June 1989, *79*, 544–51.

Kahneman, Daniel, "Comments on the Contingent Valuation Method." In Cummings, Ronald G., David S. Brookshire, and William D. Schulze, eds., *Valuing Environmental Goods: A State of the Arts Assessment of the Contingent Valuation Method.* Totowa: Rowman and Allanheld, 1986, 185–94.

Kahneman, Daniel, and Jack L. Knetsch, "Valuing Public Goods: The Purchase of Moral Satisfaction," *Journal of Environmental Economics and Management*, January 1992, *22*, 57–70.

Kahneman, Daniel and Ilana Ritov, "Determinants of Stated Willingness to Pay for Public Goods: A Study in the Headline Method," mimeo, Department of Psychology, University of California, Berkeley, 1993.

Kemp, M. A. and Maxwell, "Exploring a Budget Context for Contingent Valuation Estimates," In Hausman, J., ed., *Contingent Valuation: A Critical Assessment*, Amsterdam: North-Holland Press, 1993, 217–70.

Loomis, John, John Hoehn, and Michael Hanemann, "Testing the Fallacy of Independent Valuation and Summation in Multi-part Policies: An Empirical Test of Whether 'Too Many Proposals Pass the Benefit Cost Test,' " mimeo, University of California, Davis, 1990.

Magleby, David B., *Direct Legislation, Voting on Ballot Propositions in the United States.* Baltimore and London: The Johns Hopkins University Press, 1984.

McFadden, Daniel, and Gregory K. Leonard, "Issues in the Contingent Valuation of Environmental Goods: Methodologies for Data Collection and Analysis." In Hausman, J., ed., *Contingent Valuation: A Critical Assessment*, Amsterdam: North-Holland Press, 1993.

Milgrom, P., "Is Sympathy an Economic Value?," In Hausman, J., ed., *Contingent Valuation: A Critical Assessment.* Amsterdam: North-Holland Press, 1993, 417–42.

Mitchell, Robert Cameron and Richard T. Carson, *Using Surveys to Value Public Goods.* Washington, D.C.: Resources for the Future, 1989.

National Oceanic and Atmospheric Administration, 1993, "Report of the NOAA Panel on Contingent Valuation," *Federal Register*, 1993, *58*, 10, 4602–14.

National Oceanic and Atmospheric Administration, "National Resource Damage Assessments; Proposed Rules," *Federal Register*, 1994, *59*, 5, 1062–191.

Neill, Helen, R., et al., "Hypothetical Surveys and Real Economic Commitments," Economics Working Paper B-93-01, Department of Economics, College of Business Administration, University of South Carolina, 1993.

Samples, Karl C., and James R. Hollyer, "Contingent Valuation and Wildlife Resources in the Presence of Substitutes and Complements," In Johnson, Rebecca L., and Gary V. Johnson, eds., *Economic Valuation of Natural Resources: Issues, Theory and Applications.* Boulder: Westview Press, 1990, 177–92.

Schkade, D. A., and J. W. Payne, "Where Do the Numbers Come From? How People Respond to Contingent Valuation Questions." In Hausman, J., ed., *Contingent Valuation: A Critical Assessment.* Amsterdam: North-Holland Press, 1993, 271–304.

Schulze, William, D., et al., "Contingent Valuation of Natural Resource Damages Due to Injuries to the Upper Clark Fork River Basin," State of Montana, Natural Resource Damage Program, 1993.

Seip, Kalle, and Jon Strand, "Willingness to Pay For Environmental Goods in Norway: A Contingent Valuation Study With Real Payment," *Environmental and Resource Economics*, 1992, *2*, 91–106.

Tolley, George S., et al., "Establishing and Valuing the Effects of Improved Visibility in the Eastern United States," Report to the U.S. Environmental Protection Agency, Washington, D.C., 1983.

Urban, Glen L., Gerald M. Katz, Thomas E. Hatch, and Alvin J. Silk, "The ASSESSOR Pre-Test Market Evaluation System," *Interfaces*, 1983 *13*, 38–59.

10 Contingent Valuation and Lost Passive Use: Damages from the Exxon Valdez Oil Spill*

Richard T. Carson

Robert C. Mitchell

Michael Hanemann

Raymond J. Kopp

Stanley Presser

Paul A. Ruud

Richard T. Carson is at the University of California, San Diego; Robert C. Mitchell is at Clark University; Michael Hanemann is at the University of California, Berkeley; Raymond J. Kopp is at Resources for the Future; Stanley Presser is at the University of Maryland; and Paul A. Ruud is at the University of California, Berkeley.

1. Introduction

On the night of 24 March 1989, the Exxon Valdez left the port of Valdez, Alaska and was steaming through the Valdez Narrows on its way to the open waters of Prince William Sound. The tanker left the normal shipping lanes to avoid icebergs from the nearby Columbia Glacier and ran into the submerged rocks of Bligh Reef; its crew failed to realize how far off the shipping lanes the tanker had strayed.[1] Oil compartments ruptured, releasing 11 million gallons of Prudhoe Bay crude oil into the Prince William Sound. It was the largest tanker spill in U.S. waters and to the public it was one of the major environmental disasters in U.S. history.

"Contingent Valuation and Lost Passive Use: Damages from the Exxon Valdez Oil Spill" by Richard T. Carson, Robert C. Mitchell, Michael Hanemann, Raymond J. Kopp, Stanley Presser, and Paul A. Rudd, from *Environmental and Resource Economics*, 25: 257–286 (2003).

[1]Descriptions of the grounding of the Exxon Valdez may be found in National Safety Transportation Board (1990) and Moore (1994). A number of spill prevention and containment measures were put into place when oil first began to be shipped from Valdez. These measures were intended to reduce various types of risks that had been identified in an initial comprehensive risk assessment. That assessment had identified one of its most likely bad accidents as a tank hitting the reef next to Bligh Reef under somewhat similar conditions as the Exxon Valdez. These measures had been progressively "relaxed" over time, in part due to their expense and in part because there had not previously been any really serious accident. These measures might have prevented or largely contained the Exxon Valdez spill had they been in place at the time of the spill.

Prior to the Exxon Valdez oil spill, the estimation of passive use value (Carson, Flores and Mitchell 1999) or as it has often been previously termed, nonuse or existence value, was an area of economic research not well known to many economists working outside the area of benefit cost analysis of projects involving environmental amenities and health risks. However, based on a belief that the State of Alaska and the Federal Government intended to litigate a natural resource damage claim for lost passive use value, the attention paid to the conceptual underpinnings and estimation techniques for passive use value changed rather abruptly.

Further sparking the rapidly growing interest in passive use values was an important 1989 court opinion, *Ohio v. U.S. Department of the Interior*,[2] which remanded back to the Department of the Interior (DOI) various components of its regulations for conducting natural resource damage assessments under the Clean Water Act and the Comprehensive, Environmental Response, Compensation and Liability Act (CERCLA), commonly known as Superfund.[3] Two particularly important aspects of the court's ruling for passive use value were its findings that: (1) passive use losses were compensable under those Acts and (2) the DOI hierarchy of damage assessment techniques, which placed contingent valuation at the bottom, was unjustified.[4] Interest in passive use values was also heightening at the time of the study by the passage of the Oil Pollution Act of 1990 (OPA) and the regulations that National Oceanic and Atmospheric Administration (NOAA) enacted under it for natural resource damage assessments. The regulations stated: "NOAA believes that the trustee(s) should have the discretion to include passive use values as a component within the natural resource damage assessment determination of compensable values.[5]

This brings us to the current debate over contingent valuation. It is generally recognized that only stated preference methods (Mitchell and Carson 1989; Louviere, Hensher and Swait 2000; Carson, Flores and Meade 2001) are applicable to the estimation of passive use value. Unlike direct use of resources, where for example, one can potentially observe individuals boating and fishing and use these observations to build economic models permitting inference about the value individuals place on such activities,[6] passive

---

[2]*Ohio v. Department of Interior*, 880 F.2d 432 (D.C. Cir. 1989).

[3]See *Ohio v. Department of Interior*, 1989. The original Department of the Interior rules challenged in the *Ohio v. DOI* case were published in the *Federal Register*, vol. 51, August 1, 1986. See Kopp, Portney and Smith (1990) for a comprehensive discussion of the *Ohio* decision.

[4]Following the *Ohio* decision, the U.S. District Court of Utah in a 1992 CERCLA case rejected a proposed consent decree, in part, for failing to include lost passive use values in the determination of damage associated with groundwater contamination. See *State of Utah v. Kennecott Corporation*, No. CIV 86-0902G, United States District Court, D. Utah, September 3, 1992, Memorandum Decision and Order.

[5]This position is consistent with OPA legislative history that specifically refers to diminution in value as a part of damages and cites the *Ohio* decision definition of value, which includes both direct use and passive use.

[6]These models and methods are termed indirect approaches and include the travel cost model and the hedonic property value model. An introduction to the use of these models for the assessment of damages due to natural resource injuries can be found in McConnell (1993).

use entails no direct involvement with natural resources. As a result, economists are fond of saying passive use leaves no behavioral trace.

Contingent valuation is a survey approach designed to create the missing market for public goods by determining what people would be willing to pay (WTP) for specified changes in the quantity or quality of such goods or, more rarely, what they would be willing to accept (WTA) in compensation for well-specified degradations in the provision of these goods (Hanemann 1999; Bateman et al. 2002).[7] Contingent valuation (CV) circumvents the absence of markets for natural resource services by presenting consumers with a choice situation in which they have the opportunity to buy or sell the services in question. A CV scenario may be modeled after either a private market or a political referendum. The popular name for this form of non-market valuation arose because the elicited values are contingent upon the particular scenario described to survey respondents.

It is fair to say that the debate within the economics community, instigated by the Exxon Valdez spill and the natural resource damage provisions of various laws, includes discussions of both the conceptual underpinnings of passive use and the technique for its measurement. However, it is the measurement technique itself which has been the target of the sharpest criticism. Much of the recent criticism of CV is contained in the Exxon-sponsored conference volume, Hausman (1993), and written submissions directed to writers of natural resource damage assessment regulations in DOI and NOAA.[8] To help assess these comments, the NOAA General Counsel, Thomas Campbell, formed a panel of social scientists to explicitly consider the criticisms of contingent valuation and make recommendations to NOAA. The panel was co-chaired by Kenneth Arrow and Robert Solow and was comprised of three additional economists: Edward Leamer of the University of California, Los Angeles, Paul Portney of Resources for the Future and Roy Radner of Bell Laboratories, as well as Howard Schuman, former Director of the Survey Research Center at the University of Michigan. The panel concluded that CV studies convey "useful information" for damage assessment including lost passive use values, provided they follow a number of "stringent guidelines" (Arrow et al. 1993). The recommendations of this panel have influenced the form of both the NOAA and DOI regulations and the wider academic debate.

The results of the CV study conducted for the State of Alaska in preparation for the Exxon Valdez litigation presented here represented the contemporary state-of-the-art, and therefore, stand as a reference point that may be used to assess the criticisms of CV and perhaps the more general debate surrounding passive use. Most of the recommendations made by the NOAA panel to help insure the reliability of CV estimates of lost passive use

---

[7]A comprehensive discussion of contingent valuation is contained in Mitchell and Carson (1989).

[8]For a sense of the debate immediately post Exxon Valdez, see the 1994 *Journal of Economic Perspective* Symposium papers by Diamond and Hausman, Hanemann, and Portney. For a more recent review see Carson, Flores and Meade (2001).

had already been implemented in the Alaska study including: (1) the use of rigorous probability sampling with a high response rate, (2) in-person interviews, (3) a discrete choice referendum elicitation format, (4) accurate description of the program, (5) conservative design features, (6) checks on understanding and acceptance, (7) debriefing questions following the referendum questions, and (8) careful pretesting. As much of the debate focuses on old CV studies, or small experiments, a reference point portraying CV practice when substantial resources were available to undertake the study should enhance the quality of the debate.[9]

The plan of the paper is as follows. Section 2 discusses the design and development of the survey questionnaire used in the study. Section 3 reviews for the reader the crucial elements of the survey. In section 4 we discuss the execution of the survey including survey sampling, interviewer training, and survey administration. Section 5 presents statistical results, and section 6 contains a postscript on the Exxon Valdez settlement.

2. Survey Design and Development

The Exxon Valdez CV survey instrument was developed over an 18-month period from July 1989 to January 1991. It was designed to be administered, face-to-face, to a national sample. The central part of the survey instrument was the valuation scenario that described the damages caused by the Exxon Valdez oil spill and established a referendum market for eliciting the value respondents place on preventing a future accident that would cause an equivalent amount of damage in the Prince William Sound area. Other questions preceding and following the scenario asked about the respondent's attitudes, previous awareness of the spill, understanding of the scenario, and personal characteristics. At appropriate places during the in-person interview, display cards, photographs, and maps were shown to the respondent to supplement the information conveyed verbally by the interviewer.

2.1 Initial Development

An extensive program of instrument development research was conducted. The first stage of instrument development involved exploratory research primarily through focus groups. In the second stage, an initial draft questionnaire was produced and revised during a series of one-on-one inter-

---

[9]Due to space limitations, many details of the study and the complete survey instrument could not be incorporated into this paper. The complete text of the report can be found online at Exxon Valdez Oil Spill Trustee website: http://www.oilspill.state.ak.us/gem/facts/economic.html. The complete survey instrument including color copies of visual material used can be found at: http://www.econ.ucsd.edu/~rcarson as can the complete dataset from the study. Mitchell and Carson (1985) and Mitchell (2002) provide additional discussion of various issues involved in the design of contingent valuation surveys.

views followed by informal field testing. The third and final stage involved formal field testing and further development work, including a series of four pilot surveys.

The research goal was to develop a valid survey instrument to measure lost passive use values due to the natural resource injuries caused by the Exxon Valdez oil spill. This is a demanding task for the survey designer because the instrument had to meet multiple goals. The first was to measure only a defined set of injuries. This required carefully describing the specific injuries to be valued, the various recovery times for the injured resources, and the available substitutes, to ensure as much as possible that respondents did not value more extensive or less extensive injuries than intended.[10] Open-ended questions at various points in the valuation scenario and diagnostic questions that followed the valuation scenario were used to gauge success in meeting this goal.

The second objective was to ensure consistency with economic theory by eliciting an approximation to the monetized loss in utility suffered by the respondents as a result of the injuries caused by the spill.

The third objective was a basic survey research goal: respondents from all educational levels and varied life experiences should be able to comprehend the language, concepts, and questions used in the survey so that they could make an informed decision. The particular challenge in CV surveys is to convey to respondents what they would get, how it would be provided, and that they would have to pay for it. Given the amount of information it was necessary to convey in the survey, this required an extended period of instrument development research, which is described below. Various diagnostic checks were used in the survey to determine acceptance of scenario features.

Plausibility, the fourth objective, requires that a respondent find the scenario and the payment vehicle believable. Lack of plausibility is a major source of error in CV surveys because it keeps respondents from taking the choice situation seriously. We took various steps to enhance plausibility, including the use of WTP rather than WTA elicitation questions.[11] A referendum format asked respondents to make a judgment as to whether they would vote for or against a program that, if adopted, would cost their household a specified amount.

---

[10]The description of the injuries was based on scientific information provided to the study team by the State of Alaska. There was substantial uncertainty regarding the precise extent of some of the injuries at the time the final survey was conducted. In order to minimize the litigation risk associated with that uncertainty, the study team valued a conservative representation of the injuries. Therefore, only injury facts of which scientists were reasonably certain as of the fall of 1990 were used. When the best estimate of the actual state of affairs required a range, the conservative end of that range was used.

[11]Willingness to accept is the appropriate property right for natural resource damages. Respondents in CV surveys tend to find questions that ask them how much they would accept in compensation to voluntarily accept a loss to a public environmental good implausible for a variety or reasons (Mitchell and Carson 1989), since they do not believe they possess a personal property right to sell the good.

The fifth objective was neutrality; the wording and information in the survey instrument should not be perceived by respondents as promoting the interests of any particular party such as the oil companies, government or environmentalists.[12] The instrument's wording was critically peer reviewed at various stages in its development to help assess our success in meeting this objective. A diagnostic question about who the respondents believed was sponsoring the study was also included to see if one party was identified more than another.

The final objective was to be conservative in estimating WTP. When faced with a decision between two wording, design, or analysis options, neither of which was clearly preferred on the basis of theory or solid methodological grounds, we chose the one that would, if it had any effect, lower the aggregate WTP amount. On this basis, for example, pictures of oiled birds were not shown to respondents, a one-time payment was used rather than installment payments, and "don't know" responses were treated as "no" votes instead of dropping them from the sample.

2.2 Design Research

During the first stage of the instrument development, we conducted six focus groups (Krueger 1988)[13] in different locations around the United States. In the first groups, discussions explored participant knowledge of the Exxon Valdez spill, beliefs about the cause and nature of the harm, and perceptions of the plausibility of possible ways of preventing a future spill. Once particular patterns of understanding and knowledge were established and confirmed, new topics were introduced in subsequent groups.[14]

In the next stage, which took place in the fall of 1989, we developed a draft of the questionnaire and used it to conduct trial interviews. During these in-depth one-on-one interviews, the instrument was repeatedly revised to refine the information it presented and to improve its clarity and flow before experienced interviewers tested it in the field.

During the third stage of instrument development research, which took place from February to November 1990, we conducted four pilot surveys

---

[12]The identity of the survey's sponsor, the State of Alaska, was not revealed to either the interviewers or the respondents.

[13]This type of qualitative research is increasingly used by survey researchers in the early stages of designing contingent valuation questionnaires because they are an efficient way to explore people's beliefs, attitudes, and knowledge about the good to be valued, and to obtain their reactions to possible CV scenario elements (Morgan 1993).

[14]In later groups, elements of a possible questionnaire were described in more detail to help us understand how the participants understood these elements and how they used this information. These included the payment vehicle, duration of payments, description of the injuries, description of a plan to prevent future spills, and use of particular photographs and maps to communicate factual aspects of the scenario.

Table I Pilot Studies for Exxon Valdez Study

Pilot I	San Jose, California	February, 1990	N = 105
Pilot II	Dayton & Toledo, Ohio	May, 1990	N = 195
Pilot III	Five rural counties in Georgia	September, 1990	N = 244
Pilot IV	Dayton & Toledo, Ohio	November, 1990	N = 176

in various parts of the country.[15] The pilots allowed us to text the instrument in a setting close to that of the final survey, obtain quantitative data to assess how the survey instrument was working, and conduct split-sample experiments to investigate key design issues. The location, date, and sample size of the pilot surveys are shown in Table I.[16]

After each pilot, we analyzed the data and revised the questionnaire on the basis of the analysis and extensive interviewer debriefings. The instrument was iteratively revised and improved in this manner until we were confident it met our research objectives.

2.3 Key Design Issues

Key design issues for this study included the choice of the elicitation method, the nature of the payment vehicle, the years over which payments are collected, and whether the good is valued in a sequence which includes other goods.

With respect to the elicitation method, we determined early in the process that respondents should be asked a binary discrete choice question (Bishop and Heberlein 1979). This type of question, often called a take-it-or-leave-it question, requests the respondent give a yes-or-no response to a specific cost. A single take-it-or-leave-it referendum-like question for a public good is incentive-compatible under fairly general conditions when the government has the ability to compel payment if the policy is implemented; that is, a respondent can do no better than saying "yes" if the policy is actually preferred at the specified cost or by saying "no" if otherwise. The simple binary discrete choice elicitation has been extended to the double-bounded dichotomous choice question (Hanemann, Loomis and Kanninen

---

[15]Westat, one of the country's premier survey research organizations conducted the interviews for this study, recruited the professional interviewers (who gave face-to-face interviews at the respondent's home), prepared the interview materials based on the instrument we delivered to them, conducted the interviewer training, supervised the production of interviews in the field, and edited and validated the completed questionnaires.

[16]Pilot I reflects the first formal field test. Pilot II, a split-sample test, compared the effect of two possible payment vehicles, income taxes and oil prices. Pilot III encompassed two split-sample tests comparing: a) revised versions of the income tax and oil price payment vehicles and, b) effect of excluding an environmental item in each of questions A-1 and A-3 on the WTP estimate. Pilot IV was the last formal field test and closely resembled the final survey.

1991). Here the respondent is asked to give a yes-or-no response to a second pre-specified higher amount if the response to the initial take-it-or-leave-it question is "yes" and to a pre-specified lower amount if the initial response is "no." Using both responses substantially increases the statistical power of the WTP estimate, i.e., it tends to produce a much tighter confidence interval for the WTP estimate for any fixed sample size; however, it does so at the expense of a downward bias in the estimate because the second response is not, in general, incentive-compatible.[17]

Of the three natural choices for the payment vehicle—higher taxes, higher oil prices, and higher prices over a wider range of goods—only the first two were found to be plausible in our preliminary research. After conducting split-sample comparisons of a tax and an oil price vehicle in Pilots II and III, we decided to use the tax vehicle in the final survey for two reasons. First, the price of gasoline, the major type of oil product through which consumers would pay for the plan if we used the oil prices vehicle, had become quite unstable due to Iraq's invasion of Kuwait. It appeared likely that gasoline prices would increase rapidly in the near future when the final survey would be in the field or, perhaps, decrease if the crisis was resolved peacefully. This instability raised the prospect that if we used the oil prices vehicle, the respondents' WTP amounts might be distorted because of factors unrelated to any economic value they held for preventing future damage to Prince William Sound. Second, the two split-sample experiments showed that, if anything, the tax vehicle tended to elicit the same (Pilot III) or lower (Pilot II) amounts than those elicited by the oil prices vehicle.

With respect to the number of years over which payments are collected, three major issues were considered. First, longer payment periods mean that budget constraints, particularly for lower income households, are less binding. Second, periodic payments tend to assure respondents that the good will be provided in future years. Third, with multiple year payments some respondents may believe that it is possible for the government to recontract if better opportunities come along. There was no obvious *a priori* basis on which to choose between the lump sum and the annual payment schemes. On the basis of additional focus group work and a telephone

---

[17]This downward bias is suggested by empirical evidence and probably results from expectations formed by the initial cost estimate given to the respondent. Some respondents who vote to pay the first amount might be willing to pay the second (higher) amount but vote against the higher amount when asked because they feel that the government would waste the extra money requested. In addition, some respondents who are not willing to pay the first amount would be willing to pay the second (lower) amount but may vote against the second amount because they believe that either the government will deliver a lower quality good than that first promised or that the probability of the government delivering the good is lower at the lower price. Both of these voting patterns result in a downward bias. The extent of the bias depends on the degree to which the second amount is perceived by the respondent as being an independent cost estimate. Carson, Groves and Machina (1999) provide a formal conceptual framework for considering this issue.

survey, we chose the lump-sum payment.[18] Focus group participants were committed to making at least the initial payment and generally to paying for two or three additional years, but any payment schedule longer than that appeared to suffer from the recontracting problem. The lump-sum payment avoids this problem and has the advantage of eliminating the need to determine what rate ought to be applied to discount future payments. It also has the disadvantage of forcing a much tighter budget constraint on respondents, a conservative feature.

Finally, there were two choices related to "embedding."[19] The first was whether to value the good of primary interest by itself or in a sequence of other substitute public goods. Here economic theory provides some important guidance for the valuation of natural resource damages.[20] Due to substitution and income effects, the later in a WTP sequence a normal good is valued, the lower its value. The opposite, however, is true of a WTA sequence; the later in such a sequence a good is valued, the greater its value. These two propositions can be combined with the fact that WTA compensation for a good is greater than or equal to willingness to pay for the same good (Hanemann 1991) to show that valuing a good first (i.e., by itself) in a WTP sequence is the closest approximation to whatever sequence-specific WTA compensation measure is desired (short of being able to measure willingness to accept directly, which is generally difficult to do).

The second "embedding" choice was methodological: the design should ensure that respondents do not answer a different question than the one they are asked, whether by forgetting about their budget constraints or by letting Prince William Sound stand for all oil spills or even all environmental damage. To meet this requirement, the scenario *must* present a plausible choice situation describing the good and its method of provision in adequate detail so that the respondents know what they will and what they will not get. The design choice is whether to value multiple goods in a single survey or to value a single good and carefully differentiate it in the instrument from those other goods with which it might be confused. A survey valuing a single good was used for two reasons. First, it avoids difficulties that are introduced by valuing multiple goods. Second, well-designed single-good CV surveys have been shown to be capable of eliciting values that are sensitive to the characteristics of the good being valued (Carson and Mitchell 1995; Carson 1997; Carson, Flores and Meade 2001).

---

[18]The telephone survey valued the installation of a scrubber on a power plant in Columbus, Ohio using 500 observations in a split-sample design with a lump sum and annual payment schemes. While the results from this survey clearly rejected ($p < 0.01$) Kahneman and Knetsch's (1992, p. 63) contention that respondents do not focus on the temporal nature of the payment obligation, they were consistent with the presence of high discount rates and/or borrowing constraints observed with many consumer durables.

[19]Embedding is a term introduced into the contingent valuation literature by Kahneman to refer to various issues related to the sequencing and nesting of goods as well as a survey design problem known as part-whole bias. See Carson and Mitchell (1995) for a discussion.

[20]For discussions, see Hoehn and Randall (1989); Bishop and Welsh (1992); and Carson, Flores and Hanemann (1998).

In constructing the scenario for this study, we took several steps to minimize the possibility of respondent perceptual error in understanding the good they are being asked to value. First, we paid particular attention in the focus groups and in-depth interviews to how people think about the good we offer them. Second, we used this knowledge, in ways that will be described later, to focus the respondents' attention on what they would and would not get if the program were implemented. Third, each time we used the instrument, both during the development process and in the final interview itself, we asked open- and close-ended questions to assess how well respondents understood what we were attempting to convey in the survey. This enabled us in the analysis to identify the presence of any remaining perceptual problems and, to the extent that they were present, to determine if and how they affected the results.

3. Structure of the Final Questionnaire

CV instruments such as the one used in this study differ from ordinary public opinion surveys in several important respects. One difference is the amount of information that the interviewer conveys to the respondent during the presentation of the scenario. Almost half the length of the 40-minute interview was devoted to informing the respondent about the effects of the spill, a program that could prevent another spill with the same effects, and how the respondent could pay for this program if the respondent thought it was worth the specified cost. A second is the focus of the survey on a single question: whether the respondent would vote for or against the program. The scenario systematically builds up to this question and a series of follow-up questions explores the respondents' reasons for voting the way they did and what they had in mind when they voted. A third is the opportunity respondents were given to change their vote at a later point in the survey in case they wished to do so after further reflection.

To maintain the respondents' interest and enhance their ability to comprehend the information received during their interview, the material was presented in a carefully designed sequence interspersed with visual aids and questions. This section provides an overview of the interview. Boxed or quoted text is from the questionnaire unless otherwise indicated. Survey text in capital letters indicates interviewer instructions not read to the respondents.

3.1 Initial Questions

At the beginning of the interview, respondents did not know that the main subject matter of the survey was the Exxon Valdez oil spill.[21] This allowed us to measure respondents' attitudes about various types of public goods and their prior awareness of the spill before revealing the purpose of the survey.

---

[21]Potential respondents were told that the interview was for a study of people's views about current issues.

After these preliminary questions, the interviewer began to present the elements of the constructed market in which the respondent would later be asked to vote in favor of or against a plan costing the respondent a specific amount of money. This scenario conveyed information about Prince William Sound, the transport of oil by ship from Valdez, the Exxon Valdez spill and its effects, and an escort ship program to prevent damage from another spill that would have the same effect on the environment. At various places during the presentation of the scenario, interviewers showed respondents one of nineteen visual aids: maps, color photographs, and show cards. These materials were designed and pretested to help respondents visualize important aspects of the scenario and to understand the material being read to them.

3.2 Prince William Sound Description

After showing respondents a map that located Prince William Sound in the context of Alaska, and Alaska in the context of the United States, the Sound was described in detail with the help of another map. Box A provides a portion of the instrument that illustrates how text and photographs were integrated to convey a sense of the Sound and its features. Photographs A, B, and C were of various features of the Sound including the Columbia Glacier.

The description then turned to wildlife. During this part of the narrative respondents were shown photographs of living examples of some of the types of wildlife that were killed by the spill. To be conservative, we did not use photographs of actual animals harmed or killed by the spill.

The next section of the scenario described the spill and its impact on the shoreline. After a photograph of a tanker in the Sound, the narrative focused on the Exxon Valdez spill. A series of questions were asked at this point to keep the respondent actively involved in the survey. The interviewer then presented a map of the spill area and pointed out where the spill began, how far it traveled, and the time it took for oil to travel that far.

Another map identified the places where the shore was and was not affected in Prince William Sound. Attention was then called to the cleanup effort in the statement, "As you may know, Exxon made a large effort to clean up the oil on the beaches," and in the presentation of Photo J which showed workers washing the oil off a beach. Respondents were given specific information about the duration of the injuries: "Scientists believe that natural processes will remove almost all the remaining oil from the beaches within a few years after the spill."

3.3 Description of Wildlife

The scenario then described the effect of the spill on wildlife. Card 4 displayed information about the twelve bird species most affected by the spill. In addition to the number of dead birds recovered, it gave the total pre-spill population for each of the species to provide a perspective on the available substitutes. For example, with respect to murres, 16,600 were reported dead, and the total population of murres was described as 350,000. Box B presents the narrative that accompanied Card 4. This material communicated a number of important items.

For example, assurance was given that none of these species was threatened with extinction because our focus groups showed that this aspect of the spill injuries was important to respondents. In order to put the bird kill in perspective the text called attention to the fact that large bird kills can occur naturally. Respondents were also told that the numbers of dead birds shown on the cards are limited to those that were recovered and that the actual toll is estimated to be three to six times higher.

Mammal deaths were shown in a table on another card. As with birds, total pre-spill population estimates were provided in addition to kill estimates. Zero kill estimates were listed for three species for which no kills were reported because some pretest respondents had assumed that there were also injuries to these species.

3.4 Explanation of the Escort Ship Plan

The next portion of the scenario introduced the concept of a possible second spill like the Exxon Valdez spill and described how an escort ship program would prevent and/or contain such a spill. It was important that the program be perceived as feasible, effective, and requiring the amount of money later stated as the cost the household would pay if it was approved in the referendum. Respondents were told that if the program were put into effect, two large Coast Guard ships would escort each tanker throughout its journey in Prince William Sound. The escort ships would help prevent an accident and, if an accident occurred, they would keep even a very large spill from spreading beyond the tanker.[22]

To avoid overburdening the respondents, only information shown in our pretesting to be essential to communicating a plausible choice situation was included in the narrative. For example, mention of the requirement that all tankers should be double-hulled within the next ten years was included because during our pretests we learned that it added credibility. This information also helped to sharply define the ten-year period during which the escort ship program would operate. The narrative further noted that the plan would not provide spill protection outside Prince William Sound.

3.5 Valuation Questions

Respondents were informed that the program would be funded by a one-time tax on the oil companies that take oil out of Alaska and that households like theirs would also pay a special one-time federal tax that would

---

[22]A line drawing of an escort ship recovering oil at an oil spill proved to be very helpful in explaining how the escort program would work.

go into a Prince William Sound Protection Fund.[23] Immediately before asking the WTP questions, the interviewer presented the material shown in Box C, which was intended to reassure respondents who might not be willing to pay for the program that a no vote was socially acceptable. The reasons presented here for voting against the program came from those given by respondents during the design phase of the research.

The WTP question, A-15, used a discrete-choice referendum elicitation format to ask whether the respondent would vote for the program if it cost a specified amount that would be paid by a one-time federal tax payment. To obtain responses to a range of amounts, four different versions (A through D) of the instrument were administered to equivalent subsamples. Every respondent was also asked a follow-up amount appropriate to the version they received and their answer to the first WTP question. Those who voted "for" were asked the higher amount for question A-16 and those who voted "against" the lower amount shown for A-17.

The dollar amounts used in this study (see Table II) were based on information about the underlying WTP distribution obtained from the pilot studies.[24] They were chosen to provide reasonable efficiency in estimating key statistics, such as the median, while providing some robustness (Alberini and Carson 1993) with respect to observing a substantially different WTP distribution in the final survey.

The remainder of Section A was devoted to open-ended debriefing questions designed to provide some information about the reasons for respondent answers to the valuation questions. Respondents who said "yes" were asked: "What was it about the program that made you willing to pay for it?" Respondents answering "no" or "not sure" were asked similar questions.

Section B contained a number of questions designed to assess the beliefs respondents held about key elements of the scenario when they answered the WTP questions. Although this type of assessment is difficult to make, it can be very helpful in checking whether respondents understood the scenario and accepted its basic features. Other questions in this section measured attributes that might affect preferences for protecting the Prince William Sound environment from the effects of another oil spill.

---

[23]Pretests had shown that some respondents criticized the notion that citizens should share in paying the cost of the plan. Because this could lead respondents to reject the premise of the scenario, that they should make a judgment about what the plan is worth to them, the interviewers were instructed to say the following to those who expressed the view that Exxon or the oil companies should pay in an attempt to persuade them that the oil companies *would* pay a share: "If the program is approved, the oil companies that bring oil through the Alaska pipeline (including Exxon) *will* have to pay part of the cost by a special tax on their corporate profits."

[24]The first pilot study established a large fraction of the population was willing to pay small amounts for the program while zero percent was willing to pay $1000. After this effort was devoted to helping to get reasonable estimates of the fraction in favor at more central quantiles of the WTP distribution.

Table II Program Cost by Version and Question

Version	A-15	A-16	A-17
A	$10	$30	$5
B	$30	$60	$10
C	$60	$120	$30
D	$120	$250	$60

In addition to demographic questions, in Section C all respondents who had voted for one or more of the amounts asked about in the WTP questions were asked how strongly they favored the program if it cost this much money. Everyone who answered "not too strongly" or "not at all strongly" was then asked: "All things considered, would you like to change your vote on the program if it cost your household $__ from a vote for the program to a vote against?" The interview concluded with the question that asked for their best guess as to who "employed my company to do this study."[25]

4. Survey Execution

The survey was conducted using a multi-stage area probability sample of residential dwelling units drawn from the 50 United States and the District of Columbia. In the first stage selection, 61 counties or county groups known as primary sampling units (PSU's) were drawn with probabilities proportionate to their population counts.[26] Within these selected PSU's, 334 Census block groups were drawn with probabilities proportionate to their total population counts. The census block groups were stratified by two block characteristics: percent of the population that was black and a weighted average of the value of owner-occupied housing and the rent of renter-occupied housing. In the third stage, approximately 1,600 dwelling units were drawn from the selected blocks. All dwelling units chosen for

---

[25]Shortly after completing each interview, the interviewer completed a series of questions in Section D about the circumstances under which the interview was conducted and the interviewer's impressions about whether the respondent had any difficulty understanding the vote questions and the seriousness of the consideration the respondent gave to these questions.

[26]Before the selection was made, the 1,179 PSU's were stratified by the following 1980 Decennial Census characteristics: (1) region of the country; (2) SMSA versus non-SMSA; (3) rate of population change between 1970 and 1980; (4) percent living on a farm (for non-SMSA PSU's); (5) percent employed in manufacturing; (6) percent white; (7) percent urban; and (8) percent over age 65. Selection from strata typically increases the precision of the survey results compared to unstratified selection. For a discussion of the comparative advantages of stratified selection, see Sudman (1976). The 1980 census was used for the sample, as results from the 1990 census were not yet available.

the sample were then randomly assigned to one of the four different dollar versions of the survey instrument.

A respondent within each dwelling unit was randomly chosen for the interview. After dropping vacant dwelling units and non-English speaking households who were ineligible for the survey,[27] the survey had an overall response rate of 75.2%. This response rate compares favorably with the best academic surveys such as the University of Michigan's American National Election Surveys and the University of Chicago's General Social Survey.

As information about the survey topic was not provided to individuals until the interview was underway, willingness to pay for the Prince William Sound Program *per se* could not have directly affected whether a household responded. It is possible, however, that other characteristics (e.g., household size or, residence in large urban areas) were related to responding/non-responding status. Thus, the composition of the interviewed sample could differ from that of the random sample initially chosen. To help correct this potential problem, sample weights were constructed that incorporated both nonresponse adjustment and poststratification to household totals from the 1990 Decennial Census. The variables used were region, age, race, household size and type (married versus other). Respondents from a western state, the elderly, blacks, and single households tended to be assigned higher weights.

5. Results

5.1 Willingness to Pay Questions

Table III shows the frequencies of each response to question A-15. As expected, the percentage responding with a "for" vote declines as the amount the respondent is asked to pay increases, dropping from 67 percent in favor at $10 to 34 percent at $120.

The A-15 response can be analyzed with a binary discrete choice model, such as a probit, or it can be combined with the A-16 and A-17 responses. Treating the "not sure" responses as "no" responses results in four response types.[28] These are presented by questionnaire version in Table IV.

The yes-yes and no-no responses are the easiest to interpret because one would expect the yes-yes responses to fall as the dollar amount the respondent is asked to pay goes from $30 in version A (i.e., 45 percent say yes to $30) to $250 in version D (i.e., 14 percent say yes to $250). We would also ex-

---

[27]Due primarily to logistical and cost considerations, no foreign language versions of the questionnaire were developed. As a result, non-English speaking households were not eligible to be interviewed. Thus, we correspondingly reduced the 1990 Census estimate of the number of U.S. households (93,347,000) by 2.7%, our survey's estimate of the proportion of U.S. households that were non-English speaking. This yields a population of 90,838,000 English-speaking households to which our results may be extrapolated.

Table III A-15 Response by Version

Version	No	Not sure	Yes
A ($10)	29.92%	2.65%	67.42%
B ($30)	39.33%	8.99%	51.69%
C ($60)	43.53%	5.88%	50.59%
D ($120)	59.14%	6.61%	34.24%

Table IV Questionnaire Version by Type of Response

Version	Yes-Yes	Yes-No	No-Yes	No-No
A ($10, $30, $5)	45.08%	22.35%	3.03%	29.55%
B (30, 10, 60)	26.04%	26.04%	11.32%	36.60%
C (60, 120, 30)	21.26%	29.13%	9.84%	39.76%
D (120, 250, 60)	13.62%	20.62%	11.67%	54.09%

pect the no-no responses to increase as one moves from version A (i.e., 30 percent say no to $5) to version D (i.e., 54 percent to $60). The no-no responses to version A define the upper bound on the percentage of respondents who may not care about preventing an Exxon Valdez type oil spill. It should be noted, though, that this group of respondents is also likely to include those who do not think that the escort ship plan will work or who believe that the oil companies should pay the entire cost of the plan.

5.2 Statistical Model

The type of data gathered using the double-bounded dichotomous choice elicitation method is sometimes referred to as interval-censored survival data (Nelson 1982). Its use in CV work has been explicated at length by Carson and Steinberg (1990), Hanemann, Loomis and Kanninen (1991), Carson, Wilks and Imber (1994), and Haab and McConnell (1997) under the

---

[28]For most of the respondents giving "not sure" answers, this interpretation seems to be appropriate. Some respondents gave a "not sure" answer to A-15 and subsequently gave a "yes" answer to the substantially lower amount in A-17. Similarly, some respondents gave "yes" responses to A-15 and "not sure" responses to the higher amount in A-16. A likely interpretation is that these "not sure" responses represent respondents who were reasonably close to their indifference thresholds. Of the 141 respondents who gave one or more "not sure" responses, 111 followed this pattern. The other 30 respondents (less than 3% of the sample) gave "not sure" responses to both A-15 and A-17; these respondents may not have been capable of answering the WTP questions. We have also conservatively treated these as no-no responses.

assumption of truthful preference revelation to both questions.[29] Instead of "time," survival is defined with respect to the cost variable. A respondent willing to pay a specific amount "survives" that amount and a respondent who is not willing to pay a specified amount "fails" that amount. A yes-yes response indicates that the respondent's maximum willingness to pay lies between the A-16 amount and infinity. A yes-no response (i.e., yes to A-15 and no to A-16), indicates that the respondent's maximum WTP amount lies between the amount asked in A-15 and the amount asked in A-16. In survival analysis terms, the failure occurred between the A-15 and A-16 cost amounts. A no-yes response indicates that the respondent's maximum WTP response lies between the amount asked in A-15 and the amount asked in A-17. A no-no response indicates that the respondent's maximum willingness to pay lies between zero and the amount asked in A-17.[30] Thus, a respondent's WTP response can be shown to lie in one of the following intervals depending on the particular response pattern and questionnaire version: A: ($0–$5 [No-No]; $5–$10 [No-Yes]; $10–$30 [Yes-No]; $30–∞ [Yes-Yes]), B: (0–10; 10–30; 30–60; 60–∞), C: (0–30; 30–60; 60–120; 120–∞), D: (0–60; 60–120; 120–250; 250–∞).[31]

The survival analysis framework imposes the key assumption from economic theory that the fraction of the public in favor of the program is weakly monotonically decreasing in its cost. Effectively, the log likelihood function is defined by the difference in WTP density evaluated at two points defined by the two cost amounts the respondent was asked about with the upper end being infinity in the case of a yes-yes response and the lower end being zero in the case of a no-no response. One can maximize this likelihood function assuming a particular parametric distribution, such as the Weibull, or by using Turnbull's (1976) modification of the Kaplan-Meier estimator.[32]

---

[29]In the analysis that follows we have also assumed that respondents do not engage in non-truthful preference revelation with respect to the second choice question. The strong theoretical prediction (Carson, Groves and Machina 1999) is that the response to the second question should be inconsistent with the first. Under stronger but plausible conditions, the response to the second question will be consistent with lower willingness to pay than the first question. The empirical results obtained here are consistent with this prediction in that an analysis based upon only the first question results in a larger WTP estimate than using both questions. Useful information can be obtained from a second question without assuming consistency between questions, but the statistical modeling is much more complex and more dependent upon assumptions made (Alberini, Kanninen and Carson 1997).

[30]If the amenity being valued is a "bad" to the respondent, then the lower bound on the interval is potentially negative infinity rather than zero. While a possibility with some public goods, it is unlikely that anyone views an Exxon Valdez type oil spill as something desirable.

[31]The WTP intervals of the ten respondents who indicated that they wanted to change their votes were set from zero to the highest amount to which they had previously said they would vote "for." In addition, four respondents who did not answer the second WTP question (A-16 or A-17) had their WTP intervals based only on their response to A-15.

[32]The Weibull is the simplest distribution that allows an increasing, decreasing, or constant hazard function. It is also flexible enough to approximate several other commonly used survival distributions, such as the exponential, the Raleigh, the normal, and the smallest extreme value.

Table V Turnbull Estimation Results

Lower bound of interval	Upper bound of interval	Probability of being greater than upper bound	Change in density	Asymptotic t-value*
0	5	0.714	0.286	15.46
5	10	0.685	0.029	2.93
10	30	0.535	0.150	10.57
30	60	0.377	0.157	11.04
60	120	0.220	0.157	11.46
120	250	0.088	0.132	9.02
250	∞	0.000	0.088	Normalized

Log-Likelihood—1325.186	*Against null of no change in density

The Turnbull nonparametric approach makes no assumptions about the shape of the underlying WTP distribution. As a result, this technique only estimates the fraction of the density falling into the intervals defined by the different dollar thresholds used in A-15, A-16, and A-17. Table V shows that about 29 percent of the respondents fall into the interval $0 to $5, and that less than 9 percent are willing to pay over $250, and that the median falls into the interval $30–$60.[33] We can also use the estimates of the change in density occurring in each interval to determine a lower-bound estimate for the mean of the WTP distribution. This is done by multiplying the density estimated to be in each interval by the lower endpoint of the interval and then summing over the interval that yields a lower-bound estimate of mean WTP of $53.60.[34] Thus, any empirical distribution that produced the Turnbull interval estimates would result in an empirical estimate of the mean equal to or greater than $53.60.

---

[33]From this point on we use the household weights provided by Westat in performing any estimations. The differences between the weighted and unweighted estimates are almost always quite small, with the weighted estimates being slightly lower than the unweighted estimates. The construction of the weights is discussed at length in section 4.10 and Appendix B.3 of the original study and are based solely on Census demographic variables. Unweighted and weighted frequencies are provided in Appendix C.1.

[34]Since this estimate is a linear function of predetermined design points and a multinomial variable, a standard error for this estimate $2.71, and a 95 percent confidence interval [$48.28–$58.91] are straightforward to calculate. The Turnbull lower bound on the mean increases toward the mean from below as more design points are added. However, for a fixed sample size adding more design points causes the variance of this estimator to grow and hence this estimator can be seen to represent the commonly found bias-variance tradeoff.

Table VI Weibull Estimation Results

Parameter	Estimate	Standard error	Asymptotic t-value
Location	58.417	3.914	14.93
Scale	0.558	0.024	23.68

Median $30.30 [$26.18–$35.08]*	Mean $97.18 [$85.82–108.54]*
Log-Likelihood—1343.014	*95% Confidence Interval

Maximizing the likelihood function under the assumption of a Weibull distribution yields the estimates in Table VI and result in estimates of $30 for the median and $97 for the mean. The standard errors indicate that the parameters are estimated with reasonable precision and are reflected in the 95 percent confidence intervals for the mean and median. Figure 1 displays the Weibull survival curve. An ideal parametric fit occurs when the parametric survival curve just touches the top of each step of the non-parametric function. The Weibull is a good approximation over most of the dollar range with some indication of divergence in the two tails. This problem can be rectified by fitting a Weibull model that allows for a spike at zero.[35] That model significantly improves the fit by placing 20.6 percent of the respondents at zero and reduces the estimated mean to $79.20 with a 95 percent confidence interval of [$67.93–$90.47].[36]

5.3 A Valuation Function

A valuation function is a statistical way to relate respondents' WTP to their characteristics. They are often estimated to demonstrate the construct validity of the estimate from a CV study. In the simplest sense, the respondent's WTP or an indicator of that WTP is regressed on respondent characteristics such as income and on preferences relevant to the good being valued.

---

[35]It is possible to fit a number of other common two parameter survival distributions to our data. These tend to result in similar estimates of the median WTP but quite different estimates of the mean. The fit of the Weibull distribution is either statistically superior or indistinguishable with respect to these other distributions. More flexible three parameter distributions tend to suggest a sharper drop-off in the percent willing to pay near zero and a sharper drop-off in the right tail. As a result, estimates of mean WTP from these distributions tend to fall between the lower-bound estimate from the Turnbull estimator and that of the two parameter Weibull.

[36]The log-likelihood for the Weibull spike model (Kristrom 1997) is –1331.293 so a likelihood ratio test rejects the two parameter Weibull model in favor of the Weibull spike model at $p < 0.01$. Effectively what is happening is that the better fit near zero reduces the implied variance of the WTP distribution. This reduction in variance (reflected in a decreased scale parameter) pulls in the right tail of the distribution, and hence, reduces the estimate of mean WTP.

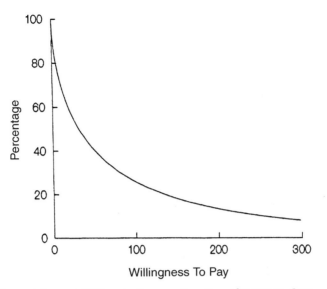

Figure 1 Percent Willing to Pay as a Function of Program Cost

A valuation function is estimated in several steps. First, for observations with missing values in predictor variables, those values must either be imputed or the observations dropped from any estimation using that variable, a generally undesirable option.[37] Next, the variables to include in the valuation function must be determined. Some variables should clearly be included, while for others, the choice is less clear. Finally, the valuation function may be used to make adjustments to WTP estimates for such things as protest responses.

A large number of possible predictors are available for use in the valuation function we wish to estimate. A few, such as income, are obvious choices. Another obvious choice is concern about the environment. Different survey questions that tap this dimension can be used to operationalize this variable in a variety of ways. Other good candidates for predictor variables include the likelihood of visiting Alaska and answers to questions that elicit the respondent's perceptions of the characteristics of the oil spill prevention plan. Also, a strong candidate is some indicator of protest responses.

We present our preferred valuation function in Table VII. The first two parameters are the scale and location parameters based on the assumption

---

[37]Because most of the missing values are on income, we have estimated an equation to predict the log of income. The estimated coefficients for this equation, which is based largely on demographic characteristics, are provided in the study report. All of the variables have the expected sign, and the equation has an R^2 of 0.46.

Table VII Weibull Valuation Function

Parameter	Estimate	Standard error	Asymptotic t-value	Covariate Mean
Location	1.637	1.641	1.00	—
Scale	0.662	0.029	22.91	—
GMORE	0.867	0.284	3.06	0.072
MORE	0.669	0.164	4.07	0.162
LESS	−0.273	0.146	−1.88	0.228
NODAM	−0.794	0.432	−1.84	0.028
MWORK	−0.862	0.131	−6.57	0.265
NWORK	−1.754	0.200	−8.79	0.073
NAME	0.203	0.134	1.51	0.520
COASTAL	0.414	0.143	2.89	0.803
WILD	0.261	0.119	2.19	0.556
STENV	0.473	0.229	2.06	0.098
LIKVIS	0.240	0.138	1.74	0.335
LINC	0.284	0.100	2.85	10.228
WHITE	0.423	0.151	2.80	0.784
PROTEST	−1.226	0.145	−8.45	0.179

Log-Likelihood—1197.728

of a Weibull survival distribution. Note that the scale parameter is a little larger than that estimated in Table VI and the location parameter is quite different because we are parameterizing the original location parameter as a function of the various covariates included in the equation. After the introduction of the covariates, a spike at zero is no longer significant, as many respondents are now predicted to have very small willingness to pay values.

The first four variables, GMORE, MORE, LESS, and NODAM, are dummy variables indicating which respondents believed that the damage likely to occur in the absence of the escort ship plan would be different from that of the Exxon Valdez spill. The coefficients on all four of these variables are significant and follow the expected rank ordering. Those respondents who think that there would be a great deal more damage, GMORE, are willing to pay quite a bit more money than the average respondent. Those who think that there will be somewhat less, but still more damage, MORE, are willing to pay less than the GMORE respondents, but still quite a bit more than the average respondent. Those who think that there would be less damage, LESS, are willing to pay less than the average respondent, and those who think that there would likely be no damage, NODAM, are willing to pay much less. These four variables taken together provide suggestive evidence of respondent sensitivity to the scope of the good valued.

The next two variables, MWORK and NWORK, indicate respondents who think that the plan will prevent less than a great deal of the damage, with MWORK indicating those who think that the plan will prevent some of the damage and NWORK indicating those who think that the plan will not reduce the damage at all. Again, both variables are significant and of the expected negative sign. The NWORK coefficient is about twice the size of the MWORK coefficient in absolute value. The MWORK and NWORK variables provide further evidence undercutting the insensitivity to scope criticism, as they suggest that respondents' valuations and expressed WTP *are* responsive to the characteristics of the good being offered; in this case, the ability of the program to actually prevent the described injuries.

NAME is a dummy variable for those respondents who spontaneously named the Exxon Valdez spill in question A-2 as one of the major environmental accidents caused by humans. As expected, this variable, which measures salience, has a positive influence on a respondent's willingness to pay. COASTAL, which is a dummy variable indicating which respondents said that protecting coastal areas from oil spills was "extremely important" or "very important" in A-3f, has a large and highly significant positive influence on a respondent's willingness to pay. Likewise, WILD, which is a dummy variable for those who felt that the government should set aside a "very large amount" or "large amount" of new land as wilderness in A-4, has a positive effect on a respondent's willingness to pay. STENV, identification of oneself as a strong environmentalist, and LIKVIS, a dummy variable for indicating that the household was "very likely" or "somewhat likely" to visit Alaska in the future, also suggest higher willingness to pay.

Respondents with higher incomes, LINC, are strongly associated with having a higher willingness to pay to prevent another Exxon Valdez type oil spill as is being WHITE. LINC is even more strongly associated with willingness to pay using the subset of respondents for whom income is not imputed. Only 3 of 1043 respondents said "yes" to an amount more than 2% of their income and only 17 said "yes" to an amount more than 1% of their income. Respondents who spontaneously protested (PROTEST) in A-14D or A-15A that Exxon should pay all of the escort ship plan costs (before being asked why they were not willing to pay in A-18), were on average willing to pay much less than those respondents with the same characteristics who did not protest (that Exxon should pay) by this point in the questionnaire.

Depending on a respondent's characteristics, the conditional median willingness to pay predicted by the valuation function varies widely; the lowest predicted value for a respondent in our sample is less than $1 and the highest is $421.

5.4 Adjustments and Sensitivity Analysis

The valuation function estimated above allows us to examine the effect that various adjustments would have on our median WTP estimate. The first type of adjustment corrects for respondent assumptions inconsistent with three important features of the scenario. Our information about these inconsistencies comes from respondent answers to questions in Section B of the survey concerning what they had in mind when they answered the WTP questions. Ideally, respondents would have based their WTP amounts on preventing damages of the same magnitude as those caused by the Exxon Valdez spill. For those respondents who did not, there are four dummy variables in our valuation function. One of these has a value of one to represent the particular deviation from this desired perception of the same damage: GMORE, MORE, LESS, and NODAM. Setting the value of these dummy variables to zero effectively forces the perceptions to the same damages. This adjustment reduces the estimate of the median household willingness to pay from $30 to $27.

Another possible adjustment is for the perceived effectiveness of the escort ship plan. Ideally, all respondents would have perceived the plan as being completely effective. One of two dummy variables in the valuation function has a value of one if a respondent indicated that the plan was not completely effective: MWORK and NWORK. Setting both of these dummy variables to zero forces the perception that the plan was completely effective. This adjustment changes the estimate of the median willingness to pay from $30 to $42.

A third adjustment is that for protest responses. The problem here is how to exactly define a protest response. The most conservative definition is the one used in the variable PROTEST in the valuation function. This indicator variable takes the value of one if the respondent volunteered that Exxon or the oil companies should pay before the respondent was asked why he was against the plan (A-18) and takes the value zero otherwise. Setting PROTEST to zero forces out that consideration and changes the estimate of the median from $30 to $37. Making all three adjustments simultaneously yields a point estimate of $48 for the median household willingness to pay to prevent an Exxon Valdez type oil spill.

We have also examined the sensitivity of the estimates to four other factors. The first of these is using only the A-15 response (rather than A-15, A-16 and A-17) since the second response may introduce some bias. Here the Turnbull estimator still places the median in the $30–$60 interval and results in a lower-bound estimate of the mean which is less than $2 lower.[38] Parametric approaches tend to result in somewhat higher esti-

---

[38]The Turnbull lower bound on the mean should approach the true mean from below as one increases the number of design points. The main reason for not using a large number of design points in conjunction with the Turnbull approach is that the variance of the estimate can increase rapidly as a fixed sample size is randomly allocated to a larger and larger number of design points. While the Turnbull estimates of the lower bound on the mean from the single and double bounded data from this study are potentially consistent with each other if the actual WTP distribution closely follows a step function, this seems unlikely. A more plausible explanation for the similarity between the two estimates is that the downward bias induced in the second question just offsets the increase in the lower bound estimate of the mean that would be found from increasing the number of design points in the double bounded framework. As such, some of the statistical gain from using the double bounded approach may be illusory, although the information from it may be useful in a more general context.

mates. The second is to drop respondents from the sample who may not have clearly understood the CV scenario posed to them. Here a number of more or less inclusive criteria can be employed based upon the interviewer evaluations and responses to particular debriefing questions. In all instances, dropping these respondents raises WTP estimates for the remaining sample. The third is to look at the sponsor question. A plurality (42%) of the respondents believed that Exxon or the oil companies sponsored the survey with the government (23%) being next. Believing that Exxon or the oil companies had sponsored the survey was not a statistically significant predictor of respondent willingness to pay.

The fourth type of sensitivity analysis is a consideration of how stable the estimates of the WTP distribution are over time. This can be done by looking at the surveys completed in Dayton-Toledo, Ohio, two pilot studies and a tracking survey conducted simultaneously with the final survey. This comparison shows that the estimates of the WTP distribution were statistically indistinguishable at three different points in time over the course of a year. The University of Chicago's National Opinion Research Center administered the final questionnaire nationally two years later and, from that data, we obtained almost identical estimates to those reported here (Carson et al. 1997).

5.5 Aggregate Lost Passive Use Value

The original study reported an estimate of $2.8 billion (1990) dollars as the lower bound on the estimated aggregate lost passive use values. This estimate was obtained by multiplying the number of English-speaking households, the population sampled, by the estimate of median WTP. This estimate was very conservative in two main ways. First, from a theoretical perspective, mean WTA (which is greater than mean WTP) is the most appropriate measure of the services lost or disrupted by the Exxon Valdez oil spill.[39] Second, median WTP is less than the mean WTP under the weak assumption that the WTP distribution is positively skewed. The advantage of the median is that it tends to be quite robustly estimated in survival models and is relatively insensitive to distributional assumptions. Since the report, substantial progress has been made on estimating non-parametric and more flexible parametric models of the WTP distribution. If one were to employ the most conservative estimate of mean WTP consistent with the non-parametric Turnbull density parameters, the estimate of aggregate lost passive use is 4.87 billion dollars.[40] Using the mean WTP estimate from the parametric three-parameter Weibull distribution yields an estimate of 7.19 billion dollars.

---

[39]The damage assessment regulations under OPA also note that WTA is the appropriate measure of damages: "Because the government is holding natural resources in trust for the public, the WTA criterion is conceptually the more appropriate measure of damages for natural resource damage claims." *Federal Register*, vol. 59, January 7, 1994, p. 1150.

[40]This number is obtained by multiplying the Turnbull lower bound mean by the number of English-speaking U.S. households (90,838,000).

These amounts reflect the public's willingness to pay to prevent another Exxon Valdez type oil spill given the scenario posed. Simultaneously adjusting the WTP estimates for protest responses, perceptions of damages larger or smaller than the Exxon Valdez spill, and for perceptions that the proposed plan would not be completely effective, results in higher estimates.

6. A Postscript

The State of Alaska and the U.S. Government settled their lawsuits against Exxon for 1 billion dollars in natural resource damages and restitution for injuries.[41] In addition, Exxon spent over 2 billion dollars on oil spill response and restoration. This compares to the 2.8 billion dollars to prevent an Exxon Valdez type oil spill put forth in the original study report. In thinking about the settlement, it may be useful to keep in mind that guidelines on natural resource damage assessment require that any money collected by the government be spent on restoration and/or the acquisition of like resources where restoration is not feasible. It is clearly possible to argue about which Exxon expenditures represented response (not to be counted toward compensable damages) and which represented restoration (counted toward compensable damages). It is also possible to be critical of the restoration effort. Much, however, has been learned since the Exxon Valdez oil spill about the effects of oil spills, how to prevent them, how to respond to them.[42]

Indeed, instances where a spill is averted receive little attention. After the Exxon Valdez oil spill, the U.S. Coast Guard put into effect an oil spill prevention and response program that strongly resembled the program described to respondents in this study. Their regulatory impact assessment for this plan was based on preventing damages of the magnitude indicated by Exxon's settlement with the government. The costs of this program have subsequently been passed on to consumers throughout the United States in the form of higher oil prices. After the plan was put into effect, a tanker had problems with its steering system after leaving Valdez and was about 100 feet from hitting the rocks when its escort ship succeeded in pushing it away (Fararo 1992). This use of the study results for a benefit-cost assessment of a program to protect *ex ante* the natural resources of Prince William Sound complete the circle between the usual policy analysis and natural resource damage assessment.[43]

---

[41]There were also a number of private claims for commercial and punitive damages brought by private parties. While many of those cases have been settled, some litigation continues as of 2003.

[42]Much has also been learned about structuring restoration and resource compensation plans. For details in this case, see http://www.oilspill.state.ak.us/.

[43]The State of California commissioned an *ex ante* study (Carson et al., forthcoming) of the benefits of preventing oil spills along California's central coast and has used it for a number of different policy purposes. This study builds upon the Exxon Valdez study reported in this paper. It incorporates a number of refinements to that survey and was intentionally designed so that its survey instrument could be more readily adaptable to other geographic areas.

The debate over CV measures of passive use and their role in the assessment of natural resource damages and public decision-making has become a major topic of debate for the economics community (Carson, Flores and Meade 2001). The Exxon Valdez represented the quintessential case in which to ignore passive use values was to effectively say that resources that the public had chosen to set aside and not develop could be harmed at little or no cost to the responsible party.

It is possible to believe that lost passive values should be compensated but not believe in using direct monetary valuation via CV. Requiring restoration of an injured resource as many critics of using monetary valuation had argued should be the remedy has been shown to be a vacuous concept when large numbers of animals are killed and ecosystems disrupted for years. While it is clearly possible to compensate the public by providing additional natural resources to compensate for the lost service flows until the resource recovers, determining the level of compensatory resources that would make the public whole effectively requires knowledge of how much monetary value the public placed on the resource (Flores and Thatcher 2002).

At the time of the Exxon Valdez oil spill it was not clear whether Admiralty law which limits damages to the value of the ship and its cargo would take precedent in determining liability over federal/state pollution statutes. The passage of the U.S. Oil Pollution Control Act of 1990 removed that ambiguity and came down clearly on the side of including passive use in assessing damages. That policy decision has not been decisively made elsewhere in the world. As such, perceived liability for a major oil spill in the United States is very high and, perhaps as a consequence, there have been no extremely large spills in the United States since the Exxon Valdez oil spill. There have been spills that might have become very large and caused widespread injuries if it had not been for the preplanned aggressive response effort undertaken.[44] This lack of extremely large oil spills in the United States for over a decade has had an interesting effect; it implies that while CV has not been used much for assessing natural resource damage of large oil spills, its potential use may be playing an important role in preventing such spills.[45] Elsewhere, the pattern of big oil spills has been largely unchanged (Chapple 2000).

---

[44]Most oil spill injuries in the U.S. since the Exxon Valdez have been short term to outdoor recreation or to small parts of larger ecosystems for which the government is the trustee. Stated preference techniques, indirect techniques like travel cost analysis, and habitat equivalence analysis have been used to help settle these cases. These spills have also caused some harm to commercial interests who can bring private lawsuits where lost profits, current or perspective, are at issue.

[45]The vast majority of CV studies have always been done for policy purposes. The number of such studies continues to grow rapidly. Carson (forthcoming) provides citations to over 5000 CV papers and studies from over 100 countries.

Acknowledgements

The authors wish to acknowledge the many contributions provided by Michael Conaway and Kerry Martin during the course of this study. Richard Bishop, Gardner Brown, Howard Schuman, Norbert Schwarz, Paul Slovic, and Robert Solow provided comments during the course of the study. We also thank Jon Krosnick, V. Kerry Smith, Jon Strand and *journal* referees who provided comments on earlier drafts. The State of Alaska provided funding for this study. Kopp acknowledges the partial support of the Alfred P. Sloan Foundation to the Welfare Economics Program at Resources for the Future. All opinions expressed in this paper are those of the authors and should not be attributed to the State of Alaska, the Alfred P. Sloan Foundation, or the authors' home institutions. The authors bear sole responsibility for any errors or omissions.

References

Alberini, Anna and Richard T. Carson (1993), "Choice of Thresholds for Efficient Binary Discrete Choice Estimation," Discussion Paper 90-34R, Department of Economics, University of California, San Diego.

Alberini, A., B. Kanninen and R. T. Carson (1997), "Modeling Response Incentives in Dichotomous Choice Contingent Valuation Data," *Land Economics* 73, 309–324.

Arrow, Kenneth, Robert Solow, Paul R. Portney, Edward E. Leamer, Roy Radner and Howard Schuman (1993), "Report of the NOAA Panel on Contingent Valuation," *Federal Register* 58, 4601–4614.

Bateman, Ian, Richard T. Carson, Brett Day, W. Michael Hanemann, Nick Hanley, Tannis Hett, Michael Jones-Lee, Graham Loomes, Susana Mourato, Ece Özdemiroglu, David Pearce, Robert Sugden and John Swanson (2002), *Economic Valuation with Stated Preference Techniques: A Manual.* Northhampton, MA: Edward Elgar.

Bishop, Richard C. and Thomas A. Heberlein (1979), "Measuring Values of Extra-Market Goods: Are Indirect Measures Biased?" *American Journal of Agricultural Economics* 61, 926–930.

Bishop, Richard C. and Michael P. Welsh (1992), "Existence Values in Benefit-Cost Analysis and Damage Assessment," *Land Economics* 68, 405–417.

Carson, Richard T. (1997), "Contingent Valuation Surveys and Tests of Insensitivity to Scope," in R. J. Kopp, W. Pommerhene and N. Schwartz (eds.), *Determining the Value of Non-Marketed Goods: Economic, Psychological, and Policy Relevant Aspects of Contingent Valuation Methods.* Boston: Kluwer.

Carson, Richard T. (forthcoming), *Contingent Valuation: A Comprehensive Bibliography and History.* Northampton, MA: Edward Elgar.

Carson, Richard T., Michael B. Conaway, W. Michael Hanemann, Jon A. Krosnick, Robert Cameron Mitchell and Stanley Presser), *Valuing Oil Spill Prevention: A Case Study of California's Central Coast.* Boston: Kluwer Academic Press, forthcoming.

Carson, Richard T., Nicholas E. Flores and W. Michael Hanemann (1998), "Sequencing and Valuing Public Goods," *Journal of Environmental Economics and Management* 36, 314–323.

Carson, Richard T., Nicholas E. Flores and Norman F. Meade (2001), "Contingent Valuation: Controversies and Evidence," *Environmental and Resource Economics* 19, 173–210

Carson, Richard T., Nicholas E. Flores and Robert C. Mitchell (1999), "The Theory and Measurement of Passive Use Value," in I. J. Bateman and K. G. Willis (eds.), *Valuing Environmental Preferences: Theory and Practice of the Contingent Valuation Method in the US, EC, and Developing Countries.* Oxford: Oxford University Press.

Carson, R. T., T. Groves and M. Machina (1999), "Incentive and Informational Properties of Preferences Questions," Plenary Address, European Association of Environmental and Resource Economists, Oslo, Norway.

Carson, Richard T., W. Michael Hanemann, Raymond J. Kopp, Jon A. Krosnick, Robert C. Mitchell, Stanley Presser, Paul A. Ruud and V. Kerry Smith (1997), "Temporal Reliability of Estimates from Contingent Valuation," *Land Economics* 73, 151–163

Carson, Richard T. and Robert Cameron Mitchell (1995), "Sequencing and Nesting in Contingent Valuation Surveys," *Journal of Environmental Economics and Management* 28, 155–173.

Carson, Richard T. and Dan Steinberg (1990), "Experimental Design for Discrete Choice Voter Preference Surveys," in *1989 Proceedings of the Survey Methodology Section of the American Statistical Association.* Washington: American Statistical Association.

Carson, Richard T., Leanne Wilks and David Imber (1994), "Valuing the Preservation of Australia's Kakadu Conservation Zone," *Oxford Economic Papers* 46(S), 727–749

Chapple, Clive (2000), "The 1990 Oil Pollution Act: Consequences for the Environment," paper presented at the Association of Environmental and Resource Economists summer workshop, La Jolla, CA.

Diamond, Peter and Jerry A. Hausman (1994), "Contingent Valuation: Is Some Number Better Than No Number," *Journal of Economic Perspectives* 8(4), 45–64.

Fararo, Kim (1992), "Near Miss in the Narrows: Oil-Laden Tanker's Tugboat Escort Puts Itself in a Hard Spot Between Middle Rock and a New Disaster," *Anchorage Daily News*, November 22, A1.

Flores, Nicholas E. and Jennifer Thatcher (2002), "Money: Who Needs It?: Natural Resource Damage Assessment," *Contemporary Economics Policy* 20, 171–178.

Haab, Timothy C. and Kenneth E. McConnell (1997), "Referendum Models and Negative Willingness to Pay: Alternative Solutions," *Journal of Environmental Economics and Management* 32, 251–270.

Hanemann, W. Michael (1991), "Willingness to Pay and Willingness to Accept: How Much Can They Differ?" *American Economic Review* 81, 635–647.

Hanemann, W. Michael (1994), "Valuing the Environment Through Contingent Valuation," *Journal of Economic Perspectives* 8(4), 19–43.

Hanemann (1999), "Neo-Classical Economic Theory and Contingent Valuation," in I. J. Bateman and K. G. Willis (eds.), *Valuing Environmental Preferences: Theory and Practice of the Contingent Valuation Method in the US, EC, and Developing Countries*. Oxford: Oxford University Press.

Hanemann, W. Michael, John Loomis and Barbara Kanninen (1991), "Statistical Efficiency of Double-Bounded Dichotomous Choice Contingent Valuation," *American Journal of Agricultural Economics* 73, 1255–1263.

Hausman, Jerry A. (ed.) (1993), *Contingent valuation: A Critical Assessment*. Amsterdam: North-Holland.

Hoehn, John P. and Alan Randall (1989), "Too Many Proposals Pass the Benefit Cost Test," *American Economic Review* 79, 544–551.

Kahneman, Daniel and Jack L. Knetsch (1992), "Valuing Public Goods: The Purchase of Moral Satisfaction," *Journal of Environmental Economics and Management* 22, 57–70.

Kopp, Raymond J., Paul R. Portney and V. Kerry Smith (1990), "The Economics of Natural Resource Damages After *Ohio v. U.S. Department of Interior*," *Environmental Law Reporter* 20(4). 10127–10131.

Kristrom, Bengt (1997), "Spike Models in Contingent Valuation", *American Journal of Agricultural Economics* 79, 1013–1023.

Krueger, Richard A. (1988), *Focus Groups: A Practical Guide for Applied Research*. Newbury Park, CA: Sage Publications.

Louviere, Jordan J., David A. Hensher and Joffre D. Swait (2000), *Stated Choice Methods: Analysis and Applications*. New York: Cambridge University Press.

McConnell, Kenneth E. (1993), "Indirect Methods for Assessing Natural Resource Damages Under CERCLA," in R. J. Kopp and V. K. Smith (eds.), *Valuing Natural Assets: The Economics of Natural Resource Damage Assessment*. Washington: Resources for the Future.

Mitchell, Robert Cameron (1995), "Current Issues in the Design, Administration, and Analysis of Contingent Valuation Surveys," in P. O. Johansson, B. Kristrom and K. G. Mäler (eds.), *Current Issues in Environmental Economics*. Manchester: Manchester University Press.

Mitchell, Robert Cameron (2002), "On Designing Constructed Markets in Valuation Surveys," *Environmental and Resource Economics* 22, 297–321.

Mitchell, Robert Cameron and Richard T. Carson (1989), *Using Surveys to Value Public Goods: The Contingent Valuation Method*. Washington: Resources for the Future.

Moore, William H. (1994), "The Grounding of the Exxon Valdez: An Examination of the Human and Organizational Factors," *Marine Technology* 31, 41–51.

Morgan, David L. (ed.) (1993), *Successful Focus Groups: Advancing the State of the Art*. Newbury Park, CA: Sage Publications.

National Transportational Safety Board (1990), *Grounding of the U.S. Tankership Exxon Valdez on Bligh Reef, Prince William Sound Near Valdez Alaska*, PB90-916405. Washington: National Safety Transportation Board.

Nelson, Wayne (1982), *Applied Life Analysis*. New York: John Wiley.

Portney, Paul R. (1994), "The Contingent Valuation Debate: Why Economists Should Care," *Journal of Economic Perspectives* 8(4), 3–17.

Sudman, Seymour (1976), *Applied Sampling*. New York: Academic.

Turnbull, Bruce W. (1976), "The Empirical Distribution Function with Arbitrarily Grouped, Censored and Truncated Data," *Journal of the Royal Statistical Society, Series B* 38, 290–295.

11 The Value of Life in Legal Contexts: Survey and Critique*

W. Kip Viscusi

W. Kip Viscusi is the John F. Cogan, Jr. Professor of Law and Economics at the Harvard Law School.

Value of life issues traditionally pertain to insurance of the losses of accident victims, for which replacement of the economic loss is often an appropriate concept. Deterrence measures of the value of life focus on risk-money tradeoffs involving small changes in risk. Using market data for risky jobs and product risk contexts often yields substantial estimates of the value of life in the range of $3 million to $9 million. These estimates are useful in providing guidance for regulatory policy and assessments of liability. However, use of these values to determine compensation, known as hedonic damages, leads to excessive insurance.

1. Introduction

Society routinely places a value on life in a variety of ways. Government regulators must make decisions regarding the level of regulatory costs that should be incurred to reduce risks to life and health. The courts provide compensation after fatalities, both to compensate families for their loss and, in some cases, to provide deterrence as well. In our daily lives, we routinely make decisions that either reduce risks of death, such as the purchase of a crashworthy car, or increase risks to our lives, such as the purchases of a small, fuel-efficient car that exposes us to the risk of injury. These choices all reflect an implicit value of life. The value attached to life and health in these various contexts has different economic content and different dollar magnitudes.

"The Value of Life in Legal Contexts: Survey and Critique," by W. Kip Viscusi, from *American Law and Economic Review*, 2(1):195–222 (2000).

*This research was supported by the Olin Center for Law, Economics, and Business and the Sheldon Seevak Research Fund.

Send correspondence to: W. Kip Viscusi, Hauser 302, Harvard Law School, Cambridge, MA 02138. Fax: (617) 495-3010; E-mail: kip@law.harvard.edu.

The natural question that arises is "Which measure of the value of life is the appropriate way for society to approach such decisions?" The key issue in selecting the pertinent value of life is to establish the purpose for which the number is intended. It is noteworthy that in no case are we asking for the amount of money a person would be willing to pay to avoid certain death or the amount that a person must be paid to accept certain death. Rather, the focus is usually either on the value of a statistical life in which the matter of concern is the risk-money tradeoff involving small mortality risks or the appropriate level of compensation after a fatality for which there is the desire to provide insurance for the survivors.

One can potentially distinguish four possible conceptualizations of the value of life. First, what is the appropriate value of life to establish efficient incentives for safety for deterrence and accident prevention? Second, what is the appropriate value of life from the standpoint of the principles of optimal insurance and appropriate compensation of accident victims? Third, if our objective is to make the victim whole, as in tort liability contexts involving nonmonetary damages, what should be the appropriate level of compensation? Unlike the property damage case in which making the victim whole is an appropriate framework for determining efficient levels of deterrence and compensation, this approach to valuing life will neither be the appropriate deterrence measure nor the appropriate insurance measure, and it has no role to play in an efficiency based value of life framework. Finally, if regulatory expenditures to save lives are very unproductive, is there any level at which their effect on risk leads to the loss of a statistical life rather than a health benefit?

2. Overview of Valuation Approaches

The Value of Statistical Lives

Economic discussions of the value of life almost invariably focus on the value of a statistical life, considering an individual facing a very small probability of death.[1] What is that person's willingness to pay to eliminate some small risk of death? For very small changes in risk, these willingness to pay measures should equal the values for people's willingness to accept increases in risk. The underlying impetus for this approach is the broader maxim in the public finance literature that the value of the benefits for any public policy consists of the willingness to pay of the citizenry for these benefits.[2] Within the context of policies that reduce risk, this value becomes the willingness to pay of those affected by the risk reduction, hence the value of the statistical life. This measure should be appropriately cast as

---

[1] For an early discussion of this principle, see Schelling (1968).

[2] For a review of these public finance principles, see Stokey and Zeckhauser (1978).

the value from the standpoint of deterrence rather than compensation. The thought experiment embodied in the methodology is a tradeoff between money and a very small risk of death. This approach considers how much individuals need to be compensated to face certain death or how much their heirs would need to be compensated after their death to provide appropriate insurance. These events involve discrete fatality outcomes, where the compensation decision is an ex post judgment. In contrast, the value of a statistical life is a prospective measure that in effect establishes the appropriate price society is willing to pay for small risk reductions.

Insurance and Human Capital Measures

Noneconomists speculating on what must be meant by the economic value of life typically think of accounting measures, such as the present value of lost earnings.[3] These human capital measures are not an appropriate guide to the value of life from the standpoint of preventing accidental deaths. As will be indicated below, statistical evidence on the value of a statistical life suggests that these values are roughly an order of magnitude greater than the present value of the earnings of the individual exposed to the risk.

In general, one's financial resources do not necessarily provide a bound on the value of a statistical life because the level of expenditure is low. It would not be entirely inconsistent for an individual to be willing to spend more than one-one thousandth of one's income to reduce the risk of death by 1/1,000. Most prospective risk reductions, whether from safer consumer products or increases in regulatory costs, involve sufficiently small probabilities of death that the budget constraints implied by one's earnings are typically not binding. Those who are more affluent will, of course, generally be willing to pay more to prevent risks to their life and health, but this is quite different from saying that one should value risks based on the proportional share of one's income that corresponds to the pertinent probability of death.

Calculation of the present value of the economic loss, including lost earnings, services, and medical expenses, is totally appropriate from the standpoint of providing insurance and compensation to the accident victim. From a theoretical standpoint, the efficient level of insurance when faced with actuarially fair insurance opportunities is to equate the marginal utility of income in the no-accident state with the marginal utility of income after an accident.[4] In situations involving financial loss, the utility function is unchanged by the accident. The prescription that marginal utility levels before the accident and after the accident be the same consequently leads

---

[3]Indeed, this approach was in fact widely used throughout the federal government. See Rice and Cooper (1967).

[4]Arrow (1971) articulates this general principle for optimal insurance for financial risks, and a large number of authors have generalized this result for state-dependent utility functions in which there is a utility function in good health and a utility function in ill health.

Marginal utility before = marginal utility after

to the full replacement of the economic loss. Doing so keeps both the utility and the marginal utility of income at the level it would have had if the accident had not occurred. From the standpoint of the accident survivors, addressing their economic loss so as to provide efficient insurance requires that they receive full compensation of the economic losses that have been incurred. The impetus for the insurance justification is to insure the accident survivors rather than provide for the welfare of the deceased.

The Make Whole Principle

In many accident contexts, the principle for setting damages is to make the victim "whole" after an economic loss by compensating for the value of the loss that has been incurred.[5] This approach not only provides for full compensation of the loss but also establishes appropriate incentives for accident avoidance in situations in which all accident losses are monetary. The underlying rationale for making individuals whole from an insurance standpoint stems from the principles for optimal insurance when actuarially fair insurance is available. Optimal insurance will provide for sufficient compensation to equate the marginal utility of income in both the accident and the no accident state of the world. Since the utility function is unchanged by an accident, as the only losses are purely financial, equating marginal utilities is tantamount to equating the overall utility level had the accident not occurred.

Making the victim whole is seldom sensible in the case of permanent health impairments or in extreme cases such as death. Money is not as valuable in promoting individual welfare after such catastrophic outcomes. This underlying assumption that health impairments diminish the marginal utility of money lies at the heart of the law and economics debate over setting the appropriate level of pain and suffering compensation. If there is no such diminution in marginal utility, then the total value of the compensation an accident victim receives for the financial loss plus any pain and suffering compensation should be sufficient to make the victim whole. For nonfatal injuries, once the financial needs are met by the compensatory award, the task of pain and suffering payments would be to make the victim indifferent to the health consequences. In the case of fatalities, it is clearly implausible to make the victim whole except in rare instances in which one's bequest motive is overwhelming. Indeed, empirical evidence in Viscusi and Moore (1989) indicates that the value placed on these bequests is in fact less than the value of consumption when one is alive, as one would expect. Purchases of life insurance are also consistent with this result, as few people provide their heirs with enough coverage to prevent any income loss.

---

[5]The idea of making the victim whole is a routine result in the case of financial losses and a desire to provide both efficient insurance and efficient deterrence. For background on these fundamental law and economic principles, see Polinsky (1989), Posner (1998), and Shavell (1987).

In most of the law and economics literature, analysts have analogized to the fatality case and have asserted that other accidents, such as brain damage and paraplegia, for example, also reduce the marginal utility of income. As a consequence, full compensation restoring the accident victim to the preaccident level of welfare is not efficient from an insurance standpoint. Whether an accident adversely affects health increases or decreases one's marginal utility is, however, an empirical question. All adverse health effects are not simply equivalent to a certain fraction of being dead. However, all available evidence suggests that such health-reducing accidents diminish the marginal utility of income. The findings for work-related accidents reported in Viscusi and Evans (1990) generate estimates of the shape of individual utility functions in the preaccident and postaccident states. Job accidents do reduce the welfare enhancing properties of income to a sufficient extent that the optimal replacement rate for the typical work injury is not 100%, but is rather 85%. Similar findings for multiple sclerosis in Sloan et al. (1998) also imply that this severe illness reduces the marginal utility of income as well. No empirical evidence has been published in the literature to suggest that accidents causing health impairments raise the marginal utility of income. There is consequently no economic justification for levels of postaccident insurance compensation that will restore the fatally injured or seriously impaired accident victims to their preaccident welfare level.

Severe illness reduces the marginal utility of income?

Risk-Risk Analysis

The final concept pertaining to the value of life emerged as a salient concern in the 1990s but can be traced back to previous economic contributions.[6] Regulations may create risks as well as reduce them. In some cases, there may be direct risk effects of the regulation. Earlier consumer product safety regulations protected children's sleepwear from fire hazards with the flame retardant chemical Tris. Unfortunately, this chemical was found to be carcinogenic, producing an unintended risk increase from the regulation. A second class of risk-risk effects is that all economic activity has associated injuries and fatalities, including that resulting from regulatory requirements. For example, regulations that stimulate manufacturing activities, such as the production of pollution control equipment, will generate injuries and deaths that occur in the normal course of all production efforts.[7]

By far the most prominent risk-risk concept, also known as health-health analysis, pertains to the health opportunity costs associated with

---

[6]The underlying rationale is that as society has become richer, preferences for safety have increased. For empirical evidence on this result see Viscusi (1978), and for further discussion of its policy implications see Wildavsky (1988).

[7]Estimates of the injury cost by industry based on this approach appear in Viscusi and Zeckhauser (1994).

regulatory expenditures. Allocating society's resources to regulation or other efforts diverts these expenditures from the usual market basket of consumer goods, which includes health care, housing, and other health-health consumption items. Economists have developed a value of life type concept with respect to such expenditures, where this value pertains not to how much it is worth to save a life. Rather, the question is what level of expenditures in terms of the cost per life saved is so high that these expenditures become counterproductive in terms of affecting personal health risk levels. This approach represents an opportunity cost measure of the value of life that will set an upper limit on the level of expenditures that could possibly be sensible even if one's sole concern were with health risks, irrespective of the cost.

3. The Value of Statistical Lives

The underlying principle for establishing the value of a statistical life is that the focus is on the risk-money tradeoff for small risks, not the value of an identified life. Consider the following thought experiment. Suppose that you are faced with a 1/10,000 risk of death. This risk is comparable to estimates of the long-run fatality risk that has faced the typical American worker. Suppose that this is a one-time-only risk that will not be repeated and that you can draw on your future resources to buy out of the risk. Also assume that the death is immediate and painless. How much would you be willing to pay to eliminate this risk?

Very few respondents indicate that they would be willing to sacrifice all of their economic resources in return for this risk reduction. As a result, life clearly has a finite value, and the only question is determining its magnitude. Similarly, few respondents indicate that they are willing to pay nothing to reduce the risk. If the risk scenario can be conveyed in a credible manner, respondents typically indicated a figure such as $500 to eliminate the risk.

How might one use such estimates to calculate the value of life? Suppose that we had 10,000 respondents, each of whom faced a 1/10,000 risk of death. Overall, there would be one statistical death expected in this group. If each person is willing to pay $500 to eliminate the risk, a total of $5 million could be raised to eliminate the one statistical death to the entire group. Thus, $5 million would be the value of a statistical life in this situation. If the respondents had indicated $200 in terms of the willingness to pay, the corresponding value of life would have been $2 million. Similarly, one can view the value of life as simply the value per unit risk, or the willingness to pay for the risk reduction divided by the probability of death, which gives the same answer as the procedure above.

Utilizing survey questions to elicit the value of life is a frequent procedure, particularly for health outcomes such as cancer deaths, for which reliable market data often do not exist. A preferable approach is to analyze tradeoffs implied by actual decisions involving real risks rather than creating hypothetical survey scenarios. While there are no explicit market trades involving the certainty of death, there are a variety of contexts in which there are transactions in which a probability of death is one component of the transaction. Purchases of cars with differing safety characteristics reflect the value that consumers place on their lives as well as fuel economy, comfort, and other attributes. Housing market decisions that expose one to various forms of pollution will reflect these valuations, as will job risk decisions of workers and purchases of safety devices, such as smoke alarms.

The principle underlying all such assessments can be traced back to Adam Smith's ([1776] 1937) analysis of compensating differentials, which was developed more than two centuries ago. Smith suggested that workers would need to be compensated for jobs that posed additional risk; otherwise, these positions would not be as attractive as safer job alternatives. In much the same way, houses in hazardous neighborhoods will command a lower price, and safer cars will command a higher price. The practical task for economists has been to identify market situations in which there is sufficient data to disentangle the risk-money tradeoff from tradeoffs involving other product attributes, whether it be fuel efficiency of automobiles or the promotion prospects of employment. The overall literature dealing with these multiple attribute concerns has been called hedonic wage analysis or hedonic price studies, as the focus is on obtaining quality-adjusted measures of prices or wages, where one of the quality components is the health and safety risk.[8]

By far the most extensive literature on money-risk tradeoffs has focused on labor market estimates. The availability of job risk data, as well as detailed information on workers and the characteristics of their employment, has enabled analysts to estimate the wage-risk tradeoffs for the United States as well as in numerous other countries. Before considering these estimates, it should be noted at the outset that there is no reason why these studies should yield the same value of life estimates. The value of life is not a natural constant, such as e or π. Rather, it simply reflects the risk-money tradeoff of the sample of the individuals being examined. People will differ in their implicit values of life depending on their willingness to bear risk, their affluence, and other factors.

Figure 1 indicates the manner in which the labor market generates wage-risk tradeoffs. The curve FF represents a market offer curve for a particular firm. For higher levels of risk, the firm is willing to offer a greater wage because the costs of workplace safety to the firm are less at higher risk levels. The additional wage premium for greater risk diminishes because the cost reductions made possible by the increase in risk decrease in size as the risk rises. The curve GG represents a different firm and its

---

[8]An early contribution to the hedonic price and wage literature is Griliches (1971). See Rosen (1986) for an extensive discussion.

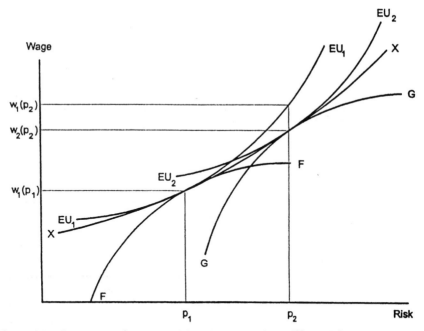

Figure 1 Market Process for Determining Compensating Differentials

associated wage offer curve. In practice, all that is relevant to any particular worker is the highest wage for any given risk level from among the various wage offer curves available in the market place.

The preferences of workers may differ as well. The curve EU_1 represents the set of points for worker 1 that yield the same level of expected utility. As the risk level increases, the wage that the worker must receive to maintain the same level of welfare, or expected utility, is higher. In addition, this compensation must rise by an increasing amount as the risk level becomes greater. The comparable constant expected utility locus for worker 2 is EU_2. Each worker has a whole set of such constant expected utility loci, where the direction of preferences is in the northwesterly direction. What is shown in Figure 1 is the constant expected utility locus for worker 1 and for worker 2 at which they are able to select the job risk-wage combination that gives them the highest level of welfare. Thus, EU_1 is tangent to the offer curve FF at the job risk level, p_1, and EU_2 is tangent to GG at the risk level p_2. The slope of the constant expected utility curves and the market offer curves are identical at these points of tangency, as the wage-risk tradeoff simultaneously reflects the wage workers require to accept small increases in risk as well as the costs to the company of altering the risk level. Statistical estimates do not isolate the tradeoff for any particular worker but instead estimate the locus of such tangencies using a curve such as XX in Figure 1. The result economists generally report is an average wage-risk tradeoff or slope of XX for the range of empirical estimates.

More specifically, economists usually estimate an equation, which in its linear form, is

$$\text{Wage} = \alpha + \beta_1 \text{ Death Risk} + \sum_{i=2}^{n} \beta_i \text{ Job and Worker Characteristics}_i + \epsilon.$$

The coefficient β_1 represents the wage-risk tradeoff, controlling for the personal characteristics of the worker and the job. If the wage and death risk variables are each in annual terms, β_1 is the implicit value of a statistical life for that sample.

These empirical estimates clearly pertain only to local rates of tradeoff for small changes in risk. Suppose, for example, that one were to ask worker 1 to move from a risk p_1 to p_2. Would it be appropriate to use the estimated market rate of tradeoff XX to determine how much wage-risk compensation worker 1 would require for such an increase in risk? Using the value of XX, one finds that instead of requiring w_1 (p_1) as the wage rate, the wage w_2 (p_2) that is sufficient to induce worker 2 to take the riskier job perhaps might suffice. However, examining EU_1, which is the locus of points that gives the worker the same level of expected utility as at the initial risk-rage position of p_1, w_1 (p_1), we find that a higher wage at w_1 (p_2) is required. Whereas market wage-risk tradeoffs are pertinent to analyzing small changes in risk, large risk increases would command a larger wage premium than the market estimates suggest. To estimate the amount of compensation required for non-incremental risk changes, one would need to know the shape of workers' utility functions, which can in fact be estimated, as was done in Viscusi and Evans (1990). For the logarithmic case, the result was that utility was equal to log Income in the injured state and 1.007 log Income in the healthy state.

Table 1 summarizes selected studies from the value of life literature, which now consists of dozens of estimates. An early influential study is that by Thaler and Rosen (1976), which found an implicit value of life of just under $1 million. However, their sample focused on workers in particularly high risk jobs, with an annual fatality risk on the order of 1/1,000. Workers who are most willing to bear risk will sort themselves into these very risky jobs and, as a result, one will find a lower value of life than in more representative samples. The estimates in Viscusi (1979) for workers facing an annual death risk of 1/10,000 indicated an implicit value of life on the order of $5 million. These estimates also appear to be sensitive to the risk measure used, as shown in Moore and Viscusi (1988a), for which the value of life obtained using the Bureau of Labor Statistics death risk measure is $3 million, whereas the value of life using the National Traumatic Occupational Fatality Survey measure is $8.8 million. Estimates for foreign countries are in a similar range, as Kniesner and Leeth (1991) found that estimates for Australia and Japan were on the order of $4 million and $9 million, respectively. Overall, these value of life estimates cluster in a range of $3–$9 million for most studies in the literature.

A wide variety of studies have also examined tradeoffs outside the labor market. In much the same way as there is a wage-risk tradeoff, one can

Table 1 Summary of Selected Value of Life Studies Based on Labor Market Data

Author (year)	Sample	Risk variable	Mean risk	Implicit value of life ($ millions)[a]
Smith (1974)	Industry data	Bureau of Labor Statistics (BLS)	NA	8.7
Smith (1976)	Current Population Survey (CPS)	BLS	0.0001	5.6
Thaler and Rosen (1976)	Survey of Economic Opportunity	Society of Actuaries	0.001	1.0
Viscusi (1978, 1979)	Survey of Working Conditions	BLS	0.0001	5.0
Brown (1980)	National Longitudinal Survey of Young Men	Society of Actuaries	0.002	1.8
Viscusi (1981)	Panel Study of Income Dynamics (PSID)	BLS	0.0001	7.9
Olson (1981)	CPS	BLS	0.0001	6.3
Arnould and Nichols (1983)	U.S. Census	Society of Actuaries	0.001	1.1
Moore and Viscusi (1988a)	PSID	BLS	0.00005	3.0
Moore and Viscusi (1988b)	PSID	National Traumatic Occupational Fatality Survey	0.00008	8.8
Kniesner and Leeth (1991)	Industry data for Japan		0.00003	9.2
Kniesner and Leeth (1991)	Industry data for Australia		0.0001	4.0
Kniesner and Leeth (1991)	CPS data for United States		0.0004	0.7

[a]Expressed in 1998 prices using the GDP deflator, as reported in the *Economic Report of the President*, 1999.

also estimate a price-risk tradeoff. Estimates in Table 2 for seatbelt use, cigarette smoking cessation, automobile safety, and housing price responses to hazardous waste risks all indicate value of life estimates that are broadly in the same range as those in labor market studies. Some of the estimates in these tables differ because in some cases very strong assumptions are needed to generate value of life estimates, and in other instances there are very strong elements of self selection that affect the value of life figures that

Table 2 Summary of Selected Price-Risk Studies Based on Product and Housing Market Data

Author (year)	Nature of risk, year	Monetary tradeoff	Implicit value of life ($ millions)[a]
Blomquist (1979)	Automobile death risks, 1972	Estimated desirability of seatbelts	1.5
Portney (1981)	Mortality effects of air pollution, 1978	Property values	1.0
Ippolito and Ippolito (1984)	Cigarette smoking risks, 1980	Monetary equivalent of risk information	0.8
Atkinson and Halvorsen (1990)	Automobile accident risks, 1986	Price of new automobiles	4.8
Dreyfus and Viscusi (1995)	Used car purchases, 1988	Price of used cars	3.4–4.8
Gayer, Hamilton, and Viscusi (forthcoming)	Cancer risks from hazardous waste sites, 1988–93	Housing price effects	4.2

[a]All estimates are in 1998 dollars.

are generated. For example, cigarette smokers would be expected to exhibit relatively low values of life, and in fact they are at the bottom end of the range of the estimates in Table 2. These findings for cigarette smokers are consistent with those in Hersch and Viscusi (1990) for nonfatal job risks, for which they found that the greatest implicit value of an injury was for individuals who wore seatbelts and did not smoke, the lowest implicit value was for people who both smoked and did not wear seatbelts, with people who engaged in only one of these risky behaviors being in the intermediate range. In short, there is substantial heterogeneity in individuals' value of life, and this heterogeneity gets reflected in people's safety decisions and in subsequent market estimates of the value of a statistical life.

Analysts have also utilized survey techniques to estimate the value of life. These approaches, which sometimes come under the heading of contingent valuation, elicit people's willingness to pay for various kinds of risk reduction. Estimates for automobile accident death risks and for cancer indicate value of life figures of the same order of magnitude as those found in labor market studies.[9] Interview studies of this kind are most useful in indicating how the value of life may vary depending on the kind of death, such as cancer versus an accidental death. They also may be instructive in indicating how the value of life differs for populations of a different age or demographic profile than the typical worker or consumer in the market-based studies.

---

[9]Results for the United Kingdom appear in Jones-Lee (1989) and for the United States appear in Viscusi, Magat, and Huber (1991). Estimates of the value of cancer appear in Magat, Viscusi, and Huber (1996).

4. Regulatory Applications of the Value of Life

A Profile of Regulatory Costs per Life

Historically, the federal government valued statistical lives saved by government policies using human capital measures. In some instances, this approach was characterized as the "cost of death," where it included both the present value of medical expenditures as well as income loss associated with death and injury. This approach shifted in the early 1980s after the Reagan administration at least nominally imposed a requirement that the agency show that the benefits of its regulatory efforts exceed the costs. In 1982 the Occupational Health and Safety Administration (OSHA) proposed a hazard communication regulation. This proposal was the most expensive regulation proposed to date in the Reagan administration. It was rejected by the Office of Management and Budget because, in its view, the associated costs exceeded the benefits. OSHA then appealed the dispute to then Vice President Bush. My reanalysis of the standard that was prepared at the request of these agencies found that the benefits exceeded the costs if one valued the lives saved using the value of life methodology rather than the cost of death. In particular, this shift alone increased projected benefits by roughly a factor of 10.[10]

The U.S. Office of Management and Budget now recommends the use of the value of life methodology for benefit assessment for all proposed federal regulations. While agencies now routinely assess benefits using these value of life figures, the results of the analysis do not always bind government policy. In most instances, the restrictive legislative mandates of the regulatory agencies require that they issue protective regulations irrespective of benefit-cost balancing. As a result, with the notable exception of the U.S. Department of Transportation, which undervalues life somewhat by using a figure of just under $3 million per life, the risk regulation agencies often issue regulations that have inordinately large costs.

Table 3 summarizes the cost effectiveness of a wide variety of regulations. The columns of the table indicate the name of the regulation, the year the regulation was issued, the pertinent agency, the cost per expected life saved, and the cost per normalized life saved. This normalization transforms all lives into accident equivalents. Thus, prevention of cancer cases generally has less of a life saving effect on a quantity-adjusted basis, where the normalization has been done based on the discounted expected number of life years saved relative to accidental deaths using a 3% rate of discount. The effect of this normalization is to make the health-oriented regulatory policies, which already are at the bottom of the table in terms of cost effectiveness, even less efficient than they would seem to be based on the unadjusted cost per life saved.

---

[10]The key results from my report prepared for Secretary of Labor Donovan, "Analysis of OMB and OSHA Evaluations of the Hazard Communication Proposal," March 15, 1982, are reported in Viscusi (1992, chap. 14). The regulation was approved the day after the report reached the White House.

Suppose that one establishes a cutoff for desirability of a policy in terms of the cost per life saved. Let all efforts with a cost exceeding $6 million per life fail a benefit-cost test and all policies with a lower cost pass such a test. A range such as this is consistent both with the results of the labor market and other value of life studies as well as with the values currently used by most federal agencies. Many regulations in Table 3, particularly those issued by the National Highway Traffic Safety Administration (NHTSA) and Federal Aviation Administration (FAA), pass a benefit-cost test. These agencies tend to be outliers because their legislative mandates do not exempt them from a benefit-cost test. Moreover, the Department of Transportation selects its regulatory interventions based on the value of life performance. Indeed, this agency consistently has used a value of life below the midpoint estimates of the value of life in labor market studies so that there may be additional transportation regulations that would be warranted but which are not now being adopted.

In contrast, the Environmental Protection Agency (EPA) and OSHA routinely issue regulations with considerable costs per life saved. For the last five regulations appearing in Table 3, the costs per life saved were on the order of $5 billion or more. Put somewhat differently, the U.S. Department of Transportation refrains from issuing regulations that are 1,000 times as cost effective as these efforts. These high levels of regulatory costs are even greater once one considers the cost per normalized life saved column in Table 3, which adjust for latency periods and the length of life saved. All regulations with higher costs than the rear lap/shoulder belts for autos regulation issued by NHTSA have costs per normalized life saved that are excessive given this measure.

Salient Policy Issues

While the value of life estimates are useful measures of the risk-money trade-off for accidental deaths to the populations exposed to these risks, because of individual heterogeneity in the value of life the appropriate measure may differ depending on the regulatory context. The first potential adjustment is with respect to individual age. Risk-reducing policies do not confer immortality, but merely extend one's life. Although there have been some estimates of the quantity-adjusted value of life in the literature[11] as well as estimates indicating how value of life estimates in surveys vary with age,[12] such quantity adjustments are still being refined. The most extreme instances of quantity adjustments arise when the regulation affects the lives of children or people with very short life expectancies, such as those with advanced respiratory ailments. Air pollution regulations promulgated by EPA are particularly affected by such concerns, since it is largely the elderly

[11]See Moore and Viscusi (1988a and 1988b) and Viscusi and Moore (1989).
[12]See, for example, the results in Jones-Lee (1989).

Table 3 Regulatory Costs and Cost-Effectiveness in Saving Lives

Regulation	Year	Agency	Cost per life saved, millions of 1995 dollars	Cost per normalized life saved, 1995 dollars
Unvented space heater ban	1980	CPSC	0.1	0.1
Aircraft cabin fire protection standard	1985	FAA	0.1	0.1
Seatbelt/air bag	1984	NHTSA	0.1	0.1
Steering column protection standards	1967	NHTSA	0.1	0.1
Underground construction standards	1989	OSHA	0.1	0.1
Trihalomethane in drinking water	1979	EPA	0.2	0.6
Aircraft seat cushion flammability	1984	FAA	0.5	0.6
Alcohol and drug controls	1985	FRA	0.5	0.6
Auto fuel-system integrity	1975	NHTSA	0.5	0.5
Auto wheel rim servicing	1984	OSHA	0.5	0.6
Aircraft floor emergency lighting	1984	FAA	0.7	0.9
Concrete and masonry construction	1988	OSHA	0.7	0.9
Crane suspended personnel platform	1988	OSHA	0.8	1.0
Passive restraints for trucks and buses	1989	NHTSA	0.8	0.8
Auto side-impact standards	1990	NHTSA	1.0	1.0
Children's sleepwear flammability ban	1973	CPSC	1.0	1.2
Auto side door supports	1970	NHTSA	1.0	1.0
Low-altitude windshear equipment and training	1988	FAA	1.6	1.9
Metal mine electrical equipment standards	1970	MSHA	1.7	2.0
Trenching and excavation standards	1989	OSHA	1.8	2.2
Traffic alert and collision avoidance systems	1988	FAA	1.8	2.2
Hazard communication standard	1983	OSHA	1.9	4.8
Trucks, buses, and MPV side-impact	1989	NHTSA	2.6	2.6
Grain dust explosion prevention standards	1987	OSHA	3.3	4.0
Rear lap/shoulder belts for autos	1989	NHTSA	3.8	3.8
Stds for radionuclides in uranium mines	1984	EPA	4.1	10.1
Benzene NESHAP (original: fugitive emissions)	1984	EPA	4.1	10.1
Ethylene dibromide in drinking water	1991	EPA	6.8	17.0
Benzene NESHAP (revised: coke by-products)	1988	EPA	7.3	18.1
Asbestos occupational exposure limit	1972	OSHA	9.9	24.7
Asbestos occupational exposure limit	1986	OSHA	88.1	220.1

Table 3 Continued

Regulation	Year	Agency	Cost per life saved, millions of 1995 dollars	Cost per normalized life saved, 1995 dollars
Benzene occupational exposure limit	1987	OSHA	10.6	26.5
Electrical equipment in coal mines	1970	MSHA	11.1	13.3
Arsenic emission standards for glass plants	1986	EPA	16.1	40.2
Ethylene oxide occupational exposure limit	1984	OSHA	24.4	61.0
Arsenic/copper NESHAP	1986	EPA	27.4	68.4
Hazardous waste listing of petroleum refining sludge	1990	EPA	32.9	82.1
Cover/move uranium mill tailings (inactive)	1983	EPA	37.7	94.3
Benzene NESHAP (revised: transfer operations)	1990	EPA	39.2	97.9
Cover/move uranium mill tailings (active sites)	1983	EPA	53.6	133.8
Acrylonitrile occupational exposure limit	1978	OSHA	61.3	153.2
Coke ovens occupational exposure limit	1976	OSHA	75.6	188.9
Lockout/tagout	1989	OSHA	84.4	102.4
Arsenic occupational exposure limit	1978	OSHA	127.3	317.9
Asbestos ban	1989	EPA	131.8	329.2
Diethylstilbestrol (DES) cattlefeed ban	1979	FDA	148.6	371.2
Benzene NESHAP (revised: waste operations)	1990	EPA	200.2	500.2
1, 2-Dechloropropane in drinking water	1991	EPA	777.4	1,942.1
Hazardous waste land disposal ban	1988	EPA	4,988.7	12,462.7
Municipal solid waste landfills	1988	EPA	22,746.8	56,826.1
Formaldehyde occupational exposure limit	1987	OSHA	102,622.8	256,372.7
Atrazine/alachlor in drinking water	1991	EPA	109,608.5	273,824.4
Hazardous waste listing for wood-preserving chemicals	1990	EPA	6,785,822.0	16,952,364.9

Source: Viscusi, Hakes, and Carlin (1997).

and young children who are protected by these efforts. Some regulatory analyses at least attempt to indicate the distribution of the populations affected and, in some cases, adjust for the amount of life expectancy lost (or more correctly, the discounted number of life years lost), but such adjustments remain controversial.

A second salient aspect of heterogeneity is with respect to income. Human capital measures for the present value of lost earnings as compensatory damages are directly proportional to one's income level. Estimates of the implicit value of job injuries also suggest that there is a strong income elasticity, which also may be close to 1.0.[13] Presumably there is similar variation in people's willingness to pay for risk reduction so that based on the usual benefit measures the value of life for more affluent populations should be greater. The government currently makes no such distinctions, a practice that in effect represents an implicit form of income redistribution.

Although income-based differences in the value of life are particularly controversial when government expenditures are involved, if the regulatory structures will impose costs that ultimately will be largely borne by the consumers themselves, they would presumably be less controversial, since they will be fostering the safety levels that an efficient market would generate, and there would be no governmental subsidy to the more affluent consumers. A case in point is that of airline safety, since airline passengers have above-average levels of income. The U.S. Department of Transportation does not, however, permit the FAA to use a higher value of life for airline safety than for other agency policies in which government funds are being expended, such as for improved guard rails on highways. In this case, however, safety regulations are not at the public's expense. They are requirements that must be paid for by the airlines and will be reflected in the ticket price.

Failure to recognize potential heterogeneity in the value of life may also lead to policies that are less protective of the environment for future generations. Society's willingness to pay for safety has been rising over time with increased affluence. Recognizing the greater value that future generations will place on environmental quality and safety will lead to more protective environmental policies than assuming these valuations would remain constant. Because future generations cannot carry out bargains with those now alive and compensate us for our protective actions, the result may be that the level of environmental quality may be lower and at a less efficient level than if such transactions could be executed.

Other refinements of the value of life that are often salient include recognition of the quality of life years at risk as well as whether the risks

---

[13]See the estimates in Viscusi and Evans (1990). For different formulations of the model, the income elasticities are 0.67 and 1.10. Also, in Viscusi (1978), I show that there are also wealth effects in the risk levels people select, as workers with greater economic resources are more likely to select safer jobs.

are voluntary and have received some form of compensation. If people have voluntarily chosen to incur risks through a market transaction, then it is often the case that this self-selection process will make those exposed to the risk a nonrandom sample of the population and hence will have a lower average value of life among their group. In addition, the fact that these individuals have received compensation for the risk may affect the perceived equity of the outcome as compared to a situation in which the risk tradeoff is similarly at the efficient level but no compensation has in fact been paid.

5. Value of Life in the Courts

Torts Cases

A routine part of wrongful death, discrimination, and wrongful discharge cases is to calculate the economic loss suffered because of the wrongful behavior. This loss amount typically is the human capital measure based on the present value of lost earnings. In the case of a person who is deceased, there is also often a subtraction for personal consumption expenditures and taxes, though these practices vary by state. These calculations are now standard practice and have become a relatively uncontroversial exercise except for differences between the experts in their projections of likely earnings trajectories and in their selection of the discount rate for bringing these projections back to their present value.

Whereas regulatory agencies have adopted the value of life methodology almost universally, the courts continue to rely on the human capital measure. The principal rationale for this continued emphasis is that the human capital approach is more pertinent to the insurance function of damages, which is to meet the economic loss of the survivors. The value of life concept can be viewed more appropriately as a deterrence concept, and awarding damages based on this amount would lead to excessive insurance as compared to what the individual would have chosen if insurance had been available before the accident on an actuarially fair basis.

Use of the value of life methodology as a substitute for the human capital measure as a compensation approach has come under the heading "hedonic damages." Numerous economists have attempted to introduce this concept in a variety of jurisdictions, but this approach has generally been rejected because of the mismatch between the value of life concept and the compensatory objectives of damages.[14] Hedonic damages are more pertinent from the standpoint of deterrence, which most courts recognize as a

---

[14]Most but not all court cases have not permitted hedonic damages to be presented. For a review of the case law in this area, see Ward (1992).

punitive damages concept, but even then there is the danger that there will be excessive insurance provided to accident victims.[15]

Value of life statistics nevertheless are useful in determining liability. In particular, a company's expenditures on safety should reflect an appropriate risk-money tradeoff. Consider the analysis prepared by Ford with respect to the gas tank design for the Ford Pinto. Although *Mother Jones* magazine received a Pulitzer Prize for an article suggesting that this analysis was prepared with reference to rear impacts that were the object of tort litigation, the assessment by Schwartz (1991) suggests that it pertained to rollover risks and regulatory matters. However, General Motors did prepare a similar analysis with respect to fires resulting from side impacts on the gas tank so that consideration of the highly publicized Ford analysis is instructive of the general approach that seems to be prevalent within the auto industry.

The cost of relocating the gas tank was $11 per unit for a total cost across the car population of $137.5 million. Relocation of the gas tank would eliminate 180 burn deaths and a similar number of burn injuries, the values for which Ford chose amounts comparable to the court awards at that time—$200,000 for a burn death and $67,000 for a serious burn injury. The result, as is shown in Table 4, is that Ford's estimate of the total benefits of relocation were just under $50 million, which is far less than the costs. If, however, Ford had used the value of life measure of $5 million for fatalities, this safety improvement alone would exceed the cost of the gas tank relocation. If, for sake of concreteness, we assume that burn injuries are half as valuable as saving lives, then the total benefits of relocating the gas tank are almost ten times greater than the cost. Focusing on court awards rather than the public's willingness to pay for greater safety will lead companies to greatly undervalue safety improvements. Liability in these contexts should be judged using value of life reference points reflecting appropriate risk-money tradeoffs rather than the much smaller human capital values that fail to reflect the full value of greater safety to those exposed to potential injury.

Risk-Risk Analysis

The very high costs per life saved of government regulations reflected in Table 3 have not gone unnoticed by the courts. In an influential opinion, U.S. Federal Court Judge Steven F. Williams indicated that such regulations may in fact be counterproductive, since the health costs of wasteful regulatory expenditures exceed the direct risks reduced.[16] This decision in

---

[15]Ideally, one would want to couple compensatory damages with a fine paid to the state to establish efficient incentives. Such a fine can, in effect, be levied through regulatory sanctions in many instances.

[16]See *UAW v. OSHA.*

Table 4 Benefits and Costs for Changes in Ford Pinto Gas Tank Design

A. Costs

Number of units	Unit cost	Total cost
11 million cars	$11	$121 million
1.5 million trucks	$11	$16.5 million
Total		$137.5 million

B. Benefits: Risks Avoided by Design Change

Outcome of faulty design	Ford's unit value	Ford's total value	Unit deterrence value	Total deterrence value
180 burn deaths	$200,000	$36 million	$5 million	$900 million
180 serious burn injuries	$67,000	$12.1 million	$2.5 million	$450 million
2,100 burned vehicles	$700	$1.5 million	$700	$1.352 billion
Total		$49.6 million		

Source: Viscusi (1991) and internal Ford engineering analysis for costs and Ford benefit values.

turn stimulated a letter from the Office of Management and Budget to OSHA, suggesting that OSHA consider this approach in its regulatory analyses.[17] To date, this methodology has not yet been adopted as official agency policy. The available evidence at that time was based on the work by Keeney (1990), who used direct estimates of the link between the mortality rate and income level leading to an estimate in the range of $7 million, or $12.5 million in 1992 prices.[18] A variety of other estimates similarly based on the correlation between income and mortality indicate that expenditures ranging from $2 million to $12 million on efforts that do not reduce health risks directly will have an opportunity cost of one statistical life.[19]

These estimates imply that expenditure levels of this amount will lead to the loss of a statistical life, whereas the value of life estimates cited above indicate that the value of life from the standpoint of saving a statistical life is $3 million to $7 million dollars. Surely these value of life estimates cannot be correct if these expenditures are only a break-even proposition in which as many statistical lives are lost as are being saved by expenditures

---

[17]See letter to Nancy Risque Rohrbach, Assistant Secretary for Policy, U.S. Department of Labor, from James B. MacRae, Jr., Acting Administrator, Office of Information and Regulatory Affairs, U.S. Office of Management and Budget, March 10, 1992.

[18]More specifically, Keeney (1990) fitted an exponential curve relating mortality risk to income using 1959 data on mortality of whites, age 25–64.

[19]For a review of the range of these studies as well as direct evidence, see Lutter and Morrall (1994) and Viscusi (1994b).

of this level.[20] To resolve these difficulties, Viscusi (1994a) developed a methodology whereby there would be a linkage between the level of expenditure that would lead to the loss of a statistical life and the value of a statistical life from the standpoint of society's willingness to pay to reduce risk. In particular, the risk-risk analysis measure of the opportunity cost of saving a life equals the estimated value of life divided by the marginal propensity to consume health-related expenditures, which he estimated to be 0.1. The result was that the level of expenditures leading to the loss of a statistical life would be $50 million.[21]

Thus far, there is general agreement on the concept,[22] but it has not yet been adopted for widespread policy use because there is not yet any consensus regarding the appropriate magnitude of the empirical value that should be used. As a practical manner, if agencies actually adopted policies based on benefit-cost analysis, the use of the risk-risk tradeoff value would become largely superfluous. This technique emerged as an alternative when the restrictive aspects of legislative provisions prevented the U.S. Office of Management and Budget from rejecting policies based on their inordinately high cost per life saved values. Even if agencies are not permitted to perform benefit-cost analysis, the reasoning was that at least on balance they should reduce death risks rather than increase them. So long as the opportunity cost in lives lost exceeds the risk gains from a policy, these efforts will not only be wasteful of financial resources but on balance will have an adverse health effect.

6. Conclusion

Noneconomists might view attaching a value to human life as the most problematic of all undertakings. Such an effort is presumably not only immoral but also unlikely to yield any estimates of practical import.

The opposite has in fact proven to be the case. The courts and regulatory agencies long used human capital measures as determinants of the appropriate value of compensation for fatalities and incorrectly used these measures to value the prevention of fatalities. The more recent literature

---

[20]There are other controversies as well. For example, improved individual health affects income level so there are problems of simultaneity in estimating the relationship between income and mortality rates.

[21]This methodology has since been refined to recognize income related expenditures that harm individual health, such as smoking and drinking. Such refinements indicate that the risk-risk analysis measure for the expenditure level that leads to the loss of a statistical life may be as low as $12 million, which is still substantially above the value of life figure for saving a statistical life. See Lutter, Morrall, and Viscusi (1999).

[22]For example, several articles in the *University of Chicago Law Review* (fall 1996) address this approach in a favorable manner.

has focused on these prevention values under the heading of the value of life, which in effect has inquired not about the value of life but rather society's willingness to pay for small risk reductions. This focus on the risk-money tradeoff for small changes in risk is analytically convenient and can be linked to market evidence for prices and wages that are in exchange for shifts in the individual risk level. Focusing on the small risk changes also leads to an appropriate match to government policies as well as most preventive risk decisions, since typically what is at stake is not the certainty of life or death but rather small incremental shifts in the probability of this adverse outcome. Estimates of the value of life in the labor market are similar to those that have been obtained for product market contexts and in interview studies. Because these values are in the millions per statistical life, there has been considerably less controversy concerning the inappropriateness of these measures that would have been the case if they had a more modest value comparable to the human capital measure for lost earnings.

The result is that value of life estimates are now used routinely in benefit analyses of risk reduction policies throughout the U.S. federal government. However, because of restrictive legislative mandates, they often do not provide the guide to policy. Attempts to use these values in court contexts for hedonic damages have largely been unsuccessful because the value of life measure is not a compensation concept but is rather a measure of the appropriate value of eliminating small risks. Adoption of this approach for determining liability would be an appropriate role for these estimates, but there is no evidence that this use of the value of life estimates has made its way into the courts.

Another value of life concept that has been at the forefront of the recent economic literature pertains to risk-risk analysis. Very wasteful expenditures may in fact have an opportunity cost in terms of lives saved, which one might view as an expenditure level that will lead to the loss of a statistical life. This concept has been the object of preliminary discussions both in the courts and the regulatory arena, but the methodology has yet to be adopted on a widespread basis.

References

Arnould, Richard, and Len M. Nichols. 1983. "Wage Risk Premiums and Workers' Compensation: A Refinement of Estimates of Compensative Wage Differentials," 91 *Journal of Political Economy* 332–40.

Arrow, Kenneth. 1971. *Essays in the Theory of Risk-Bearing*. Chicago: Markham.

Atkinson, Scott E., and Robert Halverson. 1990. "The Valuation of Risks to Life: Evidence from the Market for Automobiles," 72 *Review of Economics and Statistics* 133–36.

Blomquist, Glenn. 1979. "Value of Life Saving: Implications of Consumption Activity," 87 *Journal of Political Economy* 540–58.

Brown, Charles. 1980. "Equalizing Differences in the Labor Market," 94 *Quarterly Journal of Economics* 113–34.

Council of Economic Advisors. 1999. *Economic Report of the President*. Washington, DC: U.S. Government Printing Office.

Dreyfus, Mark, and W. Kip Viscusi. 1995. "Rates of Time Preference and Consumer Valuations of Automobile Safety and Fuel Efficiency," 38 *Journal of Law and Economics* 79–105.

Gayer, Ted, James T. Hamilton, and W. Kip Viscusi. Forthcoming. "Private Values of Risk Tradeoffs at Superfund Sites: Housing Market Evidence on Learning About Risk," *Review of Economics and Statistics*.

Griliches, Zvi, ed. 1971. *Price Indexes and Quality Change*. Cambridge, MA: Harvard University Press.

Hersch, Joni, and W. Kip Viscusi. 1990. "Cigarette Smoking, Seatbelt Use and Differences in Wage-Risk Tradeoffs," 25 *Journal of Human Resources* 202–27.

Ippolito, Pauline M., and Richard A. Ippolito. 1984. "Measuring the Value of Life Saving from Consumer Reactions to New Information," 25 *Journal of Public Economics* 53–81.

Jones-Lee, Michael W. 1989. *The Economics of Safety and Physical Risk*. Oxford: Basil Blackwell.

Keeney, Ralph L. 1990. "Mortality Risks Induced by Economic Expenditures," 10 *Risk Analysis* 147–59.

Kniesner, Thomas J., and John D. Leeth. 1991. "Compensating Wage Differentials for Fatal Injury Risk in Australia, Japan, and the United States," 41 *Journal of Risk and Uncertainty* 75–90.

Lutter, Randall, and John F. Morrall III. 1994. "Health-Health Analysis: A New Way to Evaluate Health and Safety Regulation," 8 *Journal of Risk and Uncertainty* 43–66.

Lutter, Randall, John F. Morrall III, and W. Kip Viscusi. 1999. "The Cost per Life Saved Cutoff for Safety-Enhancing Regulations," 37 *Economic Inquiry* 599–608.

Magat, Wesley, W. Kip Viscusi, and Joel Huber. 1996. "Reference Lottery Metric for Valuing Health," 42 *Management Science* 1118–29.

Moore, Michael J., and W. Kip Viscusi. 1988a. "Doubling the Estimated Value of Life: Results Using New Occupational Fatality Data," 7 *Journal of Policy Analysis and Management* 476–90.

———. 1988b. "The Quantity Adjusted Value of Life," 26 *Economic Inquiry* 369–88.

Olson, Craig A. 1981. "An Analysis of Wage Differentials Received by Workers on Dangerous Jobs," 16 *Journal of Human Resources* 167–85.

Polinsky, A. Mitchell. 1989. *An Introduction to Law and Economics*, 2nd ed. Boston: Little, Brown.

Portney, Paul R. 1981. "Housing Prices, Health Effects, and Valuing Reductions in Risk of Death," 8 *Journal of Environmental Economics and Management* 72–78.

Posner, Richard. 1998. *Economic Analysis of Law*, 5th ed. New York: Aspen.

Rice, Dorothy, and Barbara Cooper. 1967. "The Economic Value of Life," 57 *American Journal of Public Health* 1954–66.

Rosen, Sherwin. 1986. "The Theory of Equalizing Differences," in Orley Ashenfelter and Richard Layard, eds., *Handbook of Labor Economics*. Amsterdam: North-Holland.

Schelling, Thomas. 1968. "The Life You Save May Be Your Own," in S. Chase, ed., *Problems in Public Expenditure Analysis*, Washington, DC: Brookings Institution.

Schwartz, Gary T. 1991. "The Myth of the Ford Pinto Case," 43 *Rutgers Law Review* 1013–68.

Shavell, Steven. 1987. *Economic Analysis of Accident Law*. Cambridge, MA: Harvard University Press.

Sloan, Frank, W. Kip Viscusi, Harrell Chesson, C. J. Conover, and Kate Whetton-Goldstein. 1998. "Alternative Approaches to Valuing Intangible Health Losses: The Evidence from Multiple Sclerosis," 17 *Journal of Health Economics* 475–97.

Smith, Adam. [1776] 1937. *The Wealth of Nations*. New York: Modern Library.

Smith, Robert S. 1974. "The Feasibility of an 'Injury Tax' Approach to Occupational Safety," 38 *Law and Contemporary Problems* 730–44.

———. 1976. *The Occupational Safety and Health Act*. Washington, DC: American Enterprise Institute.

Stokey, Edith, and Richard J. Zeckhauser. 1978. *A Primer for Policy Analysis*. New York: Norton.

Thaler, Richard, and Sherwin Rosen. 1976. "The Value of Saving a Life: Evidence from the Labor Market," in Nestor E. Terleckyj, ed., *Household Production and Consumption*. Cambridge, MA: National Bureau of Economic Research.

Viscusi, W. Kip. 1978. "Wealth Effects and Earnings Premiums for Job Hazards," 60 *Review of Economics and Statistics* 408–16.

———. 1979. *Employment Hazards: An Investigation of Market Performance*. Cambridge, MA: Harvard University Press.

———. 1981. "Occupational Safety and Health Regulations: Its Impact and Policy Alternatives," in J. Crecine, ed., *Research in Public Policy Analysis and Management*. Vol. 2, Greenwich, CT: JAI Press.

———. 1991. *Reforming Products Liability*. Cambridge, MA: Harvard University Press.

———. 1992. *Fatal Tradeoffs: Public and Private Responsibilities for Risk*. New York: Oxford University Press.

———. 1994a. "Mortality Effects of Regulatory Costs and Policy Evaluation Criteria," 25 *Rand Journal of Economics* 94–109.

———. 1994b. "Risk-Risk Analysis," 8 *Journal of Risk and Uncertainty* 5–17.

Viscusi, W. Kip, and William Evans. 1990. "Utility Functions that Depend on Health Status: Estimates and Economic Implications," 80 *American Economic Review* 353–74.

Viscusi, W. Kip, John K. Hakes, and Alan Carlin. 1997. "Measures of Mortality," 14 *Journal of Risk and Uncertainty* 228–29.

Viscusi, W. Kip, Wesley Magat, and Joel Huber. 1991. "Pricing Environmental Health Risks: Survey Assessments of Risk-Risk and Risk-Dollar Trade-offs for Chronic Bronchitis," 21 *Journal of Environmental Economics and Management* 32–51.

Viscusi, W. Kip, and Michael J. Moore. 1989. "Rates of Time Preference and Valuations of Duration of Life," 38 *Journal of Public Economics* 297–317.

Viscusi, W. Kip, and Richard J. Zeckhauser. 1994. "The Fatality and Injury Costs of Expenditures," 8 *Journal of Risk and Uncertainty* 19–41.

Ward, John. 1992. "A Review of Case Law," in John O. Ward and Thomas R. Ireland, eds., *The New Hedonics Primer for Economists and Attorneys*, 2nd ed. Tucson, AZ: Lawyers and Judges Publishing.

Wildavsky, Aaron. 1988. *Searching for Safety*. New Brunswick, NJ: Transaction Publishers.

Case Reference

UAW v. OSHA, United States Court of Appeals for the District of Columbia Circuit, 89–1559.

IV

The Goals of Environmental Policy: Economic Efficiency and Benefit-Cost Analysis

12   Is There a Role for Benefit-Cost Analysis in Environmental, Health, and Safety Regulation?

Kenneth J. Arrow

Maureen L. Cropper

George C. Eads

Robert W. Hahn

Lester B. Lave

Roger G. Noll

Paul R. Portney

Milton Russell

Richard Schmalensee

V. Kerry Smith

Robert N. Stavins

Kenneth J. Arrow is Joan Kenney Professor of Economics Emeritus at Stanford University; Maureen L. Cropper is Professor of Economics at the University of Maryland, and Principal Economist in the Research Department of the World Bank; George C. Eads is Vice President of Charles River Associates, Washington, D.C.; Robert W. Hahn is Resident Scholar at the American Enterprise Institute, and Director of the AEI-Brookings Joint Center for Regulatory Studies; Lester B. Lave is James Higgins Professor of Economics and Finance, Professor of Urban and Public Affairs, and Professor of Engineering and Public Policy at Carnegie-Mellon University; Roger G. Noll is Morris M. Doyle Professor of Public Policy, Department of Economics and director, Stanford Center for International Development at Stanford University; Paul R. Portney is President and Senior Fellow at Resources for the Future; Milton Russell is Senior Fellow at the Joint Institute for Energy and Environment, and Professor Emeritus of Economics at the University of Tennessee; Richard Schmalensee is Dean of the Sloan School of Management at the Massachusetts Institute of Technology; V. Kerry Smith is a University Distinguished Professor at North Carolina State University; and Robert N. Stavins is Albert Pratt Professor of Business and Government, John F. Kennedy School of Government at Harvard University, and University Fellow at Resources for the Future.

The growing impact of regulations on the economy has led both Congress and the Administration to search for new ways of reforming the regulatory process. Many of these initiatives call for greater reliance on the use of economic analysis in the development and evaluation of regulations. One specific approach being advocated is benefit-cost analysis, an economic tool for comparing the desirable and undesirable impacts of proposed policies.

For environmental, health, and safety regulation, benefits are typically defined in terms of the value of having a cleaner environment or a safer workplace. Ideally, costs should be measured in the same terms: the losses implied by the increased prices that result from the costs of meeting a regulatory objective. In practice, the costs tend to be measured on the basis of direct compliance costs, with secondary consideration given to indirect costs, such as the value of time spent waiting in a motor vehicle inspection line.

The direct costs of federal environmental, health, and safety regulation appear to be on the order of $200 billion annually, or about the size of all domestic nondefense discretionary spending (1). The benefits of the regulations are less certain, but evidence suggests that some but not all recent regulations would pass a benefit-cost test (2). Moreover, a reallocation of expenditures on environmental, health, and safety regulations has the potential to save significant numbers of lives while using fewer resources (3). The estimated cost per statistical life saved has varied across regulations by a factor of more than $10 million (4), ranging from an estimated cost of $200,000 per statistical life saved with the Environmental Protection Agency's (EPA's) 1979 trihalomethane drinking water standard to more than $6.3 trillion with EPA's 1990 hazardous waste listing for wood-preserving chemicals (3, 5). Thus, a reallocation of priorities among these same regulations could save many more lives at the given cost, or alternatively, save the same number of lives at a much lower cost (6).

Most economists would argue that economic efficiency, measured as the difference between benefits and costs, ought to be one of the fundamental criteria for evaluating proposed environmental, health, and safety regulations. Because society has limited resources to spend on regulation, benefit-cost analysis can help illuminate the trade-offs involved in making different kinds of social investments. In this regard, it seems almost irresponsible to not conduct such analyses, because they can inform decisions about how scarce resources can be put to the greatest social good. Benefit-cost analysis can also help answer the question of how much regulation is enough. From an efficiency standpoint, the answer to this question is simple: regulate until the incremental benefits from regulation are just offset by the incremental costs. In practice, however, the problem is much more difficult, in large part because of inherent problems in measuring marginal benefits and costs. In addition, concerns about fairness and process may be important noneconomic factors that merit consideration. Regulatory policies inevitably involve winners and losers, even when aggregate benefits exceed aggregate costs (7).

Over the years, policy-makers have sent mixed signals regarding the use of benefit-cost analysis in policy evaluation. Congress has passed several statutes to protect health, safety, and the environment that effectively preclude the consideration of benefits and costs in the development of certain regulations, even though other statutes actually require the use of benefit-cost analysis (8). Meanwhile, former presidents Carter, Reagan, and Bush and President Clinton have all introduced formal processes for reviewing economic implications of major environmental, health, and safety regulations. Apparently the Executive Branch, charged with designing and implementing regulations, has seen a need to develop a yardstick against which the efficiency of regulatory proposals can be assessed. Benefit-cost analysis has been the yardstick of choice (9).

We suggest that benefit-cost analysis has a potentially important role to play in helping inform regulatory decision-making, although it should not be the sole basis for such decision-making. We offer the following eight principles on the appropriate use of benefit-cost analysis (10).

1. Benefit-cost analysis is useful for comparing the favorable and unfavorable effects of policies. Benefit-cost analysis can help decision-makers better understand the implications of decisions by identifying and, where appropriate, quantifying the favorable and unfavorable consequences of a proposed policy change, even when information on benefits and costs, is highly uncertain. In some cases, however, benefit-cost analysis cannot be used to conclude that the economic benefits of a decision will exceed or fall short of its costs, because there is simply too much uncertainty.

2. Decision-makers should not be precluded from considering the economic costs and benefits of different policies in the development of regulations. Agencies should be allowed to use economic analysis to help set regulatory priorities. Removing statutory prohibitions on the balancing of benefits and costs can help promote more efficient and effective regulation. Congress could further promote more effective use of resources by explicitly asking agencies to consider benefits and costs in formulating their regulatory priorities.

3. Benefit-cost analysis should be required for all major regulatory decisions. Although the precise definition of "major" requires judgment (11), this general requirement should be applied to all government agencies. The scale of a benefit-cost analysis should depend on both the stakes involved and the likelihood that the resulting information will affect the ultimate decision. For example, benefit-cost analyses of policies intended to retard or halt depletion of stratospheric ozone were worthwhile because of the large stakes involved and the potential for influencing public policy.

4. Although agencies should be required to conduct benefit-cost analyses for major decisions and to explain why they have selected actions for which reliable evidence indicates that expected benefits are significantly less than expected costs, those agencies should not be bound by strict benefit-cost tests. Factors other than aggregate economic benefits and costs, such as equity within and across generations, may be important in some decisions.

5. Benefits and costs of proposed policies should be quantified wherever possible. Best estimates should be presented along with a description of the uncertainties. In most instances, it should be possible to describe the effects of proposed policy changes in quantitative terms; however, not all impacts can be quantified, let alone be given a monetary value. Therefore, care should be taken to assure that quantitative factors do not dominate important qualitative factors in decision-making. If an agency wishes to introduce a "margin of safety" into a decision, it should do so explicitly (*12*).

Whenever possible, values used to quantify benefits and costs in monetary terms should be based on trade-offs that individuals would make, either directly or, as is often the case, indirectly in labor, housing, or other markets (*13*). Benefit-cost analysis is premised on the notion that the values to be assigned to program effects—favorable or unfavorable—should be those of the affected individuals, not the values held by economists, moral philosophers, environmentalists, or others.

6. The more external review that regulatory analyses receive, the better they are likely to be. Historically, the U.S. Office of Management and Budget has played a key role in reviewing selected major regulations, particularly those aimed at protecting the environment, health, and safety. Peer review of economic analyses should be used for regulations with potentially large economic impacts (*14*). Retrospective assessments of selected regulatory impact analyses should be carried out periodically.

7. A core set of economic assumptions should be used in calculating benefits and costs. Key variables include the social discount rate, the value of reducing risks of premature death and accidents, and the values associated with other improvements in health. It is important to be able to compare results across analyses, and a common set of economic assumptions increases the feasibility of such comparisons. In addition, a common set of appropriate economic assumptions can improve the quality of individual analyses. A single agency should establish a set of default values for typical benefits and costs and should develop a standard format for presenting results.

Both economic efficiency and intergenerational equity require that benefits and costs experienced in future years be given less weight in decision-making than those experienced today. The rate at which future benefits and costs should be discounted to present values will generally not equal the rate of return on private investment. The discount rate should instead be based on how individuals trade off current for future consumption. Given uncertainties in identifying the correct discount rate, it is appropriate to use a range of rates. Ideally, the same range of discount rates should be used in all regulatory analyses.

8. Although benefit-cost analysis should focus primarily on the overall relation between benefits and costs, a good analysis will also identify

important distributional consequences. Available data often permit reliable estimation of major policy impacts on important subgroups of the population (*15*). On the other hand, environmental, health, and safety regulations are neither effective nor efficient tolls for achieving redistributional goals.

Conclusion. Benefit-cost analysis can play an important role in legislative and regulatory policy debates on protecting and improving health, safety, and the natural environment. Although formal benefit-cost analysis should not be viewed as either necessary or sufficient for designing sensible public policy, it can provide an exceptionally useful framework for consistently organizing disparate information, and in this way, it can greatly improve the process and, hence, the outcome of policy analysis. If properly done, benefit-cost analysis can be of great help to agencies participating in the development of environmental, health, and safety regulations, and it can likewise be useful in evaluating agency decision-making and in shaping statutes.

References and Notes

1. T. D. Hopkins, "Cost of Regulation: Filling in the Gaps" (report prepared for the Regulatory Information Service Center, Rochester, NY, 1992); Office of Management and Budget, *Budget of the United States Government, Fiscal Year 1996* (Government Printing Office, Washington, DC, 1995).
2. R. W. Hahn, in *Risks, Costs, and Lives Saved: Getting Better Results from Regulation*. R. W. Hahn, Ed. (Oxford Univ. Press, Oxford, and AEI Press, Washington, DC, in press).
3. J. F. Morrall, *Regulation 10*, 25 (November–December 1986).
4. These figures represent the incremental direct cost of part or all of proposed regulations relative to specified baselines. For examinations of issues associated with estimating the full costs of environmental protection, see (*16*).
5. Office of Management and Budget, *Regulatory Program of the United States Government: April 1, 1992–March 31, 1993* (Government Printing Office, Washington, DC, 1993).
6. If the goals of a program or the level of a particular standard have been specified, economic analysis can still play an important role in evaluating the costs of various approaches for achieving these goals. Too frequently, regulation has used a one-size-fits-all or command-and-control approach to achieve specified goals. Cost-effectiveness analysis, which identifies the minimum-cost means to achieve a given goal, can aid in designing more flexible approaches, such as using markets and performance standards that reward results.
7. L. Lave, in (*2*).
8. Several statutes have been interpreted to restrict the ability of regulators to consider benefits and costs. Examples include the Federal Food, Drug, and Cosmetic Act (Delaney Clause); health standards under the Occupational Safety and Health Act; safety regulations from the National Highway and Transportation Safety Agency; the Clean Air Act; the Clean Water Act; the Resource Conservation and Recovery Act; the Safe Drinking Water Act; and the Comprehensive Environmental Response, Compensation, and Liability Act. On the other hand,

the Consumer Product Safety Act, the Toxic Substances Control Act, and the Federal Insecticide, Fungicide, and Rodenticide Act explicitly allow regulators to consider benefits and costs.

9. In particular cases, such as the phasing out of lead in gasoline and the banning of certain asbestos products, benefit-cost analysis has played an important role in decision-making (17).

10. For a more extended discussion, see (18).

11. In this context, "major" has traditionally been defined in terms of annual economic impacts on the cost side.

12. For example, potentially irreversible consequences are not outside the scope of benefit-cost analysis. The combination of irreversibilities and uncertainty can have significant effects on valuation.

13. For a conceptual overview of methods of estimating the benefits of environmental regulation and a brief survey of empirical estimates, see (19). For examinations of regulatory costs, see (16).

14. For a description of problems that arise when benefit-cost analysis is used in the absence of standardized peer review, see (20).

15. G. B. Christiansen and T. H. Tietenberg, in Handbook of Natural Resource and Energy Economics, A. V. Kneese and J. L. Sweeney, Eds. (North-Holland, Amsterdam, 1985), vol. 1, pp. 345–393.

16. R. Schmalensee, in Balancing Economic Growth and Environmental Goals, M. B. Kotowski, Ed. (American Council for Capital Formation, Center for Policy Research, Washington, DC, 1994), pp. 55–75; A. B. Jaffe, S. R. Peterson, P. R. Portney, R. N. Stavins, J. Econ. Lit. 33, 132 (1995).

17. A. Fraas, Law Contemp. Probl. 54, 113 (1991).

18. K. J. Arrow et al., Benefit-Cost Analysis in Environmental, Health, and Safety Regulation (AEI Press, Washington, DC, 1996).

19. M. L. Cropper and W. E. Oates, J. Econ. Lit. 30, 675 (1992); A. M. Freeman, The Measurement of Environmental and Resource Values (Resources for the Future, Washington, DC, 1993).

20. W. N. Grubb, D. Whittington, M. Humphries, in Environmental Policy Under Reagan's Executive Order: The Role of Benefit-Cost Analysis. V. K. Smith, Ed. (Univ. of North Carolina Press, Chapel Hill, 1984), pp. 121–164.

21. This work was sponsored by the American Enterprise Institute, the Annapolis Center, and Resources for the Future, with funding provided by the Annapolis Center. The manuscript benefited from comments from an editor and a referee, but the authors alone are responsible for the final product.

13 _An Eye on the Future_

Lawrence H. Goulder
Robert N. Stavins

Lawrence H. Goulder is in the Department of Economics and the Institute for International Studies, Stanford University. Robert N. Stavins is at the John F. Kennedy School of Government, Harvard University.

Decisions made today usually have impacts both now and in the future. But in carrying out policy evaluations to help decision-makers, economic analysts typically discount future impacts. In the environmental realm, many of the future impacts are benefits from policy-induced improvements. Thus, in the environmental-policy context, future benefits (as well as costs) are often discounted.

This is controversial, partly because discounting can seem to give insufficient weight to future benefits and thus to the well-being of future generations. But does it actually shortchange the future? As economists, we have often encountered scepticism about discounting, particularly from non-economists. Some of this scepticism seems valid, yet some reflects misconceptions about the nature and purpose of discounting. By examining here how discounting affects the evaluation of environmental policies, we hope to clarify this concept.

It helps to begin by considering the use of discounting in private investments. Here, the rationale stems from the fact that capital is productive—money earns interest. Consider a company deciding whether to invest $1 million in the purchase of a copper mine, and suppose that the most profitable strategy involves extracting the available copper three years from now, yielding revenues (net of extraction costs) of $1,150,000. Would investing in this mine make sense? Assume that the company has the alternative of putting the $1 million in the bank at 5% annual interest. Then, on a purely financial basis, the company would do better with the bank, as after three years it will have $1,157,625 ($1,000,000 × (1.05)^3), compared with only $1,150,000 if it invests in the mine.

"An Eye on the Future," by Lawrence H. Goulder and Robert N. Stavins, from _Nature_, 419:673–674 (October 2002).

Future Returns

We compared these alternatives by compounding to the future the up-front cost of the project. It is mathematically equivalent to compare the options by discounting to the present the future revenues or benefits from the mine. Discounting offers a quick way to check whether the return on a project is greater or less than the interest rate by taking future revenues and translating them into present units, using the "alternative rate of return" (the bank's rate of interest in our example) as the discount rate. So the discounted revenue in this case is $1,150,000 divided by $(1.05)^3$, or $993,413— less than the cost of the investment. Thus, the project would not earn as much as the alternative of putting money in the bank. If the discounted revenue exceeded the cost of the project, then the project would yield a higher return than the bank, and the company would be better off investing in the mine.

This simple example suggests a general formula to determine whether an investment offers a return that is greater or less than the alternative of putting money in the bank. Suppose a project involves benefits (revenues) and costs over a time span from the present (time 0) to T years from now. Let B_t and C_t refer, respectively, to the benefit and cost t years from now, and let r represent the annual rate of return on a standard investment. The present value of the net benefit (PVNB) is given by

$$\text{PVNB} = \sum_{t=0}^{T} (B_t - C_t)/(1 + r)^t$$

If this value is positive, the project will yield a return that is higher than the market interest rate.

Discounting translates future sums of money into equivalent current sums; it undoes the effects of compound interest. It is not aimed at accounting for inflation, as even if there were no inflation it would still be necessary to discount future revenues to account for the fact that a dollar today translates (through interest) into more dollars in the future.

Sums for Society

Can the same kind of thinking be applied to investments made by the public sector for the benefit of society? Consider the following hypothetical public-sector investment: a potential climate policy. Our purpose is to convey key issues in the starkest terms, so we will intentionally oversimplify some aspects of what follows. Suppose that a policy, if introduced today and maintained, would avoid significant damage to the environment and human welfare 100 years from now. The "return on investment" is the avoidance of future damage to the environment and to people's well-being. Suppose that this policy costs $4 billion to implement, and that this cost is borne in its entirety today. Suppose also that the beneficial impacts—

avoided damages to the environment—will be worth $800 billion to people alive 100 years from now. Should the policy be implemented?

The answer will depend, of course, on the evaluation criteria used. Consider first the criterion of whether the winners have the potential to compensate the losers and still be no worse off. For this condition to be met, the benefit to the winners, after being translated to equivalent dollars, needs to be larger than the losses of the losers. After compensation from winners to losers, the policy would yield what economists call a "Pareto improvement": some individuals would be better off, and no individual would be worse off.

Are the benefits great enough that the winners could potentially compensate the losers and still be no worse off? Here, discounting is helpful. If, over the next 100 years, the average rate of interest on ordinary investments is 5%, a gain of $800 billion to people 100 years from now is equivalent to $6.08 billion today. (Equivalently, $6.08 billion today, compounded at an annual interest rate of 5%, will become $800 billion in 100 years). The project satisfies the principle of potential compensation if it costs the current generation less than $6.08 billion.

Because the up-front cost of $4 billion is indeed less than this figure, the benefit to future generations is more than enough to offset the cost to the current one. More generally, a positive PVNB means that the policy has the potential to yield a Pareto improvement. More realistic policies involve costs and benefits that occur at all points in time. For these policies, discounting serves the same purpose, as we convert costs and benefits from various periods into their equivalents at a given time (such as the present, for example).

Applying a discount rate does not mean giving less weight to the welfare of future generations. Rather, the process simply converts the (full) values of the impacts that occur at different points of time into common units. In our example, the full benefit to future generations is translated into a current monetary sum, which then allows us to compare this benefit with the full cost to the present generation.

Winners and Losers

Even if one accepts the idea of discounting as a mechanism to translate impacts into equivalent monetary units, one might be uneasy about PVNB analysis, which is based on the potential Pareto improvement (PPI) criterion—whether the winners from a given policy could compensate the losers and still be better off. If a policy's benefits exceed its costs, and compensation is introduced so that no one is worse off, then the attractiveness of the policy seems clear. But if compensation is not actually made, the appeal seems considerably weaker.

In our climate-policy example, discounted benefits to future generations will exceed the loss to the current generation, so the potential exists for a Pareto improvement—the PPI criterion is met. But if future generations do not actually compensate the present one, is it still appropriate to enact the policy? Perhaps so, but many would argue that if actual compensation cannot be made, a positive PVNB has less merit as an evaluation criterion.

Suppose a proposed climate policy fails the PPI test—the future benefits are not large enough to offset current costs. Do current generations nevertheless have an obligation to undertake the policy? They might. The PPI criterion deserves to be given weight, but in almost all policy evaluations—especially when compensation is not actually carried out—it is important to consider other evaluation criteria, as there are bound to be some cases in which there are compelling reasons for adopting a policy even when the PPI criterion is not satisfied, or for rejecting a policy even when it is.

Should a lower discount rate be used to incorporate considerations of intergenerational equity more fully in the PVNB calculation? Suppose that, when the market interest rate is used for discounting, a policy that would benefit future generations fails to generate a positive PVNB. Using a lower discount rate would give greater weight to future benefits (and costs), possibly making the PVNB positive. Such adjustments are problematic, however: they blur the distinction between the PPI (efficiency) criterion and other legitimate policy-evaluation criteria, such as distributional (in this case, intergenerational) equity. In evaluating policies, it seems better to use the market interest rate so that the PVNB calculation provides a meaningful indication of whether the PPI criterion is satisfied, while at the same time judging intergenerational fairness by direct examination.

Even if one accepts the use of the PPI criterion and discounting in principle, estimates of PVNB are necessarily imprecise. There is uncertainty about the denominator—the discount rate. Theoretically, this should reflect the market interest rate but, of course, future market rates are impossible to predict. There is also considerable uncertainty about the elements in the numerator—the benefits and costs that current and future generations will experience from a policy that is introduced today. This uncertainty is derived both from scientific uncertainty about the biophysical impacts of policies and from uncertainty about future generations' tastes and preferences—how much they will value the biophysical impacts.

Much scepticism about the discounting and, more broadly, the use of benefit–cost analysis, is connected to these uncertainties. Consider the difficulties of ascertaining, for example, the benefits that future generations would enjoy from a regulation that protects certain endangered species. Some of the gain to future generations might come in the form of medical products (such as serums or vaccines) derived from the protected species, but such future impacts are impossible to predict. Moreover, benefits reflect the value that future generations will attach to the protected species—the enjoyment of observing them in the wild or just knowing of their existence. But how can we predict future generations' values? Economists and other social scientists try to infer them through surveys (such as the contingent valuation method) and by inferring preferences from individuals' behaviour. But these approaches are far from perfect, and at best they indicate only the values or tastes of people alive today.

The uncertainties are substantial and unavoidable. They do not invalidate the use of discounting or benefit–cost analysis, but they do oblige analysts to acknowledge them in their policy evaluations. It is crucial to evaluate policies using a range of values for discount rates and for future benefits and costs. We should have less confidence in a project for which the sign of the PVNB is highly sensitive to the discount rate or to small changes in projected future benefits and costs, compared with a project with a PVNB that is not very sensitive to these elements.

The Discounting Debate

The application of discounting to environmental-policy evaluation is controversial, partly because of misunderstanding outside the economics community of what discounting actually does, which is to translate the values of future impacts into equivalent values in today's monetary units. The PPI criterion, which provides the rationale for discounting and calculation of the PVNB, deserves weight in evaluating environmental policies, although it is also important to consider other criteria (such as distributional equity), especially when the potential harm to "losers" is substantial. Moreover, it is crucial to acknowledge any uncertainties about benefits, costs and interest rates. Some may argue that these complications invalidate PVNB calculations, but in our view such calculations—when carefully executed and thoughtfully interpreted—can provide useful information for making environmental-policy decisions.

Further Reading

Arrow, K. J. et al. in *Climate Change 1995: Economic and Social Dimensions of Climate Change* (eds. Bruce, J. P. et al.) 125–144 (Cambridge Univ. Press, 1996).
Arrow, K. J. et al. *Science 272*, 221–222 (1996).
Fullerton, D. & Stavins, R. *Nature 395*, 433–434 (1998).
Portney, P. R. & Weyant, J. P. *Discounting and Intergenerational Equity* (Resources for the Future, Washington DC, 1999).
Weitzman, M. L. *J. Environ. Econ. Management 36*, 201–208 (1998).

14   *Cost-Benefit Analysis:*
An Ethical Critique
(with replies) *

Steven Kelman

*Steven Kelman is Albert J. Weatherhead III and Richard W. Weatherhead
Professor of Public Management at the John F. Kennedy School of
Government, Harvard University.*

At the broadest and vaguest level, cost-benefit analysis may be regarded
simply as systematic thinking about decision-making. Who can oppose,
economists sometimes ask, efforts to think in a systematic way about the
consequences of different courses of action? The alternative, it would appear, is unexamined decision-making. But defining cost-benefit analysis
so simply leaves it with few implications for actual regulatory decision-
making. Presumably, therefore, those who urge regulators to make greater
use of the technique have a more extensive prescription in mind. I assume
here that their prescription includes the following views:

(1) There exists a strong presumption that an act should not be undertaken unless its benefits outweigh its costs.

(2) In order to determine whether benefits outweigh costs, it is desirable
to attempt to express all benefits and costs in a common scale or denominator, so that they can be compared with each other, even when
some benefits and costs are not traded on markets and hence have
no established dollar values.

(3) Getting decision-makers to make more use of cost-benefit techniques
is important enough to warrant both the expense required to gather
the data for improved cost-benefit estimation and the political efforts
needed to give the activity higher priority compared to other activities, also valuable in and of themselves.

My focus is on cost-benefit analysis as applied to environmental, safety,
and health regulation. In that context, I examine each of the above propositions from the perspective of formal ethical theory, that is, the study of
what actions it is morally right to undertake. My conclusions are:

"Cost-Benefit Analysis: An Ethical Critique," by Steven Kelman, from *AEI Journal on Government and
Society Regulation* (January/February 1981) pp. 33–40. Reprinted with permission of the American
Enterprise Institute for Public Policy Research, Washington, D.C.

*Including replies printed in the *AEI Journal*, March/April 1981 issue.

(1) In areas of environmental, safety, and health regulation, there may be many instances where a certain decision might be right even though its benefits do not outweigh its costs.

(2) There are good reasons to oppose efforts to put dollar values on non-marketed benefits and costs.

(3) Given the relative frequency of occasions in the areas of environmental, safety, and health regulation where one would not wish to use a benefits-outweigh-costs test as a decision rule, and given the reasons to oppose the monetizing of non-marketed benefits or costs that is a prerequisite for cost-benefit analysis, it is not justifiable to devote major resources to the generation of data for cost-benefit calculations or to undertake efforts to "spread the gospel" of cost-benefit analysis further.

I

How do we decide whether a given action is morally right or wrong and hence, assuming the desire to act morally, why it should be undertaken or refrained from? Like the Molière character who spoke prose without knowing it, economists who advocate use of cost-benefit analysis for public decisions are philosophers without knowing it: the answer given by cost-benefit analysis, that actions should be undertaken so as to maximize net benefits, represents one of the classic answers given by moral philosophers—that given by utilitarians. To determine whether an action is right or wrong, utilitarians tote up all the positive consequences of the action in terms of human satisfaction. The act that maximizes attainment of satisfaction under the circumstances is the right act. That the economists' answer is also the answer of one school of philosophers should not be surprising. Early on, economics was a branch of moral philosophy, and only later did it become an independent discipline.

Before proceeding further, the subtlety of the utilitarian position should be noted. The positive and negative consequences of an act for satisfaction may go beyond the act's immediate consequences. A facile version of utilitarianism would give moral sanction to a lie, for instance, if the satisfaction of an individual attained by telling the lie was greater than the suffering imposed on the lie's victim. Few utilitarians would agree. Most of them would add to the list of negative consequences the effect of the one lie on the tendency of the person who lies to tell other lies, even in instances when the lying produced less satisfaction for him than dissatisfaction for others. They would also add the negative effects of the lie on the general level of social regard for truth-telling, which has many consequences for future utility. A further consequence may be added as well. It is sometimes said that we should include in a utilitarian calculation the feeling of dissatisfaction produced in the liar (and perhaps in others) because, by telling a lie, one has "done the wrong thing." Correspondingly, in this view, among the positive consequences to be weighed into a utilitarian calculation of truth-telling is satisfaction arising from "doing the right thing." This view rests on an error, however, because it *assumes* what it is the purpose of the calculation to *determine*—that telling the truth in the instance in question is indeed the right thing to do. Economists are likely to object to this point, arguing that no feeling ought "arbitrarily" to be excluded from a complete cost-benefit calculation, including a feeling of dissatisfaction at doing the wrong thing. Indeed, the economists' cost-benefit calculations would, at least ideally, include such feelings. Note the difference between the economist's and the philosopher's cost-benefit calculations, however. The economist may choose to include feelings of dissatisfaction in his cost-benefit calculation, but what happens if somebody asks the economist, "Why is it right to evaluate an action on the basis of a cost-benefit test?" If an answer is to be given to that question (which does not normally preoccupy economists but which does concern both philosophers and the rest of us who need to be persuaded that cost-benefit analysis is right), then the circularity problem reemerges. And there is also another difficulty with counting feelings of dissatisfaction at doing the wrong thing in a cost-benefit calculation. It leads to the perverse result that under certain circumstances a lie, for example, might be morally right if the individual contemplating the lie felt no compunction about lying and morally wrong only if the individual felt such a compunction!

This error is revealing, however, because it begins to suggest a critique of utilitarianism. Utilitarianism is an important and powerful moral doctrine. But it is probably a minority position among contemporary moral philosophers. It is amazing that economists can proceed in unanimous endorsement of cost-benefit analysis as if unaware that their conceptual framework is highly controversial in the discipline from which it arose— moral philosophy.

Let us explore the critique of utilitarianism. The logical error discussed before appears to suggest that we have a notion of certain things being right or wrong that *predates* our calculation of costs and benefits. Imagine the case of an old man in Nazi Germany who is hostile to the regime. He is wondering whether he should speak out against Hitler. If he speaks out, he will lose his pension. And his action will have done nothing to increase the chances that the Nazi regime will be overthrown: he is regarded as somewhat eccentric by those around him, and nobody has ever consulted his views on political questions. Recall that one cannot add to the benefits of speaking out any satisfaction from doing "the right thing," because the purpose of the exercise is to determine whether speaking out *is* the right thing. How would the utilitarian calculation go? The benefits of the old man's speaking out would, as the example is presented, be nil, while the costs would be his loss of his pension. So the costs of the action would outweigh the benefits. By the utilitarians' cost-benefit calculation, it would be *morally wrong* for the man to speak out.

Another example: two very close friends are on an Arctic expedition together. One of them falls very sick in the snow and bitter cold, and sinks quickly before anything can be done to help him. As he is dying, he asks his friend one thing, "Please, make me a solemn promise that ten years from today you will come back to this spot and place a lighted candle here to remember me." The friend solemnly promises to do so, but does not tell a soul. Now, ten years later, the friend must decide whether to keep his promise. It would be inconvenient for him to make the long trip. Since he told nobody, his failure to go will not affect the general social faith in promise-keeping. And the incident was unique enough so that it is safe to assume that his failure to go will not encourage him to break other promises. Again, the costs of the act outweigh the benefits. A utilitarian would need to believe that it would be *morally wrong* to travel to the Arctic to light the candle.

A third example: a wave of thefts has hit a city and the police are having trouble finding any of the thieves. But they believe, correctly, that punishing someone for theft will have some deterrent effect and will decrease the number of crimes. Unable to arrest any actual perpetrator, the police chief and the prosecutor arrest a person whom they know to be innocent and, in cahoots with each other, fabricate a convincing case against him. The police chief and the prosecutor are about to retire, so the act has no effect on any future actions of theirs. The fabrication is perfectly executed, so nobody finds out about it. Is the *only* question involved in judging the act of framing the innocent man that of whether his suffering from conviction and imprisonment will be greater than the suffering avoided among potential crime victims when some crimes are deterred? A utilitarian would need to believe that it is *morally right to punish the innocent man* as long as it can be demonstrated that the suffering prevented outweighs his suffering.

And a final example: imagine two worlds, each containing the same sum total of happiness. In the first world, this total of happiness came about from a series of acts that included a number of lies and injustices (that is, the total consisted of the immediate gross sum of happiness created by certain acts, minus any long-term unhappiness occasioned by the lies and injustices). In the second world the same amount of happiness was produced by a different series of acts, none of which involved lies or injustices. Do we have any reason to prefer the one world to the other? A utilitarian would need to believe that the choice between the two worlds is a *matter of indifference.*

To those who believe that it would not be morally wrong for the old man to speak out in Nazi Germany or for the explorer to return to the Arctic to light a candle for his deceased friend, that it would not be morally right to convict the innocent man, or that the choice between the two worlds is not a matter of indifference—to those of us who believe these things, utilitarianism is insufficient as a moral view. We believe that some acts whose costs are greater than their benefits may be morally right and, contrariwise, some acts whose benefits are greater than their costs may be morally wrong.

This does not mean that the question whether benefits are greater than costs is morally irrelevant. Few would claim such. Indeed, for a broad range of individual and social decisions, whether an act's benefits outweigh its

doesn't include people's rights or duties that are right

costs is a sufficient question to ask. But not for all such decisions. These may involve situations where certain duties—duties not to lie, break promises, or kill, for example—make an act wrong, even if it would result in an excess of benefits over costs. Or they may involve instances where people's rights are at stake. We would not permit rape even if it could be demonstrated that the rapist derived enormous happiness from his act, while the victim experienced only minor displeasure. We do not do cost-benefit analyses of freedom of speech or trial by jury. The Bill of Rights was not RARGed. As the United Steelworkers noted in a comment on the Occupational Safety and Health Administration's economic analysis of its proposed rule to reduce worker exposure to carcinogenic coke-oven emissions, the Emancipation Proclamation was not subjected to an inflationary impact statement. The notion of human rights involves the idea that people may make certain claims to be allowed to act in certain ways or to be treated in certain ways, even if the sum of benefits achieved thereby does not outweigh the sum of costs. It is this view that underlies the statement that "workers have a right to a safe and healthy work place" and the expectation that OSHA's decisions will reflect that judgment.

In the most convincing versions of nonutilitarian ethics, various duties or rights are not absolute. But each has a *prima facie* moral validity so that, if duties or rights do not conflict, the morally right act is the act that reflects a duty or respects a right. If duties or rights do conflict, a moral judgment, based on conscious deliberation, must be made. Since one of the duties non-utilitarian philosophers enumerate is the duty of beneficence (the duty to maximize happiness), which in effect incorporates all of utilitarianism by reference, a non-utilitarian who is faced with conflicts between the results of cost-benefit analysis and nonutility-based considerations will need to undertake such deliberation. But in that deliberation, additional elements, which cannot be reduced to a question of whether benefits outweigh costs, have been introduced. Indeed, depending on the moral importance we attach to the right or duty involved, cost-benefit questions may, within wide ranges, become irrelevant to the outcome of the moral judgment.

In addition to questions involving duties and rights, there is a final sort of question where, in my view, the issue of whether benefits outweigh costs should not govern moral judgment. I noted earlier that, for the common run of questions facing individuals and societies, it is possible to begin and end our judgment simply by finding out if the benefits of the contemplated act outweigh the costs. This very fact means that one way to show the great importance, or value, attached to an area is to say that decisions involving the area should not be determined by cost-benefit calculations. This applies, I think, to the view many environmentalists have of decisions involving our natural environment. When officials are deciding what level of pollution will harm certain vulnerable people—such as asthmatics or the elderly—while not harming others, one issue involved may be the right of those people not to be sacrificed on the altar of somewhat higher living standards for the rest of us. But more broadly than this, many environ-mentalists fear that subjecting decisions about clean air or water to the cost-benefit tests that determine the general run of decisions removes those matters from the realm of specially valued things.

II

In order for cost-benefit calculations to be performed the way they are sup-posed to be, all costs and benefits must be expressed in a common mea-sure, typically dollars, including things not normally bought and sold on markets, and to which dollar prices are therefore not attached. The most dramatic example of such things is human life itself; but many of the other benefits achieved or preserved by environmental policy—such as peace and quiet, fresh-smelling air, swimmable rivers, spectacular vistas—are not traded on markets either.

Economists who do cost-benefit analysis regard the quest after dollar values for nonmarket things as a difficult challenge—but one to be met with relish. They have tried to develop methods for imputing a person's "willingness to pay" for such things, their approach generally involving a search for bundled goods that *are* traded on markets and that vary as to whether they include a feature that is, *by itself*, not marketed. Thus, fresh air is not marketed, but houses in different parts of Los Angeles that are similar except for the degree of smog are. Peace and quiet is not marketed, but similar houses inside and outside airport flight paths are. The risk of death is not marketed, but similar jobs that have different levels of risk are. Economists have produced many often ingenious efforts to impute dollar prices to non-marketed things by observing the premiums accorded homes in clean air areas over similar homes in dirty areas or the premiums paid for risky jobs over similar nonrisky jobs.

These ingenious efforts are subject to criticism on a number of tech-nical grounds. It may be difficult to control for all the dimensions of qual-ity other than the presence or absence of the non-marketed thing. More important, in a world where people have different preferences and are sub-ject to different constraints as they make their choices, the dollar value im-puted to the non-market things that most people would wish to avoid will be lower than otherwise, because people with unusually weak aversion to those things or usually strong constraints on their choices will be willing to take the bundled good in question at less of a discount than the average person. Thus, to use the property value discount of homes near airports as a measure of people's willingness to pay for quiet means to accept as a proxy for the rest of us the behavior of those least sensitive to noise, of air-port employees (who value the convenience of a near-airport location) or of others who are susceptible to an agent's assurances that "it's not so bad." To use the wage premiums accorded hazardous work as a measure of the value of life means to accept as proxies for the rest of us the choices of people who do not have many choices or who are exceptional risk-seekers.

A second problem is that the attempts of economists to measure people's willingness to pay for non-marketed things assume that there is no difference between the price a person would require for *giving up* something to which he has a preexisting right and the price he would pay to *gain* something to which he enjoys no right. Thus, the analysis assumes no difference between how much a homeowner would need to be paid in order to give up an unobstructed mountain view that he already enjoys and how much he would be willing to pay to get an obstruction moved once it is already in place. Available evidence suggests that most people would insist on being paid far more to assent to a worsening of their situation than they would be willing to pay to improve their situation. The difference arises from such factors as being accustomed to and psychologically attached to that which one believes one enjoys by right. But this creates a circularity problem for any attempt to use cost-benefit analysis to determine *whether* to assign to, say, the homeowner the right to an unobstructed mountain view. For willingness to pay will be different depending on whether the right is assigned initially or not. The value judgment about whether to assign the right must thus be made first. (In order to set an upper bound on the value of the benefit, one might hypothetically assign the right to the person and determine how much he would need to be paid to give it up.)

Third, the efforts of economists to impute willingness to pay invariably involve bundled goods exchanged in *private* transactions. Those who use figures garnered from such analysis to provide guidance for *public* decisions assume no difference between how people value certain things in private individual transactions and how they would wish those same things to be valued in public collective decisions. In making such assumptions, economists insidiously slip into their analysis an important and controversial value judgment, growing naturally out of the highly individualistic microeconomic tradition—namely, the view that there should be no difference between private behavior and the behavior we display in public social life. An alternative view—one that enjoys, I would suggest, wide resonance among citizens—would be that public, social decisions provide an opportunity to give certain things a higher valuation than we choose, for one reason or another, to given them in our private activities.

Thus, opponents of stricter regulation of health risks often argue that we show by our daily risk-taking behavior that we do not value life infinitely, and therefore our public decisions should not reflect the high value of life that proponents of strict regulation propose. However, an alternative view is equally plausible. Precisely because we fail, for whatever reasons, to give life-saving the value in everyday personal decisions that we in some general terms believe we should give it, we may wish our social decisions to provide us the occasion to display the reverence for life that we espouse but do not always show. By this view, people do not have fixed unambiguous "preferences" to which they give expression through private ac-

Using private behavior to model social choice

tivities and which therefore should be given expression in public decisions. Rather, they may have what they themselves regard as "higher" and "lower" preferences. The latter may come to the fore in private decisions, but people may want the former to come to the fore in public decisions. They may sometimes display racial prejudice, but support antidiscrimination laws. They may buy a certain product after seeing a seductive ad, but be skeptical enough of advertising to want the government to keep a close eye on it. In such cases, the use of private behavior to impute the values that should be entered for public decisions, as is done by using willingness to pay in private transactions, commits grievous offense against a view of the behavior of the citizen that is deeply engrained in our democratic tradition. It is a view that denudes politics of any independent role in society, reducing it to a mechanistic, mimicking recalculation based on private behavior.

Finally, one may oppose the effort to place prices on a non-market thing and hence in effect incorporate it into the market system out of a fear that the very act of doing so will reduce the thing's perceived value. To place a price on the benefit may, in other words, reduce the value of that benefit. Cost-benefit analysis thus maybe like the thermometer that, when placed in a liquid to be measured, itself changes the liquid's temperature.

Examples of the perceived cheapening of a thing's value by the very act of buying and selling it abound in everyday life and language. The disgust that accompanies the idea of buying and selling human beings is based on the sense that this would dramatically diminish human worth. Epithets such as "he prostituted himself," applied as linguistic analogies to people who have sold something, reflect the view that certain things should not be sold because doing so diminishes their value. Praise that is bought is worth little, even to the person buying it. A true anecdote is told of an economist who retired to another university community and complained that he was having difficulty making friends. The laconic response of a critical colleague—"If you want a friend why don't you buy yourself one"—illustrates in a pithy way the intuition that, for some things, the very act of placing a price on them reduces their perceived value.

The first reason that pricing something decreases its perceived value is that, in many circumstances, non-market exchange is associated with the production of certain values not associated with market exchange. These may include spontaneity and various other feelings that come from personal relationships. If a good becomes less associated with the production of positively valued feelings because of market exchange, the perceived value of the good declines to the extent that those feelings are valued. This can be seen clearly in instances where a thing may be transferred both by market and by non-market mechanisms. The willingness to pay for sex bought from a prostitute is less than the perceived value of the sex consummating love. (Imagine the reaction if a practitioner of cost-benefit analysis computed the benefits of sex based on the price of prostitute services.)

putting a price on a non-market thing
the very act diminishes its perceived value.

Furthermore, if one values in a general sense the existence of a non-market sector because of its connection with the production of certain valued feelings, then one ascribes added value to any non-marketed good simply as a repository of values represented by the non-market sector one wishes to preserve. This seems certainly to be the case for things in nature, such as pristine streams or undisturbed forests: for many people who value them, part of their value comes from their position as repositories of values the non-market sector represents.

The second way in which placing a market price on a thing decreases its perceived value is by removing the possibility of proclaiming that the thing is "not for sale," since things on the market by definition are for sale. The very statement that something is not for sale affirms, enhances, and protects a thing's value in a number of ways. To begin with, the statement is a way of showing that a thing is valued for its own sake, whereas selling a thing for money demonstrates that it was valued only instrumentally. Furthermore, to say that something cannot be transferred in that way places it in the exceptional category—which requires the person interested in obtaining that thing to be able to offer something else that is exceptional, rather than allowing him the easier alternative of obtaining the thing for money that could have been obtained in an affinity of ways. This enhances its value. If I am willing to say "You're a really kind person" to whoever pays me to do so, my praise loses the value that attaches to it from being exchangeable only for an act of kindness.

In addition, if we have already decided we value something highly, one way of stamping it with a cachet affirming its high value is to announce that it is "not for sale." Such an announcement does more, however, than just reflect a preexisting high valuation. It signals a thing's distinctive value to others and helps us persuade them to value the thing more highly than they otherwise might. It also expresses our resolution to safeguard that distinctive value. To state that something is not for sale is thus also a source of value for that thing, since if a thing's value is easy to affirm or protect, it will be worth more than an otherwise similar thing without such attributes.

If we proclaim that something is not for sale, we make a once-and-for-all judgment of its special value. When something is priced, the issue of its perceived value is constantly coming up, as a standing invitation to reconsider that original judgment. Were people constantly faced with questions such as "how much money could get you to give up your freedom of speech?" or "how much would you sell your vote for if you could?", the perceived value of the freedom to speak or the right to vote would soon become devastated as, in moments of weakness, people started saying "maybe it's not worth *so much* after all." Better not to be faced with the constant questioning in the first place. Something similar did in fact occur when the slogan "better red than dead" was launched by some pacifists during the Cold War. Critics pointed out that the very posing of this stark choice—in effect, "would you *really* be willing to give up your life in exchange for not living under communism?"—reduced the value people attached to freedom and thus diminished resistance to attacks on freedom.

Finally, of some things valued very highly it is stated that they are "priceless" or that they have "infinite value." Such expressions are reserved for a subset of things not for sale, such as life or health. Economists tend to scoff at talk of pricelessness. For them, saying that something is price-less is to state a willingness to trade off an infinite quantity of all other goods for one unit of the priceless good, a situation that empirically appears highly unlikely. For most people, however, the word priceless is preg-nant with meaning. Its value-affirming and value-protecting functions can-not be bestowed on expressions that merely denote a determinate, albeit high, valuation. John Kennedy in his inaugural address proclaimed that the nation was ready to "pay any price [and] bear any burden . . . to assure the survival and the success of liberty." Had he said instead that we were will-ing to "pay a high price" or "bear a large burden" for liberty, the statement would have rung hollow.

III

An objection that advocates of cost-benefit analysis might well make to the preceding argument should be considered. I noted earlier that, in cases where various non-utility-based duties or rights conflict with the maxi-mization of utility, it is necessary to make a deliberative judgment about what act is finally right. I also argued earlier that the search for commen-surability might not always be a desirable one, that the attempt to go be-yond expressing benefits in terms of (say) lives saved and costs in terms of dollars is not something devoutly to be wished.

In situations involving things that are not expressed in a common mea-sure, advocates of cost-benefit analysis argue that people making judgments "in effect" perform cost-benefit calculations anyway. If government regu-lators promulgate a regulation that saves 100 lives at a cost of $1 billion, they are "in effect" valuing a life at (a minimum of) $10 million, whether or not they say that they are willing to place a dollar value on a human life. Since, in this view, cost-benefit analysis "in effect" is inevitable, it might as well be made specific.

This argument misconstrues the real difference in the reasoning processes involved. In cost-benefit analysis, equivalencies are established in *advance* as one of the raw materials for the calculation. One determines costs and benefits, one determines equivalencies (to be able to put various costs and benefits into a common measure), and then one sets to toting things up—waiting, as it were, with bated breath for the results of the cal-culation to come out. The outcome is determined by the arithmetic; if the outcome is a close call or if one is not good at long division, one does not know how it will turn out until the calculation is finished. In the kind of deliberative judgment that is performed without a common measure, no establishment of equivalencies occurs in advance. Equivalencies are not aids to the decision process. In fact, the decision-maker might not even be aware of what the "in effect" equivalencies were, at least before they are revealed to him afterwards by someone pointing out what he had "in effect" done. The decision-maker would see himself as simply having made a deliberate judgment; the "in effect" equivalency number did not play a causal role in the decision but at most merely reflects it. Given this, the argument against making the process explicit is the one discussed earlier in the discussion of problems with putting specific quantified values on things that are not normally quantified—that the very act of doing so may serve to reduce the value of those things.

My own judgment is that modest efforts to assess levels of benefits and costs are justified, although I do not believe that government agencies ought to sponsor efforts to put dollar prices on non-market things. I also do not believe that the cry for more cost-benefit analysis in regulation is, on the whole, justified. If regulatory officials were so insensitive about regulatory costs that they did not provide acceptable raw material for deliberative judgments (even if not of a strictly cost-benefit nature), my conclusion might be different. But a good deal of research into costs and benefits already occurs—actually, far more in the U.S. regulatory process than in that of any other industrial society. The danger now would seem to come more from the other side.

Replies to Steven Kelman

From James V. DeLong, Vice President at the National Legal Center for the Public Interest

Steven Kelman's "Cost-Benefit Analysis—An Ethical Critique" presents so many targets that it is difficult to concentrate one's fire. However, four points seem worth particular emphasis:

(1) The decision to use cost-benefit analysis by no means implies adoption of the reductionist utilitarianism described by Kelman. It is based instead on the pragmatic conclusion that any value system one adopts is more likely to be promoted if one knows something about the consequences of the choices to be made. The effort to put dollar values on noneconomic benefits is nothing more than an effort to find some common measure for things that are not easily comparable when, in the real world, choice must be made. Its object is not to write a computer program but to improve the quality of difficult social choices under conditions of uncertainty, and no sensible analyst lets himself become the prisoner of the numbers.

in the real world, choices must be made
this is a tool to do just that

(2) Kelman repeatedly lapses into "entitlement" rhetoric, as if an assertion of a moral claim closes an argument. Even leaving aside the fundamental question of the philosophical basis of those entitlements, there are two major problems with this style of argument. First, it tends naturally toward all-encompassing claims.

Kelman quotes a common statement that "workers have a right to a safe and healthy workplace," a statement that contains no recognition that safety and health are not either/or conditions, that the most difficult questions involve gradations of risk, and that the very use of entitlement language tends to assume that a zero-risk level is the only acceptable one. Second, entitlement rhetoric is usually phrased in the passive voice, as if the speaker were arguing with some omnipotent god or government that is maliciously withholding the entitlement out of spite. In the real world, one persons' right is another's duty, and it often clarifies the discussion to focus more precisely on who owes this duty and what it is going to cost him or her. For example, the article posits that an issue in government decisions about acceptable pollution levels is "the right" of such vulnerable groups as asthmatics or the elderly "not to be sacrificed on the altar of somewhat higher living standards for the rest of us." This defends the entitlement by assuming the costs involved are both trivial and diffused. Suppose, though, that the price to be paid is not "somewhat higher living standards," but the jobs of a number of workers?

Kelman's counter to this seems to be that entitlements are not firm rights, but only presumptive ones that prevail in any clash with nonentitlements, and that when two entitlements collide the decision depends upon the "moral importance we attach to the right or duty involved." So the above collision would be resolved by deciding whether a job is an entitlement and, if it is, by then deciding whether jobs or air have greater "moral importance."

I agree that conflicts between such interests present difficult choices, but the quantitative questions, the cost-benefit questions, are hardly irrelevant to making them. Suppose taking X quantity of pollution from the air of a city will keep one asthmatic from being forced to leave town and cost 1,000 workers their jobs? Suppose it will keep 1,000 asthmatics from being forced out and cost one job? These are not equivalent choices, economically or morally, and the effort to decide them according to some abstract idea of moral importance only obscures the true nature of the moral problems involved.

(3) Kelman also develops the concept of things that are "specially valued," and that are somehow contaminated if thought about in monetary terms. As an approach to personal decision making, this is silly. There are many things one specially values—in the sense that one would find the effort to assign a market price to them ridiculous—which are nonetheless affected by economic factors. I may specially value a family relationship, but how often I phone is influenced by long-distance rates. I may specially value music, but be affected by the price of records or the cost of tickets at the Kennedy Center.

When translated to the realm of government decisions, however, the concept goes beyond silliness. It creates a political grotesquerie. People specially value many different things. Under Kelman's assumptions, people must, in creating a political coalition, recognize and accept as legitimate everyone's special value, without concern for cost. Therefore, everyone becomes entitled to as much of the thing he specially values as he says he specially values, and it is immoral to discuss vulgar questions of resource limitations. Any coalition built on such premises can go in either of two directions: It can try to incorporate so many different groups and interests that the absurdity of its internal contradictions becomes manifest. Or it can limit its membership at some point and decide that the special values of those left outside are not legitimate and should be sacrificed to the special values of those in the coalition. In the latter case, of course, those outside must be made scapegoats for any frustration of any group member's entitlement, a requirement that eventually leads to political polarization and a holy war between competing coalitions of special values.

(4) The decisions that must be made by contemporary government indeed involve painful choices. They affect both the absolute quantity and the distribution not only of goods and benefits, but also of physical and mental suffering. It is easy to understand why people would want to avoid making such choices and would rather act in ignorance than with knowledge and responsibility for the consequences of their choices. While this may be understandable, I do not regard it as an acceptable moral position. To govern is to choose, and government officials—whether elected or appointed—betray their obligations to the welfare of the people who hired them if they adopt a policy of happy ignorance and nonresponsibility for consequences.

The article concludes with the judgment that the present danger is too much cost-benefit analysis, not too little. But I find it hard to believe, looking around the modern world, that its major problem is that it suffers from an excess of rationality. The world's stock of ignorance is and will remain quite large enough without adding to it as a matter of deliberate policy.

From Robert M. Solow, Institute Professor of Economics Emeritus at the Massachusetts Institute of Technology

I am an economist who has no personal involvement in the practice of cost-benefit analysis, who happens to think that modern economics underplays the significance of ethical judgments both in its approach to policy and its account of individual and organizational behavior, and who once wrote in print:

> It may well be socially destructive to admit the routine exchangeability of certain things. We would prefer to maintain that they are beyond price (although this sometimes means only that we would prefer not to know what the price really is).

You might expect, therefore, that I would be in sympathy with Steven Kelman's ethical critique of cost-benefit analysis. But I found the article profoundly, and not entirely innocently, misleading. I would like to say why.

First of all, it is not the case that cost-benefit analysis works, or must work, by "monetizing" everything from mother love to patriotism. Cost-benefit analysis is needed only when society must give up some of one good thing in order to get more of another good thing. In other cases the decision is not problematical. The underlying rationale of cost-benefit analysis is that the cost of the good thing to be obtained is precisely the good thing that must or will be given up to obtain it. Wherever he reads "willingness to pay" and balks, Kelman should read "willingness to sacrifice" and feel better. In a choice between hospital beds and preventive treatment, lives are traded against lives. I suppose it is only natural that my brethren should get into the habit of measuring the sacrifice in terms of dollars forgone. In the typical instance in which someone actually does a cost-benefit analysis, the question to be decided is, say, whether the public should be taxed to pay for a water project—a context in which it does not seem far-fetched to ask whether the project will provide services for which the public would willingly pay what it would have to give up in taxes. But some less familiar unit of measurement could be used.

Let me add here, parenthetically, that I do agree with Kelman that there are situations in which the body politic's willingness to sacrifice may be badly measured by the sum of individuals' willingnesses to sacrifice in a completely "private" context. But that is at worst an error of technique, not a mistaken principle.

Second, Kelman hints broadly that "economists" are so morally numb as to believe that a routine cost-benefit analysis could justify killing widows and orphans, or abridging freedom of speech, or outlawing simple evidences of piety or friendship. But there is nothing in the theory or the practice of cost-benefit analysis to justify that judgment. Treatises on the subject make clear that certain ethical or political principles may irreversibly dominate the advantages and disadvantages capturable by cost-benefit analysis. Those treatises make a further point that Kelman barely touches on: since the benefits and the costs of a policy decision are usually enjoyed and incurred by different people, a distributional judgment has to be made which can override any simple-minded netting out. In addition, Kelman's point that people may put different values on the acquisition of a good for the first time and on the loss of a preexisting entitlement to the same good is not exactly a discovery. He should look up "compensating variation" and "equivalent variation" in a good economics textbook.

Third, Kelman ends by allowing that it is not a bad thing to have a modest amount of cost-benefit analysis going on. I would have supposed that was a fair description of the state of affairs. Do I detect a tendency to eat one's cost-benefit analysis and have it too? If not, what is the point of all the overkill? As a practical matter, the vacuum created by diminished reliance on cost-benefit analysis is likely to be filled by a poor substitute for ethically informed deliberation. Is the capering of Mr. Stockman more to Mr. Kelman's taste?

From Gerard Butters, Assistant Director for Consumer Protection at the Bureau of Economics, Federal Trade Commission; John Calfee, Resident Scholar at the American Enterprise Institute; and Pauline Ippolito, Associate Director for Special Projects at the Bureau of Economics, Federal Trade Commission

In his article, Steven Kelman argues against the increased use of cost-benefit analysis for regulatory decisions involving health, safety, and the environment. His basic contention is that these decisions are moral ones, and that cost-benefit analysis is therefore inappropriate because it requires the adoption of an unsatisfactory moral system. He supports his argument with a series of examples, most of which involve private decisions. In these situations, he asserts, cost-benefit advocates must renounce any moral qualms about lies, broken promises, and violations of human rights.

We disagree (and in doing so, we speak for ourselves, not for the Federal Trade Commission or its staff). Cost-benefit analysis is not a means for judging private decisions. It is a guide for decision making involving others, especially when the welfare of many individuals must be balanced. It is designed not to dictate individual values, but to take them into account when decisions must be made collectively. Its use is grounded on the principle that, in a democracy, government must act as an agent of the citizens.

We see no reason to abandon this principle when health and safety are involved. Consider, for example, a proposal to raise the existing federal standards on automobile safety. Higher standards will raise the costs, and hence the price, of cars. From our point of view, the appropriate policy judgment rests on whether customers will value the increased safety sufficiently to warrant the costs. Any violation of a cost-benefit criterion would require that consumers purchase something they would not voluntarily purchase or prevent them from purchasing something they want. One might argue, in the spirit of Kelman's analysis, that many consumers would want the government to impose a more stringent standard than they would choose for themselves. If so, how is the cost-safety trade-off that consumers really want to be determined? Any objective way of doing this would be a natural part of cost-benefit analysis.

Kelman also argues that the process of assigning a dollar value to things not traded in the marketplace is rife with indignities, flaws, and biases. Up to a point, we agree. It *is* difficult to place objective dollar values on certain intangible costs and benefits. Even with regard to intangibles which have been systematically studied, such as the "value of life," we know of no cost-benefit advocate who believes that regulatory staff economists should reduce every consideration to dollar terms and simply supply the decision maker with the bottom line. Our main concerns are twofold: (1) to make the major costs and benefits explicit so that the decision maker makes the trade-offs consciously and with the prospect of being held accountable, and (2) to encourage the move toward a more consistent set of standards.

The gains from adopting consistent regulatory standards can be dramatic. If costs and benefits are not balanced in making decisions, it is likely that the returns per dollar in terms of health and safety will be small for some programs and large for others. Such programs present opportunities for saving lives, and cost-benefit analysis will reveal them. Perhaps, as Kelman argues, there is something repugnant about assigning dollar values to lives. But the alternative can be to sacrifice lives needlessly by failing to carry out the calculations that would have revealed the means for saving them. It should be kept in mind that the avoidance of cost-benefit analysis has its own cost, which can be gauged in lives as well as in dollars.

Nonetheless, we do not dispute that cost-benefit analysis is highly imperfect. We would welcome a better guide to public policy, a guide that would be efficient, morally attractive, and certain to ensure that governments follow the dictates of the governed. Kelman's proposal is to adopt an ethical system that balances conflicts between certain unspecified "duties" and "rights" according to "deliberate reflection." But who is to do the reflecting, and on whose behalf? His guide places no clear limits on the actions of regulatory agencies. Rather than enhancing the connections between individual values and state decisions, such a vague guideline threatens to sever them. Is there a common moral standard that every regulator will magically and independently arrive at through "deliberate reflection"? We doubt it. Far more likely is a system in which bureaucratic decisions reflect the preferences, not of the citizens, but of those in a peculiar position to influence decisions. What concessions to special interests cannot be disguised by claiming that it is degrading to make explicit the trade-offs reflected in the decision? What individual crusade cannot be rationalized by an appeal to "public values" that "rise above" values revealed by individual choices?

V

The Means of Environmental Policy: Cost Effectiveness and Market-Based Instruments

15   *Economic Instruments for Environmental Regulation*

Tom H. Tietenberg

Tom H. Tietenberg is Mitchell Family Professor of Economics at Colby College.

I. Introduction

As recently as a decade ago environmental regulators and lobbying groups with a special interest in environmental protection looked upon the market system as a powerful adversary. That the market unleashed powerful forces was widely recognized and that those forces clearly acted to degrade the environment was widely lamented. Conflict and confrontation became the battle cry for those groups seeking to protect the environment as they set out to block market forces whenever possible.

Among the more enlightened participants in the environmental policy process the air of confrontation and conflict has now begun to recede in many parts of the world. Leading environmental groups and regulators have come to realize that the power of the market can be harnessed and channelled toward the achievement of environmental goals, through an economic incentives approach to regulation. Forward-looking business people have come to appreciate the fact that cost-effective regulation can make them more competitive in the global market-place than regulations which impose higher-than-necessary control costs.

The change in attitude has been triggered by a recognition that this former adversary, the market, can be turned into a powerful ally. In contrast to the traditional regulatory approach, which makes mandatory particular forms of behaviour or specific technological choices, the economic incentive approach allows more flexibility in how the environmental goal is reached. By changing the incentives an individual agent faces, the best private choice can be made to coincide with the best social choice. Rather than relying on the regulatory authority to identify the best course of action, the individual agent can use his or her typically superior information to select the best means of meeting an assigned emission reduction responsibility. This flexibility achieves environmental goals at lower cost, which, in turn, makes the goals easier to achieve and easier to establish.

"Economic Instruments for Environmental Regulation," by T. H. Tietenberg, from *Oxford Review of Economic Policy*, 6(1):17–33.

One indicator of the growing support for the use of economic incentive approaches for environmental control in the United States is the favourable treatment it has recently received both in the popular business[1] and environmental[2] press. Some public interest environmental organizations have now even adopted economic incentive approaches as a core part of their strategy for protecting the environment.[3]

In response to this support the emissions trading concept has recently been applied to reducing the lead content in gasoline, to controlling both ozone depletion and non-point sources of water pollution, and was also prominently featured in the Bush administration proposals for reducing acid rain and smog unveiled in June 1989.

Our knowledge about economic incentive approaches has grown rapidly in the two decades in which they have received serious analytical attention. Not only have the theoretical models become more focused and the empirical work more detailed, but we have now had over a decade of experience with emissions trading in the US and emission charges in Europe.

As the world community becomes increasingly conscious of both the need to tighten environmental controls and the local economic perils associated with tighter controls in a highly competitive global market-place, it seems a propitious time to stand back and to organize what we have learned about this practical and promising approach to pollution control that may be especially relevant to current circumstances. In this paper I will draw upon economic theory, empirical studies, and actual experience with implementation to provide a brief overview of some of the major lessons we have learned about two economic incentive approaches— emissions trading and emission charges—as well as their relationships to the more traditional regulatory policy.[4]

II. The Policy Context

(i) Emissions Trading

Stripped to its bare essentials, the US Clean Air Act[5] relies upon a *command-and-control* approach to controlling pollution. Ambient standards es-

---

[1]See, for example, Main (1988).

[2]See, for example, Stavins (1989).

[3]See the various issues in Volume XX of the EDF Letter, a report to members of the Environmental Defense Fund.

[4]In the limited space permitted by this paper only a few highlights can be illustrated. All of the details of the proofs and the empirical work can be found in the references listed at the end of the paper. For a comprehensive summary of this work see Tietenberg (1980), Liroff (1980), Bohm and Russell (1985), Tietenberg (1985), Liroff (1986), Dudek and Palmisano (1988), Hahn (1984), Hahn and Hester (1989a and 1989b), and Tietenberg (1989b).

[5]The US Clean Air Act (42 U.S.C. 7401–642) was first passed in 1955. The central thrust of the approach described in this paragraph was initiated by the Clean Air Act Amendments of 1970 with mid-course corrections provided by the Clean Air Act Amendments of 1977.

tablish the highest allowable concentration of the pollutant in the ambient air for each conventional pollutant. To reach these prescribed ambient standards, emission standards (legal emission ceilings) are imposed on a large number of specific emission points such as stacks, vents, or storage tanks. Following a survey of the technological options of control, the control authority selects a favoured control technology and calculates the amount of emission reduction achievable by that technology as the basis for setting the emission standard. Technologies yielding larger amounts of control (and, hence, supporting more stringent emission standards) are selected for new emitters and for existing emitters in areas where it is very difficult to meet the ambient standard. The responsibility for defining and enforcing these standards is shared in legislatively specified ways between the national government and the various state governments.

The emissions trading programme attempts to inject more flexibility into the manner in which the objectives of the Clean Air Act are met by allowing sources a much wider range of choice in how they satisfy their legal pollution control responsibilities than possible in the command-and-control approach. Any source choosing to reduce emissions at any discharge point more than required by its emission standard can apply to the control authority for certification of the excess control as an "emission reduction credit" (ERC). Defined in terms of a specific amount of a particular pollutant, the certified emissions reduction credit can be used to satisfy emission standards at other (presumably more expensive to control) discharge points controlled by the creating source or it can be sold to other sources. By making these credits transferable, the US Environmental Protection Agency (EPA) has allowed sources to find the cheapest means of satisfying their requirements, even if the cheapest means are under the control of another firm. The ERC is the currency used in emissions trading, while the offset, bubble, emissions banking, and netting policies govern how this currency can be stored and spent.[6]

The *offset policy* requires major new or expanding sources in "non-attainment" areas (those areas with air quality worse than the ambient standards) to secure sufficient offsetting emission reductions (by acquiring ERCs) from existing firms so that the air is cleaner after their entry or expansion than before.[7] Prior to this policy no new firms were allowed to enter non-attainment areas on the grounds they would interfere with attaining the ambient standards. By introducing the offset policy EPA allowed economic growth to continue while assuring progress toward attainment.

The *bubble policy* receives its unusual name from the fact that it treats multiple emission points controlled by existing emitters (as opposed to those expanding or entering an area for the first time) as if they were enclosed in a bubble. Under this policy only the total emissions of each pol-

---

[6]The details of this policy can be found in "Emissions Trading Policy Statements" 51 *Federal Register* 43829 (4 December 1986).

[7]Offsets are also required for major modifications in areas which have attained the standards if the modifications jeopardize attainment.

lutant leaving the bubble are regulated. While the total leaving the bubble must not be larger than the total permitted by adding up all the corresponding emission standards within the bubble (and in some cases the total must be 20 per cent lower), emitters are free to control some discharge points less than dictated by the corresponding emission standard as long as sufficient compensating ERCs are obtained from other discharge points within the bubble. In essence sources are free to choose the mix of control among the discharge points as long as the overall emission reduction requirements are satisfied. Multi-plant bubbles are allowed, opening the possibility for trading ERCs among very different kinds of emitters.

Netting allows modifying or expanding sources (but not new sources) to escape from the need to meet the requirements of the rather stringent new source review process (including the need to acquire offsets) so long as any net increase in emissions (counting any ERCs earned elsewhere in the plant) is below an established threshold. In so far as it allows firms to escape particular regulatory requirements by using ERCs to remain under the threshold which triggers applicability, netting is more properly considered regulatory relief than regulatory reform.

Emissions banking allows firms to store certified ERCs for subsequent use in the offset, bubble, or netting programmes or for sale to others.

Although comprehensive data on the effects of the programme do not exist because substantial proportions of it are administered by local areas and no one collects information in a systematic way, some of the major aspects of the experience are clear.[8]

- The programme has unquestionably and substantially reduced the costs of complying with the requirements of the Clean Air Act. Most estimates place the accumulated capital savings for all components of the programme at over $10 billion. This does not include the recurring savings in operating cost. On the other hand the programme has not produced the magnitude of cost savings that was anticipated by its strongest proponents at its inception.

- The level of compliance with the basic provisions of the Clean Air Act has increased. The emissions trading programme increased the possible means for compliance and sources have responded.

- Somewhere between 7,000 and 12,000 trading transactions have been consummated. Each of these transactions was voluntary and for the participants represented an improvement over the traditional regulatory approach. Several of these transactions involved the introduction of innovative control technologies.

- The vast majority of emissions trading transactions have involved large pollution sources trading emissions reduction credits either created by excess control of uniformly mixed pollutants (those for which the lo-

---

[8]See, for example, Tietenberg (1985), Hahn and Hester (1989a and 1989b), and Dudek and Palmisano (1988).

cation of emission is not an important policy concern) or involving facilities in close proximity to one another.

- Though air quality has certainly improved for most of the covered pollutants, it is virtually impossible to say how much of the improvement can be attributed to the emissions trading programme. The emissions trading programme complements the traditional regulatory approach, rather than replaces it. Therefore, while it can claim to have hastened compliance with the basic provisions of the act and in some cases to have encouraged improvements beyond the act, improved air quality resulted from the package taken together, rather than from any specific component.

(ii) Emissions Charges

Emission charges are used in both Europe and Japan, though more commonly to control water pollution than air pollution.[9] Currently effluent charges are being used to control water pollution in France, Italy, Germany, and the Netherlands. In both France and the Netherlands the charges are designed to raise revenue for the purpose of funding activities specifically designed to improve water quality.

In Germany discharges are required to meet minimum standards of waste water treatment for a number of defined pollutants. Simultaneously a fee is levied on every unit of discharge depending on the quantity and noxiousness of the effluent. Dischargers meeting or exceeding state-of-the-art effluent standards have to pay only half the normal rate.

The Italian effluent charge system was mainly designed to encourage polluters to achieve provisional effluent standards as soon as possible. The charge is nine times higher for firms that do not meet the prescribed standards than for firms that do meet them. This charge system was designed only to facilitate the transition to the prescribed standards so it is scheduled to expire once full compliance has been achieved.[10]

Air pollution emission charges have been implemented by France and Japan. The French air pollution charge was designed to encourage the early adoption of pollution control equipment with the revenues returned to those paying the charge as a subsidy for installing the equipment. In Japan the emission charge is designed to raise revenue to compensate victims of air pollution. The charge rate is determined primarily by the cost of the compensation programme in the previous year and the amount of remaining emissions over which this cost can be applied pro rata.

Charges have also been used in Sweden to increase the rate at which consumers would purchase cars equipped with a catalytic converter. Cars not equipped with a catalytic converter were taxed, while new cars equipped with a catalytic converter were subsidized.

---

[9]See Anderson et al. (1977), Brown and Johnson (1984), Bressers (1988), Vos (1989), Opschoor and Vos (1989), and Sprenger (1989).

[10]The initial deadline for expiration was 1986, but it has since been postponed.

While data are limited a few highlights seem clear.

- Economists typically envisage two types of effluent or emissions charges. The first, an efficiency charge, is designed to produce an efficient outcome by forcing the polluter to compensate completely for all damage caused. The second, a cost-effective charge, is designed to achieve a predefined ambient standard at the lowest possible control cost. In practice, few, if any, implemented programmes fit either of these designs.

- Despite being designed mainly to raise revenue, effluent charges have typically improved water quality. Though the improvements in most cases have been small, apparently due to the low level at which the effluent charge rate is set, the Netherlands, with its higher effective rates, reports rather large improvements. Air pollution charges typically have not had much effect on air quality because the rates are too low and, in the case of France, most of the revenue is returned to the polluting sources.

- The revenue from charges is typically earmarked for specific environmental purposes rather than contributed to the general revenue as a means of reducing the reliance on taxes that produce more distortions in resource allocation.

- The Swedish tax on heavily polluting vehicles and subsidy for new low polluting vehicles was very successful in introducing low polluting vehicles into the automobile population at a much faster than normal rate. The policy was not revenue neutral, however; owing to the success of the programme in altering vehicle choices, the subsidy payments greatly exceeded the tax revenue.

III. First Principles

Theory can help us understand the characteristics of these economic approaches in the most favourable circumstances for their use and assist in the process of designing the instruments for maximum effectiveness. Because of the dualistic nature of emission charges and emission reduction credits,[11] implications about emission charges and emissions trading flow from the same body of theory.

Drawing conclusions about either of these approaches from this type of analysis, however, must be done with care because operational versions typically differ considerably from the idealized versions modelled by the theory. For example, not all trades that would be allowed in an ideal emis-

---

[11]Under fairly general conditions any allocation of control responsibility achieved by an emissions trading programme could also be achieved by a suitably designed system of emission charges and vice versa.

sions trading programme are allowed in the current US emissions trading programme. Similarly the types of emissions charges actually imposed differ considerably from their ideal versions, particularly in the design of the rate structure and the process for adjusting rates over time.

Assuming all participants are cost-minimizers, a "well-defined" emissions trading or emission charge system could cost-effectively allocate the control responsibility for meeting a predefined pollution target among the various pollution sources despite incomplete information on the control possibilities by the regulatory authorities.[12]

The intuition behind this powerful proposition is not difficult to grasp. Cost-minimizing firms seek to minimize the sum of (a) either ERC acquisition costs or payments of emission charges and (b) control costs. Minimization will occur when the marginal cost of control is set equal to the emission reduction credit price or the emission charge. Since all cost-minimizing sources would choose to control until their marginal control costs were equal to the same price or charge, marginal control costs would be equalized across all discharge points, precisely the condition required for cost-effectiveness.[13]

Emission charges could also sustain a cost effective allocation of the control responsibility for meeting a predefined pollution target, but only if the control authority knew the correct level of the charge to impose or was willing to engage in an iterative trial-and-error process over time to find the correct level. Emissions trading does not face this problem because the price level is established by the market, not the control authority.[14]

Though derived in the rarified world of theory, the practical importance of this theorem should not be underestimated. Economic incentive approaches offer a unique opportunity for regulators to solve a fundamental dilemma. The control authorities' desire to allocate the responsibility for control cost-effectively is inevitably frustrated by a lack of information sufficient to achieve this objective. Economic incentive approaches create a system of incentives in which those who have the best knowledge about control opportunities, the environmental managers for the industries, are encouraged to use that knowledge to achieve environmental objectives at minimum cost. Information barriers do not preclude effective regulation.

What constitutes a "well-defined" emissions trading or emission charge system depends crucially on the attributes of the pollutant being controlled.[15]

---

[12]For the formal demonstration of this proposition see Baumol and Oates (1975), Montgomery (1972), and Tietenberg (1985).

[13]It should be noted that while the allocation is cost-effective, it is not necessarily efficient (the amount of pollution indicated by a benefit-cost comparison). It would only be efficient if the predetermined target happened to coincide with the efficient amount of pollution. Nothing guarantees this outcome.

[14]See Tietenberg (1988) for a more detailed explanation of this point.

[15]For the technical details supporting this proposition see Montgomery (1972), and Tietenberg (1985).

To be consistent with a cost-effective allocation of the control responsibility, the policy instruments would have to be defined in different ways for different types of pollutants. Two differentiating characteristics are of particular relevance. Approaches designed to control pollutants which are uniformly mixed in the atmosphere (such as volatile organic compounds, one type of precursor for ozone formation) can be defined simply in terms of a rate of emissions flow per unit time. Economic incentive approaches sharing this design characteristic are called *emission trades* or *emission charges*.

Instrument design is somewhat more difficult when the pollution target being pursued is defined in terms of concentrations measured at a number of specific receptor locations (such as particulates). In this case the cost-effective trade or charge design must take into account the *location* of the emissions (including injection height) as well as the *magnitude* of emissions. As long as the control authorities can define for each emitter a vector of transfer coefficients, which translate the effect of a unit increase of emissions by that emitter into an increase in concentration at each of the affected receptors, receptor-specific trades or charges can be defined which will allocate the responsibility cost-effectively. The design which is consistent with cost-effectiveness in this context is called an *ambient trade* or an *ambient charge*.

Unfortunately, while the design of the ambient ERC is not very complicated,[16] implementing the markets within which these ERCs would be traded is rather complicated. In particular for each unit of planned emissions an emitter would have to acquire separate ERCs for each affected receptor. When the number of receptors is large, the result is a rather complicated set of transactions. Similarly, establishing the correct rate structure for the charges in this context is particularly difficult because the set of charges which will satisfy the ambient air quality constraints is not unique; even a trial-and-error system would not necessarily result in the correct matrix of ambient charges being put into effect.

As long as markets are competitive and transactions costs are low, the trading benchmark in an emissions trading approach does not affect the ultimate cost-effective allocation of control responsibility. When markets are non-competitive or transactions costs are high, however, the final allocation of control responsibility is affected.[17] Emission charge approaches do not face this problem.

Once the control authority has decided how much pollution of each type will be allowed, it must then decide how to allocate the operating permits among the sources. In theory emission reduction credits could either be auctioned off, with the sources purchasing them from the control authority at the market-clearing price, or (as in the US programme) created

---

[16]Each permit allows the holder to degrade the concentration level at the corresponding receptor by one unit.

[17]See Hahn (1984) for the mathematical treatment of this point. Further discussions can be found in Tietenberg (1985) and Misiolek and Elder (1989).

by the sources as surplus reductions over and above a predetermined set of emissions standards. (Because this latter approach favours older sources over newer sources, it is known as "grandfathering".) The proposition suggests that either approach will ultimately result in a cost-effective allocation of the control responsibility among the various polluters as long as they are all price-takers, transactions costs are low, and ERCs are fully transferable. Any allocation of emission standards in a grandfathered approach is compatible with cost-effectiveness because the after-market in which firms can buy or sell ERCs corrects any problems with the initial allocation. This is a significant finding because it implies that under the right conditions the control authority can use this initial allocation of emissions standards to pursue distributional goals without interfering with cost-effectiveness.

When firms are price-setters rather than price-takers, however, cost-effectiveness will only be achieved if the control authority initially allocates the emission standards so a cost-effective allocation would be achieved even in the absence of any trading. (Implementing this particular allocation would, of course, require regulators to have complete information on control costs for all sources, an unlikely prospect.) In this special case cost-effectiveness would be achieved even in the presence of one or more price-setting firms because no trading would take place, eliminating the possibility of exploiting any market power.

For all other emission standard assignments an active market would exist, offering the opportunity for price-setting behaviour. The larger is the deviation of the price setting source's emission standard from its cost-effective allocation, the larger is the deviation of ultimate control costs from the least-cost allocation. When the price-setting source is initially allocated an insufficiently stringent emission standard, it can inflict higher control costs on others by withholding some ERCs from the market. When an excessively stringent emission standard is imposed on a price-setting source, however, it necessarily bears a higher control cost as the means of reducing demand (and, hence, prices) for the ERCs.

Similar problems exist when transactions costs are high. High transactions costs preclude or reduce trading activity by diminishing the gains from trade. When the costs of consummating a transaction exceed its potential gains, the incentive to participate in emissions trading is lost.

IV. Lessons from Empirical Research

A vast majority, though not all, of the relevant empirical studies have found the control costs to be substantially higher with the regulatory command-and-control system than the least cost means of allocating the control responsibility.

While theory tells us unambiguously that the command-and-control system will not be cost-effective except by coincidence, it cannot tell us the magnitude of the excess costs. The empirical work cited in Table 1 adds the important information that the excess costs are typically very large.[18] This is an important finding because it provides the motivation for introducing a reform programme; the potential social gains (in terms of reduced control cost) from breaking away from the status quo are sufficient to justify the trouble. Although the estimates of the excess costs attributable to a command and control presented in Table 1 overstate the cost savings that would be achieved by even an ideal economic incentive approach (a point discussed in more detail below), the general conclusion that the potential cost savings from adopting economic incentive approaches are large seems accurate even after correcting for overstatement.

Economic incentive approaches which raise revenue (charges or auction ERC markets) offer an additional benefit—they allow the revenue raised from these policies to substitute for revenue raised in more traditional ways. Whereas it is well known that traditional revenue-raising approaches distort resource allocation, producing inefficiency, economic incentive approaches enhance efficiency. Some empirical work based on the US economy suggests that substituting economic incentive means of raising revenue for more traditional means could produce significant efficiency gains.[19]

When high degrees of control are necessary, ERC prices or charge levels would be correspondingly high. The financial outlays associated with acquiring ERCs in an auction market or paying charges on uncontrolled emissions would be sufficiently large that sources would typically have lower financial burdens with the traditional command-and-control approach than with these particular economic incentive approaches. Only a "grandfathered" trading system would guarantee that sources would be no worse off than under the command-and-control system.[20]

Financial burden is a significant concern in a highly competitive global market-place. Firms bearing large financial burdens would be placed at a competitive disadvantage when forced to compete with firms not bearing those burdens. Their costs would be higher.

From the point of view of the source required to control its emissions, two components of financial burden are significant: (a) control costs and (b) expenditures on permits or emission charges. While only the former represent real resource costs to society as a whole (the latter are merely transferred from one group in society to another), both represent a financial burden to the source. The empirical evidence suggests that when an auction market is used to distribute ERCs (or, equivalently, when all un-

---

[18]A value of 1.0 in the last column of Table 1 would indicate that the traditional regulatory approach was cost-effective. A value of 4.0 would indicate that the traditional regulatory approach results in an allocation of the control responsibility which is four times as expensive as necessary to reach the stipulated pollution target.

[19]See Terkla (1984).

[20]See Atkinson and Tietenberg (1982, 1984), Hahn (1984), Harrison (1983), Krupnick (1986), Lyon (1982), Palmer et al. (1980), Roach et al. (1981), Seskin et al. (1983), and Shapiro and Warhit (1983) for the individual studies, and Tietenberg (1985) for a summary of the evidence.

Table 1 Empirical Studies of Air Pollution Control

Study	Pollutants Covered	Geographic Area	CAC Benchmark	Ratio of CAC Cost to Least Cost
Atkinson and Lewis	Particulates	St Louis	SIP regulations	6.00[a]
Roach et al.	Sulphur dioxide	Four corners in Utah	SIP regulations Colorado, Arizona, and New Mexico	4.25
Hahn and Noll	Sulphates standards	Los Angeles	California emission	1.07
Krupnick	Nitrogen dioxide regulations	Baltimore	Proposed RACT	5.96[b]
Seskin et al.	Nitrogen dioxide regulations	Chicago	Proposed RACT	14.40[b]
McGartland	Particulates	Baltimore	SIP regulations	4.18
Spofford	Sulphur Dioxide	Lower Delaware Valley	Uniform percentage regulations	1.78
	Particulates	Lower Delaware Valley	Uniform percentage regulations	22.00
Harrison	Airport noise	United States	Mandatory retrofit	1.72[c]
Maloney and Yandle	Hydrocarbons	All domestic DuPont plants	Uniform percentage reduction	4.15[d]
Palmer et al.	CFC emissions from non-aerosol applications	United States	Proposed emission	1.96

CAC = command and control, the traditional regulatory approach.
SIP = state implementation plan.
RACT = reasonably available control technologies, a set of standards imposed on existing sources in non-attainment areas.
[a]Based on a 40 $\mu g/m^3$ at worst receptor.
[b]Based on a short-term, one-hour average of 250 $\mu g/m^3$.
[c]Because it is a benefit-cost study instead of a cost-effectiveness study, the Harrison comparison of the command-and-control approach with the least-cost allocation involves different benefit levels. Specifically, the benefit levels associated with the least-cost allocation are only 82 per cent of those associated with the command-control allocation. To produce cost estimates based on more comparable benefits, as a first approximation the least-cost allocation was divided by 0.82 and the resulting number was compared with the command-and-control cost.
[d]Based on 85 per cent reduction of emissions from all sources.

controlled emissions are subject to an emissions charge), the ERC expenditures (charge outlays) would frequently be larger in magnitude than the control costs; the sources would spend more on ERCs (or pay more in charges) than they would on the control equipment. Under the traditional command-and-control system firms make no financial outlays to the government. Although control costs are necessarily higher with the command-and-control system than with an economic incentive approach, they are not so high as to outweigh the additional financial outlays required in an auction market permit system (or an emissions tax system). For this reason existing sources could be expected vehemently to oppose an auction market or emission charges despite their social appeal, unless the revenue derived is used in a manner which is approved by the sources, and the sources with which it competes are required to absorb similar expenses. When environmental policies are not coordinated across national boundaries, this latter condition would be particularly difficult to meet.

In the absence of either a politically popular way to use the revenue or assurances that competitors will face similar financial burdens, this political opposition could be substantially reduced by grandfathering. Under grandfathering, sources have only to purchase any additional ERCs they may need to meet their assigned emission standard (as opposed to purchasing sufficient ERCs or paying charges to cover all uncontrolled emissions in an auction market). Grandfathering is *de facto* the approach taken in the US emissions trading programme.

Grandfathering has its disadvantages. Because ERCs become very valuable, especially in the face of stringent air quality regulations, sources selling emission reduction credits would be able to command very high prices. By placing heavy restrictions on the amount of emissions, the control authority is creating wealth for existing firms *vis-à-vis* new firms.

Although reserving some ERCs for new firms is possible (by assigning more stringent emission standards than needed to reach attainment and using the "surplus" air quality to create government-held ERCs), this option is rarely exercised in practice. In the United States under the offset policy firms typically have to purchase sufficient ERCs to more than cover all uncontrolled emissions, while existing firms only have to purchase enough to comply with their assigned emission standard. Thus grandfathering imposes a bias against new sources in the sense that their financial burden is greater than that of an otherwise identical existing source, even if the two sources install exactly the same emission control devices. This new source bias could retard the introduction of new facilities and new technologies by reducing the cost advantage of building new facilities which embody the latest innovations.

While it is clear from theory that larger trading areas offer the opportunities for larger potential cost savings in an emissions trading programme, some empirical work suggests that substantial savings can be achieved in emissions trading even when the trading areas are rather small.

The point of this finding is *not* that small trading areas are fine; they do retard progress toward the standard. Rather, when political considerations allow only small trading areas or nothing, emissions trading still can play a significant role.

Sometimes political considerations demand a trading area which is smaller than the ideal design. Whether large trading areas are essential for the effective use of this policy is therefore of some relevance. In general, the larger the trading area, the larger would be the potential cost savings due to a wider set of cost reduction opportunities that would become available. The empirical question is how sensitive the cost estimates are to the size of the trading areas.

One study of utilities found that even allowing a plant to trade among discharge points within that plant could save from 30 to 60 per cent of the costs of complying with new sulphur oxide reduction regulations, compared to a situation where no trading whatsoever was permitted.[21] Expanding the trading possibilities to other utilities within the same state permitted a further reduction of 20 per cent, while allowing interstate trading permitted another 15 per cent reduction in costs. If this study is replicated in other circumstances, it would appear that even small trading areas offer the opportunity for significant cost reduction.[22]

Although only a few studies of the empirical impact of market power on emissions trading have been accomplished, their results are consistent with a finding that market power does not seem to have a large effect on regional control costs in most realistic situations.[23]

Even in areas having especially stringent controls, the available evidence suggests that price manipulation is not a serious problem. In an auction market the price-setting source reduces its financial burden by purchasing fewer ERCs in order to drive the price down. To compensate for the smaller number of ERCs purchased, the price-setting source must spend more on controlling its own pollution, limiting the gains from price manipulation. Although these actions could have a rather large impact on *regional financial burden*, they would under normal circumstances have a rather small effect on *regional control costs*. Estimates typically suggest that control costs would rise by less than 1 per cent if market power were exercised by one or more firms.

It should not be surprising that price manipulation could have rather dramatic effects on regional financial burden in an auction market, since the cost of *all* ERCs is affected, not merely those purchased by the price-setting source. The perhaps more surprising result is that control costs are quite insensitive to price-setting behaviour. This is due to the fact that the only control cost change is the net difference between the new larger control burden borne by the price searcher and the correspondingly smaller burden borne by the sources having larger-than-normal allocations of permits. Only the costs of the marginal units are affected.

Within the class of grandfathered distribution rules, some emission standard allocations create a larger potential for strategic price behaviour than others. In general the larger the divergence between the control responsibility assigned to the price-searching source by the emission standards and the cost-effective allocation of control responsibility, the larger the potential for market power. When allocated too little responsibility by the control authority, price-searching firms can exercise power on the selling side of the market, and when allocated too much, they can exercise power on the buying side of the market.

---

[21]ICF Resources, Inc. (1989).

[22]As indicated below, the fact that so many emissions trades have actually taken place within the same plant or among contiguous plants provides some confirmation for this result.

[23]For individual studies see de Lucia (1974), Hahn (1984), Stahl, Bergman and Mäler (1988), and Maloney and Yandle (1984). For a survey of the evidence see Tietenberg (1985).

According to the existing studies it takes a rather considerable divergence from the cost-effective allocation of control responsibility to produce much difference in regional control costs. In practice the deviations from the least-cost allocation caused by market power pale in comparison to the much larger potential cost reductions achievable by implementing emissions trading.[24]

V. Lessons from Implementation

Though the number of transactions consummated under the Emissions Trading Program has been large, it has been smaller than expected. Part of this failure to fulfill expectations can be explained as the result of unrealistically inflated expectations. More restrictive regulatory decisions than expected and higher than expected transaction costs also bear some responsibility.

The models used to calculate the potential cost savings were not (and are not) completely adequate guides to reality. The cost functions in these models are invariably *ex ante* cost functions. They implicitly assume that the modelled plant can be built from scratch and can incorporate the best technology. In practice, of course, many existing sources cannot retrofit these technologies and therefore their *ex post* control options are much more limited than implied by the models.

The models also assume all trades are multilateral and are simultaneously consummated, whereas actual trades are usually bilateral and sequential. The distinction is important for non-uniformly mixed pollutants;[25] bilateral trades frequently are constrained by regulatory concerns about decreasing air quality at the site of the acquiring source. Because multilateral trades would typically incorporate compensating reductions coming from other nearby sources, these concerns normally do not arise when trades are multilateral and simultaneous. In essence the models implicitly assume an idealized market process, which is only remotely approximated by actual transactions.

In addition some non-negligible proportion of the expected cost savings recorded by the models for non-uniformly mixed pollutants is attributable to the substantially larger amounts of emissions allowed by the modelled permit equilibrium.[26] For example, the cost estimates imply that the control authority is allowed to arrange the control responsibility in *any* fashion that satisfies the ambient air quality standards. In practice the mod-

---

[24]Strategic price behaviour is not the only potential source of market power problems. Firms could conceivably use permit markets to drive competitors out of business. See Misiolek and Elder (1989). For an analysis which concludes that this problem is relatively rare and can be dealt with on a case-by-case basis should it arise, see Tietenberg (1985).

[25]See Tietenberg and Atkinson (1989) for a demonstration that this is an empirically significant point.

[26]This is demonstrated in Atkinson and Tietenberg (1987).

els allocate more uncontrolled emissions to sources with tall stacks because those emissions can be exported. Exported emissions avoid control costs without affecting the readings at the local monitors. That portion of the cost savings estimated by the models in Table 1 which is due to allowing increased emissions is not acceptable to regulators. Some recent work has suggested that the benefits received from the additional emission control required by the command-and-control approach may be justified by the net benefits received.[27] The regulatory refusal to allow emission increases was apparently consistent with efficiency,[28] but it was not consistent with the magnitude of cost savings anticipated by the models.

Certain types of trades assumed permissible by the models are prohibited by actual trading rules. New sources, for example, are not allowed to satisfy the New Source Performance Standards (which imply a particular control technology) by choosing some less stringent control option and making up the difference with acquired emission reduction credits; they must install the degree of technological control necessary to meet the standard. Typically this is the same technology used by EPA to define the standard in the first place.

A lost of uncertainty is associated with emission reduction credit transactions since they depend so heavily on administrative action. All trades must be approved by the control authorities. If the authorities are not cooperative or at least consistent, the value of the created emission reduction credits could be diminished or even destroyed.

For non-uniformly mixed pollutants, trades between geographically separated sources will only be approved after dispersion modelling has been accomplished by the applicants. Not only is this modelling expensive, it frequently ends up raising questions which ultimately lead to the transaction being denied. Few trades requiring this modelling have been consummated.

Trading activity has also been inhibited by the paucity of emission banks. The US system allows states to establish emission banks, but does not require them to do so. As of 1986 only seven of the fifty states had established these banks. For sources in the rest of the states the act of creating emission credits is undervalued because the credits cannot be legally held for future use. The supply of emission reduction credits is hence less than would be estimated by the models.

The Emissions Trading Program seems to have worked particularly well for trades involving uniformly mixed pollutants and for trades of nonuniformly mixed pollutants involving contiguous discharge points.

It is not surprising that most consummated trades have been internal (where the buyer and seller share a common corporate parent) rather than

---

[27]See Oates, Portney, and McGartland (1988).

[28]Not all of the cost savings, of course, is due to the capability to increase emissions. The remaining portion of the savings, which is due to taking advantage of opportunities to control a given level of emissions at a lower cost, is still substantial and can be captured by a well-designed permit system which does not allow emissions to increase beyond the command-and-control benchmark. See the calculations in Atkinson and Tietenberg (1987).

external. Not only are the uncertainties associated with interfirm transfers avoided, but most internal trades involve contiguous facilities. Trades between contiguous facilities do not trigger a requirement for dispersion modelling.[29]

It is also not surprising that the plurality of consummated trades involve volatile organic compounds, which are uniformly mixed pollutants. Since dispersion modelling is not required for uniformly mixed pollutants even when the trading sources are somewhat distant from one another, trades involving these pollutants are cheaper to consummate. Additionally emissions trades involving uniformly mixed pollutants do not jeopardize local air quality since the location of the emissions is not a matter of policy consequence.

The establishment of the Emissions Trading Program has encouraged technological progress in pollution control. Although generally the degree of progress has been modest, it has been more dramatic in areas where emission reductions have been sufficiently stringent as to restrict the availability of emission reduction credits created by more traditional means.[30]

Theory would lead us to expect more technological progress with emissions trading than with a command-and-control policy because it changes the incentives so drastically. Under a command-and-control approach technological changes discovered by the control authority typically lead to more stringent standards (and higher costs) for the sources. Sources have little incentive to innovate and a good deal of incentive to hide potential innovations from the control authority. With emissions trading, on the other hand, innovations allowing excess reductions create saleable emission reduction credits.

The evidence suggests that the expectations based on this theory have been borne out to a limited degree in the operating programme. The most prominent example of technological change has been the substitution of water-based solvents for solvents containing volatile organic compounds. Though somewhat more expensive, this substitution made economic sense once the programme was introduced.

It should probably not be surprising that the number of new innovations stimulated by the programme is rather small. As long as cheaper ways of creating credits within existing processes (fuel substitution, for example) are available, it would be unreasonable to expect large investments in new technologies with unproven reliabilities. On the other hand as the degree of control rises and the supply of readily available credits dries up, the demand for new technologies would be expected to rise as well. This expectation seems to have been borne out in those areas where unusually low air quality or stringent regulatory rules have served to limit the available credits.[31]

---

[29]The fact that so many trades have taken place between contiguous discharge points serves as confirmation that substantial savings can be achieved even if the geographic boundaries of the trading area are quite restricted.

[30]For more details see Tietenberg (1985), Maleug (1989), and Dudek and Palmisano (1988).

[31]For the experience in California see Dudek and Palmisano (1988).

This is an important point. Those who fail to consider the dynamic advantages of an economic incentive approach sometimes suggest that if few credits would be traded, implementing a system of this type has no purpose. In fact it has a substantial purpose—the encouragement of new technologies to meet the increasingly stringent standards.

Introducing the Emissions Trading Program has provided an opportunity to control sources which can reduce emissions relatively cheaply, but which under the traditional policy were under-regulated due either to their financially precarious position or the fact that they were not subject to regulation.[32]

Due to the social distress caused by any resulting unemployment, the control authorities and the courts are understandably reluctant to enforce stringent emission standards against firms which would not be able to pass higher costs on to customers without considerable loss of production. Since many of these sources could control emissions at a lower marginal cost than other sources, their political immunity from control makes regional control costs higher than necessary; other sources have to control their own emissions to a higher degree (at a higher marginal cost) to compensate.

Due to its ability to separate the issue of who pays for the reduction from the issue of which discharge points are to be controlled, the emissions trading programme provides a way to secure those low cost reductions. The command-and-control policy would assign, as normal, a very low (perhaps zero) emission reduction to any previously unregulated firm. Once emissions trading had been established, however, it would be in the interest of this firm to control emissions further, selling the resulting emission reduction credits. As long as the revenues from the sale at least covered the cost, this transaction could profit, or at least not hurt, the seller. Because these reductions could be achieved at a lower cost than ratcheting up the degree of control on already heavily controlled sources, non-immune sources would find purchasing the credits cheaper than controlling their own emissions to a higher degree. Everyone benefits from controlling these previously under-regulated sources.

Another unique attribute of an emissions trading approach is the capability it offers sources for leasing credits.[33]

Leasing offers an enormously useful degree of flexibility which is not available with other policy approaches to pollution control. The usefulness of leasing derives from the fact that some sources, utilities in particular, have patterns of emission that vary over time while allowable emissions remain constant. In a typical situation, for example, suppose an older utility would, in the absence of control, be emitting heavily. In the normal course of a utility expansion cycle the older plant would subsequently experience substantially reduced emissions when the utility constructed a new plant and shifted a major part of the load away from the older plant to the new plant. Ultimately growth in demand on the system would increase the emis-

---

[32]See Tietenberg (1985).
[33]See Feldman and Raufer (1987) and Tietenberg (1989a).

sions again for the older plant as its capacity would once again be needed. The implication of this temporal pattern is that during the middle period, as its own emissions fell well below allowable emissions, this utility could lease excess emission credits to another facility, recalling them as its own need rose with demand growth. Indeed one empirical study of the pattern of the utility demand for and supply of acid rain reduction credits over time suggests that leasing is a critical component of any cost-effective control strategy, a component that neither the traditional approach nor emission charges can offer.[34]

Leasing also provides a way for about-to-be-retired sources to participate in the reduction programme. Under the traditional approach once the deadline for compliance had been reached the utility would either have to retire the unit early or to install expensive control equipment which would be rendered useless once the unit was retired. By leasing credits for the short period to retirement, the unit could remain in compliance without taking either of those drastic steps; it would, however, be sharing in the cost of installing the extra equipment in the leasing utility. Leased credits facilitate an efficient transition into the new regime of more stringent controls.

Unless the process to determine the level of an effluent or emissions charge includes some automatic means of temporal adjustment, the tendency is for the real rate (adjusted for inflation) to decline over time.[35] This problem is particularly serious in areas with economic growth where increasing real rates would be the desired outcome.

In contrast to emissions trading where ERC prices respond automatically to changing market conditions, emission charges have to be determined by an administrative process. When the function of the charge is to raise revenue for a particular purpose, charge rates will be determined by the costs of achieving that purpose; when the costs of achieving the purpose rise, the level of the charge must rise to secure the additional revenue.[36]

Sometimes that process produces an unintended dynamic. In Japan, for example, the charge is calculated on the basis of the amount of compensation paid to victims of air pollution in the previous year. While the amount of compensation has been increasing, the amount of emissions (the base to which the charge is applied) has been decreasing. As a result unexpectedly high charge rates are necessary in order to raise sufficient revenue for the compensation system.

In countries where the tax revenue feeds into the general budget, increases in the level of the charge require a specific administrative act. Evidently it is difficult to raise these rates in practice, since charges have commonly even failed to keep pace with inflation, much less growth in the number of sources. The unintended result is eventual environmental deterioration.

---

[34]Feldman and Raufer (1987).

[35]For further information see Vos (1989) and Sprenger (1989).

[36]While it is theoretically possible (depending on the elasticity of demand for pollution abatement) for a rise in the tax to produce less revenue, this has typically not been the case.

VI. Concluding Comments

Our experience with economic incentive programmes has demonstrated that they have had, and can continue to have, a positive role in environmental policy in the future. I would submit the issue is no longer *whether* they have a role to play, but rather *what kind* of role they should play. The available experience with operating versions of these programmes allows us to draw some specific conclusions which facilitate defining the boundaries for the optimal use of economic incentive approaches in general and for distinguishing the emissions trading and emission charges approaches in particular.

Emissions trading integrates particularly smoothly into any policy structure which is based either directly (through emission standards) or indirectly (through mandated technology or input limitations) on regulating emissions. In this case emission limitations embedded in the operating licenses can serve as the trading benchmark if grandfathering is adopted.

Emissions charges work particularly well when transactions costs associated with bargaining are high. It appears that much of the trading activity in the United States has involved large corporations. Emissions trading is probably not equally applicable to large and small pollution sources. The transaction costs are sufficiently high that only large trades can absorb them without jeopardizing the gains from trade. For this reason charges seem a more appropriate instrument when sources are individually small, but numerous (such as residences or automobiles). Charges also work well as a device for increasing the rate of adoption of new technologies and for raising revenue to subsidize environmentally benign projects.

Emissions trading seems to work especially well for uniformly mixed pollutants. No diffusion modelling is necessary and regulators do not have to worry about trades creating "hot spots" or localized areas of high pollution concentration. Trades can be on a one-to-one basis.

Because emissions trading allows the issue of who will pay for the control to be separated from who will install the control, it introduces an additional degree of flexibility. This flexibility is particularly important in nonattainment areas since marginal control costs are so high. Sources which would not normally be controlled because they could not afford to implement the controls without going out of business, can be controlled with emissions trading. The revenue derived from the sale of emission reduction credits can be used to finance the controls, effectively preventing bankruptcy.

Because it is quantity based, emissions trading also offers a unique possibility for leasing. Leasing is particularly valuable when the temporal pattern of emissions varies across sources. As discussed above this appears generally to be the case with utilities. When a firm plans to shut down one plant in the near future and to build a new one, leasing credits is a vastly superior alternative to the temporary installation of equipment in the old plant which would be useless when the plant was retired. The useful life of this temporary control equipment would be wastefully short.

We have also learned that ERC transactions have higher transactions costs than we previously understood. Regulators must validate every trade. When non-uniformly mixed pollutants are involved, the transactions costs associated with estimating the air quality effects are particularly high. Delegating responsibility for trade approval to lower levels of government may in principle speed up the approval process, but unless the bureaucrats in the lower level of government support the programme the gain may be negligible.

Emissions trading places more importance on the operating permits and emissions inventories than other approaches. To the extent those are deficient the potential for trades that protect air quality may be lost. Firms which have actual levels of emissions substantially below allowable emissions find themselves with a trading opportunity which, if exploited, could degrade air quality. The trading benchmark has to be defined carefully.

There can be little doubt that the emissions trading programme in the US has improved upon the command-and-control programme that preceded it. The documented cost savings are large and the flexibility provided has been important. Similarly emissions charges have achieved their own measure of success in Europe. To be sure the programmes are far from perfect, but the flaws should be kept in perspective. In no way should they overshadow the impressive accomplishments. Although economic incentive approaches lose their Utopian lustre upon closer inspection, they have none the less made a lasting contribution to environmental policy.

The role for economic incentive approaches should grow in the future if for no other reason than the fact that the international pollution problems which are currently commanding centre-stage fall within the domains where economic incentive policies have been most successful. Significantly many of the problems of the future, such as reducing tropospheric ozone, preventing stratospheric ozone depletion, moderating global warming, and increasing acid rain control, involve pollutants that can be treated as uniformly mixed, facilitating the use of economic incentives. In addition larger trading areas facilitate greater cost reductions than smaller trading areas. This also augers well for the use of emissions trading as part of the strategy to control many future pollution problems because the natural trading areas are all very large indeed. Acid rain, stratospheric ozone depletion, and greenhouse gases could (indeed should!) involve trading areas that transcend national boundaries. For greenhouse and ozone depletion gases, the trading areas should be global in scope. Finally, it seems clear that the pivotal role of carbon dioxide in global warming may require some fairly drastic changes in energy use, including changes in personal transportation, and ultimately land use patterns. Some form of charges could play an important role in facilitating this transformation.

We live in an age when the call for tighter environmental controls intensifies with each new discovery of yet another injury modern society is inflicting on the planet. But resistance to additional controls is also growing with the recognition that compliance with each new set of controls is more expensive than the last. While economic incentive approaches to environmental control offer no panacea, they frequently do offer a practical way to achieve environmental goals more flexibly and at lower cost than more traditional regulatory approaches. That is a compelling virtue.

References

Anderson, F. R. et al. (1977), *Environmental Improvement Through Economic Incentives*, Baltimore, The Johns Hopkins University Press for Resources for the Future, Inc.

Atkinson, S. E. and Lewis, D. H. (1974). "A Cost-Effectiveness Analysis of Alternative Air Quality Control Strategies," *Journal of Environmental Economics and Management*, 1, 237–50.

—— and Tietenberg, T. H. (1982), "The Empirical Properties of Two Classes of Designs for Transferable Discharge Permit Markets," *Journal of Environmental Economics and Management*, 9, 101–21.

—— (1984), "Approaches for Reaching Ambient Standards in Non-Attainment Areas: Financial Burden and Efficiency Considerations," *Land Economics*, 60, 148–59.

—— (1987), "Economic Implications of Emission Trading Rules for Local and Regional Pollutants," *Canadian Journal of Economics*, 20, 370–86.

Baumol, W. J., and Oates, W. E. (1975), *The Theory of Environmental Policy*, Englewood Cliffs, N.J., Prentice-Hall.

Bohm, P. and Russell, C. (1985), "Comparative Analysis of Alternative Policy Instruments," in A. V. Kneese and J. L. Sweeney (eds.), *Handbook of Natural Resource and Energy Economics*, Vol. 1, 395–460, Amsterdam, North-Holland.

Bressers, H. T. A. (1988), "A Comparison of the Effectiveness of Incentives and Directives: The Case of Dutch Water Quality Policy," *Policy Studies Review*, 7, 500–18.

Brown, G. M. Jr. and Johnson, R. W. (1984), "Pollution Control by Effluent Charges: It Works in the Federal Republic of Germany, Why Not in the United States?," *Natural Resources Journal*, 24, 929–66.

de Lucia, R. J. (1974), *An Evaluation of Marketable Effluent Permit Systems*, Report No. EPA-600/5-74-030 to the US Environmental Protection Agency (September).

Dudek, D. J. and Palmisano, J. (1988), "Emissions Trading: Why Is This Thoroughbred Hobbled?," *Columbia Journal of Environmental Law*, 13, 217–56.

Feldman, S. L. and Raufer, R. K. (1987), *Emissions Trading and Acid Rain Implementing a Market Approach to Pollution Control*, Totowa, N.J., Rowman & Littlefield.

Hahn, R. W. (1984), "Market Power and Transferable Property Rights," *Quarterly Journal of Economics*, 99, 753–65.

—— (1989), "Economic Prescriptions for Environmental Problems: How the Patient Followed the Doctor's Orders," *The Journal of Economic Perspectives*, 3, 95–114.

—— and Noll, R. G. (1982), "Designing a Market for Tradeable Emission Permits," in W. A. Magat (ed.), *Reform of Environmental Regulation*, Cambridge, Mass., Ballinger.

—— and Hester, G. L. (1989a), "Where Did All the Markets Go? An Analysis of EPA's Emission Trading Program," *Yale Journal of Regulation*, 6, 109–53.

⸻ (1989b), "Marketable Permits: Lessons from Theory and Practice," *Ecology Law Quarterly*, 16, 361–406.

Harrison, D., Jr. (1983), "Case Study 1: The Regulation of Aircraft Noise," in Thomas C. Schelling (ed.), *Incentives for Environmental Protection*, Cambridge, Mass, MIT Press.

ICF Resources, Inc. (1989), "Economic, Environmental, and Coal Market Impacts of SO2 Emissions Trading Under Alternative Acid Rain Control Proposals," a report prepared for the Regulatory Innovations Staff, USEPA (March).

Krupnick, A. J. (1986), "Costs of Alternative Policies for the Control of Nitrogen Dioxide in Baltimore," *Journal of Environmental Economics and Management*, 13, 189–97.

Liroff, R. A. (1980), *Air Pollution Offsets: Trading, Selling and Banking*, Washington, D.C., Conservation Foundation.

⸻ (1986), *Reforming Air Pollution Regulation: The Toil and Trouble of EPA's Bubble*, Washington, D.C., Conservation Foundation.

Lyon, R. M. (1982), "Auctions and Alternative Procedures for Allocating Pollution Rights," *Land Economics*, 58, 16–32.

McGartland, A. M. (1984), "Marketable Permit Systems for Air Pollution Control: an Empirical Study," Ph.D. dissertation, University of Maryland.

Main, J. (1988), "Here Comes the Big Cleanup," *Fortune*, 21 November, 102.

Maleug, David A. (1989), "Emission Trading and the Incentive to Adopt New Pollution Abatement Technology," *Journal of Environmental Economics and Management*, 16, 52–7.

Maloney, M. T. and Yandle, B. (1984), "Estimation of the Cost of Air Pollution Control Regulation," *Journal of Environmental Economics and Management*, 11, 244–63.

Misiolek, W. S. and Elder, H. W. (1989), "Exclusionary Manipulation of Markets for Pollution Rights," *Journal of Environmental Economics and Management*, 16, 156–66.

Montgomery, W. D. (1972), "Markets in Licenses and Efficient Pollution Control Programs," *Journal of Economic Theory*, 5, 395–418.

Oates, W. E., Portney, P. R., and McGartland, A. M. (1988), "The Net Benefits of Incentive-Based Regulation: The Case of Environmental Standard Setting in the Real World," Resources for the Future Working Paper December.

Opschoor, J. B. and Vos, H. B. (1989), *The Application of Economic Instruments for Environmental Protection in OECD Countries*, Paris, OECD.

Palmer, A. R., Mooz, W. E., Quinn, T. H., and Wolf, K. A. (1980), *Economic Implications of Regulating Chlorofluorocarbon Emissions from Nonaerosol Applications*, Report No. R–2524–EPA prepared for the US Environmental Protection Agency by the Rand Corporation, June.

Roach, F., Kolstad, C., Kneese, A. V., Tobin, R., and Williams, M. (1981), "Alternative Air Quality Policy Options in the Four Corners Region," *Southwestern Review*, 1, 29–58.

Seskin, E. P., Anderson, R. J., Jr., and Reid, R. O. (1983), "An Empirical Analysis of Economic Strategies for Controlling Air Pollution," *Journal of Environmental Economics and Management*, 10, 112–24.

Shapiro, M. and Warhit, E. (1983), "Marketable Permits: The Case of Chlorofluorocarbons," *Natural Resource Journal*, 23, 577–91.

Spofford, W. O., Jr. (1984), "Efficiency Properties of Alternative Source Control Policies for Meeting Ambient Air Quality Standards: An Empirical Application to the Lower Delaware Valley," Discussion paper D–118, Washington D.C., Resources for the Future, November.

Sprenger, R. U. (1989), "Economic Incentives in Environmental Policies: The Case of West Germany," a paper presented at the Symposium on Economic Instruments in Environmental Protection Policies, Stockholm, Sweden (June).

Stahl, L., Bergman, L., and Mäler, K. G. (1988), "An Experimental Game on Marketable Emission Permits for Hydro-carbons in the Gothenburg Area," Research Paper No. 6359, Stockholm School of Economics (December).

Stavins, R. N. (1989), "Harnessing Market Forces to Protect the Environment," *Environment*, 31, 4–7, 28–35.

Terkla, D. (1984), "The Efficiency Value of Effluent Tax Revenues," *Journal of Environmental Economics and Management*, 11, 107–23.

Tietenberg, T. H. (1980), "Transferable Discharge Permits and the Control of Stationary Source Air Pollution: A Survey and Synthesis," *Land Economics*, 56, 391–416.

—— (1985), *Emissions Trading: An Exercise in Reforming Pollution Policy*, Washington, D.C., Resources for the Future.

—— (1988), *Environmental and Natural Resource Economics*, 2nd edn., Glenview, Illinois, Scott, Foresman and Company.

—— (1989a), "Acid Rain Reduction Credits," *Challenge*, 32, 25–9.

—— (1989b), "Marketable Permits in the U.S.: A Decade of Experience," in Karl W. Roskamp (ed.), *Public Finance and the Performance of Enterprises*, Detroit, MI, Wayne State University Press.

—— and Atkinson, S. E. (1989), "Bilateral, Sequential Trading and the Cost-Effectiveness of the Bubble-Policy," Colby College Working Paper (August).

Vos, H. B. (1989), "The Application and Efficiency of Economic Instruments: Experiences in OECD Member Countries," a paper presented at the Symposium on Economic Instruments in Environmental Protection Policies, Stockholm, Sweden (June).

16 Environmental Policy Making in a Second-Best Setting

Lawrence H. Goulder

Lawrence H. Goulder is the Shuzo Nishihara Professor of Environmental and Resource Economics at Stanford University, Senior Fellow of the Institute for International Studies, University Fellow at Resources for the Future, and Research Associate at the National Bureau of Economic Research.

I. Introduction

Economists have long been interested in ways that taxes and other policy instruments can address environmental problems associated with externalities. This interest dates back at least to Pigou (1938), who showed that taxes could usefully internalize externalities and thereby "get the prices right"—that is, bring prices into alignment with marginal social cost. In the last two decades, there has been increased attention to other, non-tax market instruments—including tradeable emission permits and deposit-refund systems—as tools for dealing with environmental problems in an effective way.

Since the publication of Pigou's classic article, the tradition in environmental economics has been to analyze environmental policies with an almost exclusive attention to the externality of immediate concern and little attention to other distortions or market failures. However, in recent years economists have come to recognize the importance of interactions between environmental policies and other (nonenvironmental) distortions in the economy. In particular, there has been increased attention to the interconnections between environmental taxes and the distortions imposed by preexisting income or commodity taxes.

These interactions were first examined in a seminal contribution by Sandmo (1975), although the insights from this article were largely ignored until recently. Sandmo analyzed the optimal setting of commodity taxes when the production or consumption of one of the commodities generates an externality. He showed that when the government's need for revenue exceeds the level that can be generated by taxes set according to the "Pigov-

"Environmental Policy Making in a Second-Best Setting," by Lawrence H. Goulder was prepared for the University of CEMA Twentieth Anniversary Conference on Applied Economics, Buenos Aires, Argentina, November 12–14, 1998. The original version of this paper appeared in the *Journal of Applied Economics*, 1(2) (November 1998). Section II of the present paper replaces the previous, more technical version of Section II. The author is grateful to Roberton C. Williams III for very helpful comments, and to the National Science Foundation (Grant SBR9613458) and U.S. Environmental Protection Agency (Grant R825313-01) for financial support.

ian principle" (that is, set equal to the marginal environmental damages), then the optimal tax system includes taxes not only on externality-generating goods and services but on other goods and services as well. In Sandmo's analysis, the optimal tax rates on environmentally damaging activities and on ordinary activities are intimately connected.

The interconnections between ordinary and environmental taxes, so central to Sandmo's optimal tax result, also figure importantly in the analysis of the impacts of marginal (that is, less than globally optimizing) environmental reforms. A line of research conducted during this decade shows that one cannot effectively evaluate the impacts of many environmental reforms without paying attention to the magnitudes and types of existing, distortionary taxes such as income, payroll, or sales taxes. There are two important interconnections here. First, as Terkla (1984), Lee and Misiolek (1986), Oates and Schwab (1988), Oates (1993), Repetto et al. (1992), and others have emphasized, the presence of distortionary taxes introduces opportunities to use revenues from new environmental taxes to finance cuts in the marginal rates of the ordinary distortionary taxes. To the extent that revenues from the environmental tax finance marginal rate cuts of this kind, some of the distortions that the ordinary taxes would have generated are avoided. This *revenue-recycling effect* suggests that the overall *gross*[1] costs of environmental taxes will be lower in a second-best world than in a first-best setting.

However, a second interconnection works in the opposite direction. Recent work by Bovenberg and de Mooij (1994a), Bovenberg and van der Ploeg (1994), Bovenberg and Goulder (1996, 1997), Parry (1995, 1997), and others[2] points out that environmental taxes are implicit taxes on factors of production such as labor and capital. By raising the costs of production and the costs of goods in general, environmental taxes (and many other environmental regulations) reduce real after-tax factor returns much like explicit factor taxes do. Thus, environmental taxes function as increments to existing factor taxes, tending to magnify the factor market distortions already generated by preexisting factor taxes. The additional efficiency costs of environmental taxes associated with the reduction in factor returns brought about by higher costs and output prices has been called the *tax-interaction effect*.[3] The larger the rates of preexisting factor taxes, the larger the tax-interaction effect, and thus the higher the gross costs from environmental taxes and other regulations that reduce after-tax returns to factors. The tax-interaction effect implies that, for any given method of recycling the revenues, the gross costs of environmental taxes are higher in a second-best setting with preexisting factor taxes than they would be if there

---

[1]The modifier "gross" indicates that the costs do not net out the policy-generated benefits associated with an improved environment.

[2]For earlier reviews of this recent literature, see Oates (1995) and Goulder (1995a).

[3]Parry (1995) was the first to isolate the tax-interaction and revenue-recycling effects in evaluating the second-best welfare impacts of environmental taxes. He termed these the "interdependency" and "revenue" effects.

were no prior taxes on factors. As will be discussed in more detail later in this paper, the tax-interaction effect tends to be of greater magnitude than the revenue-recycling effect; that is, it is only partly offset by the revenue-recycling effect.

The revenue-recycling and tax-interaction effects are highly relevant to the evaluation of "green tax reforms." A green tax policy of particular interest is a revenue-neutral carbon tax, which would address the prospect of global climate change by discouraging combustion of fossil fuels and the associated emissions of carbon dioxide, a principal contributor to the greenhouse effect. In discussions of carbon taxes, there has been great interest in the possibility that judicious recycling of the revenues from these taxes could cause the overall gross costs of this policy to be become zero or negative. Proponents of carbon taxes certainly would welcome this result, since it implies that policy makers must only establish that there are nonnegative environment-related *benefits* from the carbon tax policy to justify the policy on efficiency grounds. Given the vast uncertainties about the environment-related benefits from carbon abatement, it would significantly reduce the information burden faced by policy makers if they simply needed to determine the sign, rather than magnitude, of the environmental benefits. If one ignores the tax-interaction effect and concentrates only on revenue-recycling (and the revenue-recycling effect), the prospects for a zero-cost carbon tax will seem quite good. But the tax-interaction effect also has a key role here and, as will be discussed below, this latter effect significantly reduces the scope for the zero-cost result.

The absence of a zero-cost result does not imply that carbon taxes are a bad idea; it only means that justifying these taxes requires attention to the magnitudes (not just the sign) of the environmental benefits. Even if revenue-neutral carbon taxes or other green tax reforms do not make environmental improvement a free lunch, they may reduce its cost enough to make it very much worth buying. Indeed, in most analyses (see below) appropriately scaled revenue-neutral green tax reforms yield environmental benefits that exceed their gross costs.

A second area where the revenue-recycling and tax-interaction effects are important is in the choice among alternative policy instruments. Consider, for example, the choice between pollution tax policies (or pollution permits policies involving the auctioning of permits by the government) and freely allocated (or "grandfathered"[4]) emissions permits. The former policies raise revenue and thus are capable of taking advantage of the revenue-recycling effect. The latter policies, in contrast, do not raise revenue and therefore cannot exploit this effect. As discussed below, the tax-

---

[4]In keeping with common practice, we use the terms "grandfathered" and "freely allocated" interchangeably. Strictly speaking, however, grandfathering is not synonymous with free allocation. Grandfathering is a legal provision whereby "old" entities (e.g., firms subject to previous environmental rules) are waived of new regulatory requirements and instead remain bound only to the earlier (and perhaps more lax) regulatory provisions.

interaction effect arises under both policies, but only under the revenue-raising policies is the (costly) tax-interaction effect offset by the revenue-recycling effect. Recent work by Parry (1997), Goulder, Parry, and Burtraw (1997), Parry, Williams, and Goulder (1999), Fullerton and Metcalf (1997), and Goulder et al. (1999) reveals that the presence or absence of the revenue-recycling effect can fundamentally affect the overall efficiency impacts of these policies.[5] In fact, when marginal benefits from pollution abatement fail to exceed a certain threshold value, pollution permit policies that fail to enjoy the revenue-recycling effect may be unable to produce any efficiency improvements, no matter what the level of pollution abatement![6] This analysis shows that the decision to give out pollution permits free rather than to auction them (or, equivalent, to employ a pollution tax) comes at a high price in terms of efficiency, and indeed may affect the sign of the overall efficiency impact. Other considerations—such as distributional consequences—may tend to support the use of grandfathered permits rather than auctioned permits or pollution taxes, but this recent literature indicates that the efficiency disadvantage of grandfathered permits is more significant than was previously recognized.

This paper examines the efficiency impacts of pollution taxes and some other pollution-control policies in a second-best setting with prior distortionary taxes in factor markets. It aims to articulate and pull together some key ideas from recent papers on this subject. The next section heuristically describes some of the main results from recent work on the efficiency effects of environmental taxes and quotas (or tradeable permits) in a second-best setting.[7] Section III then elaborates on these results, first by offering additional interpretation related to environmental taxes and the double dividend issue, and then by considering the significance of second-best issues for the choice between taxes and other, non-tax instruments for environmental protection. Section IV briefly depicts some results from investigations that apply this second-best framework to assess the efficiency impacts of environmental taxes and regulations. It first considers the impacts of revenue-neutral environmental taxes; it then examines potential impacts of pollution permits, with a focus on the efficiency implications of the decision whether to auction or freely offer the permits. The final section offers conclusions.

---

[5]Fullerton and Metcalf explain differences in efficiency outcomes in terms of whether policies generate privately-retained scarcity rents, rather than in terms of whether they exploit the revenue-recycling effect. As discussed in Section III, the two issues are intimately connected.

[6]This result, for pollution permits, was foreshadowed by Bovenberg and Goulder's (1996) finding that a carbon tax with lump-sum replacement of the revenues will be efficiency-reducing if marginal environmental benefits from carbon abatement are below a certain threshold (about $50 per ton). Parry (1997) recognized that the same formal analysis applies to the case of pollution quotas and grandfathered pollution permits; thus the same "threshold" issue arises.

[7]This section offers a nontechnical presentation of the results generated in Goulder (1998). Other sections of this paper involve only incidental changes from the corresponding sections in Goulder (1998).

II. Impacts of Environmental Taxes and Quotas in a Second-Best Setting

A. The Conventional, Partial Equilibrium Analysis of Policy Impacts

To understand how environmental policies interact with preexisting factor-market distortions, it helps to consider first the impacts of environmental policies in a setting with no prior distortionary taxes. We can then observe how the situation changes in the presence of distortionary taxes and associated factor-market distortions.

Figure 1 offers the typical partial equilibrium framework for analyzing the welfare effects of an environmental tax or quota.[8] *MC* denotes the private marginal costs of producing the given commodity, which in this example is coal. MC_{soc} represents the social marginal-cost curve, incorporating the marginal external damage (marginal external cost) *MED*. *MB* represents the marginal benefit (demand) curve. If a tax is imposed on coal equal to the marginal external damage, the welfare gain is area *B*.[9] This is the value of the environmental improvement (*A* + *B*) minus the gross costs of the tax (*A*).[10]

The same figure indicates the impacts of a quota on coal use. Suppose that the government restricts total coal use to the quantity Q_1. The government could do this, for example, by issuing licenses to coal-supplying firms, where the licenses authorize the sale of coal and where the total number of licenses limits aggregate sales to Q_1. (Assume that the licenses are given out free, rather than auctioned, so that the government does not earn revenue in issuing licenses. We will consider shortly the significance of auctioning the licenses.) The diagram indicates that the restriction in coal supply will cause the price of coal to rise by the same amount as in the case of the coal tax. Under this policy, the restriction on coal supply imposes gross costs of *A*; these gross costs are the lost potential surplus to users of coal such as steel manufacturers or electric utilities. The value of the environmental improvement is again (*A* + *B*), and thus the welfare gain is again *B*.[11]

---

[8]Here the tax is a strict Pigovian tax in that it applies to a commodity with which pollution is associated rather than directly to pollution emissions. Similarly, the quota applies to the commodity (coal) rather than to pollution emissions from coal. The lessons from this section apply equally to taxes and quotas on emissions. For a general examination of issues surrounding the choice between regulating emissions and regulating a commodity closely associated with emissions, see Bovenberg and Goulder (1999).

[9]In the case with nonconstant private marginal costs or nonconstant marginal external costs, the presentation is slightly more complicated but the results are essentially the same.

[10]The environmental economics literature often refers to *abatement costs*. These are usually defined in a way that corresponds, in Figure 1, to the entire area below the *MB* curve (including the area below the *MC* curve) over the interval from Q_0 to Q_1.

[11]The efficiency impacts of the tax and quota are the same in this example. However, this example ignores uncertainty by the regulator with regard to firms' costs of coal (or pollution) abatement. In the presence of such uncertainty, taxes and quotas generally have different impacts. See Weitzman (1974) and Stavins (1995).

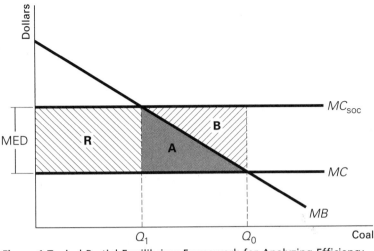

Figure 1 Typical Partial Equilibrium Framework for Analyzing Efficiency Impacts of Environmental Taxes and Quotas

B. Two Complications

Prior distortionary taxes complicate the analysis in two ways. The simple analysis usually assumes that there are no efficiency consequences associated with the transfer of the tax revenue R from those who pay the coal tax to the government and then back to the private sector.[12] However, in an economy with prior taxes, the revenues from an environmental tax can be used to finance reductions in the marginal rates of prior distortionary taxes such as income, payroll, or sales taxes. When revenues are "recycled" in this way, some of the distortions or excess burdens from prior taxes can be avoided. This beneficial efficiency impact is the revenue-recycling effect.

A second complicating effect works in the opposite direction. This second effect, the tax-interaction effect, occurs because the environmental tax or quote tends to reduce the real returns to factors such as labor and capital, discourage the supply of these factors, and thereby exacerbate preexisting distortions in factor markets. The tax-interaction effect is discussed in general terms in a number of recent studies.[13] For concreteness, in the present discussion we will illustrate the tax-interaction effect using our example with coal. In addition, we will describe the tax-interaction effect through its impact on the labor market. A recent paper by Williams (1999) shows that the tax-interaction effect applies to capital in much the same way it applies to labor.

The tax-interaction effect reflects the links from (1) the tax or quota to (2) the cost of living to (3) the real wage and finally to (4) the distortion in

---

[12]In the simplest case, the revenues are returned to the private sector in a lump-sum fashion.
[13]See Parry (1995, 1997), Goulder, Parry, and Burtraw (1997), and Goulder et al. (1999).

the labor market. As suggested by Figure 1, the tax or the quota causes the market price of coal to rise. The higher price of coal raises costs to users of coal, which implies increased prices of goods or services from coal-using industries. One might expect the price-increases to be most pronounced in the industries for which coal is a significant, direct input (e.g., electricity and steel). However, higher coal prices affect the costs and output prices of other industries too, since other industries use coal indirectly: for example, they use the steel that was made from coal. Through direct and indirect cost-impacts, the higher coal price leads to higher prices in many industries and contributes to a rise in the cost of living. This increase in the cost of living means that a given nominal wage, w, now represents a lower real wage.

By raising the costs of goods and services, environmental policies reduce the real return to labor. These policies are implicit taxes on labor (and other factors of production). These implicit taxes discourage labor (and other factor) supply, as indicated by Figure 2. In this figure, S_L and D_L represent the supply and demand curves for labor, respectively. Let τ_L denote the prior tax on labor implied by preexisting payroll or income taxes. In this setting, with a prior labor tax, the initial equilibrium labor supply is $L_1 < L_0$. The prior distortion in the labor market is given by the triangular region defined by points a, b, and c. Now consider the labor-market impact of the environmental tax or quota. By raising the cost of living and lowering the real wage, the environmental policy induces a shift in the

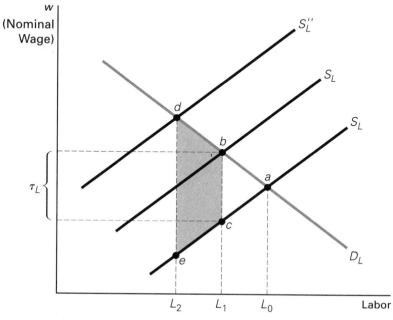

Figure 2 The Tax Interaction Effect

labor supply curve from S_L^i to S_L^{ii}. This implies a further reduction (to L_2) in the equilibrium labor supply, and a further distortion in the labor market, represented by the trapezoidal area defined by points b, d, e, and c. This area is the tax-interaction effect. As suggested by Figure 2, the tax-interaction effect is an increasing function of the size of the prior tax on labor.[14] In the limiting case where the prior tax τ_L is zero, the tax-interaction effect disappears.

Thus, in a second-best setting, two effects complicate the efficiency analysis of environmental taxes and quotas. The revenue-recycling effect tends to imply lower costs of these policies than in a "first-best" setting with no prior taxes. But the tax-interaction effect tends to imply higher costs. Which effect is stronger? In the simple models developed in recent studies, the tax-interaction effect dominates. If the good to which the environmental tax applies in an average substitute for leisure, the tax-interaction effect is stronger than the revenue-recycling effect.[15] This implies that the costs of environmental taxes and quotas are higher in the presence of prior factor taxes than in their absence—even when the revenues are recycled through cuts in marginal income tax rates.

Why is the tax-interaction effect more powerful? Note that the environmental (coal) tax affects the relative prices of goods and services. It thus "distorts" not only the labor market (by lowering the real wage) but also "distorts" consumers' choices among these goods and services.[16] Recycling the revenues helps return the real wage to its original value and thereby helps reduce the labor-market distortion, but such recycling does not undo the change in relative consumer good prices and the associated "distortion" in consumption choices. For this reason the revenue-recycling effect only partly offsets the tax-interaction effect. The revenue-neutral environmental tax policy effectively substitutes (at the margin) a narrow environmental tax for a broader income tax. This makes the tax system less efficient along the nonenvironmental dimensions captured under the notion of gross cost. (At the same time, the tax system may well be more efficient overall, once one accounts for the environment-related benefits from the tax or quota.)

Figure 3 illustrates these findings. The figure shows the marginal efficiency costs of pollution abatement, at different levels of abatement, where the efficiency costs represented here are gross (that is, exclusive) of the benefits from environmental improvement. The lowermost line depicts the marginal costs of abatement in the "first-best" setting, by which we mean an economy with no distortionary taxes. In a first-best situation, the marginal costs of abatement are the same regardless of whether an environmental tax or quota is imposed.

---

[14]See Parry (1997) for a rigorous demonstration.

[15]We discuss below the significance of the "average substitute" assumption.

[16]The word "distort" is in quotes to acknowledge that we are ignoring environment-related benefits here. While the changes in relative prices of commodities occasioned by the environmental tax may contribute to higher gross costs, these same relative price changes may bring about an overall efficiency improvement, since overall efficiency incorporates the environment-related benefits (reduced pollution) associated with the relative price changes.

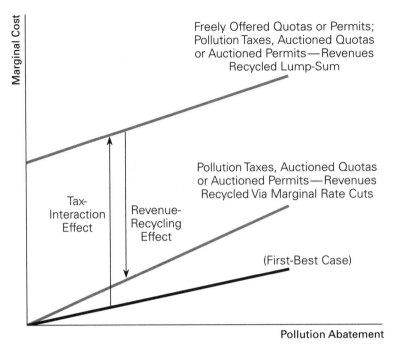

Figure 3 Marginal Costs of Pollution Abatement in First- and Second-Best Settings

The other lines represent the marginal costs in an economy with prior distortionary taxes. The top line depicts the marginal costs of abatement for policies that produce the tax-interaction effect but do not enjoy the revenue-recycling effect. Several policies fall into this category. One is the coal quota just discussed. Another is a system of tradeable coal permits, where the permits are given out free ("grandfathered"). A third is a coal tax policy in which the revenues are returned to the economy lump-sum rather than through cuts in marginal tax rates. In all of these cases, the revenue-recycling effect is absent. For these policies, at all levels of abatement, the marginal costs of abatement are higher than in the first-best case. This is the case even at incremental abatement: the second-best marginal cost curve has a positive intercept, whereas the marginal cost of incremental abatement for these policies is zero in the first-best case.[17] At any level of abatement, the tax-interaction effect is represented by the vertical distance between the top and bottom marginal cost curve.

The intercept of the top marginal cost curve represents the critical value for marginal environmental *benefits* from pollution abatement through these policies. If the marginal benefits are (always) below this value, then pollution reductions through one of these policies will always involve costs

---

[17]So long as the prior tax rate on labor is positive, the introduction of these environmental policies augments a preexisting distortion and involves a first-order (i.e., nonincremental) efficiency cost.

that exceed the benefits. Under these circumstances, these policies will be efficiency-reducing regardless of the level of abatement!

The middle line in Figure 3 represents the marginal costs of abatement for policies that exploit the revenue-recycling effect by raising revenues and using these revenues to finance cuts in the marginal rates of prior distortionary taxes. Such policies include environmental taxes, *auctioned* coal quotas or *auctioned* tradeable permits, where revenues are recycled through marginal rate cuts. The revenue-recycling effect is represented by the vertical distance between the top and middle marginal cost curves. Revenue-recycling through marginal rate reductions can significantly reduce the general-equilibrium costs of environmental regulations. At incremental abatement, the revenue-recycling effect fully offsets the tax-interaction effect; hence, the marginal cost of abatement is zero at incremental abatement (as in the first-best case). However, for larger amounts of abatement, the revenue-recycling effect only partly offsets the tax-interaction effect (for the reasons given above), and thus the costs of abatement exceed the costs of comparable abatement in a first-best setting.

Figure 3 illustrates the idea that an environmental policy's potential to yield an overall efficiency gain can depend on whether it exploits the revenue-recycling effect. By definition, a policy yields an efficiency improvement if and only if its (environment-related) benefits exceed its overall gross costs (including the net contribution of the tax-interaction and revenue-recycling effects). The revenue-recycling effect may be necessary to make net benefits positive.

The figure also indicates that second-best considerations tend to imply higher costs from environmental policies. Even so, the news for environmental policy reform is not entirely bad. Note that for policies that exploit the revenue-recycling effect, the general equilibrium marginal costs are initially zero. Note also that, in general, one would expect the (gross) marginal *benefits* from pollution-abatement to be strictly positive at initial amounts of abatement. Together, these ideas imply that these policies generally will be justified on efficiency grounds—so long as the amount of abatement is not too great. In a second-best world, there remains potential for efficiency gains through pollution taxes and other policies that deal with pollution-related externalities.

It should be noted that Figure 3 illustrates the "central case" results from analytical models—that is, the results that stem from the assumption that the good on which the environmental tax is imposed is an average substitute for leisure. Suppose instead, that this good were a weaker than average substitute for leisure, that is, a relative complement to leisure. Analytical studies indicate that in this case, for a sufficiently small environmental tax (or sufficiently small amount of abatement in Figure 3), the revenue-recycling effect will outweigh the tax-interaction effect. Under these circumstances, the costs of abatement are *lower* in a second-best world than in a first-best world—at least up to a certain level of abatement. When a good is a relative complement to leisure, the environmental tax causes a reduction in both the demand for that good and the demand for leisure. The reduced demand for leisure, or increased supply of labor, helps alleviate preexisting labor market distortion. If, on the other hand, the taxed good were a stronger than average substitute for leisure, the tax-interaction effect would overtake the revenue-recycling effect by even more than in the average-substitute case, and the costs of given amounts of abatement would be greater than in the average-substitute case. There is a lack of solid empirical information regarding the extent to which various pollution-related goods are substitutes or complements with leisure. In the absence of such information, the assumption of "average substitutability" seems reasonable. Further empirical work that clarifies these substitutability or complementarity relationships could be of great value to researchers aiming to assess the costs of environmental regulations.

III. Interpretations, Qualifications, and Extensions

A. Can Pollution Taxes Deliver a "Double Dividend"?

In recent years there has been considerable debate about the possibilities for "green tax reform," that is, the substitution of taxes on pollution for ordinary, distortionary taxes. A general argument for such reform is that it makes sense to concentrate taxes on "bads" like pollution rather than "goods" like labor effort or capital formation (saving and investment). To buttress the case for green tax reform, some analysts have argued that the revenue-neutral swap of pollution taxes for ordinary taxes will produce a "double dividend": not only (1) improve the quality of the environment but also (2) reduce certain costs of the tax system. This argument has occupied a prominent place in the debate about carbon taxes, as mentioned in the introduction. Few analysts deny the first dividend; it is the second dividend that generates controversy.

Can environmental taxes generate the second dividend? Different policy analysts have meant different things by this dividend, and this has led to confusion. Goulder (1995a) distinguishes a "strong" and "weak" version of the double dividend claim, as follows. Let $C(\tau_E, \Delta\tau_L)$ refer to the gross cost of a revenue-neutral policy involving a new environmental tax τ_E that finances the change (reduction) $\Delta\tau_L$ in preexisting distortionary taxes.[18] Let $C(\tau_E, \Delta T)$ denote the gross cost of a revenue-neutral policy in which a new environmental tax τ_E finances the lump-sum reduction in taxes, ΔT. The weak double dividend claim is:

$$C(\tau_E, \Delta\tau_L) < C(\tau_E, \Delta T)$$

---

[18]In keeping with Section II's focus on labor-market distortions, we use the subscript "L" to refer to the distortionary factor tax. The points raised here apply to economies in which there are several distortionary taxes, including taxes on capital as well as labor.

The above expression asserts that a reform in which the environmental tax's revenues are recycled through cuts in the rates of distortionary tax involves lower gross costs than a policy in which the environmental tax's revenues are returned lump-sum. This weak double-dividend claim is easy to justify: environmental taxes, with revenues devoted to cuts in distortionary taxes, do indeed lower the costs of the tax system *relative to what the costs would be if the revenues were returned lump-sum.* As shown in Goulder (1995a), the weak double-dividend claim is upheld so long as the tax τ_L is appropriately labeled as distortionary. That is, the weak claim is upheld if and only if the tax τ_L has a positive marginal excess burden.

In terms of Figure 3, the weak double-dividend claim is verified by the fact that the marginal cost curve for the environmental tax with lump-sum revenue-replacement lies above the curve for the environmental tax accompanied by cuts in the marginal rates of a distortionary tax. In essence, the weak double-dividend claim amounts to the assertion that, in terms of efficiency, it pays to take advantage of the revenue-recycling effect. Thus it is closely related to the notion that pollution taxes that finance cuts in distortionary taxes are preferable on efficiency grounds to pollution quotas or grandfathered tradeable permits.

The stronger double-dividend claim is

$$C(\tau_E, \Delta\tau_L) \leq 0$$

that is, the revenue-neutral swap of an environmental tax for existing distortionary taxes involves zero or negative gross costs. This is equivalent to asserting that the gross distortionary cost directly attributable to the environmental tax is smaller than the avoided gross distortionary cost stemming from the environmental-tax-financed cut in the distortionary tax. If this strong double-dividend claim held for a carbon tax, then, as noted in the introduction, the tax would be justified on efficiency grounds so long as the environment-related gross *benefits* from the policy were nonnegative.

Is the stronger claim justified? Figure 3 sheds light on the answer. For the strong claim to be valid, the marginal cost curve for the pollution tax accompanied by cuts in distortionary taxes would have to lie on or below the horizontal axis. Clearly the curve does not fulfill this requirement—except at zero abatement. To support the stronger double-dividend claim, the revenue-recycling effect not only would have to fully offset the tax-interaction effect, but also would have to overcome the usual, first-best abatement costs represented by the dashed line. The analytical studies referred to in Section II, which form the basis for the positions of the marginal cost curves in Figure 3, do not support such an outcome. In these studies, for anything but an infinitesimal amount of abatement (infinitesimal environmental tax) the gross costs of a revenue-neutral environmental tax reform are positive.

Some qualifications are in order. As mentioned in the previous section, in most of the aforementioned analytical models the pollution-generating (or "dirty") good is assumed to be an average substitute for leisure. If instead the pollution-generating good were a weaker than average substitute for (stronger than average complement with) leisure, then the double dividend will arise after all—for a sufficiently small environmental tax. Further empirical work to gauge the extent of substitutability or complementarity could shed much light.

Second, more complex theoretical models can provide more scope for the strong double-dividend claim than is offered here.[19] To achieve greater tractability, many of the models examining this issue consider only one factor of production—labor. In models with both capital and labor, an environmental tax reform can produce the second dividend under certain circumstances. Specifically, if the tax system initially is highly inefficient in the sense that one factor is overtaxed relative to the other,[20] and if the environmental tax reform (the combination of the tax itself and the recycling of the revenues) serves to shift the tax burden from the overtaxed to the undertaxed factor, then the reform will produce a *tax-shifting effect* that works toward a more efficient tax system. If this beneficial tax-shifting effect is large enough, it (combined with the revenue-recycling effect) can entirely compensate for usual "first-best" abatement costs and the tax-interaction effect.[21] Thus, under these circumstances, the strong double dividend materializes after all.

Most empirical studies indicate that in the United States, capital is overtaxed (in efficiency terms) relative to labor.[22] With these initial conditions, an environmental tax reform will produce a favorable tax-shifting effect if it shifts the burden away from capital and toward labor. Bovenberg and Goulder (1997) examine two environmentally motivated, revenue-neutral tax reforms—a Btu tax applied to fossil fuels and an increase in the Federal gasoline tax—and find that the latter policy produces a tax-shifting effect that significantly reduces the gross costs. However, the tax-shifting effect is generally not strong enough to make the gross costs zero or negative, except under extreme values for behavioral parameters. Although the results are somewhat mixed, other simulation studies have tended to support the idea that it is difficult to generate the strong double dividend under plausible parameter values and realistic policy specifications.[23]

The possibility of a (strong) double dividend through a powerful tax-shifting effect is illustrative of a general theme that emerges from recent theoretical work. In virtually all of the theoretical studies, a double

---

[19]Bovenberg (1996), Goulder (1995a), and Bovenberg and Goulder (1999) analyze a range of complicating issues.

[20]In efficiency terms, one factor of production is overtaxed relative to another if the tax on this factor has a larger marginal excess burden per dollar of revenue than the tax on the other factor.

[21]For a theoretical treatment of the tax-shifting issue, see Bovenberg and de Mooij (1994b), and Bovenberg and Goulder (1997).

[22]See, for example, Ballard, Shoven, and Whalley (1985), Fullerton and Mackie (1987), Jorgenson and Yun (1990), Lucas (1990), and Goulder and Thalmann (1993).

[23]Goulder (1995a) surveys these studies.

dividend becomes possible only when two general conditions are met: (1) prior to the introduction of the environmental tax reform, there is a significant inefficiency in the tax system along a nonenvironmental dimension, and (2) the environmental tax reform serves to reduce this "nonenvironmental" inefficiency. If this "non-green" benefit from green tax reform is large enough, it can compensate for the factors that work against the double dividend. The possibility of a double dividend through environmental tax policies that reduce prior inefficiencies in the relative taxation of labor and capital is an illustration of this general theme.[24]

It is important to recognize that the absence of the (strong) double dividend does not vitiate the case for green tax reform. It only means that the positive *sign* of the environmental benefits is not a sufficient condition for justifying such reform. If there is no double dividend, policy makers are obliged to consider the magnitudes of the environmental benefits and compare them with the (positive) gross costs. Also, the absence of a double dividend does not repudiate our intuition that it makes sense to orient the tax system, to a degree, on "bads" (polluting activities) rather than "goods" (labor and capital). *Even if the strong double-dividend claim fails, it is still the case that "Pigovian considerations" should be part of the design of an efficient tax system*: other things equal, the tax on a given good or activity should be higher, the larger the environmental externalities associated with that good or activity. Higher environmental benefits justify higher taxes on polluting activities. It is the larger environmental benefits—not the presumption of zero gross costs—that justify the greening of the tax system.

B. Significance of the Scale of Abatement for the Choice between Taxes and Quotas

The theoretical model indicated that the pollution taxes and auctioned permits have an efficiency advantage over pollution quotas and grandfathered pollution permits to the extent that the former policies exploit the revenue-recycling effect. However, the size of the efficiency advantage generally declines with the amount of abatement. In fact, this advantages approaches zero as the extent of abatement approaches 100 percent. This is illustrated by Figure 4, which is borrowed from Goulder, Parry, and Burtraw (1997), which we will refer to as GPB. Marginal costs rise faster for the pollution tax (or auctioned pollution permit) policy. Eventually—when the extent of abatement is substantial—marginal costs under this policy exceed those for the pollution quota (or grandfathered permit) policy.

---

[24]This theme also is illustrated in the case where the double dividend can arise because the pollution-generating good is a stronger than average complement with leisure. Ignoring environmental considerations, optimal "Ramsey" commodity taxation would tend to justify taxing this relative complement to leisure. In this setting, introducing an environmental tax both serves an environmental purpose and helps eliminate a preexisting inefficiency of the tax system along nonenvironmental dimensions. Thus the situation is conducive to a double dividend.

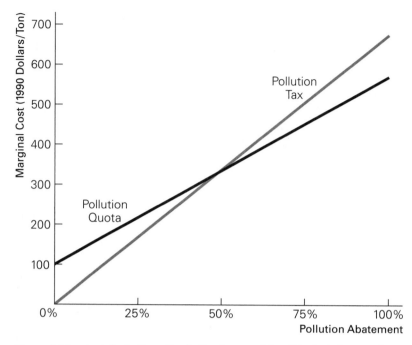

Figure 4 Marginal Costs Over the Entire Range of Possible Emissions Reductions

Why is this so? Consider the pollution tax. Because of this policy's negative impact on labor supply and on emissions, marginal tax revenue declines as the emissions tax rate rises. This means that, with greater abatement, the ability to exploit the revenue-recycling effect diminishes. Eventually, the point is reached where, at the margin, additional abatement (via an incrementally higher pollution tax) raises no more revenue than is raised under the quota policy.[25]

That is the point where the pollution tax and pollution quota marginal cost curves cross. To the right of that point, *at the margin* the tax policy is more costly than the quota policy, because at the margin it has a *negative* revenue-recycling effect (as compared with the negligible revenue-recycling effect of the quota policy). Indeed, if one pursues emissions reductions to the point of 100 percent abatement, the total costs of the two types of policies are identical. This makes sense: at 100 percent abatement neither policy earns any revenue, and thus there is no effective difference between a tax and a quota at that point. Thus the areas under the marginal cost curves from 0 to 100 percent abatement are the same for both policies.

These results demonstrate that the relative superiority (in terms of lower cost) of policies that exploit the revenue-recycling effect diminishes

---

[25]The quota policy does not necessarily raise zero revenue. This policy will tend to raise revenue insofar as quota rents are taxed, and will tend to lose revenue insofar as the policy causes a loss of overall real income and a reduction in the labor tax base.

with the extent of abatement. At low levels of abatement (as would be appropriate if marginal environmental *benefits* are low), these policies have a considerable cost advantage. But at high levels of abatement (as would be justified when marginal environmental benefits are high) the advantage of these policies is much smaller. In the limiting case of 100 percent abatement, these policies have no cost advantage.

C. Impacts of Other Environmental Policies in a Second-Best Setting

Thus far, all of the discussion in this paper has centered on pollution taxes, quotas, and permits. Recent papers by Fullerton and Metcalf (1997) and Goulder, Parry, Williams, and Burtraw (1999) examine the impacts of other policy instruments (in addition to pollution taxes and quotas) in a second-best setting.[26] Among the additional instruments considered in these recent papers are some "command-and-control" policies: namely, mandated technologies and performance standards.

Goulder et al. (1999) show that preexisting taxes also raise the costs of the command-and-control policies relative to their costs in a first-best world. Like emissions taxes and quotas, the command-and-control policies raise production costs and lead to higher output prices. If there are prior distortionary taxes in factor markets, the higher output prices produce the tax-interaction effect, which implies higher costs relative to the costs in a first-best setting.

Although second-best considerations raise the costs of all instruments, they do not increase costs in the same proportion. Indeed, when the amount of pollution-abatement is incremental or "small," preexisting taxes especially raise the costs of non-auctioned quotas or permits, and can put non-auctioned quotas or permits at a cost-disadvantage relative to command-and-control policies. Economists have long favored market-based policies as being more cost-effective than the command-and-control alternatives. Yet in a second-best setting, certain market-based policies can be at a disadvantage. The recent studies by Fullerton and Metcalf and Goulder et al. indicate that the marginal abatement costs of performance standards and technology mandates resemble those of the emissions tax in that marginal costs are zero at the first increment of abatement.[27] This contrasts with the strictly positive costs of initial abatement under a non-auctioned quota. Thus, for "low" amounts of abatement, a command-and-control policy can be less costly than grandfathered permits. However, it should be kept in mind that the command-and-control policies eventually involve higher costs as the amount of abatement becomes very extensive. As discussed in Goul-

---

[26]See also Ng (1980), who analyzed environmental subsidies in the presence of prior tax distortions.

[27]This point was first demonstrated by Fullerton and Metcalf. This was shown for a "technology restriction" policy, which was a constraint on the ratio of labor input to emissions. In their model, this is functionally equivalent to a policy involving a constraint on the ratio of emissions to output.

der et al. (1999), this reflects the inability of these alternative instruments to provide the appropriate prices of inputs and outputs.

It is worth considering further why the marginal cost curves of these alternative instruments emerge from the origin (as in the case of the pollution tax or auctioned quota—with revenues devoted to marginal rate reductions), while the marginal cost curves of grandfathered quotas (or emissions taxes with revenues returned lump sum) do not. Since the mandated technology and performance standard do not raise revenue, it is clear that raising revenue *per se* is not necessary for the zero-marginal-cost-at-initial-abatement property to obtain. One can explain these differences in terms of whether the tax-interaction and revenue-recycling effects cancel at initial abatement. At the first incremental amount of abatement, emissions taxes (with revenues returned through marginal rate cuts) produce a strictly positive tax-interaction effect that is exactly offset by the strictly negative revenue-recycling effect. Hence the marginal abatement costs are zero at initial abatement. The mandated technology and performance standard produce neither a tax-interaction effect nor a revenue-recycling effect. Hence the marginal costs of abatement are again zero at initial abatement.[28] In contrast, under grandfathered quotas there is a strictly positive tax-interaction effect and no offsetting revenue-recycling effect. Hence marginal costs are strictly positive. Thus, the tax-interaction and revenue-recycling effects can explain why marginal costs start out strictly positive under nonauctioned permits or quotas, and start out at zero under the other policies.

These differences at initial abatement can also be linked to the presence or absence of a lump-sum transfer. The government effectuates a lump-sum transfer to individuals when it introduces a pollution tax and returns the revenues lump-sum, when it implements a pollution quota (thus generating quota rents that are not entirely taxed away), or when it introduces a pollution tax and recycles the revenues through cuts in the marginal tax rate on a perfectly inelastically supplied factor of production.[29] In a second-best world, such transfers involve an efficiency cost because they must ultimately be financed through distortionary taxes. In contrast, under the pollution tax or fuels tax (with revenues financing cuts in prior taxes), or under the mandated technology or performance standard, there is no such transfer. Thus the presence or absence of a positive intercept of the marginal cost function corresponds to the presence or absence of this lump-sum transfer.[30]

---

[28]Alternatively, one can view the technology mandate as producing two tax-interaction effects and two revenue-recycling effects. As indicated by Fullerton and Metcalf, the mandated technology is equivalent to the combination of a subsidy to the use of the clean input and a tax on emissions. The subsidy and tax components respectively account for negative (in efficiency terms) and positive revenue-recycling effects, which cancel out, and positive and negative tax-interaction effects, which also cancel out (at the first unit of abatement).

[29]This last case is examined by Bovenberg and de Mooij (1996) and Williams (1998).

[30]Fullerton and Metcalf (1997) point out that pollution regulation through grandfathered permits creates scarcity rents that remain in private (that is, the regulated firm's) hands, and indicate that this accounts for the fact that the marginal costs of incremental abatement are strictly positive. The creation of scarcity rents is an example of the government's bringing about a lump-sum transfer to the private sector.

IV. Some Numerical Results

Thus far we have only considered results from analytical models. Analytical tractability comes at a price in that it necessitates the use of fairly simple models. In this section we briefly display results from some numerical models.[31]

First we present some results that pertain to the double-dividend issue. Here we display and briefly interpret results from the disaggregated computable general equilibrium model employed in Bovenberg and Goulder (1997). We will only sketch the results here; the reader is referred to the Bovenberg-Goulder article for details. In this discussion we also present a sampling of results from other numerical models.

Next we display numerical results indicating how preexisting taxes affect the choice between auctioned and grandfathered emissions permits, in the context of sulfur dioxide (SO_2) and carbon dioxide (CO_2) emissions reductions in the United States.

A. Numerical Explorations of the Double-Dividend Issue

1. Results from Bovenberg-Goulder (1997). Here we examine simulations in which a fossil fuel Btu tax or a consumer gasoline tax increase is implemented in revenue-neutral fashion, with the revenues devoted to reductions in the income tax. An important item to keep in mind when interpreting the results is the relative taxation of capital and labor. In the baseline, or reference equilibrium (and under central values for parameters), the marginal excess burden (MEB) of capital taxes is .43, while the MEB of labor taxes is .31. This means that the tax-shifting effect (see III.A above) works in favor of the second dividend when policies shift the burden of taxation from (overtaxed) capital to (undertaxed) labor. In this regard, note that while the Btu tax tends to fall more or less evenly on capital and labor, the gasoline tax tends to fall mainly on labor (by virtue of its being akin to a consumption tax). Hence the gasoline tax has more potential for tax-shifting that support the second dividend.

Figure 5 shows results when these taxes are introduced with *lump-sum* replacement of the revenues. Figure 5a shows that in the short term, the environmental (Btu and gas) taxes entail a greater GDP sacrifice than the personal income tax. Figure 5b shows that the gasoline tax has a much smaller investment cost than does the Btu tax or income tax. This reflects the fact that the gasoline tax tends to ease the tax burden on capital.

Table 1 shows the effects of these policies on factor prices and quantities. It indicates that the combination of gasoline tax increase and reduction in personal income tax reduces capital's tax burden and raises la-

---

[31]Real-world environmental taxes and other regulations involve "large," as opposed to incremental, changes in the level of pollution. Numerical simulation is usually necessary to evaluate the efficiency implications of these changes.

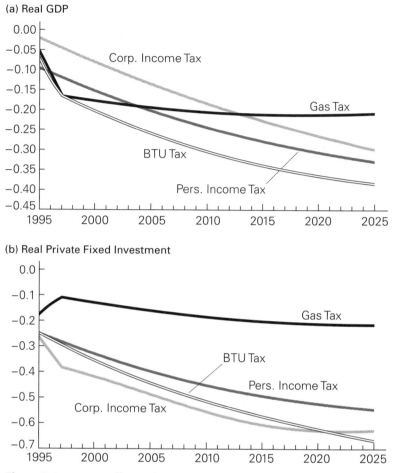

Figure 5 Aggregate Effects of Energy and Income Tax Policies (percentage changes from reference case)

bor's. In contrast, the combination of Btu tax and cut in personal income tax does not significantly alter the relative taxation of capital and labor. Thus, the revenue-neutral policy involving the gasoline tax produces a more significant tax-shifting effect.

Table 2 shows welfare effects. These are the monetary equivalent (using the equivalent variation) of the change in utility associated with the policy change. These welfare measures disregard welfare impacts associated with the changes in environmental quality; they refer only to the cost side of the benefit-cost ledger.

Comparing the left and right columns indicates the importance of the revenue-recycling effect; that is, of returning revenues through cuts in marginal tax rates instead of through lump-sum tax cuts. The welfare costs of the revenue-neutral reforms are significantly higher when revenues are returned in lump-sum fashion.

Table 1 Impacts of Taxes on Factor Prices and Supplies
(percentage changes from baseline)

	Years after Policy Introduction			
	1	*2*	*5*	*30*
"Single Tax" Policies:				
Btu Tax, Lump-Sum Repl.				
w	−0.250	−0.390	−0.446	−0.655
r	−0.083	−0.239	−0.179	−0.084
L	−0.124	−0.140	−0.121	−0.049
K	−0.017	−0.035	−0.092	−0.364
Gasoline Tax Increase, Lump-Sum Repl.				
w	−0.722	−1.069	−1.058	−0.983
r	0.095	−0.007	−0.027	−0.005
L	−0.266	−0.335	−0.331	−0.298
K	−0.011	−0.019	−0.031	−0.069
Personal Tax Increase, Lump-Sum Repl.				
w	−0.333	−0.347	−0.404	−0.655
r	−0.104	−0.108	−0.105	−0.053
L	−0.277	−0.274	−0.265	−0.212
K	−0.015	−0.030	−0.072	−0.313
Substitution of Environmental Tax *for Personal Tax:*				
Btu Tax, Personal Tax Repl.				
w	0.083	−0.042	−0.042	0.014
r	0.031	−0.125	−0.074	−0.053
L	0.157	0.139	0.149	0.163
K	−0.001	−0.005	−0.019	−0.037
Gasoline Tax Increase, Personal Tax Repl.				
w	−0.375	−0.694	−0.571	−0.307
r	0.216	0.111	0.076	0.057
L	0.013	−0.057	−0.061	−0.084
K	0.004	0.012	0.041	0.252

Note: *w*, *r*, *L*, and *K* respectively refer to the after-tax real wage, after-tax real rate of return, aggregate real labor supply, and aggregate real capital stock.

Table 2 Welfare Impacts

	Welfare Cost Per Dollar of Revenue	
	Lump-Sum Tax Replacement	*Personal Income Tax Replacement*
BTU Tax	.656	.318
Consumer-Level Gasoline Tax Increase	.594	.253
Personal Income Tax Increase	.379	—
Corporate Income Tax Increase	.438	.093

Concentrate now on the right column, which displays results from revenue-neutral policies in which the environmental tax revenues finance reductions in the personal tax. There are two main results from this column. First, the second dividend does not arise: the gross welfare costs (i.e., the costs before netting out the environmental benefits) are positive. Second, the welfare cost is lower for the gasoline tax reform, despite the narrower base of the gasoline tax. This reflects the tax-shifting effect: as Table 1 indicated, under the gasoline tax reform the tax burden is shifted from capital to labor, which tends to reduce the gross costs. However, the tax-shifting effect is not strong enough to undo the cost associated with the tax-interaction effect.

Is it possible to make the tax-shifting effect large enough to give the second dividend? Yes. The tax-shifting effect will be stronger to the extent that (1) the initial inefficiencies in the relative taxation of capital and labor are large, and (2) the policy shifts the burden from the overtaxed to the undertaxed factor. To enhance the first condition, we have performed simulations with very elastic capital supply assumptions. Specifically, we assume that the elasticity of substitution in consumption (which affects the household's interest elasticity of saving) is "high" relative to most estimates. To enhance the second condition, we consider a policy in which a gasoline tax is introduced and all the revenues from this tax are recycled through cuts in capital taxes only. This combination produces a large enough tax-shifting effect to yield the second dividend if the intertemporal elasticity of substitution is 1.8 or more. Although this shows that the second dividend can arise, producing this dividend seems to require implausibly high values for the intertemporal elasticity of substitution (most estimates are between 0 and unity)[32].

2. Results from a Sampling of Other Models.

Table 3 summarizes results from numerical studies of a revenue-neutral carbon tax policy. The table presents results from seven numerical models. These are the Goulder and Jorgenson-Wilcoxen intertemporal general equilibrium models of the United States, the Proost-Regemorter general equilibrium model of Belgium, the DRI and LINK econometric macroeconomic models of the United States, and the Shah-Larsen partial equilibrium model, which has been applied to five countries, including the United States.[33] The results in Table 3 are for the revenue-neutral combination of an environmental tax (usually a carbon tax) and reduction in the personal income tax, except in cases where this combination was not available.

---

[32]Using time-series data, Hall (1988) estimates that this elasticity is below 0.2. A cross-section analysis by Lawrance (1991) generates a central estimate of 1.1. Estimates from time-series tend to be lower than those from cross-section analyses.

[33]For a more detailed description of these models, see Goulder (1995b), Jorgenson and Wilcoxen (1990, 1996), Shackleton et al. (1996), Proost and Regemorter (1995), and Shah and Larsen (1992). The Shah-Larsen model is the simplest of the models, in part because it takes pretax factor prices as given. Despite its simplicity, the model addresses interactions between commodity and factor markets and thus incorporates some of the major efficiency connections discussed earlier.

Table 3 Numerical Assessments of Welfare Impacts of Revenue-Neutral Environmental Tax Reforms

Model	Reference	Country	Type of Environmental Tax	Method of Revenue Replacement	Welfare Effect
DRI	Shackleton et al. (1996)	U.S.	Phased-in Carbon Tax[a]	Personal Tax Cut	−0.39[b]
Goulder	Goulder (1995b)	U.S.	$25/ton Carbon Tax	Personal Tax Cut	−0.33[c]
"	Goulder (1994)	U.S.	Fossil Fuel Btu Tax	Personal Tax Cut	−0.28[c]
Jorgenson-Wilcoxen	Shackleton et al. (1996)	U.S.	Phased-in Carbon Tax[a]	Capital Tax Cut	0.19[d]
LINK	Shackleton et al. (1996)	U.S.	Phased-in Carbon Tax[a]	Personal Tax Cut	−0.51[b]
Proost-van Regemorter	Proost and van Regemorter (1995)	Belgium	Hybrid of Carbon and Energy Tax	Payroll (Social Security) Tax Cut	−3.45[d]
Shah-Larsen	Shah and Larsen (1992)	U.S.	$10/ton	Personal Tax Cut	−1049.[e]
"	"	India	"	"	−129.
"	"	Indonesia	"	"	−4.
"	"	Japan	"	"	−269.
"	"	Pakistan	"	"	−23.

Notes: [a]Beginning at $15/ton in 1990 (period 1), growing at five percent annually to $39.80 per ton in 2010 (period 21), and remaining at that level thereafter. [b]Percentage change in the present value of consumption; the model does not allow for utility-based welfare measures. [c]Welfare cost per dollar of tax revenue, as measured by the equivalent variation. [d]Equivalent variation as a percentage of benchmark private wealth. [e]Compensating variation in levels (millions of U.S. dollars).

All welfare changes abstract from changes in welfare associated with improvements in environmental quality (reductions in greenhouse gas emissions). Thus they correspond to the gross cost concept discussed above. In the Goulder, Jorgenson-Wilcoxen, and Proost-Regemorter models, welfare changes are reported in terms of the equivalent variation; in the Shah-Larsen model, the changes are based on the compensating variation.[34] In the DRI and LINK macroeconomic models, the percentage change in aggregate real consumption substitutes for a utility-based welfare measure.[35]

---

[34]The equivalent variation is the lump-sum change in wealth which, under the "business-as-usual" or base case, would leave the household as well off as in the policy-change case. Thus a positive equivalent variation indicates that the policy is welfare-improving. The compensating variation is the lump-sum change in wealth that, in the policy-change scenario, would cause the household to be as well off as in the base case. In reporting the Shah-Larsen results we adopt the convention of multiplying the compensating variation by −1, so that a positive number in the table signifies a welfare improvement here as well.

[35]The demand functions in these models are not derived from an explicit utility function. Hence they do not yield utility-based measures.

In most cases, the revenue-neutral green tax swap implies a reduction in welfare, that is, entails positive gross costs. This militates against the double dividend claim. Results from the Jorgenson-Wilcoxen model, however, support the double dividend notion. Relatively high interest elasticities of savings (a high capital supply elasticity) and the assumption of perfect capital mobility across sectors may partially explain this result, at least in the case where revenues from the carbon tax are devoted to cuts in marginal taxes on capital. These assumptions imply large marginal excess burdens from taxes on capital, considerably larger than the MEBs from labor taxes. As indicated above, if the MEB on capital significantly exceeds that on labor, and the environmental reform shifts the tax burden on to labor, the double dividend can arise. Thus, the large MEBs from capital taxes help explain why, in the Jorgenson-Wilcoxen model, a revenue-neutral combination of carbon tax and reduction in capital taxes involves negative gross costs, that is, produces a double dividend. Identifying the sources of differences in results across models is difficult, in large part because of the lack of relevant information on simulation outcomes and parameters. Relatively few studies have performed the type of analysis that exposes the channels underlying the overall impacts. There is a need for more systematic sensitivity analysis, as well as closer investigations of how structural aspects of tax policies (type of tax base, narrowness of tax base, uniformity of tax rates, etc.) influence the outcomes. In addition, key behavioral parameters need to be reported. Serious attention to these issues will help explain differences in results and, one hopes, lead to a greater consensus on likely policy impacts.

B. Preexisting Taxes and the Choice between Auctioned and Non-Auctioned Pollution Permits

Here we display numerical results that bear on the importance of preexisting taxes for the choice between auctioned and non-auctioned (or grandfathered) pollution permits. As the discussion in Section II indicates, these results display the significance of the revenue-recycling effect. Thus the principles here are somewhat broader than the choice between auctioned or grandfathered permits. The results for auctioned permits also would apply to emissions taxes that exploit the revenue-recycling effect by using the revenues to finance cuts in marginal rates of preexisting factor taxes. Likewise, the results for non-auctioned permits apply to emissions taxes that fail to exploit the revenue-recycling effect by returning the revenues in a lump-sum fashion.

1. Sulfur Dioxide Abatement. The GPB study includes an assessment of the costs of reducing emissions of sulfur dioxide (SO_2) from U.S. coal-fired electric power plants. Provisions of the 1990 Clean Air Act Amendments call for such reductions and introduce a system of grandfathered SO_2 emissions permits to achieve them.

Two questions arise. First, how much higher are the costs of reducing SO_2 emissions as a result of preexisting taxes? And how much of the increase in abatement costs could be avoided if the reductions were achieved through a policy that auctioned the permits (or imposed an SO_2 tax) and exploited the revenue-recycling effect, rather than through a policy that grandfathered the permits? Figure 6 gives GPB's best estimates of the answers to these questions. The two solid lines in the figure are the ratios of total costs in a second-best setting (with a positive preexisting tax rate on labor equal to 0.4) to total costs in a first-best setting (with no preexisting tax on labor). In the case of auctioned permits (or pollution taxes), the line is almost perfectly horizontal: this ratio is approximately constant throughout the entire range of possible emissions reductions (0 to 20 million tons). Second-best considerations raise the costs of auctioned permits by about 30 percent, regardless of the extent of emissions abatement. For the actual policy of grandfathered emissions permits, the ratio of total cost is very sensitive to the extent of abatement. Under this policy the ratio begins at infinity, in keeping with the fact that the intercept of the *marginal* cost function is positive for this policy in a second-best world and zero in a first-best world. As the level of abatement approaches 100 percent, the ratio of total costs approaches the ratio for auctioned permits. This is in keeping with the point made in Section III that the efficiency disadvantage of policies that forgo the revenue-recycling effect disappears at 100 percent abatement.

The 1990 Clean Air Act Amendments call for a 10-million-ton (or approximately 50 percent) reduction in SO_2 emissions. There may be significant distributional or political objectives that are served by grandfather-

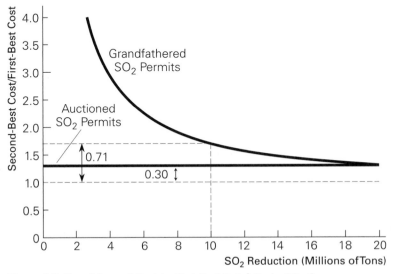

Figure 6 Ratio of Second-Best to First-Best Total Costs, SO_2 Case

ing, but Figure 6's results indicate that they come at a high price in terms of the social cost of abatement. At 10 million tons of abatement, annual total costs under the actual policy are estimated to be 71 percent (or $907 million) higher than they would be in a first-best world. As indicated in this figure, over half of this extra cost could be avoided by auctioning the permits or employing an SO_2 tax. The difference in cost between the two types of policy is $533 million.[36] These results indicate that preexisting taxes and the presence or absence of revenue-recycling have a very substantial impact on the costs of environmental policies.

Figure 7 brings in the benefit side in considering the overall efficiency gains from SO_2 abatement. The overall gains obviously depend on the marginal benefits from SO_2 reductions, and these are highly uncertain. Most estimates are in the range of $100–600 per ton, but some recent estimates are as high as $1000 per ton. The figure displays the net efficiency gains as a function of different values for the marginal benefits, ranging from zero to about $750 per ton.[37] It shows the efficiency gains that result under optimal levels of abatement, that is, abatement levels that equate marginal benefits with marginal costs. For low and intermediate values of the marginal benefits, the efficiency gains are considerably larger when SO_2 permits are auctioned than when they are grandfathered, in keeping with the lower marginal costs of abatement in the former case. Indeed, net gains under grandfathered permits are zero if marginal benefits are below $104 per ton, because in this circumstance the optimal policy is not to regulate SO_2; that is, the optimal reduction in SO_2 is zero. For very high values of the marginal benefits, there is less difference in the net efficiency gains. In fact the net efficiency gains are identical for marginal benefits greater than or equal to about $680 per ton. When marginal benefits go beyond this level, the optimal policy is to eliminate SO_2 emissions entirely. At this point it makes no difference whether permits are grandfathered or auctioned, since no permits are actually provided and thus no revenue can be raised in either case.

2. Carbon Dioxide Abatement. Recent work by Parry, Williams, and Goulder (1999) examines these issues in the context of carbon dioxide (CO_2) emissions abatement in the United States. Figures 8 and 9, based on re-

---

[36]The costs of a 10-million-ton reduction are $2182 and $1649 million under the grandfathering and auctioning of emissions allowances, respectively. Although this paper points out the efficiency drawbacks of the grandfathering element of SO_2 emissions regulation under the 1990 Clean Air Act Amendments, it is not intended to be a wholesale critique of this legislation. We would note that the 1990 legislation achieved major reforms in environmental regulation by introducing a flexible, incentive-based approach to regulation in the form of emissions allowance trading. This approach has a number of theoretical advantages over the traditional, less flexible methods (see, for example, Tietenberg [1985]), and empirical studies already indicate that this approach will yield a dramatic reduction in overall compliance costs, compared to conventional approaches (see, for example, Burtraw [1996], and Ellerman and Montero [1996]).

[37]The marginal benefits are assumed to be constant, that is, independent of the level of abatement.

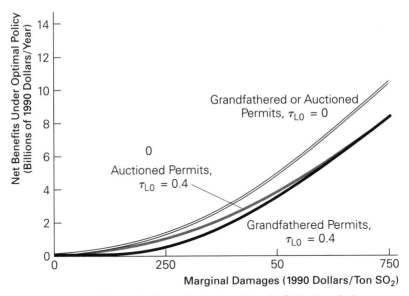

Figure 7 Net Welfare Gain from the Optimal Level of SO_2 Regulation

sults from this study, provide for CO_2 abatement policies the same sort of information as was displayed for SO_2 policies in Figures 6 and 7.

Figure 8 presents the ratio of second-best ($\tau_L = .4$) and first-best ($\tau_L = 0$) total costs, under a carbon (CO_2) tax and a carbon (CO_2) quota.[38] The carbon tax policy exploits the revenue-recycling effect: revenues from the tax are devoted to cuts in the preexisting distortionary (labor) tax. The results are qualitatively similar to the results that were shown in Figure 6. For the carbon tax, the ratio of total costs is virtually unaffected by the extent of carbon emissions abatement. For the carbon quota, in contrast, the ratio of total costs is highly sensitive to the amount of abatement, for the same reasons as were discussed earlier.

Figure 9 shows Parry, Williams, and Goulder's best estimates for net efficiency gains from carbon abatement policies, for a range of values for the marginal benefits from CO_2 abatement. Efficiency gains are considerably larger under the carbon tax than under the carbon quota. In fact, efficiency gains are zero (the optimal amount of abatement is zero) if marginal benefits are below $18 per ton. This reflects the fact that the (gross) marginal costs of CO_2 abatement begin at $18 per ton under the quota policy. Thus, any emissions abatement by way of this type of policy will be ef-

---

[38]The tax and quota policies actually would be oriented toward the use of carbon-based fuels (oil, coal, and natural gas) rather than emissions of CO_2 itself. Emissions from the combustion of these fuels are strictly proportional to carbon content, so that taxing or regulating the use of these fuels is virtually equivalent to taxing or regulating CO_2 emissions. A complication is posed by non-combustion or feedstock uses of these fuels. In the U.S. such uses represent a very small share (less than four percent) of total use.

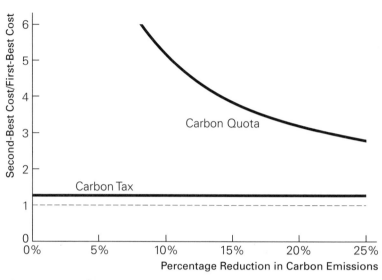

Figure 8 Ratio of Second-Best to First-Best Total Costs, CO_2 Case

ficiency-reducing if the marginal benefits are below this value. Most estimates of the marginal environmental benefits from carbon abatement obtain values below \$18 per ton.[39] Thus, these results suggest that any car-

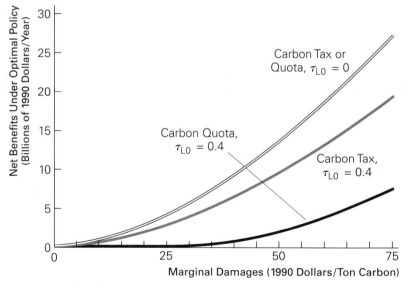

Figure 9 Net Welfare Gain from the Optimal Level of CO_2 Regulation

---

[39]See, for example, Nordhaus (1991), Peck and Teisberg (1993), and Fankhauser (1994).

bon abatement by way of a quota (or freely offered set of carbon permits) will be efficiency reducing![40]

Thus, in the context of regulating SO_2 and CO_2 emissions, second-best interactions have a very substantial effect on the gross costs and net efficiency gains. Preexisting taxes significantly raise the costs of achieving emissions reductions relative to the costs in a first-best setting. And they put policies involving emissions quotas or grandfathered permits policies at a very significant cost disadvantage relative to policies that raise revenue and finance cuts in preexisting taxes. Second-best interactions have first-order consequences.

V. Conclusions

This paper examines the significance of preexisting factor taxes for various environmental policies. It indicates that, under plausible assumptions, prior factor-market distortions raise the costs of revenue-neutral environmental policies, despite the potential to use the revenues from environmental taxes to finance cuts in the marginal rates of preexisting factor taxes. It also shows that prior factor taxes amplify the costs of other environmental policies, including pollution quotas and tradeable pollution permits, relative to what the costs would be in a first-best world.

Two effects underlie these results. The *tax-interaction effect* is the adverse impact in factor markets arising from reductions in after-tax returns to factors (labor) brought about by environmental regulation. In a world with prior taxes on factors, this effect leads to significantly higher costs of regulation relative to what would apply in a first-best world with no preexisting taxes. By generating revenues and using them to reduce preexisting tax rates, pollution taxes and auctioned pollution permits exploit a *revenue-recycling effect* that offsets some of the tax-interaction effect. In contrast, pollution quotas and grandfathered permits enjoy no such offset. Thus the costs of achieving given reductions in pollution are higher under these latter policies.

Even when they take advantage of the revenue-recycling effect, pollution abatement policies through pollution taxes or auctioned permits generally entail positive gross costs. If the good responsible for pollution emissions is an average substitute for leisure, the revenue-recycling effect only partly offsets the gross costs attributable to the tax-interaction effect. This implies that pollution-abatement through these policies is more costly in a second-best setting than it would be in a first-best world, and that the double dividend claim (in its strong form) is not upheld.

---

[40]Several studies suggest that the marginal climate-related damages increase with CO_2 concentrations. If this is the case, and if CO_2 concentrations increase through time, then marginal damages from CO_2 emissions (or marginal benefits from CO_2 emissions abatement) will increase over time. Under such circumstances the prospects for efficiency gains under a quota policy improve with time.

The interactions with factor markets affect the choice among alternative policy instruments. In particular, they put pollution quotas and grandfathered pollution permits at a serious efficiency disadvantage relative to revenue-raising policies whose revenues finance reductions in the marginal rates of existing taxes. Indeed, if the marginal environmental benefits from pollution reductions are below a certain threshold value, then *any* level of pollution abatement through quotas or grandfathered permits is efficiency-reducing. These results emerge from simple analytical models and are confirmed by numerical investigations in specific regulatory contexts.

In recognizing the efficiency advantages of these pollution-tax and auctioned-permit policies over policies involving pollution quotas or grandfathered permits, one should not lose sight of related equity issues. The decision whether to exploit the revenue-recycling effect fundamentally affects the distribution of wealth between taxpayers, on the one hand, and owners and employees of polluting firms, on the other. Clearly, there are important equity issues associated with the differences in distribution. The second-best considerations raised in this paper do not reduce the importance of the equity issues, but at the same time they indicate that the efficiency costs of forgoing the redistribution toward taxpayers are greater than what would be suggested by a first-best analysis.

The tax-interaction effect is relevant to government regulation outside the environmental area. To the extent that government regulations of international trade or agricultural production raise the costs of output and thereby reduce real factor returns, these regulations exacerbate the labor market distortions from preexisting taxes and thus involve higher social costs than would be indicated by partial equilibrium analyses.[41]

References

Ballard, Charles, L., John B. Shoven, and John Whalley, 1985. "General Equilibrium Computations of the Marginal Welfare Costs of Taxes in the U.S." *American Economic Review* 75(1):128–38.

Bovenberg, A. Lans, 1996. "Environmental Policy, Distortionary Labor Taxation, and Employment: Pollution Taxes and the Double Dividend." In Carlo Carraro, Yiannis Katsoulacos, and Anastasios Xepapadeas, eds., *Environmental Policy and Market Structure.* Dordrecht: Kluwer Academic Publishers.

Bovenberg, A. Lans, and Ruud A. de Mooij, 1994a. "Environmental Levies and Distortionary Taxation." *American Economic Review* 84(4):1085–9.

Bovenberg, A. Lans, and Ruud A. de Mooij, 1994b. "Environmental Taxation and Labor Market Distortions." *European Journal of Political Economy* 10(4):655–83.

Bovenberg, A. Lans, and Ruud A. de Mooij, 1996. "Environmental Taxation and the Double-Dividend: The Role of Factor Substitution and Capital Mobility." In C.

---

[41]Similarly, Browning (1997) finds that monopoly pricing exacerbates preexisting distortions in factor markets. Hence the efficiency costs of monopoly pricing increase with the magnitude of preexisting factor tax rates. Browning estimates that monopoly pricing in the U.S. is ten times more costly than it would be in the absence of prior factor taxes.

Carraro and D. Siniscalco, eds., *Environmental Fiscal Reform and Unemployment.* Dordrecht: Kluwer.

Bovenberg, A. Lans, and Lawrence H. Goulder, 1996. "Optimal Environmental Taxation in the Presence of Other Taxes: General Equilibrium Analyses." *American Economic Review*, September.

Bovenberg, A. Lans, and Lawrence H. Goulder, 1997. "Costs of Environmentally Motivated Taxes in the Presence of Other Taxes: General Equilibrium Analyses." *National Tax Journal*, forthcoming March 1997.

Bovenberg, A. Lans, and Lawrence H. Goulder, 1999. "Environmental Taxation." In A. Auerbach and M. Feldstein, eds., *Handbook of Public Economics.* New York: North-Holland, forthcoming.

Bovenberg, A. Lans, and F. van der Ploeg, 1994. "Environmental Policy, Public Finance, and the Labour Market in a Second-Best World." *Journal of Public Economics* 55:349–70.

Browning, E. K., 1987. "On the Marginal Welfare Cost of Taxation." *American Economic Review* 77:11–23.

Browning, E. K., 1997. "The Welfare Cost of Monopoly and Other Output Distortions." *Journal of Public Economics*, 66:127–44.

Burtraw, Dallas, 1996. "The SO_2 Emissions Trading Program: Cost Savings Without Allowance Trades," *Contemporary Economic Policy*, vol. XIV, no. 2 (April), 79–94.

Ellerman, A. Denny, and Juan Pablo Montero, 1996. "Why Are Allowance Prices So Low? An Analysis of the SO_2 Emissions Trading Program," CEEPR 96-001, Massachusetts Institute of Technology (February).

Fankhauser, Samuel, 1994. "The Social Costs of Greenhouse Gas Emissions: An Expected Value Approach." *The Energy Journal* 15:157–84.

Fullerton, Don, and J. Mackie, 1987. "Investment Allocation and Growth under the Tax Reform Act of 1986." *In Compendium of Tax Research 1987*, Office of Tax Analysis of the U.S. Department of the Treasury, Washington, D.C., pp. 131–171.

Fullerton, Don and Gilbert Metcalf, 1997. "Environmental Controls, Scarcity Rents, and Pre-Existing Distortions." NBER Working paper 6091, July.

Goulder, Lawrence H., 1994. "Energy Taxes: Traditional Efficiency Effects and Environmental Implications." In J. M. Poterba, ed., *Tax Policy and the Economy.* Cambridge: MIT Press.

Goulder, Lawrence H., 1995a. "Environmental Taxation and the 'Double Dividend': A Reader's Guide." *International Tax and Public Finance* 2(2):157–183.

Goulder, Lawrence H., 1995b. "Effects of Carbon Taxes in an Economy with Prior Tax Distortions: An Intertemporal General Equilibrium Analysis," *Journal of Environmental Economics and Management*, October.

Goulder, Lawrence H., 1998. "Environmental Policy Making in a Second-Best Setting," *Journal of Applied Economics*, 1(2).

Goulder, Lawrence H., Ian W. H. Parry, and Dallas Burtraw, 1997. "Revenue-Raising vs. Other Approaches to Environmental Protection: The Critical Significance of Pre-Existing Tax Distortions." *RAND Journal of Economics*, Winter.

Goulder, Lawrence H., Ian W. H. Parry, Roberton C. Williams III, and Dallas Burtraw, 1999. "The Cost-Effectiveness of Alternative Instruments for Environmental Protection in a Second-best Setting." *Journal of Public Economics* 72(3):329–60.

Goulder, Lawrence H., and Philippe Thalmann, 1993. "Approaches to Efficient Capital Taxation: Leveling the Playing Field vs. Living by the Golden Rule." *Journal of Public Economics* 50:169–96.

Hall, Robert, 1988. "Intertemporal Substitution in Consumption," *Journal of Political Economy* 96(2):339–57.

Jorgenson, Dale W. and Peter J. Wilcoxen, 1990. "Environmental Regulation and U.S. Economic Growth," *RAND Journal of Economics* 21(2), 314–340.

Jorgenson, Dale W. and Peter J. Wilcoxen, 1996. "Reducing U.S. Carbon Emissions: An Econometric General Equilibrium Assessment." In Darius Gaskins and John Weyant, eds., *Reducing Global Carbon Dioxide Emissions: Costs and Policy Options*. Energy Modeling Forum, Stanford University, Stanford, Calif.

Jorgenson, Dale, and Kun-Young Yun, 1990. "Tax Policy and the Cost of Capital." Oxford: Oxford University Press.

Lawrence, Emily, 1991, "Poverty and the Rate of Time Preference: Evidence from Panel Data," *Journal of Political Economy* 99(1):54–77.

Lee, Dwight R., and Walter S. Misiolek, 1986. "Substituting Pollution Taxation for General Taxation: Some Implications for Efficiency in Pollution Taxation." *Journal of Environmental Economics and Management* 13:338–347.

Lucas, Robert E., 1990. "Supply-Side Economics: An Analytical Review." *Oxford Economic Papers* 42:293–316.

Ng, Y. K., 1980. "Optimal Corrective Taxes or Subsidies when Revenue-Raising Imposes an Excess Burden." *American Economic Review* 70:744–51.

Nordhaus, William D., 1991. "To Slow or Not to Slow: The Economics of the Greenhouse Effect." *The Economic Journal* 101:920–37.

Oates, Wallace E., 1993. "Pollution Charges as a Source of Public Revenues." In Herbert Giersch, ed., *Economic Progress and Environmental Concerns*. Berlin: Springer-Verlag, pp. 135–52.

Oates, Wallace E., 1995. "Green Taxes: Can We Protect the Environment and Improve the Tax System at the Same Time?" *Southern Economic Journal* 61(4):914–922.

Oates, Wallace E., and Robert M. Schwab, 1988. "Economic Competition among Jurisdictions: Efficiency Enhancing or Distortion Inducing?" *Journal of Public Economics* 35:333–354, April.

Oates, Wallace E., and Diana L. Strassmann, 1984. "Effluent Fees and Market Structure." *Journal of Public Economics* 24:29–46.

Parry, Ian W. H., 1995. "Pollution Taxes and Revenue Recycling." *Journal of Environmental Economics and Management* 29:S64–S77.

Parry, Ian W. H., 1997. "Environmental Taxes and Quotas in the Presence of Distorting Taxes in Factor Markets." *Resource and Energy Economics* 19:203–220.

Parry, Ian W. H., Roberton Williams, and Lawrence H. Goulder, 1999. "When Can Carbon Abatement Policies Increase Welfare? The Fundamental Role of Distorted Factor Markets." *Journal of Environmental Economics and Management* 37:52–84.

Peck, Stephen C. and Thomas J. Teisberg, 1993. "Global Warming Uncertainties and the Value of Information: An Analysis Using CETA." *Resource and Energy Economics* 15:71–98.

Pigou, A. C., 1938. *The Economics of Welfare* (4th edition). London: Weidenfeld and Nicolson.

Proost, S., and D. van Regemorter, 1995. "The Double Dividend and the Role of Inequality Aversion and Macroeconomic Regimes." *International Tax and Public Finance* 2(2), August.

Repetto, Robert, Roger C. Dower, Robin Jenkins, and Jacqueline Geoghegan, 1992. *Green Fees: How a Tax Shift Can Work for the Environment and the Economy*. World Resources Institute, November.

Sandmo, Agnar, 1975. "Optimal Taxation in the Presence of Externalities." *Swedish Journal of Economics* 77.

Shackleton, Robert, Michael Shelby, Alex Cristofaro, Roger Brinner, Joyce Yanchar, Lawrence Goulder, Dale Jorgenson, Peter Wilcoxen, and Peter Pauly, 1996. "The Efficiency Value of Carbon Tax Revenues." In Darius Gaskins and John Weyant, eds., *Reducing Global Carbon Dioxide Emissions: Costs and Policy Options.* Stanford, Calif.: Energy Modeling Forum.

Shah, Anwar, and Bjorn Larsen, 1992. "Carbon Taxes, the Greenhouse Effect and Developing Countries," World Bank Policy Research Working Paper Series No. 957, The World Bank, Washington, D.C.

Stavins, Robert N., 1995. "Transactions Costs and Tradeable Permits." *Journal of Environmental Economics and Management* 29, 133–147.

Terkla, David, 1984. "The Efficiency Value of Effluent Tax Revenues." *Journal of Environmental Economics and Management* 11:107–23.

Tietenberg, T. H., 1985. *Emissions Trading: An Exercise In Reforming Pollution Policy.* Washington D.C.: Resources for the Future.

Weitzman, Martin L., 1974. "Prices vs. Quantities." *Review of Economic Studies* 41, 477–491.

Williams, Roberton C. III, 1998. "Revisiting the Cost of Protectionism: The Role of Tax Distortions in the Labor Market." *Journal of International Economics*, forthcoming.

Williams, Roberton C. III, 1999. "Tax-Interactions in a Dynamic Model with Capital Accumulation." Working paper, Stanford University.

17 What Can We Learn from the Grand Policy Experiment? Lessons from SO₂ Allowance Trading*

Robert N. Stavins

Robert N. Stavins is Albert Pratt Professor of Business and Government at the John F. Kennedy School of Government, Harvard University, and University Fellow at Resources for the Future.

Economists consistently have urged the use of "market-based" or "economic-incentive" instruments—principally pollution taxes and systems of tradeable permits—to address environmental problems, rather than so-called "command-and-control" instruments, such as design standards, which require the use of particular technologies, or performance standards, which prescribe the maximum amount of pollution that individual sources can emit. At least in theory, a well-designed pollution tax (Pigou, 1920) or tradeable permit system (Crocker, 1966; Dales, 1968; Montgomery, 1972) will minimize the aggregate cost of achieving a given level of environmental protection (Baumol and Oates, 1988), and provide dynamic incentives for the adoption and diffusion of cheaper and better pollution control technologies (Milliman and Prince, 1989).

Despite such advantages, market-based environmental instruments have been used far less frequently than command-and-control standards. In particular, while taxes have been imposed on certain products that are linked to pollution, like gasoline and chemicals, this has typically been done as a way of raising revenue, such as with gas taxes to fund highway construction or chemical taxes to fund cleanup of Superfund toxic waste sites, rather than as incentive devices intended to reduce externalities (Barthold, 1994). But over the past 25 years, the political process has gradually become more receptive to market-oriented environmental tools. Beginning in the 1970s, the Environmental Protection Agency (EPA) offered states the option of employing variants of tradeable permits for the control of local-

"What Can We Learn from the Grand Policy Experiment? Lessons from SO₂ Allowance Trading," by Robert N. Stavins, from *Journal of Economic Perspectives*, 12(3):69–88 (Summer 1998).

*I am indebted to Peter Zapfel for excellent research assistance, and Elizabeth Bailey, Dallas Burtraw, Brad De Long, Denny Ellerman, Lawrence Goulder, Robert Hahn, Paul Joskow, Alan Krueger, Richard Schmalensee, and (especially) Timothy Taylor for valuable comments on a previous version of this article. Any remaining errors are my own.

ized air pollutants. Tradeable-permit systems were used in the 1980s to phase leaded gasoline out of the market and to phase out ozone-depleting chlorofluorocarbons (CFCs). But by far the most ambitious application of these instruments has been for the control of acid rain under Title IV of the Clean Air Act amendments of 1990, which established a sulfur dioxide (SO_2) allowance trading program intended to cut nationwide emissions of SO_2 by 50 percent below 1980 levels by the year 2000.

This essay seeks to identify lessons that can be learned from this grand experiment in economically-oriented environmental policy. Since the SO_2 allowance trading program became binding only in 1995, it might seem premature to search for lessons for future policy. This would be true, were one to consider this policy experiment in isolation. But the SO_2 allowance trading program did not emerge into a policy vacuum; rather, it is but one step in the evolution of market-based environmental policies. Considered in this context, the time is ripe not only for an interim appraisal, but for reflection on what we have learned.

I begin with a brief description of the SO_2 allowance trading system and its performance, relying on the accompanying article by Richard Schmalensee and his colleagues to provide details. I then address questions of positive political economy; for example, given the historical support for command-and-control environmental policy instruments, why was allowance trading adopted for acid-rain control in 1990? Subsequently, I consider normative lessons for the design and implementation of market-oriented environmental policies, and offer some conclusions.

The SO_2 Allowance Trading System and Its Performance

Title IV of the Clean Air Act amendments of 1990 sought to reduce SO_2 emissions by 10 million tons from 1980 levels. The first phase of SO_2 emissions reduction was achieved in 1995, with a second phase of reduction to be accomplished by the year 2000.[1] In Phase I, individual emissions limits were assigned to the 263 most SO_2-emissions intensive generating units at 110 electric utility plants operated by 61 electric utilities, and located largely at coal-fired power plants east of the Mississippi River. EPA allocated each affected unit, on an annual basis, a specified number of allowances related to its share of heat input during the baseline period from 1985–87, plus bonus allowances available under a variety of provisions. After January 1, 1995, these units could emit sulfur dioxide only if they had adequate allowances to cover their emissions. Under Phase II of the program, begin-

---

[1]The law also sought to reduce nitrogen oxide (NO_x) emissions by 2 million tons annually from 1980 levels. A proposal for trading between SO_2 and NO_x was eliminated by Congress.

ning January 1, 2000, almost all fossil-fuel electric power plants will be brought within the system.

Cost-effectiveness is promoted by permitting allowance holders to transfer their permits among one another, so that those who can reduce emissions at the lowest cost have an incentive to do so and sell their allowances to those for whom reducing the cost would be greater. Allowances can also be "banked" for later use. The anticipated result is that marginal abatement costs will be equated across sources, thus achieving aggregate abatement at minimum total cost. In addition to the private market for bilateral trades, an annual auction of allowances withheld from utilities (about 3 percent of total allowances) was established by EPA, with revenues distributed to utilities on the basis of their original allocations. Also, utilities can offer allowances for sale at the annual government-sponsored auction. Finally, compliance is encouraged by a penalty of $2,000 per ton of emissions that exceed any year's allowances, along with a requirement that such excesses be offset the following year.

The SO_2 allowance trading program has performed successfully. Targeted emissions-reductions have been achieved and exceeded; in fact, because of excess reductions in 1995 and 1996 (and because of bonus allowances distributed by the government), utilities have built up an allowance bank of more than six million tons (U.S. Environmental Protection Agency, 1997). Total abatement costs have been significantly less than what they would have been in the absence of the trading provisions. Trading volume has increased over the life of the program, with EPA having recorded more than four million tons of allowance transfers in 1996 among economically unrelated parties (U.S. Environmental Protection Agency, 1997). This robust market has resulted in cost savings of up to $1 billion annually, compared with the cost of command-and-control regulatory alternatives that were considered by Congress in prior years (Kennedy, 1986).

Prospective analysis in 1990 suggested that the program's benefits would approximately equal its costs (Portney, 1990), but recent analysis indicates that benefits will exceed costs by a very significant margin (Burtraw, Krupnick, Mansur, Austin and Farell, 1997). Although the original motivation of the acid-rain control program was to reduce acidification of forest and aquatic ecosystems, the bulk of the benefits result from reduced human risk of premature mortality through reduced exposure to sulfates.

Positive Political Economy Lessons

To understand why the SO_2 allowance trading system was adopted in its particular form in 1990, it is useful to examine first the factors that led to the dominance of command-and-control over market-based instruments in the previous 20 years. To do this, I consider the demand for environmental policy instruments by individuals, firms, and interest groups, and their supply by the legislature and regulatory agencies. This "political market" framework is developed by Keohane, Revesz and Stavins (1997).

Why Have Command-and-Control Instruments Dominated Environmental Regulations?

The short answer is that command-and-control instruments have predominated because all of the main parties involved had reasons to favor them: affected firms, environmental advocacy groups, organized labor, legislators, and bureaucrats.

On the regulatory demand side, affected firms and their trade associations tended to prefer command-and-control instruments because standards can improve a firm's competitive position, while often costing a firm less than pollution taxes or tradeable permits. Command-and-control standards are inevitably set up with extensive input from existing industry and trade associations, which frequently obtain more stringent requirements for new sources and other advantages for existing firms. In contrast, auctioned permits and pollution taxes require firms to pay not only abatement costs to reduce pollution to some level, but also regulatory costs associated with emissions beyond that level, in the form either of permit purchases or tax payments. Because market-based instruments focus on the quantity of pollution, not on who generates it or the methods used to reduce it, these instruments can make the detailed lobbying role of trade associations less important.

For a long time, most environmental advocacy groups were actively hostile towards market-based instruments, for several reasons. A first reason was philosophical: environmentalists frequently portrayed pollution taxes and tradeable permits as "licenses to pollute." Although such ethical objections to the use of market-based environmental strategies have greatly diminished, they have not disappeared completely (Sandel, 1997). A second concern was that damages from pollution—to human health and ecological well-being—were difficult or impossible to quantify and monetize, and thus could not be summed up in a marginal damage function or captured by a Pigovian tax rate (Kelman, 1981). Third, environmental organizations have opposed market-based schemes out of a fear that permit levels and tax rates—once implemented—would be more difficult to tighten over time than command-and-control standards. If permits are given the status of "property rights," then any subsequent attempt by government to reduce pollution levels further could meet with demands for compensation.[2] Similarly, increasing pollution tax rates may be unlikely because raising tax rates is always politically difficult. A related strategic issue is that

---

[2]This concern was alleviated in the SO_2 provisions of the Clean Air Act Amendments of 1990 by an explicit statutory provision that permits do not represent property rights.

moving to tax-based environmental regulation would shift authority from environment committees in the Congress, frequently dominated by pro-environment legislators, to tax-writing committees, which are generally more conservative (Kelman, 1981).[3]

Finally, environmental organizations have objected to decentralized instruments on the grounds that even if emission taxes or tradeable permits reduce overall levels of emissions, they can lead to localized "hot spots" with relatively high levels of ambient pollution. In cases where this is a reasonable concern, it can be addressed in theory, through the use of "ambient permits" or through charge systems that are keyed to changes in ambient conditions at specified locations (Revesz, 1996). Despite the extensive theoretical literature on such ambient systems going back to Montgomery (1972), they have never been implemented, with the partial exception of a two-zone trading system in Los Angeles under the new RECLAIM program.

Organized labor has also been active in some environmental policy debates. In the case of restrictions on clean air, organized labor has taken the side of the United Mine Workers, whose members are heavily concentrated in eastern mines that produce higher-sulfur coal, and have therefore opposed pollution-control measures that would increase incentives for using low-sulfur coal from the largely nonunionized (and less labor-intensive) mines in the Powder River Basin of Wyoming and Montana. In the 1977 debates over amendments to the Clean Air Act, organized labor fought to include a command-and-control standard that effectively required scrubbing, thereby seeking to discourage switching to cleaner western coal (Ackerman and Hassler, 1981). Likewise, the United Mine Workers opposed the SO_2 allowance trading system in 1990 because of a fear that it would encourage a shift to western low-sulfur coal from non-unionized mines.

Turning to the supply side of environmental regulation, legislators have had a number of reasons to find command-and-control standards attractive. First, many legislators and their staffs are trained in law, which predisposes them to favor legalistic regulatory approaches. Second, standards tend to help hide the costs of pollution control (McCubbins and Sullivan, 1984), while market-based instruments generally impose those costs more directly. Compare, for example, the tone of public debates associated with proposed increases in gasoline taxes with those regarding commensurate increases in the stringency of the Corporate Average Fuel Economy standards for new cars.

Third, standards offers greater opportunities for symbolic politics, because strict standards—strong statements of support for environmental protection—can readily be combined with less visible exemptions or with lax enforcement measures. As one recent example of this pattern (albeit from the executive rather than the legislative branch), the Clinton admin-

---

[3]These strategic arguments refer, for the most part, to pollution taxes, not to market-based instruments in general. Indeed, as I discuss later, one reason some environmental groups have come to endorse the tradeable permits approach is that it promises the cost savings of taxes, without the drawbacks that environmentalists associate with tax instruments.

istration announced with much fanfare in June 1997 that it would tighten regulations of particulates and ambient ozone, but the new requirements do not take effect for eight years! Congress has frequently prescribed administrative rules and procedures to protect intended beneficiaries of legislation by constraining the scope of executive intervention (McCubbins, Noll and Weingast, 1987). Such stacking of the deck is more likely to be successful in the context of command-and-control legislation, since market-based instruments leave the allocation of costs and benefits up to the market, treating polluters identically.[4] Of course, the underlying reason why symbolic politics works is that voters have limited information, and so respond to gestures, while remaining relatively unaware of details.

Fourth, if politicians are risk averse, they will prefer instruments that involve more certain effects.[5] The flexibility inherent in market-based instruments creates uncertainty about distributional impacts and local levels of environmental quality. Typically, legislators in a representative democracy are more concerned with the geographic distribution of costs and benefits than with comparisons of total benefits and costs. Hence, aggregate cost-effectiveness—the major advantage of market-based instruments—is likely to play a less significant role in the legislative calculus than whether a politician is getting a good deal for constituents (Shepsle and Weingast, 1984). Politicians are also likely to oppose instruments that can induce firms to close and relocate, leading to localized unemployment. Although there will be winners as well as losers from such relocation, potential losers are likely to be more certain of their status than potential gainers.

Finally, legislators are wary of enacting programs that are likely to be undermined by bureaucrats in their implementation. And bureaucrats are less likely to undermine legislative decisions if their own preferences over policy instruments are accommodated. Bureaucratic preferences—at least in the past—were not supportive of market-based instruments, on several grounds: bureaucrats were familiar with command-and-control approaches; market-based instruments do not require the same kinds of technical expertise that agencies have developed under command-and-control regulation; and market-based instruments can imply a scaled-down role for the agency by shifting decision-making from the bureaucracy to the private sector. In other words, government bureaucrats—like their counterparts in environmental advocacy groups and trade associations—might be expected to oppose market-based instruments to prevent their expertise from becoming obsolete and to preserve their human capital. More recently, however, this same incentive has helped lead EPA staff involved in the SO_2 trading program to become strong proponents of trading for other air pollution problems.

---

[4]But the Congress has nevertheless tried. Joskow and Schmalensee (1998) examine Congressional attempts along these lines in the SO_2 allowance trading program.

[5]"Legislators are likely to behave as if they are risk averse, even if they are personally risk neutral, if their constituents punish unpredictable policy choices or their reelection probability is nearly unity" (McCubbins, Noll and Weingast, 1989, p. 437).

Why Has the Chosen Form of Market-Based Approaches Always Been Freely Allocated Tradeable Permits?

Economic theory suggests that the choice between tradeable permits and pollution taxes should be based upon case-specific factors, but when market-based instruments have been adopted in the United States, they have virtually always taken the form of tradeable permits rather than emission taxes. As already noted, taxes that are related to sources of pollution, like gasoline taxes, serve primarily as revenue-raising instruments, rather than environmental taxes designed to reduce an externality.[6] Moreover, the initial allocation of such permits has always been through free initial distribution, rather than through auctions, despite the apparent economic superiority of the latter mechanism in terms of economic efficiency (Fullerton and Metcalf, 1997; Goulder, Parry, and Burtraw, 1997; Stavins, 1995). The EPA does have an annual auction of SO_2 allowances, but this represents less than 2 percent of the total allocation (Bailey, 1996). While the EPA auctions may have helped in establishing the market for SO_2 allowances, they are a trivial part of the overall program (Joskow, Schmalensee and Bailey, 1996).

Again, many actors in the system have reasons to favor freely allocated tradeable permits over other market-based instruments. On the regulatory demand side, existing firms favor freely allocated tradeable permits because they convey rents to them. Moreover, like stringent command-and-control standards for new sources, but unlike auctioned permits or taxes, freely allocated permits give rise to entry barriers, since new entrants must purchase permits from existing holders. Thus, the rents conveyed to the private sector by freely allocated tradeable permits are, in effect, sustainable.

Environmental advocacy groups have generally supported command-and-control approaches, but given the choice between tradeable permits and emission taxes, these groups strongly prefer the former. Environmental advocates have a strong incentive to avoid policy instruments that make the costs of environmental protection highly visible to consumers and voters; and taxes make those costs more explicit than permits.[7] Also, environmental advocates prefer permit schemes because they specify the quantity of pollution reduction that will be achieved, in contrast with the indirect effect of pollution taxes. Overall, some environmental groups have come to endorse the tradeable permits approach because it promises the cost sav-

---

[6]This pattern holds in Europe, as well. There, environmental taxes have been far more prevalent than tradeable permits, but the taxes employed have typically been two low to induce pollution abatement (Cansier and Krumm, 1997).

[7]For this same reason, private industry may strategically choose to endorse a pollution tax approach, in the hope that consequent public opposition will result in the setting of a less stringent environmental goal. This may seem farfetched, but it appears to be precisely what happened in the closing days of the 1990 Clean Air Act debate in the U.S. Senate. When it had become clear that a 10 million ton SO_2 allowance trading system was about to be passed, electric utilities suddenly proposed an SO_2 emissions tax as an alternative policy instrument.

ings of pollution taxes, without the drawbacks that environmentalists associate with environmental tax instruments.

Freely allocated tradeable permits are easier for legislators to supply than taxes or auctioned permits, again because the costs imposed on industry are less visible and less burdensome, since no money is exchanged at the time of the initial permit allocation. Also, freely allocated permits offer a much greater degree of political control over the distributional effects of regulation, facilitating the formation of majority coalitions. Joskow and Schmalensee (1998) examined the political process of allocating SO_2 allowances in the 1990 amendments, and found that allocating permits on the basis of prior emissions can produce fairly clear winners and losers among firms and states. An auction allows no such political maneuvering.

Why Was a Market-Based Approach Adopted for SO_2 Emissions in 1990?

By the late 1980s, there had already been a significant shift of the political center toward a more favorable view of using markets to solve social problems. The Bush administration, which proposed the SO_2 allowance trading program and then championed it through an initially resistant Democratic Congress, deserves much of the credit here. The ideas of "fiscally responsible environmental protection" and "harnessing market forces to protect the environment" fit well with its quintessentially moderate Republicanism. (The Reagan administration enthusiastically embraced a market-oriented ideology, but demonstrated little interest in employing actual market-based policies in the environmental area.) More broadly, support for market-oriented solutions to various social problems had been increasing across the political spectrum as early as the Carter administration, as evidenced by deliberations and action regarding deregulation of the airline, telecommunications, trucking, railroad, and banking industries. Indeed, by 1990, the phrase "market-based environmental policy" had evolved from being politically problematic to politically attractive. Even leading liberal environmental advocates like Rep. Henry Waxman began to characterize their clean air proposals as using "economic-incentive mechanisms," even if the actual proposals continued to be of the conventional, command-and-control variety.

Given the historical opposition to market-oriented pollution control policies, how can we explain the adoption of the SO_2 allowance trading program in 1990? More broadly, why has there been increased openness to the use of market-based approaches?

For economists, it would be gratifying to believe that increased understanding of market-based instruments had played a large part in fostering their increased political acceptance, but how important has this really been? In 1981, Steven Kelman surveyed Congressional staff members, and found that Republican support and Democratic opposition to market-based environmental policy instruments was based largely on ideological grounds, with little awareness or understanding of the advantages or disadvantages of the various instruments. What would happen if we were to replicate Kelman's (1981) survey today? My hypothesis is that we would find increased support from Republicans, greatly increased support from Democrats, but insufficient improvements in understanding to explain these changes.[8] So what else has mattered?

One factor has surely been increased pollution control costs, which have led to greater demand for cost-effective instruments. By 1990, U.S. pollution control costs had reached $125 billion annually, nearly a tripling of real costs from 1972 levels (U.S. Environmental Protection Agency, 1990). In the case of SO_2 control, it was well known that utilities faced very different marginal abatement costs and would want to use varying abatement methods, because of differences in the ages of plants and their proximity to sources of low-sulfur coal. EPA estimates in the late 1980s were that a well-functioning tradeable-permit program would save 50 percent on costs that would otherwise exceed $6 billion annually if a dictated technological solution were implemented (ICF, 1989).

A second factor that was important in the 1990 Clean Air Act debates was strong and vocal support for the SO_2 allowance trading system from parts of the environmental community, particularly the Environmental Defense Fund (EDF), which had already become a champion of market-based approaches to environmental protection in other, less nationally prominent domains, such as water marketing in California. By supporting allowance trading, EDF solidified its reputation as a pragmatic environmental organization willing to adopt new strategies involving less confrontation with private industry, and distinguished itself from other groups (Keohane, Revesz and Stavins, 1997). When the memberships (and financial resources) of other environmental advocacy groups subsequently declined with the election of the environment-friendly Clinton-Gore administration, EDF continued to prosper and grow (Lowry, 1993).

A third key factor in 1990 was the fact that the SO_2 allowance trading program was designed to reduce emissions, not simply to reallocate them cost-effectively. In 1990, EDF was able to make powerful arguments for tradeable permits on the grounds that the use of a cost-effective instrument would make it politically feasible to achieve greater reductions in SO_2 emissions than would otherwise be possible. Market-based instruments are most likely to be politically acceptable if they can achieve environmental improvements which otherwise are not politically or economically feasible. It is not coincidental that the earlier (and successful) lead and chlorofluorocarbon permit trading programs also aimed at reducing emissions, while EPA's attempts to reform local air quality regulation through its Emissions Trading Program without incremental improvements in air quality have been troubled and halting.

---

[8]But there has been some increased understanding of market-based approaches to environmental protection among policymakers and their staffs, due in part to the economics training that is now common in law schools, and the proliferation of schools of public policy.

Fourth, many of the economists involved in the deliberations regarding the SO_2 allowance system took the approach of accepting—implicitly or otherwise—a political goal of reducing SO_2 emissions by 10 million tons. Rather than debating the costs and benefits of that goal, they simply focused on the cost-effective means of achieving it. Separating the benefit-cost calculation about the goals from the instruments used to achieve the goal was important to avoid splintering support for an SO_2 trading program. As evidenced by the failed Republican attempts at "regulatory reform" in 1996, the notion of using explicit benefit-cost calculations as the basis for judging regulations remains highly controversial in political circles. Of course, even if the strategy worked out well in the SO_2 case, there are limitations to the wisdom of separating ends and means: one risks designing a fast train to the wrong station.

Fifth, it is important to note that acid rain was effectively an unregulated problem until the SO_2 allowance trading program of 1990. Hence, there were no existing constituencies for the status quo approach, because there *was* no status quo approach. The demand for a market-based instrument is likely to be greatest and the political opportunity costs of legislators providing support are likely to be least when the status quo instrument is essentially nonexistent. This implies that we should be more optimistic about introducing such market-based instruments for "new" problems, such as global climate change, than for existing, highly regulated problems, such as abandoned hazardous waste sites.

Finally, a caveat is in order. The adoption of the SO_2 allowance trading program for acid rain control—like any major innovation in public policy—can partly be attributed to a healthy dose of chance that placed specific persons in key positions, in this case at the White House, EPA, the Congress, and environmental organizations. Within the White House, among the most active and influential enthusiasts of market-based environmental instruments were Counsel Boyden Gray and his Deputy John Schmitz; Domestic Policy Adviser Roger Porter; Council of Economic Advisers (CEA) Member Richard Schmalensee; CEA Senior Staff Economist Robert Hahn; and Office of Management and Budget Associate Director Robert Grady. At EPA, Administrator William Reilly—a "card-carrying environmentalist"—enjoyed valuable credibility with environmental advocacy groups; Deputy Administrator Henry Habicht was a key supporter of market-based instruments; and Assistant Administrator William Rosenberg was an early convert. In the Congress, Senators Timothy Wirth and John Heinz provided high-profile, bipartisan support for the SO_2 allowance trading system and, more broadly, for a variety of market-based instruments for environmental problems through their "Project 88" (Stavins, 1988). Within the environmental community, EDF Executive Director Fred Krupp, Senior Economist Daniel Dudek, and Staff Attorney Joseph Goffman worked closely with the White House to develop the allowance trading proposal.

Normative Lessons

Within the context of 30 years of federal environmental regulation, characterized by sporadic but increasing reliance on market-based policy instruments, I consider normative lessons from the design and implementation of the SO_2 allowance trading system for design and implementation of tradeable permit systems, analysis of prospective and adopted systems, and identification of new applications.

Lessons for Design and Implementation of Tradeable Permit Systems

The performance of the SO_2 allowance trading system to date provides valuable evidence for environmentalists and others who have been resistant to these innovations that market-based instruments can achieve major cost savings while accomplishing their environmental objectives (Ellerman et al., 1997; U.S. General Accounting Office, 1995). Likewise, we have seen that the system can be implemented without a surge of lawsuits, partly because it was well designed (Burtraw and Swift, 1996) and partly because issues of distributional equity were handled through a congressionally imposed allocation. The system's performance also offers lessons about the importance of flexibility, simplicity, the role of monitoring and enforcement, and the capabilities of the private sector to make markets of this sort work.

In regard to flexibility, tradeable permit systems should be designed to allow for a broad set of compliance alternatives, in terms of both timing and technological options. Allowing flexible timing and intertemporal trading of the allowances—that is, "banking" allowances for future use—has played a very important role in the program's performance (Ellerman et al., 1997), much as it did in the lead rights trading program a decade earlier (Kerr and Maré, 1997). The permit system was based on emissions of SO_2, as opposed to sulfur content of fuels, so that both scrubbing and fuel-switching were feasible options. Moreover, one of the most significant benefits of the trading system was simply that technology standards requiring scrubbing of SO_2 were thereby avoided. This allowed midwestern utilities to take advantage of lower rail rates (brought about by railroad deregulation) to reduce their SO_2 emissions by increasing their use of low-sulfur coal from Wyoming and Montana, an approach that would not have been possible if scrubber requirements had been in place. Also, a less flexible system would not have led to the technological change that may have been induced in scrubber performance and rail transport (Burtraw, 1996; Ellerman and Montero, 1996; Bohi and Burtraw, 1997). Likewise, the economic incentives provided by the trading system have led to induced process innovations in the form of bundling of allowances with coal supplies (Doucet and Strauss, 1994) and the installation of emission reduction technology in exchange for generated allowances (Dudek and Goffman, 1995). The flexibility of the allowance trading system accommodates the dynamic market changes that are occurring because of electric utility deregulation, allowing shifts in industry structure and production methods while assuring that total emissions do not increase.

In regard to simplicity, a unique formula for allocating permits based upon historical data is relatively difficult to contest or manipulate. More generally, trading rules should be clearly defined up front, without ambiguity. For example, there should be no requirements for prior government approval of individual trades. Such requirements hampered EPA's Emissions Trading Program in the 1970s, while the lack of such requirements was an important factor in the success of lead trading (Hahn and Hester, 1989). In the case of SO_2 trading, the absence of requirements for prior approval has reduced uncertainty for utilities and administrative costs for government, and contributed to low transactions costs (Rico, 1995).

Considerations of simplicity and the experience of the SO_2 allowance system also argue for using absolute baselines, not relative ones, as the point of departure for tradeable permit programs. The difference is that with an absolute baseline (so-called "cap-and-trade"), sources are each allocated some number of permits (the total of which is the "cap"); with a relative baseline, reductions are credited from an unspecified baseline. The problem is that without a specified baseline, reductions must be credited relative to an unobservable hypothetical—what the source would have emitted in the absence of the regulation. A hybrid system—where a cap-and-trade program is combined with voluntary "opt-in provisions"—creates the possibility for "paper trades," where a regulated source is credited for an emissions reduction (by an unregulated source) that would have taken place in any event (Montero, 1997). The result is a decrease in aggregate costs among regulated sources, but this is partly due to an unintentional increase in the total emissions cap (Atkeson, 1997). As was experienced with EPA's Emissions Trading Program, relative baselines create significant transaction costs by essentially requiring prior approval of trades as the authority investigates the claimed counterfactual from which reductions are calculated and credits generated (Nichols, Farr and Hester, 1996).

The SO_2 program has also brought home the importance of monitoring and enforcement provisions. In 1990, environmental advocates insisted on continuous emissions monitoring (Burtraw and Swift, 1996), which helps build market confidence (McLean, 1995). The costs of such monitoring, however, are significant. On the enforcement side, the Act's stiff penalties have provided sufficient incentive for the very high degree of compliance that has been achieved.

Another normative lesson is linked with positive issues. Above we emphasized the political advantages of freely allocated permit systems, as employed with SO_2. But the same characteristic that makes such allocation attractive in positive political economy terms—the conveyance of scarcity rents to the private sector—also makes free allocation problematic in normative, efficiency terms (Fullerton and Metcalf, 1997). Goulder, Parry, and Burtraw (1997) estimate that the costs of SO_2 allowance trading would be 25 percent less if permits were auctioned rather than freely allocated, because auctioning yields revenues that can be used to finance reductions in pre-existing distortionary taxes. Furthermore, in the presence of some forms of transaction costs, the post-trading equilibrium—and hence aggregate abatement costs—are sensitive to the initial permit allocation (Stavins, 1995). For both reasons, a successful attempt to establish a politically viable program through a specific initial permit allocation can result in a program that is significantly more costly than anticipated.

Finally, the SO_2 program's performance demonstrates that the private sector can fulfill brokerage needs, providing price information and matching trading partners, despite claims to the contrary when the program was enacted. Entrepreneurs have stepped in to make available a variety of services, including private brokerage, electronic bid/ask bulletin boards, and allowance price forecasts. The annual EPA auctions may have served the purpose of helping to reveal market valuations of allowances, but bilateral trading has also informed the auctions (Joskow, Schmalensee and Bailey, 1996).

Lessons for Analysis of Tradeable Permit Systems

When assessing trading programs, economists have typically employed some measure in which gains from trade are estimated for moving from conventional standards to marketable permits. Aggregate cost savings are the best yardstick for measuring success, not number of trades or total trading volume (Hahn and May, 1994).

The challenge for analysts is to compare realistic versions of both tradeable permit systems and "likely alternatives," not idealized versions of either. It is not enough to analyze static gains from trade (Hahn and Stavins, 1992). For example, the gains from banking allowances should also be modeled (unless this is not permitted in practice). It can also be important to allow for the effects of alternative instruments on technology innovation and diffusion (Milliman and Prince, 1989; Jaffe and Stavins, 1995; Doucet and Strauss, 1994; Dudek and Goffman, 1995), especially when permit trading programs impose significant costs over long time horizons (Newell, Jaffe and Stavins, 1997).

More generally, it is important to consider the effects of the pre-existing regulatory environment. The level of pre-existing factor taxes can affect the total costs of regulation (Goulder, Parry and Burtraw, 1997). Also, because SO_2 is both a transboundary precursor of acid rain and a local air pollutant regulated under a separate part of the Clean Air Act, "local" environmental regulations have sometimes prevented utilities from acquiring allowances rather than carrying out emissions reductions (Conrad and Kohn, 1996). Moreover, because electricity generation and distribution have been regulated by state commissions, a prospective analysis of SO_2 trading should consider the incentives these commissions may have to influence the level of allowance trading.[9]

---

[9]Also, rate-of-return regulation that employs capital investments as a baseline might be expected to lead electric utilities to bias their SO_2 compliance choices toward investments in scrubbers, for example, and away from allowance transactions (Averch and Johnson, 1962).

A set of theoretical arguments suggests that state public utility commissions may have incentives to erect such barriers. Coal interests in some midwestern and eastern states, where high-sulfur coal is mined, were opposed to the concept of allowance trading because it would permit utilities to switch to cleaner western coal. Hence, it is reasonable to suspect that those same interests would pressure state regulatory commissions to erect direct or indirect barriers to trading (Bohi and Burtraw, 1992; Burtraw, 1996). However, the only rigorous analysis that has been carried out of this contention suggests that such pressures have not, if applied, been effective (Bailey, 1996). In any event, it is clear that state regulatory commissions have not encouraged utilities to engage in allowance trading, either (Bohi, 1994). The commissions have been reactive, rather than proactive in terms of accounting and tax treatment of allowance transactions (Rose, 1997), restricting themselves to reviewing and approving plans submitted by utilities. Only the Georgia Public Service Commission has actively ordered utilities in its jurisdiction to monitor the allowance market and purchase allowances when prices are below compliance costs.

It has also been suggested that many electric utilities have been reluctant to consider new options, which is consistent with their reputation as firms that seek to minimize risk, rather than cost (Rose, 1997), but this may change due to the heightened role of competition brought about by electricity deregulation. Also, long-term contractual precommitments have tied many utilities to plans conceived before allowance trading was an option (Coggins and Swinton, 1996). Finally, some utilities may be reluctant to make serious investments in allowances in the face of future regulatory uncertainty (U.S. Energy Information Administration, 1997).

Issues such as these must be taken into account in the analysis of any pollution control program, whether it is market-oriented or command-and-control in nature.

Lessons for Identifying New Applications

Market-based policy instruments are now considered for each and every environmental problem that is raised, ranging from endangered species preservation to what may be the greatest of environmental problems, the greenhouse effect and global climate change. Our experiences with SO_2 trading—and with the earlier programs of lead and chlorofluorocarbon trading—offer some guidance to the conditions under which tradeable permits are likely to work well, and when they may face greater difficulties.

First, SO_2 trading is a case where the cost of abating pollution differs widely among sources, and where a market-based system is therefore likely to have greater gains, relative to conventional, command-and-control regulations (Newell and Stavins, 1997). It was clear early on that SO_2 abatement cost heterogeneity was great, because of differences in ages of plants and their proximity to sources of low-sulfur coal. But where abatement costs are more uniform across sources, the political costs of enacting an allowance trading approach are less likely to be justifiable.

Second, the greater the degree to which pollutants mix in the receiving airshed or watershed, the more attractive a tradeable emission permit (or emission tax) system will be, relative to a conventional uniform standard. This is because taxes or tradeable permits can lead to localized "hot spots" with relatively high levels of ambient pollution. This is a significant distributional issue. Some acid-rain receiving states have attempted to erect barriers to those trades that could increase deposition within their borders.[10] It can also become an efficiency issue, if damages are nonlinearly related to pollutant concentrations.

Third, the efficiency of a tradeable permit system will depend on the pattern of costs and benefits. If uncertainty about marginal abatement costs is significant, and if marginal abatement costs are quite flat and marginal benefits of abatement fall relatively quickly, then a quantity instrument, such as tradeable permits, will be more efficient than a price instrument, such as an emission tax (Weitzman, 1974). Furthermore, when there is also uncertainty about marginal benefits, and marginal benefits are positively correlated with marginal costs (which, it turns out, is a relatively common occurrence for a variety of pollution problems), then there is an additional argument in favor of the relative efficiency of quantity instruments.[11]

Fourth, tradeable permits will work best when transaction costs are low, and the SO_2 experiment shows that if properly designed, private markets will tend to render transaction costs minimal. Finally, considerations of political feasibility point to the wisdom of proposing trading instruments when they can be used to facilitate emissions reductions, as was done with SO_2 allowances and lead rights trading. Policy instruments that appear impeccable from the vantage point of Cambridge, Massachusetts, but consistently prove infeasible in Washington, D.C., can hardly be considered "optimal."

Many of these issues can be illuminated by considering a concrete example: the current interest in applying tradeable permits to the task of cutting carbon dioxide (CO_2) emissions to reduce the risk of global climate change. It is immediately obvious that the number and diversity of sources of CO_2 emissions due to fossil fuel combustion are vastly greater than in the case of SO_2 emissions as a precursor of acid rain, where the focus can be placed on a few hundred electric utility plants (Environmental Law Institute, 1997).

---

[10]For example, as recently as the summer of 1997, legislation emerged in the New York State legislature that would penalize utilities for selling allowances to companies "accused of exacerbating New York's acid rain problem" (*Boston Globe*, June 26, 1997, on-line). Under the legislation, if a trade were found to be "detrimental to environmentally sensitive areas," the Public Service Commission would be directed to impose a fine three times the value of the trade.

[11]One generator of stochastic shocks that frequently affects both marginal benefits and marginal costs—with the same sign—is the weather. For further explanation and specific examples, see Stavins (1996).

Any pollution-control program must face the possibility of "emissions leakage" from regulated to unregulated sources. This could be a problem for meeting domestic targets for CO_2 emissions reduction, but it would be a vastly greater problem for an international program, where emissions would tend to increase in nonparticipant countries. This also raises serious concerns with provisions in the Kyoto Protocol for industrialized countries to participate in a CO_2 cap-and-trade program, while non-participant (developing) nations retain the option of joining the system on a project-by-project basis, an approach commonly known as "joint implementation." As emphasized earlier, provisions in tradeable permit programs that allow for unregulated sources to "opt in" can lower aggregate costs by substituting low-cost for high-cost control, but may also have the unintended effect of increasing aggregate emissions beyond what they would otherwise have been. This is because there is an incentive for adverse selection: sources in developing countries that would reduce their emissions, opt in, and receive "excess allowances" would tend to be those that would have reduced their emissions in any case.

To the limited degree that any previous trading program can serve as a model for the case of global climate change, some attention should be given to the tradeable-permit system that accomplished the U.S. phaseout of leaded gasoline. The currency of that system was not lead oxide emissions from motor vehicles, but the lead content of gasoline. So too, in the case of global climate, great savings in monitoring and enforcement costs could be had by adopting *input* trading linked to the carbon content of fossil fuels. This is reasonable in the climate case, since—unlike in the SO_2 case—CO_2 emissions are roughly proportional to the carbon content of fossil fuels and scrubbing alternatives are largely unavailable, at least at present. On the other hand, natural sequestration of CO_2 from the atmosphere by expanding forested areas is available (even in the United States) at reasonable cost (Stavins, 1997) and is explicitly counted toward compliance with the targets of the Kyoto Protocol. Hence, it will be important to combine any carbon trading (or carbon tax) program with a carbon sequestration program, possibly denominated by forested areas.

In terms of carbon permit allocation mechanisms, auctions would have the advantage that revenues could be used to finance reductions in distortionary taxes. Although free allocation of carbon permits might meet with less political resistance, such free allocation could increase regulatory costs enough that the sign of the efficiency impact would be reversed from positive to negative net benefits (Parry, Williams and Goulder 1997).

Finally, developing a tradeable permit system in the area of global climate change would surely bring forth an entirely new set of economic, political, and institutional challenges, particularly with regard to enforcement problems (Schmalensee, 1996; Stavins, 1998). But it is also true that the diversity of sources of CO_2 emissions and the magnitude of likely abatement costs make it equally clear that only a market-based instrument— some form of carbon rights trading or (probably revenue-neutral) carbon taxes—will be capable of achieving the domestic targets that may eventually be forthcoming from international agreements.

Conclusion

Given that the SO_2 allowance-trading program became fully binding only in 1995, we should be cautious when drawing conclusions about lessons to be learned from the program's development or its performance. A number of important questions remain. For example, little is known empirically about the impact of trading on technological change. Also, much more empirical research is needed on how the pre-existing regulatory environment affects the operation of permit trading programs. Moreover, all the successes with tradeable permits have involved air pollution: acid rain, leaded gasoline, and chlorofluorocarbons. Our experience (and success rate) with water pollution is much more limited (Hahn, 1989), and in other areas, we have no experience at all. Even for air pollution problems, the tremendous differences between SO_2 and acid rain, on the one hand, and the combustion of fossil fuels and global climate change, on the other, indicate that any rush to judgement regarding global climate policy instruments is unwarranted.

Despite these and other uncertainties, market-based instruments for environmental protection—and, in particular, tradeable permit systems—now enjoy proven successes in reducing pollution at low cost. Such cost effectiveness is the primary focus of economists when evaluating public policies, but the political system clearly gives much greater weight to distributional concerns. In the Congressional deliberations that led up to the Clean Air Act amendments of 1990, considerable pressures were brought to bear to allow less switching from high-sulfur to low-sulfur coal to benefit regions dependent on high-sulfur coal mining. Such provisions would have increased compliance costs for midwestern coal-burning utilities (U.S. Congressional Budget Office, 1986), encouraged political pressures for nationwide cost sharing, and greatly reduced the cost-effectiveness of the system. In this way, individual constituencies, each fighting for its own version of distributional equity, negate efficiency and cost effectiveness. In the pursuit of obtaining nicely shaped pieces of the proverbial pie, we all too often end up with a systematically smaller pie. That this did not happen in 1990 was the exception, not the rule.

There are sound reasons why the political world has been slow to embrace the use of market-based instruments for environmental protection, including the ways economists have packaged and promoted their ideas in the past: failing to separate means (cost-effective instruments) from ends (efficiency); and treating environmental problems as little more than "externalities calling for corrective taxes." Much of the resistance has also been due, of course, to the very nature of the political process and the incentives it provides to both politicians and interest groups to favor command-and-control methods instead of market-based approaches.

But despite this history, market-based instruments have moved center stage, and policy debates look very different from the time when these ideas were characterized as "licenses to pollute" or dismissed as completely impractical. Of course, no single policy instrument—whether market-based or conventional—will be appropriate for all environmental problems. Which instrument is best in any given situation depends upon characteristics of the specific environmental problem, and the social, political, and economic context in which the instrument is to be implemented.

References

Ackerman, Bruce A., and William T. Hassler, *Clean Coal/Dirty Air*. New Haven: Yale University Press, 1981.

Atkeson, Erica, "Joint Implementation: Lessons from Title IV's Voluntary Compliance Programs," Working Paper 97–003, MIT Center for Energy and Environmental Policy Research, May 1997.

Averch, Harvey, and Leland L. Johnson, "Behavior of the Firm under Regulatory Constraint," *American Economic Review*, 1962, *52*, 1053–69.

Bailey, Elizabeth M., "Allowance Trading Activity and State Regulatory Rulings: Evidence from the US Acid Rain Program," Working Paper 96–002, MIT Center for Energy and Environmental Policy Research, March 1996.

Barthold, Thomas A., "Issues in the Design of Environmental Excise Taxes," *Journal of Economic Perspectives*, Winter 1994, *8*:1, 133–51.

Baumol, William J., and Wallace E. Oates, *The Theory of Environmental Policy*. Second edition. New York: Cambridge University Press, 1988.

Bohi, Douglas R., "Utilities and State Regulators Are Failing to Take Advantage of Emissions Allowance Trading," *The Electricity Journal*, March 1994, *7*:2, 20–27.

Bohi, Douglas R., and Dallas Burtraw, "Utility Investment Behavior and the Emission Trading Market," *Resources and Energy*, April 1992, *14*:1/2, 129–53.

Bohi, Douglas R., and Dallas Burtraw, "SO_2 Allowance Trading: How Do Expectations and Experience Measure Up?" *Electricity Journal*, August/September 1997, 67–75.

Burtraw, Dallas, "The SO_2 Emissions Trading Program: Cost Savings Without Allowance Trades," *Contemporary Economic Policy*, April 1996, *14*, 79–94.

Burtraw, Dallas, Alan Krupnick, Erin Mansur, David Austin, and Deidre Farrell, "The Costs and Benefits of Reducing Acid Rain," Discussion Paper 97–31-REV, Resources for the Future, Washington, D.C., September 1997.

Burtraw, Dallas, and Byron Swift, "A New Standard of Performance: An Analysis of the Clean Air Act's Acid Rain Program," *Environmental Law Reporter News & Analysis*, August 1996, *26*:8, 10411–423.

Cansier, Dieter, and Raimund Krumm, "Air Pollutant Taxation: An Empirical Survey," *Ecological Economics*, 1997, *23*:1, 59–70.

Coggins, Jay S., and John R. Swinton, "The Price of Pollution: A Dual Approach to Valuing SO_2 Allowances," *Journal of Environmental Economics and Management*, January 1996, *30*:1, 58–72.

Conrad, Klaus, and Robert E. Kohn, "The US Market for SO_2 Permits: Policy Implications of the Low Price and Trading Volume," *Energy Policy*, 1996, *24*:12, 1051–59.

Crocker, Thomas D., "The Structuring of Atmospheric Pollution Control Systems." In Harold Wolozin, ed. *The Economics of Air Pollution*. New York: Norton, 1966.

Dales, John H., *Pollution, Property, and Prices*. Toronto: University of Toronto Press, 1968.

Doucet, Joseph A., and Todd Strauss, "On the Bundling of Coal and Sulphur Dioxide Emissions Allowances," *Energy Policy*, September 1994, *22*:9, 764–70.

Dudek, Daniel J., and Joseph Goffman, "The Clean Air Act Acid Rain Program: Lessons for Success in Creating a New Paradigm," 85th Annual Meeting of the Air & Waste Management Association, 95-RA120.06, San Antonio, Texas, 1995.

Ellerman, A. Denny, and Juan Pablo Montero, "Why are Allowance Prices so Low? An Analysis of the SO_2 Emissions Trading Program," Working Paper 96–001, MIT Center for Energy and Environmental Policy Research, February 1996.

Ellerman, A. Denny, Richard Schmalensee, Paul J. Joskow, Juan Pablo Montero, and Elizabeth M. Bailey, *Emissions Trading Under the U.S. Acid Rain Program: Evaluation of Compliance Costs and Allowance Market Performance.* Cambridge: MIT Center for Energy and Environmental Policy Research, October 1997.

Environmental Law Institute, "Implementing an Emissions Cap and Allowance Trading System for Greenhouse Gases: Lessons from the Acid Rain Program," Research Report, Washington, D.C., September 1997.

Fullerton, Don, and Gilbert Metcalf, "Environmental Controls, Scarcity Rents, and Pre-Existing Distortions," NBER Working Paper 6091, July 1997.

Goulder, Lawrence H., Ian W. H. Parry, and Dallas Burtraw, "Revenue-Raising vs. Other Approaches to Environmental Protection: The Critical Significance of Pre-Existing Tax Distortions," *RAND Journal of Economics*, Winter 1997, *28*:4, 708–31.

Hahn, Robert W., "Economic Prescriptions for Environmental Problems: How the Patient Followed the Doctor's Orders," *Journal of Economic Perspectives*, Spring 1989, *3*:2, 95–114.

Hahn, Robert W., and Gordon L. Hester, "Marketable Permits: Lessons for Theory and Practice," *Ecology Law Quarterly*, 1989, *16*:2, 361–406.

Hahn, Robert W., and Carol A. May, "The Behavior of the Allowance Market: Theory and Evidence," *The Electricity Journal*, March 1994, 7:2, 28–37.

Hahn, Robert W., and Robert N. Stavins, "Economic Incentives for Environmental Protection: Integrating Theory and Practice," *American Economic Review*, 1992, *82*, 464–68.

ICF, Inc., "Economic Analysis of Title V (Acid Rain Provisions) of the Administration's Proposed Clean Air Act Amendments (H.R. 3030/S. 1490)." Prepared for the U.S. Environmental Protection Agency, Washington, D.C., 1989.

Jaffe, Adam B., and Robert N. Stavins, "Dynamic Incentives of Environmental Regulations: The Effects of Alternative Policy Instruments on Technological Diffusion." *Journal of Environmental Economics and Management*, November 1995, *29*:3, S43–S63.

Joskow, Paul L., and Richard Schmalensee, "The Political Economy of Market-Based Environmental Policy: The U.S. Acid Rain Program," *Journal of Law and Economics*, April 1998, *41*, 89–135.

Joskow, Paul L., Richard Schmalensee, and Elizabeth M. Bailey, "Auction Design and the Market for Sulfur Dioxide Emissions," National Bureau of Economic Research Working Paper No. 5745, Cambridge, September 1996.

Kelman, Steven P., *What Price Incentives?* Boston: Auburn House, 1981.

Kennedy, David M., *Controlling Acid Rain, 1986.* Case Study C15-86-699.0. Cambridge: John F. Kennedy School of Government. Harvard University, 1986.

Kerr, Suzi, and David Maré, "Efficient Regulation Through Tradeable Permit Markets: The United States Lead Phasedown," Department of Agricultural and Resource Economics, University of Maryland, College Park, Working Paper 96–06, January 1997.

Keohane, Nathaniel O., Richard L. Revesz, and Robert N. Stavins, "The Positive Political Economy of Instrument Choice in Environmental Policy." In Paul Portney and Robert Schwab, eds. *Environmental Economics and Public Policy*. London: Edward Elgar, Ltd., 1997.

Lowry, Robert C., "The Political Economy of Environmental Citizen Groups," unpublished Ph.D. thesis, Harvard University, 1993.

McCubbins, Matthew D., Roger G. Noll, and Barry R. Weingast, "Administrative Procedures as Instruments of Political Control," *Journal of Law, Economics and Organization*, 1987, *3*, 243–77.

McCubbins, Matthew D., Roger G. Noll, and Barry R. Weingast, "Structure and Process, Politics and Policy: Administrative Arrangements and the Political Control of Agencies," *Virginia Law Review*, 1989, *75*, 431–82.

McCubbins, Matthew and Terry Sullivan, "Constituency Influences on Legislative Policy Choice," *Quality and Quantity*, 1984, *18*, 299–319.

McLean, Brian J., "Lessons Learned Implementing Title IV of the Clean Air Act," 85th Annual Meeting of the Air & Waste Management Association, 95-RA120.04, San Antonio, Texas, 1995.

Milliman, Scott R., and Raymond Prince, "Firm Incentives to Promote Technological Changes in Pollution Control," *Journal of Environmental Economics and Management*, 1989, *17*, 247–65.

Montgomery, W. David, "Markets in Licenses and Efficient Pollution Control Programs," *Journal of Economic Theory*, 1972, 395–418.

Montero, Juan-Pablo, "Volunteering for Market-Based Environmental Regulation: The Substitution Provision of the SO_2 Emissions Trading Program," Working Paper 97–001, MIT Center for Energy and Environmental Policy Research, January 1997.

Newell Richard G., Adam B. Jaffe, and Robert N. Stavins, "Environmental Policy and Technological Change: The Effects of Economic Incentives and Direct Regulation on Energy-Saving Innovation," paper presented at the 1997 Allied Social Science Association meeting, New Orleans, January 1997.

Newell, Richard G., and Robert N. Stavins, "Abatement Cost Heterogeneity and Potential Gains from Market-Based Instruments." Working paper, John F. Kennedy School of Government, Harvard University, June 1997.

Nichols, Albert L., John G. Farr, and Gordon Hester, "Trading and the Timing of Emissions: Evidence from the Ozone Transport Region," National Economic Research Associates, Cambridge, Massachusetts, Draft of September 9, 1996.

Parry, Ian, Roberton Williams, and Lawrence Goulder, "When Can Carbon Abatement Policies Increase Welfare? The Fundamental Role of Distorted Factor Markets," Working paper, Resources for the Future and Stanford University, September 1997.

Pigou, Arthur Cecil, *The Economics of Welfare*. London: Macmillan and Company, 1920.

Portney, Paul R., "Policy Watch: Economics and the Clean Air Act," *Journal of Economic Perspectives*, Fall 1990, *4*:4, 173–81.

Revesz, Richard L., "Federalism and Interstate Environmental Externalities," *University of Pennsylvania Law Review*, 1996, *144*, 2341.

Rico, Renee, "The U.S. Allowance Trading System for Sulfur Dioxide: An Update of Market Experience," *Environmental and Resource Economics*, March 1995, *5*:2, 115–29.

Rose, Kenneth, "Implementing an Emissions Trading Program in an Economically Regulated Industry: Lessons from the SO_2 Trading Program." In R. Kosobud, and J. Zimmermann, eds. *Market Based Approaches to Environmental Policy: Regulatory Innovations to the Fore*. New York: Van Nostrand Reinhold, 1997.

Sandel, Michael J., "It's Immoral to Buy the Right to Pollute," *New York Times*, December 15, 1997, p. A29.

Schmalensee, Richard, "Greenhouse Policy Architecture and Institutions," MIT Joint Program on the Science and Policy of Global Change, Report 13, November 1996.

Shepsle, Kenneth A., and Barry R. Weingast, "Political Solutions to Market Problems," *American Political Science Review*, 1984, *78*, 417–34.

Stavins, Robert N., "Transaction Costs and Tradable Permits," *Journal of Environmental Economics and Management*, September 1995, *29*, 133–48.

Stavins, Robert N., "Correlated Uncertainty and Policy Instrument Choice," *Journal of Environmental Economics and Management*, 1996, *30*, 218–32.

Stavins, Robert N., "The Costs of Carbon Sequestration: A Revealed-Preference Approach." Working paper, John F. Kennedy School of Government, Harvard University, November 1997.

Stavins, Robert N., "Policy Instruments for Climate Change: How Can National Governments Address a Global Problem," *The University of Chicago Legal Forum*, forthcoming 1998.

Stavins, Robert N., ed., *Project 88—Harnessing Market Forces to Protect Our Environment: Initiatives for the New President.* A Public Policy Study sponsored by Senator Timothy E. Wirth, Colorado, and Senator John Heinz, Pennsylvania. Washington, D.C.: December 1988.

U.S. Congressional Budget Office, *Curbing Acid Rain: Costs, Budget, and Coal-Market Effects.* Washington, D.C., 1986.

U.S. Energy Information Administration, "The Effects of Title IV of the Clean Air Act Amendments of 1990 on Electric Utilities: An Update," DOE/EIA-0582, March 1997, Washington, D.C.

U.S. Environmental Protection Agency, *Environmental Investments: The Cost of a Clean Environment.* Washington, D.C.: U.S. Environmental Protection Agency, 1990.

U.S. Environmental Protection Agency, "1996 Compliance Record: Acid Rain Program," EPA 430-R-97-025, June 1997, Office of Air and Radiation, Washington, D.C.

U.S. General Accounting Office, "Air Pollution: Allowance Trading Offers an Opportunity to Reduce Emissions at Less Cost," GAO/RCED-95-30, Washington, D.C., 1995.

Weitzman, Martin L., "Prices vs. Quantities," *Review of Economic Studies*, 1974, *41*, 477–91.

18   *It's Immoral to Buy the Right to Pollute (with replies)* *

Michael J. Sandel

Michael J. Sandel is the Anne T. and Robert M. Bass Professor of Government at Harvard University.

At the conference on global warming in Kyoto, Japan, the United States found itself at toggerheads with developing nations on two important issues: The United States wanted those countries to commit themselves to restraints on emissions, and it wanted any agreement to include a trading scheme that would let countries buy and sell the right to pollute.

The Administration was right on the first point, but wrong on the second. Creating an international market in emission credits would make it easier for us to meet our obligations under the treaty but undermine the ethic we should be trying to foster on the environment.

Indeed, China and India threatened to torpedo the talks over the issue. They were afraid that such trading would enable rich countries to buy their way out of commitments to reduce greenhouse gases. In the end, the developing nations agreed to allow some emissions trading among developed countries, with details to be negotiated next year.

The Clinton Administration has made emission trading a centerpiece of its environmental policy. Creating an international market for emissions, it argues, is a more efficient way to reduce pollution than imposing fixed levels for each country.

Trading in greenhouse gases could also make compliance cheaper and less painful for the United States, which could pay to reduce some other country's carbon dioxide emissions rather than reduce its own. For example, the United States might find it cheaper (and more politically palatable) to pay to update an old coal-burning factory in a developing country than to tax gas-guzzling sports utility vehicles at home.

Since the aim is to limit the global level of these gases, one might ask, what difference does it make which places on the planet send less carbon to the sky?

It may make no difference from the standpoint of the heavens, but it does make a political difference. Despite the efficiency of international emissions trading, such a system is objectionable for three reasons.

"It's Immoral to Buy the Right to Pollute," editorial by Michael J. Sandel, from *New York Times*, December 15, 1997, p. A29.

*Including replies printed in *New York Times*, Dec. 17, 1997.

First, it creates loopholes that could enable wealthy countries to evade their obligations. Under the Kyoto formula, for example, the United States could take advantage of the fact that Russia has already reduced its emissions 30 percent since 1990, not through energy efficiencies but through economic decline. The United States could buy excess credits from Russia, and count them toward meeting our obligations under the treaty.

Second, turning pollution into a commodity to be bought and sold removes the moral stigma that is properly associated with it, if a company or a country is fined for spewing excessive pollutants into the air, the community conveys its judgment that the polluter has done something wrong. A fee, on the other hand, makes pollution just another cost of doing business, like wages, benefits and rent.

The distinction between a fine and a fee for despoiling the environment is not one we should give up too easily. Suppose there were a $100 fine for throwing a beer can into the Grand Canyon, and a wealthy hiker decided to pay $100 for the convenience. Would there be nothing wrong in his treating the fine as if it were simply an expensive dumping charge?

Or consider the fine for parking in a place reserved for the disabled. If a busy contractor needs to park near his building site and is willing to pay the fine, is there nothing wrong with his treating that space as an expensive parking lot?

In effacing the distinction between a fine and a fee, emission trading is like a recent proposal to open carpool lanes on Los Angeles freeways to drivers without passengers who are willing to pay a fee. Such drivers are now fined for slipping into carpool lanes; under the market proposal, they would enjoy a quicker commute without opprobrium.

A third objection to emission trading among countries is that it may undermine the sense of shared responsibility that increased global cooperation requires.

Consider an illustration drawn from an autumn ritual: raking fallen leaves into great piles and lighting bonfires. Imagine a neighborhood where each family agrees to have only one small bonfire a year. But they also agree that families can buy and sell their bonfire permits as they choose.

The family in the mansion on the hill buys permits from its neighbors— paying them, in effect, to lug their leaves to the town compost heap. The market works, and pollution is reduced, but without the spirit of shared sacrifice that might have been produced had no market intervened.

Those who have sold their permits and those who have bought them, come to regard the bonfires less as an offense against clean air than as a luxury, a status symbol that can be bought and sold. And the resentment against the family in the mansion makes future, more demanding forms of cooperation more difficult to achieve.

Of course, many countries that attended the Kyoto conference have already made cooperation elusive. They have not yet agreed to restrict their emissions at all. Their refusal undermines the prospect of a global environmental ethic as surely as does our pollution trading scheme.

But the United States would have more suasion if these developing countries could not rightly complain that trading in emissions allows wealthy nations to buy their way out of global obligation.

Replies to Michael J. Sandel

From Steven Shavell, Professor of Law and Economics at Harvard Law School

Michael J. Sandel ("It's Immoral to Buy the Right to Pollute," Op-Ed, Dec. 15) discounts the great benefits of trade in pollution rights and advances flawed arguments against it.

Suppose a rich country like the United States would have to spend $50 billion annually to reduce its carbon dioxide emissions by some amount, whereas China could reduce its emissions by this same amount more cheaply, at a cost of $5 billion (say, by installing simple smoke scrubbers in its coal-burning factories).

If trade in emissions credits were allowed, both China and the United States would be better off.

The United States could pay China $30 billion for the right to emit carbon dioxide. This would make China $25 billion better off: it would receive $30 billion and spend only $5 billion to prevent the emissions. The United States would pay $30 billion rather than spend $50 billion to abate the emissions.

And trade would probably lead ultimately to less pollution. When countries know that they can make profits or that ceilings on pollution are easier to meet, they will be more likely to agree to reduce the total amount of permitted pollution over time.

From Robert N. Stavins, Albert Pratt Professor of Business and Government at the John F. Kennedy School of Government, Harvard University, and University Fellow at Resources for the Future

The ink is barely dry on the Kyoto protocol, but Michael J. Sandel argues that the agreement's emissions trading provisions, supported by the Clinton Administration, will foster "immoral" behavior (Op-Ed, Dec. 15).

Was it immoral when the United States used a tradable permit system among refineries to phase leaded gasoline out of the market in the 1980's more rapidly than anyone had anticipated and at a savings of $250 million a year?

Replies to editorial, by Steven Shavell, Robert N. Stavins, Sanford Gaines, and Eric Maskin, from *New York Times*, December 17, 1997.

Is it now immoral that we are reducing acid rain by half through a tradable permit system among electrical utilities, reducing emissions (sulfur dioxide) faster than anyone had predicted and saving up to $1 billion a year for electricity consumers? Is that why the Environmental Defense Fund and others have worked so tirelessly and effectively to implement these emissions-trading programs?

From Sanford E. Gaines, Professor of Law at the University of Houston

Michael J. Sandel (Op-Ed, Dec. 15) invokes the moral argument against emissions trading in the context of reducing greenhouse gas emissions. Maintaining a moral stigma on pollution makes sense for hazardous substances where polluters have choices, for reducing the pollution. But global warming is not such a situation. Does Mr. Sandel really believe he is behaving immorally when he cooks his dinner, switches on a light or turns on a computer to write an Op-Ed article? These activities result in emissions of carbon dioxide. Or is it his utility that should be stigmatized, perhaps for not using nuclear power?

To reduce greenhouse gas emissions, producers and consumers alike need to adopt new technologies. That's a perfect situation to use the power of the market. Mr. Sandel should reserve his moral outrage for those who don't even want the chance to buy the right to pollute because they refuse to accept that the planet can no longer afford cheap energy.

From Eric S. Maskin, Louis Berkman Professor of Economics at Harvard University

Michael J. Sandel (Op-Ed, Dec. 15) neglects an important distinction in his argument against tradable emissions credits. The examples he gives of immoral acts—throwing beer cans into the Grand Canyon or parking in spots reserved for the disabled—are discrete choices: one can do them or not do them, and society can therefore reasonably ban them outright.

But virtually any manufacturing activity entails the creation of some pollution. So the question is not will we pollute, but rather how much. Further, if there is to be pollution, shouldn't we try to trade it off against its economic consequences? Such a trade-off is facilitated by tradable rights.

VI

Trade, Growth, and the Environment

19 The Environment and Globalization*

Jeffrey A. Frankel

Harpel Professor of Capital Formation and Growth at the Kennedy School of Government, Harvard University, Cambridge, MA.

Introduction

At the Ministerial meeting of the World Trade Organization in Seattle in November 1999, some protestors wore turtle costumes while launching the first of the big anti-globalization demonstrations. These demonstrators were concerned that international trade in shrimp was harming sea turtles by ensnaring them in nets. They felt that a WTO panel had, in the name of free trade, negated the ability of the United States to protect the turtles, simultaneously undermining the international environment and national sovereignty.

Subsequently, anti-globalization protests became common at meetings of multinational organizations. Perhaps no aspect of globalization worries the critics more than its implications for the environment. The concern is understandable. It is widely (if not universally) accepted that the direct effects of globalization on the economy are positive, as measured by Gross Domestic Product. Concerns rise more with regard to "non-economic" effects of globalization.[1] Of these, some, such as labor rights, might be considered to be a subject properly of national sovereignty, with each nation bearing the responsibility of deciding to what extent it wishes to protect its own labor force, based on its own values, capabilities, and politics. When we turn to influences on the environment, however, the case for countries sticking their noses into each other's business is stronger. We all share a common planet.

Pollution and other forms of environmental degradation are the classic instance of what economists call an externality. This term means that

"The Environment and Globalization," by Jeffrey A. Frankel, in *Globalization: What's New,* ed. Michael Weinstein (New York: Columbia University Press, forthcoming)

*The author would like to thank Steve Charnovitz, Dan Esty, Don Fullerton, Rob Stavins, and Michael Weinstein for useful comments; Anne Lebrun for research assistance; and the Savitz Research Fund for support.

[1] The quotation marks are necessary around "non-economic," because economists' conceptual framework fully incorporates such objectives as environmental quality, even though pollution is an externality that is not measured by GDP. For further reading on how economists think about the environment, see Hanley, Shogren, and White (1997) or Stavins (2000).

individual people and firms, and sometimes even individual countries, lack the incentive to restrain their pollution, because under a market system the costs are borne primarily by others, rather than by themselves. The phrase "tragedy of the commons" was originally coined in the context of a village's shared pasture land, which would inevitably be over-grazed if each farmer were allowed free and unrestricted use. It captures the idea that we will foul our shared air and water supplies and deplete our natural resources unless somehow we are individually faced with the costs of our actions.

A central question for this chapter is whether globalization helps or hurts in achieving the best tradeoff between environmental and economic goals. Do international trade and investment allow countries to achieve more economic growth for any given level of environmental quality? Or do they undermine environmental quality for any given rate of economic growth? Globalization is a complex trend, encompassing many forces and many effects. It would be surprising if all of them were always unfavorable to the environment, or all of them favorable. The highest priority should be to determine ways in which globalization can be successfully harnessed to promote protection of the environment, along with other shared objectives, as opposed to degradation of the environment.[2]

One point to be emphasized here is that it is an illusion to think that environmental issues could be effectively addressed if each country were insulated against incursions into its national sovereignty at the hands of international trade or the WTO. Increasingly, people living in one country want to protect the air, water, forests, and animals not just in their *own* countries, but also in *other* countries as well. To do so international cooperation is required. National sovereignty is the obstacle to such efforts, not the ally. Multilateral institutions are a potential ally, not the obstacle.

In the course of this chapter, we encounter three ways in which globalization can be a means of environmental improvement. So the author hopes to convince the reader, at any rate. Each has a component that is new.

First is the exercise of *consumer power*. There is the beginning of a worldwide trend toward labeling, codes of corporate conduct, and other ways that environmentally conscious consumers can use their purchasing power to give expression and weight to their wishes. These tools would not exist without international trade. American citizens would have little way to dissuade Mexican fishermen from using dolphin-unfriendly nets if Americans did not import tuna to begin with. The attraction of labeling is that it suits a decentralized world, where we have both national sovereignty and consumer sovereignty. Nevertheless, labeling cannot be a completely laissez faire affair. For it to work, there need to be some rules or standards. Otherwise, any producer could inaccurately label its product as environmentally pure, and any country could unfairly put a pejorative label on imports from rival producers. This consideration leads to the second respect in which globalization can be a means of environmental improvement.

---

[2]The literature on trade and the environment is surveyed in Dean (1992, 2001) and Copeland and Taylor (2003b).

International environmental issues require international cooperation, a system in which countries interact under a set of *multilateral rules* determined in multilateral negotiations and monitored by multilateral institutions. This is just as true in the case of environmental objectives, which are increasingly cross-border, as of other objectives. It is true that in the past, the economic objectives of international trade have been pursued more effectively by the GATT and other multilateral organizations than have environmental objectives. But multilateral institutions can be made a means of environmental protection. This will sound like pie-in-the-sky to the many who have been taken in by the mantra that recent WTO panel decisions have overruled legislative efforts to protect the environment. But the WTO has actually moved importantly in the environmentalists' direction in recent years.

The front lines of multilateral governance currently concern—not illusory alternatives of an all-powerful WTO versus none at all—but rather questions about how reasonably to balance both economic and environmental objectives. One question under debate is whether countries are to be allowed to adopt laws that may be trade restricting, but that have as their objective influencing other countries' processes and production methods (PPMs), such as their fishermen's use of nets. While the issue is still controversial, the WTO has moved clearly in the direction of answering this question in the affirmative, that is, asserting in panel decisions countries' ability to adopt such laws. The only "catch" is that the measures cannot be unnecessarily unilateral or discriminatory. The environmentalist community has almost entirely failed to notice this major favorable development, because of confusion over the latter qualification. But not only is the qualification what a reasonable person would want, it is secondary to the primary issue of countries' rights under the trading system to implement such laws. By ignoring their victory on the main issue, environmentalists risk losing the opportunity to consolidate it. Some players, particularly poor countries, would love to deny the precedent set in these panel decisions and to return to a system where other countries cannot restrict trade in pursuit of PPMs.

Third, countries can learn from others' experiences. There has recently accumulated *statistical evidence* on how globalization and growth tend to affect environmental objectives on average, even without multilateral institutions. Looking for patterns in the data across countries in recent decades can help us answer some important questions. Increased international trade turns out to have been beneficial for some environmental measures, such as SO_2 pollution. There is little evidence to support the contrary fear that international competition in practice works to lower environmental standards overall. Rather, globalization can aid the process whereby economic growth enables people to demand higher environmental quality. To be sure, effective government regulation is probably required if this demand is ever to be translated into actual improvement; the environment cannot take care of itself. But the statistical evidence says that high-income countries do indeed eventually tend to use some of their wealth to clean up the environment, on average, for measures such as SO_2 pollution. For the increasingly important category of global environmental externalities, however, such as emission of greenhouse gases, regulation at the national level is not enough.

These three new reasons to think that globalization can be beneficial for the environment—consumer power, multilateralism, and cross-country statistical evidence—are very different in nature. But in each case what is striking is how little the facts correspond to the suspicions of critics that turning back the clock on globalization would somehow allow them to achieve environmental goals. The rise in globalization, with the attempts at international environmental accord and quasi-judicial oversight, is less a threat to the environment than an ally. It is unfettered national sovereignty that poses the larger threat.

This chapter will try to lay out the key conceptual points concerning the relationship of economic globalization and the environment and to summarize the available empirical evidence, with an emphasis on what is new. We begin by clarifying some basic issues, such as defining objectives, before going on to consider the impact of globalization.

Objectives

It is important to begin a consideration of these issues by making clear that both economic income and environmental quality are worthy objectives. Individuals may disagree on the weight that should be placed on one objective or another. But we should not let such disagreements lead to deadlocked political outcomes in which the economy and the environment are both worse off than necessary. Can globalization be made to improve the environment that comes with a given level of income in market-measured terms? Many seem to believe that globalization necessarily makes things worse. If Mexico grows rapidly, is an increase in pollution inevitable? Is it likely, on average? If that growth arises from globalization, rather than from domestic sources, does that make environmental damage more likely? Less likely? Are there policies that can simultaneously promote *both* economic growth and an improved environment? These are the questions of interest.

Two Objectives: GDP and the Environment

An extreme version of environmental activism would argue that we should turn back the clock on industrialization—that it is worth deliberately impoverishing ourselves—if that is what it takes to save the environment. If the human species still consisted of a few million hunter-gatherers, human-made pollution would be close to zero. Thomas Malthus, writing in the early 19th century, predicted that geometric growth in population and in the economy would eventually and inevitably run into the natural resource limits of the carrying capacity of the planet.[3] In the 1960s, the Club of Rome picked up where Malthus had left off, warning that environmental disaster was coming soon. Some adherents to this school might favor the deliberate reversal of industrialization—reducing market-measured income below current levels in order to save the environment.[4]

But environmental concerns have become more mainstream since the 1960s. We have all had time to think about it. Most people believe that both a clean environment and economic growth are desirable, that we can have a combination of both, and it is a matter of finding the best tradeoff. Indeed, that is one possible interpretation of the popular phrase "sustainable development."

To evaluate the costs and benefits of globalization with regard to the environment, it is important to be precise conceptually, for example to make the distinction between effects on the environment that come *via* rapid economic growth and those that come *for a given level* of economic output.

We have a single concept, GDP, that attempts to measure the aggregate value of goods and services that are sold in the marketplace and that does a relatively good job of it. Measurement of environmental quality is much less well advanced. There are many different aspects of the environment that we care about, and it is hard to know how to combine them into a single overall measure. It would be harder still to agree on how to combine such a measure with GDP to get a measure of overall welfare. Proponents of so-called green GDP accounting have tried to do exactly that, but so far the enterprise is very incomplete. For the time being, the best we can do is look at a variety of separate measures capturing various aspects of the environment.

A Classification of Environmental Objectives

For the purpose of this chapter, it is useful to array different aspects of the environment according to the extent to which damage is localized around specific sources, as opposed to spilling out over a geographically more extensive area.

The first category of environmental damage is pollution that is *internal* to the household or firm. Perhaps 80 percent (by population) of world exposure to particulates is indoor pollution in poor countries—smoke from indoor cooking fires—which need not involve any externality.[5] There may be a role for dissemination of information regarding long-term health impacts that are not immediately evident. Nevertheless, what households in

---

[3]Malthus was an economist. A contemporary commentator reacted by calling economics the dismal science. This description has stuck, long after ecology or environmental science broke off as independent fields of study, fields that in fact make economists look like sunny optimists by comparison.

[4]Meadows et al. (1972), and Daly (1993). For a general survey of the issues, see Esty (2001).

[5]Chaudhuri and Pfaff (2002) cite Smith (1993, p. 551).

such countries are primarily lacking is the economic resources to afford stoves that run on cleaner fuels.[6] In the case of internal pollution, higher incomes directly allow the solution of the problem.

Some other categories of environmental damage pose potential externalities, but could be internalized by assigning property rights. If a company has clear title to a depletable natural resource such as an oil well, it has some incentive to keep some of the oil for the future, rather than pumping it all today.[7] The biggest problems arise when the legal system fails to enforce clear divisions of property rights. Tropical forest land that anyone can enter to chop down trees will be rapidly over-logged. Many poor countries lack the institutional and economic resources to enforce laws protecting such resources. Often corrupt arms of the government themselves collude in the plundering. Another example is the dumping of waste. If someone agreed to be paid to let his land be used as a waste disposal site, voluntarily and without hidden adverse effects, economics says that there would not necessarily be anything wrong with the arrangement. Waste has to go somewhere. But the situation would be different if the government of a poor undemocratic country were to agree to be paid to accept waste that then hurt the environment and health of residents who lacked the information or political clout to participate in the policy decision or to share in the benefits.

A second category, *national externalities*, includes most kinds of air pollution and water pollution, the latter a particularly great health hazard in the third world. The pollution is external to the individual firm or household, and often external to the state or province as well, but most of the damage is felt within the country in question. Intervention by the government is necessary to control such pollution. There is no reason why each national government cannot undertake the necessary regulation on its own, though the adequacy of economic resources to pay the costs of the regulation is again an issue.

A third category is *international externalities*. Increasingly, as we will see, environmental problems cross national boundaries. Acid rain is an example. In these cases, some cooperation among countries is necessary. The strongest examples are purely *global externalities*: chemicals that deplete the stratospheric ozone layer, greenhouse gases that lead to global climate change, and habitat destruction that impairs biological diversity. Individual countries should not expect to be able to do much about global externalities on their own. These distinctions will turn out to be important.

---

[6]Some health risks in industrial production are analogous. Workers in every country voluntarily accept dangerous jobs, e.g., in mining, because they pay better than other jobs that are available to someone with the same set of skills.

[7]Even when property rights are not in doubt and there is no externality, a common environmental concern is that the welfare of future generations does not receive enough weight, because they are not here to represent themselves. From the economists' viewpoint, the question is whether the interest rate that enters firms' decisions incorporates the correct *discount rate*. This topic is beyond the scope of this chapter, but Goulder and Stavins (2002) provide a concise survey.

The Relationship between Economic Production and the Environment

Scholars often catalog three intermediating variables or channels of influence that can determine the aggregate economic impacts of trade or growth on the environment.

- First is the *scale* of economic activity: For physical reasons, more output means more pollution, other things equal. But other things are usually not equal.

- Second is the *composition* of economic activity: Trade and growth can shift the composition of output, for example, among the agricultural, manufacturing, and service sectors. Because environmental damage per unit of output varies across these sectors, the aggregate can shift.

- Third are the *techniques* of economic activity: Often the same commodity can be produced through a variety of different techniques, some cleaner than others. Electric power, for example, can be generated by a very wide range of fuels and techniques.[8] To the extent trade or growth involves the adoption of cleaner techniques, pollution per unit of GDP will fall.

The positive effects of international trade and investment on GDP have been fairly well established by researchers, both theoretically and empirically. The relationship between GDP and the environment is not quite as well understood and is certainly less of a constant relationship. The relationship is rarely monotonic: Sometimes a country's growth is first bad for the environment and later good. The reason is the three conflicting forces that were just noted. On the one hand, when GDP increases, the greater scale of production leads directly to more pollution and other environmental degradation. On the other hand, there tend to be favorable shifts in the composition of output and in the techniques of production. The question is whether the latter two effects can outweigh the first.

The Environmental Kuznets Curve

A look at data across countries or across time allows some rough generalization as to the usual outcome of these conflicting effects. For some important environmental measures, a U-shaped relationship appears: At

---

[8]The most important alternatives are
- coal-fired plants (the dirtiest fuel, though there is a little scope for mitigating the damage, through low-sulphur coal, scrubbers, and perhaps someday new carbon-sequestration technologies);
- petroleum products (not quite as dirty);
- solar (very clean, but much more expensive); and
- hydro and nuclear (very clean with respect to pollution, but controversial on other environmental grounds).

relatively low levels of income per capita, growth leads to greater environmental damage, until it levels off at an intermediate level of income, after which further growth leads to improvements in the environment. This empirical relationship is known as the environmental Kuznets curve. The label is by analogy with the original Kuznets curve, which was a U-shaped relationship between average income and inequality. The World Bank (1992) and Grossman and Krueger (1993, 1995) brought to public attention this statistical finding for a cross section of countries.[9] Grossman and Krueger (1995) estimated that SO_2 pollution peaked when a country's income was about \$5,000–\$6,000 per capita (in 1985 dollars). Most developing countries have not yet reached this threshold.

For countries where a long enough time series of data is available, there is also some evidence that the same U-shaped relationship can hold across time. The air in London was far more polluted in the 1950s than it is today. (The infamous "pea soup" fogs were from pollution.) The same pattern has held in Tokyo, Los Angeles, and other cities. A similar pattern holds typically with respect to deforestation in rich countries: The percentage of US land that was forested fell in the 18th century and first half of the 19th century but rose in the 20th century.[10]

The idea behind the environmental Kuznets curve is that growth is bad for air and water pollution at the initial stages of industrialization, but later on reduces pollution, as countries become rich enough to pay to clean up their environments. The dominant theoretical explanation is that production technology makes some pollution inevitable, but that demand for environmental quality rises with income. The standard rationale is thus that, at higher levels of income per capita, growth raises the public's demand for environmental quality, which can translate into environmental regulation. Environmental regulation, if effective, then translates into a cleaner environment. It operates largely through the techniques channel, encouraging or requiring the use of cleaner production techniques for given products, although regulation might also have a composition effect:

---

[9]Grossman and Krueger (1993, 1995) found the Kuznets curve pattern for urban air pollution (SO_2 and smoke) and several measures of water pollution. Selden and Song (1994) found the pattern for SO_2, suspended particulate matter (PM), NO_x, and carbon monoxide. Shafik (1994) found evidence of the U shape for deforestation, suspended PM, and SO_2, but not for water pollution and some other measures. Among more recent studies, Hilton and Levinson (1998) found the U-shaped relationship for automotive lead emissions and Bradford, Schlieckert and Shore (2000) found some evidence of the environmental Kuznets curve for arsenic, COD, dissolved oxygen, lead, and SO_2, while obtaining more negative results in the cases of PM and some other measures of pollution. Bimonte (2001) found the relationship for the percentage of land that is protected area, within national territory. Harbaugh, Levinson, and Wilson (2000) pointed out that the relationship is very sensitive with respect, for example, to functional form and updating of the data set. The evidence is generally against the proposition that the curve turns down in the case of CO_2 (e.g., Holtz-Eakin and Selden, 1995), as is discussed later.

[10]Cropper and Griffiths (1994) find little evidence across countries of an EKC for forest growth. But Foster and Rosenzweig (2003) find supportive evidence in the time series for India.

raising the price of polluting goods and services relative to clean ones and thus encouraging consumers to buy more of the latter.[11]

It would be inaccurate to portray the environmental Kuznets curve as demonstrating—or even claiming—that if countries promote growth, the environment will eventually take care of itself. Only if pollution is largely confined within the home or within the firm does that Panglossian view necessarily apply.[12] Most pollution, such as SO_2, NO_x, etc., is external to the home or firm. For such externalities, higher income and a popular desire to clean up the environment are not enough. There must also be effective government regulation, which usually requires a democratic system to translate the popular will into action (something that was missing in the Soviet Union, for example), as well as the rule of law and reasonably intelligent mechanisms of regulation. The empirical evidence confirms that the participation of well-functioning democratic governments is an important part of the process. That is at the national level. The requirements for dealing with cross-border externalities are greater still.

Another possible explanation for the pattern of the environmental Kuznets curve is that it works naturally via the composition of output. In theory, the pattern could result from the usual stages of economic development: the transition from an agrarian economy to manufacturing, and then from manufacturing to services. Services tend to generate less pollution than heavy manufacturing.[13] This explanation is less likely than the conventional view to require the mechanism of effective government regulation. If the Kuznets curve in practice resulted solely from this composition effect, however, then high incomes should lead to a better environment even when externalities arise at the international level, which is not the case. No Kuznets curve has yet appeared for carbon dioxide, for example. Even though emissions per unit of GDP do tend to fall, this is not enough to reduce overall emissions, in the absence of a multilateral effort.

Regulation

It will help if we clarify one more fundamental set of issues before we turn to the main subject, the role of globalization per se.

It is logical to expect environmental regulation to cost something, to have a negative effect on measured productivity and income per capita.

---

[11]Theoretical derivations of the environmental Kuznets curve include Andreoni and Levinson (2001), Jaeger and Kolpin (2000), Selden and Song (1995), and Stokey (1998), among others.

[12]Chaudhuri and Pfaff (2002) find a U-shaped relationship between income and the generation of indoor smoke, across households. In the poorest households, rising incomes mean more cooking and more indoor pollution. Still-higher incomes allow a switch to cleaner fuels. Individual families make the switch on their own, as they gain the wherewithal to do so. Government intervention is not required.

[13]Arrow et al. (1995), Panayotou (1993).

"There is no free lunch," Milton Friedman famously said. Most tangible good things in life cost something, and for many kinds of regulation, if effective, people will readily agree that the cost is worth paying. Cost-benefit tests and cost-minimization strategies are economists' tools for trying to make sure that policies deliver the best environment for a given economic cost or the lowest economic cost for a given environmental goal. Taxes on energy, for example, particularly on hydrocarbon fuels, are quite an efficient mode of environmental regulation (if the revenue is "recycled" efficiently). Fuel efficiency standards are somewhat less efficient. (Differentiated CAFE standards for vehicles, for example, probably encouraged the birth of the SUV craze.) And crude "command and control" methods are less efficient still. (Government mandates regarding what specific technologies firms must use, for example, deny firms the flexibility to find better ways to achieve a given goal.) Some environmental regulations, when legislated or implemented poorly, can impose very large and unnecessary economic costs on firms, and workers, and consumers.

Occasionally policy measures have both environmental and economic benefits. Usually these "win-win" ideas constitute the elimination of some previously existing distortion in public policy. Many countries have historically subsidized the use of coal. The United States subsidizes mining and cattle grazing on federal land, and sometimes logging and oil drilling as well, not to mention water use. Other countries have substantial subsidies for ocean fishing. Elimination of such subsidies would improve the environment and save money at the same time—not just for the federal budget, but for people's real income in the aggregate as well. Admittedly the economists' approach—taxing gasoline or making ranchers pay for grazing rights—is often extremely unpopular politically.

Another idea that would have economic and environmental benefits simultaneously would be to remove all barriers against international trade in environmental equipment and services, such as those involved in renewable energy generation, smokestack scrubbing, or waste treatment facilities. There would again be a double payoff: the growth-enhancing effect of elimination barriers to exports (in a sector where the United States is likely to be able to develop a comparative advantage), together with the environment-enhancing effect of facilitating imports of the inputs that go into environmental protection. A precedent is the removal of barriers to the imports of fuel-efficient cars from Japan, which was a clear case of simultaneously promoting free trade and clean air.

A different school of thought claims that opportunities for saving money while simultaneously saving the environment are common rather than rare. The *Porter hypothesis* holds that a tightening of environmental regulation stimulates technological innovation and thereby has positive effects on both the economy and the environment—for example, saving money by saving energy.[14] The analytical rationale for this view is not always made clear.

---

[14]Porter and van der Linde (1995).

(Is the claim that a change in regulation, regardless in what direction, stimulates innovation, or is there something special about environmental regulation? Is there something special about the energy sector?) Its proponents cite a number of real-world examples where a new environmental initiative turned out to be profitable for a given firm or industry. Such cases surely exist, but there is little reason to think that a link between regulation and productivity growth holds as a matter of generality. The hypothesis is perhaps better understood as making a point regarding "first mover advantage." That is, if the world is in the future to be moving in a particular direction, such as toward more environmentally friendly energy sources, then a country that innovates new products and new technologies of this sort before others do will be in a position to sell the fruits to the latecomers.

Effects of Openness to Trade

The central topic of this chapter is the implications of trade for the environment. Some effects come via economic growth, and some come even for a given level of income. In both cases, the effects can be either beneficial or detrimental. Probably the strongest effects of trade are the first sort, via income. Much like saving and investment, technological progress, and other sources of growth, trade tends to raise income. As we have seen, higher income in turn has an effect on some environmental measures that is initially adverse but, according to the environmental Kuznets curve, eventually turns favorable.

What about effects of trade that do not operate via economic growth? They can be classified in three categories: systemwide effects that are adverse, systemwide effects that are beneficial, and effects that vary across countries depending on local "comparative advantage."

Race to the Bottom

The *"race to the bottom"* hypothesis is perhaps the strongest basis for fearing that international trade and investment specifically (rather than industrialization generally) will put downward pressure on countries' environmental standards and thus damage the environment across the global system. Leaders of industry, and of the unions whose members are employed in industry, are always concerned about competition from abroad. When domestic regulation raises their costs, they fear that they will lose competitiveness against firms in other countries. They warn of a loss of sales, employment, and investment to foreign competitors.[15] Thus domestic producers often sound the

---

[15]Levinson and Taylor (2001) find that those U.S. industries experiencing the largest rise in environmental control costs have indeed also experienced the largest increases in net imports.

competitiveness alarm as a way of applying political pressure on their governments to minimize the burden of regulation.[16]

To some, the phrase "race to the bottom" connotes that the equilibrium will be a world of little or no regulation. Others emphasize that, in practice, it is not necessarily a matter of globalization leading to environmental standards that actually decline over time, but rather retarding the gradual raising of environmental standards that would otherwise occur. Either way, the concern is that, to the extent that countries are open to international trade and investment, environmental standards will be lower than they would otherwise be. But how important is this in practice? Some economists' research suggests that environmental regulation is not one of the more important determinants of firms' ability to compete internationally. When deciding where to locate, multinational firms seem to pay more attention to such issues as labor costs and market access than to the stringency of local environmental regulation.[17]

Once again, it is important to distinguish (1) the fear that globalization will lead to a race to the bottom in regulatory standards from (2) fears that the environment will be damaged by the very process of industrialization and economic growth itself. Opening national economies to international trade and investment could play a role in both cases, but the two possible channels are very different. In the first case, the race to the bottom hypothesis, the claim is that openness undermines environmental standards even for a given path of economic growth. This would be a damning conclusion from the standpoint of globalization, because it would imply that by limiting trade and investment in some way, we might be able to attain a better environment for any given level of GDP. In the second case, the implication would be that openness affects the environment only in the way that investment, or education, or productivity growth, or any other source of growth affects the environment, by moving the economy along the environmental Kuznets curve. Trying to restrict trade and investment would be a less attractive strategy in this case, because it would amount to deliberate self-impoverishment.

---

[16]What is competitiveness? Economists tend to argue that concerns regarding international competitiveness, if interpreted as fears of trade deficits, are misplaced, which would seem to imply they should not affect rational policy-making. (Or else, to the extent competitiveness concerns can be interpreted as downward pressure on regulation commensurate with cost considerations, economists figure that they may be appropriate and efficient.) But Esty and Gerardin (1998, pp. 17–21) point out that competitiveness fears, under actual political economy conditions, may inhibit environmental regulation even if they are not fully rational. Ederington and Minier (2002) find econometrically that countries do indeed use environmental regulation to reduce trade flows—that they tend to adopt less stringent environmental regulations for their import-competing industries than for others.

[17]Jaffe, Peterson, Portney and Stavins (1995), Grossman and Krueger (1993), Low and Yeats (1992), and Tobey (1990). Other empirical researchers, however, have found more of an effect of environmental regulation on direct investment decisions: Lee and Roland-Holst (1997) and Smarzynska and Wei (2001). Theoretical analyses include Copeland and Taylor (1994, 1995, 2001) and Liddle (2001).

Gains from Trade

While the possibility that exposure to international competition might have an adverse effect on environmental regulation is familiar, less widely recognized and more surprising is the possibility of effects in the beneficial direction, which we will call the "gains from trade hypothesis." Trade allows countries to attain more of what they want, which includes environmental goods in addition to market-measured output.

How could openness have a positive effect on environmental quality, once we set aside the possibility of accelerating progress down the beneficial slope of the environmental Kuznets curve? A first possibility concerns technological and managerial innovation. Openness encourages ongoing innovation.[18] It then seems possible that openness could encourage innovation beneficial to environmental improvement well as economic progress. A second possibility is an international ratcheting up of environmental standards.[19] The largest political jurisdiction can set the pace for others. Within the United States, it is called the "California effect": When the largest state sets high standards for auto pollution control equipment, for example, the result may be similar standards in other states as well. The United States can play the same role globally.

Multinational corporations (MNCs) are often the vehicle for these effects. They tend to bring clean state-of-the-art production techniques from high-standard countries of origin, to host countries where they are not yet known, for several reasons:

> First, many companies find that the efficiency of having a single set of management practices, pollution control technologies, and training programmes geared to a common set of standards outweighs any cost advantage that might be obtained by scaling back on environmental investments at overseas facilities. Second, multinational enterprises often operate on a large scale, and recognise that their visibility makes them especially attractive targets for local enforcement officials . . .
> Third, the prospect of liability for failing to meet standards often motivates better environmental performance . . . (Esty and Gentry 1997, p. 161)

The claim is not that all multinational corporations apply the highest environmental standards when operating in other countries. Rather the claim is that the standards tend on average to be higher than if the host country were undertaking the same activity on its own.[20]

Corporate codes of conduct, as under the U.N. Global Compact promoted by Kofi Annan, offer a new way that residents of some countries

---

[18]Trade speeds the absorption of frontier technologies and best-practice management. This explains why countries that trade more appear to experience a sustained increase in growth rather than just the one-time increase in the level of real income predicted by classical trade theory.

[19]E.g., Vogel (1995), Braithwaite and Drahos (2000), Porter (1990, 1991) and Porter and van der Linde (1995). This ratcheting up may be more effective for product standards than for standards regarding processes and production methods.

[20]Esty and Gentry (1997, pp. 157, 161, 163) and Schmidheiny (1992).

can pursue environmental goals in other countries.[21] Formal international cooperation among governments is another way that interdependence can lead to higher environmental standards rather than lower.[22]

Furthermore, because trade offers consumers the opportunity to consume goods of greater variety, it allows countries to attain higher levels of welfare (for any given level of domestically produced output), which, as before, will raise the demand for environmental quality. Again, if the appropriate institutions are in place, this demand for higher environmental quality will translate into effective regulation and the desired reduction in pollution.

Attempts to Evaluate the Overall Effects of Trade on the Environment

If a set of countries opens up to trade, is it on average likely to have a positive or negative effect on the environment (for a given level of income)? Which tend in practice to dominate, the unfavorable "race to the bottom" effects or the favorable "gains from trade" effects? Econometrics can help answer the question.

Statistically, some measures of environmental quality are positively correlated with the level of trade. Figure 1 shows a rough inverse correlation between countries' openness to trade and their levels of SO_2 pollution. But the causality is complex, running in many directions simultaneously. One would not want to claim that trade leads to a cleaner environment, if in reality they are both responding to some other third factor, such as economic growth or democracy.[23]

Eiras and Schaeffer (2001, p. 4) find: "In countries with an open economy, the average environmental sustainability score is more than 30 percent higher than the scores of countries with moderately open economies, and almost twice as high as those of countries with closed economies." Does this mean that trade is good for the environment? Not necessarily. It might be a result of the Porter hypothesis—environmental regulation stimulates productivity—together with the positive effect of income on trade. Or it might be because democracy leads to higher levels of environmental regulation, and democracy is causally intertwined with income and trade. As noted, democracy raises the demand for environmental regulation. Figure 1 suggests that the relationship between SO_2 concentrations and openness remains clear even if one controls for the beneficial effect of democracy. But there remain other possible third factors.

---

[21]Ruggie (2002).

[22]Neumayer (2002). Multilateral environmental agreements (MEAs) are discussed in a subsequent section.

[23]Barrett and Graddy (2000) is one of several studies to find that an increase in civil and political freedoms significantly reduces some measures of pollution.

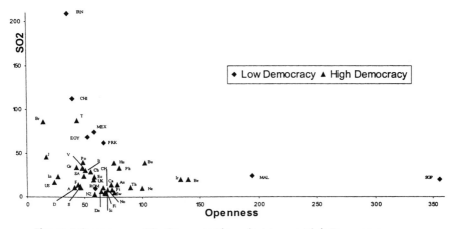

Figure 1 Openness vs SO₂ Concentrations, in Low- vs High-Democracy Regimes, 1990

A number of studies have sought to isolate the independent effect of openness. Lucas et al. (1992) studied the toxic intensity implied by the composition of manufacturing output in a sample of 80 countries and found that a high degree of trade-distorting policies increases pollution in rapidly growing countries. Harbaugh, Levinson, and Wilson (2000) report in passing a beneficial effect of trade on the environment, after controlling for income. Dean (2002) found a detrimental direct effect of liberalization for a given level of income, via the terms of trade, though this is outweighed by a beneficial indirect effect via income. Antweiler, Copeland, and Taylor (2001) and Copeland and Taylor (2001, 2003a) represent an extensive body of empirical research explicitly focused on the effects of trade on the environment. They conclude that trade liberalization that raises the scale of economic activity by 1 percent works to raise SO₂ concentrations by ¼ to ½ percent via the scale channel, but that the accompanying technique channel reduces concentrations by 1¼ to 1½, so that the overall effect is beneficial.

None of these studies makes allowances for the problem that trade may be the *result* of other factors rather than the cause. Antweiler et al. point out this potential weakness.[24] Frankel and Rose (2003) attempt to disentangle

---

[24]A few authors have sought to address some aspects of the problem of endogeneity. Levinson (1999) shows that controlling for endogeneity of environmental regulation can change results, in his study of hazardous waste trade. Dean (2002) treats income as endogenous in her study of the effect of trade liberalization on water pollution across Chinese provinces. But the existing research does not directly address the problem that trade may be simultaneously determined with income and environmental outcomes.

the various causal relationships. The study focuses on exogenous variation in trade across countries attributable to factors such as geographical location. It finds effects on several measures of air pollution (particularly SO_2 and NO_x concentrations), for a given level of income, that are more good than bad. This suggests that the "gains from trade" effects may be at least as powerful as the "race to the bottom" effect. The findings are not as optimistic for other measures of environmental quality, however, particularly emissions of CO_2.

Differential Effects Arising from Comparative Advantage

So far we have considered only effects that could be expected to hold for the average country, to the extent that it is open to international trade and investment. What if the environment improves in some open countries and worsens in others? An oft-expressed concern is that, to the extent that countries are open to international trade and investment, some will specialize in producing dirty products and export them to other countries. Such countries could be said to exploit a comparative advantage in pollution. The prediction is that the environment will be damaged in this set of countries, as compared to what would happen without trade. The environment will be *cleaner* in the second set of countries, those that specialize in clean production and instead import the dirty products from the other countries. Leaving aside the possibility of a race to the bottom effect, the worldwide environment on average might even benefit somewhat, just as aggregate output should benefit, because of the gains from trade. But not everyone would approve of such a bargain.

What determines whether a given country is expected to be in the set of economies specializing in clean or dirty environmental production? There are several possible determinants of comparative advantage.

Endowments and comparative advantage. First, trade patterns could be determined by endowments of capital and labor, as in the standard neoclassical theory of trade, attributed to Heckscher, Ohlin, and Samuelson. Assume manufacturing is more polluting than alternative economic activities, such as services. (If the alternative sector, say agriculture, is instead just as polluting as manufacturing, then trade has no overall implications for the environment.) Since manufacturing is capital intensive, the country with the high capital/labor ratio—say Japan—will specialize in the dirty manufactured goods, while countries with low capital/labor ratios—say China—will specialize in cleaner goods.

For example, Grossman and Krueger predicted that NAFTA might reduce overall pollution in Mexico and raise it in the United States and Canada, because of the composition effect: Mexico has a comparative advantage in agriculture and labor-intensive manufacturing, which are relatively cleaner, versus the northern comparative advantage in more capital intensive sectors. This composition effect runs in the opposite direction from the usual worry, that trade would turn Mexico into a pollution haven as a result of high demand for environmental quality in the United States. That theory is discussed in the next section, below.

Second, comparative advantage could be determined by endowments of natural resources. A country with abundant hardwood forests will tend to export them if given the opportunity to do so. Here there cannot be much doubt that trade is indeed likely to damage the environment of such countries. True, in theory, if clear property rights can be allocated and enforced, someone will have the proper incentive to conserve these natural resources for the future. In practice, it seldom works this way. Poor miners and farmers cannot be kept out of large tracts of primitive forest. And even if there were clear property rights over the natural resources, private firms would not have the correct incentives to constrain external side effects of logging and mining, such as air and water pollution, soil erosion, loss of species, and so on. Government regulation is called for, but is often stymied by the problems of inadequate resources, at best, and corruption, at worst.

Pollution havens. Third, comparative advantage could be deliberately created by differences in environmental regulation itself. This is the pollution haven hypothesis. The motivation for varying levels of regulation could be differences in demand for environmental quality, arising, for example, from differences in income per capita. Or the motivation could be differences in the supply of environmental quality, arising, for example, from differences in population density.

Many object to an "eco dumping" system according to which economic integration results in some countries exporting pollution to others, even if the overall global level of pollution does not rise.[25] They find distasteful the idea that the impersonal market system would deliberately allocate environmental damage to an "underdeveloped" country. A chief economist of the World Bank once signed his name to an internal memo with economists' language that read (in the summary sentence of its most inflammatory passage) "Just between you and me, shouldn't the World Bank be encouraging *more* migration of the dirty industries to the LDCs?" After the memo was leaked, public perceptions of the young Larry Summers were damaged for years.

There is a little empirical evidence, but not much, to support the hypothesis that countries that have a particularly high demand for environmental quality—the rich countries—currently specialize in products that can be produced cleanly and let the poor countries produce and sell the products that require pollution.[26] For the specific case of SO_2, the evidence

---

[25]The desire to "harmonize" environmental regulation across countries, and the arguments against it, are analyzed by Bhagwati and Srinivasan (1996).

[26]Suri and Chapman (1998) find that middle-income countries' growth only leads to lower domestic pollution if they increase imports of manufactures. Muradian, O'Connor, and Martinez-Alier (2001) find evidence that the imports of rich countries embody more air pollution than their exports. Ederington, Levinson and Minier (2003) find that pollution abatement costs are relevant for only a small sub-set of trade: imports from developing countries in sectors that are especially mobile geographically.

appears to be, if anything, that trade leads to a reallocation of pollution from the poor country to the rich country, rather than the other way around.[27] This is consistent with the finding of Antweiler, Copeland, and Taylor (2001) that trade has a significantly less favorable effect on SO_2 emissions in rich countries than in poor countries. Their explanation is that rich countries have higher capital/labor ratios, capital-intensive industries are more polluting, and this factor-based pollution-haven effect dominates the income-based pollution-haven effect.

Does Most U.S. Trade and FDI Take Place with Low-Standard Countries?

To listen to some American discussion of globalization, one would think that the typical partner in U.S. trade and investment is a poor country with low environmental or labor standards. If so, it would help explain the fear that opening to international trade and investment in general puts downward pressure on U.S. standards. In fact, less than half of U.S. trade and investment takes place with partners who have lower wages and lower incomes than we do. Our most important partners have long been Canada, Japan, and the European Union (though Mexico has now become important as well). These trading partners sometimes regard *the United States* as the low-standard country.

Does Economic Globalization Conflict with Environmental Regulation?

There is a popular sense that globalization is a powerful force undermining environmental regulation. This can be the case in some circumstances. The "race to the bottom" phenomenon can potentially put downward pressure on the regulatory standards of countries that complete internationally in trade and investment. But, as an argument against globalization, it leaves much out.

First is the point that, for most of us, environmental quality is one goal, but not the only goal. As already noted, we care also about income, and trade is one means of promoting economic growth. The goals often need to be balanced against each other.

Environmental concerns can be an excuse for protectionism. If policymakers give in to protectionist arguments and erect trade barriers, we will enjoy less growth in trade and income. We will not even necessarily end up with a better environment. Import-competing corporations (or their workers), in sectors that may themselves not be particularly friendly to the

---

[27]Frankel and Rose (2003). We do not find significant evidence of other pollution-haven effects, based on population density or factor endowments, or for other pollutants.

environment, sometimes seek to erect or retain barriers to imports in the name of environmental protection, when in reality it is their own pocket-books they are trying to protect. In other words, environmentalism is an excuse for protectionism.

Often, the problem is less sinister, but more complex. To see how the political economy works, let us begin with the point that most policy debates are settled as the outcome of a complicated mix of multiple countervailing arguments and domestic interest groups on both sides. Most of the major viewpoints are in some way represented "at the table" in the federal government decision-making process. In the case of environmental measures, there are often adversely affected industry groups sitting across the table from the environmentalists, and they have an effect on the final political outcome. But when the commodity in question happens to be produced by firms in foreign countries, then that point of view largely disappears from the table around which the decision is made. If the issue is big enough, the State Department may weigh in to explain the potential costs facing foreign countries. But, understandably, the foreigners receive less weight in the policy process than would the identical firms if they were American. The result is that the environmental policies that are adopted on average can discriminate against foreign firms relative to domestic firms, without anyone ever deliberately having supported a measure out of protectionist intent.

One possible example is the strong opposition in Europe to genetically modified organisms (GMOs). A Biosafety Agreement was negotiated in Montreal, January 29, 2000, in which the United States felt it had to agree to label grain shipments that might in part be bio-engineered and to allow countries to block imports of GMOs.[28] In some ways, these negotiations might serve as a useful model for compromise in other areas.[29] But why have Europeans decided so definitively that they want to keep out genetically modified varieties of corn, despite the emergence of little or no scientific evidence against them as of yet, where American consumers are far less agitated? Is it because Europeans are predisposed to have higher standards for environmental issues? Perhaps.[30] An important part of the explanation, however, is that Monsanto and other U.S. technology companies and U.S. farmers are the ones who developed the technology and produce the stuff, not European companies or European farmers. Thus it

---

[28]*The Economist*, February 5, 2000. So far, the United States has been reluctant to bring the GMO case to the WTO, out of a fear that the outcome might be a political failure even if a legal success. As Victor and Runge (2002, 112–113) argue, the Europeans were sufficiently traumatized in the 1990s by a series of scandals in the regulation of their food, such as the UK government's failure to stop "Mad Cow" disease, that an attempt by the United States to use the WTO dispute settlement process to pry the European market open for GMOs would be counterproductive, regardless of the scientific evidence. But the United States may go ahead anyway.

[29]Environmental NGOs were allowed inside the meeting hall, a new precedent. *FT*, February 1, 2000.

[30]But it is interesting that some health issues have gone the other way. The United States has in the past cared more about feared carcinogens than Europeans. The United States requires cheese to be pasteurized, and the EU does not (Vogel, 1995).

is American producers, not Europeans, who stand to lose from the European squeamishness. European agriculture need not consciously launch a campaign against GMOs. All that the European movement needed was an absence around the table of producers who would be adversely affected by a ban. But the result is to reduce trade, hurt American producers, and benefit European farmers.

Whatever the source of different perceptions across countries, it is important to have a set of internationally agreed rules to govern trade and if possible a mechanism for settling disputes that arise. That is the role of the WTO. The need for such an institution does not vanish when environmental issues are a part of the dispute. Certainly if one cares at all about trade and growth, then one cannot automatically sign on to each and every campaign seeking to block trade on environmental grounds. But even if one cares solely about the environment, claims need to be evaluated through some sort of neutral process. One can be easily misled; corporations make dubious claims to environmental motivations in, for example, seeking federal support of "clean coal" research or ethanol production. Most of the time, there is no substitute for investigating the details and merits of the case in question. One should not presume that an interest group's claims are right just because that group happens to be of one's own nationality.

The Impossible Trinity of Global Environmental Regulation

The concerns of anti-globalizers can be understood by means of a trilemma of regulation, called the principle of the "impossible trinity of global governance" (see Figure 2). In designing a system of global governance, three kinds of goals are desirable. First, *globalization* is desirable, other things equal, for its economic benefits if nothing else. Second, *regulation* is desirable when it comes to externalities like pollution or other social goals not adequately addressed by the marketplace. Third, national *sovereignty* is desirable, because different countries have different needs or preferences and also because nations take pride in their political independence. The principle of the impossible trinity points out that it is feasible to design a system with any two of these attributes, but not with all three.

The three attributes are represented as the sides of the triangle in the accompanying figure. The lower left corner represents a system of complete laissez faire. The private market is given responsibility for everything. With no government regulation, there is nothing to coordinate internationally, and thus no loss in national sovereignty. If another country wants to make the mistake of heavy-handed intervention, that is its affair. One can imagine Friederich von Hayek, Ayn Rand, or Milton Friedman favoring the laissez faire corner.

The lower right corner represents a system of regulation at the global level. While there are not many "world federalists" around today, a proposal to establish a powerful world environment organization would be a step in this direction.

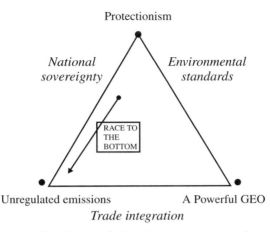

Figure 2 The Impossible Trinity of Global Environment Regulation

The top corner represents isolationism. Only if countries cut themselves off from trade, investment, and other international interactions can they preserve complete national sovereignty, while practicing whatever kind of regulation they wish. Two candidates in the year 2000 U.S. presidential election, Ralph Nader and Pat Buchanan, seemed to want to move in this direction.

The environmental concerns created by globalization can be understood in terms of this diagram. The process of international economic integration is moving the United States and most other countries downward in the graph, toward the bottom side of the triangle. As a result, globalization is creating a growing conflict between the needs of environmental regulation and the demands of national sovereignty, or so goes the theory. National sovereignty has been winning, which means that the movement has been toward the lower left corner. The claim is that globalization has undermined the ability of sovereign governments to impose the level of environmental standards they would like.

Although the impossible trinity can be a useful way to think about the potential for globalization to undercut national environmental regulation, it can be very misleading in some contexts. There are two main reasons for this. First, even for environmental externalities that are largely confined within countries, such as local air pollution, there is little empirical evidence that the "race to the bottom" hypothesis in fact holds, i.e., that international trade and investment in fact put significant downward pressure on environmental regulation in the aggregate. Indeed, international trade and activities of multinational corporations may sometimes put upward pressure on environmental standards. Second, and more importantly, some environmental issues spill over across national borders even in the absence of international trade and investment, making it difficult for individual countries to address them through independent regulation.

Environmental Concerns Cross National Borders

Even those who do not care about trade at all should appreciate the role of international agreements and institutions. The reason is the increasing importance of major sources of environmental damage that cross national borders and that would do so even if there were no such thing as international trade. Some externalities have long spilled over from each country to its neighbors—such as SO_2 pollution, which is responsible for acid rain, or water pollution, which flows downriver. They can be addressed by negotiations between the two countries involved (e.g., United States and Canada). An increasing number of environmental externalities are truly global, however. The best examples are greenhouse gases. A ton of carbon dioxide creates the same global warming potential regardless where in the world it is emitted. Other good examples of direct global externalities are stratospheric ozone depletion, depletion of ocean fish stocks, and threats to biodiversity.

Even localized environmental damage, such as deforestation, is increasingly seen as a valid object of international concern. A distinction is traditional between trade measures that target specific undesirable products, such as asbestos, and those that target *processes and production methods*, such as the use of prison labor in the manufacture of the commodity in question. It is clear that a country concerned about its own health or environment has the right to tax or ban products that it regards as harmful, so long as it does not discriminate against foreign producers. Indeed, such bans are less liable to become a vehicle for surreptitious protectionism than are attempts to pass judgment on other countries' production methods that are unrelated to the physical attributes of the product itself. But is it legitimate for importing countries also to discriminate according to how a given product was produced? Some ask what business is it of others whether the producing country wants to use its own prison labor, or cut down its own forests, or pollute its own environment?[31]

Often an international externality can be easily identified. Forests absorb carbon dioxide (a process called "sequestration," or creating carbon sinks), so logging contributes to global climate change. An endangered species may contain a unique genetic element that someday could be useful to international scientists. Desertification can lead to social instability and political conflict, which can in turn produce problems for international

---

[31]See Charnovitz (2002a) on the history, law, and analysis of PPMs, and for other references. He argues that the public failure to understand environment-friendly developments in the late 1990s within GATT/WTO jurisprudence regarding PPMs is now an obstacle to further progress (e.g., in the WTO Committee on Trade and Environment, pp. 64, 103–104).

security. Thus environmental damage in one country can have indirect effects on others.

But foreign residents increasingly care about localized environmental damage as well, even when they live far away and even when there is no evident link to their interests. The idea of "non-use value" is that many people place value on keeping, for example, a river canyon unspoiled, even if they know they will never see it. While the methodology of estimating the value according to what people say they would pay ("contingent valuation") is fraught with problems, the basic principle of non-use value is now widely accepted. This means that citizens in one country may have a stake in whether another country dams up a gorge, kills its wildlife, or pollutes its air and water.

Reversing Globalization Would Not End the Tension of Regulation vs. Sovereignty

Thus, for an increasingly important set of environmental issues, the idea that individual countries could properly address the issues if left on their own is myth. If countries do not cooperate through multilateral institutions, each will be tempted to free ride on the efforts of others, and little will get done. Globalization and multilateral institutions are not the obstacle—and the appeal of national sovereignty is not an ally—in international efforts to protect the environment. Rather, environmentalists need global agreements and global agencies if they are going to get other countries to do the things they want them to do. It is the appeal of national sovereignty that is the obstacle.

The mistake of blaming all ills on globalization and multilateral institutions such as the WTO has yielded some very strange bedfellows. Environmentally concerned protestors have been treating labor unions and poor countries as comrades in arms, proud of the fact that a disparate set of groups have supposedly been brought together by a shared opposition to globalization. But in fact, some of these groups are on the other side of the environmental issue. U.S. labor unions are strong opponents of the Kyoto Protocol on Global Climate Change. Poor countries tend to be strong opponents of international environmental agreements in general. Both groups cite national sovereignty in support of their positions. It is particularly puzzling that some environmentalists see pro-sovereignty supporters as natural allies, when so many environmental problems can be addressed only by means of multilateral institutions that in fact infringe on national sovereignty.

If labor unions and environmentalists can come together on an issue, that is fine. *But they have to agree on that issue.* They should share something more than an emotional antipathy to some particular multilateral institution: They should want the institution to move in the same direction, not opposite directions. They don't have to get into fine details, if they don't want to. But if, for example, one group thinks that the proper response to

globalization is that the multilateral institutions should exercise less invasion of national sovereignty in the pursuit of environmental regulation and
the other thinks the institutions should exercise more invasion of national
sovereignty in that pursuit, then they are in truth hardly allies.

International Agreements and Institutions

Environmentalists are keen to interject themselves into the WTO. Those
who live in the world of international trade negotiations tell those who live
in the environmentalist world that their concerns may be valid, but that
they should address them outside the WTO, in their own, separate, negotiations and their own multilateral agencies.[32]

Multilateral Environmental Organizations

The one multilateral organization dedicated to environmental issues in general, the United Nations Environmental Program, is universally considered
small and weak, even by the standards of UN agencies. Some may favor
beefing it up. Most feel that it is not fixable, that—to begin with—it would
have to be based somewhere like Geneva in order to be taken seriously, not
in Nairobi as now. On these grounds, some have proposed a new, powerful, multilateral world environment organization.[33] Daniel Esty (1994) proposed that it be called the Global Environmental Organization, providing
the appropriate acronym GEO. But the source of the problem is not some
accident of bureaucratic design history or geography. The problem, rather,
is that there is very little support among the world's governments for a powerful multilateral agency in the area of the environment. They fear infringement on their sovereignty.

One can say that in concentrating their fire on the WTO, environmental activists are adopting a strategy of taking the multilateral trading system hostage. They envy the relative success of the WTO system. They are
aware that international environmental treaties, even if successfully negotiated and ratified, may be toothless. The agreements made at Rio de Janeiro
in 1992 are an example. The activists would ideally like to adopt trade sanctions as a means of enforcement, as does the WTO itself.

Such proposals do not explain attempts to take globalization hostage
more broadly, for example by demonstrations at WTO ministerial meetings. There is nothing in the WTO to block multilateral environmental

---

[32]The most prominent and articulate spokesman of the viewpoint opposing linkage between
trade and unrelated issues is Jadgish Bhagwati (2000).

[33]Charnovitz (2002b) surveys the proposals. Juma (2000) argues in opposition, on the grounds
that decentralized agreements can do the job better.

treaties from adopting penalties against relevant trade with non-members. Indeed, the Montreal Protocol on stratospheric ozone depletion has such trade controls, ran into no problems under international trade rules, and is generally considered to have been successful in achieving its goals. Admittedly there is strong resistance to using trade to overcome the free rider problem. Most governments do not favor international environmental agreement that are so aggressive as to include trade sanctions. Again, the failure does not mean that globalization and global institutions like the WTO are the problem. More likely it is the other way around: Globalization is the ally, and national sovereignty is the obstacle.

Bilateral and Regional RTAs

Regional and bilateral agreements, such as the European Union or the Australia–New Zealand Closer Economic Relationship, have incorporated environmental components more often than have multilateral agreements. Whether because of cultural homogeneity or the small numbers involved, a group consisting of a few neighbors is usually readier to contemplate the sort of "deep integration" required for harmonization of environmental standards than are negotiators in groups with more than 100 diverse members, such as the WTO.

In the public debate over the North American Free Trade Agreement, one of the most prominent concerns of opponents was the pollution that had already accompanied industrialization in northern Mexico, particularly among the maquilladoras along the border, which in turn was a result of the ability to trade with the United States. The final agreement departed from previous U.S. trade agreements, and those in most other parts of the world, by taking into account environmental concerns, at least in a small way. The preamble includes environmentally friendly language, such as a stipulation that the NAFTA goals are to be pursued "in a manner consistent with environmental protection and conservation." Chapter 7B allows the member countries to continue adopting sanitary and phyto-sanitary standards. Chapter 9 allows countries to set whatever environmental standards they want, provided only that they do not discriminate or discourage trade unnecessarily.[34]

Nevertheless, environmental groups were unhappy with the subsequent outcome. Proposed side agreements, for example, to establish a bank to finance environmental cleanup along the border received a lot of attention during Bill Clinton's presidential campaign and during the subsequent NAFTA ratification campaign. Followup after the NAFTA went into effect in 1994, however, was disappointing.

Meanwhile, provisions under Chapter 11, which governs direct investment, have turned out to be important. On the one hand, the text reads

---

[34]Hufbauer, Esty, Orejas, Rubio, and Schott (2000).

"the Parties recognize that it is inappropriate to encourage investment by relaxing domestic health, safety or environmental measures." On the other hand, protection of the rights of investors has confirmed some environmentalists' fears particularly a case brought by a Canadian company called Metalclad under the dispute settlement mechanism. Under a clause that forbids a signatory from taking measures "tantamount to nationalization or expropriation" of firms from other member countries, Metalclad in August 2000 won a judgment from a NAFTA tribunal against local Mexican regulators' attempt to close its hazardous waste disposal plant without compensation. The finding that Mexican regulation had denied a foreign firm fair and equitable treatment was potentially an important precedent under the NAFTA.[35] But it would be strange, even from a pro-business viewpoint, if an American or Canadian firm were extensively protected against regulatory "takings" in Mexico when it would not be in its country of origin.

The NAFTA experience reinforced environmentalists' concerns with trade agreements. They urged the U.S. government to bring environmental issues inside trade negotiations, for example, forbidding parties in trade agreements from relaxing environmental regulation in order to seek competitive advantage. A preferential trading arrangement negotiated by the United States at the end of the Clinton Administration, the Jordan-U.S. free trade agreement, incorporated such environmental provisions directly in the text, rather than as a side agreement, a precedent that was hoped to establish a "template" or precedent for future agreements. In addition, an executive order now requires that the government prepare an "environmental impact statement" whenever negotiating new trade agreements in the future, to guard against possible inadvertent side effects adverse to the environment.[36]

The Failed Multilateral Agreement on Investment

The first time that NGOs using Internet-age methods successfully mobilized to block a major multilateral economic agreement was not in Seattle in 1999, but rather the preceding campaign against the Multilateral Agreement on Investment (MAI). Efforts to agree on rules governing cross-border investment tend to founder as soon as the circle of countries is broadened beyond a small regional grouping. The MAI was an attempt to negotiate such rules among the industrialized countries, at the OECD (Organization for Economic Cooperation and Development). Notwithstanding the weakness of the negotiated text and the seeming obscurity of the issue, environmentalist and other NGOs were energized by claims that the MAI would handcuff countries' regulatory efforts, and the MAI was not ratified.

---

[35]Ibid. pp. 8–14

[36]The executive order was issued by President Clinton in 1999. But President George W. Bush announced he would continue to abide by it, e.g., in preparing possible free-trade agreements with Singapore, Chile, and the Americas. Martin Crutsinger, AP 4/21/2001 [e.g., *Boston Globe*].

The WTO and Some Panel Cases

In the postwar period, the vehicle for conducting the multilateral negotiations that succeeded in bringing down trade barriers in many countries was the General Agreement on Tariffs and Trade. An important outcome of the Uruguay Round of negotiations was the replacement of the GATT organization with a real agency, the World Trade Organization, which came into existence in 1995. One reason why the change was important is that the new institution featured a dispute settlement mechanism, whose findings were to be binding on the member countries. Previously, a party that did not like the ruling of a GATT panel could reject it.

Why do so many environmentalists apparently feel that the still-young WTO is a hostile power? Allegations concern lack of democratic accountability and negative effects on the environment. It is difficult to see how these allegations could apply to the process of setting WTO rules themselves. Regarding the alleged lack of democracy, the GATT and WTO are in principle one-country one-vote bodies that make decisions by consensus. Clearly in practice, some countries—particularly the United States—matter far more than others. But consider what it would mean to make this process more democratic. It would presumably mean giving less weight to U.S. views and more to the views, for example, of India, the world's most populous democracy. But, given India's preferences and its aversion to "eco-imperialism," this would indisputably mean giving *less* attention in the WTO to environmental goals, not more.

The allegation that the GATT and WTO are hostile to environmental measures could conceivably arise from the core provisions of the GATT, which prohibit a member country from discriminating against the exports of another, in favor of "like products" made either by a third country (that is the Most Favored Nation provision of Article I) or by domestic producers (the national treatment provision of Article III). But Article XX allows for exceptions to the non-discrimination principle for environmental reasons (among others), provided that the measures in question are not "a means of arbitrary or unjustifiable discrimination" or a "disguised restriction on international trade." (Umbrella clauses allow countries to take actions to protect human, animal or plant life or health, and to conserve exhaustible natural resources.).

Under the GATT, there was ambiguity of interpretation as to what was to happen when Article XX conflicted with the non-discrimination article. To clarify the matter, in the preamble of the articles agreed at Marrakech establishing the WTO, language was added specifying that its objectives were not limited to promoting trade but included also optimal use of the world's resources, sustainable development, and environmental protection. Environmental objectives are also recognized specifically in the WTO agreements dealing with product standards, food safety, intellectual property protection, etc.

The protests are in a sense a puzzle. It would be easy to understand a political campaign in favor of the WTO taking a more aggressive pro-environment stance. But how does one explain the common view in the protest movement that the WTO currently is actively harmful to the environment?

When members of the protest movement identify specifics, they usually mention the rulings of WTO panels under the dispute settlement mechanism. The panels are quasi-judicial tribunals, whose job is to rule in disputes whether parties are abiding by the rules that they have already agreed to. Like most judicial proceedings, the panels themselves are not intended to be democratic. The rulings to date do not show a pattern of having been dominated by any particular country or interest group. There have been three or four fairly prominent WTO panel rulings that concern the environment in some way. Most within the environmentalist and NGO community have at some point acquired the belief that these rulings told the United States, or other defendant country, that their attempts to protect the environment must be repealed. The mystery is why this impression is so widespread, because it has little basis in fact.

The four WTO cases that will be briefly reviewed here are Canadian asbestos, Venezuelan reformulated gasoline, U.S. hormone-fed beef, and Asian shrimp and turtles. We will also touch on the Mexican tuna-dolphin case. Each of the cases involves an environmental measure that the producer plaintiff alleged to have trade-distorting effects. The complaints were not based, however, on the allegation that the goal of the measure was not valid or that protectionism was the original motivation of the measure. In most of the cases, the allegation was that discrimination against foreigners was an incidental, and unnecessary, feature of the environmental measure.

Canadian asbestos. One case is considered a clear win for the environmentalists. The WTO appellate body in 2001 upheld a French ban on asbestos products, against a challenge by Canada, which had been exporting to France. This ruling made real the WTO claim that its charter gives priority to health, safety, and environmental requirements, in that for such purposes GATT Article XX explicitly allows exceptions to the Most Favored Nation and national treatment rules.[37]

Venezuelan reformulated gasoline. In the reformulated gasoline case, Venezuela successfully claimed that U.S. law violated national treatment, i.e., discriminated in favor of domestic producers (with regard to whether refineries were allowed to use individual composition baselines when measuring pollution reduction). The case was unusual in that the intent to discriminate had at the time of passage been made explicit by U.S. administration officials seeking to please a domestic interest group. If the WTO had ruled in the U.S. favor, it would have been saying that it was fine for a country to discriminate needlessly and explicitly against foreign producers so long as the law came under an environmental label. Those who oppose this

---

[37]*New York Times*, July 25, 2000.

panel decision provide ready-made ammunition for the viewpoint that environmental activism is a false disguise worn by protectionist interests.

The United States was not blocked in implementing its targets, under the Clean Air Act, as commonly charged. Rather, the offending regulation was easily changed so as to be nondiscriminatory and thus to be permissible under the rules agreed by members of the WTO. This case sent precisely the right message to the world's governments, that environmental measures should not and need not discriminate against foreign producers.

Hormone-fed beef. What happens if the commodity in question is produced entirely, or almost entirely, by foreign producers, so that it cannot be conclusively demonstrated whether a ban, or other penalty, is or is not discriminatory? The WTO has attempted to maintain the rule that such measures are fine so long as a scientific study has supported the claimed environmental or health benefits of the measure. In the hormone-fed beef case, the WTO ruled against an EU ban on beef raised with growth hormones because the EU conspicuously failed to produce a science-based risk assessment showing that it might be dangerous. It thus resembles the case of the EU moratorium on GMOs.

These are genuinely difficult cases. On the one hand, where popular beliefs regarding a scientific question vary widely, a useful role for a multilateral institution could be to rule on the scientific merits. Or, at least, a useful role could be, as under the current WTO procedures, to rule on whether the country seeking to impose the regulation has carried out internally a reasonable study of the scientific merits. This logic suggests overruling the EU bans. On the other hand, the world may not be ready for even this mild level of loss of national sovereignty. If a nation's intent is to protect its health or environment, even if the measure has little scientific basis and even if its primary burden would fall on foreign producers, perhaps ensuring that the ban does not unnecessarily discriminate among producing countries is the best that can be done.

Despite the WTO ruling on hormone-fed beef, the Europeans did not cancel the ban. Their strategy, which they justify with the name "precautionary principle," is to continue to study the matter before allowing the product in. The precautionary principle, as the Europeans apply it, says to prohibit new technologies that have not yet been proven safe, even if there is no evidence that they are dangerous.[38] A compromise would be to allow

---

[38]Does the precautionary principle derive from risk aversion? Someone should point out that risk aversion in the presence of uncertainty is not necessarily sufficient to justify it. For poor residents of developing countries, the risk may be higher from drought or pests or disease in their crops, or from existing pesticides, than from the new GMOs that are designed to combat them more safely. Does the precautionary principle say that society should persist with what is natural and traditional, even if the current state of scientific evidence suggests a better, artificial, substitute? Then Asian men concerned about maintaining virility should continue to buy powdered rhino horn rather than switching to Viagra. (Gollier, 2001, offers another economist's perspective on the precautionary principle.)

imports of American beef subject to labeling requirements, as in the Montreal agreement on GMOs, thus letting the consumer decide.

Shrimp-turtle. Perceptions regarding the WTO panel ruling on a dispute about shrimp imports and the protection of sea turtles probably vary more widely than on any other case. The perception among many environmentalists is that the panel ruling struck down a U.S. law to protect sea turtles that are caught in the nets of shrimp fishermen in the Indian Ocean. (The provision was pursuant to the U.S. Endangered Species Act.) In reality, the dispute resembled the gasoline case in the respect that the ban on imports from countries without adequate regulatory regimes in place was unnecessarily selective and restrictive. The WTO panel and appellate body decided that the U.S. application of the law, in a complex variety of ways, was arbitrarily and unjustifiably discriminatory against the four plaintiff countries (Asian shrimp suppliers). The United States had unilaterally and inflexibly banned shrimp imports from countries that did not have in place for all production a specific turtle-protection regime of its own liking, one that mandated Turtle Excluder Devices.[39]

The case could in fact be considered a victory for the environmentalists, in that the WTO panel and the appeals body in 1998 explicitly stated that the United States could pursue the protection of endangered sea turtles against foreign fishermen. The United States subsequently allowed more flexibility in its regulation and made good-faith efforts to negotiate an agreement with the Asian producers, which it could have done in the first place. The WTO panel and appellate body in 2001 found the new U.S. regime to be WTO compliant.[40] The case set a precedent in clarifying support for the principle that the WTO rules allow countries to pass judgment on other countries' processes and production methods, even if it means using trade controls to do so, provided only that the measures are not unnecessarily discriminatory.[41]

Tuna-dolphin. In an earlier attempt to protect another large flippered sea animal, the United States (under the Marine Mammal Protection Act) had banned imports of tuna from countries that allowed the fishermen to use

---

[39]For example, the Asian suppliers had been given only four months' notice, thus discriminating against them and in favor of Caribbean suppliers. (The U.S. measure has also been pronounced unnecessarily restrictive in another sense: the majority of suppliers in India raise shrimp by aquaculture, where no sea turtles are endangered. Jagdish Bhagwati, *Financial Times*, December 21, 1999.)

[40]Charnovitz (2002a, pp. 98–99).

[41]For a full explanation of the legal issues, see Charnovitz (2002a). Also Michael Weinstein, "Greens and Globalization: Declaring Defeat in the Face of Victory," *New York Times*, April 22, 2001. Charnovitz and Weinstein (2001) argue that the environmentalists fail to realize the progress they have made in recent WTO panel cases and may thereby miss an opportunity to consolidate those gains. It is not only environmentalists who are under the impression that the GATT rules do not allow PPMs. Some developing countries also claim that PPMs violate the GATT. The motive of the first group is to fight the GATT, while the motive of the second group is to fight PPMs.

nets that also caught dolphins. Mexico brought a case before the GATT, as this pre-dated the WTO, and the GATT panel ruled against the U.S. law. Its report was never adopted. The parties instead in effect worked out their differences bilaterally, "out of court." The case could be considered a setback for trade-sensitive environmental measures, at least unilateral ones, but a setback that was to prove temporary. That the GATT ruling in the tuna case did not affirm the right of the United States to use trade bans to protect the dolphins shows how much the environmentalist cause has progressed under the WTO, in the subsequent gasoline, shrimp-turtle, and asbestos cases.

A system for labeling tuna in the U.S. market as either "dolphin safe" or not was later found consistent with the GATT. The American consumer response turned out to be sufficiently great to accomplish the desired purpose. Since 1990, the major companies have sold only the dolphin-safe kind of tuna. The moral is not just that the goal of protecting the dolphins was accomplished despite globalization in its GATT incarnation. The moral is, rather, that *globalization was instrumental in the protection of the dolphins.* The goal could not have been accomplished without international trade, because American citizens would have had no effective way of putting pressure on Mexico. Leaving the U.S. government free to regulate its own fishermen would not have helped.[42]

Multilateral Environmental Agreements

When it comes to global externalities such as endangered species, stratospheric ozone depletion, and global climate change, it is particularly clear that the problem cannot be addressed by a system where each country pursues environmental measures on its own. Multilateral negotiations, agreements, and institutions are required. Furthermore, the point is not simply that global regulatory measures are necessary in any effort to combat the effects of economic globalization. If countries had industrialized in isolation, without any international trade or investment among them, they would still be emitting greenhouse gases, and we would still need a globally coordinated response.

Multilateral environmental agreements (MEAs), even if they involve trade-restricting measures, are viewed more favorably under the international rules than unilateral environmental measures. Leaving aside the

---

[42]Thomas Friedman, *New York Times,* December 8, 1999, p. A31. Presumably, in the absence of the opportunity to export to the United States, Mexican fisherman would not have caught as many tuna for the domestic market alone, which would have limited the dolphin casualties somewhat. It is not known whether the much-reduced number of dolphins still killed under the current system is less than in the hypothetical no-trade case. But working through the channel of voting power represented by U.S. imports was surely a better way to have accomplished the goal. Telling Mexican fisherman they must remain poor and telling American consumers that they couldn't eat tuna would have been a less satisfactory solution to the problem.

Law of the Sea, the Basel Convention on Hazardous Wastes, and a large number of relatively more minor agreements, three MEAs merit particular mention.

The Convention on International Trade in Endangered Species (CITES) was negotiated in 1973. Although it lacks the teeth that many would like, it was notable as a precedent establishing that MEAs are compatible with the GATT even if they restrict trade. An interesting issue relevant for species protection is whether a plan of using animals to support the economic livelihood of local residents can be a more sustainable form of protection than attempts to leave them untouched altogether.

The Montreal Protocol on Substances that Deplete the Ozone Layer is the most successful example of an MEA, as it has resulted in the phasing out of most use of CFCs (chlorofluorocarbons) and other ozone-depleting chemicals. The success of this agreement is partly attributable to the enforcement role played by trade penalties: the protocol prohibits trade in controlled substances with countries that do not participate. This created the necessary incentive to push those developing countries that otherwise might have been reluctant into joining. If substantial numbers of countries had nevertheless remained outside the protocol, the trade controls would have also accomplished the second objective—minimizing *leakage,* that is, the migration of production of banned substances to non-participating countries.[43] The protocol was helped to succeed in that there were a relatively small number of producers. It also helped that there turned out to be good substitutes for the banned substances, though that was not known until the ban was tried.[44] One might say it also helped bolster the principle that PPM-targeted measures were not necessarily incompatible with the GATT: the agreement threatened non-participants not only with a ban on trade in ozone-depleting chemicals themselves, but also a potential ban on trade in goods manufactured with such chemicals in the sense that governments were required to determine the feasibility of such a ban. But it never went further than that.

The Kyoto Protocol on Global Climate Change, negotiated in 1997, is the most ambitious attempt at a multilateral environment agreement to date. This is not the place to discuss the Kyoto Protocol at length. The task of addressing climate change while satisfying the political constraints of the various factions (particularly, the United States, EU, and developing countries) was an inherently impossible task. Most economists emphasize that the agreement as it was written at Kyoto would impose large economic costs on the United States and other countries, while making only a minor dent in the problem. The Clinton Administration's interpretation of the protocol insisted on so-called flexibility mechanisms, such as international trading of emission permits, to bring the economic costs down

---

[43]Brack (1996).
[44]Parson (2002).

to a modest range.[45] This interpretation was rejected by the Europeans at the Hague in November 2000. Without the flexibility mechanisms, the United Sates would be out of the protocol, even if the subsequent administration had been more environmentally friendly than it was. (Ironically, now that European and other countries are trying to go ahead without the United States, they are finding that they cannot manage without such trading mechanisms.)

Even most of those who for one reason or another do not believe that Kyoto was a useful step, however, must acknowledge that multilateral agreements will be necessary if the problem of global climate change is to be tackled. The current U.S. administration has yet to face up to this. The point for present purposes is that a system in which each country insists, based on an appeal to national sovereignty, that it be left to formulate environmental policies on its own, would be a world in which global externalities like greenhouse gas emissions would not be effectively addressed.

Summary of Conclusions

The relationship between globalization and the environment is too complex to sum up in a single judgment—whether "good" or "bad." In many respects, global trade and investment operate like other sources of economic growth. They tend to raise income as measured in the marketplace. On the one hand, the higher scale of output can mean more pollution, deforestation, and other kinds of environmental damage. On the other hand, changes in the composition and techniques of economic activity can lower the damage relative to income. Although it is not possible to generalize universally about the net effect of these channels, it is possible to put forward general answers to some major relevant questions.

- A key question is whether openness to international trade undermines national attempts at environmental regulation, through a "race to the bottom" effect. This no doubt happens sometimes. But there is little statistical evidence, across countries, that the unfavorable effects on

---

[45]The author was one of the few economists sympathetic to the Clinton Administration policy on the Kyoto Protocol. Two claims: (1) Quantitative targets a la Kyoto are the "least impossible" way politically to structure an international agreement (see Frankel, 2003, for my response to the arguments of Cooper, 1998, Nordhaus, 2001, and Schelling, 2002, against assignment of quantitative targets). And (2) Bill Clinton's approach—signing the treaty but announcing his intention not to submit for ratification unless the Europeans agreed to unrestricted international trading of emission permits and unless developing countries agreed to participate in the system—was the least impossible way, subject to the existing political constraints, of demonstrating U.S. willingness to address climate change. It was our hope that when the world is ready to make a more serious attempt, it will build on the good aspects of the Kyoto Protocol, particularly the role for international permit trading and other flexibility mechanisms.

average outweigh favorable "gains from trade" effects on measures of pollution, such as SO_2 concentrations. If anything, the answer seems to be that favorable effects dominate.

- Perceptions that WTO panel rulings have interfered with the ability of individual countries to pursue environmental goals are poorly informed. In cases such as Canadian asbestos, Venezuelan gasoline, and Asian shrimp, the rulings have confirmed that countries can enact environmental measures, even if they affect trade and even if they concern others' processes and production methods, provided the measures do not unnecessarily discriminate among producer countries.

- People care about both the environment and the economy. As their real income rises, their demand for environmental quality rises. Under the right conditions, this can translate into environmental progress. The right conditions include democracy, effective regulation, and externalities that are largely confined within national borders and are therefore amenable to national regulation.

- Increasingly, however, environmental problems do in fact spill across national borders. The strongest examples are pure global externalities such as global climate change and ozone depletion. Economic growth alone will not address such problems, in a system where each country acts individually, due to the free rider problem. International institutions are required. This would be equally true in the absence of international trade.

- Indeed, trade offers a handle whereby citizens of one country can exercise a role in environmental problems of other countries that they would otherwise not have. Consumer labeling campaigns and corporate codes of conduct are examples.

- Many aspects of the environment that might have been considered purely domestic matters in the past, or that foreign residents might not even have known about, are increasingly of concern to those living in other countries. It again follows that if the issues are to be addressed, then multilateral institutions are the vehicle and expressions of national sovereignty are the obstacle, not the other way around. Indeed, if one broadens the definition of globalization, beyond international trade and investment, to include the globalization of ideas and of NGO activities, then one can see the international environmental movement as itself an example of globalization.

References

Andreoni, James, and Arik Levinson. 2001. "The Simple Analytics of the Environmental Kuznets Curve," NBER Working Paper no. 6739. *Journal of Public Economics* 80, May, 269–286.

Antweiler, Werner, Brian Copeland, and M. Scott Taylor. 2001. "Is Free Trade Good for the Environment?" NBER Working Paper No. 6707. *American Economic Review* 91, no. 4, September, 877–908.

Arrow, K., R. Bolin, P. Costanza, P. Dasgupta, C. Folke, C. S. Holling, B. O. Jansson, S. Levin, K. G. Mäler, C. Perrings, and D. Pimentel. 1995. "Economic Growth, Carrying Capacity, and the Environment," *Science* 268, April 28, 520–521.

Barrett, Scott, and Kathryn Graddy. 2000. "Freedom, Growth, and the Environment," *Environment and Development Economics* 5, 433–456.

Bhagwati, Jadgish. 2000. "On Thinking Clearly About the Linkage Between Trade and the Environment," in *The Wind of the Hundred Days: How Washington Mismanaged Globalization*, Cambridge: MIT Press.

Bhagwati, Jadgish, and T. N. Srinivasan. 1996. "Trade and the Environment: Does Environmental Diversity Detract from the Case for Free Trade," in *Fair Trade and Harmonization*, Vol. 1: *Economic Analysis*, Jadgish Bhagwati and Robert Hudec eds. Cambridge: MIT Press, pp. 159–223.

Bimonte, Salvatore. 2001. "Model of Growth and Environmental Quality, A New Evidence of the Environmental Kuznets Curve," Universita degli Studi di Siena, Quaderni, no. 321, April.

Brack, Duncan. 1996. *International Trade and the Montreal Protocol*, London: The Royal Institute of International Affairs and Earthscan Publications, Ltd.

Bradford, David, Rebecca Schlieckert and Stephen Shore. 2000. "The Environmental Kuznets Curve: Exploring a Fresh Specification," NBER Working Paper no. 8001. Forthcoming, *Topics in Economic Analysis and Policy*.

Braithwaite, John, and Peter Drahos. 2000. *Global Business Regulation*, UK: Cambridge University Press.

Charnovitz, Steve. 2002a. "The Law of Environmental 'PPMs' in the WTO: Debunking the Myth of Illegality," *Yale Journal of International Law* 27, no. 1, Winter, pp. 59–110.

Charnovitz, Steve. 2002b. "A World Environment Organization," *Columbia Journal of Environmental Law* 27, no. 2, 323–362.

Charnovitz, Steve, and Michael Weinstein. 2001. "The Greening of the WTO," *Foreign Affairs* 80, no. 6, 147–156.

Chaudhuri, Shubham, and Alexander Pfaff. 2002. "Economic Growth and the Environment: What Can We Learn from Household Data?" Columbia University, February.

Cooper, Richard. 1998. "Why Kyoto Won't Work," *Foreign Affairs*, March/April.

Copeland, Brian, and M. Scott Taylor. 1994. "North-South Trade and the Environment," *Quarterly Journal of Economics* 109, 755–787.

Copeland, Brian, and M. Scott Taylor. 1995. "Trade and the Environment: A Partial Synthesis," *American Journal of Agricultural Economics* 77, 765–771.

Copeland, Brian, and M. Scott Taylor. 2001. "International Trade and the Environment: A Framework for Analysis," NBER Working Paper No. 8540, October.

Copeland, Brian, and M. Scott Taylor. 2003a. *Trade and the Environment: Theory and Evidence*, Princeton: Princeton University Press.

Copeland, Brian, and M. Scott Taylor. 2003b. "Trade, Growth and the Environment." NBER Working Paper No. 9823, July.

Cropper, Maureen, and Charles Griffiths. 1994. "The Interaction of Population Growth and Environmental Quality," *American Economic Review* 84, no. 2, May, 250–254.

Daly, Herman. 1993. "The Perils of Free Trade," *Scientific American*, November, 51–55.

Dean, Judy. 1992. "Trade and the Environment: A Survey of the Literature," in Patrick Low, ed., *International Trade and the Environment*. World Bank Discussion Paper No. 159.

Dean, Judy. 2001. "Overview," in *International Trade and the Environment*, J. Dean, ed., International Library of Environmental Economics and Policy Series, (UK: Ashgate Publishing).

Dean, Judy. 2002. "Does Trade Liberalization Harm the Environment? A New Test," *Canadian Journal of Economics* 35, no. 4, 819–842 November.

Dua, Andre, and Daniel Esty, 1997, *Sustaining the Asia Pacific Miracle: Environmental Protection and Economic Integration*, Institute for International Economics: Washington DC.

Ederington, Josh, and Jenny Minier. 2002. "Is Environmental Policy a Secondary Trade Barrier? An Empirical Analysis," University of Miami; *Canadian Journal of Economics*, forthcoming.

Ederington, Josh, Arik Levinson, and Jenny Minier. 2003. "Footloose and Pollution-Free," NBER Working Paper No. 9718, May.

Eiras, Ana, and Brett Schaefer. 2001. "Trade: The Best Way to Protect the Environment," *Backgrounder*, The Heritage Foundation no. 1480, September 27.

Esty, Daniel. 1994. *Greening the GATT: Trade, Environment, and the Future*, Washington, DC: Institute for International Economics.

Esty, Daniel. 2001. "Bridging the Trade-Environment Divide," *Journal of Economic Perspectives*, Summer 15, no. 3, 113–130.

Esty, Daniel, and Bradford Gentry. 1997. "Foreign Investment, Globalisation, and the Environment," in *Globalization and the Environment*, Tom Jones ed. Paris: Organization for Economic Cooperation and Development.

Esty, Daniel, and Damien Giradin. 1998. "Environmental Protection and International Competitiveness: A Conceptual Framework," *Journal of World Trade* 32, no. 3, June, 5–46.

Esty, Daniel, and Michael Porter. 2001. "Measuring National Environmental Performance and Its Determinants," Yale Law School and Harvard Business School, April.

Foster, Andrew, and Mark Rosenzweig. 2003. "Economic Growth and the Rise of Forests," *Quarterly Journal of Economics* 118, issue 2, May, 601–638.

Frankel, Jeffrey. 2003. "You're Getting Warmer: The Most Feasible Path for Addressing Global Climate Change Does Run Through Kyoto," Fondazione Eni Enrico Mattei, Milan, Italy; forthcoming in *Trade and the Environment in the Perspective of the EU Enlargement*, edited John Maxwell, with Marialuisa Tamborra, London: Edward Elgar Publishers, Ltd.

Frankel, Jeffrey, and Andrew Rose. 2003. "Is Trade Good or Bad for the Environment? Sorting Out the Causality," RWP03-038, Kennedy School, Harvard University, September. Revised version of NBER Working Paper 9201. *Review of Economics and Statistics*, forthcoming.

Gollier, Christian. 2001. "Should We Beware the Precautionary Principle?" *Economic Policy* 33, October, 303–327.

Goulder, Lawrence, and Robert Stavins. 2002. "An Eye on the Future," *Nature*, 419, October 17, 673–674.

Grossman, Gene, and Alan Krueger. 1993. "Environmental Impacts of a North American Free Trade Agreement," in *The U.S.-Mexico Free Trade Agreement*, Peter Garber, ed., Cambridge MA: MIT Press.

Grossman, Gene, and Alan Krueger. 1995. "Economic Growth and the Environment," *Quarterly Journal of Economics*, 110, no. 2, May 1995, pp. 353–377.

Hanley, Nick, Jason Shogren, and Ben White, *Environmental Economics in Theory and Practice*, New York: Oxford University Press, 1997.

Harbaugh, William, Arik Levinson, and David Wilson. 2000. "Reexamining the Empirical Evidence for an Environmental Kuznets Curve," NBER Working Paper No. 7711, May.

Hilton, F. G. Hank, and Arik Levinson. 1998. "Factoring the Environmental Kuznets Curve: Evidence from Automotive Lead Emissions," *Journal of Environmental Economics and Management* 35, 126–141.

Holtz-Eakin and T. Selden. 1995. "Stoking the Fires? CO2 Emissions and Economic Growth," *Journal of Public Economics* 57, May, 85–101.

Hufbauer, Gary, Daniel Esty, Diana Orejas, Luis Rubio, and Jeffrey Schott. 2000. *NAFTA and the Environment: Seven Years Later*, Policy Analyses in International Economics No. 61, Washington, DC: Institute for International Economics, October.

Jaeger, William, and Van Kolpin. 2000. "Economic Growth and Environmental Resource Allocation," Williams University and University of Oregon, August 22.

Jaffe, Adam, S. R. Peterson, Paul Portney, and Robert Stavins. 1995. "Environmental Regulation and the Competitiveness of U.S. Manufacturing: What Does the Evidence Tell Us?" *Journal of Economic Literature* 33, 132–163.

Juma, Calestous. 2000. "The Perils of Centralizing Global Environmental Governance" *Environment* 42, no. 9, November, 44–45.

Lee, Hiro, and David Roland-Holst, "The Environment and Welfare Implications of Trade and Tax Policy," *Journal of Development Economics*, February 1997, 52, 65–82.

Levinson, Arik. 1999. "State Taxes and Interstate Hazardous Waste Shipments," *American Economic Review* 89, no. 3, June.

Levinson, Arik, and M. Scott Taylor. 2001. "Trade and the Environment: Unmasking the Pollution Haven Effect," Georgetown University and University of Wisconsin.

Liddle, Brantley. 2001. "Free Trade and the Environment-Development System," *Ecological Economics* 39, 21–36.

Low, P., and A. Yeats. 1992. "Do 'Dirty' Industries Migrate?" in *International Trade and the Environment*, P. Low ed., 89–104. Geneva: World Bank, 1992.

Lucas, Robert E. B., David Wheeler, and Hememala Hettige. 1992. "Economic Development, Environmental Regulation and the International Migration of Toxic Industrial Pollution: 1960–1988," in Patrick Low, editor, *International Trade and the Environment*, World Bank Discussion Papers no. 159 (The World Bank: Washington DC).

Meadows, Donella, Dennis Meadows, Jorgen Randres, and William Behrens. 1972. *The Limits to Growth*, New York: Universe Books.

Muradian, Roldan, Martin O'Connor, and Joan Martinez-Alier. 2001. "Embodied Pollution in Trade: Estimating the 'Environmental Load Displacement' of Industrialised Countries," FEEM Working Paper No. 57, July, Milan.

Neumayer, Eric. 2002. "Does Trade Openness Promote Multilateral Environmental Cooperation?" *The World Economy* 25, no. 6, 812–832.

Nordhaus, William. 2001. "After Kyoto: Alternative Mechanisms to Control Global Warming," American Economic Association, Atlanta, GA, January 4.

Panayotou, Theo. 1993. "Empirical Tests and Policy Analysis of Environmental Degradation at Different Stages of Development," Working Paper WP238, Technology and Employment Programme (Geneva: International Labor Office).

Parson, Edward. 2002. *Protecting the Ozone Layer: Science, Strategy, and Negotiation in the Shaping of a Global Environmental Regime*, Oxford University Press, forthcoming.

Porter, Michael. 1990. *The Competitive Advantage of Nations* New York: The Free Press, Macmillan.

Porter, Michael. 1991. "America's Green Strategy," *Scientific American*, April.

Porter, Michael, and Claas van der Linde. 1995. "Toward a New Conception of the Environment-Competitiveness Relationship," *Journal of Economic Perspectives* 9, No. 4.

Ruggie, John. 2002. "Trade, Sustainability and Global Governance," *Columbia Journal of Environmental Law* 27, no. 297–307.

Schelling, Thomas. 2002. "What Makes Greenhouse Sense?" *Foreign Affairs* 81, no. 3, May/June.

Schmidheiny, Stephan. *Changing Course: A Global Business Perspective on Development and the Environment*. Cambridge: The MIT Press, 1992.

Selden, Thomas, and Daqing Song. 1994. "Environmental Quality and Development: Is There a Kuznets Curve for Air Pollution Emissions," *Journal of Environmental Economics and Management* 27, 147–162.

Selden, Thomas, and Daqing Song. 1995. "Neoclassical Growth, the J Curve for Abatement, and the Inverted U Curve for Pollution," *Journal of Environmental Economics and Management* 29, 162–168.

Shafik, Nemat. 1994. "Economic Development and Environmental Quality: An Econometric Analysis," *Oxford Economic Papers* 46, 757–773.

Smarzynska, Beata, and Shang-Jin Wei. 2001. "Pollution Havens and Foreign Direct Investment: Dirty Secret or Popular Myth?" NBER Working Paper No. 8465, September.

Smith, Kirk. "Fuel Combustion, Air Pollution Exposure, and Health: The Situation in Developing Countries," *Annual Review of Energy and Environment*, 1993, 18, 529–566.

Stavins, Robert. 2000. *Economics of the Environment: Selected Readings*, 4th ed, Norton.

Stokey, Nancy. 1998. "Are There Limits to Growth," *International Economic Review* 39, no. 1, February, 1–31.

Suri, Vivek, and Duane Chapman. 1998. "Economic Growth, Trade and Energy: Implications for the Environmental Kuznet Curve," *Ecological Economics* 25, 2, May, 147–160.

Tobey, James A. 1990. "The Effects of Domestic Environmental Policies on Patterns of World Trade: An Empirical Test," *Kyklos* 43, 191–209.

Victor, David, and C. Ford Runge. 2002. "Farming the Genetic Frontier," *Foreign Affairs* 81, no. 3 pp. 107–121.

Vogel, David. 1995. *Trading Up: Consumer and Environmental Regulation in a Global Economy*, Cambridge: Harvard University Press.

World Bank. 1992. *Development and the Environment*, World Development Report.

20 Confronting the Environmental Kuznets Curve*

Susmita Dasgupta, Benoit Laplante, Hua Wang, and David Wheeler

Susmita Dasgupta, Benoit Laplante, Hua Wang, and David Wheeler are Economists, Development Research Group, World Bank, Washington, D.C.

The environmental Kuznets curve posits an inverted-U relationship between pollution and economic development. Kuznets's name was apparently attached to the curve by Grossman and Krueger (1993), who noted its resemblance to Kuznets's inverted-U relationship between income inequality and development. In the first stage of industrialization, pollution in the environmental Kuznets curve world grows rapidly because people are more interested in jobs and income than clean air and water, communities are too poor to pay for abatement, and environmental regulation is correspondingly weak. The balance shifts as income rises. Leading industrial sectors become cleaner, people value the environment more highly, and regulatory institutions become more effective. Along the curve, pollution levels off in the middle-income range and then falls toward pre-industrial levels in wealthy societies.

The environmental Kuznets curve model has elicited conflicting reactions from researchers and policymakers. Applied econometricians have generally accepted the basic tenets of the model and focused on measuring its parameters. Their regressions, typically fitted to cross-sectional observations across countries or regions, suggest that air and water pollution increase with development until per capita income reaches a range of $5000 to $8000. When income rises beyond that level, pollution starts to decline, as shown in the "conventional EKC" line in Figure 1. In developing countries, some policymakers have interpreted such results as conveying a message about priorities: Grow first, then clean up.

Numerous critics have challenged the conventional environmental Kuznets curve, both as a representation of what actually happens in the

"Confronting the Environmental Kuznets Curve," by Susmita Dasgupta, Benoit Laplante, Hua Wang, and David Wheeler, from *Journal of Economic Perspectives*, 16(1):147–168 (Winter 2002).

*Particular thanks to David Shaman and Yasmin D'Souza for their support, and to Shakeb Afsah, Hemamala Hettige, Mainul Huq, Muthukumara Mani, Craig Meisner, Kiran Pendey and Sheoli Pargal for valuable contributions to the research and policy initiatives reviewed in this paper. Thanks also to Timothy Taylor, Alan Krueger, Brad De Long and Michael Waldman for valuable comments on an earlier draft.

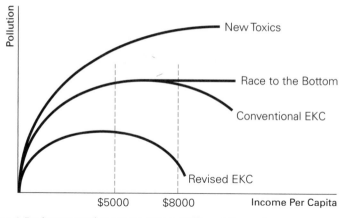

Figure 1 Environmental Kuznets Curve: Different Scenarios

development process and as a policy prescription. Some pessimistic critics argue that cross-sectional evidence for the environmental Kuznets curve is nothing more than a snapshot of a dynamic process. Over time, they claim, the curve will rise to a horizontal line at maximum existing pollution levels, as globalization promotes a "race to the bottom" in environmental standards, as shown in Figure 1. Other pessimists hold that, even if certain pollutants are reduced as income increases, industrial society continuously creates new, unregulated and potentially toxic pollutants. In their view, the overall environmental risks from these new pollutants may continue to grow even if some sources of pollution are reduced, as shown by the "new toxics" line in Figure 1. Although both pessimistic schools make plausible claims, neither has bolstered them with much empirical research.

In contrast, recent empirical work has fostered an optimistic critique of the conventional environmental Kuznets curve. The new results suggest that the level of the curve is actually dropping and shifting to the left, as growth generates less pollution in the early stages of industrialization and pollution begins falling at lower income levels, as shown by the "revised EKC" in Figure 1.

The stakes in the environmental Kuznets curve debate are high. Per capita GDP in 1998 (in purchasing power parity dollars) was $1440 in the nations of sub-Saharan Africa, $2060 in India, $2407 in Indonesia, and $3051 in China (World Bank, 2000). Since these societies are nowhere near the income range associated with maximum pollution on the conventional environmental Kuznets curve, a literal interpretation of the curve would imply substantial increases in pollution during the next few decades. Moreover, empirical research suggests that pollution costs are already quite high in these countries. For example, recent World Bank estimates of mortality and morbidity from urban air pollution in India and China suggest annual losses in the range of 2–3 percent of GDP (Bolt, Hamilton, Pandey and Wheeler, 2001).

The stakes are not trivial for industrial societies, either. Those who believe in the "race to the bottom" model repeatedly advocate trade and investment restrictions that will eliminate the putative cost advantage of "pollution havens" in the developing world. If their assessment of the situation is correct, then industrial society faces two unpalatable options: Protect environmental gains by moving back toward autarky, but reducing global income in the process, or accept much higher global pollution under unrestrained globalization. Moreover, industrialized countries surely must consider the daunting possibility that they are not actually making progress against pollution as their incomes rise, but instead are reducing only a few measured and well-known pollutants while facing new and potentially greater environmental concerns.

In this paper, we review the arguments and the evidence on the position, shape and mutability of the environmental Kuznets curve. We ultimately side with the optimists—but with some reservations.

Theory and Measurement of the Relationship between Economic Development and Environmental Quality

Numerous theoretical and empirical papers have considered the broad relationship between economic development and environmental quality. The focus of the theoretical papers has mainly been to derive transition paths for pollution, abatement effort, and development under alternative assumptions about social welfare functions, pollution damage, the cost of abatement, and the productivity of capital. This theoretical work has shown that an environmental Kuznets curve can result if a few plausible conditions are satisfied as income increases in a society: specifically, the marginal utility of consumption is constant or falling; the disutility of pollution is rising; the marginal damage of pollution is rising; and the marginal cost of abating pollution is rising. Most theoretical models implicitly assume the existence of public agencies that regulate pollution with full information about the benefits and costs of pollution control. In addition, they assume that the pollution externality is local, not cross-border. In the latter case, there would be little local incentive to internalize the externality.

López (1994) uses a fairly general theoretical model to show that if producers pay the social marginal cost of pollution, then the relationship between emissions and income depends on the properties of technology and preferences. If preferences are homothetic, so that percentage increases in income lead to identical percentage increases in what is consumed, then an increase in output will result in an increase in pollution. But if preferences are nonhomothetic, so that the proportion of household spending on different items changes as income rises, then the response of pollution to growth will depend on the degree of relative risk-aversion and the elasticity of substitution in production between pollution and conventional inputs.

Selden and Song (1995) derive an inverted-U curve for the relationship between optimal pollution and the capital stock, assuming that optimal abatement is zero until a given capital stock is achieved, and that it rises thereafter at an increasing rate. John and Pecchenino (1994), John, Pecchenino, Schimmelpfennig and Schreft (1995), and McConnell (1997) derive similar inverted-U curves by using overlapping generations models. Recent analytical work by López and Mitra (2000) suggests that corruption may also account for part of the observed relationship between development and environmental quality. Their results show that for any level of per capita income, the pollution level corresponding to corrupt behavior is always above the socially optimal level. Further, they show that the turning point of the environmental Kuznets curve takes place at income and pollution levels above those corresponding to the social optimum.

Numerous empirical studies have tested the environmental Kuznets curve model. The typical approach has been to regress cross-country measures of ambient air and water quality on various specifications of income per capita. For their data on pollution, these studies often rely on information from the Global Environmental Monitoring System (GEMS), an effort sponsored by the United Nations that has gathered pollution data from developed and developing countries. The GEMS database includes information on contamination from commonly regulated air and water pollutants. Stern, Auld, Common and Sanyal (1998) have supplemented the GEMS data with a more detailed accounting of airborne sulfur emissions. Although greenhouse gases have not been included in the GEMS database, carbon dioxide emissions estimates for most developed and developing countries are available from the U.S. Oak Ridge National Laboratories (Marland, Boden and Andres, 2001).

Empirical researchers are far from agreement that the environmental Kuznets curve provides a good fit to the available data, even for conventional pollutants. In one of the most comprehensive reviews of the empirical literature, Stern (1998) argues that the evidence for the inverted-U relationship applies only to a subset of environmental measures; for example, air pollutants such as suspended particulates and sulfur dioxide. Since Grossman and Krueger (1993) find that suspended particulates decline monotonically with income, even Stern's subset is open to contest. In related work, Stern, Auld, Common and Sanyal (1998) find that sulfur emissions increase through the existing income range. Results for water pollution are similarly mixed.

Empirical work in this area is proceeding in a number of directions. First, international organizations such as the United Nations Environment Programme and the World Bank are sponsoring collection of more data on environmental quality in developing countries. As more data is collected, new opportunities will open up for studying the relationship between economic development and environmental quality. In the meantime, it is useful to think about how to compensate for incomplete monitoring information. For example, Selden and Song (1994) develop estimates of air emissions based on national fuel-use data and fuel-specific pollution parameters that are roughly adjusted for conditions in countries at varying income levels.

A second issue is that for many pollutants data is scarce everywhere, not just in developing countries. The GEMS effort has focused on a few "criteria" pollutants, so-designated because legal statutes have required regulators to specify their damaging characteristics. Criteria air pollutants, for example, have generally included ozone, carbon monoxide, suspended particulates, sulfur dioxide, lead and nitrogen oxide. A far broader class of emissions, known as toxic pollutants, includes materials that cause death, disease or birth defects in exposed organisms. Among the hundreds of unregulated toxic pollutants that have been subjected to laboratory analysis, the quantities and exposures necessary to produce damaging effects have been shown to vary widely. Literally thousands of potentially toxic materials remain untested and unregulated.

Data gathering in this area has started, as some countries have mandated public reports of toxic emissions by industrial facilities. For example, the United States has a Toxic Release Inventory; Canada has a National Pollutant Release Inventory; the United Kingdom has a Pollutant Inventory; and Australia has a National Pollutant Inventory. Using sectoral estimates of toxic emissions relative to level of output, developed from U.S. data by Hettige, Martin, Singh and Wheeler (1995), researchers have estimated toxic emissions in eastern Europe (Laplante and Smits, 1998) and Latin America (Hettige and Wheeler, 1996; Dasgupta, Laplante and Meisner, 2001). However, the underlying scarcity of data has as yet made it impossible to do more than speculate about the shape of an environmental Kuznets curve for toxics.

A third empirical issue involves thinking about the curvature of the environmental Kuznets curve. In most cases, the implied relationship between income growth and pollution is sensitive to inclusion of higher-order polynomial terms in per capita income whose significance varies widely.

Fourth, it is useful to compare the results of time series studies where the environmental evidence is available. De Bruyn, van den Bergh and Opschoor (1998) estimate time series models individually for Netherlands, Germany, the United Kingdom and the United States and show that economic growth has had a positive effect on emissions of carbon dioxide, nitrogen oxides, and sulfur dioxide. They argue that conventional cross-section estimation techniques have generated spurious estimates of the environmental Kuznets curve because they do not adequately capture the dynamic process involved.

Given the data limitations, concerns over appropriate functional forms, and choices between cross-section and time series analysis, structural interpretations of the environmental Kuznets curve have remained largely ad hoc. In view of these uncertainties, few researchers have taken the next step and begun to study the sources of change in the marginal relationship between economic development and pollution.

How the Environmental Kuznets Curve Can Become Lower and Flatter

Research on the environmental Kuznets curve has suggested that its shape is not likely to be fixed. Instead, the relationship between growth in per capita income and environmental quality will be determined by how many parties react to economic growth and its side effects—including citizens, businesses, policymakers, regulators, nongovernmental organizations, and other market participants. A body of recent research has investigated these connections. The theme that emerges from this research is that it is quite plausible for developing societies to have improvements in environmental quality. It also seems likely that because of growing public concern and research knowledge about environmental quality and regulation, countries may be able to experience an environmental Kuznets curve that is lower and flatter than the conventional measures would suggest. That is, they may be able to develop from low levels of per capita income with little or no degradation in environmental quality, and then at some point to experience improvements in both income and environmental quality.

The Primary Role of Environmental Regulation

In principle, observed changes in pollution as per capita income rises could come from several different sources: shifts in the scale and sectoral composition of output, changes in technology within sectors, or the impact of regulation on pollution abatement (Grossman and Krueger, 1993). The absence of appropriate microdata across countries has precluded a systematic empirical approach to this decomposition. However, the available evidence suggests that regulation is the dominant factor in explaining the decline in pollution as countries grow beyond middle-income status.

For instance, Panayotou (1997) estimates a decomposition equation for a sample of 30 developed and developing countries for the period 1982–1994. He incorporates policy considerations into the income-environmental relationship while decomposing it into scale, sectoral composition and pollution intensity (or pollution per unit of output) effects. His main finding, at least for ambient sulfur dioxide levels, is that effective policies and institutions can significantly reduce environmental degradation at low income levels and speed up improvements at higher income levels, thereby lowering the environmental Kuznets curve and reducing the environmental cost of growth. However, the estimated equation is not derived from any formal structural equation. In addition, in the absence of actual measures of environmental regulations, Panayotou uses indices of contract enforcement and bureaucratic efficiency as proxies. De Bruyn (1997) decomposes the growth-environment relationship in a sample of OECD and former socialist economies, using a divisia index methodology. Analyzing changes in sulfur dioxide pollution, he finds a significant role for environmental policy, but not for structural change in the economy. In a cross-country study of water pollution abatement, Mani, Hettige and Wheeler (2000) find that while

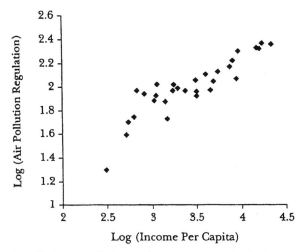

Figure 2 Air Pollution Regulation and Income Per Capita in 31 Countries

Source: Dasgupta, Mody, Roy and Wheeler (2001).

some of the improvement in water quality with increases in per capita income is attributable to sectoral composition and technology effects, the main factor is stricter environmental regulation.

There appear to be three main reasons that richer countries regulate pollution more strictly. First, pollution damage gets higher priority after society has completed basic investments in health and education. Second, higher-income societies have more plentiful technical personnel and budgets for monitoring and enforcement activities. Third, higher income and education empower local communities to enforce higher environmental standards, whatever stance is taken by the national government (Dasgupta and Wheeler, 1997; Pargal and Wheeler, 1996; Dean, 1999). The result of these mutually reinforcing factors, as shown in Figure 2, is a very close relationship between national pollution regulation and income per capita (Dasgupta, Mody, Roy and Wheeler, 2001).

Economic Liberalization

During the past two decades, many countries have liberalized their economies by reducing government subsidies, dismantling price controls, privatizing state enterprises and removing barriers to trade and investment. Easterly (2001) provides strong evidence that measures of financial depth and price distortion have improved significantly for developing countries since 1980. The result has been an adjustment toward economic activities that reflect comparative advantage at undistorted factor and product prices, which in turn can affect the level of pollution in an economy by shifting the sectoral composition.

One result has been growth of labor-intensive assembly activities such as garment production. These activities are seldom pollution-intensive, although there are some notable exceptions such as electronics assembly that employs toxic cleaning solvents and fabric production that generates organic water pollution and toxic pollution from chemical dyes (Hettige, Martin, Singh and Wheeler, 1995). Another likely area of comparative advantage is information services with relatively low skill requirements, such as records maintenance for internationally distributed information-processing services. Such activities are typically not very polluting. More environmentally sensitive areas of comparative advantage include large-scale agriculture and production that exploits local natural resources such as forest products, basic metals and chemicals (Lee and Roland-Holst, 1997). These industries are often heavy polluters, because they produce large volumes of waste residuals and frequently employ toxic chemicals.

Elimination of government subsidies often has an environmentally beneficial effect in this context. The heaviest polluters often receive subsidies, because they operate in sectors such as steel and petrochemicals where state intervention has been common. Privatization and reduction of subsidies tend to reduce the scale of such activities, while expanding production in the assembly and service sectors that emit fewer pollutants (Dasgupta, Wang and Wheeler, 1997; Lucas, Hettige and Wheeler, 1992; Jha, Markandya and Vossenaar, 1999; Birdsall and Wheeler, 1993). Elimination of energy subsidies increases energy efficiency, shifts industry away from energy-intensive sectors, and reduces demand for pollution-intensive power (Vukina, Beghin and Solakoglu, 1999; World Bank, 1999). However, higher energy prices also induce shifts from capital- and energy-intensive production techniques to labor- and materials-intensive techniques, which are often more pollution-intensive in other ways (Mani, Hettige and Wheeler, 2000).

Economic liberalization also has a common effect, at least in pollution-intensive sectors, of enlarging the market share of larger plants that operate at more efficient scale (Wheeler, 2000; Hettige, Dasgupta and Wheeler, 2000). This change often involves a shift toward publicly held firms at the expense of family firms. The improvement in efficiency means less pollution per unit of production, although larger plants may also concentrate pollution in a certain locality (Lucas, Dasgupta and Wheeler, 2001). In China, state-owned enterprises have much higher costs for reducing air pollution because they are operated less efficiently. Figure 3 displays recent econometric estimates of control costs for sulfur dioxide air pollution in large Chinese factories (Dasgupta, Wang and Wheeler, 1997).[1]

---

[1] Xu, Gau, Dockery and Chen (1994) have shown that atmospheric sulfur dioxide concentrations are highly correlated with damage from respiratory disease in China. Sulfur dioxide and other oxides of sulfur combine with oxygen to form sulfates and with water vapor to form aerosols of sulfurous and sulfuric acid. Much of the health damage from sulfur dioxide seems to come from fine particulates in the form of sulfates.

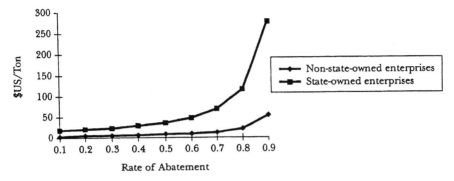

Figure 3 Sulfur Dioxide Marginal Abatement Costs: Large Chinese Factories

Source: World Bank (1999).

The level of polluting emissions also reflects managers' technology decisions. In the OECD countries, innovations have generated significantly cleaner technologies that are available at incremental cost to producers in developing countries. Even in weakly regulated economies, many firms have adopted these cleaner technologies because they are more profitable. Increased openness to trade also tends to lower the price of cleaner imported technologies, while increasing the competitive pressure to adopt them if they are also more efficient (Reppelin-Hill, 1999; Huq, Martin and Wheeler, 1993; Martin and Wheeler, 1992). Thus, firms in relatively open developing economies adopt cleaner technologies more quickly (Birdsall and Wheeler, 1993; Huq, Martin and Wheeler, 1993).

While liberalization can certainly improve environmental conditions, it is no panacea. The evidence suggests that in a rapidly growing economy, the effect of lower pollution per unit of output as a result of greater efficiency is generally overwhelmed by the rise in overall pollution as a result of rising output (Beghin, Roland-Holst and van der Mensbrugghe, 1997; Dessus and Bussolo, 1998; Lee and Roland-Holst, 1997). Thus, total pollution will grow unless environmental regulation is strengthened (Mani, Hettige and Wheeler, 2000).

Pervasive Informal Regulation

Low-income communities frequently penalize dangerous polluters, even when formal regulation is weak or absent. Abundant evidence from Asia and Latin America shows that neighboring communities can strongly influence factories' environmental performance (Pargal and Wheeler, 1996; Hettige, Huq, Pargal and Wheeler, 1996; Huq and Wheeler, 1992; Hartman, Huq and Wheeler, 1997). Where formal regulators are present, communities use the political process to influence the strictness of enforcement. Where regulators are absent or ineffective, nongovernmental organizations and community groups—including religious institutions, social organizations, citizens' movements, and politicians—pursue informal regulation. Although these pressures vary from region to region, the pattern everywhere is similar: Factories negotiate directly with local actors in response to threats of social, political or physical sanctions if they fail to compensate the community or to reduce emissions.

The response of factories can take many forms. Cribb (1990) cites the case of a cement factory in Jakarta that—without admitting liability for the dust it generates—"compensates local people with an ex gratia payment of Rp. 5000 and a tin of evaporated milk every month." Agarwal, Chopra and Sharma (1982) describe a situation where, confronted by community complaints, a paper mill in India installed pollution abatement equipment—and to compensate residents for remaining damage, the mill also constructed a Hindu temple. If all else fails, community action can also trigger physical removal of the problem. In Rio de Janeiro, a neighborhood association protest against a polluting tannery led managers to relocate it to the city's outskirts (Stotz, 1991). Mark Clifford (1990) has reported in the *Far Eastern Economic Review* that community action prevented the opening of a chemical complex in Korea until appropriate pollution control equipment was installed. Indeed, communities sometimes resort to extreme measures. Cribb (1990) has recounted an Indonesian incident "reported from Banjaran near Jakarta in 1980 when local farmers burned a government-owned chemical factory that had been polluting their irrigation channels."

Such examples are not limited to developing countries, of course. They also play an important role in the work of Coase (1960), who called traditional regulation into question by noting that pollution victims, as well as regulators, can take action if they perceive that the benefits outweigh the costs. Of course, the victims need information about pollution risks to take appropriate action. In most cases, such information can only be gathered by public authorities that have a legal mandate to collect it. We will return to this issue in our discussion of public disclosure as a new regulatory instrument in developing countries.

Pressure from Market Agents

Market agents can also play an important role in creating pressures for environmental protection. Bankers may refuse to extend credit because they are worried about environmental liability; consumers may avoid the products of firms that are known to be heavy polluters.

The evidence suggests that multinational firms are important players in this context. These firms operate under close scrutiny from consumers and environmental organizations in the high-income economies. Investors also appear to play an important role in encouraging clean production. Heavy emissions may signal to investors that a firm's production techniques are inefficient. Investors also weigh potential financial losses from regulatory penalties and liability settlements. The U.S. and Canadian stock markets react significantly to environmental news, generating gains from good news and losses from bad news in the range of 1–2 percent (Muoghalu, Robison and Glascock, 1990; Lanoie and Laplante, 1994; Klassen and McLaughlin, 1996; Hamilton, 1995; Lanoie, Laplante and Roy, 1998). One recent study found that firms whose bad environmental press has the greatest impact on stock prices subsequently reduce emissions the most (Konar and Cohen, 1997). Similar effects of environmental news on stock prices have been identified in Argentina, Chile, Mexico and the Philippines (Dasgupta, Laplante and Mamingi, 2001). In fact, the market responses in these countries are much larger than those reported for U.S. and Canadian firms: Stock price gains average 20 percent in response to good news and losses range from 4–15 percent in the wake of bad news.

Multinationals have responded to such factors. A recent study of 89 U.S.-based manufacturing and mining multinationals with branches in developing countries found that nearly 60 percent adhere to a stringent internal standard that reflects OECD norms, while the others enforce local standards (Dowell, Hart and Yeung, 2000). Controlling for other factors such as physical assets and capital structure, the study found that firms with uniform internal standards had an average market value $10.4 billion higher than their counterparts. Indeed, multinational firms operating in low-income economies are often environmentally friendlier than domestically owned firms. For example, a careful audit of Indonesian factories undertaken in 1995 found that almost 70 percent of domestic plants failed to comply with Indonesian water pollution regulations, while around 80 percent of the multinational plants were fully compliant (Afsah and Vincent, 1997).

Better Methods of Environmental Regulation

Poor countries with weak regulatory institutions can reduce pollution significantly by following a few basic principles. The first is focus. In many areas, relatively few sources are responsible for most of the pollution (Hettige, Martin, Singh and Wheeler, 1995; World Bank, 1999). Therefore, emissions can be significantly reduced by targeting regulatory monitoring and enforcement on those dominant sources.

Notable inroads against pollution have also been made where environmental agencies in developing countries have begun moving away from traditional command-and-control policies toward market-oriented forms of regulation. Pollution charges have proven feasible in developing countries, with successful implementation in China (Wang and Wheeler, 1996), Colombia, Malaysia and Philippines (World Bank, 1999). In Colombia, for example, the recent implementation of water pollution charges in the Rio Negro Basin reduced organic discharges from factories by 52 percent during the program's first year of operation. No participating factory seems to have experienced financial difficulties in the process (World Bank, 1999). A pollution charge program in the Laguna Bay region of Philippines reduced organic pollution by 88 percent during its first two years of operation (World Bank, 1999). Similar conclusions have emerged from studies of regulation and control costs in Malaysia (Jha, Markandya and Vossenaar, 1999; Khalid and Braden, 1993).

Better Information

Until recently, relatively little was known about the economic damage associated with pollution in developing countries. During the past few years, however, economic analyses have repeatedly shown that large cities in developing countries suffer very high costs from pollution, even when damage is evaluated at conservative estimates of local opportunity costs (Dasgupta, Wang and Wheeler, 1997; Von Amsberg, 1997; Calkins, 1994). Such evidence has induced rapid strengthening of pollution control in the large cities of China, Brazil, Mexico and other developing countries.

This improved information combines with pressures from citizens, government, nongovernmental organizations and market agents to create pressures for rapid enactment of stricter environmental regulations. Strong results have also been obtained by programs that provide accessible public information about polluters, pollution damages, local environmental quality and the cost of pollution abatement. Such programs significantly improve the ability of local communities to protect themselves, the ability of national regulators to enforce decent environmental standards, and the ability of market agents to reward clean firms and punish heavy polluters.

International institutions such as the World Bank have begun supporting this idea in collaborative programs with environmental agencies in Indonesia, Philippines, China, India, Thailand, Vietnam, Mexico, Colombia, Brazil and elsewhere.[2] In Indonesia and Philippines, pilot public disclosure programs have reduced emissions from hundreds of large water polluters by 40–50 percent during a two-year period (Afsah and Vincent, 1997; World Bank, 1999). After the success of a pilot public disclosure program in two Chinese cities, the approach is now being extended to an entire province, Jiangsu, with a population of approximately 100 million.

Cautionary Notes

In light of recent research and policy experience, the most plausible long-run forecast is for rising, not falling, environmental quality in both high- and low-income economies. Indeed, it is likely that the environmental Kuznets curve has begun to flatten downward under the combined impact of economic liberalization, improved information, and more stringent and

---

[2]For more information about these programs, see the World Bank's "New Ideas in Pollution Regulation" website at (http://www.worldbank.org/nipr).

cost-effective approaches to regulating pollution under developing-country conditions. But although we are sanguine about the prospects for combining economic growth and environmental protection, we remain cautious optimists. At least four plausible concerns have been raised.

Will Countries Need to Suffer Lower Environmental Quality in the Short and Medium Run?

The conventional environmental Kuznets curve implies that vast areas of the world—including much of Asia and Africa—will have to experience rising pollution levels until their per capita incomes rise significantly. However, there is no evidence to support the view that this would be economically advantageous. Several benefit-cost analyses have made a persuasive case for stricter pollution control, even in very low income economies. In China, for example, a recent study has shown that the economic returns to pollution abatement would justify significant tightening of regulation (Dasgupta, Wang and Wheeler, 1997). Studies in Indonesia (Calkins, 1994) and Brazil (Von Amsberg, 1997) have produced similar conclusions.

Countries whose economic policies induce a rapid expansion of income and employment may experience severe environmental damage unless appropriate environmental regulations are enacted and enforced. Economic analysis can be employed to justify environmental regulatory policies that result in a flatter and lower environmental Kuznets curve.

Globalization and the Risk of a Race to the Bottom

Perhaps the most commonly heard critique of the environmental Kuznets curve is that even if such a relationship existed in the past, it is unlikely to exist in the future because of the pressures that global competition places on environmental regulations. In the "race to the bottom" scenario, relatively high environmental standards in high-income economies impose high costs on polluters. Shareholders then drive firms to relocate to low-income countries, whose people are so eager for jobs and income that their environmental regulations are weak or nonexistent. Rising capital outflows force governments in high-income countries to begin relaxing environmental standards. As the ensuing race to the bottom accelerates, the environmental Kuznets curve flattens and rises toward the highest existing level of pollution.

In the United States, political opponents of the World Trade Organization (WTO) frequently invoke elements of this model. For example, Congressman David Bonior (1999) offered the following critique: "The WTO, as currently structured, threatens to undo internationally everything we have achieved nationally—every environmental protection, every consumer safeguard, every labor victory." Herman Daly (2000), an economist at the University of Maryland's School of Public Affairs, has recently provided a forceful statement of the race to the bottom model.

Proponents of this model often recommend high environmental standards that would be uniform around the world. For countries that are unwilling or unable to enforce such standards, tariffs or other restrictions and penalties would be imposed on exports of their pollution-intensive products to neutralize their cost advantage as "pollution havens." Proponents of free trade naturally view these prescriptions as anathema, arguing that their main impact would be denial of jobs and income to the world's poorest people.

The race to the bottom model has an air of plausibility. It does appear that polluting activities in high-income economies face higher regulatory costs than their counterparts in developing countries (Jaffe, Peterson, Portney and Stavins, 1995; Mani and Wheeler, 1998). This creates an incentive for at least some highly polluting industries to relocate. But how substantial is this incentive compared to the other location incentives faced by businesses? To what extent have countries actually been reducing their environmental standards to provide such location incentives?

Research in both high- and low-income countries suggests that pollution control does not impose high costs on business firms. Jaffe, Peterson, Portney and Stavins (1995) and others have shown that compliance costs for OECD industries are surprisingly small, despite the use of command-and-control regulations that are economically inefficient. Firms in developing countries frequently have even lower abatement costs, because the labor and materials used for pollution control are less costly than in the OECD economies.

Numerous studies have suggested that, in comparison with other factors considered by businesses, pollution-control costs are not major determinants of relocation (Eskeland and Harrison, 1997; Albrecht, 1998; Levinson, 1997; Van Beers and van den Bergh, 1997; Tobey, 1990; Janicke, Binder and Monch, 1997). More important factors include distance to market and infrastructure quality and cost (Mody and Wheeler, 1992). In a study of Mexican *maquiladora* plants, Grossman and Krueger (1993) found that pollution abatement costs were not a major determinant of imports from Mexico, while their unskilled labor component was of paramount importance. Most OECD-based multinationals maintain nearly uniform environmental standards in their national and international plants. They do so to realize economies in engineering standards for design, equipment purchases and maintenance; to reduce potential liability from regulatory action; and to guard against reputational damage in local and international markets (Dowell, Hart and Yeung, 2000).

In fairness, the evidence also suggests that pollution havens can emerge in extreme cases (Xing and Kolstad, 1995). During the 1970s, for example, environmental regulation tightened dramatically in the OECD economies with no countervailing change in developing countries. The regulatory cost differential was apparently sufficient to generate a significant surge in production and exports of pollution-intensive products from developing countries. Since then, however, regulatory changes in the developing countries have narrowed the gap and apparently stopped the net migration of polluting industries (Mani and Wheeler, 1998). This pattern of tighter environmental regulations in low-income countries runs counter to the "race to the bottom" scenario.

Indeed, the scenario in which more heavily polluting industries locate in low-income countries and export back to high-income countries appears to be an incorrect description of actual patterns. In recent times, developing country imports from high-income economies have been more pollution-intensive than their exports to those economies (Mani and Wheeler, 1998; Albrecht, 1998).

In short, there are many reasons to be dubious about the race to the bottom model. But perhaps the most powerful challenge to the model is a direct assessment of its simple and robust prediction: After decades of increasing capital mobility and economic liberalization, the race to the bottom should already be underway and pollution should be increasing everywhere. It should be rising in poor countries because they are pollution havens, and in high-income economies because they are relaxing standards to remain cost-competitive. Wheeler (2001) has tested these propositions using data on foreign investment and urban air quality in China, Mexico and Brazil. Together, these three countries received 60 percent of the total foreign direct investment for developing countries in 1998. If the race to the bottom model is correct, then air pollution should be rising in all three countries. Moreover, air quality should be deteriorating in U.S. cities, since U.S. industrial imports from all three countries have been expanding for decades.

As Figures 4 and 5 indicate, the converse is true: Instead of racing toward the bottom, major urban areas in China, Brazil, Mexico and the United States have all experienced significant improvements in air quality, as measured by concentrations of fine particulate matter (PM-10) or suspended particulate matter (SPM). Further research is necessary before any definitive conclusions can be drawn, because similar comparisons are currently unavailable for other pollutants. At present, however, the available evidence strongly suggests that the pessimism of the race to the bottom model is unwarranted.

Are Other Pollutants Rising? The Case of Toxic Chemicals

Even if one accepts the evidence that growth in per capita income can be accompanied by reductions in well-known conventional pollutants, there is still a question about whether other less-known pollutants and environmental hazards may be rising with levels of per capita income.

One recent focus has been on emissions of toxic organic chemicals into the air and water. Although some toxic chemicals are monitored in some industrialized countries, they remain largely unregulated almost everywhere. Thornton (2000) argues that conventional regulation has failed to control the proliferation of organic chlorine compounds that are carcinogenic and mutagenic. He recommends banning the whole family of chlorine compounds,

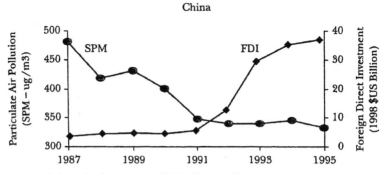

Notes: SPM is suspended particulate matter. FDI is foreign direct investment.

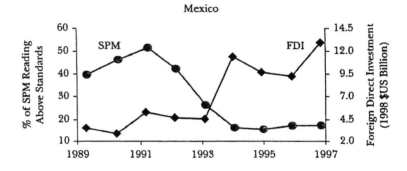

Notes: SPM is suspended particulate matter. FDI is foreign direct investment.

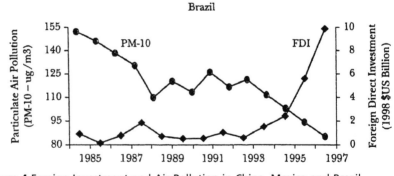

Figure 4 Foreign Investment and Air Pollution in China, Mexico and Brazil

Source: Wheeler (2001).

which would be economically disruptive, to put it mildly. The international community has begun responding to such thinking for some "persistent" organic pollutants that are among the organochlorines known to be most

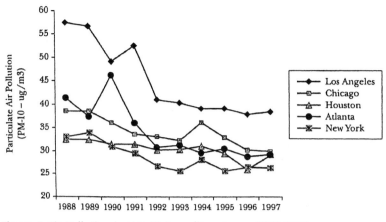

Figure 5 Air Pollution in U.S. Metropolitan Areas, 1988–1997

Source: Wheeler (2001).

dangerous, because they accumulate in plant and animal life. In May 2001, 127 countries signed a treaty to ban international production and trade in twelve persistent organic pollutants, including PCBs, dioxins, DDT and other pesticides that have been shown to contribute to birth defects and cancer ("U.N. Treaty on Chemicals," 2001).

Such concerns raise the possibility that economic development will always be accompanied by environmental risks that are either newly discovered or generated by the use of new materials and technologies. If this proves to be the case, the recent treaty banning production and sale of persistent organic pollutants may be a harbinger of broader regulatory changes that will affect both developed and developing countries.

This issue provides a useful reminder that our understanding of environmental problems and remedies must develop over time. It seems unlikely that addressing pollution from organochlorines and other toxics will require measures as radical as those suggested by Thornton (2000). However, it will clearly be inappropriate to declare conventional environmental protection a success if it reduces a limited list of conventional pollutants while ignoring an ever-growing list of toxic pollutants that may pose threats to future generations as well as this one.

Building Regulatory Capability

If per capita income and environmental quality are to increase together, developing countries will require effective regulatory capabilities. These capabilities include not only appropriate legal measures for regulation, but also effective monitoring and enforcement of regulatory compliance. Better environmental governance, broadly understood, involves the enactment of liberalizing economic measures that affect pollution through their impact on an economy's sectoral composition and efficiency. It also includes the capability to develop and disseminate information about environmental quality and pollution sources, even if such information may embarrass certain government officials in the short run. Much of the pessimism about the prospects for environmental quality in developing countries is not about whether a win-win outcome is technically possible for the economy and the environment, but whether these societies have the institutional capabilities necessary for achieving such an outcome.

The evidence on how regulatory capability can be developed is sparse, but the World Bank's indicators of institutional and policy development provide grounds for moderate optimism. It appears that productive public policy is correlated with economic development—but that there is considerable variation in the relationship. Some excellent economic performers have quite poor regulatory capability by international standards. In turn, general policy indicators predict environmental policy performance very well, but some countries with low overall policy ratings have proven capable of focused efforts to protect critical environmental assets. The most pronounced outliers are mostly countries where specific natural resources are important determinants of tourist revenue, such as Maldives, Seychelles, Belize, Ecuador and Bhutan. Apparently, even poorly administered societies can strengthen regulation when environmental damage is clear, costly, and concentrated in a few sites. But these exceptions aside, it seems unlikely that broader environmental regulation will outpace more general institutional reform. A full response to the environmental challenge of globalization will therefore require serious attention to long-run development of public sector administrative and decision-making capacity.

Sustaining effective environmental regulation will also require the design of appropriate financing mechanisms, some of which may depart from theoretically optimal measures under the conditions that prevail in developing countries. For example, Colombia's successful pollution charge program became politically feasible only after regulators, industrialists, and public sewerage authorities agreed to use part of the revenues to support local regulatory agencies and to invest the rest in local environmental projects. Although traditional public finance theory does not support earmarking revenues in this way, rather than balancing costs and benefits of all spending choices, the program's results have clearly compensated for this conceptual flaw. Local financing may also prove to be critical during future recessions, when Colombia's central government may reduce support for national monitoring and enforcement of regulations. However, accepting political reality does not imply uncritical acceptance of any funding scheme. The designers of Colombia's system have stressed the application of clear benefit-cost criteria to local financing of pollution reduction projects.

International Assistance

We believe that the international community can play a valuable role in lowering and flattening the environmental Kuznets curve by financing appropriate training, policy reforms, information gathering and public environmental education. In our view, a steadily accumulating body of research and program experience suggests two keys to rapid progress on this front. The first is support for programs that provide public, easily accessible information about polluters, pollution damages, local environmental quality and the cost of pollution abatement. The second is support for development of stronger regulatory institutions and cost-effective measures to reduce pollution. Sustained support is critical, because institutional development takes time.

We also believe that trade and aid sanctions are inappropriate and ineffective levers for narrowing the regulatory gap between low- and high-income countries. Such sanctions are unjust because they penalize both poor workers and the many firms in developing countries that have excellent environmental performance despite weak regulation (Huq and Wheeler, 1992; Hartman, Huq and Wheeler, 1997; Afsah and Vincent, 1997; World Bank, 1999). In any case, weak regulatory institutions would prevent governments of low-income countries from delivering on promises of OECD-level regulation, even if they were willing to make them. A similar caveat applies to multilateral institutions such as the World Bank, whose operating rules now mandate accounting for environmental risks in economic reform programs. While it is important to avoid serious pollution damage during rapid liberalization, it is also critical to support carefully targeted pollution control programs whose long-run resource requirements are feasible for the recipient countries.

References

Afsah, S. and J. Vincent. 1997. "Putting Pressure on Polluters: Indonesia's PROPER Program." Case study for the HIID 1997 Asia Environmental Economics Policy Seminar. Harvard Institute for International Development, March.

Agarwal, A., R. Chopra and K. Sharma. 1982. *The State of India's Environment 1982*. New Delhi, India: Centre for Science and Environment.

Albrecht, J. 1998. "Environmental Policy and Inward Investment Position of U.S. Dirty Industries." *Intereconomics*. July/August, pp. 186–94.

Beghin, J., D. Roland-Holst and D. van der Mensbrugghe. 1997. "Trade and Environment Linkages: Piecemeal Reform and Optimal Intervention." *Canadian Journal of Economics*. 30:2, pp. 442–55.

Birdsall, N. and D. Wheeler. 1993. "Trade Policy and Industrial Pollution in Latin America: Where are the Pollution Havens?" *Journal of Environment and Development*. Winter, 2:1, pp. 137–49.

Bolt, K., K. Hamilton, K. Pandey and D. Wheeler. 2001. "The Cost of Air Pollution in Developing Countries: New Estimates for Urban Areas." World Bank Development Research Group Working Paper, forthcoming.

Bonior, D. 1999. "Defending Democracy in the New Global Economy." Statement to an AFL-CIO conference on workers' rights, trade development, and the WTO. Seattle, Washington, December.

Calkins, R. 1994. *Indonesia: Environment and Development*. Washington: World Bank.

CETESB. 1986. "Restoring the Serra do Mar." São Paulo: Companhia de Tecnologia de Saneamento Ambiental (CETESB).

CETESB. 1990. "Cubatão: A Change of Air." São Paulo: Companhia de Tecnologia de Saneamento Ambiental (CETESB).

CETESB. 1994. "Acao da CETESB em Cubatão: Situacao em Junho de 1994." São Paulo: Companhia de Tecnologia de Saneamento Ambiental (CETESB).

Clifford, M. 1990. "Kicking up a Stink: South Korean Government Reels from Anti-Pollution Backlash." *Far Eastern Economic Review*. October 18, pp. 72–3.

Coase, R. 1960. "The Problem of Social Cost." *Journal of Law and Economics*. October, 3, pp. 1–44.

Cribb, R. 1990. "The Politics of Pollution Control in Indonesia." *Asian Survey*. 30, pp. 1123–35.

Daly, H. 2000. "Globalization." Presented at the 50th Anniversary Conference of the Aspen Institute. Aspen, Colorado, August.

Dasgupta, S., B. Laplante and N. Mamingi. 2001. "Capital Market Responses to Environmental Performance in Developing Countries." *Journal of Environmental Economics and Management*. Forthcoming.

Dasgupta, S., B. Laplante and C. Meisner. 2001. "Accounting for Toxicity Risks in Pollution Control: Does It Matter?" *Journal of Environmental Management*. Forthcoming.

Dasgupta, S., A. Mody, S. Roy and D. Wheeler. 2001. "Environmental Regulation and Development: A Cross-Country Empirical Analysis." *Oxford Development Studies*. June, 29:2, pp. 173–87.

Dasgupta, S., H. Wang and D. Wheeler. 1997. "Surviving Success: Policy Reform and the Future of Industrial Pollution in China." World Bank Policy Research Department Working Paper No. 1856, October.

Dasgupta, S. and D. Wheeler. 1997. "Citizen Complaints as Environmental Indicators: Evidence from China." World Bank, Policy Research Department Working Paper No. 1704, January.

De Bruyn, S. M. 1997. "Explaining the Environmental Kuznets Curve: Structural Change and International Agreements in Reducing Sulphur Emissions." *Environment and Development Economics*. 2:4, pp. 485–503.

De Bruyn, S. M., J. C. J. M. van den Bergh and J. B. Opschoor. 1998. "Economic Growth and Emissions: Reconsidering the Empirical Basis of Environmental Kuznets Curves." *Ecological Economics*. 25:2, pp. 161–75.

Dean, J. M. 1999. "Testing the Impact of Trade Liberalization on the Environment: Theory and Evidence," in *Trade, Global Policy and the Environment*. P. Fredriksson, ed. Washington, D.C.: World Bank, pp. 55–63.

Dessus, S. and M. Bussolo. 1998. "Is There a Trade-off Between Trade Liberalization and Pollution Abatement? A Computable General Equilibrium Assessment Applied to Costa Rica." *Journal of Policy Modeling*. 20:1, pp. 11–31.

Dowell, G., S. Hart and B. Yeung. 2000. "Do Corporate Global Environmental Standards Create or Destroy Market Value?" *Management Science*. August, 46:8, pp. 1059–74.

Easterly, W. 2001. "The Lost Decades: Developing Countries' Stagnation in Spite of Policy Reform 1980–1998." *Journal of Economic Growth*. June, 6:2, pp. 135–57. Available in draft online at (http://www.worldbank.org/research/growth/padate.htm).

Eskeland, G. and A. Harrison. 1997. "Moving to Greener Pastures? Multinationals and the Pollution-Haven Hypothesis." World Bank Policy Research Department Working Paper No. 1744.

Grossman, G. and A. Krueger. 1993. "Environmental Impacts of the North American Free Trade Agreement," in *The U.S.-Mexico Free Trade Agreement*. P. Garber, ed. Cambridge: MIT Press, pp. 13–56.

Hamilton, J. 1995. "Pollution as News: Media and Stock Market Reactions to the Toxic Release Inventory Data." *Journal of Environmental Economics and Management*. 28:1, pp. 98–113.

Hartman, R., M. Huq and D. Wheeler. 1997. "Why Paper Mills Clean Up: Determinants of Pollution Abatement in Four Asian Countries." World Bank, Policy Research Department Working Paper No. 1710.

Hettige, H., M. Huq, S. Pargal and D. Wheeler. 1996. "Determinants of Pollution Abatement in Developing Countries: Evidence from South and Southeast Asia.: *World Development*. 24:12, pp. 1891–904.

Hettige, M. and D. Wheeler. 1996. "An Environmental Performance Analysis System for Industrial Plants in Mexico." Development Research Group, World Bank, Washington, D.C., mimeo.

Hettige, H., P. Martin, M. Singh and D. Wheeler. 1995. "IPPS: The Industrial Pollution Projection System." World Bank, Policy Research Department Working Paper No. 1431.

Hettige, M., S. Dasgupta and D. Wheeler. 2000. "What Improves Environmental Compliance? Evidence from Mexican Industry." *Journal of Environmental Economics and Management*. 39:1, pp. 39–66.

Huq, M., P. Martin and D. Wheeler. 1993. "Process Change, Economic Policy, and Industrial Pollution: Cross Country Evidence from the Wood Pulp and Steel Industries." Presented at the Annual Meetings, American Economic Association, Anaheim, California, January.

Huq, M. and D. Wheeler. 1992. "Pollution Reduction Without Formal Regulation: Evidence from Bangladesh." World Bank Environment Department Working Paper No. 1993-39.

Jaffe, A., S. Peterson, P. Portney, and R. Stavins. 1995. "Environmental Regulation and the Competitiveness of U.S. Manufacturing: What Does the Evidence Tell Us?" *Journal of Economic Literature*. 33:1, pp. 132–63.

Janicke, M., M. Binder and H. Monch. 1997. " 'Dirty Industries': Patterns of Change in Industrial Countries." *Environmental and Resource Economics*. 9:4, pp. 467–91.

Jha, V., A. Markandya and R. Vossenaar. 1999. *Reconciling Trade and the Environment: Lessons from Case Studies in Developing Countries*. Northampton, Mass.: Edward Elgar Publishing Co.

John, A. and R. Pecchenino. 1994. "An Overlapping Generations Model of Growth and the Environment." *Economic Journal*. November, 104, pp. 1393–410.

John, A., R. Pecchenino, D. Schimmelpfennig and S. Schreft. 1995. "Short-Lived Agents and the Long-Lived Environment." *Journal of Public Economics*. 58:1, pp. 127–41.

Khalid, R. and J. B. Braden. 1993. "Welfare Effects of Environmental Regulation in an Open Economy: The Case of Malaysian Palm Oil." *Journal of Agricultural Economics*. January, 44, pp. 25–37.

Klassen, R. D. and C. P. McLaughlin. 1996. "The Impact of Environmental Management on Firm Performance." *Management Science*. 42:8, pp. 1199–214.

Konar, S. and M. Cohen. 1997. "Information as Regulation: The Effect of Community Right to Know Laws on Toxic Emissions." *Journal of Environmental Economics and Management*. January, 32, pp. 109–24.

Lanoie, P. and B. Laplante. 1994. "The Market Response to Environmental Incidents in Canada: A Theoretical and Empirical Analysis." *Southern Economic Journal*. 60, pp. 657–72.

Lanoie, P., B. Laplante and M. Roy. 1998. "Can Capital Markets Create Incentives for Pollution Control?" *Ecological Economics*. July, 26, pp. 31–41.

Laplante, B. and K. Smits. 1998. "Estimating Industrial Pollution in Latvia." ECSSD Rural Development and Environment Sector, Working Paper 4, The World Bank, Washington, D.C., mimeo.

Lee, H. and D. Roland-Holst. 1997. "The Environment and Welfare Implications of Trade and Tax Policy." *Journal of Development Economics*. February, 52, pp. 65–82.

Levinson, A. 1997. "Environmental Regulations and Industry Location: International and Domestic Evidence," in *Fair Trade and Harmonization: Prerequisites for Free Trade?* J. N. Bhagwati and R. E. Hudec, eds. Cambridge: MIT Press, pp. 429–58.

López, R. 1994. "The Environment as a Factor of Production: The Effects of Economic Growth and Trade Liberalization." *Journal of Environmental Economics and Management*. 27:2, pp. 163–84.

López, R. and S. Mitra. 2000. "Corruption, Pollution, and the Kuznets Environment Curve." *Journal of Environmental Economics and Management*. 40:2, pp. 137–50.

Lucas, R., H. Hettige and D. Wheeler. 1992. "The Toxic Intensity of Industrial Production: Global Patterns, Trends, and Trade Policy." *American Economic Review Papers and Proceedings*. May, 82:2, p. 478–81.

Lucas, R., S. Dasgupta and D. Wheeler. 2001. "Plant Size, Industrial Air Pollution and Local Incomes: Evidence from Brazil and Mexico." *Environment and Development Economics*. Forthcoming.

Mani, M. S. and D. Wheeler. 1998. "In Search of Pollution Havens? Dirty Industry in the World Economy, 1960–1995." *Journal of Environment and Development*. September, 7:3, pp. 215–47.

Mani, M., H. Hettige and D. Wheeler. 2000. "Industrial Pollution in Economic Development: The Environmental Kuznets Curve Revisited." *Journal of Development Economics*. 2:2, pp. 445–76.

Marland, G., T. Boden and R. Andres. 2001. "Global, Regional, and National Fossil Fuel CO2 Emissions." Carbon Dioxide Information Analysis Center, Oak Ridge National Laboratory, U.S. Department of Energy, Oak Ridge, Tennessee (available online at <http://cdiac.esd.ornl.gov/trends/emis/meth_reg.htm>).

Martin, P. and D. Wheeler. 1992. "Prices, Policies, and the International Diffusion of Clean Technology: The Case of Wood Pulp Production," in *International Trade and the Environment*. Patrick Low, ed. Washington, D.C.: World Bank, pp. 197–224.

McConnell, K. E. 1997. "Income and the Demand for Environmental Quality." *Environment and Development Economics*. 2:4, pp. 383–99.

Mody, A. and D. Wheeler. 1992. "International Investment Location Decisions: The Case of U.S. Firms.: *Journal of International Economics*. 3, pp. 57–76.

Muoghalu, M., D. Robison and J. Glascock. 1990. "Hazardous Waste Lawsuits, Stockholder Returns, and Deterrence." *Southern Economic Journal*. October, 57, pp. 357–70.

Panayotou, T. 1997. "Demystifying the Environmental Kuznets Curve: Turning a Black Box into a Policy Tool." *Environment and Development Economics*. 2:4, pp. 465–84.

Pargal, S. and D. Wheeler. 1996. "Informal Regulation of Industrial Pollution in Developing Countries: Evidence from Indonesia." *Journal of Political Economy*. 104:6, pp. 1314–27.

Reppelin-Hill, V. 1999. "Trade and Environment: An Empirical Analysis of the Technology Effect in the Steel Industry." *Journal of Environmental Economics and Management*. 38:3, pp. 283–301.

Samet, J., F. Dominici, F. Curriero, I. Coursac and S. Zeger. 2000. "Fine Particulate Air Pollution and Mortality in 20 U.S. Cities, 1987–1994." *New England Journal of Medicine*. 343:24, pp. 1742–49.

Selden, T. and D. Song. 1994. "Environmental Quality and Development: Is There a Kuznets Curve for Air Pollution Emissions?" *Journal of Environmental Economics and Management*. 27:2, pp. 147–62.

Selden, T. and D. Song. 1995. "Neoclassical Growth, the J Curve for Abatement, and the Inverted U Curve for Pollution." *Journal of Environmental Economics and Management*. 29:2, pp. 162–68.

Stern, D. I. 1998. "Progress on the Environmental Kuznets Curve?" *Environment and Development Economics*. 3:2, pp. 175–98.

Stern, D. I., A. Auld, M. S. Common and K. K. Sanyal. 1998. "Is There an Environmental Kuznets Curve for Sulfur?" Working Papers in Ecological Economics, 9804, Center for Resource and Environmental Studies, Australian National University, Canberra.

Stotz, E. 1991. "Luta Pela Saude Ambiental: A AMAP Contra Cortume Carioca, S.A., Una Experiencia Vitoriosa," V. V. Valla and E. N. Stotz, eds. Participacao Popular, Educacao e Saude, Rio de Janeiro, pp. 133–60.

Thornton, J. 2000. *Pandora's Poison: Chlorine, Health, and a New Environmental Strategy*. Cambridge: MIT Press.

Tobey, J. A. 1990. "The Effects of Domestic Environmental Policies on Patterns of World Trade: An Empirical Test." *Kyklos*. 43:2, pp. 191–209.

"U.N. Treaty On Chemicals Is Approved." 2001. *Washington Post*. May 23, Page A30.

Van Beers, C. and J. C. J. M. Van den Bergh. 1997. "An Empirical Multi-Country Analysis of the Impact of Environmental Regulations on Trade Flows." *Kyklos*. 50:1, pp. 29–46.

Von Amsberg, J. 1997. "Brazil: Managing Pollution Problems, The Brown Environmental Agenda." World Bank Report #16635-BR, June.

Vukina, T., J. C. Beghin and E. G. Solakoglu. 1999. "Transition to Markets and the Environment: Effects of the Change in the Composition of Manufacturing Output." *Environment and Development Economics*. 4:4, pp. 582–98.

Wang, H. and D. Wheeler. 1996. "Pricing Industrial Pollution in China: An Econometric Analysis of the Levy System." World Bank, Policy Research Department Working Paper No. 1644.

Wheeler, D. 1997. "Information in Pollution Management: The New Model," in "Brazil: Managing Pollution Problems, The Brown Environmental Agenda." World Bank Report.

Wheeler, D. 2000. "Racing to the Bottom? Foreign Investment and Air Pollution in Developing Countries." World Bank Development Research Group Working Paper No. 2524.

Wheeler, D. 2001. "Racing to the Bottom? Foreign Investment and Air Pollution in Developing Countries." *Journal of Environment and Development*. 10:3, pp. 225–45.

World Bank. 1999. *Greening Industry: New Roles for Communities, Markets and Governments*. New York: Oxford/World Bank.

World Bank. 2000. *World Development Indicators*. Washington, D.C.: World Bank.

Xing, Y. and C. Kolstad. 1995. "Do Lax Environmental Regulations Attract Foreign Investments?" University of California, Santa Barbara, Working Papers in Economics: 06/95, May.

Xu, X., J. Gao, D. Dockery and Y. Chen. 1994. "Air Pollution and Daily Mortality in Residential Areas of Beijing, China." *Archives of Environmental Health*. 49:4, pp. 216–22.

21 Creating Incentives for Cooperation: Strategic Choices

Scott Barrett

Scott Barrett is a professor of Environmental Economics and International Political Economy at Johns Hopkins University.

There is a world of difference between the provision of national public goods and transnational public goods. National public goods are mainly provided by the state. Indeed, part of the reason states exist is to supply public goods. The state is unique among institutions in having the authority to coerce—an authority usually needed if public goods are to be supplied efficiently. For example, a state's first priority is to protect its citizens, and national defense is a national public good. It is a public good because protection of one citizen does not diminish the protection afforded to others and because no citizen can be excluded from being protected. It is a national public good because it is supplied only to citizens of the state. International collective defense, such as that provided by the North Atlantic Treaty Organization, is a transnational public good. National defense is costly and is financed by taxes, not voluntary donations. Citizens are required to pay taxes; if they do not, they are sent to prison. Conscription may also be deemed necessary to national defense and is another example of the state's coercive power.

Why does the state coerce? It does so because if goods like national defense were financed entirely by voluntary contributions, not enough money would be made available and the goods would be underprovided. (If people can benefit without having to pay, why should they pay?) The provision of public goods thus requires getting the incentives right. The state typically solves this problem by means of its visible—and sometimes very heavy—hand.[1]

"Creating Incentives for International Cooperation: Strategic Choices," in I. Kaul, P. Conceição, K. Le Goulven, and R. U. Mendoza (eds.), *Providing Global Public Goods: Managing Globalization*, New York: Oxford University Press, 2002, pp. 308–328.

[1]The need for coercion is not always apparent. Ostrom (1990), for example, shows that community groups can often manage common property resources efficiently without direct interference by the state. Yet even in these cases, state coercion plays a role. First, effective management by the community depends on noncommunity members being excluded from using the resources. For common property resources, exclusion is often enforced by the state. For public goods, of course, exclusion is not possible. Second, the state must recognize the community's authority to govern its affairs. Third, community groups are almost always homogeneous assemblages. Nations exist because of the differences that divide people. Baland and Platteau (1996) argue that even such community-based mechanisms work best in conjunction with the visible hand of government.

The provision of transnational (regional and global) public goods also poses a challenge for incentives. The difference between national and transnational public goods lies in the institutional response. There is no world government with the authority to coerce states into supplying transnational public goods. Sovereignty safeguards the independence of individual states in this sphere as in others. A state can be pressured but not forced to contribute to the supply of a transnational public good. Provision of transnational public goods must be voluntary.

How can the incentive problem be resolved for transnational public goods, especially global public goods? Unilateralism can provide an alternative to world government—but only when a country's self-interest in a good is so strong that it will provide it regardless of whether others contribute. Another alternative is voluntary international cooperation achieved by restructuring incentives, typically through strategy. This chapter explains the considerations that matter when devising incentive-based cooperation strategies (see Barrett forthcoming for a more comprehensive treatment of this topic).

The chapter is divided into two main sections. The first examines different incentive structures that can underlie the provision of global public goods. The second shows how these structures could be manipulated to foster international cooperation and increase the provision of these goods. The concluding section summarizes the chapter's main messages.

Incentive Structures for the Provision of Global Public Goods

Not all public goods are alike (Sandler 1992, 1998, 2001, in this volume). Some global public goods have close substitutes in national public goods. In such cases national provision, or self-provision, can discourage international cooperation. Other global public goods yield countries such huge benefits relative to the costs of provision that they will supply them unilaterally.[2] Coordination of national policies can help provide some global public goods. For others, international cooperation—and enforcement—is needed. This section analyzes these different incentives for and approaches to provision—and shows that where incentives differ, the remedies for underprovision also differ.

Self-Provision and Cooperative Provision

The provision of national and transnational public goods is often interrelated. When a transnational public good is undersupplied, increased provision of a national public good may help compensate. But provision of a

---

[2]Olson (1965) calls such countries "privileged."

national public good can also undermine incentives to supply a transnational public good. That is, national and transnational public goods may be substitutes.

Consider efforts to control measles, a highly infectious disease that kills up to 1 million children a year in developing countries but that rarely infects (and almost never kills) children of privilege. Thanks to extensive childhood vaccination campaigns, measles is no longer endemic in industrial countries. A few cases occur in the United States every year, but these are imported. National elimination of the disease is a national public good. But it has implications for other countries. Once industrial countries have immunized their children against measles, they have fewer incentives to help control the disease abroad.

There may still be a collective benefit from global eradication, which would obviate the need for national vaccinations. But the risk that a disease will be reintroduced, accidentally or maliciously, means that countries should probably maintain surveillance programs and vaccine stockpiles—dulling incentives to invest in global eradication. The global eradication of smallpox remains perhaps the greatest achievement of international cooperation. But its success has been blighted by current worries about bioterrorist attack. Sadly, this is what makes smallpox eradication a bittersweet victory (Committee on the Assessment of Future Scientific Needs for Live Variola Virus 1999).

For countries that can afford national immunizations, helping to control a disease abroad may best be described as an act of charity.[3] Indeed, major donors to the Global Polio Eradication Initiative include Rotary International, the United Nations Foundation, and the Bill and Melinda Gates Foundation (see http://www.polioeradication.org/). These organizations are presumably investing in this initiative not just because they think the effort worthy, but also because they do not believe that governments will foot the entire bill. Given that the global public good of polio eradication is underprovided, the efforts of these institutions are to be welcomed. But at the same time, the involvement of these institutions is an indicator of underprovision by nation-states—an outcome not entirely to be cheered.

As it turns out, the measles problem is different in developing countries. In industrial countries children are exposed to measles when they are school-aged. In developing countries children are exposed much earlier. Newborns inherit from their mothers a natural immunity to measles. But this immunity wears off when babies are about 9 months old—making the timing of vaccination tricky. If the vaccine is given too early, it will not take effect, and the baby will be vulnerable when the inherited immunity wears off. If the vaccine is given too late, the baby may already have been exposed. Getting the timing right is hard enough for a single baby—and

---

[3]To the extent that the citizens of all countries care about the well-being of the citizens of other countries, assistance to reduce child mortality in developing countries may be a transnational public good.

even harder for an entire population. In developing countries vaccines are normally given to all children of a given age cohort (but not precisely the same age) on national immunization days—usually once or twice a year. This kind of program works well for some diseases but leaves too many children vulnerable to measles.

Obviously it would be desirable to have a vaccine that could be given early and that would "switch on" when the inherited immunity has worn off. But such a vaccine would mainly benefit children in developing countries, and has not yet been developed. Knowledge of how to make such a vaccine would be another transnational public good, and could dramatically increase the supply of the global public good of measles eradication.

Global climate change provides another example of how national protection diminishes the incentive to supply a transnational public good. Climate change mitigation is a global public good. But countries can reduce the damage from climate change by investing in adaptation—building sea walls (a local public good), changing the varieties of seeds planted (private goods), and so on. Having this option reduces national returns to mitigation efforts. As a result countries do not sufficiently reduce their greenhouse gas emissions (a global public bad); instead they spend too much on adaptation. This approach is inefficient and especially harmful to countries least able to adapt.

To sum up, when provision of a global public good is inadequate, countries have incentives to take defensive measures at home. This is to be welcomed given that global (cooperative) provision is inadequate. But the ability to take defensive measures at home also dulls the incentive to provide the global public good, and this outcome can be inefficient. In a sense some global public goods (including measles eradication) are underprovided because they are not public enough. This leaves the countries that are least able to act at home the most vulnerable.

Unilateral (Best Shot) Provision

Some global public goods, called best shot public goods, only need to be supplied by one country (see Sandler 1998 and in this volume). These goods will be supplied without the need for international cooperation as long as the national benefit of their provision exceeds the cost for the providing country. An example is the knowledge supplied by some government-funded research—leading, for example, to the development of safe, effective vaccines for diseases such as polio (Stiglitz 1999). Countries fund such research primarily to benefit their own citizens, but the knowledge acquired can be used around the world.

However, public goods do not always have to be supplied by the state. (Coercion is not essential to the supply of all public goods, even transnational public goods.) Edward Jenner, a British physician, discovered that vaccination with cowpox provided lasting immunity to smallpox. This discovery, one of the most important in the history of science, was made by an inquisitive doctor, apparently without state funding.

Basic research and development is an essential part of innovation and is typically provided by the state either directly (as with the research conducted by the U.S. National Institutes of Health) or indirectly (as with university research). But some research and development, as well as most product development, is usually left to the private sector. Thus the push of state-funded research is complemented by the pull of the market and the patent system.

The patent system has recently attracted much attention. As discussed by Correa (in this volume), AIDS-suppressing antiretroviral drugs are available worldwide. But the drugs are too expensive for millions of HIV-infected people in developing countries, and the companies that make the drugs have been pressured to lower their prices. The pressure is coming from different directions. It is coming from public protests in developing countries. It is coming from copycat producers, who can offer essentially the same drugs at much lower prices. And it is coming from countries threatening to force manufacturers to license their drug recipes on favorable terms to domestic producers or to allow parallel imports.

The marginal cost of making a drug is usually very low—perhaps pennies a pill. The high cost is in carrying out the research and testing needed to develop a drug and bring it to market. Static efficiency demands that drugs be sold at marginal cost, an outcome more or less guaranteed by competition. But if there is competition in drug manufacturing, research and development will be unprofitable. Dynamic efficiency demands that companies have the incentive to invest their capital, at considerable risk, in the development of new drugs. The patent system provides this incentive by essentially granting a monopoly on new drugs for the short to medium term. Thus it sacrifices static efficiency for dynamic efficiency.

Two problems can result. The first is that the drug is priced so that some people cannot afford it—a problem for intragenerational equity as well as static efficiency. The second is that if the patent system were not respected, pharmaceutical companies would have little incentive to develop new drugs—a problem for intergenerational equity as well as dynamic efficiency. Discussions in the media have focused almost exclusively on the first problem.

But the problem is actually more complicated. Monopolies maximize profits by selling goods to different people at different prices. Thus drug companies in industrial countries would probably like nothing better than to sell their drugs at low prices in developing countries. As long as a drug's price exceeds its marginal cost, its manufacturer would make money. The problem is that international arbitrage undercuts manufacturers' ability to do this. A secondary market may develop, with drugs sold cheaply in Africa being shipped back to a higher-price market. A related problem is that drug companies may have trouble defending their prices to bodies such as the U.S. Congress. It is not difficult to imagine a congressperson asking the chief executive officer of a pharmaceutical company why U.S. consumers are being charged so much more for a drug than foreign consumers.

Price discrimination is good for the consumers who pay the lowest price and bad for the consumers who pay the highest price. But such discrimination is often good for overall efficiency. Hence an insistence by industrial countries that drugs sell for the same price worldwide may impair efficiency. For the moment, stopgap measures are being taken to address these pricing problems, but in the future a fair, efficient international regime for drug pricing needs to be established.[4] (Even the United States arm-twisted the manufacturer of the antibiotic Cipro into lowering its price in the wake of the October 2001 anthrax attacks.)

Dependence on the Weakest Link

All disease eradication campaigns begin with the disease being eliminated from a certain area, such as the Western Hemisphere. As a campaign advances, the disease is eliminated from other regions and, finally, from particular countries. The disease will usually have a few last strongholds, such as countries being torn apart by civil war or very poor countries with inadequate public health and transportation infrastructure. The challenge is not how to eliminate the disease in the first few countries. The real challenge always lies in eliminating the disease in the last country. Almost by definition, this is where elimination is hardest to achieve. And this is where the eradication effort will succeed or fail. If the disease cannot be eliminated in the last country, it cannot be eradicated (globally) at all.

Now imagine a world where all countries are more or less alike. For each country the cost of eliminating the disease locally far exceeds the benefit—not least because, even if the disease is eliminated locally, vaccination efforts will have to continue indefinitely. But for all countries collectively the benefit of global eradication far exceeds the cost of local elimination. In that case, if every country believes that all others will eliminate the disease, each has an incentive to eliminate it at home. These are weakest link games, where the weakest link in the chain determines whether the chain will hold when put to the test (see Sandler 1992, 1998, and in this volume).

The problem just described may also be a coordination game (see Sandler 1992). In a coordination game each country wants to do what all other countries are doing. If all others are not eliminating the disease at home, then each will not eliminate the disease at home—because, by assumption, the cost of doing so will exceed the local benefit. But if all others are eliminating the disease at home, then each will eliminate the disease at home—because doing so will ensure that the disease is eliminated globally and (again, by assumption) the benefit of global elimination exceeds the cost of local elimination for each country.

---

[4]International spillovers complicate the pricing problem, however. To the extent that antiretrovirals suppress the transmission of HIV, their use in one country will benefit others. But misuse of such drugs may also hasten resistance, imposing a cost on other countries. What is needed is not just a policy for pricing and trade but an effective global infrastructure for public health.

Because they do not require enforcement, coordination problems are easier for the international system to deal with than cooperation problems (discussed in the next section). The assurance by others that a disease will be eliminated at home is sufficient to impel every country to eliminate the disease. To be sure, there is no guarantee that eradication will be sustained by the international system. But if countries recognize a problem together, there is a good chance they will succeed. What each country needs is an assurance that others will coordinate. Unfortunately, coordination will not always suffice. Eradication will sometimes require international enforcement, the focus of the discussion below (see also Barrett 2002).

Summation Public Goods

The final kind of public good is the hardest for the international system to supply. These are goods where the total supply is the sum of the amounts supplied by individual countries. An example is climate change mitigation. Climate change depends on the total greenhouse gases in the atmosphere, not the releases of individual countries. Each country has a unilateral incentive to supply only limited quantities of these kinds of public goods. But all countries would be better off if every country supplied more. These are prisoner's dilemma games (see Sandler 1998).

Countries have mixed motives in prisoner's dilemma games. Each would prefer that others supply the good. But each also recognizes that if everyone depended on others to supply the good, the result would be bad for everyone. Thus there is a collective advantage in collective provision. The challenge is enforcing an agreement for collective provision. Sovereignty means that countries do not have to become parties to such agreements. Supplying summation public goods requires restructuring incentives, the subject of the next section.

Strategies for Restructuring Incentives

The preceding analysis shows that a strategic approach is required to foster international cooperation in the provision of public goods. Different players may have different priorities for a certain global public good, and the properties of global public goods vary. For both reasons a remedy that works for one good may not work for another.

Threshold Effects

In many cases it may benefit a country to take action X only if enough other countries (or certain other countries) do the same; otherwise it may benefit every country to take action Y. That is, there may be threshold effects.

If such effects are strong enough, they may tip the balance from noncooperative to cooperative behavior (see Schelling 1978 and Gladwell 2000).

Such a situation may be especially likely where countries are interconnected. An example is the decision of which side of the road to drive on. In most countries people drive on the right. Countries that drive on the left usually do so because they are not interconnected with countries that drive on the right. In Britain and Australia (a former British colony) people drive on the left; in Canada (another former British colony) they drive on the right. Britain and Australia are islands; their roads are not interconnected with other countries. Canada, by contrast, shares a long border with a large neighbor (the United States) that drives on the right.

Whether to drive on the right or the left is a standard, and standards are public goods. (One person's use of a standard does not preclude others from using it, and no one can be excluded from using it.) Other examples include the location of a car's steering wheel (chosen according to whether the car is driven on the left or the right) and its bumper height (which should be similar for all cars because otherwise a collision would cause greater damage to both vehicles).

In networks every country has an incentive to adopt the same standards as others. That is, there is a tendency toward harmonization. An important example is the use of unleaded gasoline and catalytic converters in automobiles (Heal 1999). Catalytic converters can only reduce harmful emissions from vehicles fueled by unleaded gasoline. A country can require the use of unleaded gasoline at home, but if the residents of that country drive to neighboring countries that do not use unleaded gasoline, the catalytic converters will soon become damaged. Thus highly interconnected countries will want to adopt the same standards. This is a major reason for EU directives on the environment.

Importantly, however, catalytic converters are quickly becoming an international standard. This is happening for several reasons. One is interconnectedness—a consequence of globalization. Another is economies of scale. It is much cheaper for a manufacturer to produce cars fitted with catalytic converters for the home market if it is already producing such cars for export. A final reason is that catalytic converters will help reduce pollution emissions at home. Thus the local government may require that all new cars be fitted with catalytic converters.

So far, so good. But standards can also pose problems for efficiency. One is that the wrong standard may get chosen. And because of interconnectedness, a country will want to use the wrong standard if its neighbors do so. Another problem is that, once a standard has been adopted, it may be hard for a new standard to gain a foothold. A new international agreement on vehicle standards has been negotiated to deal with this last problem.[5]

---

[5]This is the 1998 Agreement Concerning the Establishing of Global Technical Regulations for Wheeled Vehicles, Equipment and Parts Which Can Be Fitted and/or Used on Wheeled Vehicles.

Reciprocity

A strategy of reciprocity is often of limited effectiveness in enforcing an agreement to cooperate. The main reason is that when a country is punished for not cooperating, the countries that impose the punishment hurt themselves in the bargain.

Consider the control of pollution at sea by oil tankers. Most people think that oil spills are accidents. But historically that has not been the case: most oil used to be released deliberately. After a tanker unloaded its cargo, it needed to take on ballast to make the return journey, and so filled its tanks with water. Yet before returning home to reload a cargo of oil, it emptied its ballast into the sea. Because the ballast water was held in the same tanks as the oil, oil-water mixtures were released.[6]

In the 1920s maritime nations began trying to negotiate a treaty that would limit oil pollution at sea. They failed, largely because they could not devise a means for enforcing an agreement (Mitchell 1994)—just the kind of result one would expect from a prisoner's dilemma situation. Realizing that they could all do better by cooperating, maritime nations met to negotiate an agreement. But being unable to enforce the agreement, it never entered into force.

However, the real problem here requires a more subtle analysis. As is well known, if a game is repeated, it may be possible for countries to prop up a degree of cooperation through a strategy of reciprocity. The countries could agree that, should any country fail to behave in the manner prescribed by the treaty, the others will reciprocate and release their oil at sea. But to implement this strategy it must be possible to observe the actions of all the players, and tanker skippers could unload their ballast when no one was looking. Another difficulty is that the threat to reciprocate may not be credible. After all, when other countries release their oil at sea, they harm not just the party they intend to punish, but also themselves.

This is the problem with using such strategies to promote the supply of transnational public goods. When relations are bilateral, reciprocity works fine. The multilateral trading rules of the World Trade Organization (WTO), for example, allow a country to retaliate in the event of a trade rule being broken by another WTO member. The act of trade (as distinguished from the multilateral trading rules) is a bilateral exchange. The country harmed by a rule violation experiences a national (private) cost and can similarly punish the violator without affecting third parties or the overall trade agreement.

For this reason it is natural to contemplate the trade weapon as a means of enforcing cooperative agreements. The International Commission for the Conservation of Atlantic Tunas (ICCAT; http://www.iccat.org) provides an example. Tunas are highly migratory. They also spend much of their lives

---

[6]By a similar means, biological specimens are transported around the world, sometimes leading to ecologically destabilizing invasions; see Elton's (2000) classic study.

beyond countries' exclusive economic zones. Open access fishing has depleted tuna populations and so reduced the value of the fishery.[7] ICCAT has tried to correct the overfishing but has run into two familiar problems. Some fishing nations have declined to join the agreement (a problem of nonparticipation), and some parties to the agreement have refused to comply with ICCAT rulings (a problem of noncompliance).

To address the second problem, ICCAT decided that tuna and swordfish imports from noncomplying countries should be banned by other ICCAT members. The advantage of this strategy is that it is credible; it really is in the interests of these nations to ban the imports (the ban is certainly popular with the member's fishermen). The disadvantage is that the import ban may not cause serious harm to the offending nations. Most countries are not ICCAT members, so a country that chooses to violate ICCAT rules can still serve a huge market. To change behavior, sanctions must be both credible and severe.

Participation and Compliance

ICCAT's problems notwithstanding, international agreements enjoy almost universal compliance. But does this mean, as Chayes and Chayes (1995) argue, that compliance is not a problem? Or does it mean, as Downs, Rocke, and Barsoom (1996) contend, that countries only negotiate and participate in treaties that they would comply with anyway?

The answer is not immediately obvious. But it is important to frame the problem correctly. Compliance cannot be divorced from participation; they are linked problems. But compliance and participation cannot be conflated; they are different problems. If the two problems are distinguished yet analyzed together, it turns out that compliance must be enforced but that participation is the binding constraint on cooperation (Barrett 1999c).

The reasoning is as follows. The problem with enforcement is that when cooperating countries punish noncooperating countries by cutting back on their provision of a public good, they harm themselves. The bigger the deviation that must be deterred, the larger must be the punishment—but larger punishments are the first to bump up against the credibility constraint. The biggest deviation that can credibly be contemplated is withdrawal from a treaty. Obviously this must be deterred. But once nonparticipation has been deterred, smaller acts of noncompliance will be easy to deter through the credible threat of smaller punishments. Hence once nonparticipation can be deterred, noncompliance can be deterred free of charge.

---

[7]International fisheries are common property resources and thus a type of impure public good—nonexcludable but rival in consumption. Conservation by each country benefits the others that share the resource. But the two problems are otherwise different. Consumption of a fish by one party depletes the resource, leaving one less fish for others. In both cases, however, there is an incentive to free ride, and this is the feature of the fisheries problem focused on here.

There is another way of looking at this issue. International law does not compel countries to belong to ICCAT. So, countries that belong to ICCAT but that are failing to comply can withdraw from the agreement. When they do so, they are free (more or less) to act as they please. But under current ICCAT rules they will be treated the same whether they withdraw or fail to comply (either way, they will be subject to the same trade restrictions). This probably explains why noncomplying countries have not withdrawn from this agreement. At the same time, ICCAT actions have done little to change behavior. They are likely to have an effect only on countries that trade extensively with other ICCAT members.

The Kyoto Protocol provides another illustration of the difficulty in enforcing international cooperation. The agreement negotiated in December 1997 left many details unsettled. At the conference of the parties held in The Hague in November 2000, a proposal was made for enforcing compliance with the treaty's main provisions. The proposal said that in the event that a country did not meet the emission targets that had been set for it in the first control period (2008–12), it would be required to reduce its emissions by an additional amount in the next control period. Not only would this country have to make up for its previous shortfall, but it would also have to reduce its emissions by an additional amount. (At the meetings held in Bonn in 2001, it was agreed that this amount should be 30 percent of the initial shortfall.) And if the country did not comply with this requirement, then in the third control period it would have to make up for the previous shortfalls and pay yet another penalty.

There are a number of problems with this approach, each on its own enough to weaken the agreement—and all taken as a group enough to undermine it entirely. First, the punishment for noncompliance is always deferred, and a punishment that is always deferred is never carried out. Second, countries that fail to meet their emission limits are expected to punish themselves. There is no mechanism in the current agreement that would punish a country for failing to punish itself for failing to comply. Third, the emission limits for future control periods have not been decided. They are thus endogenous to this process. A country that is having problems complying, whether for lack of trying or for more legitimate reasons, can therefore negotiate higher future emission ceilings, effectively relaxing the constraint of the compliance penalty. Fourth, the Kyoto Protocol already says that any binding compliance mechanisms cannot apply except by means of an amendment. An amendment is basically a new treaty. Hence not only would the compliance mechanisms proposed thus far not work, but they could not even be applied to the first control period. At best they could only be incorporated in a follow-on protocol, and thus apply only beginning with the second control period. Finally, and perhaps most important, the Kyoto Protocol does little to promote participation (Barrett 1999b). Thus a country worried about future compliance and enforcement can take the safe option of not ratifying the agreement.

Strategic Substitutes and Complements

In a (one shot) prisoner's dilemma game, every country wants to not supply the good regardless of what other countries do. This is in contrast to a coordination game, where each country's best strategy depends on what other countries do.

Other situations require different strategies. In some cases where one country provides a public good, others become more inclined to do so. In these cases provision is a strategic complement. Such positive feedback facilitates the supply of transnational public goods. If there is no threshold, formal cooperation may not even be needed (see Heal 1994).

But in other cases feedback may be negative. As one country supplies a public good, others may respond by supplying less. In these situations provision is a strategic substitute. A treaty may help, but it may not be able to sustain full cooperation (see Barrett 1994).

These kinds of interdependencies are common. Take the example of disease control. As the prevalence of a disease falls globally, the risk of infection to any one country falls. After one country controls a disease, others may relax their controls. Eradication, by contrast, has the opposite effect. As explained previously, the benefit to one country of eradicating a disease may increase (nonlinearly) with the number of others that eradicate it.

One way of facilitating cooperation is to change the rules of the game. In the cooperation games described above, cooperation entails direct provision of the public good, and punishment strategies are limited to reducing provision levels. But the International Convention for the Prevention of Pollution from Ships (the MARPOL agreement) suggests a different approach. As noted, direct attempts failed to reduce oil dumping at sea. So, in the early 1970s a different approach was tried. The MARPOL agreement requires oil tankers to have separate tanks for ballast water and oil. As a result monitoring at sea is no longer a problem; port inspections of hulls are sufficient (Mitchell 1994). Moreover, coastal countries—seeking to prevent harmful oil releases—have strong incentives to ban from their ports ships not fitted with separate ballast tanks. Finally, ship owners have an incentive to adopt this standard because otherwise they would be shut out of major ports. By focusing on the technical standard of separate ballast tanks, the oil dumping problem was transformed: the underlying prisoner's dilemma game was turned into a coordination game.

The shift to separate ballast tanks required an international agreement. If only one country had adopted the new tanker standard, it is unlikely that others would have followed—and deliberate oil releases at sea would hardly have been reduced. Only if enough countries adopted the new standard would there be a strong enough incentive for all countries to do so, and only in that case would oceans be protected. The strategic challenge for the MARPOL agreement was not just to negotiate standards rather than emission limits. It was also to ensure that the threshold for coordination would be crossed—or that the demand for separate ballast tanks would be tipped.

Trade Linkages and Leakages

As noted, there are strong reasons for linking the provision of a public good to international trade. In fact, nearly every successful incentive restructuring has exploited trade linkages. Participation in the MARPOL agreement, for example, is encouraged by a trade restriction. To enforce the agreement, ports merely need to ban entry by oil tankers that violate it. Enforcement is facilitated by the fact that the agreement is linked to bilateral relationships between the port state and the flag state.

The Montreal Protocol on Substances that Deplete the Ozone Layer, perhaps the most successful international treaty ever adopted, functions in a similar way. The treaty restricts trade in ozone-depleting substances and in products containing them. Once again, it works by transforming the game (Barrett 1999b).

Ozone protection is a summation public good and so vulnerable to the usual free rider incentives. Imagine now a situation in which some countries reduce their emissions of ozone-depleting substances. Comparative advantage in using or producing such substances may then shift to other countries—a phenomenon known as trade leakage. As a result of some countries reducing their emissions, other countries may increase theirs. In this case the linkage to trade actually weakens the incentive to supply the public good unilaterally.

But once the parties to the Montreal Protocol agreed to ban trade in ozone-depleting substances and products containing them, countries that failed to participate in the treaty would suffer a loss in trade. If only a few countries had participated, this loss might not have been enough to make participation attractive to others. But once enough countries signed the agreement, the loss became big enough to foster participation. Again, there was a tipping point or threshold to be crossed. Even if the sanction did not make free riders want to participate, it at least stopped the trade leakage.

Ironically, although the trade leakage undermined unilateral attempts to provide the public good, it helped multilateral efforts (Barrett 1999a). The underlying prisoner's dilemma was transformed into a coordination game. If enough countries supply the good, all countries want to supply it. But how did supporters of the treaty ensure that enough countries would supply the good? The answer is simple: the treaty merely had to state that it became binding on parties only if it was ratified by a certain number of countries (and in some cases by certain countries). Thus the minimum participation level served as a coordinating device (Barrett 1997).

Carrots and Sticks

Punishments are negative incentives. Can positive incentives work too? Positive incentives are needed when countries are asymmetric; they ensure that every country gains from an agreement. For example, when the parties to the North Pacific Fur Seal Treaty of 1911 struck a deal banning the hunting of seals at sea, the oceanic sealing nations—Canada and Japan—had to be compensated for agreeing to close their industries. The compensation came partly in cash and partly in shares of pelts from seals killed on land by Japan, Russia, and the United States (Mirovitskaya, Clark, and Purvey 1993).

Side payments are also made by the Montreal Protocol Fund. This agreement treats developing countries differently from industrial countries in two ways. First, in allowing more time before achieving the same ultimate goal of eliminating the production and consumption of ozone-destroying chemicals. Second, in compensating developing countries for the agreed incremental costs of compliance. Together these features give expression to the notion that industrial and developing countries have shared but distinct responsibilities.

It might seem that this formula should work more generally. But there is reason to think that the Montreal Protocol may be a special case (Barrett 1999b). Countries are strongly asymmetric in their responsibilities for the depletion of the ozone layer. When the protocol was written, developing countries were not important to ozone layer protection in the short run; they used little of the offending chemicals and produced even less. In the long run, however, these countries would be very important, partly because their consumption of chlorofluorocarbons (CFCs) was predicted to increase dramatically. Moreover, production might have shifted to these countries if the Montreal Protocol only restricted production in industrial countries (leakage). Thus industrial countries knew that they had to negotiate an agreement attracting close to full participation.

But while industrial countries very much wanted developing countries to participate, developing countries had few compelling reasons to do so. Many were not especially concerned about ozone depletion—because they had different priorities, because ozone depletion would be worse near the poles than near the equator, and because ozone depletion would affect fair-skinned people more than dark-skinned people.

This asymmetry meant that developing countries could credibly claim to prefer not to participate. The cooperation problem facing industrial countries was not so much how to agree to cut their emissions. Rather, the problem was to agree to supply the funds needed to pay developing countries to prevent their emissions from rising. This asymmetry ratcheted up the cooperation problem (Barrett 2001). Where asymmetries are less stark, this opportunity to expand cooperation will not exist. When one country pays another to participate, the gains from an agreement are redistributed. The country that is paid gains, but the country that pays loses.

Is the offer to pay incremental costs fair? It might not seem to be. Though determining incremental costs is as much art as science, the basic concept means that developing countries should be compensated for complying but given no surplus (in the form of cash payments or technology transfers) on top of that. This might seem to give the entire surplus to industrial countries. But there is a difference between the marginal and the total surplus. Because the offer to pay incremental costs is made to every developing country, each will gain a surplus in benefits from ozone protection. As noted, developing countries benefit less from ozone protection than do industrial countries—but they do benefit. Ozone depletion suppresses the immune system, causes cataracts, and reduces the productivity of agriculture and fisheries. The offer to pay incremental costs would have a nonmarginal effect on each developing country if it was accepted by all of them.

Informal Institutions

The state is the primary actor in international affairs. But it is not the only actor. Nor is it a monolith, as the discussion to this point has implicitly assumed.

The introduction to this chapter noted how the state uses its power to supply national public goods. Other sections have emphasized the importance of treaties in supplying transnational public goods. But states and treaties are formal means of supplying public goods, and their effectiveness significantly depends on informal mechanisms.

Perhaps the best illustration is the study by Putnam, Leonardi, and Nanetti (1993) of northern and southern Italy after World War II. Both regions were given the same formal institutions, but the north achieved a much faster economic transformation. The reason seems to be that citizens of the north made better use of formal institutions. They read newspapers, voted, and complained when public services fell short of expectations. Formal institutions work best when they are used, but their use poses a collective action problem and needs to be supported informally—by a culture of civic engagement.

Effective treaty-making also requires civic involvement. Concerned citizens must learn about what is going on in the world, form judgments on what should and should not be done about important issues, and convey those preferences to their representatives. The Mine Ban Treaty is probably the best example of a treaty taking strength from global civic engagement. The International Campaign to Ban Landmines, a nongovernmental organization affiliated with more than a thousand civil society organizations, spearheaded the effort. The campaign influenced the negotiation and ratification of the treaty and in 1997 won the Nobel Peace Prize.

Nationally, there is a link between political institutions and the supply of public goods. Democracies are more likely than dictatorships to supply the kinds of goods that most benefit citizens. For example, Barrett and Graddy (2000) find that local air and water quality is higher in countries with greater civil and political freedoms, even after controlling for differences in income and geography. Presumably there is also a link between these institutions and the provision of transnational public goods. The evidence for this is mixed, however (see Congleton 1992; Murdock and Sandler 1997; Murdoch, Sandler and Sargent 1997; Fredriksson and Gaston 1999). One reason may be that the decision to participate in a treaty is strategic: participation depends on what other countries do and on what a treaty requires of its parties.

Treaty remedies are also more effective if monitoring of compliance is supported by civil organizations. A recent example is the ICCAT treaty, discussed previously. To monitor compliance, fishermen are expected to monitor the behavior of others at sea and report suspected breaches of the treaty back to their national authorities.

Some businesses have voluntarily pledged to reduce their greenhouse gas emissions. A few have even established internal systems for emissions trading.[8] By doing so, these companies are demonstrating their concern for the environment. They are acknowledging their responsibility to contribute to the global mitigation effort. They are learning how emissions trading can be made to work. And they may be anticipating first mover advantages. Such actions and intentions are to be welcomed. But it would be wrong to believe that this behavior will do much to help the environment.

If the aim of the Framework Convention on Climate Change is to be realized—that is, if atmospheric concentrations of greenhouse gases are to be stabilized at an acceptable level, whatever that may be—the global economy will need to be restructured. Market forces have sparked technological revolutions in the past. But in the case of climate change, new technologies have to be developed and adopted even while cheap fossil fuel energy remains abundant.

Even in the case of stratospheric ozone depletion, where CFC substitutes cost only a little more than the ozone-destroying chemicals they were meant to replace, government intervention—and especially international cooperation—was needed to effect a transformation. For climate change the need for government regulation and international cooperation is much greater because the costs of substituting away from carbon-based fuels are much larger. Indeed, international cooperation was relatively easy to effect in the case of ozone depletion precisely because the costs of ozone protection were low (Barrett 1999b). Global climate change poses a much greater challenge to the international system.

Application to Global Climate Change

If international cooperation is needed to mitigate global climate change but the Kyoto Protocol's enforcement mechanisms are inadequate, what should be done? The first thing to understand about international cooperation is that it may not be possible to sustain a first best outcome every time. The Kyoto Protocol was designed to be a kind of first best remedy. Its overall emissions reduction target is justified by cost-benefit analysis, and the treaty incorporates "flexible mechanisms" aimed at minimizing the costs of achieving this target (Barrett 1999b). However, the treaty negotiated in

---

[8]The companies most prominent in this area are the 36 members of the Business Environmental Leadership Council, a group affiliated with the Pew Center on Global Climate Change.

December 1997 ignored enforcement.[9] This was something that the negotiators thought they could add later. But this problem should be viewed from the other direction. Negotiators should first ask what can be enforced, then build a treaty around that. Enforcement is the main challenge, and it needs to be addressed directly.

Two aspects of global climate change make enforcement of a Kyoto-like treaty difficult. The first is that abatement is costly. The second is that climate change is a global problem. Costly abatement makes nonparticipation (noncompliance) attractive to every country. The global nature of the problem means that the stiff punishments needed to deter nonparticipation and noncompliance will not be credible. The Montreal Protocol worked because abatement was not very costly and because trade restrictions could be used to promote participation. With climate change the situation is not so accommodating.

The MARPOL agreement (on the design of oil tankers) may be a better model for addressing global climate change. Recall that international negotiations first tried to control oil pollution at sea by setting limits on oil dumping. That approach failed because the limits could not be monitored or enforced. The MARPOL agreement took the radical step of focusing instead on a technology standard. A treaty on climate change should do something similar.

A superior climate change treaty should:

- Promote cooperative research and development on technologies needed to substitute away from carbon-based fuels or to safely capture and store carbon. Climate change is a long-term problem that requires a long-term solution.

- Based on the fruits of this collaborative research and development, create follow-on protocols that establish technology standards for electricity generation, carbon capture and storage, and vehicles. Technology standards are easy to monitor and, unlike emission limits, create positive feedback. If there are network externalities, the more countries that embrace a standard, the greater will be the incentive for others to adopt the same standard. Technology standards also establish automatic, easily administered trade restrictions that conform to the rules of the World Trade Organization.

- Promote transfers of these technologies to developing countries. Climate change is a global problem and requires global action. But it is unreasonable to expect—and unfair to ask—developing countries to foot the bill for their abatement efforts. As with the Montreal Protocol, abatement should be facilitated by a system of transfers.

---

[9]The treaty has other flaws. Its "flexible mechanisms" are likely to be saddled with large transactions costs, preventing cost-effective implementation. The treaty also requires that substantial emission cuts be made in the short term—even though costs would be much lower (without much sacrifice in benefits) if abatement were postponed until capital could be turned over more cheaply.

- Establish a protocol for the short run. Because of the enforcement problem, legally binding emission limits should be abandoned. Instead countries should pledge to take certain actions—such as instituting carbon taxes, raising energy efficiency standards, and subsidizing renewable energy. The Kyoto Protocol has not only failed to support international cooperation, it has also taken pressure off countries to do much unilaterally.

- Recognize that climate change will likely occur no matter what is done to mitigate it. As a result some countries will suffer related damages. Developing countries are more vulnerable, yet they contributed little to the problem. Thus industrial countries have a responsibility to reduce the damages suffered by developing countries and to ease their adjustment. Designing such transfers will not be easy, not least because it will be impossible to determine whether any particular change in the climate was caused by humans. Still, this problem needs to be acknowledged and addressed.

Although this proposal would improve matters, it falls short of an ideal treaty on climate change. But it is not meant to be ideal. The ideal outcome for climate change is unlikely to be enforceable, and an outcome that cannot be enforced cannot be attained. The above proposal is enforceable (as well as fair and oriented to the long term). Thus it is attainable. Though not ideal, it may be the best climate outcome that the international system is capable of sustaining.

Conclusion

Some transnational public goods are supplied unilaterally. But many are not, and so require multilateral efforts to restructure incentives for their provision. Because of the constraint of sovereignty, this is a colossal institutional challenge.

There is no universal solution. Different public goods pose different problems and require different remedies. Some problems pose a challenge only for coordination. Because coordination does not require enforcement, these problems are relatively easy for the international system to fix.

Enforcement is a bigger challenge because sovereignty requires that multilateral approaches be self-enforcing. Strategy must be used to restructure the game, perhaps changing it from one requiring cooperation (and hence enforcement) to one requiring only coordination. This can sometimes be achieved by carefully choosing the instrument of policy. The MARPOL agreement, for example, shows how relying on a technical standard (on the design of oil tankers) rather than an emissions standard (on the dumping of oil) completely changed the game of reducing oil pollution at sea.

In other cases the switch from a cooperation to a coordination game can be achieved by linking the provision of public goods to international trade. The Montreal Protocol, for example, was transformed into a coordination game by imposing the credible threat of restricting trade with nonparties. Finally, cash payments and technology transfers can help when there are substantial asymmetries. This was another approach used by the Montreal Protocol. It was this combination of strategies that helped ensure protection of the stratospheric ozone layer.

Unfortunately, these successes are special cases. Too often, multilateralism fails or succeeds only partially. Remedies that work for one problem do not work for another. The international regime for regulating catches of Atlantic tuna, for example, has incorporated trade restrictions as a means of enforcing both compliance and participation. However, it is not clear that this approach will work because it is relatively easy for some countries to reduce the impact of the restrictions. The Kyoto Protocol was styled after the Montreal Protocol in that it established targets and timetables for reducing emissions of a global public bad. The difference is that the Montreal Protocol was able to enforce both participation and compliance by means of a trade restriction. The Kyoto Protocol has tried an alternative approach to enforcement—one that is almost certain to fail. The alternative treaty design proposed above has a greater chance of success.

This might seem a depressing note on which to end. But the international system is resilient—and occasionally ingenious—and with each failure new approaches are tried. Regulation of oil pollution at sea, for example, started out on the wrong foot but was adjusted after this failure became apparent. And although trade restrictions on tuna imports may not work as intended, they are being buttressed by other approaches. For example, the 1993 Agreement to Promote Compliance with International Conservation and Management Measures by Fishing Vessels on the High Seas acknowledges that all states have a duty not to undermine the conservation objectives of fisheries agreements. This agreement has not entered into force. But were it to do so and to attract substantial participation, countries would be further constrained from acting as they please on the high seas.

The international system is not static: it evolves. The challenge is to use strategy to ensure that it evolves toward greater provision of transnational public goods. An important first step is to know well the good in question, particularly its underlying incentive structures.

References

Baland, Jean-Marie, and Jean-Philippe Platteau. 1996. *Halting Degradation of Natural Resources: Is There a Role for Rural Communities?* New York: Food and Agriculture Organization of the United Nations.

Barrett, Scott. 1994. "Self-Enforcing International Environmental Agreements." *Oxford Economic Papers* 46: 878–94.

———. 1997. "The Strategy of Trade Sanctions in International Environmental Agreements." *Resource and Energy Economics* 19 (4): 345–61.

———. 1999a. "The Credibility of Trade Sanctions in International Environmental Agreements." In Per G. Fredriksson, ed., *Trade, Global Policy, and the Environment.* World Bank Discussion Paper 402. Washington, D.C.

———. 1999b. "Montreal versus Kyoto: International Cooperation and the Global Environment." In Inge Kaul, Isabelle Grunberg, and Marc A. Stern, eds., *Global Public Goods: International Cooperation in the 21st Century.* New York: Oxford University Press.

———. 1999c. "A Theory of Full International Cooperation." *Journal of Theoretical Politics* 11 (4): 519–41.

———. 2001. "International Cooperation for Sale." *European Economic Review* 45 (10): 1835–50.

———. 2002. "Global Disease Eradication." Johns Hopkins University, School of Advanced International Studies, Washington, D.C.

———. Forthcoming. *Environment and Statecraft: The Strategy of Environmental Treaty-Making.* Oxford: Oxford University Press.

Barrett, Scott, and Kathryn Graddy. 2000. "Freedom, Growth, and the Environment." *Environment and Development Economics* 5: 433–56.

Committee on the Assessment of Future Scientific Needs for Live Variola Virus. 1999. *Assessment of Future Scientific Needs for Live Variola Virus.* Washington, D.C.: National Academy Press.

Chayes, Abram, and Antonia Handler Chayes. 1995. *The New Sovereignty.* Cambridge, Mass.: Harvard University Press.

Congleton, Roger D. 1992. "Political Institutions and Pollution Control." *Review of Economics and Statistics* 74 (3): 412–21.

Downs, George W., David M. Rocke, and Peter N. Barsoom. 1996. "Is the Good News about Compliance Good News about Cooperation?" *International Organization* 50 (3): 379–406.

Elton, Charles S. 2000. *The Ecology of Invasions by Animals and Plants.* Chicago: University of Chicago Press.

Fredriksson, Per G., and Noel Gaston 1999. "The Importance of Trade for Ratification of the 1992 Climate Change Convention." In Per G. Fredriksson, ed., *Trade, Global Policy, and the Environment.* World Bank Discussion Paper 402. Washington, D.C.

Gladwell, Malcolm. 2000. *The Tipping Point: How Little Things Can Make a Big Difference.* Boston: Little, Brown & Company.

Heal, Geoffrey. 1994. "Formation of International Environmental Agreements." In Carlo Carraro, ed., *Trade, Innovation, Environment.* Dordrecht, the Netherlands: Kluwer Academic Publishers.

———. 1999. "New Strategies for the Provision of Global Public Goods: Learning from International Environmental Challenges." In Inge Kaul, Isabelle Grunberg, and Marc A. Stern, eds., *Global Public Goods: International Cooperation in the 21st Century.* New York: Oxford University Press.

Mirovitskaya, Natalia S., Margaret Clark, and Ronald G. Purvey. 1993. "North Pacific Fur Seals: Regime Formation as a Means of Resolving Conflict." In O. R. Young and G. Osherenko, eds., *Polar Politics: Creating International Environmental Regimes.* Ithaca, N.Y.: Cornell University Press.

Mitchell, Ronald B. 1994. *Intentional Oil Pollution at Sea: Environmental Policy and Treaty Compliance.* Cambridge, Mass.: MIT Press.

Murdoch, James C., and Todd Sandler. 1997. "The Voluntary Provision of a Pure Public Good: The Case of Reduced CFC Emissions and the Montreal Protocol." *Journal of Public Economics* 63 (3): 331–49.

Murdoch, James C., Todd Sandler, and Keith Sargent. 1997. "A Tale of Two Collectives: Sulphur versus Nitrogen Oxides Emission Reduction in Europe." *Economica* 64 (254): 281–301.

Olson, Mancur. 1965. *The Logic of Collective Action: Public Goods and the Theory of Groups.* Cambridge, Mass.: Harvard University Press.

Ostrom, Elinor. 1990. *Governing the Commons: The Evolution of Institutions for Collective Action.* Cambridge: Cambridge University Press.

Putnam, Robert D., with Robert Leonardi, and Rafaella Y. Nanetti. 1993. *Making Democracy Work: Civic Traditions in Modern Italy.* Princeton, N.J.: Princeton University Press.

Sandler, Todd. 1992. *Collective Action: Theory and Applications.* Ann Arbor: University of Michigan Press.

———. 1998. "Global and Regional Public Goods: A Prognosis for Collective Action." *Fiscal Studies* 19 (3): 221–47.

———. 2001. "Financing Global and International Public Goods." In Christopher D. Gerrard, Marco Ferroni, and Ashoka Mody, eds., *Global Public Policies and Programs: Implications for Financing and Evaluation.* Washington, D.C.: World Bank.

Schelling, Thomas C. 1978. *Micromotives and Macrobehavior.* New York: W. W. Norton.

Stiglitz, Joseph E. 1999. "Knowledge as a Public Good." In Inge Kaul, Isabelle Grunberg, and Marc A. Stern, eds., *Global Public Goods: International Cooperation in the 21st Century.* New York: Oxford University Press.

VII

Global Climate Change

22　Reflections on the Economics of Climate Change

William D. Nordhaus

William D. Nordhaus is A. Whitney Griswold Professor of Economics and on the staff of the Cowles Foundation, Yale University.

Albert Einstein's reaction to quantum mechanics was "God does not play dice with the universe." Yet mankind *is* playing dice with the natural environment through a multitude of interventions—injecting into the atmosphere trace gases like the greenhouse gases or ozone-depleting chemicals, engineering massive land-use changes such as deforestation, depleting multitudes of species in their natural habitats even while creating transgenic ones in the laboratory, and accumulating sufficient nuclear weapons to destroy human civilizations. As natural or social scientists, we need to understand the human sources of these global changes, the potential damage they cause to natural and economic systems, and the most efficient ways of alleviating or removing the dangers. Just as towns in times past decided on the management of their grazing or water resources, so must we today and in the future learn to use wisely and to protect economically our common geophysical and biological resources. This task of understanding and controlling interventions on a global scale can be called managing the global commons.

The issue analyzed in this symposium is the threat of greenhouse warming. Climatologists and other scientists warn that the accumulation of carbon dioxide (CO_2) and other greenhouse gases is likely to lead to global warming and other significant climatic changes over the next century. Many scientific bodies, along with a growing chorus of environmental groups and governments, are calling for severe curbs on the emissions of greenhouse gases. In response, governments have recently approved a framework treaty on climate change to monitor trends and natural efforts, and this treaty formed the centerpiece of the Earth Summit held in Rio in June 1992.[1]

Natural scientists have pondered the question of greenhouse warming for a century. Only recently have economists begun to tackle the issue, studying the impacts of climate change, the costs of slowing climate change,

---

"Reflections on the Economics of Climate Change," by William D. Nordhaus from *Journal of Economic Perspectives*, 7(4):11–25 (Fall 1993).

[1]Formally known as the United Nations Conference on Environment and Development (UNCED), the Earth Summit was the culmination of an effort to reach international agreements on climate, forest, biodiversity and biotechnology, as well as to develop principles for environmentally sound economic development.

and alternative approaches for implementing policies. The intellectual challenge here is daunting for those who take policy analysis seriously, raising formidable issues of data, modeling, uncertainty, international coordination, and institutional design. In addition, the economic stakes are enormous, involving investments on the order of hundreds of billions of dollars a year to slow or prevent climate change.

My purpose here is to provide a non-technical introduction to the economics of climate change. I will sketch the scientific background and uncertainties, survey the results of existing studies of the impacts of climate change, present a summary of a study of efficient policies to slow global warming, and end with the uncertainties that haunt the entire field.

The Scientific Background

What is the greenhouse effect? It is the process by which radiatively active gases like CO_2 selectively absorb radiation at different points of the spectrum and thereby warm the surface of the earth. The greenhouse gases are transparent to incoming solar radiation but absorb significant amounts of outgoing radiation. There is no debate about the importance of the greenhouse effect, without which the Earth's climate would resemble the moon's.[2]

Concern about the greenhouse effect arises because human activities are currently raising atmospheric concentrations of greenhouse gases. The major anthropogenic greenhouse gases are carbon dioxide (emitted primarily from the combustion of fossil fuels), methane, and chlorofluorocarbons (CFCs)—but of these CO_2 is likely to be the most significant over the coming decades. Scientific monitoring has firmly established the buildup of the major greenhouse gases over the last century. Using the standard but problematical metric of the "CO_2 equivalent" of greenhouse gases,[3] atmospheric concentrations of greenhouse gases have risen by over half of the preindustrial level of CO_2.

While the historical record is well established, there is great uncertainty about the potential for future climate change. On the basis of climate models, scientists project that a doubling of the atmospheric concentrations of CO_2 will in equilibrium lead to a warming of the earth's surface of 1 to 5 degree Celsius; other projected and equally uncertain effects include an increase in precipitation and evaporation, a small rise in sea level over the next century, and the potential for hotter and drier weather in midcontinental regions such as the U.S. midwest. Atmospheric scientists have

---

[2]A non-technical description of the science underlying the greenhouse effect is contained in National Academy of Sciences (1992). A thorough survey, full of interesting figures and background, is contained in IPCC (1990).

[3]Because greenhouse gases have differing lifetimes, combining them into a single index of their "CO_2 equivalent" poses complex scientific and economic questions, as Schmalensee (1993) shows.

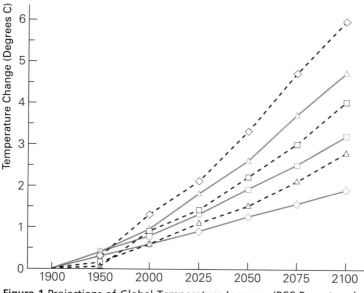

Figure 1 Projections of Global Temperature Increase: IPCC Report and DICE Model

Note: IPCC Report is from Intergovernmental Panel on Climate Change (1990), while DICE model is from Nordhaus (1993a). The dashed lines are from IPCC Report and represent, from top to bottom, high estimate, best estimate, and low estimate. The solid lines are from the DICE model and represent, from top to bottom, the 90th, 50th, and 10th percentiles of calculated temperature increases from 500 Monte Carlo runs. In both cases, the changes represent temperature increases from 1900.

engaged in a spirited debate about the climatic impact of increasing greenhouse-gas concentrations, but it is unlikely that the uncertainties will be resolved until this vast geophysical experiment has run its course.

To translate these equilibrium results into a projection of future climate change requires a scenario for emissions and concentrations. Using rudimentary economic modeling, the Intergovernmental Panel on Climate Change (or IPCC), an international panel of distinguished scientists, projected that "business as usual" would produce a 3 to 6 degree C warming in 2100 (relative to 1900) with the best guess being 4 degrees C. The dashed lines in Figure 1 show the high, best, and low estimates from the IPCC.

I have recently used a dynamic optimization model (the DICE model, described more fully later in this paper) to develop a distribution of future temperature increases. Figure 1 shows as solid lines the 10th, 50th, and 90th percentiles of the temperature-increase distribution from the DICE model. In general, economic models project rising relative energy prices and slowing economic growth in the coming decades; as a result, they tend to show lower emissions and temperature trends than the extrapolative approaches often used in the scientific community and exemplified by the IPCC projections. However, virtually all projections are worrisome because climate appears to be heading out of the historical range of temperatures witnessed during the span of human civilizations.

Climate models resemble large macroeconomic models in their ability to answer virtually any question that modelers care to ask. However, the reliability of climate models for global climate changes is unproven, and climate modelers do not expect to be able to forecast regional climates accurately in the foreseeable future. Some believe that there may be "regime changes" in which the climate flips from one locally stable equilibrium to another, say because of changes in ocean circulation. Elaborating bigger and better models will provide fruitful full employment for climatologists well into the next century.

Impacts of Climate Change

What are the likely impacts of projected climate changes over the next century? To begin, we should recognize that in the long march of economic development, technology has increasingly insulated humans and economic activity from the vagaries of climate. Two centuries ago, work and recreation were dictated by the cycles of daylight, the seasons, and the agricultural growing season.

Today, thanks to modern technology, humans live and thrive in virtually every climate on earth. For the bulk of economic activity, variables like wages, unionization, labor-force skills, and political factors swamp climatic considerations. When a manufacturing firm decides between investing in Hong Kong and Moscow, climate will probably not even be on the list of factors considered. Moreover, the process of economic development and technological change tend progressively to reduce climate sensitivity as the share of agriculture in output and employment declines and as capital-intensive space heating and cooling, enclosed shopping malls, artificial snow, and accurate weather or hurricane forecasting reduces the vulnerability of economic activity to weather.

In thinking about the impact of climate change, one must recognize that the variable focussed on in most analyses—globally averaged surface temperature—has little salience for impacts. Rather, variables that accompany or are the result of temperature changes—precipitation, water levels, extremes of droughts or freezes, and thresholds like the freezing point or the level of dikes and levees—will drive the socioeconomic impacts. Mean temperature is chosen because it is a useful *index* of climate change that is highly correlated with or determines the more important variables. Moreover, it must be emphasized that impact studies are in their infancy and that studies of low-income regions are virtually non-existent.

Existing research uses a wide variety of approaches including time-series analysis, engineering studies, and historical analogs. Climate change is likely to have different effects on different sectors and in different coun-

Table 1 Comparison of Estimates of Impact of Global Warming on the United States: Impact on Incomes of CO_2 Doubling
(*in billions of 1988 U.S. dollars per year*)

	Nordhaus	*Cline*	*Fankhauser*
Heavily affected sectors			
Agriculture	1	15.2	7.4
Coastal areas	10.7	2.5	2.3
Energy	0.5	9	0
Other sectors	38.1		
Wetland and species loss	b	7.1	14.8
Health and amenity	b	8.4	30.3
Other	b	11.2	12.1
Total: billions of $	50.3	53.4	66.9
(*Percent of output*)	*1.0*	*1.1*	*1.3*

[a]References are Nordhaus (1991), Cline (1992), Fankhauser (1993).
[b]These are included in the total for "other sectors."

tries.[4] In general, those sectors of the economy that depend heavily on unmanaged ecosystems—that is, are heavily dependent upon naturally occurring rainfall, runoff, or temperatures—will be most sensitive to climate change. Agriculture, forestry, outdoor recreation, and coastal activities fall in this category. Countries like Japan or the United States are relatively insulated from climate change while developing countries like India are more vulnerable.

This survey of impacts will concentrate primarily upon the United States, because that is where the evidence is most abundant. In reality, most of the U.S. economy has little direct interaction with climate. For example, cardiovascular surgery and parallel supercomputing are undertaken in carefully controlled environments and are unlikely to be directly affected by climate change. More generally, underground mining, most services, communications, and manufacturing are sectors likely to be largely unaffected by climate change—sectors that comprise around 85 percent of GDP.

A few studies have estimated the impact of an equilibrium CO_2 doubling (2.5 to 3 degrees C) on the United States, and the results of three such surveys are shown in Table 1. The first column of Table 1 shows the results of Nordhaus (1991) updated to 1988 prices. The other two comprehensive studies by Cline (1992) and Fankhauser (1993) use largely the same data base but extend the Nordhaus analysis to other sectors. The convention used in most damage studies is to calculate impacts in terms of today's level and composition of output. Hence, the $53 billion estimate of damage from CO_2 doubling estimated by Cline and shown in Table 1 su-

---

[4]An early review, emphasizing the potential costs of climate change, is contained in EPA (1989). A more balanced approach, emphasizing the potential for adaptation, is contained in National Academy of Sciences (1992).

perimposes the estimated impacts that would occur roughly a century from now upon today's economy.

Cline has performed the most detailed economic analysis of the potential impact of climate change on a number of market and non-market sectors, and the overall results are shown in the second column of Table 1. While Cline examined a wide variety of possible impacts, many of the estimates are extremely tenuous and may lean toward overestimating the impacts. For example, Cline's estimates of the impact of losses from storms assume that storms become more severe, whereas both the IPCC and the National Academy studies concluded that the effect of warming on storm intensity is ambiguous. Another example is leisure activities, where he includes only losses to skiing but excludes any gains from the much larger warm-weather industries such as camping, boating, and swimming. In agriculture, Cline relies on estimates that involve little or no adaptation. For health effects, Cline bases his estimates on a study that virtually ignores adaptation. For species loss, Cline takes a very costly decision (that of the Northern spotted owl) and uses that as the basis for valuation. Even with this tendency to see the pessimistic side of global warming, Cline's estimates of impacts are only marginally above those found in other studies (1.1 percent of GNP for a 2.5 degree C warming in Cline, as opposed to 1 percent of GNP for a 3 degree of warming in Nordhaus).

A third approach is a compilation by Fankhauser (1993). This study employs much the same methodology as Nordhaus and Cline but uses additional studies and extends the analysis to the OECD countries and to the world. Fankhauser's results are very close to those in earlier studies, finding a 1.3 percent impact of a 3 degree warming for the United States.

A full assessment of the impact of greenhouse warming must, of course, include regions outside the United States. To date, studies for other countries are fragmentary, and it is not possible to make any general conclusions at this time. A preliminary reading is that other advanced industrial countries will experience modest impacts similar to those of the United States, and some may even have net economic benefits; for example, Fankhauser (1993) extends his analysis and estimates losses from CO_2 doubling of 1.4 percent to OECD countries and 1.5 for the world. Another estimate, more qualitative in nature, is an intensive survey of experts on the economic impacts of climate change (Nordhaus, 1993b). For a 3 degree C warming in 2090, the median response was an economic loss of 1.8 percent of world output. However, there is great uncertainty: the median estimate of the 10th percentile of outcomes is for no impact, while the median estimate of the 90th percentile of outcomes is for a 5.5 percent loss of world output.

All these studies indicate the great uncertainty about the impact of climate change. More recent analysis suggests that the studies reported in Table 1 may well overestimate the impact of climate change because they ignore many ways in which economies can adapt to changing climate. One kind of adaptation ignored in most studies is the buffering of shocks by trade. A study by Reilly and Hohmann (1993) begins with the results of agricultural production-function studies such as those used in Table 1; these studies estimate the impact of climate change on crop yields in individual regions. These yield estimates are then imbedded in a model of international trade. Reilly and Hohmann find that trade tends to reduce the economic impacts by a factor of from five to ten as reactions of supply and demand buffer production shocks. For example, the estimated impact of a substantial (30 percent) yield shock in temperate regions, buffered by the adaptive response in markets, produces a negligible impact on incomes: 0.06 percent of income for the U.S. and 0.08 percent loss for the world over a period of nearly a century. This careful study is a good lesson on how impact estimates often tend to exaggerate losses while ignoring gains and adaptations.[5]

Another approach to measuring impacts is a "Ricardian" analysis that estimates the rents to climate in particular climate zones and then uses these to estimate the impact of climate change on income. The Ricardian approach is useful because it allows all forms of adaptation, whereas the production-function approaches omit all but a few forms of adaptation to changing climate. A study by Mendelsohn, Nordhaus, and Shaw (1993a, b) developed such an approach by examining the impact of climate on U.S. agriculture. This study uses cross-sectional data on climate, farm-land prices, and other economic and geophysical data for almost 3000 counties in the United States.

Applying the model to a global-warming scenario found a range of impacts. The traditional analysis of global warming analyzes the impact upon the grains. Under this approach, the Ricardian model finds annual losses ranging from $6 to $8 billion annually (without CO_2 fertilization in 1988 prices at 1988 levels of farm income). This can be related to gross farm income in 1982 of $175 billion. Strikingly different results emerge if we use a broader approach which includes all agricultural crops. For these, the net impact of warming is slightly positive, ranging from a loss of $0.7 billion to a *gain* of $2 billion per year. The differing results arise because the broader approach weights relatively more heavily the irrigated lands of the American West and South that thrive in a Mediterranean and subtropical climate, a climate that will become relatively more abundant with a warmer climate.

---

[5]One might suspect that there is often an unconscious impulse to find costs and ignore benefits of climate change. A comparison of two sets of studies is instructive in this respect. Almost two decades ago, a series of studies was undertaken to investigate the impact of flights in the stratosphere on global *cooling*. Studies by d'Arge and others (summarized in National Research Council, 1979) found that global cooling of 1°C would impose costs in a number of areas. Of the nine areas of costs identified in the global cooling studies (agriculture, forest products, marine resources, health, locational preferences, fuel demand, housing, public expenditures, and aesthetics), only two were examined in the 1989 EPA study of global warming and *none* were calculated by the EPA to produce benefits. The largest estimated cost in the global cooling studies was the amenity effect of cooling, determined through regional wage differentials. This topic was completely ignored in the EPA studies. One is tempted to say that environmental impact studies can find the cloud behind every silver lining.

The one area where our information is particularly sparse is for developing countries. Small and poor countries, particularly ones with low population mobility in narrowly restricted climatic zone, may be severely affected. Much more work on the potential impact of climate change on developing countries needs to be done.

The Balancing Act in Climate Change Policies

The greenhouse effect is the granddaddy of public goods problems—emissions affect climate globally for centuries to come. Because of the climate externality, individuals will not produce the efficient quantity of greenhouse gases. An important goal of economic research is to examine policies that will find the right balance, on the margin, of costs of action to slow climate change and the benefits of reducing future damages from climate change.

The benefits of emissions reductions come when lower emissions reduce future climate-induced damages. To translate these into a marginal benefit function, it is necessary to follow the emissions through greenhouse-gas concentrations to economic impacts, and then take the present value of the impact of an emission of an additional unit. Graphically, we can depict the marginal damages averted per unit of emissions reduction as the downward-sloping marginal benefit (MB) curve in Figure 2.

The second relationship is the marginal cost of emissions reduction, which portrays the costs that the economy undertakes to reduce a unit of greenhouse-gas emissions (or the equivalent in other policies that would

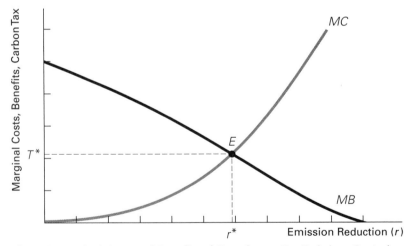

Figure 2 Marginal Costs and Benefits of Greenhouse-Gas Emissions Controls
Note: Efficient policy comes at point E, where marginal cost of further emissions reduction (MC) equals marginal benefit of emissions reductions in slowing climate change (MB). T^* is the efficient carbon tax while r^* is the efficient reduction rate.

slow greenhouse warming). A wide variety of approaches are available to slow climate change. Most policy discussion has focussed on reducing CO_2 emissions by reducing the consumption of fossil fuels through energy conservation, alternative energy sources (some would even contemplate nuclear power), and other measures. Such policies could be implemented through carbon taxes of the kind James Poterba analyzes in this symposium, while some prefer regulations such as tradable emissions permits. Other approaches include reforestation to remove CO_2 from the atmosphere and putting even more stringent controls on CFCs.

Another option, definitely not in the environmentally correct package, would be to offset greenhouse warming through climatic engineering, primarily through measures to change the albedo (reflectivity) of the earth. Such options include injection particles that would increase the backscattering or reflecting of incoming sunlight or stimulate absorption of carbon. Two particularly interesting proposals include shooting smart mirrors into space with 16-inch naval rifles or seeding the oceans with iron to accelerate carbon sequestration.[6] Whatever the approach, economists emphasize the importance of cost-effectiveness—structuring policies to get the maximal reduction in harmful climatic change for a given level of expenditure. Figure 2 shows schematically the marginal cost of cost-effective emissions reductions as MC.

The shape of the cost function for reducing CO_2 emissions has been thoroughly studied, and the effort discussed by John Weyant in this symposium represents the most careful comparative examination of the results of different models. In addition, policies should include other cost-effective measures, and a recent National Academy of Sciences Panel (1992) has compared the costs of a wide variety of measures, including rough estimates of the costs of climate engineering.

From an economic point of view, efficient policies are ones in which the marginal costs are balanced with the marginal benefits of emissions reductions. Figure 2 shows schematically how the efficient rate of emissions reduction and the optimal carbon tax are determined. The pure market solution comes with emissions reductions at 0, where MB is far above the zero MC. Point E represents the efficient point at which marginal abatement costs equal marginal benefits from slowing climate change. The policy can be represented by the efficient fractional reduction in emissions, r^* on the horizontal axis, or by the optimal carbon tax, T^* on the vertical axis.

Empirical Modeling of Optimal Policies

Sketching the optimal policy in Figure 2 demands little more than pencil, paper, and a rudimentary understanding of economics. To move from theory to useful empirical models requires understanding a wide variety of

---

[6]The issues of geoengineering are discussed in National Academy of Sciences (1992, Chapter 28).

empirical economic and geophysical relationships. Work has progressed to the point where the economics and natural science can be integrated to estimate optimal control strategies. In one study, I developed a simple cost-benefit analysis for determining the optimal steady-state control of CO_2 and other greenhouse gases based on the comparative statics framework shown in Figure 2 (Nordhaus, 1991). This earlier study came to a middle-of-the-road conclusion that the threat of greenhouse warming was sufficient to justify low-cost steps to slow the pace of climate change.

A more complete elaboration has been made using an approach I call the "DICE model," shorthand for a Dynamic Integrated Model of Climate and the Economy.[7] The DICE model is a global dynamic optimization model for estimating the optimal path of reductions of greenhouse-gas emissions. The basic approach is to calculate the optimal path for both capital accumulation and reductions of greenhouse-gas emissions in the framework of the Ramsey (1928) model of intertemporal choice. The resulting trajectory can be interpreted as the most efficient path for slowing climate change given inputs and technologies; an alternative interpretation is as a competitive market equilibrium in which externalities or spillover effects are corrected using the appropriate social prices for greenhouse-gas emissions.

The DICE model asks whether to consume goods and services, invest in productive capital, or slow climate change via reducing greenhouse-gas emissions. The optimal path chosen is one that maximizes an objective function that is the discounted sum of the utilities of per capita consumption. Consumption and investment are constrained by a conventional set of economic relationships (Cobb-Douglas production function, capital-balance equation, and so forth) and by a newly developed set of aggregate geophysical constraints (interrelating economic activity, greenhouse-gas emissions and concentrations, climate change, costs of abatement, and impacts from climate change).

To give the flavor of the results from the DICE model, consider the economic optimum and compare it to two alternative policies that have been proposed by governments or by the environmental community. The three options are (1) economic optimization as described in the previous paragraph; (2) stabilizing greenhouse-gas emissions at 1990 levels, a target that was endorsed at the Rio Earth Summit by the United States and other governments; and (3) stabilizing climate so that the change in global average temperature is limited to no more than 0.2 degrees C per decade with an ultimate limitation of 1.5 degrees C (compare this with the projections in Figure 1).

Solving the DICE model for the three policies just described produces a time sequence of consumption, investment, greenhouse-gas emissions, and carbon taxes. The carbon taxes can be interpreted as the taxes on green-

---

[7]The basic model and results are presented in Nordhaus (1992a, b), while complete documentation and analysis are forthcoming in Nordhaus (1993a).

house-gas emissions (or the regulatory equivalent, say in auctionable emissions rights) that would lead to the emissions that would attain the policy objectives just described.

Figure 3 shows the resulting carbon taxes. For calibration purposes, in the United States, a carbon tax of $100 per ton would raise coal prices by about $70 per ton, or 300 percent; would increase oil prices by about $8 per barrel; and would raise around $200 billion of revenues (before taking account of emissions reductions). The economic optimum produces relatively modest carbon taxes, rising from around $5 per ton carbon to around $20 per ton by the end of the next century. The stabilization scenarios require must more stringent restraints. For emissions stabilization, the carbon tax would rise from around $40 per ton of carbon currently to around $500 per ton late in the next century; climate stabilization involves current carbon taxes over $100 per ton carbon today rising to nearly $1000 per ton by the end of the next century.

The DICE model can also be used to inquire into the estimated net economic impact of alternative policies. For the global economy, the economic optimum has a net benefit over no controls for the global economy (in terms of the discounted present value measured in 1990 consumption units) of $270 billion. On the other hand, stabilizing emissions or climate imposes major net economic costs. Stabilizing emissions leads to a net present-value loss of around $7 trillion relative to the optimum, while attempting to stabilize climate would have a net present-value cost of around $41 trillion. If these present value figures are converted into consumption annuities using an annuity rate of 4 percent per annum, these strategies represent, respectively, a gain of 0.05 percent and losses of 1.4 and 8.2 per-

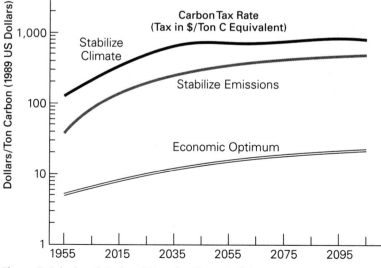

Figure 3 Calculated Carbon Taxes for Three Policies

cent of today's annual gross world output. It would take a major misestimate of either the costs of emissions reductions or of climate-change damages to make the stabilization options economically advantageous.

Several other economic studies have also calculated efficient approaches to slowing global warming. The studies of Manne and Richels (1990, 1992), Peck and Teisberg (1992), and Kolstad (1993) find conclusions roughly similar to those reported here. Other studies—those of Kolstad (1993) as well as earlier studies by the present author (1979, 1991)—also determine the optimal emissions control rates and carbon taxes and show optimal policies in the general range of those determined here.

Two studies derive quite different results, one more optimistic, one more pessimistic. The study by Jorgenson and Wilcoxen (1991) most strikingly shows a lower set of carbon taxes needed to stabilize greenhouse-gas emissions than those shown here; the reason for the lower carbon taxes seems to reside largely in the slow projected economic growth. By contrast, the study by Cline (1992) proposes much higher control rates. The more stringent controls in the Cline study are due to a number of features—primarily because the Cline result is not grounded in explicit intertemporal optimization and assumes a rate of time preference that is lower than would be consistent with observed real interest rates. Clearly, if we arbitrarily assume a near-zero discount rate (as Cline does), society will undertake massive investments in tangible, human, and environmental capital; who will do all this saving is an unanswered question.

Uncertainties and Anxieties

Most economic studies of the impacts and policies concerning climate change are based on scenarios like the smooth and gradual warming depicted in Figure 1. And, as indicated in the last section, the conclusion that emerges from most economic studies is to impose modest restraints, pack up our tools, and concentrate on more pressing problems. Given the high costs of controls and the modest projected impacts of a 1 to 3 degree C warming over the next half century, how high should global warming be on an international agenda that includes exploding population in the South, nuclear proliferation in the Middle East, collapsing economies in eastern Europe, increasing cycles of poverty and drug use along with stagnating incomes in the West, and sporadic outbreaks of violence and civil war just about everywhere? Given the modest estimated impact of climate change along with these other urgent concerns, we might conclude that global warming should be demoted to a second-tier issue.

Yet, even for those who downplay the urgency of the most likely scenarios for climate change, a deeper anxiety remains about future uncertainties and surprises. Scientists raise the specter of shifting currents turning Europe into Alaska, of mid-continental drying transforming grain belts into deserts, of great rivers drying up as snow packs disappear, of severe storms wiping out whole populations of low-lying regions, of surging ice sheets raising ocean levels by 20 to 50 feet, of northward migration of old or new tropical pests and diseases decimating the temperature regions, of environmentally induced migration overrunning borders in search of livable land. Given the potential for catastrophic surprises, perhaps we should conclude that the major concern lies in the uncertainties and imponderable impacts of climate change rather than in the smooth changes foreseen by the global models.

At present, we do not have the scientific basis for making a firm judgment of the likelihood of one of these catastrophic outcomes. In the survey discussed above (Nordhaus, 1993b), experts were asked about the probability of a 25 percent sustained loss in global income from a 3-degree C warming in 2090 (scenario A) and a 6-degree warming in 2175 (scenario B). The median estimated probability of this catastrophic outcome was 0.5 percent for scenario A and 3 percent for scenario B. On the other hand, the assessment of the catastrophic scenarios varied greatly across respondents and particularly across disciplines. For scenario B, according to the most pessimistic quartile of respondents, the mean probability of this catastrophic outcome was 40 percent. The more pessimistic assessments generally came from natural scientists while the more sanguine views were held by mainstream economists.

Once the door is open to consider catastrophic changes, a whole new debate is engaged. If we do not know how human activities will affect the thin layer of life-supporting activities that gave birth to and nurture human civilization, and if we cannot reliably judge how potential geophysical changes will affect civilization or the world around us, can we use the plain vanilla cost-benefit analysis (or even the Häagen-Dazs variety in dynamic optimization models)? Should we be ultraconservative and tilt toward preserving the natural world at the expense of economic growth and development? Do we dare put human betterment before the preservation of natural systems and trust that human ingenuity will bail us out should Nature deal us a nasty hand?

Faced with this dilemma, we might be tempted to say that such questions are beyond the capability of rational analysis and turn the decisions over to philosophers and politicians. Rather, I believe that natural and social sciences have a central role to play in analyzing potential future outcomes and delineating potential responses. Society often requires that decisions be made in the absence of complete information, whether the decisions be military strategy, oil drilling, or research and development. In each case, a reasoned decision process involves listing the events that may occur, estimating the consequences of the events, judging the probabilities that each of the events will occur, weighing the expected value of the consequences against the expected costs under different courses of action, and choosing the action that maximizes the expected value or utility of the outcome.

Reasoned decision-making under uncertainty is no different for climate-change policy than for other areas, although it may be more complex and require crossing traditional disciplinary boundaries more often.

In thinking through the appropriate treatment of future surprises, to the natural scientists falls the crucial task of sorting through the apocalyptic scenarios and obtaining rough judgments as to the likelihood of different geophysical outcomes so as to distinguish between the likely, plausible, possible, and virtually impossible. To the social scientists falls the issue of assessing the probabilities, determining the values of different outcomes, and devising sensible strategies in the face of such massive uncertainties. To our leaders falls the burden of ultimately deciding how to balance future perils against present costs. For all, this is a fruitful use of our collective talents, full of intellectual challenges and practical payoffs.

References

Cline, William, *The Economics of Global Warming*. Washington D.C.: Institute of International Economics, 1992.

EPA, "U.S. Environmental Protection Agency," *The Potential Effects of Global Climate Change on the United States: Report to Congress*. EPA-230-05-89-050, December 1989.

Fankhauser, Samuel, "The Economic Costs of Global Warming: Some Monetary Estimates." In Kaya, Y., N. Nakicenovic, W. D. Nordhaus, and F. L. Toth, eds., *Costs, Impacts, and Benefits of CO_2 Mitigation*, Laxenburg, Austria: International Institute for Applied Systems Analysis, CP-93-2, 1993, 85–105.

Gaskins, Darius W., and John P. Weyant, "Model Comparisons of the Costs of Reducing CO_2 Emissions," *American Economic Review Papers and Proceedings*, May 1993, 83:2, 318–30.

IPCC, Intergovernmental Panel on Climate Change. *Climate Change: The IPCC Scientific Assessment*. J. T. Houghton, G. J. Jenkins, and J. J. Ephraums, eds., New York: Cambridge University Press, 1990.

Jorgenson, Dale W., and Peter J. Wilcoxen, "Reducing U.S. Carbon Dioxide Emissions: The Cost of Different Goals." In Moronery, John R., ed., *Energy, Growth, and the Environment*. Greenwich: JAI Press, 1991, 125–28.

Kolstad, Charles D., "Looking vs. Leaping: The Timing of CO_2 Control in the Face of Uncertainty and Learning." In Kaya Y., N. Nakicenovic, W. D. Nordhaus, and F. L. Toth, eds., *Costs, Impacts, and Benefits of CO_2 Mitigation*. Laxenburg, Austria: International Institute for Applied Systems Analysis, CP-93-2, 1993, 63–82.

Manne, Alan S., and Richard G. Richels, "CO_2 Emission Limits: An Economic Cost Analysis for the USA," *The Energy Journal*, April 1990, *11*:2, 51–74.

Manne, Alan S., and Richard G. Richels, *Buying Greenhouse Insurance: The Economic Costs of CO_2 Emission Limits*. Cambridge: MIT Press, 1992.

Mendelsohn, Robert, William Nordhaus, and Dai Gee Shaw, "The Impact of Climate on Agriculture: A Ricardian Approach." In Kaya, Y., N. Nakicenovic, W. D. Nordhaus, and F. L. Toth, eds., *Costs, Impacts, and Benefits of CO_2 Mitigation*. Laxenburg, Austria: International Institute for Applied Systems Analysis, CP-93-2, 1993a, 173–207.

Mendelsohn, Robert, William D. Nordhaus, and Dai Gee Shaw, "The Impact of Global Warming on Agriculture: A Ricardian Approach," *American Economic Review*, forthcoming 1993b.

National Academy of Sciences (NAS), Committee on Science, Engineering, and Public Policy, *Policy Implications of Greenhouse Warming: Mitigation, Adaptation, and the Science Base*. Washington, D.C.: National Academy Press, 1992.

National Research Council, *Carbon Dioxide and Climate: A Scientific Assessment*. Washington, D.C.: National Academy Press, 1979.

Nordhaus, William D., *The Efficient Use of Energy Resources*. New Haven: Yale University Press, 1979.

Nordhaus, William D., "To Slow or Not to Slow: The Economics of the Greenhouse Effect," *The Economic Journal*, July 1991, *101*, 920–37.

Nordhaus, William D., "How Much Should We Invest in Preserving Our Current Climate?" In Giersch, Herbert, ed., *Economic Progress and Environmental Concerns*. Berlin: Verlag-Springer, 1992a, 255–99.

Nordhaus, William D., "An Optimal Transition Path for Slowing Climate Change," *Science*, November 1992b, *258*, 1315–19.

Nordhaus, William D., *Managing the Global Commons: The Economics of Climate Change*. Cambridge: MIT Press, forthcoming 1993a.

Nordhaus, William D., "Survey on Uncertainties Associated with Future Climate Change," Yale University, processed mimeo, April 1993b.

Peck, Stephen C., and Thomas J. Teisberg, "CETA: A Model for Carbon Emissions Trajectory Assessment," *The Energy Journal*, 1992, *13*:1, 55–77.

Ramsey, Frank P., "A Mathematical Theory of Saving," *The Economic Journal*, December 1928, *38*, 543–59.

Reilly, John, and Neil Hohmann, "Climate Change and Agriculture: The Role of International Trade," *American Economic Review Papers and Proceedings*, May 1993, *83*:2, 306–23.

Schmalensee, Richard, "Comparing Greenhouse Gases for Policy Purposes," *The Energy Journal*, 1993, *14*:1, 245–55.

23 *The Cost of Combating Global Warming: Facing the Tradeoffs*

Thomas C. Schelling

Thomas C. Schelling is Distinguished University Professor of Economics and Public Affairs emeritus at the University of Maryland.

At international conferences, people speaking for the developing world insist that it is the developed nations that feel endangered by carbon emissions and want to retard elsewhere the kind of development that has been enjoyed by Western Europe, North America, and Japan. A reduction in carbon emissions in the developing world, they assert, will have to be at the expense of the rich nations. Their diagnosis is wrong, but their conclusion is right. Any costs of mitigating climate change during the coming decades will surely be borne by the high-income countries. But the benefits, despite what spokespeople for the developing world say, will overwhelmingly accrue to future generations in the developing world. Any action combating global warming will be, intended or not, a foreign aid program.

The Chinese, Indonesians, or Bangladeshis are not going to divert resources from their own development to reduce the greenhouse effect, which is caused by the presence of carbon-based gases in the earth's atmosphere. This is a prediction, but it is also sound advice. Their best defense against climate change and vulnerability to weather in general is their own development, reducing their reliance on agriculture and other such outdoor livelihoods. Furthermore, they have immediate environmental problems—air and water pollution, poor sanitation, disease—that demand earlier attention.

There are three reasons the beneficiaries will be in the developing countries, which will be much more developed when the impact of climate change is felt. The first is simple: that is where most people live—four-fifths now, nine-tenths in 75 years.

Second, these economies may still be vulnerable, in a way the developed economies are not, by the time climate change occurs. In the developed world hardly any component of the national income is affected by climate. Agriculture is practically the only sector of the economy affected by climate, and it contributes only a small percentage—three percent in the

"The Costs of Combatting Global Warming: Facing the "Tradeoffs," by Thomas C. Schelling from *Foreign Affairs*, 76(6):8–14 (Nov./Dec. 1997).

United States—of national income. If agricultural productivity were drastically reduced by climate change, the cost of living would rise by one or two percent, and at a time when per capita income will likely have doubled. In developing countries, in contrast, as much as a third of GNP and half the population currently depends on agriculture. They may still be vulnerable to climate change for many years to come.

Third, although most of these populations should be immensely better off in 50 years, many will still be poorer than the rich countries are now. The contribution to their welfare by reduced climate change will therefore be greater than any costs the developing world bears in reducing emissions.

I say all this with apparent confidence, so let me rehearse the uncertainties, which have remained essentially the same for a decade and a half. Arbitrarily adopting a doubling of greenhouse gases as a benchmark, a committee of the U.S. National Academy of Sciences estimated in 1979 that the change in average global surface atmospheric temperature could be anywhere from 1.5 to 4.5 degrees Celsius. (Note that the upper estimate is three times the lower.) This range of uncertainty has still not officially been reduced.

More important than the average warming is the effect it may have on climates. Things will not just get warmer, climatologists predict; some places will, but others will get cooler, wetter, drier, or cloudier. The average warming is merely the engine that will drive the changes. The term "global warming" is mischievous in suggesting that hot summers are what it is all about.

The temperature gradient from equator to pole is a main driving force in the circulation of the atmosphere and oceans, and a change in that gradient will be as important as the change in average temperature. Climatologists have to translate changes in temperature at various latitudes, altitudes, and seasons into changes in weather and climate in different localities. That is another source of uncertainty. Mountains, for example, are hard to work into climate models. Not many people live high in the mountains, so why worry? But India, Pakistan, Bangladesh, and Burma depend on snowfall in the Himalayas for their irrigation.

A further question gets little attention: what will the world be like 75 years from now, when changes in climate may have become serious? If we look back to 1920 and conjecture about what environmental problems then might be affected by climate changes over the coming 75 years, one problem high on the list would be mud. This was the era of muddy roads and narrow tires. Cars had to be pulled out by horses. People could not ride bicycles, and walking in the stuff was arduous. One might think, "If things get wetter or drier the mud problem will get worse or better." It might not occur to anyone that by the 1990s most of the country would be paved.

If the climate changes expected 75 years from now were to happen immediately, the most dramatic consequences would be in the incidence of parasitic and other tropical diseases. Temperature and moisture affect malaria, river blindness, schistosomiasis, dengue fever, and infantile diarrhea, all vastly more dangerous than the radioactive and chemical hazards that worry people in the developed countries.

Alarmists have weighed in with dire predictions of how a warming of tropical and subtropical regions will aggravate the scourge of tropical diseases. But any changes in temperature and moisture need to be superimposed on those areas as they are likely to be 50 or 75 years from now, with better sanitation, nutrition and medical and environmental technology, cleaner water, and the potential eradication of vector-borne diseases.

Malaysia and Singapore have identical climates. There is malaria in Malaysia, but hardly any in Singapore, and any malaria in Singapore gets sophisticated treatment. By the time Malaysia catches up to where Singapore is now, many tropical diseases may have been tamed. One invasive tropical creature, the guinea worm, is already expected to follow smallpox into extinction.

The Marshall Model

The modern era of greenhouse concern dates from the 1992 Rio Conference, attended by President Bush, which produced a "framework convention" for the pursuit of reduced carbon emissions. A sequel is set for Kyoto in December. Countries from the Organization for Economic Cooperation and Development (OECD) are groping for criteria and procedures to determine "targets and timetables." There are proposals for the formal allocation of enforceable quotas, possibly with trading of emission rights. There is disappointment with the lack of convincing progress in the five years since Rio. Many people wonder whether Kyoto will settle anything.

It will not. But five years is to soon to be disappointed. Nothing like a carbon emissions regime has ever been attempted, and it is no country's individual interest to do much about emissions: the atmosphere is a global common where everybody's emissions mingle with everybody else's. The burden to be shared is large, there are no accepted standards of fairness, nations differ greatly in their dependence on fossil fuels, and any regime to be taken seriously has to promise to survive a long time.

There are few precedents. The U.N. budget required a negotiated formula, but adherence is conspicuously imperfect, and the current budget, even including peacekeeping, is two orders of magnitude smaller than what a serious carbon regime would require. The costs in reduced productivity are estimated at two percent of GNP—forever. Two percent of GNP seems politically unmanageable in many countries.

Still, if one plots the curve of U.S. per capita GNP over the coming century with and without the two percent permanent loss, the difference is about the thickness of a line drawn with a number two pencil, and the doubled per capita income that might have been achieved by 2060 is reached in 2062. If someone could wave a wand and phase in, over a few years, a climate-mitigation program that depressed our GNP by two percent in perpetuity, no one would notice the difference.

The only experience commensurate with carbon reduction was division of aid in the Marshall Plan. In 1949–50 there was $4 billion to share. The percentage of European GNP that this amounted to depends on hypothetical exchange rates appropriate to the period, but it was well over two percent, although differing drastically among the countries. The United States insisted that the Europeans divide the aid themselves, and gave them most of a year to prepare.

The procedure was what I call "multilateral reciprocal scrutiny." Each country prepared detailed national accounts showing consumption, investment, dollar earnings and imports, intra-European trade, specifics like per capita fuel and meat consumption, taxes, and government expenditures—anything that might justify a share of U.S. aid. There was never a formula. There were not even criteria; there were "considerations." There was no notion that aid should be allocated to maximize recovery, equalize standards of living, balance improvements in consumption levels, or meet any other objective. Each country made its claim for aid on whatever grounds it chose. Each was queried and cross-examined about dollar-export potential, domestic substitutes for dollar imports, dietary standards, rate of livestock recovery, severity of gasoline rationing, and anything pertinent to dollar requirements. The objective was consensus on how to divide the precious $4 billion.

Although they did not succeed, they were close enough for arbitration by a committee of two people to produce an acceptable division. After the Korean War, when NATO replaced recovery as the objective, the same procedure was used. Again consensus was not reached, but again there was enough agreement for arbitration by a committee of three to decide not only the division of aid but military burdens to be assumed. Multilateral reciprocal scrutiny proved effective, no doubt because an unprecedented camaraderie had been cultivated during the Marshall Plan. And remember, consensus had to be reached by countries as different in their development, war damage, politics, and cultures as Turkey, Norway, Italy, and France. A similar procedure recently led to the European Union's schedule of carbon reductions for its member countries. A difference is that in the Marshall Plan it was for keeps!

Did the Marshall Plan succeed despite, or because of, its lack of formal quantitative criteria and its reliance on looser, more open-ended, pragmatic modes of discourse and argument? In the time available, plan participants could not have agreed on formal criteria. In the end they had to be satisfied with a division. Any argument over variables and parameters would have been self-serving arguments once removed; arguing explicitly over shares was more direct and candid. Had the process gone on several years, more formal criteria might have been forged. The same may occur eventually with carbon emissions.

Setting the Ceiling

Two thousand American economists recently recommended that national emission quotas promptly be negotiated, with purchase and sale of emission rights allowed to assure a fair geographic distribution of reductions. This appears to be the U.S. position for the meeting in Kyoto. It is an elegant idea. But its feasibility is suspect, at least for the present.

One cannot envision national representatives calmly sitting down to divide up rights in perpetuity worth more than a trillion dollars. It is also hard to imagine an enforcement mechanism acceptable to the U.S. Senate. I do not even foresee agreement on what concentration of greenhouse gases will ultimately be tolerable. Without that, any trajectory of global emissions had to be transitory, in which case renegotiation is bound to be anticipated, and no prudent nation is likely to sell its surplus emissions when doing so is clear evidence that it was originally allowed more than it needed.

The current focus of international negotiation is extremely short-term. That is probably appropriate, but the long term needs to be acknowledged and kept in mind. If carbon-induced climate change proves serious, it will be the ultimate concentration of greenhouse gases in the atmosphere that matters. The objective should be to stabilize that final concentration at a level compatible with tolerable climate change. Emissions of the carbon-based gases are the current focus of attention, but the question of concentration is what needs to be settled.

If scientists knew the upper limit to what the earth's climate system could tolerate, that limit could serve as the concentration target. It would probably not matter much climatically how that limit was approached. The optimal trajectory would probably include a continuing rise in annual emissions for a few decades, followed by a significant decline as the world approached a sustainable low level compatible with the ceiling on concentration. That is no argument for present inaction: future technologies that people will rely on to save energy or make energy less carbon-intensive 10, 20, or 30 years from now will depend on much more vigorous research and development, much of it at public expense, than governments and private institutions are doing or even contemplating now.

The ceiling is variously proposed as 450, 550, 650, or 750 parts per million, compared with about 360 parts per million today. The Intergovernmental Panel on Climate Change, the scientific advisory body associated with these conferences, has rendered no opinion on what level of concentration might ultimately become intolerable. Without that decision, there can be no long-range plan.

In the short run, there will almost certainly be innumerable modest but worthwhile opportunities for reducing carbon emissions. National representatives from the developed countries are counting on it. They are proposing reductions of 10 or 15 percent in annual emissions for most developed countries during the coming decade or so. If such reductions are seriously pursued—an open question—a rising trend in emissions would be superimposed on a short-term effort to limit actual emissions.

A program of short-term reductions would help governments learn more about emissions and how much they can be reduced by different measures. But the prevailing sentiment seems to be that emissions can be brought down and kept down in the OECD countries. It is not yet politically correct to acknowledge that global emissions are bound to increase for many decades, especially as nations like China experience economic growth and greater energy use.

When the OECD countries do get serious about combating climate change, they should focus on actions—policies, programs, taxes, subsidies, regulations, investments, energy technology research and development—that governments can actually take or bring about that will affect emissions. Commitments to targets and timetables are inherently flawed. They are pegged some years into the future, generally the further the better. Moreover, most governments cannot predict their policies' impact on emissions.

To pick an unrealistic example, if the United States committed itself to raising the tax on gasoline by ten cents per gallon per year for the next 15 years, any agency could discern whether the tax actually went up a dime per year, and the U.S. government would know exactly what it was committed to doing. But nobody can predict what that tax would do to emissions by the end of 15 years.

Greenhouse Politics

Slowing global warming is a political problem. The cost will be relatively low: a few trillion dollars over the next 30 or 40 years, out of an OECD gross product rising from $15 trillion to $30 trillion or $40 trillion annually. But any greenhouse program that is not outrageously inefficient will have to address carbon emissions in China, whose current emissions are half the United States' but will be several times the U.S. level in 2050 if left unchecked. The OECD countries can curtail their own emissions through regulation, which, although inefficient, is politically more acceptable than taxes because the costs remain invisible. The developed-country expense of curtailing Chinese emissions will require visible transfers of budgeted resources. it will look like the foreign aid it actually is, although it will benefit China no more than India or Nigeria. Building non-carbon or carbon-efficient electric power in China will look like aid to China, not climate relief for the world.

There remains a nagging issue that is never addressed at meetings on global warming policy. The future beneficiaries of these policies in developing countries will almost certainly be better off than their grandparents, today's residents of those countries. Alternative uses of resources devoted to ameliorating climate change should be considered. Namely, does it make more sense to invest directly in the development of these countries?

There are two issues here. One is whether, in benefits three or four generations hence, the return for investing directly in public health, education, water resources, infrastructure, industry, agricultural productivity, and family planning is as great as that for investing in reduced climate change. The second is whether the benefits accrue earlier, to people who more desperately need the help. Is there something escapist about discussing two percent of GNP to be invested in the welfare of future generations when nothing is done for their contemporary ancestors, a third of whom are so undernourished that a case of measles can kill?

If there were aid to divide between Bangladesh and Singapore, would anybody propose giving any of it to Singapore? In 50 or 75 years, when climate change may be a significant reality, Bangladesh probably will have progressed to the level of Singapore today. Should anyone propose investing heavily in the welfare of those future Bangladeshis when the alternative is to help Bangladesh today? People worry that the sea level may rise half a meter in the next century from global warming and that large populated areas of Bangladesh may flood. But Bangladesh already suffers terrible floods.

The need for greenhouse gas abatement cannot logically be separated from the developing world's need for immediate economic improvement. The tradeoff should be faced. It probably won't be.

24   *Kyoto's Unfinished Business*

Henry D. Jacoby

Ronald G. Prinn

Richard Schmalensee

Henry D. Jacoby is a Professor of Management Economics and Codirector of the Joint Program on the Science and Policy of Global Change at the Massachusetts Institute of Technology; Ronald G. Prinn is the TEPCO Professor of Atmospheric Chemistry, Codirector of the Joint Program on the Science and Policy of Global Change, and Director of the Center for Global Change Science at MIT; Richard Schmalensee is the John C. Head III Dean and Professor of Economics of the Sloan School of Management at the Massachusetts Institute of Technology.

Taking the Long View on Global Warming

Even well-informed observers disagree about what the Kyoto Protocol on Climate Change will accomplish. Some gaze at its text and see a battle won. They cheer the fact that the generally richer nations participating in the protocol agreed to cut their collective emissions of the greenhouse gases that cause global warming to about five percent less than 1990 levels by early in the next century. These optimists also applaud features of the Kyoto accord designed to hold down the costs of achieving these reductions. In computing their emissions, nations can include changes in the six major greenhouse gases emitted because of human activity, not just carbon dioxide, the most important of the six. In addition, countries can factor in reduced carbon dioxide levels from changes in land use and new forestry techniques that take the gas out of the atmosphere. Groups of participating nations may comply jointly and reallocate commitments among themselves, as the European Union (EU) plans to do within a European "bubble," and there is agreement in principle to some form of emissions trading. Joint implementation, under which agents in one country can get credit for reductions they achieve in another, is to be permitted between participating nations, and a new Clean Development Mechanism will provide access to these opportunities in nonparticipating countries, mainly in the developing world. Finally, emissions targets are not rigidly tied to a single year, but to averages over a five-year "commitment period" from 2008 to 2012.

Pessimists, on the other hand, see Kyoto as a costly defeat. They note that there is no solid proof that human-induced climate change will occur or

"Kyoto's Unfinished Business," by Henry D. Jacoby, Ronald G. Prinn, and Richard Schmalensee, from *Foreign Affairs*, 77(4):54–66 (July/August 1998).

that its adverse effects would be serious were it to happen. At the same time, the expense of reducing greenhouse gas emissions to meet the Kyoto targets will be substantial, and pessimists believe that the effort will make participating countries less competitive. In the darkest interpretation, the Kyoto agreement is a pact among rich nations that will cripple their economies for decades to come, made simply because today's political leaders needed to burnish their environmental credentials.

Neither of these schools of thought is correct. Still a third group, whose views are much closer to the mark, believes that Kyoto mainly postpones much-needed work on what may prove a very serious long-term challenge. To them, Kyoto is a quick political fix for a problem created at the First Conference of Parties to the Climate Convention held in Berlin in 1995. The so-called Berlin mandate instructed negotiators to seek short-term, legally binding targets and timetables for emission control for participating countries only. In the run-up to Kyoto, many leaders publicly committed themselves to this idea. Not surprisingly, avoiding embarrassment on this score became the dominant focus of the negotiations. As a result, this group argues, the Kyoto agreement allows political leaders to declare success, but it does not address the larger climate issues at stake.

Even worse, these skeptics fear that by following the Berlin mandate, negotiators at Kyoto may have made it harder, not easier, to meet the long-term challenge. Now the next decade may be spent haggling over these short-term commitments, thereby diverting attention from more important century-scale issues and postponing the involvement of the developing world. The Kyoto agreement might fail to meet even its immediate goals if the lack of domestic support in the United States prevents ratification, which in turn would rationalize inaction by other participating nations. The entire international response to climate change could be discredited, thus increasing the difficulty of collective action in the future, no matter how serious the problem turns out to be.

To some degree, these widely divergent analyses of the Kyoto achievement reflect differing interpretations of its text, key parts of which are still the subject of strong and sometimes bitter international disagreement. Some of these points will be taken up again at the Fourth Conference of the Parties in November, but others may take years to resolve. What is in dispute is not merely the Kyoto text, of course, but the underlying science and economics of global warming. Above all, for the journey from Kyoto to succeed, policymakers will need to spend more time thinking of the long term.

A Global Warming Primer

To start with the basics, climate change can be driven by an imbalance between the energy the earth receives from the sun, largely as visible light, and the energy it radiates back to space as invisible infrared light. The "greenhouse effect" is caused by the presence in the air of gases and clouds that absorb some of the infrared light flowing upward and radiate it back downward. The warming influence of this re-radiated energy is opposed by substances at the surface and in the atmosphere that reflect sunlight directly back into space. These include snow and desert sand, as well as clouds and aerosols. (Aerosols are tiny, submicroscopic solid or liquid particles suspended in the air, such as smoke and fog.)

Water vapor and clouds, which typically remain in the atmosphere for a week or so, are responsible for most of the re-radiated infrared light. Central to the climate change debate, however, are less important but much longer-lasting greenhouse gases, most notably carbon dioxide. Atmospheric concentrations of carbon dioxide and other long-lived greenhouse gases have increased substantially over the past century. As this has happened, the flow of infrared energy to space has been reduced, so that, all else being equal, the earth receives slightly more energy than it radiates to space. This imbalance tends to raise temperatures at the earth's surface. These aspects of the greenhouse effect are not controversial. It is also generally accepted that emissions of carbon dioxide from the combustion of fossil fuels (primarily coal, oil, and natural gas) are the most significant way humans can increase the greenhouse effect, and that this emitted carbon dioxide remains in the atmosphere for a long time, on the order of a century or so.

What is much more uncertain, and the cause of serious scientific debate, is the response of the complex system that determines our climate to changes in the concentrations of greenhouse gases in the atmosphere. Some poorly understood processes in the climate system tend to amplify the warming effect of greenhouse gases, while others, equally poorly understood, tend to counteract or dampen it. Any global warming will likely be delayed because it takes a lot of heat to warm the oceans, but it is not known just how rapidly heat is carried into the ocean depths.

To predict climate, scientists must use mathematical models whose complexity taxes the capabilities of even the world's largest computers. These models are based on incomplete knowledge about the key factors that influence climate, including clouds, ocean circulation, the natural cycles of greenhouse gases, natural aerosols like those produced by volcanic gases, and man-made aerosols like smog. Today's climate models cannot reproduce the succession of ice ages and warm periods over the last 250,000 years, let alone the smaller climatic fluctuations observed over the last century. In addition, climate models are driven by forecasts of greenhouse gas emissions, which in turn rest on highly uncertain long-term predictions of population trends, economic growth, and technological advances.

Burning Down the House?

To help quantify the uncertainty in climate prediction, we and our MIT colleagues have developed a model of global economic development, climate processes, and ecosystems. We have produced seven forecasts of cli-

mate change over the next century, each of which assumes no action to restrict future greenhouse gas emissions and can be defended as possible
given current knowledge. These forecasts involve changes in global average surface temperature between 1990 and 2100 as small as two degrees
Fahrenheit or as large as nine degrees Fahrenheit (roughly one to five degrees centigrade). We cannot sort out which of these paths (or other possible ones) we are heading along, although we are less likely to be on one
of the extreme ones. There may be other paths involving rapid climate
changes driven by purely natural processes that are not well handled by
any current climate models.

Unfortunately, we know even less about the likely impact of climate
change. Warming may increase storm damage, for instance, but it may
also decrease it. Very little is known about the likely impact on human
health or the ability of unmanaged ecosystems to adapt to shifting conditions. Civilization and natural systems have coped with climate change
in the past and can, to at least some degree, adapt. What we do know
suggests that the changes summarized by the lowest of the seven forecasts would do little harm and might even benefit some countries. Most
analysts would agree, however, that the highest of our seven forecasts
implies significant risks to a variety of important natural processes including ocean circulation, polar glaciers, and unmanaged ecosystems, as
well as agriculture and other human activities. Indeed, for policymakers,
the most important finding of climate research to date may be that the
range of possible outcomes is so wide. Sound policy decisions must take
account of this profound uncertainty, and it is plainly vital to accelerate
research aimed at reducing it.

An important complement to the work on forecasts is the search for
what has been called a fingerprint—evidence that would clearly reveal human influence on climate. In its 1995 report, the Intergovernmental Panel
on Climate Change (IPCC) declared in its *Summary for Policymakers* that
"the balance of evidence suggests a discernible human influence on climate." Several scientists, however, subsequently questioned the scientific
basis of this summary and the certainty it conveyed. Hence the hunt for
definitive evidence of human-induced climate change remains an important research area—mainly because the stronger the human influence on
climate, the earlier it will be possible to detect its "signal" despite the "noise"
of natural variability in climate over time. The larger the proven human
influence on climate, the stronger will be the case for substantial reductions in greenhouse gas emissions.

The current debate about detection does not justify inaction. As our
range of forecasts indicates, we know enough to conclude that human activity may produce significant global warming, with substantial adverse impacts. It would be irresponsible to ignore such a risk, just as it would be
irresponsible to do nothing when you smell smoke at home until and unless you see flames. It would also be irresponsible, of course, to call the
fire department and hose down all your belongings at the slightest whiff
of what might be smoke.

What It Takes

The ultimate goal of the climate treaty to which the Kyoto protocol is attached is stabilizing atmospheric concentrations of greenhouse gases at levels that will avoid "danger" to economies and ecosystems. No one knows what the appropriate levels might be, or even if the implicit notion of a sharp line between danger and safety makes sense. The nature of the potential task can be explored, however, by studying an EU recommendation that countries stabilize the amount of carbon dioxide in the atmosphere at roughly twice preindustrial levels, in the long run. Doing this would slow climate change but, according to most climate models, not stop it. For the middle range of MIT model forecasts, following the IPCC path to stabilization at the EU target would lower projected warming between now and 2100 by only about 30 percent, although it would produce a larger percentage reduction in the following century.

Following this EU recommendation would require very sharp cuts in global carbon dioxide emissions, however, and the current signatories to the Kyoto protocol could not do the job by themselves. If the nonparticipating nations were to accept no restrictions, net emissions by participating nations would somehow have to become negative by around the middle of the next century. Even a total ban on use of fossil fuels by all industrialized countries would not reach the target.

Of course, if the nations currently participating in Kyoto reduce their emissions, other nations might also eventually agree to lower theirs. Unfortunately, income growth in the most populous nonparticipating countries—including China, India, Indonesia, and Brazil—seems unlikely to encourage voluntary efforts until the latter part of the next century. Until then, these nations will naturally be more concerned with feeding their children than with protecting their grandchildren from potential global warming. Thus, if the relatively rich participating countries want to stabilize atmospheric concentrations of greenhouse gases, they will have to pay at least some poor countries to reduce their emissions. Achievement of substantial reduction in this way implies international transfers of wealth on a scale well beyond anything in recorded history.

There is no effective political support for such a herculean effort, particularly in the United States. Given the uncertainties discussed above, such an effort would make little economic sense in any event. The groundwork, however, must be laid now to preserve any hope of someday mounting such a response. Future generations will find three legacies especially valuable: participation of all countries in climate-related actions, development of new technologies to lower the cost of emissions control, and the creation of institutions for cost-effective multinational action.

First, a substantial reduction in global emissions will require something close to worldwide participation, so it is essential to build a climate agreement that can encompass countries not currently participating in Kyoto—including most of the developing world. Such an accord must include a way for these countries to gradually accept the burdens of emissions control. Equally important, it must also anticipate a regime to govern climate-related transfers of resources to countries that cannot bear the cost of emissions reduction.

An exclusive emphasis on the relatively wealthy nations participating in Kyoto is a double-edged sword. If rich nations do not control their emissions, poorer ones are unlikely even to consider slowing theirs. But carbon dioxide emission controls will raise the cost in participating countries of manufacturing those goods whose production requires substantial energy. For these products, industries in developing countries will gain an advantage over industries in countries that abide by Kyoto. Once they have invested in production facilities, nonparticipating nations will be more reluctant to take emission-control measures that threaten these activities.

Second, it will be nearly impossible to slow warming appreciably without condemning much of the world to poverty unless energy sources that emit little or no carbon dioxide become competitive with conventional fossil fuels. Only a large R&D effort can have any hope of bringing this about, although it would be cheap relative to the cost of dramatic reductions in carbon dioxide emissions using current technologies. The range of technological options is wide—from using solar power to produce electricity to converting fossil fuels to hydrogen fuel and storing (underground or deep in the ocean) the carbon dioxide produced as a byproduct. Few of the alternatives currently under discussion, however, can be widely used at reasonable costs without fundamental improvements.

Finally, since climate change will be a high-stakes global issue for many decades, the world must begin to develop international institutions that will facilitate policies that minimize the cost of reducing greenhouse gas emissions. For starters, this requires solving the monitoring and enforcement problems necessary to implement efficient international trading of rights to emit greenhouse gases (or to implement internationally harmonized taxes on greenhouse gas emissions). It also requires an institutional structure that can exploit the cheapest abatement opportunities, wherever they may be found, and a decision-making process that can adjust policies to reflect changes in scientific knowledge and economic development.

This is a tall order. The international trade regime developed under the General Agreement on Tariffs and Trade, now the World Trade Organization, hints at the difficulties involved. This regime grew and evolved over time, adding countries and goods along the way, peacefully resolving conflicts between national economic interests, and contributing importantly to global economic growth. By the standards of international affairs, the WTO has been a stunning success, but it took 50 years of hard work—even given an intelligent, forward-looking design at the outset.

A Kyoto Report Card

Kyoto's results are mixed. The agreement failed miserably at including poorer countries. Until the last minute, the negotiating text at Kyoto contained a provision allowing a nonparticipating nation to choose, at any time and on a voluntary basis, a level of emissions control it felt was appropriate to its circumstances. This "opt-in" provision made sense as an opening to wider participation, particularly since some nonparticipating nations, like Singapore, are wealthier than some participants, like Romania. Several nonparticipating countries supported the idea, but the provision was struck from the protocol because key developing countries—especially China and India—strongly opposed adding any avenues that could lead to emissions limits for them. For their part, the developed countries were unwilling to risk deadlock on this issue and let Beijing and New Delhi have their way.

Investment in research and development on new long-term technical options was not even discussed. One phrase calling for parties to "cooperate in scientific and technical research" was tucked away in the text, but that was all; no nation was obliged to devote any resources to R&D. Politicians love to call for more research instead of more regulation, but there is little commitment to the long-term development of greenhouse-friendly technology by those countries most capable of producing it.

The news from Kyoto is more encouraging regarding provisions to facilitate flexible, cost-efficient policies for controlling emissions. Including multiple gases was a step in the right direction. In principle, schemes like the Clean Development Mechanism may encourage making emissions reductions wherever they are least expensive. But these systems give credit for specific emissions reductions, and U.S. experience with similar policies indicates that the administrative and transaction costs of the required project-by-project approval process are likely to limit their benefits substantially. Most important, the Kyoto provision that in principle allows the trading of rights to emit greenhouse gases, if implemented effectively, would yield major reductions in cost.

Other features built into Kyoto to create more flexibility give less cause for celebration. The provision for multicountry "bubbles," within which national emissions limits can be adjusted as long as the total is kept constant, is an artifact of short-term political convenience. The creation of such a bubble for the EU is entirely consistent with other EU institutions. It provides a mechanism for differentiation within the EU while its leaders seek uniform commitments from non-Europeans. The application of the idea to other groups of nations emerged as Washington's defensive response to widespread and continuing opposition to emissions trading. If full-fledged trading were ultimately lost, at least some flexibility might be gained in the short term through government-to-government shifting of quotas. While such arrangements may reduce costs over the next few years, they will not provide flexibility in the long run, and they might make it harder to realize the benefits of full global trading by balkanizing the market.

The inclusion in the Kyoto protocol of credits for "carbon sinks"—increases in the removal of carbon dioxide from the atmosphere because of post-1990 changes in land use and forestry practices—is another double-edged sword. In principle, measures to encourage the use of these sinks should be covered by Kyoto because they may be cost-effective for some countries. Land vegetation is already removing carbon from the atmosphere, on balance, probably spurred by increased plant growth caused by rising atmospheric carbon dioxide. The uncertainties are great, but central estimates in the IPCC report indicate that for the world as a whole, the net removal of carbon dioxide from the atmosphere in this way amounts to about 30 percent of current emissions from the burning of fossil fuels. For countries with large forests, such as the United States, Canada, and Russia, biological sinks may play an important role in their emissions accounting. With stakes this large, and with ambiguity inherent in the protocol's definitions of the 1990 baseline and of increases in removal by sinks, fierce debates about measurement and accounting are already under way. The sinks issue could easily become a troubling diversion.

Finally, it is important to be clear-eyed about the risks involved in the core agreement of the Kyoto protocol: national targets and the 2008–12 timetable. On the positive side, the Kyoto targets are a start toward a long-term solution. If participating countries meet the 5 percent reduction goal and stabilize their emissions at that level for the rest of the century, then—with no restrictions on nonparticipating nations—warming by 2100 will be reduced by about 16 percent. Also, these initial cuts could have important symbolic value, providing incentives for R&D and laying the groundwork for broader national participation. The risk is that these advantages will be lost, and worse, if the emissions reductions agreed to in Kyoto are not met—as they probably will not be. The longer any nation delays adopting serious controls on greenhouse gas emissions, the higher the cost of meeting its Kyoto obligations and the more difficult it will be to generate the requisite domestic political support. The current U.S. policy involves a long delay, which is likely to discourage earlier action by other participating nations fearing a loss of international competitiveness.

The current U.S. climate plan has two main provisions. First, the Clinton administration has asked Congress for $6.3 billion over five years for a technology initiative offering tax incentives and R&D expenditures "to encourage energy efficiency and the use of cleaner energy sources." Second, after a "decade of experience, a decade of data, a decade of technological innovation," the plan holds that whatever administration is in office in 2007 will cap U.S. greenhouse gas emissions and institute a domestic system of tradable rights to emit. Unfortunately, under current policy, the end of the "decade of opportunity" is likely to find U.S. emissions 20 to 25 percent above the 1990 level. The International Energy Agency estimates that by 2000 the United States' emissions will be 16 percent higher than they were in 1990, and climbing. It is simply laughable to forecast that

Washington would then impose a cap on emissions stringent enough to turn the energy economy around in three to five years. Moreover, the administration has promised not to send the Kyoto protocol to the Senate for ratification until developing nations commit to "substantial participation." It is not easy to see when such a condition might be met, particularly if vigorous U.S. action is in any way needed to involve the developing world.

Thus, Kyoto is likely to yield far less than the targeted emissions reduction. That failure will most likely be papered over with creative accounting, shifting definitions of carbon sinks, and so on. If this happens, the credibility of the international process for addressing climate change will be at risk. Other outcomes are possible, of course. Other nations may decide to move forward with emissions control despite U.S. inaction. Changes in U.S. public opinion may accelerate domestic action. Small investments in research may yield unexpectedly large near-term payoffs. Slow economic growth may hold emissions down. Still, even meeting the aggregate Kyoto target will be a hollow victory if it requires spending economic resources and political capital that would be better used to prepare for the vastly greater reductions in global emissions that may be required in the future.

Now, the Hard Part

Even though the dust has not settled from the struggle in Kyoto, preparations have begun for the Fourth Conference of the Parties (COP-4) in November. Its focus should be on the longer term.

It is most important to try again to develop a system that can include developing countries and, if necessary, transfer substantial resources to help them participate in a global effort to control emissions. Two opportunities are apparent, one recently rejected at Kyoto and the other only recently advanced there. First is an amendment to Kyoto that restores the provision that would allow nonparticipating countries to volunteer to control their emissions under flexible terms. For any nation seriously concerned with climate change, this should be a necessary condition for ratification of the Kyoto protocol. If the developing countries' opposition to even voluntary action cannot be overcome, it is probably better to scrap Kyoto and start negotiations again when opinions have changed.

Given success on this point, there may then be room for progress on negotiating the details of the Clean Development Mechanism. The protocol suggests that the "operating entities" that will decide how much credit will be given for specific emission reduction projects under the CDM might serve as intermediaries, helping to reduce transaction costs. If so, the CDM might help bring developing countries into the fold. Most studies find that emissions can be least expensively reduced in those countries, so that nonparticipating nations could, in principle, make a great deal of money selling emissions reductions to participating nations. On the other hand, the

U.S. regulatory experience suggests that because it is hard to estimate precisely what emissions would have been in the absence of particular investments, the CDM could also produce red tape and plenty of administrative jobs but have scant impact on emissions. Much depends on the details to be worked out in COP-4. If those negotiations produce a heavily bureaucratic structure, perhaps burdened with taxes on trades in emissions reduction credits, it may be better to reject this proposal and begin anew.

Dealing seriously with climate change requires a substantial R&D program to produce new technologies that could bring about deep global emissions reductions and still allow robust economic growth. Such an effort should involve several wealthy participating nations. Candidate technologies include nuclear, solar, hydroelectric, geothermal, and hydrogen from fossil fuel. Methods for safe and economical long-term storage of carbon in subterranean reservoirs, the deep ocean, and forests are also important research areas, as are technologies that enhance energy efficiency. In contrast, the U.S. "technology initiative" concentrates on subsidizing the adoption of existing technologies but would spend little in the search for long-term breakthroughs. Efforts elsewhere are similarly dwarfed by the challenge.

Finally, a well-designed, durable institutional structure can significantly reduce the cost of limits on global emissions. Here, the key piece of unfinished business from Kyoto is implementing a system for trading the rights to emit greenhouse gases among participating nations. In negotiating the details of this system, now scheduled for COP-4, a focus on clear definitions, vigilant monitoring, and strict enforcement is essential. Otherwise, the market should be left unfettered. Many nations oppose trading in any form; others want to restrict its use in meeting emissions commitments. If they make it impossible to implement a plausible framework for international trading of emission rights, the Kyoto protocol is headed for a dead end, obviating the point of ratifying it.

The challenge will be developing a framework for international decision-making that can work for several decades. Building these three legacies—inclusion of the developing world, R&D, and flexible provisions for emissions reductions—will be a huge undertaking. But since no serious response to climate change is possible without them, the task merits the same sense of urgency that motivated Kyoto. When it comes to climate change, the world's work has just begun.

25   *The Role of Economics in Climate Change Policy**

Warwick J. McKibbin and Peter J. Wilcoxen

Warwick J. McKibbin is Professor of International Economics in the Research School of Pacific and Asian Studies, Australia National University, Canberra, Australia. Peter J. Wilcoxen is Associate Professor of Economics and Public Administration at The Maxwell School, Syracuse University. Both authors are also Non-Resident Senior Fellows, Brookings Institution, Washington, D.C.

Many policy problems have frustratingly long histories of inefficient regulation that can be difficult or impossible to reverse, even where large efficiency gains might be had from doing so. Climate change is an exception, however, because little real action has been undertaken to date. It presents an unusual opportunity for an efficient economic policy to be employed right from the beginning. However, the opportunity could easily be lost. Ongoing negotiations conducted under the auspices of the United Nations Framework Convention on Climate Change have so far produced the Kyoto Protocol, a deeply flawed agreement that manages to be both economically inefficient and politically impractical.

In this article, we examine the key economic characteristics of climate change and argue that economic theory provides good guidance on the design of an efficient and politically realistic policy. Because climate change involves vast uncertainties and has potentially enormous distributional effects, neither of the standard market-based environmental policy instruments is a viable approach: a tradable permit system would be inefficient, and an emissions tax would be politically unrealistic. However, a hybrid policy, combining the best features of the two, would be an efficient and practical approach. We then compare our hybrid proposal to the Kyoto Protocol and argue that it overcomes the Protocol's shortcomings.

The Only Certainty Is Uncertainty

At the heart of the climate change debate are two undisputed facts. The first is that certain gases in the atmosphere are transparent to ultraviolet light but absorb infrared radiation. The most famous of these gases is carbon

"The Role of Economics in Climate Change Policy," by Warwick J. McKibbin and Peter J. Wilcoxen, from *Journal of Economic Perspectives*, 16(2):107–129 (Spring 2002).

*We are grateful to J. Bradford De Long, Michael Waldman and Timothy Taylor for many helpful comments on an earlier draft of this paper.

dioxide, but water vapor, methane, nitrous oxide, chlorofluorocarbons and various other gases have the same property. Energy from the sun, in the form of ultraviolet light, passes through the carbon dioxide unimpeded and is absorbed by objects on the ground. As the objects become warm, they release the energy as infrared radiation. If the atmosphere held no carbon dioxide, most of the infrared energy would escape back into space. The carbon dioxide, however, absorbs the infrared and reradiates it back toward the surface, thus raising global temperatures. This mechanism is known as the "greenhouse effect," because it traps energy near the Earth's surface in a manner somewhat analogous to the way glass keeps a greenhouse warm. Carbon dioxide and other gases contributing to this effect are called "greenhouse gases."

The second undisputed fact is that the concentration of many greenhouse gases has been increasing rapidly due to human activity. Every year, fossil fuel use adds about six billion metric tons of carbon—in the form of carbon dioxide—to the atmosphere. As shown in Table 1, emissions are largest in industrialized countries, but growing most rapidly in the developing world (Energy Information Administration, 1999). Once emitted, carbon dioxide remains in the atmosphere for as long as 200 years. As a result, the atmospheric concentration of carbon dioxide—and hence its effect on temperature—reflects the stock of accumulated emissions over decades. Studies of ice cores from Antarctica show that carbon dioxide levels varied between 270 and 290 parts per million for thousands of years before the beginning of the Industrial Revolution.[1] By 1998, however, the concentration had risen to 365 parts per million, an increase of 30 percent.

Human activity has increased the concentration of other greenhouse gases as well. The concentration of methane—emitted as a byproduct of agriculture, natural gas production and landfills—has risen by 150 percent: from 700 parts per billion to 1,745 parts per billion in 1998. The concentration of nitrous oxide has also risen over the same time frame, although by a more modest 17 percent. Finally, chlorofluorocarbons comprise only a small fraction of the atmosphere, but they are entirely the result of human activity and are especially effective at trapping infrared energy. Together, the increased concentrations of methane, nitrous oxide and chlorofluorocarbons contribute about two-thirds as much heat-trapping capacity to the atmosphere as the increase in carbon dioxide.

Beyond these two points, controversy arises. Although greenhouse gases can trap energy and make the atmosphere warmer, and the concentration

---

[1] The scientific literature on the causes of climate change, its potential effects on natural ecosystems and human populations, and on policies that might be used in response has been exhaustively surveyed by the Intergovernmental Panel on Climate Change (IPCC). The IPCC was created in 1988 under the joint sponsorship of the World Meteorological Organization and the United Nations Environment Programme. To date, it has conducted three assessments of the literature, each involving hundreds of natural and social scientists from around the world. These figures, and others in the paper that are not specifically attributed to another source, are drawn from the IPCC's most recent study, the *Third Assessment Report*, which was completed in 2001.

Table I Recent Carbon Emissions by Region and Country
(millions of metric tons of carbon)

Region	Carbon (MMT)		Percentage of 1999 Total	Increase from 1990 to 1999
	1990	*1999*		
North America	1567	1772	29%	13%
Canada	128	151	2%	18%
Mexico	84	101	2%	20%
United States	1355	1520	25%	12%
Central and South America	192	267	4%	39%
Brazil	63	89	1%	41%
Other	129	178	3%	38%
Western Europe	1006	1015	17%	1%
Germany	271	230	4%	−15%
United Kingdon	164	152	2%	−7%
Other	571	633	10%	11%
Eastern Europe and the Former USSR	1298	789	13%	−39%
Russia	647	400	7%	−38%
Other	651	389	6%	−40%
Middle East	203	287	5%	41%
Africa	198	237	4%	20%
Far East and Oceania	1410	1776	29%	26%
Australia	72	94	2%	31%
China	617	669	11%	8%
India	156	243	4%	56%
Japan	269	307	5%	14%
Other	296	463	8%	56%
World Total	5873	6143	100%	5%

of those gases has been increasing, it is far from clear what those facts mean for global temperatures. A long list of scientific uncertainties makes it difficult to say precisely how much warming will result from a given increase in greenhouse gas concentrations, or when such warming will occur or how it will affect different regions and ecosystems.

One challenge for climatologists has been understanding the link between temperature change and atmospheric water vapor. On one hand, higher temperatures increase the rate of evaporation and allow the atmosphere to hold more water vapor. Since water vapor is itself a greenhouse gas, this could lead to a feedback cycle that exacerbates any temperature increase caused by carbon dioxide. On the other hand, a given increase in atmospheric capacity to hold water vapor does not necessarily imply an equal increase in water vapor, since much of the atmosphere is not saturated.

A closely related uncertainty is the role of clouds. Clouds reflect ultraviolet radiation, thus reducing the amount of solar radiation reaching the ground, so an increase in cloud cover could tend to reduce the greenhouse effect. At the same time, clouds absorb and reradiate infrared, which tends to increase the greenhouse effect. Which effect dominates depends heavily on factors that vary from one location to another: the altitude and thickness of the cloud, the amount of water vapor in the atmosphere and the presence of ice crystals or aerosols (tiny airborne particles or droplets) in the area. Given current knowledge, it is not possible to say for certain whether cloud formation is likely to amplify or to attenuate temperature changes from other sources.

Another problem is determining how quickly ocean temperatures will respond to global warming. Water has a high capacity for holding heat, and the volume of sea water is enormous, so the oceans will tend to slow climate change by absorbing excess heat from the atmosphere. This effect delays warming, but does not prevent it: eventually the oceans will warm enough to return to thermal equilibrium with the atmosphere. However, the time required to reach equilibrium depends on many complicated interactions, such as the mixing of different layers of sea water, that are not completely understood and are difficult to model.

Yet another important uncertainty arises because the role of aerosols in the atmosphere is poorly understood. Aerosols originate from a variety of sources: dust storms, volcanoes, fossil fuel combustion and the burning of forests or other organic material. These tiny particles or droplets reflect a portion of incoming solar radiation, which tends to reduce climate change, but they also absorb infrared, which tends to increase it. The concentration of aerosols in the atmosphere seems to be increasing, and this increase may have partially offset the increase in carbon dioxide during the last century (Intergovernmental Panel on Climate Change, 2001c).

These uncertainties are very difficult to resolve, but scientists have nonetheless attempted to estimate the effect of greenhouse gases on climate. The earliest effort was in 1895, by a Swedish chemist named Svante Arrhenius who used a very simple model with limited data to show that the presence of carbon dioxide in the atmosphere raises the Earth's surface temperature substantially. Arrhenius calculated that removing all carbon dioxide from the atmosphere would lower global temperatures by about 31°C (56°F). The direct effect of removing the carbon dioxide would be to lower temperatures by 21°C (38°F). In addition, the cooler air would hold less water vapor, which would lower temperatures by another 10°C (18°F). For comparison, the actual global average temperature is about 14°C (57°F), and a change of this magnitude would give Los Angeles a climate roughly like that of Nome, Alaska. Arrhenius also calculated that doubling the concentration of carbon dioxide in the atmosphere from preindustrial levels—which on current projections is likely to happen sometime between 2050 and 2100—would raise global average temperatures by 4 to 6°C.

Today, elaborate climate models that capture many more physical and chemical interactions suggest that doubling carbon dioxide concentrations would raise global average temperatures by 1.5 to 4.5°C. Although the magnitude of warming remains uncertain, there is no serious scientific disagreement about the underlying problem: no climate models predict zero warming, and no one seriously suggests that greenhouse gas concentrations can continue to increase without eventually producing some degree of warming.

Estimating the impact of past greenhouse gas emissions on current global temperatures has proven equally difficult. In spite of articles in the popular press that report every hot summer as evidence of global warming and every cold winter as evidence against it, it is quite hard to prove that global warming has begun. Normal variations in global temperatures are large, and it is very difficult to tell whether actual increases in temperature are outside the usual range and, thus, hard to tell how much warming may have occurred.

What's more, temperature measurements themselves can be suspect, in part because over the years, people have measured temperatures with different kinds of instruments, at different locations and even at different altitudes. One example of this problem is the "urban heat island effect." Over time, temperature measurements have become increasingly concentrated in cities, which tend to be warmer than their surroundings. Without correcting for this effect, average temperatures appear to have increased much more than they actually have.

Current evidence seems to suggest that climate change can be detected in historical data, although climatologists are far from unanimous. In an exhaustive survey of the literature, the Intergovernmental Panel on Climate Change (2001c) concluded that during the twentieth century, global average surface temperatures increased by 0.6 ± 0.2°C and that "most of the observed warming over the last 50 years is likely to have been due to the increase in [anthropogenic] greenhouse gas emissions," where "likely" is defined to mean a 66 to 90 percent probability. This conclusion is suggestive, but it would be a substantial overstatement of current scientific knowledge to conclude that anthropogenic warming has been measured accurately in historical data. At the same time, the underlying problems of measurement and causality make it equally difficult to prove that global warming has *not* begun to occur.

In truth, it is impossible to say exactly how much warming has occurred to date or how much will occur in the next century. Current research summarized by the Intergovernmental Panel on Climate Change (2001c) finds that the concentration of carbon dioxide in the atmosphere in 2100 is likely to exceed preindustrial levels by 75 to 350 percent. This enormous range of uncertainty is very difficult to resolve. Predicting the emissions of carbon dioxide depends heavily on many factors—population growth, technical change, income growth and energy prices, among other things—none of which are easy to predict themselves. Other greenhouse gas concentrations are likely to increase as well, although by amounts that are equally difficult to predict. Predictions of global average surface temperatures in 2100 range from increases of 1.4°C to 5.8°C above 1990, and even that large range does not include all identifiable uncertainties. Given the complexity of the processes involved, scientists will probably be unable to reduce this uncertainty for decades.

Moreover, climatology is only one of several sources of uncertainty that are important for climate change policy. Even if temperature changes could be predicted perfectly, many of the physical and ecological consequences of temperature change are less well understood than climatology.

Some consequences of global warming are clear, although their magnitude is uncertain. Global warming is expected to cause sea levels to rise between 9 and 88 cm (3.5 inches to 2.9 feet) by 2100. Much of this increase is due to thermal expansion of the upper layers of water in the oceans, with a smaller but significant contribution from melting of glaciers. Contrary to science fiction accounts of global warming, the polar ice caps are unlikely to have a major effect on sea level. Warming is likely to reduce the amount of ice in Greenland, but to increase it in the Antarctic, which is thought likely to receive an increase in precipitation. Two events that would cause a catastrophic rise in sea level—complete melting of the Greenland ice sheet or disintegration of the West Antarctic Ice Sheet, either of which would raise the sea level by three meters—are now thought to be very unlikely before 2100.

Table 2 gives a brief summary of other possible effects of global warming on the climate. Where possible, the relative certainty of each effect is indicated following the terminology of the Intergovernmental Panel on Climate Change (2001c): "very likely" means a 90 to 99 percent chance, "likely" means a 66 to 90 percent chance, "medium" means a 33 to 66 percent chance and "unlikely" means a 10 to 33 percent chance. These levels of certainty roughly indicate the amount of agreement among climatologists and are not formal probability estimates. Moreover, these effects on climate change will vary by region.

These changes in climate are likely to produce a variety of effects on ecosystems and human activities, as summarized in Table 3. All of these effects are less certain than the changes in climate discussed above: they depend on the amount of warming, which is uncertain, but they also involve additional uncertainties. For example, the agricultural damage done by climate change depends on the costs of adapting crops and farming methods, which vary across region and are largely unknown. Moreover, climate change can actually be good for agriculture in certain circumstances: some crops benefit more from higher carbon dioxide levels than they are hurt by temperature and precipitation changes. Most uncertain of all are the values to assign to changes that are not mediated by markets, such as the extinction of a species or a change in an ecosystem. Economists do not even agree on the methodology to be used in these cases, much less on the estimates themselves.[2]

---

[2]The main method used to determine what people are willing to pay for environmental goods that they don't use directly is "contingent valuation," which involves estimating people's willingness to pay based on their answers to opinion surveys. However, contingent valuation has some serious problems: see Diamond and Hausman (1994) in the *Journal of Economic Perspectives* for a detailed critique.

Table 2 Possible Climatic Consequences of Higher Global Temperatures

Extreme weather events
  Increase in frequency of heat waves; higher risk of summer droughts over
    continental areas at midlatitudes; more intense precipitation. (Likely to very likely)

Tropical storm intensity
  Higher peak wind speeds and more intense precipitation in cyclones, hurricanes and
    typhoons. (Likely)

Patterns of precipitation
  Increase in average global evaporation and precipitation, but with substantial
    regional variability.

Midlatitude storm intensity
  Changes cannot be determined from current climate models.

Atlantic thermohaline circulation
  Differences in water temperature and salinity produce the Gulf Stream and other
    currents that bring warm surface water to the North Atlantic. Without these
    currents, the climate in northern Europe would be significantly colder. Current
    climate models show that this circulation is likely to weaken over the next 100
    years, but not enough to cause a negative net temperature change in Europe: the
    increase due to global warming exceeds the reduction due to changes in currents.

Decomposition of methane hydrates
  Deep ocean sediments contain an enormous reservoir of methane in the form of
    frozen deposits called hydrates. If ocean temperatures warmed enough to allow
    these deposits to thaw, there would be a dramatic increase in atmospheric
    greenhouse gas concentrations. However, recent studies indicate that the
    temperature changes expected from global warming over at least the next
    100 years will be too small to trigger such an event.

Overall, the Intergovernmental Panel on Climate Change (2001a) concludes with "medium confidence" (33 to 67 percent) that the aggregate market sector impacts of a small increase in global temperatures could be "plus
or minus a few percent of world GDP." The effects tend to be small—or
even positive—in developed countries. Developing countries are more vulnerable to climate change and are likely to suffer more adverse impacts.
Larger temperature increases would cause aggregate effects to become increasingly detrimental in all countries.[3]

The cost of reducing greenhouse gas emissions is also uncertain. A variety of studies have been done, most focusing on the near-term costs—
through 2010 or 2020—of one of two policies: reducing emissions to 1990
levels or implementing the 1997 Kyoto Protocol (which will be discussed in
detail below). The studies typically determine the marginal cost of reducing

---

[3]Aggregate GDP is far from ideal as a measure of welfare, especially when applied to something
as heterogeneous as the world economy. We cite these figures to indicate the uncertainties involved
in measuring the effects of climate change rather than to endorse GDP as a welfare measure. Other
frameworks that incorporate equity, sustainability and development concerns are discussed in Intergovernmental Panel on Climate Change (2001b).

Table 3 Possible Effects of Climate Change

Energy demand
    Increased energy demand for cooling; reduced demand for heating. (Very likely)
    Net effect varies by region and climate change scenario.

Coastal zone inundation
    Low-lying coastal areas in developing countries would be inundated by sea level
    rise: a 45 cm rise would inundate 11 percent of Bangladesh and affect 5.5 million
    people; with a 100 cm rise, inundation increases to 21 percent and the population
    affected to 13.5 million. Indonesia and Vietnam would also be severely affected,
    as well as a number of small island countries. (Likely)

Exposure to storm surge
    Global population affected by flooding during coastal storms will increase by 75 to
    200 million.

Human Health
    Increased heat-related injuries and mortality and decreased cold-related ones. For
    developed countries in temperate regions, evidence suggests a net improvement.
    (Medium) Moderate increase in global population exposed to malaria, dengue
    fever and other insect-borne disease. (Medium to likely) Increase in prevalence of
    water-borne diseases, such as cholera. (Medium) Increase in ground-level ozone.
    (Medium)

Water supplies
    Many arid areas will have a net decrease in available water.

Agriculture
    Many crops in temperate regions benefit from higher carbon dioxide concentrations
    for moderate increases in temperature, but would be hurt by larger increases.
    Effect varies strongly by region and crop. Tropical crops would generally be hurt.
    Small positive effect in developed countries; small negative effect in developing
    countries. Low to medium confidence: 5 to 67 percent.

Extinction of species
    Species that are endangered or vulnerable will become rarer or extinct. The number
    of species affected depends on the amount of warming and regional changes in
    precipitation. (Likely)

Ecosystem loss
    How ecosystems respond to long-term changes is poorly understood. Climate change
    will affect the mix of plant and animal species in ecosystems. (Likely to occur, but
    with a substantial lag)

---

emissions by calculating the carbon tax—a tax levied on fossil fuels in proportion to their carbon content—that would be needed to drive emissions
down to a specified level. A ton of coal contains 0.65 tons of carbon, so a
$1 per ton carbon tax would translate into a tax of $0.65 per ton of coal;
the same tax would add $0.14 to the price of a barrel of crude oil and $0.02
to the price of a thousand cubic feet of natural gas.

The results vary substantially across models. For example, the carbon
tax needed in the United States to reduce greenhouse gas emissions to 93
percent of 1990 levels by 2010 (as would be required by the Kyoto Proto-

col) ranges from $94 to $400 (in 2000 U.S. dollars) per ton of carbon.[4] To put this in perspective, the tax on a barrel of crude oil would be $13 to $55, which would raise the price of a $20 barrel of oil by 65 to 275 percent. The tax on a ton of coal would be $60 to $260, raising the price of a $22 ton of coal by 270 to 1,180 percent. The range of estimates for the carbon tax needed to reduce emissions in European OECD countries is even larger: $25 to $825 per ton of carbon.

The wide range of these estimates is due to uncertainties about a variety of key economic parameters and variables. Some of the uncertainties are relatively straightforward econometric issues, like variation in estimates of the short-term price elasticity of demand for gasoline. Other variables, however, are much more difficult to pin down. Population growth and the rates of productivity growth in individual industries are key determinants of the cost of reducing greenhouse gas emissions, but neither can be projected with much confidence very far into the future.

In short, uncertainty is the single most important attribute of climate change as a policy problem. From climatology to economics, the uncertainties in climate change are pervasive, large in magnitude and very difficult to resolve. Before presenting our version of a policy to address these uncertainties, however, it is important to discuss a second important attribute of climate change policy: distribution effects. Any serious climate change policy will need widespread participation over a long time. The key to assuring participation is to be realistic about distributional issues in the design of the policy.

A Hardheaded Look at Distributional Issues

Greenhouse gas emissions originate throughout the world, and most countries will eventually need to participate in any solution. A treaty that makes heavy demands on national sovereignty, or that requires large transfers of wealth from one part of the world to another, is unlikely to be ratified or, if ratified, is likely to be repudiated sooner or later. No international agency can coerce countries to comply with a climate change agreement they find significantly inconsistent with their national interest.

Unfortunately, much of the debate over the distributional aspects of climate change policy has focused on a different question: Which countries should be held responsible for reducing climate change? Some argue that industrialized countries are obligated to do the most to avoid climate change

---

[4]The figures in this paragraph are drawn from Energy Modeling Forum 16, a multimodel evaluation of the Kyoto Protocol. The results of the study appear in a 1999 special issue of the *Energy Journal* and were heavily used in Intergovernmental Panel on Climate Change (2001c).

because their emissions have caused most of the increase in greenhouse gas concentrations to date. Others argue that developing countries account for a large and growing share of emissions and that no climate policy will succeed without significant participation by the developing world. Both of these positions are true, but neither is a realistic basis for designing a policy that sovereign nations will have to ratify and to implement.

In addition, an international agreement should be explicitly designed to make it easy for governments to address domestic distributional concerns in a flexible and transparent manner. For example, a policy involving tradable permits gives governments a distributional instrument—the initial allocation of permits—that would be absent under a pure emissions tax. Tradable permits would allow a government to provide "transition relief" easily and transparently to an industry by granting firms enough permits to cover a large share of their initial emissions. From the industry's point of view, the policy would be a flexible form of grandfathering. In contrast, if the international policy were a pure emissions tax, the compensation scheme would have to be a system of side payments, entirely separate from the treaty, that would be more difficult to negotiate at the domestic level and far less transparent internationally.

Designing a Practical Climate Policy

The uncertainties associated with climate change have polarized public debate. Some observers argue that the uncertainties are too large to justify immediate action—that climate change is an "unproved theory"—and that the best response is to do more climate research and wait for the uncertainties to be resolved. Other observers take the opposite position that the risks from global warming are so severe that substantial cuts should be made in greenhouse gas emissions immediately, regardless of the cost. Neither position is appropriate. On one hand, increasing the concentration of greenhouse gases in the atmosphere exposes the world to the risk of an adverse change in the climate, even though the distribution of that risk is poorly understood. Enough is known to justify reducing greenhouse gas emissions, particularly to preserve the option of avoiding an irreversible change in the climate. On the other hand, too little is known about the causes and consequences of climate change to justify a draconian cut in emissions. Given the uncertainties, a prudent approach would be to abate emissions where possible at modest cost.

Minimizing the cost of abating a given amount of greenhouse emissions requires that all sources clean up amounts that cause their marginal costs of abatement to be equated. To achieve this, the standard economic policy prescription would be a market-based instrument, such as a tax on emissions or a tradable permit system for emission rights. In the absence of uncertainty, the efficient level of abatement could be achieved under either policy, although the distributional effects of tax and emissions trading policies would be very different. Under uncertainty, however, the situation becomes more complicated. Weitzman (1974) showed that taxes and permits are *not* equivalent when marginal benefits and costs are uncertain and that the relative slopes of the two curves determine which policy will be better.

To see why this is so, consider a hypothetical air pollutant. The pollutant is dangerous only at high levels: it causes no damage at all when daily emissions are below 100 tons, but each ton emitted beyond that causes $10 worth of health problems. Emissions are currently 150 tons per day, so the marginal benefit of abatement would be $10 (the damage avoided) for each of the first 50 tons eliminated. Beyond that point, however, the marginal benefit of abatement would drop to zero: emissions would be below the 100 ton threshold and no longer causing any damage. This is an example of a steep marginal benefit curve: at the threshold, marginal benefits go rapidly from $10 to zero. Finally, suppose that the pollutant can be cleaned up with constant returns to scale—the marginal cost curve is flat—but the precise cost is uncertain: all that is known is that the cost of clean-up is less than $10 per ton.

Given this information, the efficient amount of pollution is 100 tons. Above 100 tons, the damage of an additional ton is higher than the cost of abating it; below 100 tons, further reductions produce no additional benefit. In this situation, a permit policy would be far better than an emissions tax. By issuing permits for 100 tons of emissions, the government could be sure of achieving the efficient outcome: for any marginal cost below $10, the permit system will keep emissions from exceeding the threshold. A tax, on the other hand, would be a terrible policy. Suppose the government imposed a $5 tax and the marginal cost of abatement turned out to be $6. In that case, firms would choose to pay the tax rather than do any abatement, and emissions would remain at 150 tons. If costs turned out to be low, say $4, the situation would be no better: in that case, firms would clean up everything and emissions would drop to zero. This example captures the essence of the advantage permits have over taxes when marginal benefits are steep and marginal costs are flat: in that situation, it is important to get the quantity of emissions down to a threshold. A permit policy does exactly that.

In the opposite situation, when marginal costs are rising sharply and marginal benefits are flat, a tax would be a better policy. This case is shown graphically in Figure 1. The horizontal axis shows the quantity of abatement and is normalized so that complete elimination of the pollutant requires 100 units of abatement. The marginal benefit of abatement, MB, is flat, and the marginal cost of abatement is believed—at the time of regulation—to rise sharply, as shown by MC_1 in the left panel. Without regulation, firms would do no abatement, and the quantity on the horizontal axis would be zero. If the government imposes a permit policy, it can guarantee a certain level of abatement—say, Q_1^a. But if marginal costs are uncertain, Q_1^a may not turn out to be the efficient outcome. For example, suppose that marginal costs

As designed for expected
marginal cost curve MC_1

After implementation, if costs
turn out higher than expected

Figure 1 A Permit Policy Under Uncertainty

turn out to be higher than expected. That situation is shown in the right panel of Figure 1, where the true marginal cost curve is shown by MC_2. Because abatement is more expensive than expected, efficiency would require doing less of it: Q_2^a instead of Q_1^a. If firms were forced to abate to Q_1^a, the price of a permit would rise substantially, to P_3. The costs of the excess abatement would exceed the benefits by shaded triangle D in the diagram.

The potential inefficiency of a permit system is intuitively understood by many participants in the climate change debate. A noneconomist might sum up a permit system by describing it as a policy that "caps emissions regardless of cost." The language differs from what an economist would use, but the point is the same.

In this example, a tax policy would have been a much wiser choice. Suppose that in the initial situation, with the low expected marginal cost curve, a tax had been imposed equal to P_1. Once firms discovered that the true marginal cost curve they faced was substantially higher than expected, the level of abatement would drop to Q_3^a—slightly too low, but with a much smaller welfare loss (triangle T) than the permit policy would have produced. The tax is more efficient because it more closely approximates the flat marginal benefit curve.

Applying this analysis to climate change suggests that a tax is likely to be far more efficient than a permit system. All evidence to date suggests that the marginal cost curve for reducing greenhouse gas emissions is very steep, at least for developed countries. At the same time, the nature of climate change indicates that the marginal benefit curve for reducing emissions will be very flat. The damages from climate change are caused by the overall stock of greenhouse gases in the atmosphere, which is the accumulation of many years of emissions. Greenhouse gases remain in the atmosphere for a long time: up to 200 years for carbon dioxide, 114 years for nitrous oxide, 45 to 260 years for chlorofluorocarbons and up to 50,000 years for perfluoromethane (CF_4). As a result, the marginal damage curve for emissions of a gas in any given year will be flat: the first ton and the last ton emitted in that year will have very similar effects on the atmospheric concentration of the gas and hence will cause very similar damages.[5] For example, any single year's emissions of carbon dioxide will be on the order of 1 percent of the excess carbon dioxide in the atmosphere. Within that 1 percent, the damages caused by a ton of emissions will be essentially constant.

Although a tax would be more efficient than a permit system for controlling greenhouse gas emissions (given flat marginal benefits, rising marginal costs and high levels of uncertainty), a tax has a major political liability: it would induce large transfers of income from firms to the government. In fact, firms would end up paying far more in taxes than they spent on reducing emissions. For example, suppose that a particular firm was initially emitting Q tons of carbon dioxide and that its efficient abatement (where the marginal cost of abatement equaled the marginal benefit) was 20 percent. Under an efficient tax, T, the firm would eliminate $0.2Q$ tons of emissions at a cost no larger than $0.2QT$ (the firm would never pay more to abate its emissions than it would save in taxes, and it might pay much less if the marginal cost of abating the initial units of pollution was quite low). However, the firm would have to pay taxes on its remaining emissions, and its tax bill would be $0.8QT$, at least four times what it spent on abatement. The political problem is not just that firms dislike paying taxes; rather, it is that the transfers would be so much larger than the abatement costs that they would completely dominate the political debate. A firm that might be willing to pay $1 million to reduce its emissions by 20 percent would almost certainly be hostile to a policy that required it to pay $1 million plus an additional $4 million in taxes. The problem is not unique to climate change and is probably the most important reason that Pigouvian taxes have rarely been used to control environmental problems.

Although marketable pollution permits and pollution taxes can have serious economic and political disadvantages when used alone, those problems can be mitigated by a hybrid policy that combines the best elements of both.[6] For efficiency, the hybrid policy should act like an emissions tax at the margin: it should provide incentives for abating emissions that can be cleaned up at low cost, while also allowing flexibility in total abatement if costs turn out to be high. For political viability, the hybrid should avoid unnecessarily large transfers and have the distributional flexibility of a permit system.

---

[5]For more discussion of the benefits of abating emissions of stock pollutants, see Newell and Pizer (1998).

[6]A hybrid policy was first proposed by Roberts and Spence (1976).

One hybrid policy with these features would combine a fixed number of tradable, long-term emissions permits with an elastic supply of short-term permits, good only for one year. Each country participating in the policy would be allowed to distribute a specified number of long-term emissions permits, possibly an amount equal to the country's 1990 emissions. The permits could be bought, sold or leased without restriction, and each one would allow the holder to emit one ton of carbon per year. We will refer to these as "perpetual permits," although in principle, they could have long but finite lives. The permits could be given away, auctioned or distributed in any other way the government of each country saw fit. Once distributed, the permits could be traded among firms or bought and retired by environmental groups. In addition, each government would be allowed to sell additional short-term permits for a specified fee, say for $10 per ton of carbon. To put the fee in perspective, $10 dollars per ton of carbon is equivalent to a tax of $6.50 per ton of coal and $1.40 per barrel of crude oil; other things equal, the price of a $22 ton of coal would rise by about 30 percent, and the price of a $20 barrel of oil would rise by 7 percent. Firms within a country would be required to have a total number of emissions permits, in any mixture of long- and short-term permits, equal to the amount of emissions they produce in a year.

To see how the policy would work, consider the supply of permits available for use in any given year. There will be an inelastic supply of Q_T perpetual permits for lease, where Q_T is the number of such permits outstanding. This is shown in Figure 2 by vertical line S_P. There will also be an elastic supply of annual permits available from the government at price P_T. This is shown by horizontal line S_A in the figure. The total supply of permits is the horizontal sum of S_P and S_A, which is shown by the right-turn supply curve in the figure.

The demand for permits will be determined by the marginal cost of abating emissions. Figure 2 shows two possible market equilibria that could result from combining the supply curve for permits with two possible demand curves. If abatement costs turn out to be relatively low, so that permit demand is given by curve D_1, the equilibrium permit price would be P_1, which is below the price of an annual permit, P_T. In this case, only perpetual permits would be supplied, and emissions would be reduced to Q_T. If abatement costs turn out to be relatively high, so that permit demand is given by curve D_2, the price of a permit would be driven up to P_T. Annual permits would be sold, and the total number of permits demanded would be Q_2.

This hybrid plan combines the key advantages of tax and permit policies. Like a tax, it places an upper limit on the marginal cost of abatement. Firms will never have to pay more than P_T, the price of an annual permit, to abate a unit of pollution, so no country would need to fear that the policy would strangle its economy in a vain attempt to meet unexpectedly expensive pollution targets. Because the total supply of permits would not be fixed, the policy would not guarantee precisely how much abatement would be done. However, it would ensure that the abatement done within a given

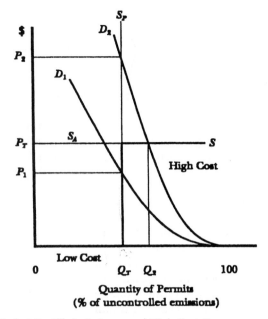

Figure 2 Market Equilibria in Low- and High-Cost Cases

country would be done at minimum cost. Moreover, marginal abatement costs would be equalized across all countries where the price of a permit rose to P_T.

The hybrid policy also avoids many of the distributional issues of an emissions tax. The block of perpetual permits could be distributed by the government to avoid the large transfers associated with a pure emissions tax. Moreover, any transfers that do occur (as a result of permit trades) take place within the private sector, rather than between the private sector and the government. The policy also minimizes transfers across national borders, because each national government can supply as many permits as desired at the capped price P_T, so purchasing permits from abroad becomes unnecessary.

The hybrid policy has built-in incentives for monitoring and enforcement. Since governments would receive revenue from selling annual permits, they would have an incentive to enforce the policy. In addition, firms will have an incentive to monitor one another, because any cheating by one firm would put its competitors at a disadvantage and would also diminish the value of permits held by other firms. With these built-in incentives for monitoring, little or no international monitoring would be needed.

Another benefit of the policy is that it would provide valuable information about the true marginal abatement cost curve. Many economists believe that reducing emissions of greenhouse gases would be quite costly, but others argue that emissions can be reduced substantially at low cost. A hybrid policy would help show which argument is correct.

The hybrid policy would be flexible and decentralized. The price charged for annual permits could be adjusted as needed when better information becomes available. It would be easy to add countries to the system over time: those interested in joining would only have to adopt the policy domestically—no international negotiations would be required. That flexibility is crucial, because it is clear from the history of climate negotiations that only a few countries would be willing to implement a significant global warming treaty in the near future. Furthermore, countries could withdraw from the system without debasing the value of the permits in those countries that continued to participate. This advantage is very important: under a pure system of internationally tradable permits, the addition or withdrawal of any country would cause the world demand and supply of permits to shift, possibly leading to large swings in the price of the permits.

A final benefit is that the policy would be very transparent: to firms, it would look like a form of grandfathering.

Overall, a hybrid policy is an efficient and politically realistic approach to climate change.[7] It does not require a major sacrifice of sovereignty by participating countries, and it reduces greenhouse gas emissions without requiring countries to commit to rigid emissions targets that must be achieved at any cost. Together, these features remove the most formidable obstacles to the development of a sound international climate change policy.

Where Does Climate Change Policy Stand Now?

International negotiations on climate change policy began in earnest in 1992 at the Rio Earth Summit organized by the United Nations. The result of the summit was the United Nations Framework Convention on Climate Change (UNFCCC), which was signed and ratified by most of the countries in the world. The goal of the UNFCCC was to stabilize emissions of greenhouse gases at 1990 levels by the year 2000 through voluntary measures taken by individual countries. In the subsequent decade, few substantive policies were implemented, and global emissions of greenhouse gases rose considerably. From that perspective, the UNFCCC has failed to achieve its goal. However, the convention did set up a mechanism under which negotiations could continue as periodic "Conference of the Parties" (COP) meetings. Between 1997 and 2001, there were seven COP meetings. They are commonly referred to by number, COP1, COP2 and so on, and they are summarized in Table 4.

---

[7]For more information about a hybrid approach to climate change policy, see McKibbin and Wilcoxen (1997a; b). This approach has also been endorsed by Kopp, Morgenstern and Pizer (1997) and Victor (2001).

Table 4 Chronology of Major International Negotiations on Climate Change

1992: Earth Summit, Rio de Janeiro
Produced the United Nations Framework Convention on Climate Change (UNFCCC), a landmark agreement with the goal of "preventing dangerous anthropogenic interference with the Earth's climate system." Industrial countries listed in the treaty's "Annex I" were to adopt policies aimed at reducing their emissions to 1990 levels by the year 2000. However, no specific policies were required, and Annex I countries were only obligated to "aim" to reduce their emissions, not actually to reduce them. The UNFCCC was signed by 153 countries and entered into force on March 24, 1994. It was ratified by the United States in October 1992.

1995: COP1, Berlin
Adopted the "Berlin Mandate," a declaration that the UNFCCC would have little effect on greenhouse gas emissions unless Annex I countries were held to "quantified limitation and reduction objectives within specified time-frames," an approach now described as setting "targets and timetables" for emissions reduction. Established a two-year "analytical and assessment phase" to negotiate a comprehensive set of "policies and measures" that should be taken by Annex I countries. No new commitments or obligations were imposed on countries outside Annex I.

1996: COP2, Geneva
Called for the establishment of legally binding emissions targets as proposed at COP1. Rejected the COP1 proposal that uniform policies be imposed in favor of allowing Annex I countries the flexibility to develop their own policies.

1997: COP3, Kyoto
Adopted the "Kyoto Protocol," in which most Annex I countries were assigned legally binding emissions targets to be achieved by 2008–2012. The average target was about 95 percent of the country's emissions in 1990. Many details of implementation were left for future negotiations.

1998: COP4, Buenos Aires
Adopted a two-year plan of action to design mechanisms for implementing the Kyoto Protocol. Issues discussed included financial transfers and Clean Development Mechanism (CDM) for developing country participation. Also discussed issues for incorporating "carbon sinks."

1999: COP5, Bonn
Primarily devoted to monitoring progress on the work program adopted at COP4.

2000: COP6, The Hague
Intended to finalize details on implementation of the Kyoto Protocol. Negotiations ended without agreement. Many issues were unresolved: how the mechanisms in the Protocol would operate; what measures would be used to enforce compliance; how large allowances would be for "sinks" that remove carbon dioxide from the atmosphere; and whether there would be restrictions on the use of the Protocol's flexibility mechanisms.

2001: COP6bis, Bonn (July)
Continuation of COP6 following the stalemate at The Hague. However, President Bush declared in March 2001 that the United States would not participate in the Kyoto Protocol. Other Annex I countries agreed to proceed without the United States. Large sink allowances were granted to Japan and Canada. Produced a set of recommendations on implementing the Protocol that were to be discussed at COP7.

Table 4 Continued

2001: COP7, Marrakesh (October)

Formally adopted most of the recommendations of COP6. Finalized rules for use of flexibility mechanisms, especially the Clean Development Mechanism. Also, established a "Compliance Committee" to "facilitate, promote and enforce" compliance with the Protocol. In the event of noncompliance, the "Enforcement Branch" of the Compliance Committee may deduct 1.3 times the amount of the violation from the violator's emissions allowance for the next commitment period. The violator may also be barred from using the flexibility mechanisms. Also finalized the accounting procedures to be used for sinks.

The main decision reached at COP1 in 1995 was that the UNFCCC would have little effect on greenhouse gas emissions unless individual countries were held to "quantified limitation and reduction objectives within specified time-frames," an approach now described as setting "targets and timetables" for emissions reduction. All subsequent COP meetings have been devoted to designing an international treaty along those lines, in which participating countries would agree to achieve specific targets for emissions of greenhouse gases by a given date. The result is the Kyoto Protocol, which was initially adopted at COP3 in 1997 and has been revised and refined in subsequent meetings.

The key feature of the Kyoto Protocol is an appendix, known as "Annex B," that specifies annual greenhouse gas emissions limits for 38 industrialized countries—essentially the developed members of the OECD plus about a dozen countries that were formerly part of the Soviet Union.[8] Each country's limit is expressed as a percentage of its emissions in 1990 (a few countries are allowed to use a different year). The limits range from 92 to 110 percent: 92 percent for most European countries, 93 percent for the United States, 94 percent for Canada and Japan, 100 percent for Russia, 110 percent for Iceland and various other values for other countries. If all Annex B countries complied with the Protocol, emissions for the group as a whole would end up 5 percent below the corresponding value from 1990.

The Protocol considers a country's greenhouse gas emissions to be the number of metric tons of carbon dioxide that would produce the same total amount of warming as the country's actual emissions of six gases—carbon dioxide, methane, nitrous oxide, hydrofluorocarbons, perfluorocarbons

---

[8]The countries listed in Annex B are a subset of a group of industrial countries identified in Annex I of the original UNFCCC. Annex B excludes Belarus, which had not ratified the UNFCCC by the time COP3 was held, and Turkey, which requested that it be removed from Annex I. Strictly speaking, the Kyoto Protocol limits the emissions of UNFCCC Annex I countries to the values given in the Protocol's Annex B. However, we will refer to the group of countries having limits as simply "Annex B countries."

and sulfur hexafluoride—plus the carbon dioxide equivalent to the net effect of any changes in the country's land use and forestry on greenhouse gas concentrations. The latter is included to allow countries to offset part of their fossil fuel emissions by planting trees or undertaking other activities—collectively known as "sinks"—that remove carbon dioxide from the atmosphere. Each country's base year emissions are multiplied by its Annex B percentage limit to give its initial allotment of "Assigned Amount Units," which are essentially tradable permits for greenhouse gas emissions.

The Protocol provides three "flexibility mechanisms" that an Annex B country can use: emissions trading, "Joint Implementation" and the "Clean Development Mechanism." Emissions trading is straightforward: one Annex B country may buy unused permits from another. Joint Implementation is a bit more complicated, but essentially allows one Annex B country to undertake an emissions reduction project in another Annex B country in exchange for some of the second country's emissions permits. Both mechanisms involve only Annex B countries and reallocate permits without affecting total Annex B emissions. The Clean Development Mechanism, in contrast, is designed to extend participation in the Protocol to non-Annex B countries. Under this mechanism, an Annex B country can receive emissions credits for undertaking a suitable emissions-reducing project in a non-Annex B host country. The project must be certified by an independent agency to reduce the host country's emissions beyond what would have occurred otherwise. It is by far the most complicated of the Protocol's flexibility mechanisms: the Clean Development Mechanism rules approved at COP7 run to 28 pages, compared with 5 pages for emissions trading. The complexity is largely due to the inherent difficulty of establishing what emissions would have been in the absence of a given emissions reduction project.

Countries having too few permits or credits in 2012 to cover their emissions during 2008–2012 would be out of compliance with the Protocol. In the event of noncompliance, the "Enforcement Branch" of the Compliance Committee may deduct 1.3 times the amount of the violation from the violator's emissions allowance for the next commitment period (possibly 2013–2017). The violator may also be barred from using the flexibility mechanisms.

Although the Kyoto Protocol was signed in 1997, it has yet to enter into force. The Protocol specifies that two conditions must be met before it becomes binding: it must be ratified by at least 55 countries, and it must be ratified by countries accounting for at least 55 percent of Annex B emissions. By the end of 2001, however, the Protocol had been ratified by only 40 countries and not by a single member of Annex B. Moreover, the United States withdrew from negotiations in March 2001, making the second condition especially difficult to satisfy. The United States alone accounts for about 33 percent of 1990 Annex B emissions; without it, the withdrawal of countries accounting for an additional 13 percent of emissions would render the 55 percent condition impossible to meet.

Problems w/ Kyoto

Even if it did enter into force, the post-COP7 Kyoto Protocol would have much less effect on worldwide greenhouse gas emissions than originally intended. In addition to the departure of the United States, the Protocol's targets were weakened during COP6 and COP7, which granted large allowances for "sinks" to Canada, Japan and Russia. Years of negotiation, in other words, have produced only a weak protocol that is unlikely to enter into force. The reason is that the fundamental approach underlying the Kyoto Protocol, setting targets and timetables for emissions reductions, is seriously flawed. We will briefly outline four key problems.

First, the Kyoto Protocol would force emissions below 1990 levels and hold them there without regard to the costs and benefits of doing so. Studies to date provide little justification for that particular target. The Protocol would only reduce the rate of warming slightly, not prevent it entirely. As a result, the Protocol's benefits are only a fraction of the estimated damages from uncontrolled warming. In addition, the Protocol's effect on temperatures is decades away, while its costs would begin immediately. Thus, for most developed countries, including the United States, the Protocol provides only small environmental benefits, but imposes significant costs. For example, Nordhaus and Boyer (1999) find that the Protocol does not "bear any relation to an economically oriented strategy that would balance the costs and benefits of greenhouse gas reductions." They calculate that the worldwide present value cost of the Kyoto Protocol would be $800 billion to $1,500 billion if it were implemented as efficiently as possible, while they estimate the present value of benefits to be $120 billion. Other studies reach similar conclusions. Tol (1999), for example, finds that the Kyoto Protocol would have a net present value cost in excess of $2.5 trillion and comments that "the emissions targets agreed in the Kyoto Protocol are irreconcilable with economic rationality."

Second, the principal international policy instrument of the Kyoto Protocol would be a system of internationally tradable emissions permits (although countries could take other domestic actions to reduce greenhouse gases as well). International permit trading runs the risk of being highly inefficient, given uncertainties in the marginal cost of abating greenhouse gas emissions. But international permit trading has a more serious political flaw: it would probably generate large transfers of wealth between countries. After all, trading and transfers are inextricably linked: if trading is likely to be important for efficiency, it is also likely to produce large transfers. Consider a rough calculation. In 1990, the United States emitted about 1,340 million tons of carbon in the form of carbon dioxide. Carbon emissions are expected to grow over time, so suppose that by 2010, the United States ended up needing to import permits equal to about 20 percent of 1990 emissions, or about 268 million tons. There is enormous uncertainty about what the price of an international carbon permit might be, but $100 to $200 a ton is well within the range of estimates. At such a price, U.S. firms would need to spend $27 billion to $54 billion to buy pollution permits from abroad every year. That amount exceeds the $26 billion that manufacturing firms spent to operate all pollution abatement equipment in 1994 (the most recent year for which data is available from the U.S. Bureau of the Census, 1996), and it dwarfs the $8 billion spent by the U.S. government in 2000 for international development and humanitarian and foreign aid (U.S. Office of Management and Budget, 2001). Transfers of wealth of this magnitude nearly guarantee the treaty would never be implemented.

A third problem with the Kyoto Protocol is that it would put enormous stress on the world trade system. The balance of trade for a developed country that imported permits would deteriorate substantially, possibly leading to increased volatility in exchange rates. Developing countries that exported permits under the Clean Development Mechanism would see their exchange rates appreciate, causing their other export industries to decline or to collapse. Moreover, revenue from the Clean Development Mechanism would come with strings attached: much of it would have to be invested in improved energy technology to reduce emissions. Since this strategy is unlikely to be ideal for long-term economic development, it would make the policy unattractive to developing countries. In fact, one of the main reasons that the Kyoto Protocol only set up a system of trading among the Annex B countries (the developed economies and the former Soviet Union) is because developing countries have been so unenthusiastic about international permit trading. However, permit trading among Annex B countries would do little to lower abatement costs, since the countries have fairly similar technology.

A fourth problem with the Kyoto Protocol is that no individual government has an incentive to police the agreement. After all, monitoring polluters is expensive, and punishing violators imposes costs on domestic residents in exchange for global climate benefits that, by their nature, will accrue largely to foreigners. Governments will have a strong temptation to look the other way when firms exceed their emissions permits. For the treaty to be viable, however, each participating country would need to be confident that the other participants were enforcing it. The Kyoto approach can only work if it includes an elaborate and expensive international mechanism for monitoring and enforcement.

Ironically, even if the Kyoto Protocol were ratified immediately, it does not actually constrain emissions for years. Emissions from the United Kingdom, Germany and especially Russia are below 1990 levels already, as was shown in Table 1. The reasons are varied, but have nothing to do with climate change policy: emissions in the United Kingdom dropped as a result of changes in its coal industry begun under the Thatcher government; German emissions fell because reunification led quickly to the elimination of many energy-inefficient activities in what was once East Germany; and Russian emissions were reduced because the Russian economy collapsed in the 1990s. As a result, total emissions from Annex B countries are currently below 1990 levels. If the Protocol goes forward without the United States, emissions from the remaining countries would be about 400 million metric tons below the target. It is unlikely that emissions would be significantly constrained during the Protocol's first commitment period, 2008 to 2012. Moreover, the Protocol's emissions targets apply *only* to the 2008–2012 period: limits for future periods remain to be negotiated. If the Protocol fails to constrain emissions in the first commitment period, it will have done nothing to reduce the risks posed by climate change.

All in all, the Kyoto Protocol is an impractical policy focused on achieving an unrealistic and inappropriate goal. The Bonn and Marrakesh revisions in 2001 postponed the Protocol's collapse by reducing its stringency, but did nothing to address the underlying design flaws. Further negotiations will accomplish little of substance as long as they remain focused on establishing a targets-and-timetables approach to climate change policy.

Conclusion

Because so little real action has been taken on climate change to date, an opportunity remains for an efficient and practical policy to be adopted. A hybrid climate change policy has much to offer. It is flexible enough to deal with the enormous uncertainties regarding climate change. It provides individual governments with an instrument to limit and to channel the distributional effects of the policy, reducing the obstacles to ratification. Moreover, it creates incentives for governments to monitor and to enforce the policy within their own borders. It is a practical policy that would reduce greenhouse gases in a cost-effective manner.

International negotiations to date have produced a very different policy, the Kyoto Protocol, which is deeply flawed. The Protocol fails to acknowledge the uncertainties surrounding climate change and requires countries to commit themselves to achieving rigid targets and timetables for emissions reductions, even though the cost of doing so could be very high, and the benefits are uncertain. The Protocol never had any real chance of ratification by the U.S. Senate and, in mid-2001, was rejected by the Bush administration. Negotiations over the Protocol's details continue to be held, but the Protocol appears increasingly unlikely to have any effect or even to enter into force.

With leadership by the United States, however, climate policy could be shifted in a more practical and efficient direction. A good first step would be for the United States, perhaps joined by other large emitters, to adopt a modified form of the hybrid policy unilaterally. The government could immediately distribute perpetual emissions permits equal to the U.S. commitment under the Kyoto Protocol, but with one important caveat: firms would not be *required* to hold emissions permits unless an international agreement were reached on climate change. Essentially, the government would distribute contingent property rights for greenhouse gas emissions. Such a step would be in the self-interest of the United States, because it would allow financial markets to help manage the risks of climate policy. For example, a firm worried that it would be unable to comply with a future climate regulation could reduce its risk by buying extra permits, or even options on extra permits, as a hedge. A firm able to reduce its emissions at low cost could sell permits (or options) now. Of course, pricing these permits would present a short-run challenge for financial markets, since the price would need to reflect if or when carbon emissions will be regulated. But financial markets confront this kind of problem every day. Within a very short time, an active market would develop with prices that reflected both the likelihood of a policy taking effect and its probable stringency. Indeed, active markets have already been formed for trading privately created emissions permits. Such a step might jump-start and redirect the course of international climate change negotiations.

Climate change is a serious environmental risk that will likely grow in importance over the coming decades. There is still an opportunity for climate change policy to take an efficient and practical form, but leadership will be needed to keep the opportunity from being lost.

References

Diamond, Peter A. and Jerry A. Hausman. 1994. "Contingent Valuation: Is Some Number Better than No Number?" *Journal of Economic Perspectives*. Fall, 8:4, pp. 45–64.

Energy Information Administration. 1999. *International Energy Annual 1999*. Washington, D.C.: U.S. Government Printing Office.

Energy Journal. 1999. "Special Issue: The Costs of the Kyoto Protocol: A Multi-Model Evaluation." May, 3.

Intergovernmental Panel on Climate Change. 2001a. *Climate Change 2001: Impacts, Adaptation and Vulnerability*. Cambridge: Cambridge University Press.

Intergovernmental Panel on Climate Change. 2001b. *Climate Change 2001: Mitigation*. Cambridge: Cambridge University Press.

Intergovernmental Panel on Climate Change. 2001c. *Climate Change 2001: The Scientific Basis*. Cambridge: Cambridge University Press.

Kopp, Raymond, Richard Morgenstern and William A. Pizer. 1997. "Something for Everyone: A Climate Policy that Both Environmentalists and Industry Can Live With." *Weathervane*. Resources for the Future, Washington, D.C., September 29.

McKibbin, Warwick J. and Peter J. Wilcoxen. 1997a. "A Better Way to Slow Global Climate Change." *Brookings Policy Brief*. June, 17.

McKibbin, Warwick J. and Peter J. Wilcoxen. 1997b. "Salvaging the Kyoto Climate Change Negotiations." *Brookings Policy Brief*. November, 27.

National Climate Data Center. 1999. "Climate of 1998: Annual Review." U.S. National Oceanic and Atmospheric Administration.

Newell, Richard G. and William A. Pizer. 1998. "Regulating Stock Externalities under Uncertainty." Discussion Paper 99–10, Resources for the Future, Washington, D.C.

Nordhaus, William D. 1991. "The Cost of Slowing Climate Change: A Survey." *Energy Journal* 12:1, pp. 37–65.

Nordhaus, William D. 1993. "Reflections on the Economics of Climate Change." *Journal of Economic Perspectives*. Fall, 7:4, pp. 11–25.

Nordhaus, William D. and Joseph G. Boyer. 1999. "Requiem for Kyoto: An Economic Analysis." *Energy Journal*. Special Issue, pp. 93–130.

Roberts, Marc J. and A. Michael Spence. 1976. "Effluent Charges and Licenses under Uncertainty." *Journal of Public Economics*. April/May, 5:3–4, pp. 193–208.

Tol, Richard S. J. 1999. "Kyoto, Efficiency, and Cost-Effectiveness: Applications of FUND." *Energy Journal*. Special Issue, pp. 131–56.

U.S. Bureau of the Census. 1996. *Pollution Abatement Cost and Expenditures, 1994*. Current Industrial Reports MA200(94)-1, Washington, D.C.: U.S. Government Printing Office.

U.S. Office of Management and Budget. 2001. *Budget of the United States Government, Fiscal Year 2002*. Washington, D.C.: U. S. Government Printing Office.

Victor, David. 2001. *The Collapse of the Kyoto Protocol and the Struggle to Control Global Warming*. Council on Foreign Relations. Princeton and Oxford: Oxford University Press.

Weitzman, Martin L. 1974. "Prices vs. Quantities." *Review of Economic Studies*. October, 41:4, pp. 477–91.

VIII

Ecological Values and Sustainability

26 Sustainability: An Economist's Perspective

Robert M. Solow

Robert M. Solow is Institute Professor of Economics Emeritus at the Massachusetts Institute of Technology.

This talk is different from anything else anyone has heard at Woods Hole; certainly for the last two days. Three people have asked me, "Do you plan to use any transparencies or slides?" Three times I said, "No," and three times I was met with this blank stare of disbelief. I actually have some beautiful aerial photographs of Prince William Sound that I could have brought along to show you, and I also have a spectacular picture of Michael Jordan in full flight that you would have liked to have seen. But in fact I don't need or want any slides or transparencies. I want to talk to you about an idea. The notion of sustainability or sustainable growth (although, as you will see, it has nothing necessarily to do with growth) has infiltrated discussions of long-run economic policy in the last few years. It is very hard to be against sustainability. In fact, the less you know about it, the better it sounds. That is true of lots of ideas. The questions that come to be connected with sustainable development or sustainable growth or just sustainability are genuine and deeply felt and very complex. The combination of deep feeling and complexity breeds buzzwords, and sustainability has certainly become a buzzword. What I thought I might do, when I was invited to talk to a group like this, was to try to talk out loud about how one might think straight about the concept of sustainability, what it might mean and what its implications (not for daily life but for your annual vote or your concern for economic policy) might be.

Definitions are usually boring. That is probably true here too. But here it matters a lot. Some people say they don't know what sustainability means, but it sounds good. I've seen things on restaurant menus that strike me the same way. I took these two parts of a definition from a UNESCO document: ". . . every generation should leave water, air and soil resources as pure and unpolluted as when it came on earth." Alternatively, it was suggested that "each generation should leave undiminished all the species of animals it found existing on earth." I suppose that sounds good, as it is meant to. But I believe that kind of thought is fundamentally the wrong

This paper was presented as the Eighteenth J. Seward Johnson Lecture to the Marine Policy Center, Woods Hole Oceanographic Institution, at Woods Hole, Massachusetts, on June 14, 1991. *National Geographic Research and Exploration,* 8:10–21 (1992).

way to go in thinking about this issue. I must also say that there are some much more carefully thought out definitions and discussions, say by the U.N. Environment Programme and the World Conservation Union. They all turn out to be vague; in a way, the message I want to leave with you today is that sustainability is an essentially vague concept, and it would be wrong to think of it as being precise, or even capable of being made precise. It is therefore probably not in any clear way an exact guide to policy. Nevertheless, it is not at all useless.

Pretty clearly the notion of sustainability is about our obligation to the future. It says something about a moral obligation that we are supposed to have for future generations. I think it is very important to keep in mind—I'm talking like a philosopher for the next few sentences and I don't really know how to do that—that you can't be morally obligated to do something that is not feasible. Could I be morally obligated to be like Peter Pan and flap my wings and fly around the room? The answer is clearly not. I can't have a moral obligation like that because I am not capable of flapping my arms and flying around the room. If I fail to carry out a moral obligation, you must be entitled to blame me. You could properly say unkind things about me. But you couldn't possibly say unkind things about me for not flying around the room like Peter Pan because you know, as well as I do, that I can't do it.

If you define sustainability as an obligation to leave the world as we found it in detail, I think that's glib but essentially unfeasible. It is, when you think about it, not even desirable. To carry out literally the injunction of UNESCO would mean to make no use of mineral resources; it would mean to do no permanent construction or semi-permanent construction; build no roads; build no dams; build no piers. A mooring would be all right but not a pier. Apart from being essentially an injunction to do something that is not feasible, it asks us to do something that is not, on reflection, desirable. I doubt that I would feel myself better off if I had found the world exactly as the Iroquois left it. It is not clear that one would really want to do that.

To make something reasonable and useful out of the idea of sustainability, I think you have to try a different kind of definition. The best thing I could think of is to say that it is an obligation to conduct ourselves so that we leave to the future the option or the capacity to be as well off as we are. It is not clear to me that one can be more precise than that. Sustainability is an injunction not to satisfy ourselves by impoverishing our successors. That sounds good too, but I want you to realize how problematic it is—how hard it is to make anything precise or checkable out of that thought. If we try to look far ahead, as presumably we ought to if we are trying to obey the injunction to sustainability, we realize that the tastes, the preferences, of future generations are something that we don't know about. Nor do we know anything very much about the technology that will be available to people 100 years from now. Put yourself in the position of someone in 1880 trying to imagine what life would be like in 1980 and you will see how wrong you would be. I think all we can do in this respect is to imagine people in the future being much like ourselves and attributing to them, imputing to them, whatever technology we can "reasonably" extrapolate—whatever that means. I am trying to emphasize the vagueness but not the meaningless of that concept. It is not meaningless, it is just inevitably vague.

We are entitled to please ourselves, according to this definition, so long as it is not at the expense (in the sense that I stated) of future well-being. You have to take into account, in thinking about sustainability, the resources that we use up and the resources that we leave behind, but also the sort of environment we leave behind including the built environment, including productive capacity (plant and equipment) and including technological knowledge. *To talk about sustainability in that way is not at all empty.* It attracts your attention, first, to what history tells us is an important fact, namely, that goods and services can be substituted for one another. If you don't eat one species of fish, you can eat another species of fish. Resources are, to use a favorite word of economists, fungible in a certain sense. They can take the place of each other. That is extremely important because it suggests that we do not owe to the future any particular thing. There is no specific object that the goal of sustainability, the obligation of sustainability, requires us to leave untouched.

What about nature? What about wilderness or unspoiled nature? I think that we ought, in our policy choices, to embody our desire for unspoiled nature as a component of well-being. But we have to recognize that different amenities really are, to some extent, substitutable for one another, and we should be as inclusive as possible in our calculations. It is perfectly okay, it is perfectly logical and rational, to argue for the preservation of a particular species or the preservation of a particular landscape. But that has to be done on its own, for its own sake, because this landscape is intrinsically what we want or this species is intrinsically important to preserve, not under the heading of sustainability. Sustainability doesn't require that any *particular* species of owl or any *particular* species of fish or any *particular* tract of forest be preserved. Substitutability is also important on the production side. We know that one kind of input can be substituted for another in production. There is no reason for our society to feel guilty about using up aluminum as long as we leave behind a capacity to perform the same or analogous functions using other kinds of materials—plastics or other natural or artificial materials. In making policy decisions we can take advantage of the principle of substitutability, remembering that what we are obligated to leave behind is a generalized capacity to create well-being, not any particular thing or any particular natural resource.

If you approach the problem that way in trying to make plans and make policies, it is certain that there will be mistakes. We will impute to the future tastes that they don't have or we will impute to them technological capacities that they won't have or we will fail to impute to them tastes and technological capacities that they do have. The set of possible mistakes is usually pretty symmetric.

That suggests to me the importance of choosing robust policies whenever we can. We should choose policies that will be appropriate over as wide a range of possible circumstances as we can imagine. But it would be wrong for policy to be paralyzed by the notion that one can make mistakes. Liability to error is the law of life. And, as most people around Woods Hole know, you choose policies to avoid potentially catastrophic errors, if you can. You insure whenever you can, but that's it.

The way I have put this, and I meant to do so, emphasizes that sustainability is about distributional equity. It is about who gets what. It is about the sharing of well-being between present people and future people. I have also emphasized the need to keep in mind, in making plans, that we don't know what they will do, what they will like, what they will want. And, to be honest, it is none of our business.

It is often asked whether, at this level, the goal or obligation of sustainability can be left entirely to the market. It seems to me that there is no reason to believe in a doctrinaire way that it can. The future is not adequately represented in the market, at least not the far future. If you remember that our societies live with real interest rates of the order of 5 or 6 percent, you will realize that that means that the dollar a generation from now, thirty years from now, is worth 25 cents today. That kind of discount seems to me to be much sharper than we would seriously propose in our public capacity, as citizens thinking about our obligation to the future. It seems to me to be a stronger discount than most of us would like to make. It is fair to say that those people a few generations hence are not adequately represented in today's market. They don't participate in it, and therefore there is no doctrinaire reason for saying, "Oh well, ordinary supply and demand, ordinary market behavior, will take care of whatever obligation we have to the future."

Now, in principle, government could serve as a trustee, as a representative for future interests. Policy actions, taxes, subsidies, regulations could, in principle, correct for the excessive present-mindedness of ordinary people like ourselves in our daily business. Of course, we are not sure that government will do a good job. If often seems that the rate at which governments discount the future is rather sharper than that at which the bond market does. So we can't be sure that public policy will do a good job. That is why we talk about it in a democracy. We are trying to think about collective decisions for the future, and discussions like this, not with just me talking, are the way in which policies of that kind ought to be thrashed out.

Just to give you some idea of how uncertain both private and public behavior can be in an issue like this, let me ask you to think about the past, not about the future. You could make a good case that our ancestors, who were considerably poorer than we are, whose standard of living was considerably less than our own, were probably excessively generous in providing for us. They cut down a lot of trees, but they saved a lot and they built a lot of railroad rights-of-way. Both private and publicly they probably did better by us than a sort of fair-minded judge in thinking about the equity (whether they got their share and we got our share or whether we profited at their expense) would have required. It would have been okay for them to save a little less, to enjoy a little more and given us a little less of a start than our generation has had. I don't think there is any simple generalization that will serve to guide policy about these issues. There is every reason to discuss economic policy and social policy from this point of view, and anything else is likely to be ideology rather than analysis.

Once you take the point of view that I have been urging on you in thinking about sustainability as a matter of distributional equity between the present and the future, you can see that it becomes a problem about saving and investment. It becomes a problem about the choice between current consumption and providing for the future.

There is a sort of dual connection—a connection that need not be intrinsic but is there—between environmental issues and sustainability issues. The environment needs protection by public policy because each of us knows that by burdening the environment, by damaging it, we can profit and have some of the cost, perhaps most of the cost, borne by others. Sustainability is a problem precisely because each of us knows or realizes that we can profit at the expense of the future rather than at the expense of our contemporaries and the environment. We free-ride on each other and we free-ride on the future.

Environmental policy is important for both reasons. One of the ways we free-ride on the future is by burdening the environment. And so current environmental protection—this is what I meant by a dual connection—will almost certainly contribute quite a lot to sustainability. Although, I want to warn you, not automatically. Current environmental protection contributes to sustainability if it comes at the expense of current consumption. Not if it comes at the expense of investment, of additions to future capacity. So, there are no absolutes. There is nothing precise about this notion but there are perhaps approximate guides to public policy that come out of this way of reasoning about the idea of sustainability. A correct principle, a correct general guide is that when we use up something—and by we I mean our society, our country, our civilization, however broadly you want to think—when we use up something that is irreplaceable, whether it is minerals or a fish species, or an environmental amenity, then we should be thinking about providing a substitute of equal value, and the vagueness comes in the notion of value. The something that we provide in exchange could be knowledge, could be technology. It needn't even be a physical object.

Let me give you an excellent example from the recent past of a case of good thought along these lines and also a case of bad thought along these lines. Commercially usable volumes of oil were discovered in the North Sea some years ago. The two main beneficiaries of North Sea oil were the United Kingdom and Norway. It is only right to say that the United Kingdom dissipated North Sea oil, wasted it, used it up in consumption and on employment. If I meet Mrs. Thatcher in heaven, since that is where I intend to go, the biggest thing I will tax her with is that she blew North Sea oil. Here was an assert that by happenstance the U.K. acquired. If the sort of general approach to sustainability that I have been suggesting to you had been taken by the Thatcher government, someone would have said, "It's okay we are going to use up the oil, that's what it is for, but we will make sure that we provide something else in exchange, that we guide those resources, at least in large part, into investment in capacity in the future." That did not happen. As I said, if you ask where (and by the way the curve of production from the North Sea fields is already on the way down; that asset is on its way to exhaustion) it went, it went into maintaining consumption in the United Kingdom and, at the same time, into unemployment.

Norway, on the other hand, went about it in the typical sober way you expect of good Scandinavians. The Norwegians said, here is a wasting asset. Here is an asset that we are going to use up. Scandinavians are also slightly masochistic, as you know. They said the one thing we must avoid is blowing this; the one thing we must avoid is a binge. They tried very hard to convert a large fraction of the revenues, of the rentals, of the royalties from North Sea oil into investment. I confess I don't know how well they succeeded but I am willing to bet that they did a better job of it than the United Kingdom.

This brings me to the one piece of technical economics that I want to mention. There is a neat analytical result in economics (mainly done by John Hartwick of Queen's University in Canada) which studies an economy that takes what we call the rentals, the pure return to a non-renewable resource, and invests those rentals.[1] That is, it uses up a natural asset like the North Sea oil field, but makes a point of investing whatever revenues intrinsically inhere to the oil itself. That policy can be shown to have neat sustainability properties. In a simple sort of economy, it will guarantee a perpetually constant capacity to consume. By the way, it is a very simple rule, and it is really true only for very simple economies; but it has the advantage, first of all, of sounding right, of sounding like justice, and secondly, of being practical. It is a calculation that could be made. It is a calculation that we don't make and I am going to suggest in a minute that we should be making it. You might want to do better. You might feel so good about your great-grandchildren that you would like to do better than invest the rents on the non-renewable resources that you use up. But in any case, it is, at a minimum, a policy that one could pursue for the sake of sustainability. I want to remind you again that most environmental protection can be regarded as an act of investment. If we were to think that our obligation to the future is in principle discharged by seeing that the return to non-renewable resources is funnelled into capital formation, any kind of capital formation—plant and equipment, research and development, physical oceanography, economics or environmental investment—we could have some feeling that we were about on the right track.

---

[1] John M. Hartwick, "Substitution among exhaustible resources and intergenerational equity," *Review of Economic Studies* 45(2): 347–543 (June 1978).

Now I want to mention what strikes me as sort of a paradox—as a difficulty with a concept of sustainability. I said, I kind of insisted, that you should think about it as a matter of equity, as a matter of distributional equity, as a matter of choice of how productive capacity should be shared between us and them, them being the future. Once you think about it that way you are almost forced logically to think about equity not between periods of time but equity right now. There is something inconsistent about people who profess to be terribly concerned about the welfare of future generations but do not seem to be terribly concerned about the welfare of poor people today. You will see in a way why this comes to be a paradox. The only reason for thinking that sustainability is a problem is that you think that some people are likely to be shortchanged, namely, in the future. Then I think you really are obligated to ask, "Well, is anybody being shortchanged right now?"

The paradox arises because if you are concerned about people who are currently poor, it will turn out that your concern for them will translate into an increase in current consumption, not into an increase in investment. The logic of sustainability says, "You ought to be thinking about poor people today, and thinking about poor people today will be disadvantageous from the point of view of sustainability." Intellectually, there is no difficulty in resolving that paradox, but practically there is every difficulty in the world in resolving that paradox. And I don't have the vaguest notion of how it can be done in practice.

The most dramatic way in which I can remind you of the nature of that paradox is to think about what it will mean for, say, CO_2 discharge when the Chinese start to burn their coal in a very large way; and, then, while you are interested in moral obligation, I think you should invent for yourself how you are going to explain to the Chinese that they shouldn't burn the coal, even living at their standard of living they shouldn't burn the coal, because the CO_2 might conceivably damage somebody in 50 or 100 years.

Actually the record of the U.S. is not very good on either the intergenerational equity of the intra-generational equity front. We tolerate, for a rich society, quite a lot of poverty, and at the same time we don't save or invest a lot. I've just spent some time in West Germany, and there is considerably less apparent poverty in the former Federal Republic than there is here; and at the same time they are investing a larger fraction of their GNP than we are by a large margin.

It would not be very hard for us to do better. One thing we might do, for starters, is to make a comprehensive accounting of rents on non-renewable resources. It is something that we do not do. There is nothing in the national accounts of the U.S. which will tell you what fraction of the national income is the return to the using up of non-renewable resources. If we were to make that accounting, then we would have a better idea than we have now as to whether we are at least meeting that minimal obligation to channel those rents into saving and investment. And I also suggested that careful attention to current environmental protection is another way that is very likely to slip in some advantage in the way of sustainability, provided it is at the expense of current consumption and not at the expense of other forms of investment.

I have left out of this talk, as some of you may have noticed until now, any mention of population growth; and I did that on purpose, although it might be the natural first order concern if you are thinking about sustainability issues. Control of population growth would probably be the best available policy on behalf of sustainability. You know that, I know that, and I have no particular competence to discuss it any further; so I won't, except to remind you that rapid population growth is fundamentally a Third World phenomenon, not a developed country phenomenon. So once again, you are up against the paradox that people in poor countries have children as insurance policies for their own old age. It is very hard to preach to them not to do that. On the other hand, if they continue to do that, then you have probably the largest, single danger to sustainability of the world economy.

All that remains for me is to summarize. What I have been trying to say goes roughly as follows. Sustainability as a moral obligation is a general obligation not a specific one. It is not an obligation to preserve this or preserve that. It is an obligation, if you want to make sense out of it, to preserve the capacity to be well off, to be as well off as we. That does not preclude preserving specific resources, if they have an independent value and no good substitutes. But we shouldn't kid ourselves, that is part of the value of specific resources. It is not a consequence of any interest in sustainability. Secondly, an interest in sustainability speaks for investment generally. I mentioned that directing the rents on non-renewable resources into investment is a good rule of thumb, a reasonable and dependable starting point. But what sustainability speaks for is investment, investment of any kind. In particular, environmental investment seems to me to correlate well with concerns about sustainability and so, of course, does reliance on renewable resources as a substitute for non-renewable ones. Third, there is something faintly phony about deep concern for the future combined with callousness about the state of the world today. The catch is that today's poor want consumption not investment. So the conflict is pretty deep and there is unlikely to be any easy to way resolve it. Fourth, research is a good thing. Knowledge on the whole is an environmentally neutral asset that we can contribute to the future. I said that in thinking about sustainability you want to be as inclusive as you can. Investment in the broader sense and investment in knowledge, especially technological and scientific knowledge, is an environmentally clean an asset as we know. And the last thing I want to say is, don't forget that sustainability is a vague concept. It is intrinsically inexact. It is not something that can be measured out in coffee spoons. It is not something that you could be numerically accurate about. It is, at best, a general guide to policies that have to do with investment, conservation and resource use. And we shouldn't pretend that it is anything other than that.

Thank you very much.

References

World Commission on Environment and Development, *Our Common Future* (The Brundtland Report). Oxford: Oxford University Press, 1987.

World Conservation Union, *Caring for the Earth*. Gland, Switzerland, 1991; see especially p. 10.

World Resources Institute, *World Resources 1992–93: Toward Sustainable Development*. New York: Oxford University Press, 1992. See especially Ch. 1.

27 *Economics of the Endangered Species Act**

Gardner M. Brown Jr.
Jason F. Shogren

Gardner M. Brown Jr. is Professor of Economics, University of Washington, Seattle. Jason F. Shogren is the Stroock Distinguished Professor of Natural Resource Conservation and Management, University of Wyoming, Laramie.

The Endangered Species Act of 1973 addresses the market failure associated with the unpriced social benefits of such species. Robert Barnwell Roosevelt might have been envisioning such an act in his 1865 book *Superior Fishing*, where he wrote: "By these means can the seductive little beauties, whether of the feathered, furred, or scaly tribe . . . be preserved through endless time in undiminished abundance, furnishing the incentive that leads us away from our dull books or wearying cares, the crowded streets, the congregations of eager men, the trials and excitement of business, . . . strengthening our nerves, renewing our hold of life, and elevating our moral nature."

The Endangered Species Act is probably the most comprehensive of all our environmental laws. It is often portrayed as the exemplar of "prohibitive policy . . . one of the most extreme forms of government intervention" (Yaffee, 1982). As such, it is no wonder the Act has proven controversial. Although the benefits of protecting endangered species accrue to the entire nation, a significant fraction of the costs imposed by the Act are borne by private landowners. About 90 percent of the nearly 1,100 species of plants and animals listed as endangered or threatened under the Act are found on private land. The combination of broad benefits and concentrated costs can fan political firestorms, and many landowners complain that the costs of complying with the Act are too high (GAO, 1995a). The pressure to answer the question of whether these costs exceed the social benefits has thrust economics into the heat of the debate over reauthorization of the Endangered Species Act.

"Economics of the Endangered Species Act," by Gardner M. Brown Jr. and Jason F. Shogren, *Journal of Economic Perspectives,* 12 (3): 3–20 (Summer 1998).

*We are grateful to Tom Crocker, Brad De Long, Jon Goldstein, Mark Plummer, Timothy Taylor, and John Tschirhart for helpful comments. Thanks to the Bugas, Lowham, and Stroock Funds at the University of Wyoming for the research support.

Economists have not been especially welcome in this debate. Many natural scientists and ecologists view the methods and mindset of economists with grave suspicion. When initially enacting the Endangered Species Act in 1973, Congress explicitly noted that economic criteria would not be included in either the listing or the designation of proposed critical habitat (Souder, 1993). This perpetuated a theme found in earlier environmental legislation. The Supreme Court agreed with this view in the 1978 case, *Tennessee Valley Authority v. Hill* (437 U.S. 187, 184 (1978)): "the value of endangered species is incalculable," and "it is clear from the Act's legislative history that Congress intended to halt and reverse the trend toward species extinction—whatever the cost."

But the realities of private incentives and social tradeoffs cannot be banished by legislative or judicial fiat. While the 1978 amendments to the Endangered Species Act acknowledge economic reality, conflict over the magnitude of these tradeoffs has delayed reauthorization since 1992. Congress has kept the Act afloat and funded through continuing resolutions. Not surprisingly, the numerous bills proposed over the last six sessions divide into two camps: bills to strengthen the Act by emphasizing endangered species recovery over extinction risk (for example, H.R. 2351); and bills to weaken the Act by bringing more attention to the needs of businesses and landowners (for example, S.1180). The Clinton administration has not pushed hard either: Interior Secretary Bruce Babbitt (1997) reasoned that since "no one had ever really tried to make the Act work, [we wanted to] dust off the Act and bring it to life . . . to prove how we can both protect the environment and permit sound economic development."

Answering the question of whether the government can pull these two camps together to make the Endangered Species Act less adversarial and more protective of endangered species requires insight into the underlying incentives at play. Unless government codifies efforts to make landowners feel like partners in species protection, the prognosis for a reformed Act is not good. By exploring and illuminating these issues, economists can help to raise the chances that when society imposes and bears costs for protecting endangered species, it is more likely to succeed.

The Endangered Species Act and the Reality of Endangered Species

Species extinction is not a new phenomenon. On a geologic time scale, five or more mass extinction episodes have been responsible for the loss of up to 84 percent of the genera or families that have ever existed (Jablonski, 1991). Species extinction by humans also is not a new event. Prehistoric colonization of Pacific islands destroyed an estimated 2,000 species of birds, equal to about 20 percent of the presently known number (Steadman, 1995). At least 15 genera of large animals were lost due to aboriginal colonization of Australia (Martin and Steadman, in press). In North America, 34 genera of large animals were lost as a result of Amerindian arrival (Martin and Steadman, in press); 68 species of birds and mammals have been threatened with extinction since the 16th century, and half of them have gone extinct (Belovsky et al., 1994).

What is new is the current rate of human-induced extinction, which appears far higher than would be implied by the past fossil record. Conservative estimates of global rates of extinction for various groups of species vary from 10 to 1,000 times the natural rates that would currently prevail (NRC, 1995; Nott et al., 1995). The wide range arises in part because of substantial uncertainty about the number of species and inadequate monitoring of known species.

In passing the Endangered Species Act in 1973, the U.S. Congress recognized in section 2 of the Act that species have "ecological, educational, historical, recreational and scientific value" inadequately accounted for in the process of "economic growth and development." The 1973 Act strengthened the Endangered Species Conservation Act of 1969, which, in turn, was passed to improve the Endangered Species Preservation Act of 1966. The 1973 Act was triggered partially by a dispute between the Departments of Defense and Interior over the listing of sperm whales that prohibited the use of sperm whale oil in submarines (Mann and Plummer, 1995, p. 155). The 1973 Act is potentially the broadest and most powerful step in the long and continuing process of protecting fish, wildlife and plants through national legislation.

The purpose of the Endangered Species Act and its subsequent amendments is "to provide a means whereby the ecosystems upon which endangered species and threatened species depend may be conserved" and to provide a program to conserve these species. Notice the direct reference to ecosystems, rather than just to species.[1] Natural scientists, with rare exceptions, believe the rightful objects to save are habitats or ecosystems because of their intrinsic value and because they enhance species survival. For economists, this poses additional analytical difficulties. Thinking about valuing a species is hard enough; valuing a complex combination of many species and their interactions within the context of a certain location—an ecosystem—generally should be more difficult.

The Act directs the Secretary of the Interior, through the branch of the Fish and Wildlife Service, and the Secretary of Commerce, through the National Marine Fisheries Service, to carry through the administrative process

---

[1]According to the ad hoc Committee on Endangered Species appointed by the Ecological Society of America (Carroll et al., 1996), the meaning of "species" in the Act "is somewhat imprecise, but the wording recognizes that a species is made up of an assemblage of individuals that collectively express genetic, morphological, and behavioral variation, and that this variation is the basis of evolutionary change and adaptation." A species includes any subspecies of fish or wildlife including invertebrates such as insects, crustaceans, and mollusks, or plant including fungi. For vertebrates, any distinct population segment of a species—one with unique morphological features or genetic traits—qualifies, although distinction is to be judged on a case-by-case basis.

supporting the Act. The administrative process involves a series of steps: i) listing a species as "endangered" or "threatened"—endangered being the more severe threat; ii) designating critical habitats for its survival; iii) prohibiting activities that enhance extinction, and creating and executing a recovery plan; and iv) removing a species from the list when it no longer is in danger.

The intention of the Endangered Species Act is to save *all* species. There is no explicit recognition of relative costs and benefits in the 1973 Act.[2] A species with high economic cost of recovery and possibly low economic benefits has the same standing as a species with palpably large economic benefits and small costs. Recovery plans are designed by natural scientists, specialists of the species and its habitat, assisted by applied mathematicians and ecological model builders. Recovery plans are typically designed with little regard for total or marginal economic benefits relative to costs, nor with much regard for ecological-economic interactions, including the relative value of information that allows policymakers to discriminate among alternative recovery plans.

But while the rhetoric of the Act offers no way of discriminating between environmental priorities, constraints on regulatory budgets and time make it inevitable that such priorities will be set, at least implicitly. The funds available to preserve species in the United States are clearly inadequate for the task. Of the 1,104 species in the United States listed as threatened (228) or endangered (876) as of July 1997, slightly over 40 percent have approved recovery plans, as shown in Table 1.[3] Since approval is a quite separate matter from adequate appropriations for the recovery plan, the status of some of these species has deteriorated and the survival prospects for slightly under 60 percent are deteriorating. Moreover, recovery plans are often not developed for years, if at all. Biological analysis of recovery plans and goals suggest that more than half of listed vertebrates would remain in serious risk of extinction even after meeting population targets in their recovery plans (Carroll et al., 1996; Tear et al., 1993).

---

[2]Mann and Plummer (1995, pp. 156–63) have an excellent account of the political environment surrounding the endangered species debate, or lack of it, in the early 1970s. The Act looked to most on Capital Hill like feel-good legislation in which everyone could support bald eagles without any perceived downside risk. Economic considerations were absent for two key reasons: commerce and industry were disengaged, and advocates removed a critical word from the final language—*practicable*. *Practicable* was the safety valve in early bills that allowed for economic balance when needed. Only after the Fish and Wildlife Service started applying the law did Congress realize the implications of its own words.

[3]Table 1 shows the FWS listings of threatened and endangered species outside the United States. Drafters of the Act included this provision to raise domestic awareness of extinction abroad. The Act allows the United States to promulgate import restrictions based on its own findings regarding foreign species status; and to provide financial assistance to foreign conservation programs. All this is intertwined with the Convention on International Trade in Endangered Species of Wild Fauna and Flora (CITES) of 1973, which is implemented through the Act. The foreign species listed in Table 1 represent a fraction of the over 30,000 CITES-listed endangered species worldwide.

Table I Box Score of Threatened and Endangered Species (as of July 31, 1997)

Group	Endangered US	Endangered Foreign	Threatened US	Threatened Foreign	Total Species	Species with Plans
Mammals	57	251	7	16	331	39
Birds	75	178	15	6	274	72
Reptiles	14	65	18	14	111	30
Amphibians	9	8	7	1	25	11
Fishes	67	11	41	0	119	74
Snails	15	1	7	0	23	18
Clams	56	2	6	0	64	44
Crustaceans	15	0	3	0	18	6
Insects	24	4	9	0	37	21
Arachnids	5	0	0	0	5	4
Animal Subtotal	337	520	113	37	1007	319
Flowering Plants	511	1	113	0	625	360
Conifers	2	0	0	2	4	1
Ferns & others	26	0	2	0	28	20
Plant Subtotal	539	1	115	2	657	381
Grand Total	876	521	228	39	1664	700[a]

Source: United States Fish and Wildlife Services, a Division of Endangered Species (1997).
[a]There are 457 approved recovery plans—some plans cover more than one species, and some species have more than one plan.

Matters are worse than this. There are nearly 200 species for which sufficient data exist on vulnerability to warrant endangered or threatened status, but the budgets for listing are inadequate to consummate the task. The current budgetary limits allow listing species at a rate of about 100 per year. Moreover, a list to 3,600 "indefinite" species designated as possibly threatened or endangered was eliminated two years ago, because the list caused "confusion about the conservation status of these taxa [species]" (61 Federal Register 7596–7597, 1996). The list of 3,600 created a cloud of uncertainty about the economic viability of the habitats affecting the species in limbo. The list was excised because landowners' complained to their congressional representatives about the economic costs of this uncertainty.

Species also bear risk due to budget constraints. Since owning land which is hospitable to an endangered species can dramatically circumscribe any development plans for that land, owners have an incentive to destroy the habitat before listing occurs, sometimes known as the "shoot, shovel, and shut-up" strategy. The print media routinely report cases of habitat destruction triggered by an anticipation of listing. For example, just ten days before the golden-cheeked warbler was rated by the Fish and Wildlife Service, a firm owned by Ross Perot hired migrant workers with chain saws to destroy hundreds of acres of oak and juniper warbler habitat (Mann and

Plummer, 1995). Wilcove et al. (1996) cite this incentive as "one reason why so many species are teetering on the very brink of extinction by the time they receive protection."

With no specific priorities for listing species as endangered, economists are not surprised that the employees in the Office of Endangered Species proceeded by listing the species that they liked best despite the prescription against ranking in the Act. A survey of their preferences demonstrated that they ranked mammals and birds above fish, amphibians, and reptiles (Brown, 1990), and these preferences reflect the rankings of which species are actually listed (Metrick and Weitzman, 1996). The few listed arachnids suggests they have relatively few to champion their case for candidacy. Attitudes toward invertebrates are often downright hostile as they are often perceived to be associated with disease and agricultural damage, and they appear to lack individual identity or consciousness (Kellert, 1993).

In 1982, Congress remedied this non-scientific choice method by requiring no favoritism in listing among types of species. Since 1982, the conditions for scientific "objectivity" seem to have been met in the sense that listings are highly correlated with the degree of endangerment of the species, except for amphibians, whose chance of listing remains below other species (Cash, 1997). There is no reason to believe, however, that the degree of endangerment is highly correlated with the expected net economic benefits of preservation—regardless of how one chooses to measure the benefits and costs.

Although in the early years of the Endangered Species Act no official priorities existed for which species should be listed, Congress did require several years after the passage of the act that expenditures on species should vary with a priority system in which "degree of threat," "recovery potential," "taxonomy," and "conflict with development" are ordered into a 18-point scale (Simon et al., 1995). The purpose of the system was to prevent favoritism for expenditures on larger mammals and birds, sometimes known as "megafauna." Preferences are not an ingredient of science. In fact, expenditures on species have not been correlated with the 18-point index for each species, but instead are correlated with a measure of whether a species is in conflict with construction or other forms of economic activity and with a measure of megafauna (Metrick and Weitzman, 1996). Researchers have yet to establish that recovery expenditures by federal agencies are driven by "science," the only allowable criterion stipulated by Congress.

Although economic considerations are implicit in many of the decisions about whether species should be listed as endangered (or some milder category) and what sort of recovery plan should be established, the explicit legal role for economic considerations only enters the picture explicitly when the designation of critical habitat for the recovery plan is made. Critical habitat is land essential for the survival of a species—a more precise meaning is not made clear in the Act. Such land triggers a duty for all federal agencies to consult the Fish and Wildlife Service about the appropriateness of a particular land use.

Under a set of 1978 amendments to the Act, the Secretary of the Interior (Sec. 4) may "take into consideration the economic impact, and any other relevant impact, of specifying any particular area as critical habitat" for a threatened or endangered species, and can exclude an area from critical habitat designation if the benefits of exclusion outweigh the benefits to specifying the critical habit, "unless failure to designate leads to extinction." Under the same amendments (Sec. 7), it is possible for a federal agency, the governor of a state, or a permit or license applicant to apply to the Secretary of the Interior for an exemption from the Act. The Secretary then submits a report to a committee, sometimes called the "God Squad," that discusses, among other things, the availability of reasonable and prudent alternatives to the agency's proposed action, and "the nature and extent of the benefits" of the action and proposed alternatives (Anderson, in press). Not surprisingly, the designation of land as "critical habitat" is often controversial and arduous, because private parties seek not to have their lands designated in this way (NRC, 1995). But since nearly 80 percent of all species have no critical habitat designation, this pathway to account for economic considerations is inactive in many cases.

The power of the Endangered Species Act rests with its far-reaching provisions to constrain the activities of private parties and public agencies. Private parties cannot "take" a listed species. A "take" includes "to harass, harm, . . . wound," and harm encompasses habitat modification.[4] Parties caught violating the proscriptions of the Act are punished by more than a slap on the wrist. Of those prosecuted on criminal charges for illegal takings, one-fourth went to jail for between 10 to 1,170 days, one-fourth paid fines from $1000 to $50,000, and many others were put on probation (GAO, 1995a).

Private parties can avoid these perils by requesting an "incidental take" provision. A person can qualify for an incidental take by submitting and receiving approval of a habitat conservation plan, which specifies how the habitat will be developed in a way that must minimize the "impact of a taking" and "not appreciably" impinge on the probability of survival or recovery. Private parties can be very much affected by how stringently the "harass" and "harm" wording is interpreted. In the past, critics of the Act have cited some impressive examples of government dedication to the letter of the law that may seem to go beyond common sense (Mann and Plummer, 1995). As an illustration that is perhaps not representative, a timber company was prohibited from harvesting timber on 72 acres because a pair of northern spotted owls were located on public land 1.6 miles away, but within the protected "owl circle," an area the size of about 6,500 football fields (Sugg, 1994). To date, 31 habitat conservation plans have been approved

---

[4]Critics of the Endangered Species Act were encouraged in 1994, when the U.S. Court of Appeals for the District of Columbia ruled in *Babbitt versus Sweet Home Chapter of Communities for a Greater Oregon* (1994 U.S. App. LEX 15 4341) that the Fish and Wildlife Service had misinterpreted "harm," but friends of the Act breathed a sigh of relief when the Supreme Court overruled that decision in 1995 (115 S. Ct. 2407 [1995]; NRC, 1995).

and 200 are waiting approval or being developed (GAO, 1995a; U.S. Fish and Wildlife Service/National Marine Fisheries Service, 1997).

Performance of the Act

Has the Endangered Species Act slowed the perceived trends in extinction? The question is difficult to answer, in part because the 25 years since the passage of the Act is a brief period to judge whether trends in extinction rates have changed, and because the ecological literature is by no means decided on a clear technical definition of "recovery" (Tear et al., 1993). Measuring the effectiveness of the Act requires one to decide when to declare victory. Should it be when a listed species is taken off the list? When a declining trend is reversed? When the rate of extinction is slowed? When critical habitat is protected so as to prevent species from declining to the point of being considered for listing? Although the answers to these questions are unclear and notwithstanding our pleasure from keeping favorite species like the bald eagle around, only one with modest expectations would give the Endangered Species Act a high performance rating.

Since the inception of the Act in 1973, 11 species of more than 1,000 listed have recovered and have been removed form the list, including the eastern states brown pelican, Utah's Rydberg milk-vetch, and the California gray whale. Species downlisted to threatened from endangered include the Aleutian Canada goose, greenback cutthroat trout, Virginia round-leaf birch and bald eagle (U.S. Fish and Wildlife Service, 1996). According to the Environmental Defense Fund, less than 10 percent of the listed species have exhibited an improved status and the status of four times that amount is declining. For example, the population of Attwater's prairie-chicken, listed in 1967, has dropped to 42 in 1996 from 2,254 birds in 1975. The ratio of declining species to improving species is 1.5 to 1 on federal lands, and 9 to 1 on private lands.

Funding for the endangered species program of the Fish and Wildlife Service has failed to keep pace with the number of listed species, with the result that the real budget per species is 60 percent of its 1976 level. The Office of Endangered Species has inadequate funds to assay the status of about one-third of the listed species (Wilcove et al., 1996).

Economic Benefits and Costs of the Endangered Species Act

Most of the services provided by endangered species, including their corresponding levels of biological diversity, are not priced by the market. Some people see no need to quantify the benefits of these services, which in their view are either obvious or impossible to capture—so that measurement is either unnecessary or futile (for example, Roughgarden, 1995, p. 153). In this view, it is enough that natural science dictates a target, so that planners can go about their attempts to establish a level of preservation that guarantees survival of the species in question (Ciriacy-Wantrup, 1952).

Essentially, the approach of the Act that prohibits any activity that harms a listed species puts a very large or infinite value on avoiding extinction. This view places endangered species beyond the reach of economic tradeoffs, and the economist is relegated to helping find the least cost solution to achieve a biological-based standard. Others take an opposing approach. They want hard evidence that the benefits of preservation exceed the alternative uses of these resources (Epstein, 1995, p. 278). From this view, comparing the costs and benefits of endangered species protection is only logical: resources are scarce, and some attempt should be made to balance the costs and benefits so that policymakers are allocating funds to their highest valued use, given plausible adjustments for uncertainty in ecosystem functions and irreversibility.

What is known about the private and social benefits of the Endangered Species Act? The private benefits derived from species protection include commercial use, consumptive use, and recreation.

One commercial use that has received considerable popular attention are possible new pharmaceutical products. Examples include the drug vincristine used to treat leukemia, derived from the rare plant called the rosy periwinkle, and the Pacific yew tree that produces taxol used in ovarian cancer treatment, a market estimated to reach $1 billion in 1996 (Norton, 1995). Taxol provided the template for a synthetic drug which replaced it. Some people use these examples as compelling evidence that justifies saving the totality of the world's variety of genetic and biochemical resources—after all, who knows where the next breakthrough to cure cancer or AIDS may come from? With new and future breakthroughs in biotechnology, so the argument goes, preserving all parts of nature only makes common sense because there is no end to the potential beneficial uses of rare species.

While no substitute exists for biodiversity as a whole, measuring commercial value requires insight into substitution possibilities and the marginal contribution that each species makes to finding a new and useful product. The expected value of a marginal species equals the expected payoff from testing it times the probability that all other species fail to provide the desired product. If one species substitutes for another in potential market success, the marginal value of an extensive genetic exploration declines as the odds increase that a firm will find a profitable species quickly. Simpson et al. (1996) provide an example which helps to illuminate the range of potential values. They make a variety of more-or-less plausible assumptions: for example, one scenario suggests that there is a 95 percent chance of getting 10 new products by sampling 250,000 species; that once a new product is identified, a $300 million investment will yield $450 million from the new product; and so on. At one end of their range of estimated values, the maximum value of saving a marginal species is estimated at slightly less than $10,000; however, when there are more species to choose from and the chances of finding a successful product are higher, the expected value of preserving a marginal species can be less than one cent. Although the value of some species is enhanced by introducing prior knowledge about the likely significance of species or ecosystems, the associated cost is to reduce the value of other species (Rausser and Small, 1997). As such, it is doubtful that the bio-prospector will be the savior of endangered species, and it will be some time before we understand ecosystem functions well enough to measure accurately the marginal value product of ecosystem components contributing to market goods.

Commercial and recreational harvesting of species are perhaps the most straightforward commercial benefit to estimate given a tangible market price. Angler and hunting expenditures amounted to about $60 billion in 1996 (U.S. Fish and Wildlife Service, 1997). Commercial and recreational salmon fishing in the Pacific Northwest helps support 60,000 jobs and over $1 billion in personal income in the regional economy (Irvin, 1995). Ecotourism is another economic benefit—many people are willing to pay to view rare species, like the $200 million California whale-watching industry. Global ecotourism expenditures have been estimated at $90–$200 billion in 1988, with about 15 percent spent in North America (Filion et al., 1994). But the ecotourist is also unlikely to be a broadbased savior for endangered species: not many endangered or threatened insects or funguses will qualify for preservation on these grounds.

Estimating the social value of endangered species protection is even more challenging. Most economists now acknowledge that people might have preferences about protecting species and related services they will rarely ever, if at all, see or use (Krutilla, 1967). The main point of contention is over trying to put a monetary value on these preferences. The primary tools for trying to accomplish this are public opinion surveys, known as contingent evaluation surveys, which use a sequence of questions to put a monetary value on personal preferences. As one might expect, this method is highly contentious, because people are responding to a survey rather than facing their own budget constraint and actually spending their own money.[5]

For endangered species, the reported results from this literature suggest that the average person's *lump sum* willingness to pay for sea turtle or bald eagle preservation ranges from $12.99 to $254; and that individual *annual* willingness to pay ranges from $6 for striped shiner to $95 for northern spotted owl preservation (Loomis and White, 1996). A piecemeal species-by-species approach, however, most likely overestimates economic benefits. To illustrate, if one summed the stated preferences from various endangered species surveys as a crude measure of benefits, the average

---

[5]For an overview of the arguments in this journal, see the Symposium on Contingent Valuation in the Fall 1994 issue, with articles by Paul Portney, Michael Hanemann, and Peter Diamond and Jerry Hausman.

person was willing to pay about $1000 to protect 18 different species. Multiplying $1000 by the number of U.S. households suggests that we would be willing to pay over 1 percent of GDP to preserve less than 2 percent of the endangered species. Many will find these values to be suspiciously high.

Contingent valuation surveys have other notable problems. Critics complain that hypothetical surveys often elicit surrogate preferences for environmental protection in general, rather than for the specific species in question.[6] For example, McClelland et al. (1992) found that up to one-half of the reported values for a specific environmental charge can be attributed to surrogate values. The fraction appears to depend on the contextual information provided in the survey. In addition, most people are unfamiliar with the services provided by endangered species. A recent survey found that over 70 percent of Scottish citizens were completely unfamiliar with the meaning of biodiversity (Hanley and Spash, 1993), and there is little reason to expect substantially more knowledge in the United States (Coursey, 1997). These problems suggest that measuring the benefits of endangered species protection remain elusive and contentious. Tests of the internal and external consistency of stated preferences are a high research priority (Diamond, 1996).

Moreover, most contingent value experiments have attempted to put a value on what might be called "charismatic megafauna"—mainly large animals that many people already see clearly and fondly in their mind's eye—not on the thousands of other species that comprise an ecosystem, but whose existence is unknown to most people. Nevertheless, valuing low-profile species would seem to be a natural outcome of valuing high-profile species, to the extent that high-profile species depend on low-profile ones. The high-profile species' derived demands for the low-profile species implies certain values for the low profile species as "intermediate goods" (Crocker and Tschirhart, 1992).

It seems implausible that private benefits of preserving endangered species, including commercial and consumptive use, will be sufficient to justify preservation efforts that would be as extensive as many would like to see. Despite the extraordinary analytical difficulties associated with measuring the social value that should be placed on preserving each species, determining at least a plausible range for these values would seem to be essential if we are to make judgments about the benefits of preservation.

The benefit side could be sidestepped to some extent by turning to measures like the costs per species saved. But the costs are not much easier to get a handle on, as they are often illustrative but not representative. The opportunity costs of the Endangered Species Act include the foregone opportunities due to restrictions on the use of property due to listings, designation of critical habitat, and recovery plans. Opportunity costs also include the reduced economic rents from restricted or altered development

---

[6]These surrogate preferences are variously called the part-whole bias, or embedding effect. See the exchange between Kahneman and Knetsch (1992) and Smith (1992).

projects, agriculture production, timber harvesting, minerals extraction, recreation activities, wages lost by displaced workers who remain unemployed or who are re-employed at lower wages, lower consumer surplus due to higher prices, and lower capital asset value.

Opportunity costs have been estimated for a few high-profile, regional conflicts. For example, the Bonneville Power Administration estimated that its expenditure on salmon conservation was about $350 million in 1994 (1 percent of 1994 revenues), of which about $300 million represented the opportunity cost of lost power revenues (NRC, 1995). Another study estimated that a recovery plan that increased the survival odds of the northern spotted owl to 91 percent, preserving about 1900 owl pairs, would decrease economic welfare by $33 billion (1990 dollars), excluding ecosystem and preservation benefits, with a disproportionate share of the losses borne by the regional producers of intermediate wood products (Montgomery et al, 1994). If the recovery plan tried to achieve a goal of a 95 percent survival odds with 2400 owl pairs, costs increased to $46 billion. For perspective, the value of rights to cut the old growth timber on the 6,500 football field area necessary to support one owl pair is more than $650 million. The cost could be reduced by 50 percent if some of the owl's range was reduced (Montgomery, 1995), but the Act requires that species be preserved throughout their spatial range.

Opportunity costs have also been estimated for critical habitat designation in a few cases: the Virgin River basin for the wound fin, Virgin River chub, and Virgin spinedace; and Colorado River basin for the razorback sucker, humpback chub, Colorado squawfish, and bonytail (Brookshire et al., 1994, 1995). Several conclusions emerge from these studies. The difference in economic output for a region (in this case, say a county) with and without critical habitat designation is relatively small, often measuring in the range of one-fiftieth of a percentage point. The impact of critical habitat designation on regional income, tax revenues, and employment is similar. But the impact of critical habitat designation is not evenly distributed across regions and states; for example, a given streamflow requirement may have a negative impact on recreation, electric power production, and future consumptive use in some states, but enhance these activities in other states.

The transaction costs of dealing with habitat conservation plans would be another element of the costs. The private transaction costs for dealing with the Act include the time and money spent applying for permits and licenses, redesigning plans, and legal fees. Estimates of these costs for the Act do not exist. As a crude comparison, the Comprehensive Environmental Response, Compensation, and Liability Act of 1980, or Superfund, generates private party transaction costs of about 30 cents on the dollar (Dixon, 1995). Since the Endangered Species Act does not employ the same far-reaching liability system of Superfund, its transaction costs should be considerably smaller.

Finally, estimates of opportunity costs also exist with regard to public resources devoted to endangered species. In a General Accounting Office report on 58 approved recovery plans, 34 of the plans had a total cost estimate for carrying out the recovery, 23 plans had cost estimates for the initial years of recovery, and one had a cost estimate for one part of a twelve-part plan (GAO, 1995b). Of the 34 total cost estimates for public agencies, estimates ranged from a 1994 cost of $145,000 for the White River spinedace to a 1991 estimate of about $154 million for the green sea turtle and loggerhead turtle. The total estimated cost for the 34 species was approximately $700 million. For the 23 plans with initial three-year estimates, costs range from a 1990 estimate of $57,000 for the Florida scrub jay to a 1991 estimate of $49.1 million for the black-capped vireo (a bird). The three-year total cost for the 23 species was over $350 million in the early 1990s (a figure not adjusted to current dollars). For the "high-priority" actions, the total estimated costs is about $223 million for three years.

Of the money actually expended on endangered species recovery by federal and state agencies between 1989 and 1991, over 50 percent was spent on the top ten species: bald eagle ($31.3 million), northern spotted owl ($26.4 million), Florida scrub jay ($19.9 million), west Indian manatee ($17.3 million), red-cockaded woodpecker ($15.1 million), Florida panther ($13.6 million), grizzly bear ($12.6 million), least Bell's vireo ($12.5 million), American peregrine falcon ($11.6 million), and whooping crane ($10.8 million) (Metrick and Weitzman, 1996). Over 95 percent of identifiable expenditures have been on vertebrates, suggesting that visceral identification with certain species has influenced resource allocation decisions more than scientific characteristics such as degree of threat or recovery potential.

How do these cost estimates translate into national levels? We do not know—no nationwide estimate exists of whether the Act has shaved percentage points off the gross domestic product. One study explored the association between the Act and economic growth by looking for a connection across the 50 states in the number of species listings in each state and either construction employment or gross state product between 1975 and 1990 (Meyer, 1995). Although no negative relationship was found—for example, Alabama had 70 listed species and a booming economy, while Louisiana had 21 listings and a dormant economy—this study made no effort to estimate national opportunity costs. Surely the impact of the Act is less than that estimated for generic environmental regulation and global climate change policy, and estimates in this area range from 0.2 percent to 1 percent losses in annual GDP (Jorgenson and Wilcoxon, 1990; Weyant, 1996).

Moreover, a national cost estimate might not be necessary right now. America is a large nation, and domestic and foreign substitutes exist for many goods and services affected by the Act. Rather, people are concerned with the redistribution of wealth in regional conflicts like the Northern spotted owl. The political process of "managing the losers" seems to be the question of today. National cost estimates, however, might be the question of tomorrow—especially if the pace of urban expansion accelerates beyond the estimated 900,000 acres converted every year (Council on Environmental Quality, 1997); or if a modicum of respect drops anchor on wide-eyed schemes like those proposing to set aside half the land area of the 48 contiguous states as nature reserves for endangered species (Noss and Cooperrider, 1994).

Improving the Endangered Species Act

Economics can and should contribute to the debate over reauthorization of the Endangered Species Act.

First, economists can frame the endangered species debate in benefit-cost terms. Such calculations are bound to be uncomfortable and controversial, especially since the overwhelming fraction of benefits from the preservation of endangered species are likely to be in the nature of public goods whose benefits are received in the future. But it is doubtful whether encyclopedic species protection regardless of cost is even possible, and if possible, whether it holds a moral trump card over all other priorities such as the health and welfare of today's children (Guha, 1997). Economists naturally seek criteria and conduct analyses which permit a discrimination among species in recognition of the existence of budget constraints. Of course, anyone who offers analysis which leads to an increased risk of a species becoming extinct will suffer attacks, but the present system is assuredly allowing many such actions, without the meliorating grace of admitting or examining them openly.

The administration of the Endangered Species Act could also take a more proactive role by moving away from the approach of identifying species and recovery plans one at a time, and moving toward identifying critical habitat for listed and unlisted species, and then designing a voluntary compensation scheme for critical habitat that cuts across the holdings of public and private landowners. This would be in keeping with the original intention of the law, which, as described earlier, placed an emphasis on preserving ecosystems, not just species. Andrew Metrick and Martin Weitzman take up the question of how to conceptualize the issue of endangered species protection in their paper in this symposium—and offer a somewhat discouraging evaluation of how the key elements that should be represented in such calculations are not being taken into account in the present administration of the Endangered Species Act.

A second task for economists in reform of the Endangered Species Act is to point out that whether and which species are or soon will be endangered are not purely ecological questions, but are in part economic questions too. After all, economic variables influence the likelihood of extinction—and even evolution (Munro, 1997). Species are more likely to be endangered the more they conflict with economic development that causes, say, habitat fragmentation. Species are less threatened the greater the conservation efforts. Since development and conservation decisions depend on economic parameters such as relative prices and income, so does the probability of species extinction. Economists must continue to stress to the natural sciences that economic parameters affect their ability to estimate the risk of extinction accurately.

Third, the net benefits of the Endangered Species Act might be dramatically increased if an amended Act provides economic rewards to landowners for good stewardship of actual and prospective habitat and species thereon. More than 90 percent of the listed species had some of their habitat on private land as of 1993 and more than one-third were completely on non-federal lands (GAO, 1995a), so the cooperation of private landowners is vital to the preservation of endangered species. Without such cooperation, landowners have strong incentives to minimize the risk of economic loss to a taking under the Act by hindering the gathering of information about species on their land, or at the extreme, by destroying potential habitat overtly before the species are listed and covertly afterwards. As an example, one owner of 7,200 acres of timber had to forgo harvest on 1,560.8 acres to protect 12 colonies or red-cockaded woodpeckers. To avoid further restriction if the woodpeckers expanded to new territory, the owner, who was actually fairly conservation-oriented, said he would "start massive clearcutting," halving the rotation time to 40 years. Since habitat for the woodpecker often occurs when the existing tree cavities are destroyed by frequent burns and rot, this action would not destroy habitat, but would avoid creating any additional habitat (Stroup, 1995).

A variety of compensation schemes are possible: direct compensation from the government to owners of land that is taken; tradable rights in habitat, under which those who wish to develop land would buy permits from those who would then not be able to develop;[7] insurance programs under which landowners are compensated if endangered species impose costs on them, like the fund created by Defenders of Wildlife under which rangers are compensated when wolves destroy livestock (Goldstein and Heintz, 1993); or tax breaks to allow large chunks of land to be preserved, rather than broken up to pay federal estate taxes (Wilcove et al., 1996). In our view, any such system should be voluntary for the private landowners, flexible enough to accommodate a single large or several small reserves, provide incentives for the landowner to reveal private information on the owner's ability to profit from the land, account for the deadweight loss of the funds used to compensate acre setasides, and account for the shadow value of a constraint that sets minimum odds of survival (Smith and Shogren, 1998).

None of the methods of using compensation to align the incentives of private landowners with the preservation of endangered species is simple or straightforward to implement. Compensation for private landowners could be subject to concocted claims and possibly extensive litigation; some of the compensation schemes proposed in recent bills to reauthorize the Endangered Species Act seem especially ill-conceived (Goldstein, 1996). Trading habitat requires ways of measuring what quantity and quality of habitat is "equivalent"—not a simple task. Widespread use of the insurance mechanism may be curtailed because of the costs of ascertaining the true losses to property owners, and the moral hazard problem that insured owners will have less reason to avoid damage. It is not obvious that tax

---

[7]The Environmental Defense Fund goes further in substitution possibilities when it proposes that a landowner who wants to destroy habitat for one species can do so by buying equivalent habitat for another species (Wilcove et al., 1996).

breaks for preserving large estates would generate more benefits than simply buying the land, or allowing it to be sold with some sort of easement, and the political attractiveness of providing additional tax breaks to wealthy landowners is questionable.

The pros and cons of these sorts of voluntary incentive programs are currently being discussed more by natural scientists than by economists (for example, Eisner et al., 1995), but economists can make a contribution by providing a better understanding of the economic nature of these schemes. In this symposium, the paper by Robert Innes, Stephen Polasky and John Tschirhart addresses the question of how various requirements for compensation would affect incentives for landowners and for the government.

Finally, these general steps that should be taken to improve the Endangered Species Act will involve a modest addition to government expenditures. Over the last couple of decades, budgets for administering the Act have not grown to match the perceived problem.

At present, the Endangered Species Act sets a lofty rhetorical goal of saving every species, while making no distinctions among species except those governed by "science," a term left largely undefined. It is driven by the belief that risk of extinction is a question best left to the natural sciences; if economics is allowed in the door at all, it is relegated to the task of managing the risk levels determined by others (Carroll et al., 1996). The Act largely ignores the importance of the incentives facing private landowners. These are shortcomings that economists are well-suited to address.

References

Anderson, S., "The Evolution of the Endangered Species Act." In Shogren, J., ed., *Private Property and the Endangered Species Act. Saving Habitats, Protecting Homes.* Austin, TX: University of Texas Press (in press).

Babbitt, B., *To Reauthorize the Endangered Species Act. Why, Where and How We Should Translate Our Success Stories into Law.* Speech to the National Press Club, Washington, DC, July 17, 1997.

Belovsky, G., J. Bissonette, R. Dueser, T. Edwards, Jr., C. M. Lueke, M. E. Ritchie, J. B. Slade, and F. H. Wagner, "Management of Small Populations: Concepts Affecting the Recovery of Endangered Species," *Wildlife Society Bulletin*, 1994, 22, 307–16.

Brookshire, D., M. McKee, and C. Schmidt, *Draft Economic Analysis of Critical Habitat Designation in The Virgin River Basin for the Woundfin, Virgin River Chub, and Virgin Spinedace.* Report to the U.S. Fish and Wildlife Service, 1995.

Brookshire, D., M. McKee, and G. Watts, *An Economic Analysis of Critical Habitat Designation in Colorado River Basin for the Razorback Sucker, Humpback Chub, Colorado Squawfish, and Bonytail.* Final Report to the U.S. Fish and Wildlife Service, 1994.

Brown, Jr., G., "Valuation of Genetic Resources." In Orians, G., G. Brown, W. Kunin and J. Swierzbinski, eds., *The Preservation and Valuation of Biological Resources.* Seattle, WA: University of Washington Press, 1990, 203–29.

Carroll, R., C. Augspurger, A. Dobson, J. Franklin, G. Orians, W. Reid, R. Tracy, D. Wilcove, and J. Wilson, "Strengthening the Use of Science in Achieving the Goals of the Endangered Species Act: An Assessment by the Ecological Society of America," *Ecological Applications*, 1996, *6*, 1–11.

Cash, D., *Science, Politics, and Environmental Risk: Regulatory Decision Making in the U.S. Endangered Species Act*. photocopy, JFK School of Government, Harvard University, 1997.

Ciriacy-Wantrup S., *Resource Conservation: Economics and Policies*. Berkeley, CA: University of California, 1952.

Council on Environmental Quality, *Environmental Quality. 25th Anniversary Report*. 1994–95. Washington, DC, 1997.

Coursey, D., *The Panitae of Environmental Value Estimates*. A paper presented at *Social Order and Endangered Species Preservation*, Centennial, Wyoming, April 1997.

Crocker, T., and J. Tschirhart, "Ecosystems, Externalities, and Economics," *Environmental and Resource Economics*, 1992, *2*, 551–67.

Diamond, P., "Testing the Internal Consistency of Contingent Valuation Surveys," *Journal of Environmental Economics and Management*, 1996, *30*, 337–47.

Dixon, L., "The Transaction Costs Generated by Superfund's Liability Approach." In R. Revesz and R. Stewart, eds., *Analyzing Superfund. Economics, Science, and Law*. Washington, DC: Resources for the Future, 1995.

Eisner, T., J. Lubchenco, E. O. Wilson, D. Wilcove, and M. Bean, "Building a Scientifically Sound Policy for Protecting Endangered Species," *Science*, 1995, *268*, 1231–32.

Epstein, R., *Simple Rules for a Complex World*. Cambridge: Harvard University Press, 1995.

Federal Register, 1996, 7596, 7597.

Filion, F., J. Foley, and A. Jacquemot, "The Economics of Global Ecotourism." In M. Munasinghe and J. McNeely, eds., *Protected Area Economics and Policy. Linking Conservation and Sustainable Development*. Washington, DC: World Bank, 1994.

Goldstein, J., "Whose Land is it Anyway?" *Choices*, 1996, second quarter, 4–8.

Goldstein, J., and H. Heintz, Jr., "Incentives for Private Conservation of Species and Habitat: An Economic Perspective," Office of Policy Analysis, U.S. Department of Interior, 1993.

Guha, R., "The Authoritarian Biologist and the Arrogance of Anti-Humanism. Wildlife Conservation in the Third World," *The Ecologist*, 1997, *27*, 14–20.

Hanley, N., and C. Spash, *The Value of Biodiversity in British Forests*. Report to the Scottish Forestry Commission, University of Sterling, Scotland, 1993.

Irvin, W.R., *Statement to United States Senate Committee on Environmental And Public Works, Subcommittee on Drinking Water, Fisheries, and Wildlife*. July 13, 1995.

Jablonski, D., "Extinctions: A Palentological Perspective," *Science*, 1991, *253*, 754–57.

Jorgenson, D., and P. Wilcoxon, "Environmental Regulation and U.S. Economic Growth," *Rand Journal of Economics*, 1990, *21*, 314–40.

Kahneman, D., and J. Knetsch, "Valuing Public Goods: The Purchase of Moral Satisfaction," *Journal of Environmental Economics and Management*, 1992, *22*, 57–70.

Kellert, S., "Values and Perceptions of Invertebrates," *Conservation Biology*, 1993, *7*, 845–55.

Krutilla, J., "Conservation Reconsidered," *American Economic Review*, 1967, *57*, 787–96.

Loomis, J., and D. White, *Economic Benefits of Rare and Endangered Species: Summary and Meta Analysis*. Photocopy, Colorado State University, 1996.

Mann, C., and M. Plummer, *Noah's Choice*. New York, NY: A. Knopf, 1995.

Martin, P., and D. Steadman, *Late Quaternary Extinctions*. New York, NY: Plenum Press, in press.

McClelland, W., W. Schulze, J. Lazo, D. Walurang, J. Doyle, S. Eliot, and J. Irwin, *Methods for Measuring Non-Use Values: A Contingent Valuation Study of Groundwater Cleanup*. Center for Economic Analysis, Boulder, CO, 1992.

Metrick, A., and M. Weitzman, "Patterns of Behavior in Endangered Species Preservation," *Land Economics*, 1996, 72, 1–16.

Meyer, S., *Endangered Species Listings and State Economic Performance*. Working paper, MIT, 1995.

Montgomery, C., "Economic Analysis of the Spatial Dimensions of Species Preservation: The Distribution of Northern Spotted Owl Habitat," *Forest Science*, 1995, 41, 67–83.

Montgomery, C., G. Brown, Jr., and M. Darius, "The Marginal Cost of Species Preservation: The Northern Spotted Owl," *Journal of Environmental Economics and Management*, 1994, 26, 111–28.

Munro, A., "Economics and Biological Evolution," *Environment and Resource Economics*, 1997, 9, 429–49.

National Research Council, *Science and the Endangered Species Act*. National Academy Press, Washington, DC, 1995.

Norton, R., "Owls, Trees, and Ovarian Cancer," *Fortune*, 1995, 2/5, 49.

Noss, R., and A. Cooperrider, *Saving Nature's Legacy: Protecting and Restoring Biodiversity*. Washington, DC: Island Press, 1994.

Nott, M., E. Rogers, and S. Pimm, "Modern Extinctions in the Kilo-death Range," *Current Biology*, 1995, 5, 14–17.

Rausser, G., and A. Small, *Bioprospecting with Prior Ecological Information*. Giannini Foundation working paper no. 819, University of California, Berkeley, 1997.

Roughgarden, J., "Can Economics Protect Biodiversity?" In Swanson, T., ed., *The Economics and Ecology of Biodiversity Decline*. Cambridge: Cambridge University Press, 1995, 149–54.

Simon, B., C. Leff, and H. Doerksen, "Allocating Scarce Resources for Endangered Species Protection," *Journal of Policy Analysis and Management*, 1995, 14, 415–32.

Simpson, R., R. Sedjo, and J. Reid, "Valuing Biodiversity for Use in Pharmaceutical Research," *Journal of Political Economy*, 1996, 104, 163–85.

Smith, R., and J. Shogren, *Voluntary Incentive Design for Endangered Species Protection*. Working paper, University of Minnesota, St. Paul, MN, 1998.

Smith, V.K., "Arbitrary Values, Good Causes, and Premature Verdicts," *Journal of Environmental Economics and Management*, 1992, 22, 71–89.

Souder, J., "Chasing Armadillos Down Yellow Lines: Economics in the Endangered Species Act," *Natural Resources Journal*, 1993, 33, 1095–1139.

Steadman, D., "Prehistoric Extinction of South Pacific Birds: Biodiversity Meets Zoo Archaeology," *Science*, 1995, 267, 1123–31.

Stroup, R., *The Endangered Species Act: Making Innocent Species the Enemy*. PERC Series, PS-3, Bozeman, MT: Political Economy Research Center, 1995.

Sugg, I., "Rule of Law: Worried About That Owl on Your Land? Here's Good News," *Wall Street Journal*, April 6, 1994.

Tear, T., J. Scott, P. Hayward, and B. Griffith, "Status and Prospects for Success of the Endangered Species Act: A Look at Recovery Plans," *Science*, 1993, 262, 976–77.

U.S. Fish and Wildlife Service (FWS), *Endangered and Threatened Wildlife and Plants*. Washington, DC, October 1996.

U.S. Fish and Wildlife Service (FWS), *1996 National Survey of Fishing, Hunting and Wildlife—Associated Recreation: National Overview*. Washington, DC, 1997.

U.S. Fish and Wildlife Service/National Marine Fisheries Service (FWS/NMFS), *Making the ESA Work Better: Implementing the 10 Point Plan and Beyond*. Washington, DC, 1997.

U.S. General Accounting Office (GAO), *Endangered Species Act: Information on Species Protection on Nonfederal Lands*. Washington, DC, GAO/RCED-95-16, 1995a.

U.S. General Accounting Office (GAO), *Correspondence to Representative Don Young on Estimated Recovery Costs of Endangered Species*. Washington, DC, B-270461, 1995b.

Weyant, J., "Introduction and Overview," *EMF 12*. Energy Modeling Forum, Stanford University, 1996.

Wilcove, D., M. Bean, R. Binnie, and M. McMillan, *Rebuilding the Ark*. Environmental Defense Fund, New York, NY, 1996.

Yaffee, S., *Prohibitive Policy: Implementing the Federal Endangered Species Act*. Cambridge, MA: MIT Press, 1982.

28 Conflicts and Choices in Biodiversity Preservation*

Andrew Metrick
Martin L. Weitzman

Andrew Metrick is Associate Professor of Finance at the Wharton School of the University of Pennsylvania; and Martin L. Weitzman is Ernest E. Monrad Professor of Economics at Harvard University.

Decisions about endangered species reflect the values, perceptions, uncertainties, and contradictions of the society that makes them. The defining limitation of the economics of biodiversity preservation is the lack of a common denominator or natural anchor. As a society, we have not even come close to defining what is the objective. What *is* biodiversity? In what units is it to be measured? By contrast, even such a morally loaded field as health economics has at least adopted, in practice, a common denominator of human lives saved as a natural anchor. Until we as a society—in the United States narrowly, and more broadly on the planet Earth—decide what is our objective, all the scientific data imaginable will not help economists to guide policy. At the end of the day, all the brave talk about "win-win" situations, which simultaneously produce sustainable development and conserve biodiversity, will not help us to sort out how many children's hospitals should be sacrificed in the name of preserving natural habitats. The core of the problem is conceptual. We have to make up our minds here what it is we are optimizing. This is the essential problem confounding the preservation of biodiversity today.

We start the paper by showing, in a simple constrained optimization problem, exactly where biodiversity appears in a plausible objective function. Then we indicate for this version the basic properties of a solution. The relevant solution concept is cast in the form of a cost-benefit ranking criterion. We then use this ranking criterion, and this theory, as a vehicle for introducing a normative discussion about the economics of biodiversity preservation. Next, we turn to a positive "revealed preference" analysis of the economics of biodiversity preservation, as acted out in U.S. fed-

"Conflicts and Choices in Biodiversity Preservation," by Andrew Metrick and Martin L. Weitzman from *Journal of Economic Perspectives*, 12(3):21–34 (Summer 1998).

*We thank Judson Jaffe for research assistance, and Brad De Long, J.R. DeShazo, Alan Krueger, Rob Stavins, and seminar participants at Stanford for helpful comments. We are especially grateful to Timothy Taylor, whose help in rewriting this final version went far beyond the usual editorial obligations. We also acknowledge support under National Science Foundation grant SBR-9422772.

eral and state government decisions about the preservation of species under the Endangered Species Act. We conclude with a discussion of how economic analysis can help to uncover difficulties in the objectives and in the decision-making process about biodiversity.

The Economics of Diversity Preservation

The analytics of the preservation of biodiversity is plagued by the absence of a workable cost-effectiveness framework, within which, at least in principle, basic questions can be posed and answered. Current approaches to endangered species protection seem almost completely lacking in theoretical underpinnings that might reasonably guide policy. This section introduces a simple analytical framework that we believe represents a useful way of thinking about the economics of diversity. Rather than presenting a broad survey of the literature, we here attempt to home in on what we consider to be the characteristic features of the underlying problem—in the form of a specific model which will lead us to what we call the Noah's Ark Problem.[1] The main underlying issue is how to determine basic priorities for maintaining or increasing diversity. Seen this way, the central task is to develop a cost-effectiveness formula or criterion that can be used to rank priorities among biodiversity-preserving projects under a limited budget constraint.

In talking about biodiversity preservation, there is always a question about what is the appropriate level of discourse. In principle, the basic unit could be at the level of the molecule, cell, organ, individual, species, habitat, ecosystem, or other levels as well. For the purposes of this paper, we take the underlying unit of analysis to be the species, although we believe that the same basic issues and themes of the paper will arise at any level.

Our key point of departure involves conceptualizing the underlying conservation unit—the species—as if it were a library. A library, of course, is full of books, and the books can be thought of as roughly analogous to the genes (or other key characteristics) of the species itself. Naturally, the book collections in various libraries may overlap to some degree. In turn, a book/gene can be thought of as a container of information. To continue the metaphor, a library is at some risk of burning down, with possible loss of the building and the book collection that it houses. Various preventive measures can be undertaken that lower the probability of a fire, such as investing in fire extinguishers—at a cost. Concentrating on the question of how best to allocate scarce fire prevention resources among the various species/libraries allows for a crisp formulation of the generic problem of optimally conserving diversity under a budget constraint.

---

[1]This approach is developed rigorously in Weitzman (1998). There are other approaches in the literature. Solow, Polasky, and Broadus (1993) were the first to present the problem of what to protect as an economic issue. See also Weitzman (1992, 1993), Polasky and Solow (1995), and Crozier (1992).

The critical part of the preservation problem is specifying the exact form of the objective function. Recognizing that no single form will satisfy everybody, there are, nevertheless, two broad classes of benefits that belong in the objective function: direct utility from each library, and indirect utility coming from the overall "diversity" of library books. We can define the diversity more explicitly to be the number of different books, or the set consisting of the union of all books, in all the existing libraries. These two categories of benefits are sufficiently universal that virtually all justifications for preservation can be fit within them. Thus, in our setup, the value of a library consists of two components: the building itself and the collection of books that it houses. Each library is housed in a building that has some inherent value as a structure; in the species interpretation, this represents the direct utility of how much we like or value the existence of that species per se. Such valuations can come from many different sources, including commercial values, aesthetic values, and even moral or religious values.

Turning now to the book collections within each library, we would like to express their value in comparable units. But why do we care about the diversity of libraries or books in the first place? Two basic answers are possible. We might like many different books per se, just as we might like many different colors simply because of the more colorful world their sheer variety creates. This would be a kind of aesthetic value of diversity. Or we might want to have different books for the utilitarian reason that they are a potential source of future ideas about new medicines, foods, or whatever. This might be called the information content of a book collection. However, at a sufficiently high level of abstraction, these two answers blur into each other, and become essentially the same. In both cases, the reduced form is that we care about having a large number of different books, or separate prices of information.

The Noah's Ark Problem is intended to be an allegory or parable that renders a vivid image of the core problem of preserving the maximum degree of diversity (plus direct utility) under a budget constraint. The parable goes as follows. Noah knows that a flood is coming. An Ark is available to help save some species/libraries. In a world of unlimited resources, the entire set of species might be saved. Unfortunately, Noah's Ark has a limited capacity; in the Bible, the capacity is given as $300 \times 50 \times 30 = 450,000$ cubed-cubits. Noah must choose which species/libraries are to be afforded more protection—and which less—when there are not enough resources around to protect everything fully. Boarding the Ark is a metaphor for investing in a conservation project, like habitat protection, that improves the survivability of a particular species/library. One especially grim version of the Noah's Ark Problem would make the choice a matter of life or death, meaning that all species/libraries that Noah does not take abroad are doomed. We might call this the Old Testament specification. But it is also possible to conceive of a gentler scenario, in which Noah's decision to take a species/library on board raises somewhat its probability of survival—but the species/library has some lesser (but still positive) chance of surviving the flood regardless.

Let us suppose further that although Noah wishes to solve this problem, he does not want to mess around with an overly elaborate and complicated algorithm. Noah is a practical outdoors man. He needs robustness and rugged performance in the field. As he stands at the door of the ark, Noah wants to use a simple priority ranking list from which he can check off one species at a time for boarding. Noah wishes to have a robust rule in the form of a basic ordinal ranking system so that he can board first species #1, then species #2, then species #3, and so forth, until he runs out of space on the ark, whereupon he battens down the hatches and casts off.

Can we help Noah? Is the concept of such a ranking system sensible? Can there exist such a simple boarding rule, which correctly prioritizes each species? If so, what sort of formula should determine Noah's ranking list for achieving an optimal ark-full of species/libraries? The answer to these questions is essentially positive. Our approach here generates a methodology that has the feel of traditional cost-effectiveness approach and can deal with the conservation of diversity. Here, we will focus on a more intuitive form of the criteria, which is at least useful in suggesting the four fundamental ingredients on which Noah should focus when determining conservation priorities.

Noah will begin with the two broad classes of benefits already defined: direct utility from each species/library, and indirect utility coming from the overall diversity of genes/books. The utility of each species/library will be measured as a combination of commercial, recreational and, yes, emotional reactions to a given species. This will pose difficulties in practice, of course, but conceptually it is reasonably straightforward.

However, thinking about the concept of diversity and how to measure it is much less conceptually straightforward. This component of the objective function represents the non-standard part of the optimization problem. (Otherwise, the Noah's Ark Problem is just a straightforward capital-budgeting problem—just rank and board each species by its expected increase in direct utility per unit of space on the Ark.) In fact, the reader might be forgiven for thinking that the notion of the diversity contributed by a species is sufficiently unorthodox that it is difficult to say anything both general and interesting about the solution to the problem. Fortunately, it turns out that by imposing some further structure on the problem, a quite striking characterization is possible.

We now suppose that the book collections are as if they were acquired by an evolutionary branching process with a corresponding evolutionary tree structure. This critical assumption permits a crisp solution—and besides, it seems warranted in the present context. The particular branching process described here is called the *evolutionary library model*, and it is patterned on the classic paradigm of descent with modification that underlies biological species evolution. The evolutionary library model explains the existence of the current library assemblage as a result of three types of evolutionary-historical events.

1. Each existing library acquires new books at any time by independent sampling, at its own rate, out of an infinitely large pool of different books. The independent acquisition of different new books by each library corresponds to the evolution of genetic traits when species are reproductively isolated, with no gene pool mixing by lateral transfer.

2. New libraries can be created by a speciation event. A new branch library can be founded by adopting a complete copy of the current collection of an existing library, as if all of the existing library's books were cloned or photocopied. Henceforth, however, this new library will become reproductively isolated and acquire its new books independently, as described a moment ago.

3. Libraries can go extinct. When a library is extinguished, its entire collection of books is lost. Thus, libraries that have already gone extinct in the past do not show up in the set of currently existing libraries.

The evolutionary library model naturally generates a corresponding evolutionary tree. When a tree structure is present, it seems to induce a way of visualizing and comprehending intuitively relationships among objects that are quite subtle or complicated to describe without the tree. "Tree thinking" represents a prime example of how one picture may be worth a thousand words.

Now let us return to the question of how much a given species/library contributes to distinctiveness or diversity. It is natural to identify the distinctiveness of a library/species with its distance from its nearest neighbor or closest relative—which here means the number of books independently acquired since being split off from its most recent common-ancestor library. In the tree corresponding to an evolutionary branching model, the distinctiveness of a library is represented geometrically by its branch length off the rest of the evolutionary tree. When a species/library goes extinct, the loss of diversity is the length of its branch, which is being snapped off from the rest of the tree. Although this image obviously does not resolve all questions about how to measure diversity in practice, it does open up a way of considering how to do so.

Noah will thus begin by viewing the overall value of a species/library as a sum of two components: 1) the direct utility of the species/library; and 2) the diversity added by the genes/books of this particular species/library. However, there are yet two more considerations that must enter the picture. Any reasonable benefit calculation must weigh the enhanced survivability of the species from being boarded. This gain will be measured by estimating the difference in probability of survival if taken aboard the Ark minus probability of survival if *not* taken aboard. Noah should then calculate the expected gain of taking the species/library aboard the Ark by multiplying the change in survival probability times the sum of direct utility plus diversity value. Finally, Noah must weigh the expected gains against the costs. For the biblical Ark, costs are measured in units of cubed-cubits. In the world today, the relevant concept is the opportunity cost of the project extending an enhanced measure of protection to a particular species/library. If the expected gains are divided by the costs, then Noah will have expected gains per dollar expended.

Now we have at hand the outline of an answer to the Noah's Ark Problem.[2] Noah should take species/libraries on board the Ark in the order of their gains in utility plus diversity, weighted by the increase in their probability of survival, per dollar of cost.[3] A small amount of notation can help make this point concisely. Let the index i stand for a species/library. Consider the following four concepts:

D_i = *distinctiveness* of i = how unique or different is i

U_i = direct *utility* of i = how much we like or value i *per se*

ΔP_i = by how much can the *survivability* of i actually be improved

C_i = how much does it *cost* to improve the survivability of i by ΔP_i

Then we have the following mathematical result. Provided ΔP_i is "relatively small" (for all i) in the usual sense of the prototypical small project justifying cost-benefit investment methodology locally, then a priority ranking based on the criterion:

$$R_i = [D_i + U_i]\left(\frac{\Delta P_i}{C_i}\right)$$

is justified in the sense of giving an arbitrarily close first-order approximation to an optimal policy.[4]

Of course, it will not be easy in practice to quantify the four variables: utility of a species, distinctiveness of a species from other species, increased probability of survival, and cost of increasing the survivability of the species. Nor will it be easy to combine these variables routinely into a simple ranking formula. The real world is more than a match for any model. Instead, the worth of this kind of result is to suggest a framework and to organize a way of conceptualizing biodiversity preservation—a way which begins with this special, but not unreasonable, case, and leads to intuitively plausible results. Perhaps one could come away with a sense that when mak-

---

[2] For an explicit and rigorous derivation of the main result within the optimization framework presented here, along with a detailed discussion of related issues, see Weitzman (1998).

[3] The argument here does assume that the cost of saving a species is "relatively small," so that many species can be saved. As a result, when one gets down to the choice of the last species to board the Ark, it may be that there isn't enough room (or money left) for the next species in line according to its ranking, and so one has to skip down the line a little to find a species where there is enough room (or money left) to accommodate it. However, if the costs of saving a species are "relatively small," then a priority ranking based on the criterion here will be justified in the sense of giving an arbitrarily close first-order approximation to an optimal policy.

[4] We again refer the reader to Weitzman (1998) for a formal derivation of the result.

ing conservation decisions in the name of preserving diversity, it might seem like a good idea at least to consider these four factors—especially in a policy world so otherwise lacking clear guidelines for endangered species protection.

The Endangered Species Act: What Are We Preserving?

We have argued in the previous section that four factors—*utility* of a species; *distinctiveness* of a species from other species; increase in *survivability* of a species following a conservation plan; *cost* of enhancing survivability— should all play a role in biodiversity preservation. Together, these four factors are used to compute Noah's ranking. But which of the factors actually matter in practice? On what species do we in the United States actually spend our scarce time, energy and money? In this section, we attempt to address such questions by looking at quantifiable actions taken in association with the Endangered Species Act.

Our strategy here will be to look at a number of actual empirical bureaucratic variables that have been gathered and catalogued as a result of the Endangered Species Act and its amendments. These variables can be used as proxies for the four theoretical variables that should be important in the analysis. In the discussion to follow, we explore some of the key places where the process of the Endangered Species Act gives rise to data that can help to answer the questions posed above. With these data in hand, we will then use several proxies for Noah's ranking as the dependent variable regressed on proxy variables for utility of a species, diversity of a species, increased probability of survival, and cost of this increased survival probability as our explanatory variables.[5] This regression framework will allow us to identify what factors really seem to matter for the decisions made about preservation of endangered species.[6]

The journey of a species towards protected status begins when some individual or organization, public or private, suggests formally to the Fish and Wildlife Service, a division of the Department of Interior, that a species should be listed under the Endangered Species Act. To be more specific, several different taxonomic units are eligible for protection under the act, including species, subspecies, and (for vertebrates) "populations." For the sake of simplicity, however, we will typically refer to all of the above as "species," except in the discussion of proxy variables for diversity, when the distinction between species and subspecies will make a conceptual dif-

---

[5]All of the variables used in this paper can be found in the DEMES database, which is described and documented in Cash et al. (1997). Readers desiring further information on the variables used in these analyses should contact the authors to obtain the reference.

[6]Similar empirical studies of the Endangered Species Act can be found in Mann and Plummer (1993), Tear et al. (1993), Metrick and Weitzman (1996) and Cash (1997).

ference. Once a species has been nominated, the Fish and Wildlife Service then calls on scientific sources, both internal and external to the organization, to determine whether the species is a viable candidate for protection. If the scientific data support listing, then the species may be officially proposed to be listed.

After a species is proposed, there is a 60-day period for public comments, during which any interested parties can go on the record with their opinions about the proposed listing. Virtually all species that reach this stage are eventually listed. Listed species enjoy special protections from harm, and must have official recovery plans created by the Fish and Wildlife Service. Listed species are also eligible for public spending on their recovery. In a 1989 amendment to the Endangered Species Act, Congress required the Fish and Wildlife Service to collect annual spending information from all federal and state authorities and to impute such spending as if on a species-by-species basis. Several steps in this process offer the opportunity to obtain quantitative proxies for Noah's ranking.

A first proxy variable for Noah's rankings is the log of the number of favorable public comments made during the proposal stage. These comments are collected by the Fish and Wildlife Service. Afterwards, summary statistics—that is, number favorable, number unfavorable, number neutral, and total number—are published in the Federal Register. The list of taxa that have received the highest number of favorable public comments reads like a *Who's Who* of the political-environmental landscape, with the northern spotted owl handily topping the list. Naturally, such controversial projects achieve a large number of favorable and unfavorable comments, so focusing only on the favorable side may miss part of the story. However, in a spirit of simplicity, we take these favorable comments as a ranking proxy and do not attempt to explain the complex relationship between the different types of comments.

A second proxy variable for Noah's ranking is the listing decision itself. In our regressions, this will be a dummy variable, taking a value of 1 if a species is listed, and 0 otherwise. Although this variable is not a continuous one, in the way we would expect Noah's rankings to be, it does make sense as an on/off variable for whether a species has been boarded onto the Ark. Since the Ark-boarding policy does use a simple cutoff in which species are either on or off the boat according to Noah's ranking, the use of the on/off decision is a natural proxy. (It also fits in well with similar studies looking for latent rankings, like the decision to buy a car or enter the work force.)

Finally, as a third proxy for Noah's ranking, we use the amount of public money spent from 1989 to 1993 on the recovery of the species. The total amount spent each year has been steadily increasing, and the five-year overall total is $914 million. Four species have each had over $50 million spent on them over this period—chinook salmon, red-cockaded woodpecker, northern spotted owl, and bald eagle—and these four together make up about one-third of the total spending. Most species have had at least some funds spent on them; of the 229 vertebrate species listed as of 1989, all but five have at least $100 of reported spending.[7] Only the costs that can be attributed to individual species are included in our totals.

We use these three different proxies for Noah's ranking because, while each seems reasonable, none seems perfect. If forced to choose a single proxy, we believe that spending is the most appropriate measure of the three because it strikes us as the most direct and least noisy measure of preservation attention.

We next try to identify proxies for our four key decision variables. We first look for proxies for the utility term. It is obviously not possible to quantify every way that humans derive utility from other species. In seeking proxy variables for utility, we choose to focus on the elements that are associated with the class of "charismatic megafauna," a term applied to describe large, popular animals. To get at this effect, we include dummy variables for each taxonomic class within the vertebrates: MAMMAL, BIRD, REPTILE, AMPHIBIAN, and FISH. For the "megafauna" portion, we use the log of the length of a representative individual of the species.

Our next right-hand-side variable is diversity. The contribution of a species to diversity can be quantified, as in the tree diagram of the evolutionary library model, by its genetic distance from other species. This measure can be roughly approximated by its taxonomic uniqueness. We use two dummy variables to capture this idea of distinctiveness. One variable, labeled UNIQUE, takes on a value of 1 if the species is the sole representative of its genus, where a genus is the taxonomic unit immediately above species, and 0 otherwise. A second dummy variable, labeled SUBSPECIES, takes on a value of 1 if a "species" is in fact from the lower taxonomic classification of subspecies or population, and 0 otherwise.

Next, as a proxy measure of a species' survivability or marginal recoverability, we use absolute endangerment. The variable we use comes from the Nature Conservancy, which ranks a comprehensive list of all U.S. vertebrate species (but not subspecies or populations) into a scale from 1 to 5, with 1 being the most endangered and 5 being the least endangered.[8] As long as the most endangered species are also those that would benefit most from small recovery projects—which is all that marginal endangerment means—then this will be a reasonable proxy. One could argue that early intervention is more cost effective, but that is not really the issue here. It is certainly true that there are several examples of species near extinction being saved. These are the cases where, by definition, the gain in survivability has been the highest. These may have been costly projects, but cost is a separate element of the decision.

---

[7]We add $100 to each species reported spending so that we can take the log of the total; this $100 can be thought of as each species' share of a small portion of the program's overhead.

[8]We again refer the reader to Cash et al. (1997) for a complete description of these variables and their sources. The ENDANGERMENT variable used in this paper is of a 1993 vintage, which is slightly different than the most recent measures. We use the 1993 variable because we want to come as close as possible to capturing the endangerment level at the time that the relevant cost decisions were made.

The Fish and Wildlife Service has itself recognized the importance of several of these factors, and they have established a formal priority system to rank species for recovery projects. Their priority system takes into account four factors; in decreasing order of importance they are: "degree of threat," "recovery potential," "taxonomy," and "conflict with development." The first three factors are combined by the Fish and Wildlife Service to form a ranking from 1 to 18 (lower numbers imply higher priority). The fourth factor, which indicates whether or not the recovery of a species conflicts with other public or private development plans, is meant to serve as a tiebreaker among species having the same priority ranking—with those species in conflict with development receiving the advantage. This "conflict" variable can be thought of as a proxy for cost—in this case, an opportunity cost. This proxy gives us at least one representative for each of the four variables in the conceptual solution to the Noah's Ark Problem. In our final test, we include both the priority ranking and the conflict tiebreaker as additional explanatory variables. The formal Fish and Wildlife Service priority system implies that conflict should have a positive effect on spending—a cost-benefit calculation would suggest otherwise.

The results of several regressions using these variables are summarized in Table 1. In all cases, comprehensive data collection is made possible only by restricting the sample to vertebrates; plants and non-vertebrate animals are excluded because of data limitations. We acknowledge that there are many econometric difficulties here: variables are measured at different times, many important considerations are omitted due to data constraints, our proxies are imperfect. For these reasons, we adopt a reduced-form approach and do not claim any structural interpretations. Rather, we hope that readers agree with us that the patterns of behavior are striking enough to yield insights despite the obvious difficulties.

In the regression in the first column, the dependent variable LNCOMMENTS is the log of the number of positive comments received after the species has been proposed. The sample includes all 142 vertebrate full species, subspecies, and populations that have been listed since 1975, when the data first become available. Using the taxonomic class dummies (MAMMAL, BIRD, REPTILE, and AMPHIBIAN—all interpreted relative to FISH, the left-out variable), along with SIZE, ENDANGERMENT, and UNIQUE as explanatory variables, we find only ENDANGERMENT to be significant at the 5 percent level. Note, however, that the coefficient on ENDANGERMENT would appear to be of the wrong sign; the more highly endangered a species is, the fewer favorable comments that it receives. (Recall that the most endangered species receive ENDANGERMENT ratings of 1, and the least endangered species receive ratings of 5.) One interpretation of this coefficient is that species which are not truly endangered must be very "charismatic" to have survived so far in the process, and this same charisma is driving the number of favorable comments. This explanation—that certain key variables proxying for charisma are likely to have been omitted—is a common theme in interpreting the results of these regressions.

Table 1 Regression Results

Regression #	1	2	3	4
Dependent Variable	LNCOMMENTS	LISTED	LNSPEND	LNSPEND
MAMMAL	−0.11	0.87*	0.73	0.42
BIRD	0.63	1.21**	0.39	0.59
REPTILE	−0.55	0.82	−1.79**	−1.71**
AMPHIBIAN	0.48	−1.51**	−0.71	−0.78
ENDANGERMENT	0.31*	−1.43**	0.62**	0.85**
SIZE	0.03	0.29*	0.86**	0.66**
UNIQUE	0.33	0.85**	0.06	—
SUBSPECIES	—	—	−0.52	—
PRIORITY	—	—	—	−0.10*
CONFLICT	—	—	—	1.19**
CONSTANT	1.24**	0.97*	9.17**	9.39**
Method of Estimation	OLS	Logit	OLS	OLS
Number of Obs.	142	509	229	229
R^2	.07	.25	.31	.41

Notes: Dependent variables and samples for each regression are (1) LNCOMMENTS: the log of total favorable comments received during the public comments period, as published in the Federal Register, the sample includes the 142 vertebrate species listed after 1975; (2) LISTED: 1 if a species is listed (as of 1997) under the ESA and 0 otherwise; the sample includes all vertebrate full species that were ranked G1, G2 or G3 by the Nature Conservancy as of 1993. (3) and (4) LNSPEND: the log of total government spending from 1989 to 1993. The sample includes all taxonomic units (species, subspecies, and populations) that were listed as of 1989. Independent variables: MAMMAL, BIRD, REPTILE, and AMPHIBIAN are dummy variables which equal 1 when the species is a member of that taxonomic class and 0 otherwise. (Coefficients can be interpreted relative to FISH, the excluded dummy variable.) ENDANGERMENT is the Nature Conservancy's Global Endangerment Rank as of 1993. SIZE is the log of the physical length for a typical individual of the species. UNIQUE is a dummy variable equal to 1 if the species is the only species in its genus. SUBSPECIES is a dummy variable equal to 1 if the taxonomic unit is below the level of full species. PRIORITY is the FWS 1–18 priority ranking for the species. CONFLICT is the FWS priority tiebreaker indicating whether or not a species is in conflict with development. (*) and (**) indicate that the relevant coefficient is significant at the five percent and one percent levels, respectively. Please see Cash et al. (1997) for a detailed description of the variables used in these estimations.

In the regression of the second column, the dependent variable is LISTED: a dummy equal to 1 if a species has been listed, and 0 otherwise. The sample includes all vertebrate full species with ENDANGERMENT rankings of 1, 2 or 3. We restrict the sample in this way so that it includes virtually all species that may reasonably be considered candidates for listing; rankings of 4 or 5 are essentially never considered in the first place. Subspecies or populations are not included in the sample because there is no comprehensive database of unlisted units below the level of full species. Several of the factors discussed above appear to play some role in the listing decision. Some dummies for taxonomic class are significant (relative to the excluded dummy for FISH): positive for MAMMAL and BIRD, and negative for AMPHIBIAN. Taxonomic uniqueness appears to play a positive role in the likelihood of listing, as does SIZE and ENDANGERMENT. All in all, the decision of what to place on the official endangerment list seems consistent with our conceptual framework.

The regression in the third column uses the log of the sum of public spending from 1989 to 1993, LNSPEND, as the dependent variable. Here, we use the same regressors as before, with the addition of SUBSPECIES, the dummy variable indicating that the taxnomic unit is below the level of a full species. The sample includes all protected taxonomic units (species, subspecies, and populations) that were listed as of the end of 1989, when the spending data was first collected. There are two important results from this regression. First, the coefficient on SIZE is large and significant. Since the SIZE variable is the log of physical length, its coefficient may be interpreted as an elasticity; it implies an 8.6 percent increase in spending for a 10 percent increase in length. Even more striking, however, is the positive and significant coefficient on ENDANGERMENT. As with the counterintuitive results for the regression in the first column, this sign implies that the more highly endangered a species is, the *less* attention it receives. (Again recall that the most endangered species receive ENDANGERMENT ratings of 1, and the least endangered species receive ratings of 5.) We have argued elsewhere that this result suggests either terribly perverse priority setting, or, more likely, an overpowering role for omitted unobservable charisma-like factors negatively correlated with ENDANGERMENT (Metrick and Weitzman, 1996). In either case, it is difficult to reconcile the sign of the ENDANGERMENT coefficient with the belief that more spending should go to the more highly endangered species, other things being equal. Owing to our belief that spending is the best proxy we have for Noah's ranking, we believe that this regression provides the most striking empirical results in the paper.

The regression in the fourth column is similar to the one in the third column, but adds the regressors PRIORITY (the Fish and Wildlife Service priority ranking from 1 to 18) and CONFLICT (a dummy equal to 1 if the species is in conflict with development according to the Fish and Wildlife Service), while dropping UNIQUE and SUBSPECIES since they are part of the PRIORITY calculation. The results show that while the Fish and Wildlife Service is following their system to some degree, the role played by CONFLICT is far larger than might be anticipated. In fact, this ostensibly least important criterion in the system, supposedly just a tiebreaker, dominates the other three. Although the sign of the CONFLICT coefficient is consistent with the intention of the Fish and Wildlife priority system, its magnitude is out of proportion. Furthermore, the sign on this coefficient is not consistent with the cost-benefit formula laid out earlier; apparently, the Fish and Wildlife Service gives priority to species with high opportunity costs. We believe that the setting of CONFLICT may be endogenous, and that the results of this regression suggest a commingling of supposed objective evaluation of endangerment levels with the preference-based spending decision. In turn, this suggests that the country might better be served by separating the intelligence-gathering and policy-making arms of the Fish and Wildlife Service.

What have we learned from these empirical exercises? First, charismatic megafauna effects do seem to matter a lot; in fact, there is strong evidence that people weigh utility the heaviest of the four criteria. Second, survivability, diversity, and costs do not seem to play their "expected" role in spending decisions. Third, the (ostensibly) scientific part of the priority system seems to be influenced by the same subjective factors that influence spending.

Conclusion

The core of the problem of biodiversity preservation today lies in specifying the objective that we are trying to preserve. We cannot evaluate the overall performance of conservation agencies, like the U.S. Fish and Wildlife Service, without specifying much more clearly what is the "output" on which they are to be graded.

At the end of the day, we must make up our minds about what is the objective function before we can properly use scientific information or formulate rational policies for good stewardship. This means confronting honestly the core problem of economic tradeoffs—because good stewardship of natural habitats, like almost everything else we want in this world, is subject to budget constraints. The evidence suggests that our actual behavior may not reflect a reasoned cost-benefit calculation. If this is true, then we should fix it. If it is not, then we should be honest about our desire to have "charismatic megafauna" effects dominate our decisions.

References

Cash, David, "Science, Politics, and Environmental Risk: Regulatory Decisionmaking in the U.S. Endangered Species Act," Manuscript, J.F.K. School of Government, Harvard University, 1997.

Cash, David, J.R. DeShazo, Andrew Metrick, Todd Schatzki, Stuart Shapiro, and Martin Weitzman, "Database on the Economics and Management of Endangered Species (DEMES)," Manuscript, Department of Economics, Harvard University, 1997.

Crozier, Ross H., "Genetic Diversity and the Agony of Choice," *Biological Conservation*, 1992, *61*, 11–15.

Mann, Charles J., and Mark L. Plummer, "Federal Expenditures on Endangered Species Recovery," Unpublished Manuscript, 1993.

Metrick, Andrew, and Martin L. Weitzman, "Patterns of Behavior in Endangered Species Preservation," *Land Economics*, 1996, *72*:1, 1–16.

Polasky, Stephan, and Andrew Solow, "On the Value of a Collection of Species," *Journal of Environmental Economics and Management*, 1995, *29*, 298–303.

Schatzki, Todd, and Stuart Shapiro, "Ruled or Ruling? Agency Discretion in the Endangered Species Act," Manuscript, J.F.K. School of Government, Harvard University, 1997.

Simpson, R. David, Roger Sedjo, and J. Reid, "Valuing Biodiversity for Use in Pharmaceutical Research," *Journal of Political Economy*, 1996, *104*:1, 163–85.

Solow, Andrew, Stephan Polasky, and James Broadus, "Searching for Uncertain Benefits and the Conservation of Biological Diversity," *Environmental and Resource Economics*, April 1993, 3:2, 171–81.

Tear, Timothy H., J. Michael Scott, Patricia H. Hayward, and Brad Griffith, "Status and Prospects for Success of the Endangered Species Act: A Look at Recovery Plans," *Science*, 1993, 976–77.

Weitzman, Martin L., "On Diversity," *Quarterly Journal of Economics*, May 1992, *107*:2, 363–405.

Weitzman, Martin L., "What to Preserve? An Application of Diversity Theory to Crane Conservation," *Quarterly Journal of Economics*, February 1993, *108*:1, 157–83.

Weitzman, Martin L., "The Noah's Ark Problem," forthcoming in *Econometrica*, 1998.

IX

Economics and Environmental Policy Making

29 The Choice of Regulatory Instruments in Environmental Policy*

Nathaniel O. Keohane

Richard L. Revesz

Robert N. Stavins

Nathaniel O. Keohane is an Assistant Professor of Economics at the Yale School of Management; Richard L. Revesz is Dean and Lawrence King Professor of Law, New York University School of Law; Robert N. Stavins is Albert Pratt Professor of Business and Government at John F. Kennedy School of Government, Harvard University, and University Fellow, Resources for the Future.

I. Introduction

The design of environmental policy requires answers to two central questions: (1) what is the desired level of environmental protection?; and (2) what policy instruments should be used to achieve this level of protection? With respect to the second question, thirty years of positive political reality in the United States has diverged strikingly from the recommendations of normative economic theory. The purpose of this Article is to explain why.

Four gaps between normative theory and positive reality merit particular attention. First, so-called "command-and-control" instruments (such as design standards requiring a particular technology's usage, or performance standards prescribing the maximum amount of pollution that a source can emit)[1] are used to a significantly greater degree than "market-based" or "economic-incentive" instruments (principally pollution taxes or

"The Choice of Regulatory Instruments in Environmental Policy," by Nathaniel O. Keohane, Richard L. Revesz, and Robert N. Stevens from *Harvard Environmental Law Review*, 22:313–367 (1998).

*Helpful comments on a previous version of the Article were provided by: David Charny, Cary Coglianese, John Ferejohn, Don Fullerton, Robert Hahn, James Hamilton, Robert Keohane, David King, Lewis Kornhauser, Robert Lowry, Roger Noll, Kenneth Shepsle, and Richard Stewart. Financial support was provided by the Dean's Research Fund, John F. Kennedy School of Government, and the Filomen D'Agostino and Max E. Greenberg Research Fund at the New York University School of Law. The authors alone are responsible for any errors.

[1]Performance standards could specify an absolute quantity of permissible emissions (that is, a given quantity of emissions per unit of time), but more typically these standards establish allowable emissions in proportional terms (that is, quantity of emissions per unit of product output or per unit of a particular input). This Article uses the term "standard" to refer somewhat generically to command-and-control approaches. Except where stated otherwise, the Article refers to proportional performance standards.

charges[2] and systems of tradeable permits[3]), despite economists' consistent endorsement of the latter.

At least in theory, market-based instruments minimize the aggregate cost of achieving a given level of environmental protection,[4] and provide dynamic incentives for the adoption and diffusion of cheaper and better control technologies.[5] Despite these advantages, market-based instruments have been used far less frequently than command-and-control standards.[6] For example, the cores of the Clean Air Act ("CAA")[7] and Clean Water Act ("CWA")[8] consist of federally prescribed emission and effluent standards, set by reference to the levels that can be achieved through the use of the "best available technology."[9]

Second, when command-and-control standards have been used, the required level of pollution abatement has generally been far more stringent for new pollution sources than for existing ones, possibly worsening pollution by encouraging firms to keep older, dirtier plants in operation.[10]

---

[2]The development of the notion of a corrective tax on pollution is generally credited to Pigou. See generally Arthur Cecil Pigou, *The Economics of Welfare* (1920).

[3]John Dales initially proposed a system of tradeable permits to control pollution. See generally John H. Dales, *Pollution, Property, & Prices* (1968). David Montgomery then formalized this system. See generally W. David Montgomery, "Markets in Licenses and Efficient Pollution Control Programs," 5 *J. Econ. Theory* 395 (1972). However, much of the literature can be traced back to Ronald Coase. See Ronald H. Coase, "The Problem of Social Cost," 3 *J.L. & Econ.* 1, 39–44 (1960).

[4]As is well known, a necessary condition for the achievement of such cost-minimization is that the marginal costs of abatement be equal for all sources. See William J. Baumol & Wallace E. Oates, *The Theory of Environmental Policy* 177 (1988). In theory, pollution taxes and systems of marketable permits induce this effect, at least under specified conditions.

[5]Market-based systems can provide continuous dynamic incentives for adoption of superior technologies, since under such systems it is always in the interest of firms to clean up more if sufficiently inexpensive cleanup technologies can be identified. See Scott R. Milliman & Raymond Prince, "Firm Incentives to Promote Technological Change in Pollution Control," 17 *J. Envtl. Econ. & Mgmt.* 247, 257–61 (1989); Adam B. Jaffe & Robert N. Stavins, "Dynamic Incentives of Environmental Regulation: The Effects of Alternative Policy Instruments and Technology Diffusion," 29 *J. Envtl. Econ. & Mgmt.* S43, S43–S46 (1995).

[6]Office of Tech. Assessment, Tech. Assessment Board of the 103d Congress, *Environmental Policy Tools: A User's Guide* 27–28 (1995).

[7]See 42 U.S.C. § 7411(a),(b) (1994).

[8]See 33 U.S.C. §§ 1311(b), 1316 (1994).

[9]We use this label as a generic one. The various statutory schemes employ somewhat different formulations. See, e.g., 33 U.S.C. § 1311(b)(1)(A) (1994) ("best practicable control technology"); id. § 1311(b)(2)(A) ("best available technology"); id. § 1316(a)(1) ("best available demonstrated control technology"); 42 U.S.C. § 7411(a)(1) (1994) ("best system of emission reduction"); id. § 7479(3) ("best available control technology").

[10]New plants ought to have somewhat more stringent standards because their abatement costs are lower, although such standards should be linked with actual abatement costs, not with the proxy of plant vintage. When new source standards are sufficiently more stringent, however, they can give rise to an "old-plant" effect, precluding plant replacements that would otherwise take place. See Matthew D. McCubbins et al., "Structure and Process, Politics, and Policy: Administrative Arrangements and the Political Control of Agencies," 75 *Va. L. Rev.* 431, 467 (1989); Richard B. Stewart, "Regulation, Innovation, and Administrative Law: A Conceptual Framework," 69 *Cal. L. Rev.* 1259, 1270–71 (1981). Empirical evidence shows that differential environmental regulations lengthen the time before plants are retired. See Michael T. Maloney & Gordon L. Brady, "Capital Turnover and Marketable Pollution Rights," 31 *J.L. & Econ.* 203, 206 (1988); Randy Nelson et al., "Differential Environmental Regulation: Effects on Electric Utility Capital Turnover and Emissions," 75 *Rev. Econ. & Stat.* 368, 373 (1993).

The federal environmental statutes further these disparities by bifurcating the regulatory requirements that apply to new and existing sources. For example, under the Clean Air Act, emission standards for new sources are set federally, whereas the corresponding standards for existing sources are set by the states.[11] Similarly, the CAA's Prevention of Significant Deterioration ("PSD") program,[12] which applies to areas with air that is cleaner than the National Ambient Air Quality Standards ("NAAQS),[13] imposes additional emission standards only on new sources.[14] The Clean Water Act sets effluent limitations for both new and existing sources, but these limitations are governed by different statutory provisions.[15]

Third, in the relatively rare instances in which they have been adopted, market-based instruments have nearly always taken the form of tradeable permits rather than emission taxes,[16] although economic theory suggests that the optimal choice between tradeable permits and emission taxes is dependent upon case-specific factors.[17] Moreover, the initial allocation of such permits has been through "grandfathering," or free initial distribution based on existing levels of pollution,[18] rather than through auctions, de-

---

[11]Compare 42 U.S.C. § 7411(a), (b) (1994) (defining federal standards for new sources) with id. § 7410(a) (requiring state plans for existing sources).

[12]See 42 U.S.C. §§ 7470–7479 (1994).

[13]See id. § 7471.

[14]See id. § 7475(a).

[15]Compare 33 U.S.C. § 1316 (1994) (prescribing standards for new sources) with id. § 1311(b) (setting standards for existing sources).

[16]Taxes (so-called unit charges) have been used in some communities for municipal solid waste collection. See Office of Tech. Assessment, supra note 6, at 119–21. Gasoline taxes serve primarily as revenue-raising instruments, rather than environmental (Pigouvian) taxes per se. Interestingly, the European experience is the reverse: environmental taxes are far more prevalent than tradeable permits, although the taxes employed have typically been too low to induce much pollution abatement. See Richard B. Stewart, "Economic Incentives for Environmental Protection: Opportunities and Obstacles" 42 (1996) (unpublished manuscript, on file with New York University). A more comprehensive positive analysis of instrument choice than we provide here would seek to explain this difference between the European and U.S. experiences.

[17]With perfect information, tradeable permits sold at auction have the same effect as a tax. Under conditions of uncertainty, the relative efficiency of tradeable permits and fixed tax rates depends upon the relative slopes of the relevant marginal benefit and marginal cost functions. See Martin L. Weitzman, "Prices v. Quantities," 41 *Rev. Econ. Stud.* 477, 485–90 (1974); Gary W. Yohe, "Towards a General Comparison of Price Controls and Quantity Controls Under Uncertainty," 45 *Rev. Econ. Stud.* 229, 238 (1978); Robert N. Stavins, "Correlated Uncertainty and Policy Instrument Choice," 30 *J. Envtl. Econ. & Mgmt.* 218, 219–25 (1996).

In theory, a hybrid system that incorporates aspects and attributes of both a simple linear tax or a simple tradeable permit system will be preferable, under conditions of uncertainty, to either alone. See Marc J. Roberts & Michael Spence, "Effluent Charges and Licenses Under Uncertain," 5 *J. Pub. Econ.* 193, 196–97 (1976); Louis Kaplow & Steven Shavell, "On the Superiority of Corrective Taxes to Quantity Regulation" 12–14 (National Bureau of Econ. Research Working Paper No. 6251, 1997).

[18]Mandated by the Clean Air Act amendments of 1990, the sulfur dioxide ("SO_2") allowance program (a tradeable permit program to reduce acid rain) provides for annual auctions in addition to grandfathering. However, such auctions involve less than three percent of the total allocation. See Elizabeth M. Bailey, "Allowance Trading Activity and State Regulatory Rulings: Evidence from the U.S. Acid Rain Program" 4 (Mass. Inst. of Tech. Working Paper No. MIT-CEEPR 96-002, 1996). These auctions have proven to be a trivial part of the overall program. See Paul L. Joskow et al., "Auction Design and the Market for Sulfur Dioxide Emissions" 27–28 (National Bureau of Econ. Research Working Paper No. 5745, 1996).

spite the apparently superior mechanism of auctions.[19] Despite diversity of available market-based instruments (taxes, revenue-neutral taxes, auctioned permits, and grandfathered permits)[20] and the numerous tradeoffs that exist in normative economic terms, the U.S. experience has been dominated by one choice: grandfathered permits.

Notably, the acid rain provision of the Clean Air Act allocates, without charge, marketable permits for sulfur dioxide emissions to current emitters.[21] Similarly, grandfathered marketable permits are created by the offset mechanism of the nonattainment provision of the CAA.[22] This mechanism permits existing sources to reduce their emissions and sell the resulting reduction to new sources attempting to locate in the area.[23]

---

[19]With perfect information and no transactions costs, trading will result in the economically efficient outcome independently of the initial distribution of permits. See W. David Montgomery, "Markets in Licenses and Efficient Pollution Control Programs" 5 *J. Econ. Theory* 395, 409 (1972); Coase, supra note 3, at 15; Robert W. Hahn & Roger G. Noll, "Designing a Market for Tradeable Emission Permits." in *Reform of Environmental Regulation* 120–21 (Wesley Magat ed., 1982). Under more realistic scenarios, however, there are compelling arguments for the superiority of auctioned permits. First, auctions are more cost-effective in the presence of certain kinds of transactions costs. See Robert N. Stavins, "Transaction Costs and Tradeable Permits," 29 *J. Envtl. Econ. & Mgmt.* 133, 146 (1995). Second, the revenue raised by an auction mechanism can be used to finance a reduction in some distortionary tax. See Lawrence H. Goulder et al., "Revenue-Raising vs. Other Approaches to Environmental Protection: The Critical Significance of Pre-Existing Tax Distortions" 1 (National Bureau of Econ. Research Working Paper No. 5641, 1996). Instruments that restrict pollution production (such as tradeable permits) can create entry barriers that raise product prices, reduce the real wage, and exacerbate preexisting labor supply distortions. However, this effect can be offset if the government auctions the permits, retains the scarcity rents, and recycles the revenue by reducing distortionary labor taxes. See Don Fullerton & Gilbert Metcalf, "Environmental Regulation in a Second-Best World" 6, 25 (1996) (unpublished manuscript, on file with authors). Third, auctions provide greater incentives for firms to develop substitutes for regulated products, by requiring firms to pay for permits rather than giving them rents. See Robert W. Hahn & Albert M. McGartland, "The Political Economy of Instrument Choice: An Examination of the U.S. Role in Implementing the Montreal Protocol, " 83 *Nw. U. L. Rev.* 592, 604 (1989). Fourth, the revenue raised by auctions may provide administrative agencies with an incentive to monitor compliance. See Bruce A. Ackerman & Richard B. Stewart, "Reforming Environmental Law," 37 *Stan. L. Rev.* 1333, 1344–46 (1985). Fifth, grandfathering, if accepted as general practice, could lead unregulated firms to increase their emissions in order to maximize the pollution rights that they obtain if there is a transition to a market-based system. See Donald N. Dewees, "Instrument Choice in Environmental Policy," 21 *Econ. Inquiry* 53, 62–63 (1983).

[20]In a straightforward scheme of effluent taxes, a constant tax is levied on each unit of pollution. In a revenue-neutral framework, the tax revenues are then rebated to the payors, by some method other than the amount of their pollution. In marketable permit schemes, the initial allocation can be performed through an auction, or through grandfathering. In a deterministic setting and abstracting from a set of other issues, a revenue-neutral emission tax can be designed which is equivalent to a grandfathered tradeable permit system. Likewise, under such conditions, a simple emission tax will be roughly equivalent to an auctioned permit system.

[21]See 42 U.S.C. § 7651(b) (1994). The amount of the allocation is capped in Phase I, which is currently in effect, at 2.5 pounds of sulfur dioxide per million BTUs of fuel input consumed. In Phase II, which goes into effect in the year 2000, the cap will be 1.2 pounds of sulfur dioxide per million BTUs of fuel input consumed. See Paul L. Joskow & Richard Schmalensee, "The Political Economy of Market-based Environmental Policy: The 1990 U.S. Acid Rain Program," 41 *J.L. & Econ.* (forthcoming April 1998) (manuscript at 94–95, on file with authors).

[22]See 42 U.S.C. § 7503(a)(1)(A) (1994).

[23]See id. at § 7503(c)(1).

Fourth and finally, there has been a conceptual gap between prior and current political practice. In recent years, the political process has been more receptive to market-based instruments,[24] even though they continue to be a small part of the overall portfolio of existing environmental laws and regulations. After being largely ignored for so long, why have incentive-based instruments begun to gain acceptance in recent years?

Commentators have advanced various explanations for the existence of these four gaps between normative theory and positive reality. While some explanations emerge from formal theories, others take the form of informal hypotheses, purporting to explain certain aspects of environmental policy, but not as a part of a formal theory of political behavior. This Article reviews, evaluates, and extends these explanations. Moreover, this Article places these disparate explanations within the framework of an equilibrium model of instrument choice in environmental policy, based upon the metaphor of a political market.

Informed by intellectual traditions within economics, political science, and law, this framework organizes and synthesizes existing theories and empirical evidence about observed departures of normative prescription from political reality. The scope of the Article, however, is limited in a number of respects. The emphasis is on the control of pollution rather than the management of natural resources. The Article treats Congress, rather than administrative agencies, as the locus of instrument choice decisions; it views legislators (rather than regulators) as the "suppliers" of regulation.[25] Moreover, the Article focuses exclusively on the choice among the policy instruments used to achieve a given level of environmental protection, ranging from tradeable permits to taxes to standards. It does not explore the related issues of how the level of protection is chosen or enforced. Nor does it address why Congress chooses to delegate authority to administrative agencies in the first place.[26] Finally, the Article's outlook is positive, not normative: it seeks to understand why the current set of tools exists, rather than which tools are desirable.

---

[24]Beginning in the 1970s, the U.S. Environmental Protection Agency ("EPA") allowed states to implement trading schemes, as alternatives to command-and-control regulation, in their State Implementation Plans under the Clean Air Act. See Robert W. Hahn, "Economic Prescriptions for Environmental Problems: How the Patient Followed the Doctor's Orders," *J. Econ. Persp.*, Spring 1989, at 95, 101. More significantly, tradeable permit systems were used in the 1980s to accomplish the phasedown of lead in gasoline. See Suzi Kerr & David Maré, "Efficient Regulation Through Tradeable Permit Markets: The United States Lead Phasedown" 3–6 (U. Md. C. Park Working Paper No. 96-06, 1997). Moreover, such systems facilitated the phasedown of ozone-depleting chlorofluorocarbons ("CFCs") and are projected to cut nationwide SO_2 emissions by 50% by the year 2005, see Office of Air Radiation, U.S. Environmental Protection Agency, *1995 Compliance Results: Acid Rain Program* 10–11 (1996), as well as achieving ambient ozone reductions in the northeast and implementing stricter local air pollution controls in the Los Angeles metropolitan region.

[25]We do not intend, however, to deny the importance of executive branch departments and administrative agencies, such as the EPA. For example, the intra-firm emission trading programs of the 1970s were largely the direct creation of EPA.

[26]See generally Morris P. Fiorina, "Legislative Choice of Regulatory Forms: Legal Process or Administrative Process?," 39 *Pub. Choice* 33 (1982).

Part II of the Article reviews the relevant intellectual traditions in economics, political science, and law. Part III presents the key features of our equilibrium framework. Part IV considers the demand for environmental policy instruments, while Part V examines the supply side. Finally, Part VI presents some conclusions.

II. Intellectual Traditions

Positive theories of policy instrument choice find their roots in the broader study of government regulation, a vast literature which has been reviewed elsewhere.[27] For the purposes of this Article, the literature can be divided into three approaches for explaining government regulation: demand-driven explanations, supply-driven explanations, and explanations incorporating the interaction between demand and supply.

A. Demand-Side Analyses

Explanations that focus heavily on the demand for regulation are grounded largely in economics. Not surprisingly, economists have generally concentrated on the demand for economic (rather than social) regulation, devoting most attention to the interests of affected firms. The "economic theory of regulation," initiated by George Stigler[28] and developed further by Richard Posner,[29] Sam Peltzman,[30] and Gary Becker,[31] suggests that much regulation is not imposed on firms but rather demanded by them, as a means of harnessing the coercive power of the state to restrict entry, support prices, or provide direct cash subsidies.[32] A related strand of literature has likewise emphasized rent-seeking behavior.[33]

---

[27]See generally Thomas Romer & Howard Rosenthal, "Modern Political Economy and the Study of Regulation," in *Public Regulation: New Perspectives on Institutions and Policies* 73 (Elizabeth E. Bailey ed., 1987).

[28]See generally George J. Stigler, "The Theory of Economic Regulation," 2 *Bell J. Econ.* 3 (1971).

[29]See generally Richard A. Posner, "Theories of Economic Regulation," 5 *Bell J. Econ.* 335 (1974).

[30]See generally Sam Peltzman, "Toward a More General Theory of Regulation," 19 *J.L. & Econ.* 211 (1976).

[31]See generally Gary S. Becker, "A Theory of Competition Among Pressure Groups for Political Influence," 98 *Q.J. Econ.* 371 (1983).

[32]Stigler's influential paper has been characterized as breaking with a previously dominant view (among economists) that regulation is initiated to correct market imperfections. See Stigler, supra note 28, at 3; see also Posner, supra note 29, at 343. It is worth nothing that as far back as E.E. Schattschneider, political scientists recognized the importance of economic interests among groups pressuring Congress. See E.E. Schattschneider, *Politics, Pressures, and the Tariff* 4 (1935). The "capture theory of regulation" in political science was already well developed by the time of Stigler's work. Stigler's main contribution was less his recognition that economic interests will seek favorable regulation than his introduction of that insight into the economics literature and his application of economic models of behavior (i.e., treating political parties as resource maximizers) to explain policy formulation.

[33]See generally James M. Buchanan & Gordon Tullock, *The Calculus of Consent* (1962); Gordon Tullock, "The Welfare Cost of Tariffs, Monopolies, and Theft," 5 *W. Econ. J.* 224 (1967).

In a number of these economic analyses, the supply side (i.e., the political process itself) is virtually ignored.[34] One paper typifying this demand-driven approach has examined private industry's preferences for regulation and has simply assumed that those policy preferences will prevail.[35] Similarly, another model of the resource allocation decisions of competing interest groups has assumed that the policy outcome depends solely on the relative pressures exerted by interest groups.[36]

Even when they model political processes, economic explanations of regulation have often remained driven by the demand of firms. In Stigler's analysis[37] and Peltzman's elaboration,[38] the state enacts the program of the industry (or, more generally, of the interest group) offering the most resources to the governing party; in other words, regulation goes to the "highest bidder."[39] Thus, private industry will tend to be regulated where and when the benefits to firms from government regulation are highly concentrated, but the costs are widely dispersed.[40] The "government" simply acts to maximize an exogenous "political support function" and thus caters to the more powerful group. Following a conceptually similar tack, another model pictures a single policymaker's decision as responding to a weighted sum of industry interests and environmental interests.[41]

Political actors are included in these analyses, but they are treated as economic agents reacting somewhat mechanically to the resources or the demands of interest groups. In many cases, as in the Stigler-Peltzman model, they have no interest other than collecting political contributions. Moreover, government is treated as a monolith, controlled by a single political party, with regulatory agencies and legislatures combined into a single unit. These accounts leave no room for constituency pressures, variation among legislators, slack between legislative direction and the actions of administrative agencies, or other supply-side phenomena.

---

[34]See generally Jean-Jacque Laffont & Jean Tirole, *A Theory of Incentives in Procurement and Regulation* (1993); Romer & Rosenthal, supra note 27.

[35]See James M. Buchanan & Gordon Tullock, "Polluters' Profits and Political Response: Direct Controls Versus Taxes," 65 *Am. Econ. Rev.* 139, 142 (1975).

[36]See Becker, supra note 31, at 392.

[37]See Stigler, supra note 28, at 12.

[38]See Peltzman, supra note 30, at 214.

[39]The Stigler-Peltzman model is essentially a policy auction. See Stigler, supra note 28, at 12–13; Peltzman, supra note 30, at 212.

[40]Peanut regulation provides an excellent example of the effect of concentrated benefits and diffuse costs. Quotas, import restrictions, and price supports combined in 1982–1987 to transfer an average of $255 million a year from consumers to producers, with a deadweight loss of $34 million. The annual cost to each consumer was only $1.23; each peanut farmer, on the other hand, gained $11,100. Peanut farmers clearly had an incentive to preserve the program, while any individual consumer had little to gain from dismantling it. See W. Kip Viscusi et al., *Economics of Regulation and Antitrust* 331 (1995).

[41]See generally Robert W. Hahn, "The Political Economy of Environmental Regulation: Towards a Unifying Framework," 65 *Pub. Choice* 21 (1990).

B. Supply-Side Analyses

By contrast, political scientists and economists studying the supply side of regulation (and of legislation more generally) have focused on the voting behavior of legislators and the institutional structure of the legislature. The approach typically used by political scientists to explain voting behavior is based upon interview and survey data. On the basis of these sources, Congressmen are seen to be most influenced by colleagues and constituents in deciding how to vote.[42] An alternative approach analyzes roll-call data to estimate the relative importance of ideology, constituent interests, and interest groups in legislative voting.[43] One study found that legislators base their votes not only on the economic interests of their constituents (as the economic theory of regulation assumes), but also on their ideologies.[44] Some scholars, notably Michael Munger and his colleagues, have sought to explain voting behavior by explicitly linking it to campaign contributions.[45] However, just as the Stigler-Peltzman model incorporates politicians but remains fundamentally demand-driven, their approach acknowledges the role of interest groups but is driven by supply-side factors. Some mention is made of the costs to legislators of supplying legislation to interest groups, but the models focus on estimating a "supply price" determined solely by the characteristics of legislators.[46]

A second line of inquiry on the supply side has investigated the role of institutional structure in the legislature. The policy outcome in Congress depends not only on the voting preferences of individual legislators, but also on features such as decision rules, the order of voting, and especially the powers of committees (and their chairmen) to control the agenda of the legislature.[47] Further, expectations of subsequent problems of oversee-

---

[42]See John W. Kingdon, *Congressmen's Voting Decisions* 17 (1989).

[43]See generally Joseph P. Kalt & Mark A. Zupan, "Capture and Ideology in the Economic Theory of Politics," 74 *Am. Econ. Rev.* 279 (1984); James B. Kau & Paul H. Rubin, "Self-Interest, Ideology, and Logrolling in Congressional Voting," 22 *J.L. & Econ.* 365 (1979); Sam Peltzman, "Constituent Interest and Congressional Voting," 27 *J.L. & Econ.* 181 (1984).

[44]See Kalt & Zupan, supra note 43, at 298. Their econometric analysis has been criticized by John Jackson and John Kingdon. See John E. Jackson & John W. Kingdon, "Ideology, Interest Group Scores, and Legislative Votes," 36 *Am. J. Pol. Sci.* 805, 806 (1992).

[45]See generally Arthur T. Denzau & Michael C. Munger, "Legislators and Interest Groups: How Unorganized Interests Get Represented," 80 *Am. Pol. Sci. Rev.* 89 (1986); see also Kevin B. Grier & Michael C. Munger, "Comparing Interest Group PAC Contributions to House and Senate Incumbents, 1980–1986," 55 *J. Pol.* 615, 625–40 (1993).

[46]In empirical studies of interest group contributions, a number of researchers seem to have in mind a "market model" of interest group contributions to legislators where interest groups offer campaign contributions and votes in return for political support. See Jonathan I. Silberman & Garey C. Durden, "Determining Legislative Preferences on the Minimum Wage: An Economic Approach," 84 *J. Pol. Econ.* 317, 328 (1976); Garey C. Durden et al., "The Effects of Interest Group Pressure on Coal Strip-Mining Legislation," 72 *Soc. Sci. Q.* 239, 249 (1991).

[47]See generally Kenneth A. Shepsle & Barry R. Weingast, "Positive Theories of Congressional Institutions," 19 *Legis. Stud. Q.* 149 (1994) (reviewing recent literature on congressional institutions).

ing implementation of regulatory policy by administrative agencies may influence legislators in their choice of regulatory procedures and instruments.[48]

C. Equilibrium Analyses

Compared to the above, relatively few works have taken an equilibrium approach by considering the interaction of the supply and demand for regulation. Those considering such linkages have typically focused on the role of campaign contributions. Several researchers have modeled campaign contributions from profit-maximizing firms to vote-maximizing politicians,[49] where candidates choose optimal policy positions that balance the need to get votes (by moving towards the policy preferences of voters) and the need to secure campaign funds (by moving towards the preferences of contributors).[50] In a similar vein, some analysts have employed game-theoretic models to link campaign contributions by interest groups and policy positions adopted by legislators.[51]

One group considered legislative outcomes directly, modeling the determination of campaign contributions, legislators' floor votes, and constituents' votes, but without advancing a theoretical model of legislative behavior.[52] Another research has explicitly considered the interaction of interest group demand and the legislative supply of policy instruments.[53] In his model, the choice of regulatory instrument is the equilibrium of a game between interest groups (who choose how much to allocate to lobbying in support of their preferred instrument) and legislators (who vote for the instrument that maximizes their support, taking into account the contributions from the interest groups).

Despite the relative scarcity of equilibrium models of positive political economy, the metaphor of a "political market" has frequently been employed in the public choice literature. The works using the market metaphor seem to have had three distinct markets in mind. One market is the market for votes *within* a legislature: legislators are at once demanders and suppliers of votes as they engage in vote trading and

---

[48]See Matthew D. McCubbins et al., "Administrative Procedures as Instruments of Political Control," 3 *J.L. Econ. & Org.* 243, 252–53 (1987); McCubbins et al., supra note 10, at 481.

[49]See generally Uri Ben-Zion & Zeev Eytan, "On Money, Votes, and Policy in a Democratic Society," 17 *Pub. Choice* 1 (1974).

[50]Bental and Ben-Zion extend the model to consider the case where politicians derive utility from adopting a platform close to their personal policy preferences. See Benjamin Bental & Uri Ben-zion, "Political Contribution and Policy—Some Extensions," 24 *Pub. Choice* 1, 1–4 (1975).

[51]See David Austen-Smith, "Interest Groups, Campaign Contributions, and Probabilistic Voting," 54 *Pub. Choice* 123, 128–34 (1987).

[52]See James B. Kau et al., "A General Equilibrium Model of Congressional Voting," 97 *Q.J. Econ.* 271, 288–89 (1982).

[53]See Jose Edgardo L. Campos, "Legislative Institutions, Lobbying, and the Endogenous Choice of Regulatory Instruments: A Political Economy Approach to Instrument Choice," 5 *J.L. Econ. & Org.* 333, 348–49 (1989).

logrolling.[54] Other market models focus on the distribution of wealth resulting *from* legislation: the demanders are the beneficiaries of legislation and the suppliers are the losers, with politicians serving as brokers between the two groups.[55] This Article employs what is perhaps the most prevalent conception of the "political market," one which focuses on the exchange between legislators and constituents or interest groups.[56]

The remainder of this Article develops a new model of a political market involving legislators, constituents, and interest groups in the context of instrument choice in environmental policy. This market framework supplements existing work by simultaneously considering the demand for regulation, the supply of regulatory options, and the equilibrium outcome, that is, the choice of policy instrument in the legislature. In this way, the Article strives to synthesize prior research from the demand side and supply side, using it as a foundation for our own equilibrium framework. This Article also seeks to suggest a richer sense of the supply side than is found in existing equilibrium models,[57] incorporating legislator ideology as well as a fuller description of the opportunity costs of supplying legislation.[58]

III. A Market Framework for Examining Instrument Choice

To develop a framework within which various existing positive political economy theories can be synthesized, consider a "political market" embodied in a legislature and focused on a single "commodity," namely leg-

---

[54]In a "logroll," or vote trade, several legislators might arrange to vote for each others' bills, so that each legislator secures her most preferred outcome in return for supporting other legislators' bills (which she may oppose only slightly if at all). For example, a series of public works projects might prompt a logroll, since each in the series matters a great deal to the representative whose district receives the funds, but is insignificant to other legislators.

[55]See *Public Choice Theory* at xviii (Charles K. Rowley ed., 1993).

[56]In previous work, the identity of demanders and suppliers has varied; the market has been in electoral votes (with legislators "paying" for votes with legislation) and in legislation (with voters paying for the policies with their votes). Peltzman, for one, was clear that the demanders were constituents and the suppliers legislators: "[t]he essential commodity being transacted in the political market is a transfer of wealth, with constituents on the demand side and their political representatives on the supply side." See Peltzman, supra note 30, at 212. In this Article's framework, the market is in units of effective political support (for particular public policies).

[57]See, e.g., Campos, supra note 53, at 338–48.

[58]As noted above, Congress is seen as the locus of policy instrument choice. Extending the framework to cover regulatory agencies and the courts would introduce several interesting but complex issues. For regulatory agencies, for example, it is important to deal with issues such as the principal-agent relationship between the agency and Congress; the degree and nature of congressional oversight; the possibly conflicting goals of the agency head and career bureaucrats; the objective function of the bureaucrats (for example, job security, power, protection of expertise); and the way in which policy demands provide payoffs to the agency.

islators' support for a given instrument in a specific policy context.[59] A schematic view of this political market is provided in Figure 1. Demand for various degrees of support comes from diverse interest groups, including environmental advocacy organizations, private firms, and trade associations. The currency in this market takes the form of resources (monetary and other contributions, and/or endorsements or other forms of support) that can facilitate legislators' reelections. The aggregation of these individual demands is not a simple sum, because the public good nature of regulation means that interest groups can free-ride on the demands of others.

Next, it is assumed that each individual legislator seeks to maximize her expected utility, which involves the satisfaction that comes from being

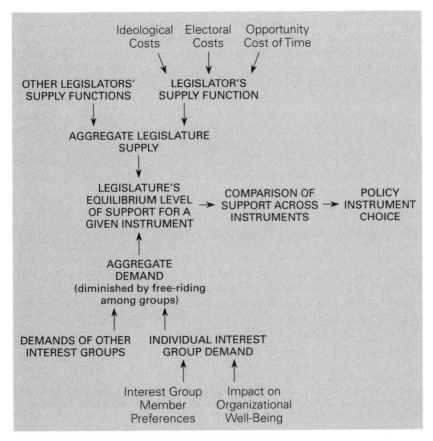

Figure 1 An Equilibrium Framework for Examining the Political Market

---

[59]"Specific policy context" simply refers to the fact that the demand for instruments and the supply of instrument options are both linked to the specific environmental problems for which the instruments are being considered. Also, as discussed below, the legislature in this framework selects a policy instrument from among a range of options, including alternative policy instruments plus the status quo.

a member of the legislature, now and in the future. The result is the legislator's political-support supply function, the shape of which is determined by her ideological predisposition, her perception of her constituents' preferences, and the increasing opportunity cost of providing additional support for the policy instrument (in terms of expended effort, foregone future electoral votes in her home district, and discomfort associated with departures from her ideology). Since each legislator supplies units of a homogeneous product called "effective support" (at differing costs), the individual legislators' supply functions combine to yield an aggregate supply function at the level of the legislature.

Thus, for each instrument, a competitive equilibrium in the legislature is given by the intersection between the aggregate political-support supply function and the aggregation of relevant demands.[60] Levels of effective support provided by individual members of the legislature are hence equivalent to the amounts they are willing to provide at the competitive equilibrium "price," the points of intersection of their supply functions with the infinitely elastic demand they face. The aggregate support is simply the sum over legislators of their individual levels of effective support. The legislative outcome, i.e., the choice of a policy instrument, then depends upon the relative degrees of support generated for alternative policy instruments.

The following sections describe the political market's commodity and currency, and then turn to more detailed expositions of the origins of regulatory demand and supply, respectively. Finally, the Article discusses the nature of political market equilibria and the legislative outcomes that result.

A. The Political Market's Commodity and Currency

Each legislator supplies some degree of support for a given regulatory instrument. Interest groups seek to secure support from legislators in the political market. The commodity of support is seen to be *homogeneous* among legislators. That is, the support produced by one legislator is equivalent to (a perfect substitute for) support produced by any other legislator. This commodity may be characterized as "effective support."[61] It is a measure of impact (output), not of effort (input).

---

[60]It is implicitly assumed that the effective support provided by individual legislators can be observed. This is a reasonable assumption in many but not all situations. Future work should explicitly incorporate this uncertainty.

[61]It might be argued that interest groups ultimately care about votes, which at the level of an individual legislator reduces to a binary variable. But there are several reasons to focus on support, rather than on votes alone. First, this approach facilitates comparisons among several instruments, since the outcome of the legislative process is the instrument that garners the most effective support. Second, empirical analysis has largely failed to link campaign contribution with legislators' votes, see Richard L. Hall & Frank W. Wayman, "Buying Time: Moneyed Interests and the Mobilization of Bias in Congressional Committees," 84 *Am. Pol. Sci. Rev.* 797, 813 (1990), while campaign contributions have been found to be highly correlated with legislators' participation in committees, itself closely linked with the notion of "effective support[.]" See Grier & Munger, supra

To be sure, different legislators require different amounts of effort to produce a unit of effective support. These variations in productivity are due to such factors as the size and effectiveness of members' staffs, their seniority, their committee assignments, and their leadership positions, including committee chairs. Moreover, a legislator's effort may encompass a much larger range of activities than simply voting for a given instrument: among other things, a legislator might hold hearings, attend committee markup meetings, draft or sponsor legislation, insert statements into committee reports, propose amendments, seek to influence colleagues, or make behind-the-scenes deals.[62]

The political currency in this market is seen as the resources necessary for the legislator's reelection: not only votes, but also monetary and other contributions.[63] An environmental interest group, for example, may publicly endorse a candidate for office, or may volunteer time and effort to mobilize votes in a legislator's district. Other forms of "payment" to legislators (such as time spent drafting legislation or policy information for the legislator) are also valued by a legislator seeking reelection, since association with the interest group may increase the legislator's support, and the time saved by the legislator may be spent on activities that generate home district votes. Incorporating home district votes, financial contributions,

---

note 45, at 641; Jonathan I. Silberman & Garey C. Durden, "Determining Legislative Preferences on the Minimum Wage: An Economic Approach," 84 *J. Pol. Econ.* 317, 326–27 (1976). Third, the fate of most prospective legislation is determined before it reaches the floor for a vote. The agenda-setting powers of committees make them virtual arbiters of whether or not bills reach the floor for voting. See Kenneth A. Shepsle & Barry R. Weingast, "The Institutional Foundations of Committee Power," 81 *Am. Pol. Sci. Rev.* 85, 87 (1987). Once a bill reaches the floor, norms of deference may lead many members of Congress to follow committee recommendations, either because of implicit logrolls among committees, see Barry R. Weingast & William J. Marshall, "The Industrial Organization of Congress, or, Why Legislatures, Like Firms, Are Not Organized as Markets," 96 *J. Pol. Econ.* 132, 157–58 (1988), or because of recognition of committees' greater expertise. See Kingdon, supra note 42, at 133.

    Votes of committee members are usually less critical than the intensity of members' support. See Richard L. Hall, "Participation and Purpose in Committee Decision Making," 81 *Am. Pol. Sci. Rev.* 105, 105–06 (1987); David R. Mayhew, *Congress: The Electoral Connection* 92 (1974). Hence, securing the support of a relatively small number of legislators (each of whom is a highly efficient producer of effective support) may be the primary goal of interest groups, even though the groups ultimately care about the outcome of floor votes. This reality is captured by the above framework, with its focus on levels of "effective support."

    [62]One set of researchers describes the range of services legislators can offer interest groups. See Denzau & Munger, supra note 45, at 91. Another group analyzes a similar measure of legislator participation, which they call "political support effort." See Silberman & Durden, supra note 61, at 318. Notably, these models generally treat as an output what in this framework is an input: namely, the effort exerted by the legislator to produce effective support. The above framework incorporates differences among legislators in effectiveness and productivity into the supply side (production of effective support) rather than the demand side (demand of interest groups for support from different legislators). For further discussion of the ways in which members of Congress participate in policy making, especially in committee, see Hall, supra note 61, at 106–08; Richard L. Hall, *Participation in Congress* 40–48 (1996); Hall & Wayman, supra note 61, at 804–15.

    [63]Monetary contributions can be used to finance advertising campaigns, literature production and distribution, and other activities that increase the probability of a legislator being reelected.

and nonmonetary contributions in the currency of "resources," the model adopts a monetary numeraire for convenience.

B. Origins of Demand for Environmental Policy Instruments

The Article now explores the nature of demand by firms and individuals, dividing the latter category into three overlapping groups (consumers, workers, and environmentalists), and then considers the role of interest groups in the political market.[64]

1. Firms and Individuals. Firms are affected by environmental regulation through the costs they incur to produce goods and services. Consider a price-taking firm[65] that wishes to maximize its profit from producing a single product and that employs a set of factors in its production, each of which has some cost associated with it. One of these input factors is the set of relevant features of the regulatory environment. In seeking to maximize profits, the firm chooses levels of all its inputs, including the efforts it puts into securing its desired regulatory environment. By solving this maximization problem, the firm derives its demand functions for all its inputs, including its demand for the environmental policy instrument. In this simple model, individual firms have a decreasing marginal willingness to pay to secure particular policy instruments.[66] At a minimum, a firm's demand for a policy instrument is a function of output and input prices, including the "price of legislators' support."[67]

The choice of environmental policy instruments can also have an effect on individuals. For example, individuals can be affected by the level of environmental quality that results from the use of a particular instrument,[68]

---

[64]Of course, individuals and interest groups also play a role on the "supply side" of the political market by affecting legislators' electoral prospects. Individuals vote, while interest groups may spend resources to influence that vote directly (for example, by disseminating information about a legislator's voting record on an issue). Stated in terms of our framework, individuals and interest groups not only exhibit a demand function, but also may also shift legislators' supply functions. See infra Part III.C. This Article attempts to draw a conceptual distinction between these two facets of individual and interest group involvement.

[65]In a competitive market economy, individual firms cannot independently set the price that they will charge (only monopolists can do this); rather, they must accept or "take" the price given by the competitively determined supply-demand equilibrium, and then decide how much to supply at that price.

[66]The maximized objective function is the firm's profit function. Hotelling's Lemma (a basic microeconomic theorem) establishes that the factor demand functions are downward sloping as long as the profit function is convex.

[67]This stylized framework implicitly assumes that firms are profit-maximizing (or cost-minimizing) atomistic units, and thus that there is no significant principal-agent slack between managers and shareholders. There is little doubt that this assumption departs from reality in many cases, but we leave its investigation to future research.

[68]Although attention has been restricted at the outset to the policy instruments used to achieve a given level of protection, the choice of cost-effective instruments can lead to the adoption of more stringent environmental standards, as noted below.

or by the costs of environmental protection as reflected in the prices of the goods and services they buy. Individuals might even derive some direct utility from knowing that a particular type of policy instrument was employed. These effects can be reflected in a utility function, which the consumer maximizes subject to a budgetary constraint. The result is a set of demand functions for all private and public goods, including demand functions for any environmental policy instruments that affect the individual's utility either directly or indirectly. Thus, like firms, individuals can have a decreasing marginal willingness to pay to secure particular policy instruments.[69] Their demand for a policy instrument is a function of their income and of the relative prices of relevant goods, including the price of securing support for their preferred instrument.

Moreover, individuals can be categorized as "consumers," "environmentalists," and "workers"; these three categories are neither mutually exclusive nor exhaustive. Individuals are "consumers" to the degree that the choice of environmental policy instrument affects them through its impact on the prices of goods and services, "environmentalists" to the degree that they are affected by the impact of instrument choice on the level of environmental quality, and "workers" to the degree that they are affected by environmental policy through its impact on the demand for labor, and hence their wages.

2. Interest Groups. Because there are significant costs of lobbying and because the target of demand (i.e., the public policy) is a public good,[70] an individual and even a firm will receive relatively small rewards for any direct lobbying efforts. For individuals, the marginal costs of lobbying are likely to outweigh the perceived marginal benefits over much of the relevant range of lobbying activity, such that individuals will undersupply lobbying, hoping instead to free ride on the efforts of others. Although some large firms maintain offices in Washington, D.C., to facilitate direct lobbying of Congress, most of the demand for public policies from both firms and individuals is transmitted through organized interest groups.

---

[69]The maximized utility function is the individual's indirect utility function. By Roy's Identity (a basic microeconomic truism), the demand functions are derived as downward sloping, as long as the utility functions has the usual properties. It is possible that over a certain region the demand function will be increasing. For example, a unit of support for an instrument will be virtually worthless at very low levels of support, since adoption of that instrument will be extremely unlikely. Assume, however, that the demand function is decreasing over the politically relevant range, in which adoption of the instrument is a realistic possibility. It might be argued that if a legislature were composed of a single legislator and there was perfect information, demand functions for political support would (in the case of support relevant for voting) be a step function with a single step: interest groups would have no willingness-to-pay below some level of (adequate) support, and no willingness-to-pay above a sufficient level of support. But in a multi-member body, more support from individual legislators can always be worth something, and if there is uncertainty about how much support is sufficient, the demand function is likely to be downward sloping over at least some range.

[70]Regulation may not always be nonexclusive. Loopholes, narrowly applying clauses in statutes, and bureaucratic exemptions can all afford special treatment for some firms or narrowly defined categories of consumers. This possibility may provide enough incentive for some individual firms to lobby.

The free-riding problem standing in the way of individual lobbying efforts can also be a significant obstacle to the formation of interest groups.[71] For an interest group to organize, it must overcome the free-riding problem by offering its members enough benefits to make the costs of membership worthwhile. For a citizen group, such as an environmental advocacy organization, these benefits are likely to include: "material incentives," such as newsletters, workshops, or gifts, "solidary incentives," namely the benefits derived from social interaction; and "purposive incentives," such as the personal satisfaction derived from membership in an organization whose activities one supports.[72]

Among citizen groups, taxpayer and consumer organizations may face greater free-riding problems than environmental groups:[73] their lobbying actions are likely to have an even wider range of potential beneficiaries; they may be able to offer fewer material incentives; and they lack the compelling moral mission that may drive the purposive incentives motivating members of environmental groups.

To overcome their own set of free-rider problems, trade associations can offer a range of benefits to member firms that nonmembers do not enjoy, including: influence over policy goals; information on policy developments; reports on economic trends; and participation in an annual convention.[74] Compared with citizen groups, trade associations may have significant advantages in overcoming free-riding: they are usually smaller, making the contributions of each member more significant; and even substantial annual dues may be negligible costs for member firms.[75] Hence, private industry interests may be over-represented in the political process relative to citizen groups.

Importantly, interest groups do not simply aggregate the political demands of their members. Indeed, an interest group's utility maximization function may diverge significantly from those of its members as a result of a principal-agent problem: the members (and donors) are principals who contract with their agent—the interest group (or, more precisely, its professional staff)—to represent their views to the legislature.[76] As in many

---

[71]See Mancur Olson, *The Logic of Collective Action: Public Goods and the Theory of Groups* 43–44 (1965).

[72]See Lawrence S. Rothenberg, *Linking Citizens to Government: Interest Group Politics at Common Cause* 66 (1992); James Q. Wilson, *Political Organizations* 33–35 (1995).

[73]Notably, labor unions are able to overcome free-riding problems through mandatory dues payments. See Olson, supra note 71, at 76; Wilson, supra note 72, at 119. To the extent that these funds are used for lobbying efforts, unions might be expected to be especially well-represented in the political arena. Yet, since unions dedicate most of their campaign contributions to securing favorable labor policy, unions as a group have only rarely been influential (or even active) in environmental policy debates.

[74]See Olson, supra note 71, at 139–41.

[75]See Wilson, supra note 72, at 144.

[76]In the typical principal-agent relationship, the principals (in this case, the firms) know their own interests and wish to ensure that the agent (here the trade association) acts in accordance with those interests. It is conceivable, however, that interest group staff may be leading the charge for policy changes that will benefit member firms, while those firms remain largely ignorant about the policy issues at stake. See Raymond A. Bauer et al., *American Business and Public Policy* 331 (1963).

such contractual relationships, the output exerted by the agents may not be directly observable or controllable by the principal. This principal-agent problem is probably far more serious for environmental advocacy groups than for private industry trade associations.[77]

Principal-agent slack between what the members want and what the interest group actually does arises because the organization's staff has its own self interests. A trade association, for example, may not only want to maximize the profits of its member firms; it may also seek to expand its membership or to increase revenue from member dues. Similarly, the objective function of an environmental group may include not only the level of environmental quality, but also factors such as membership size, budget, and reputation among various constituencies that affect the organization's health and viability.[78]

With these competing interests and constraints in mind, an interest group must decide how to allocate its scarce resources as it lobbies the legislature for its preferred outcome. The total benefits to an interest group of the legislature's support for an instrument rise with the degree of support offered, but there are increasing marginal returns. As in the case of individuals and firms, a unit increased in support when the legislature is already very favorably disposed to one's position is worth less than a unit increase in support by a lukewarm or previously unsupportive legislature. This characteristic produces a downward-sloping demand function: an interest group's marginal willingness-to-pay for support decreases as the legislature's total support increases.

C. Origins of Supply of Environmental Policy Instruments

The Article now considers a legislator who derives utility from a number of relevant interests: making public policy, doing good things for the country or for her district, satisfying ideological beliefs, having prestige and the perquisites of office, and so on. To continue getting utility from these fac-

---

[77]An environmental organization may have a hundred thousand members or more scattered across the country, paying scant attention to the operational proprieties of the organization (let alone the details of its day-to-day activities). Trade associations, on the other hand, may be dominated by a large producer, with an incentive to monitor the association's activities, and their boards of directors may be made up of executives from member firms. Moreover, trade associations have many fewer members, and therefore the stake of each in the organization is greater, and monitoring is more likely to be worthwhile. On the other hand, trade associations have their own set of problems. Among these are the possible necessity of obtaining an expression of consensus from member firms prior to undertaking specific lobbying efforts.

[78]One researcher treats the agency problem in environmental groups extensively, arguing that, because members and patrons cannot observe the outputs or effort of their agents directly, they must instead make funding and membership decisions based on a group's inputs: its expenditures on lobbying, member materials, advertising, and fund raising. See Robert C. Lowry, "The Political Economy of Environmental Citizen Groups" 94–96 (1993) (unpublished Ph.D. dissertation, Harvard University) (on file with the Harvard University Library).

tors, the legislator must be reelected. Assuming that legislators seek to maximize their expected utility, a legislator will choose her level of support for a proposed policy instrument based on the effort required to provide that support, the inherent satisfaction she derives from providing that level of support, and the effects her position will likely have on her chances of reelection.[79]

Accordingly, the legislator's supply function consists of three components: (1) the opportunity cost of efforts required to provide a given degree of support for a policy instrument; (2) the psychological cost of supporting an instrument despite one's ideological beliefs;[80] and (3) the opportunity cost (in terms of reduced probability of reelection) of supporting an instrument not favored by one's electoral constituency in terms of reduced probability of reelection.[81]

The first component emerges from the individual legislator's productivity in providing support. As indicated in Figure 2, the legislator's input is "effort"[82] and the relevant output is "effective support." Some legislators may produce "effective support" more efficiently with a given amount of effort thanks to the size and effectiveness of their staffs, their seniority in the legislature, and their membership and leadership on relevant committees. By placing a value on the opportunity cost of time and effort, an opportunity cost function can be derived (Figure 3), and from that, the related marginal opportunity cost of effort, represented by the upward-sloping line emanating from the origin in Figure 4.[83]

Next, assuming that a legislator derives disutility from acting inconsistently with her ideology, the psychological cost of supporting a policy inconsistent with one's ideological beliefs can be introduced into the framework. As suggested above, this cost would be negative (a benefit) if one were ideologically predisposed to favor the particular policy. In either case, it is conceivable that these marginal psychological costs might be increas-

---

[79]This notion of legislators' goals is consistent with other descriptions of Representatives as having three basic objectives: reelection, influence within the House, and good public policy. See Richard F. Fenno, Jr., *Home Style: House Members in Their Districts* 137 (1978). In our framework, "influence within the House" and "good public policy" are combined in "being a legislator." If the legislator wishes to continue to be a legislator in the future, she will also value reelection.

[80]If supporting the instrument is consistent with one's ideological beliefs, then this is a "negative cost," i.e., a benefit.

[81]This is also a "negative cost" (benefit) if supporting the instrument is consistent with one's constituents' positions.

[82]This includes the use of other resources, but may be thought of as being denominated in units of time.

[83]In the face of the overwhelming claims on her time and resources—both in Washington and in her home districts—a member's time and effort carries a significant opportunity cost. See Bauer, supra note 76, at 412–13; Kingdon, supra note 42, at 216; Fenno, supra note 79, at 141. Effort invested in providing support for one bill could have been spent working on other legislation that would satisfy ideological goals, reflect voters' objectives, and/or attract votes, dollars, and other resources; or visiting the home district and supplying constituency services such as help in dealing with the bureaucracy. See Denzau & Munger, supra note 45, at 92–96; Grier & Munger, supra note 45, at 618. Note that the marginal cost function is assumed in the figure to be linear, simply to keep the explication simple.

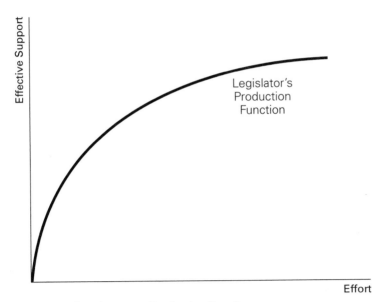

Figure 2 Political-Support Production Function

ing or decreasing (in absolute value) with the degree of support, but for ease of presentation we portray this marginal cost as constant in Figure 4. In this case, the legislator's ideology has no effect on the slope of the combined marginal cost function; rather, ideology shifts the function upwards (for inconsistency with ideology) or downwards (for consistency with ideology).

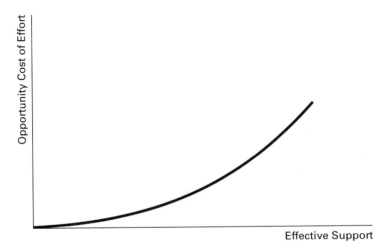

Figure 3 Political-Support Cost Function

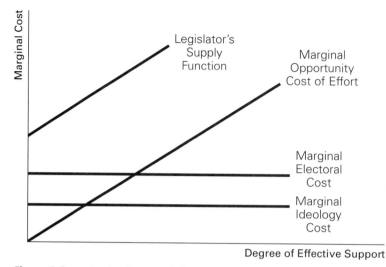

Figure 4 Opportunity Costs and the Supply of Political Support by an Individual Legislator

Finally, the framework incorporates the third component of the legislator's supply function: the opportunity cost corresponding to the reduced probability of reelection given the support of an instrument not favored by one's electoral constituency. Lost votes from constituents unhappy with the legislator's position would directly affect the legislator's chances of reelection, whereas protest and grassroots efforts by interest groups unhappy with the legislator's position could indirectly affect constituents' assessment of the legislator.[84] Again, this is a "negative cost" if supporting the instrument is consistent with one's constituents' positions.[85] As with ideological costs, although these marginal electoral opportunity costs could be increasing or decreasing with the level of the legislator's support, they are drawn as constant (and positive) in Figure 4, to keep things simple.[86]

---

[84]Members of Congress tend to take into account the preferences of the people who voted for them, i.e., their "supporting coalition," see Kingdon, supra note 42, at 60, or their "reelection constituency," see Fenno, supra note 79, at 8. A conservative legislator whose reelection constituency is anti-regulatory, for example, will not be affected by a minority group of environmentalists calling for command-and-control regulation.

[85]Departing from the preferences of constituents reduces the probability of the legislator's reelection. This reduced probability can be evaluated in terms of the resources required to maintain a constant probability of reelection.

[86]Figure 4 represents both ideological costs and electoral costs as being positive; support for the policy is essentially inconsistent both with the legislator's own ideology and her constituents' preferences. It is not inconceivable that these could be of opposite sign, but in a representative democracy, that would be the exception, not the rule. As stated by one author, "If your conscience and your district disagree too often,' members like to say, 'you're in the wrong business.' " Fenno, supra note 79, at 142.

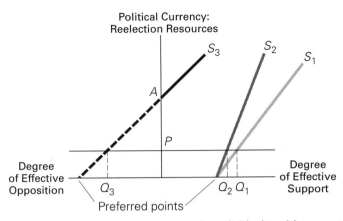

Figure 5 Supplies of Political Support by Individual Legislators

Accordingly, the overall (individual) marginal cost function, or the legislator's supply-of-support function, is simply the vertical summation of these three components: opportunity costs of effort, ideological costs, and constituency costs (Figure 4). The amount of support for a policy instrument that a legislator would supply in the absence of any contributions helpful to advancing the member's goals (including her reelection) is represented in Figure 5 as the "preferred point," the intersection of the supply function with the horizontal axis. In this framework, the legislator can be induced to offer progressively greater degrees of support from this preferred point through offers of "political compensation" that offset the legislator's respective opportunity costs.

Thus, the legislator has an upward-sloping marginal opportunity-cost or supply function, beginning at her preferred degree of support along the horizontal axis. The intersection of the supply function with the horizontal axis can take place at either a positive or a negative degree of support (see S_1 and S_3, respectively, in Figure 5). A politician who is strongly opposed to a given instrument will have a supply function with a negative intercept on the horizontal axis (and a positive intercept on the vertical axis). For such a legislator, a positive, non-marginal shadow price[87] of political compensation is required for any positive degree of support to be forthcoming (see point A in Figure 5).

The legislator's supply function is affected by several exogenous factors. First, an exogenous increase in the negative impact of a given instrument on a legislator's constituents (for example, the construction in the legislator's district of a new factory that would have to pay pollution taxes)

---

[87]The shadow price refers to the implicit price or the marginal valuation of the good or service in question.

may increase the legislator's opportunity costs of supporting that instrument. Conversely, an exogenous increase in the benefits of an instrument to the legislator's constituents (for example, the expansion of a firm in the district that produced a mandated abatement technology) would decrease the legislator's opportunity costs.

Second, the position of the legislator's political party is also relevant. Parties supply funds and organizational support in reelection campaigns. Moreover, leadership posts in the party offer opportunities for increased effectiveness in the legislature. Obviously, parties are likely to be more generous with legislators who are loyal.[88]

Third, the actions of other legislators will have a bearing on the costs of supplying support thanks to the possibilities for vote trading. For example, one legislator may care a great deal about the chosen level of environmental protection, while having only a slight preference for standards over taxes; another legislator may care less about the exact level but have a strong preference for taxes over standards, given her own market-oriented ideology. In a logroll, both legislators could gain from vote trading, with such a logroll affecting both legislators' costs of supplying support for a given instrument.

Fourth and finally, it is both the intent and the consequence of some lobbying activities to shift legislators' supply functions. In other words, in addition to being the primary demanders for alternative forms of regulation, organized interest groups can also play a role in determining the position and shape of legislators' supply functions. Lobbyists might attempt to: affect a legislator's ideologically based perception of the merits of a proposed policy instrument;[89] affect a legislator's perceptions of her constituents' policy preferences;[90] and/or affect a legislator's effort-support production function through provision of information or technical support.[91]

D. Formation of Equilibria and Legislative Outcomes

Up to this point, this Article has focused on the origins of supply and demand for a single policy instrument. However, in many contexts, there will be a *set* of possible instruments considered for achieving a given policy goal: for example, a standard, a tax, and a system of tradeable permits. In addition, there will exist the possibility of doing nothing, i.e., maintaining the status quo. Hence if N alternative instruments are under consideration,

---

[88]Party leaders may conceivably also become effective demanders for policy instrument support by offering various resources to legislators in exchange for support, in which case the parties are essentially functioning as interest groups.

[89]See Kingdon, supra note 42, at 141–42.

[90]See David Austen-Smith & John R. Wright, "Counteractive Lobbying," 38 *Am. J. Pol. Sci.* 25, 29–30 (1994).

[91]See Bauer, supra note 76, at 354–57.

then there will be N + 1 possible choices of action.[92] Each option can define a "political market" for effective support.[93] On the demand side, each policy instrument may have an associated set of interest groups seeking to secure support for it. Moreover, on the supply side, each policy instrument gives rise to its own set of legislator supply functions.[94]

The legislative outcome is the choice of one of the N + 1 alternatives arising from the interactions of interest groups' demands for and legislators' supplies of support for alternative instruments. The degree of aggregate support for each instrument results from an equilibrium established in the legislature, and the outcome in the legislature favors the policy instrument with the greatest degree of total support.

The following sections examine the component parts of this process. First, the nature of the aggregation of demand for a policy instrument across interested individuals and groups, and the aggregation of supplies of support for a policy instrument across members of the legislature, is considered. Then, the formation of equilibria in the legislature for alternative policy instruments and the consequent choice of political outcome is examined. Finally, alternative approaches to modeling this political market are discussed.

1. Aggregation of Demand for Policy Instrument Support. Typically, more than one interest group will be pressing for support from the legislature. How is such interest group demand to be aggregated? In the classic model associated with Stigler[95] and Peltzman,[96] the "winner takes all": the highest bidder wins and gains control over regulation. In another model, competing interest groups participate in a zero-sum game along a single dimension: one group is taxed, the other subsidized, and each tries to improve its lot at the expense of the other.[97] In an actual legislature, interest groups may be opposed to one another or aligned in support of the same instrument.

The most obvious approach for aggregating the demand functions of interest groups might be simply to sum, at each level of willingness-to-pay, the degrees of support that each group demands at that price. Such demand aggregation makes sense for private goods, but the support the legislature provides is essentially a public good. Hence, an efficient approach might involve taking a given level of support and vertically summing what

---

[92]The choice set of instruments is simply taken as given. Important questions remain regarding how it is determined, but these are beyond the scope of this Article.

[93]An interest group can demand and a legislator can supply support for more than one instrument. Although this may at first seem counterintuitive, recall that each legislator's supply function for a given instrument may include the possibility of opposition.

[94]A single legislator may be more efficient at producing support for one instrument than for another and may even have different ideological attitudes towards different instruments. Moreover, the preferences of her reelection constituency may vary across instruments.

[95]See Stigler, supra note 28, at 12–13.

[96]See Peltzman, supra note 30, at 212.

[97]See Becker, supra note 31, at 373–76.

each interest group is (marginally) willing to pay for that degree of support. But such an efficient approach is unlikely to reflect positive reality, as long as free-rider problems among interest groups exist. Therefore, the aggregate demand thus calculated represents the upper bound of actual aggregate demand, that is, the demand experienced in the absence of free-riding.

2. Aggregation of Supply of Policy Instrument Options. In this framework, the degree of support by individual legislators is denominated in terms of homogenous units of "effective support," with differences among legislators already incorporated into the underlying production functions with respect to individual marginal opportunity costs of effort (as well as individual marginal ideological and electoral costs). Therefore, the legislature's supply function can be derived by horizontally summing the supply functions of individual legislators. As noted above, some legislators' supply functions may extend to the left of the vertical axis (for example, S_3 in Figure 5), corresponding to opposition to the instrument in question. Therefore, when the individual legislator supply functions are horizontally added, the aggregate supply function for the legislature represents the relevant net supply of support. Like the supply function for an individual legislator, the aggregate supply function for some instruments may intersect the vertical axis at a positive price.

3. Equilibrium Support in the Legislature for a Policy Instrument. The model treats the legislature as a competitive market for the support of policy instruments. Given the homogeneity of the commodity demanded and supplied, the number of members in the two houses of Congress, and the number of active interest groups, perfect competition is a reasonable first approximation. Under that assumption, the equilibrium, aggregate level of "effective support" provided for the policy instrument is the level for which aggregate supply equals aggregate demand (Q^* in Figure 6). This level is associated with a shadow price (P in Figure 6) representing the aggregate marginal willingness to pay for support in the legislature's equilibrium.

There are two cases of interest in which the aggregate supply and demand functions do not intersect in the politically relevant positive orthant, the northeast part of the graph where both price and quantity are positive. In one case, the demand function intersects the horizontal axis to the left of the legislature's "aggregate preferred point" (see the gap between points B and E_A in Figure 7). In that instance, the maximum support demanded in aggregate by interest groups (at zero price) is lower than the amount that the legislature would provide on its own. In this case of "excess supply," it is reasonable to assume that the legislature would provide support at its preferred point (E_A). With the likelihood of free-riding among interest groups, it would not be surprising if the aggregate demand by interest groups often fell short of the support a strongly committed legislature would provide absent any lobbying. In the above case, the competitive equilibrium price is zero, with each legislator providing support at her own preferred point.

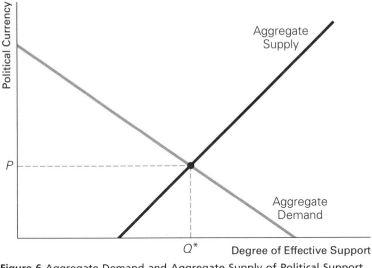

Figure 6 Aggregate Demand and Aggregate Supply of Political Support and the Formation of a Legislative Equilibrium

A second special case arises when a legislature so strongly opposes a policy that its upward-sloping aggregate supply function intersects the vertical axis at a positive price (point C in Figure 7). In this case, the supply function could conceivably lie entirely above the interest groups' aggregate demand function. The political price that such a legislature would require

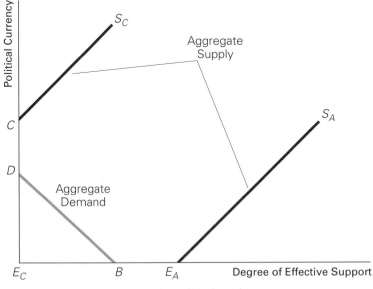

Figure 7 Degenerate Cases in the Political Market

for a positive degree of support is simply greater than the interest groups' overall reservation price for obtaining such support (point D in Figure 7).

In this competitive political market framework, an individual legislator will tend to supply support for a particular policy instrument up to the point where her marginal opportunity costs of doing so are equivalent to the infinitely elastic demand for support she faces from interest groups, represented by the horizontal line through the point P in Figure 5 (derived with the equilibrium in Figure 6). Thus, a set of legislators with supply functions represented by S_1, S_2, and S_3 (Figure 5), would provide effective support of Q_1, Q_2, and Q_3, respectively.

The legislator with supply function S_3 provides a negative level of support, i.e., opposition. An interest group might benefit from contributing to this legislator in the hope of reducing her degree of active opposition,[98] just as it can benefit by increasing the support of a "friendly" legislator. It would take a level of demand (and political compensation) equivalent to point A in Figure 5 to move this same legislator to a position of inaction or indifference. On the other hand, legislators such as those represented by S_1 and S_2 in Figure 5 derive benefits (negative costs) from supporting an instrument, no matter what the position of relevant interest groups. Not surprisingly, such friendly legislators supply even greater levels of support in response to interest group demand.

4. Legislative Outcomes.

4. Legislative Outcomes. The previous section discussed the equilibrium level of support for a policy instrument by a single legislator. The next step, then, is to ask how these individual levels of support translate into policy outcomes. One could imagine summing the individual levels of support across legislators to find the aggregate support for an instrument. Such an approach is insufficient, however, because it ignores institutional processes (for example, various kinds of voting rules) that influence collective decisions. In moving from individual support to policy outcomes, therefore, the analysis must take institutional features of the legislature into account.

First, the committee structure of Congress (especially in the House of Representatives) gives different legislators widely different levels of influence over policy.[99] Thus, legislators vary greatly in the effectiveness of the

---

[98]Hall and Wayman examine legislator participation in committees, and argue that interest groups give contributions to "hostile" legislators in order to reduce their participation, i.e., their opposition. See Hall & Wayman, supra note 61, at 803.

[99]Norms of deference, backed up by repeated interactions and the threat of retaliation, give members of committees and subcommittees significant influence over policies under their jurisdiction. See Shepsle & Weingast, supra note 61, at 88–89; Weingast & Marshall, supra note 61, at 158. Agenda-setting or "gate keeping" powers give committees the right to send bills to the floor or table them in committee. Standing committees are also heavily represented on the conference committees that are established to reconcile differences between the chambers before final passage. Power is particularly concentrated in the hands of committee chairs, who hold sway over the committees' agendas and the bills reported to the floor. Given the importance of committee composition, policy outcomes may differ markedly from the preferences of the legislature as a whole; given low committee turnover and the importance of seniority, the status quo may persist long after support in the full legislature has ebbed. See Kenneth A. Shepsle & Barry R. Weingast, "Political Solutions to Market Problems," 78 *Am. Pol. Sci. Rev.* 417, 429 (1984).

support they can supply for a given instrument. However, with the framework's focus on degrees of *effective* support, this reality is already incorporated (through the political support production functions) and has no effect on the appropriate aggregation; it remains one of simple summation of individual equilibria.

Second, legislative outcomes are affected by voting rules. The number of votes necessary for passage (taking into account the veto power of the executive) determines the level and distribution of support needed to pass a bill.[100] Furthermore, the order of voting on amendments and the nature of the final vote also affect the outcome.[101] The question is then how support translates into votes. Whereas the model's "degree of support" is a continuous variable, it produces a binary variable: a vote. Any empirical implementation of this framework would need to address this linkage.[102] For the purposes of this Article, focus can be confined to the reality that, in general, the policy instrument chosen will be the alternative garnering the greatest aggregate support.

5. Alternative Equilibrium Frameworks. Alternative conceptual frameworks of the political market are possible. One potential approach would give greater emphasis to the differences existing among individual legislators in terms of the nature of support they can provide. Thus, instead of quantifying support in terms of perfectly homogenous units of "effective support," the "uniqueness" of support from any single legislator (particularly from powerful members of the legislature) would be interpreted as leading to a set of monopoly political markets, rather than to a single competitive political market.

At one extreme, each member of the legislature is assumed to be a monopoly supplier of her unique type of support and is thus facing a downward-sloping demand for her support. As such, there would exist a set of monopoly equilibria, one for each member of the legislature. In their respective equilibria, each member equates her marginal cost (individual supply function) with the "marginal revenue" function associated with the policy demands she faces, and determines her equilibrium (and utility-maximizing) level of support.

The extreme case of multiple monopoly suppliers appears less reasonable than the perfectly competitive case as an approximation of political reality. However, it does illustrate the potential for alternative models of imperfect competition that may be superior for capturing important characteristics of political markets. Various models of cooperative and noncooperative oligopoly might capture significant elements of legislative rela-

---

[100]In the U.S. Congress, a bill needs a bare majority in the House of Representatives, but may have to clear a higher hurdle in the Senate to bring closure to debate. If the President vetoes the bill, of course, two-thirds majorities in both houses are required to enact legislation.

[101]If modified by successful amendments, a bill will be considered in opposition to the status quo in the final vote. This arrangement favors the status quo and requires that each bill be compared ultimately with the status quo rather than with other alternatives.

[102]Discrete-choice econometric models theoretically based on the existence of an unobserved latent variable are obvious candidates.

tionships.[103] Such explorations will not be dealt with here. Instead, in order to develop a conceptual framework within which existing political economy theories can be organized and synthesized, the basic competitive framework is examined further.

IV. Demand for Environmental Policy Instruments

Demand-side explanations for the choice among environmental policy instruments can be separated into four sectors of regulatory demand: firms, environmentalists, labor, and consumers.

A. Firms

Firms tend to demand the policy instruments promising the highest profits (or the lowest losses) from regulation. While all environmental regulation imposes costs of compliance on firms, not all instruments impose the same costs to achieve a given regulatory goal. Positive political economy explanations of firm demand for environmental regulation can be divided into three principal categories: firm preferences for particular instruments given lower aggregate costs of compliance compared to the industry as a whole; the presence of rents and entry barriers; and differential costs of compliance across firms in a given industry.[104]

1. Lower Aggregate Costs to an Industry as a Whole. All else being equal, firms will tend to prefer regulatory instruments with lower aggregate costs for the industry as a whole. As market-based approaches are likely more cost-effective than command-and-control instruments, the above would suggest that private industry as a whole would generally prefer market-based approaches. However, a crucial distinction exists between the aggregate cost for society and the aggregate cost for private industry. By de-

---

[103]For example, the respective roles played by committee chairs and members may be modeled as a monopolist operating in the context of a competitive fringe.

[104]There are other plausible explanations for firms' preferences. Firms may simply support the continuation of the status quo, which is generally the command-and-control approach, because replacing familiar policies with new instruments can mean that existing expertise within firms becomes less valued. See Steven P. Kelman, *What Price Incentives?* 118–22 (1981); Stewart, supra note 16, at 40. For example, lobbyists—the agents in a principal-agent relationship—may be rationally expected to resist the dissipation of their human capital. See Robert W. Hahn & Robert N. Stavins, "Incentive-based Environmental Regulation: A New Era from an Old Idea," 18 *Ecology L.Q.* 1, 24 (1991). It has also been suggested that market-based instruments may be opposed simply because they are not well understood, and there is at least anecdotal evidence that this has been the case. See Kelman at 96, above; W.P. Welch, "The Political Feasibility of Full Ownership Property Rights: The Case of Pollution and Fisheries," 16 *Pol'y Sci.* 165, 175 (1983). Such lack of understanding can also affect the supply side, and we discuss this later.

finition, cost-effective instruments minimize costs to society; they may how-ever vary in proportion of costs imposed on polluters. Accordingly, the use of market-based instruments does not guarantee that firms' compliance costs will be less than the compliance costs of command-and-control reg-ulation.

It would then follow that firms would oppose regulatory instruments that shift a greater cost burden onto industry. For instance, the virtually unanimous opposition by private industry to pollution taxes results from the fact that, under such schemes, firms pay not only their private costs of compliance, but also the costs of tax payments to the government for any residual emissions.[105] Similarly, under tradeable permit schemes, firms bear equivalent costs if the initial distribution of the permits is through an auction. In contrast, under a tradeable permit scheme with grandfathered permits, existing firms do not bear any cost for their residual emissions.[106]

The above suggests that private industry as a whole would prefer grand-fathered permits *and* standards to other instruments, since grandfathered permits are cost-effective and the burden placed on industry (at least on existing firms) is minimized. Emissions standards are usually worse for in-dustry in terms of the total-cost criterion, but are likely to be preferred by firms to auctioned permits or taxes.

2. Generation of Rents and Erection of Entry Barriers. Certain types of regulation can actually augment firms' profits through the generation of rents and the erection of entry barriers. In general, firms earn rents if a regulatory instrument drives price above average cost. Assume the case of a command-and-control standard that sets an allowable level of aggregate pollution for each firm, where firms can meet the standard only by reduc-ing output.[107] Assume further that the industry is initially made up of many identical firms, each facing an identical demand, with classical average and marginal cost functions. In the absence of regulation, each firm would pro-duce at the intersection of its marginal and average cost curves, making zero profits. The environmental standard reduces total production and therefore raises price along the aggregate demand curve. If the environ-mental restriction is not exceptionally severe, the new price will be above average cost for all firms. Firms, therefore, earn rent: the difference be-tween the price they receive for their product and their cost of production.

---

[105]On this point, see Kelman, supra note 104, at 120; see also Frank S. Arnold, *Economic Analy-sis of Environmental Policy and Regulation* 227 (1995); Robert W. Crandall, *Controlling Industrial Pol-lution* 70 (1983); Robert W. Hahn & Roger G. Noll, "Environmental Markets in the Year 2000," 3 *J. Risk Uncertainty* 351, 359 (1990). Actually, firms pay less than the full amount of the tax, since a share is passed on to consumers.

[106]Grandfathering distributes the rents from permits to firms that participate in the initial al-location, in contrast with an auction. See Donald N. Dewees, "Instrument Choice in Environmental Policy," 21 *Econ. Inquiry* 53, 59 (1983); Gary W. Yohe, "Polluters' Profits and Political Response: Di-rect Control Versus Taxes: Comment," 66 *Am. Econ. Rev.* 981, 981 (1976).

[107]See James M. Buchanan & Gordon Tullock, "Polluters' Profits and Political Response: Direct Control Versus Taxes," 65 *Am. Econ. Rev.* 139, 140 (1975).

If entry is prohibited, existing firms will continue earning rents into the future; even if not, rents will last until enough new firms enter to reestablish competitive equilibrium at the new price. Hence, in the above model, firms may prefer standards to no regulation at all, and firms will prefer standards to taxes, since a tax charges for a resource that otherwise would be free.[108]

Firms, however, are not limited to the single response of cutting output. They can also reduce emissions by adopting new technologies or by changing their input mix. In this more general and realistic scenario, depending on the stringency of the standards and other factors, command-and-control standards can still have the effect of providing rents to regulated firms.[109] Here, too, under certain conditions, firms may prefer command-and-control standards to no regulation at all.[110]

It is important to note that the enhanced industry profitability resulting from rents will be sustainable over the long term *only* in the presence of entry restrictions. Thus, firms regulated by a rent-generating instrument, such as command-and-control standards, will benefit if that instrument is linked to a mechanism that imposes barriers to entry. In theory, such a mechanism might prohibit new entry outright; a more politically feasible approach would impose higher costs on new entrants.[111]

The above body of theory explains why private firms (and their trade associations) may have a strong preference for command-and-control standards, which may create rents, and especially for considerably more stringent command-and-control standards for new pollution sources, which create barriers to entry.[112] The indication that firms would support this form of regulation

---

[108]Even if the restriction is severe enough to impose losses on firms, they will prefer standards to taxes, which impose new costs. In the long run, under a tax scheme, firms will exit the industry until a new zero-profit equilibrium is reached; in the short term, firms will lose money. The tax reduces each firm's present value of income, whether it remains in the industry or exits. Firms will therefore oppose the introduction of pollution taxes.

[109]See Michael T. Maloney & Robert E. McCormick, "A Positive Theory of Environmental Quality Regulation," 25 *J.L. & Econ.* 99, 105 (1982).

[110]Pollution restrictions raise both the average and marginal cost curves. Each firm will produce at the level where restricted marginal cost intersects the per-firm demand curve. If the minimum average cost under regulation is to the left of this point, the price (marginal cost) will exceed average cost, and firms will earn rents. Maloney and McCormick identified three conditions that are sufficient for regulation to enhance producer profits: (1) output under regulation corresponds to some cost-minimizing level of output in the absence of regulation; (2) pollution increases with output; and (3) average costs increase more at higher levels of output under regulation. See id. at 104. The necessary and sufficient condition for higher profits is that the intersection of average and marginal cost under regulation lie to the left of the firm's demand curve.

[111]See Stigler, supra note 28, at 3, 5; Eric Rasmusen & Mark Zupan, "Extending the Economic Theory of Regulation to the Form of Policy," 72 *Pub. Choic* 167, 187–89 (1991).

[112]Other barriers to entry result, for example, from the permitting requirements for new sources under the PSD and non-attainment programs under the Clean Air Act, as well as by non-attainment programs' offset requirements for new sources. The positive significance of scarcity rents as a major explanation for the prevalence of particular forms of environmental regulation has important normative implications as well. This is because, in the presence of pre-existing tax distortions, the distribution of these rents can have efficiency implications. See Fullerton & Metcalf, supra note 19, at 44–45. It is ironic that the mechanism that facilitates political acceptance of some environmental policies (transmission of scarcity rents to the regulated sector) may also undo some or all of the welfare gains that would have been forthcoming.

begins to explain the prevalence of such instruments in U.S. environmental law. Furthermore, the theory indicates that, under certain conditions, the regulated industry would be better off than without regulation.

Although the theoretical arguments are strong, there are no conclusive empirical validations of these demand-side propositions. Direct empirical tests of firm demand for regulatory instruments (such as analyses of resources devoted to lobbying for such instruments as a function of firms' stakes in an issue) are virtually nonexistent. Instead, most empirical work in this area simply seeks to measure the benefits an industry receives under regulation. Thus, the work examines not instrument demand itself, but rather the presumed product of such demand.[113]

The above discussion also provides a positive political economy explanation for why market-based instruments have virtually always taken the form of grandfathered tradeable permits, or at least why private firms should be expected to have strong demands for this means of permit allocation. In tradeable permit schemes, grandfathering not only conveys scarcity rents to firms, since existing polluters are granted valuable economic resources for free, but also provides entry barriers, in that new entrants must purchase permits from existing holders.[114]

The preceding discussion does not provide a compelling explanation for the prevalence of command-and-control standards over grandfathered tradeable permits. In principle, either instrument could provide sustainable rents to existing firms. The theory needs to be extended to explain this phenomenon.

3. Differential Costs across Firms in an Industry. An alternative explanation for the landscape of environmental policy instruments arises from the existence of differential costs of environmental compliance across firms. Due to this heterogeneity, a firm may support policy instruments that impose costs on it, as long as those costs affect it less than the industry average, giving it a competitive advantage.[115] For example, firms which could

---

[113]Several researchers employed financial market event analysis in two regulatory cases to test whether the value of regulated firms (measured by stock market prices) was positively affected by the announcement of regulation, as the economic theory of regulation would suggest. They found that cotton dust standards promulgated by the U.S. Occupational, Safety, and Health Administration ("OSHA") raised the asset value of cotton producers, which is consistent with the notion that regulation increased firms' profits by creating rents. See Maloney & McCormick, supra note 109, at 122. However, a more comprehensive study reached the opposite conclusion. See John S. Hughes et al., "The Economic Consequences of the OSHA Cotton Dust Standards: An Analysis of Stock Market Price Behavior," 29 *J.L. Econ.* 29, 58–59 (1986).

[114]One research group provided anecdotal evidence for rent-seeking in the decision making process over EPA's implementation of the Montreal Protocol restricting the use and production of CFCs. See Hahn & McGartland, supra note 19, at 601–10. They argue that a rent-seeking model explains the positions of large producers supporting grandfathered tradeable permits and opposing other implementation schemes, including an auction proposal. See id.

[115]See Robert A. Leone & John E. Jackson, *Studies in Public Regulation* 231, 247 (Gary Fromm ed. 1981); Sharon Oster, "The Strategic Use of Regulatory Investment by Industry Sub-groups," 20 *Econ. Inquiry* 604, 606 (1982).

reduce lead content at relatively low costs (thanks to large refineries) tended to support the gradeable permit system by which the leaded content of gasoline was reduced in the 1980s,[116] while firms with less efficient, smaller refineries were vehemently opposed.[117] Other empirical work, however, has cast doubt on the proposition that firms advocate instruments based on inter-industry or intra-industry transfers.[118]

Another form of cost differential arises as a result of barriers to entry. It is important to maintain the distinction between the entry of new firms and the expansion of existing firms. Entry barriers from environmental regulation generally apply to both situations. Within an industry, firms with no plans to expand would derive greater benefit from entry barriers, potentially discouraging further growth by their competitors.

Conversely, firms with ambitious expansion plans relative to their existing operations would benefit from weaker barriers. Such firms would also try to structure barriers in a manner giving them an advantage relative to newcomers. For example, the "bubble" program of the Clean Air Act creates barriers that are less onerous for existing firms because firms are allowed to engage in intra-firm emissions trading.[119] Under this program, a firm can reduce the emissions of an existing source by an amount at least equal to the emissions of the new source, instead of having to take the more costly step of meeting the command-and-control standard otherwise applicable to new sources.[120] The CAA's banking policies, which allow intra-firm trading across time periods, also make expansion by an incumbent easier than entry by a new firm.

The mechanism for allocating tradeable permits might also produce different winners and losers within an industry. Under a grandfathering

---

[116]See Kerr & Maré, supra note 24, at 31.

[117]See Small Refiner Lead Phasedown Task Force v. EPA, 705 F.2d 506, 514 (D.C. Cir. 1983) (discussing small refineries' opposition). Another example of such intra-industry differentials, and the resulting splintering of lobbying strategy, occurred when the National Coal Association ("NCA") divided over the question of scrubber requirements in clean air legislation. A universal scrubber requirement would have preserved demand for eastern coal, which had higher sulfur content than its cleaner western competition. The NCA split between eastern and western coal producers and stayed out of the debates leading up to the 1977 Clean Air Act Amendments. See Bruce A. Ackerman & William T. Hassler, *Clean Coal/Dirty Air* 31 (1981). Similarly, the largest producers of CFCs (DuPont and Imperial Chemical Industries) supported a ban on CFCs mainly because they were the firms best able to develop substitutes. See Kenneth A. Oye & James H. Maxwell, "Self-Interest and Environmental Management," in *Local Commons and Global Interdependence: Heterogeneity and Cooperation in Two Domains* 191, 198 (Robert O. Keohane & Elinor Ostrom eds., 1995).

[118]Several researchers found that legislators with a paper producer in their districts voted against water pollution control legislation, regardless of whether the producer stood to gain or lose relative to its competitors. See Leone & Jackson, supra note 115, at 247. These authors note that firms may oppose regulation out of uncertainty concerning how the legislation will be implemented, since cost predictions depend on subsequent rulemaking decisions by administrative agencies. Id. at 248.

[119]See 51 Fed. Reg. 43,814, 43,830 (1986). The bubble program typically permits only geographically contiguous trades. Thus, even among existing firms with expansion plans, the benefits of the program depend on where the expansion is contemplated.

[120]Inter-firm trading (as opposed to only intra-firm trading) would eliminate this advantage. See 51 Fed. Reg. 43,814, 43,847–48 (1986).

scheme that allocates permits on the basis of emissions at the time of the scheme's establishment, firms investing in pollution abatement prior to regulation stand to lose relative to their more heavily polluting competitors.[121] Although such investing and expanding firms might conceivably prefer the allocation of permits by means of an initial auction,[122] smaller firms often prefer grandfathering out of concern that auctions will be dominated by larger players.[123]

B. Environmental Organizations

As noted above, the utility of an environmental advocacy group will probably be affected by both the organization's well-being and the level of environmental quality. First, organizational well-being may be measured partly by budgetary resources, which are a function of donor contributions. This financial concern can affect an organization's demand for specific policy instruments if such support attracts members, persuades donors to make contributions, or, more broadly, increases the visibility and prestige of the organization. Hence, an organization's demand for a given policy instrument is likely to be affected by several factors, all else being equal: the likelihood that the instrument will be chosen by policymakers;[124] the degree to which the organization is clearly identified with supporting the instrument; the magnitude of potential funding gains from distinguishing the organization from other environmental groups; and the ability to offer

---

[121]See Hahn & Noll, supra note 105, at 359.

[122]Some supporting evidence is provided by the establishment of a market in takeoff and landing slots at the nation's busiest airports. Since 1968, peak-hour takeoffs and landings have been restricted at LaGuardia, John F. Kennedy, O'Hare, and Washington National Airports. Until 1986, these slots were allocated by a scheduling committee composed of the airlines using a given airport. In that year, the Federal Aviation Administration ("FAA") replaced the committee allocation system with a system of grandfathered tradeable permits. See "Government Policies on the Transfer of Operating Rights Granted by the Federal Government: Hearings before the Subcomm. on Aviation of the House Comm. on Pub. Works and Transp." 99th Cong. 2–4 (1985) (statement of Rep. Norman Y. Mineta). In the months before the proposal was to go into effect, Congress held hearings and considered whether to overrule the FAA. At the hearings, large airlines, which already held most of the slots, supported grandfathering. See, e.g., id. at 55–56 (statement of Robert L. Crandall, CEO, American Airlines); id. at 96 (statement of Steven G. Rothmeier, CEO, Northwest Airlines). In contrast, upstart airlines looking to expand but having few slots, such as People Express, Republic, and Western, vigorously opposed grandfathering, calling for a large percentage of existing slots to be auctioned or distributed by lottery. See, e.g., id. at 71 (statement of Robert E. Cohn, CEO, People Express); id. at 372 (statement of A.B. Magary, Marketing VP, Republic Airlines).

[123]See Hahn & McGartland, supra note 19, at 606. Similarly, since the transition to a grandfathered-permits system is likely to involve less uncertainty than an auction, it might receive disproportionate support from risk-averse firms. Id. at 605.

[124]There is an important distinction between advocacy groups' strategic and tactical decisions. An environmental organization's strategic decision to express demand for a policy instrument and get it on the agenda for consideration tends to be positively related to perceived probability of success, whereas the tactical decision to express demand for an instrument already on the agenda may well be negatively related to probability of success.

donors and members a compelling environmental quality argument in support of the instrument.

A prominent example is provided by the Environmental Defense Fund's ("EDF") enthusiastic and effective support of the SO_2 allowance trading system adopted as part of the Clean Air Act Amendments of 1990. With the Bush Administration eager to back up the President's claim of being "the environmental President," and with key senior staff in the Administration having strong predispositions to the use of market-based approaches, the proposal had a strong chance of success. EDF had already become a champion of market-based approaches to environmental protection in other, less nationally prominent, domains. Now it faced an opportunity to strengthen that position and solidify its reputation as a pragmatic environmental organization willing to adopt new strategies involving less confrontation with private industry. By supporting tradeable permits, EDF could seize a market niche in the environmental movement, distinguishing itself further from other groups. Importantly, EDF was able to make a powerful argument for tradeable permits on environmental, as opposed to economic, grounds: the use of a cost-effective instrument would make it politically possible to achieve greater reductions in sulfur dioxide emissions than would otherwise be the case.[125]

EDF is an outlier in this realm. Most environmental advocacy groups have been relatively hostile towards market-based instruments. This should not be terribly surprising. Because of their interest in strengthening environmental protection, environmental organizations might be expected to prefer command-and-control approaches to market-based schemes for philosophical, strategic, and technical reasons. On philosophical grounds, environmentalists have portrayed pollution taxes and tradeable permits as "license[s] to pollute."[126] Moreover, they have voiced concerns that damages from pollution—to human health and to ecological well-being—are so difficult or impossible to quantify and monetize that the harm cannot be calculated through a marginal damage function or captured by a Pigouvian tax rate.[127]

Second, environmental organizations may oppose market-based schemes on strategic grounds. Once implemented, permit levels and tax rates may be more difficult to alter than command-and-control standards. If permits are given the status of "property rights," an attempt to reduce pollution levels in the future may meet with "takings" claims and demands for government compensation.[128] This concern, however, can be alleviated by an explicit statutory provision (like that contained in the acid rain provisions of the Clean Air Act Amendments of 1990) stating that permits do

---

[125]See Hahn & Stavins, supra note 104, at 33 n. 180.

[126]See Kelman, supra note 104, at 44. This criticism overlooks the fact that under conventional command-and-control regulations, firms receive these same licenses to pollute for free. See Hahn & Stavins, supra note 104, at 37.

[127]See Kelman, supra note 104, at 54–55.

[128]See Hahn & Noll, supra note 105, at 359.

not represent property rights,[129] or by "sunset" provisions that specify a particular period of time during which a permit is valid.

Likewise, in the case of pollution taxes, if increased tax rates become desirable in response to new information about a pollutant or about the response of firms to the existing taxes, adjustment may be unlikely because raising tax rates is politically difficult. Furthermore, taxes have long been treated as "political footballs" in the United States (or as in the recent case of efforts to reduce gasoline taxes). Hence, environmental organizations might oppose pollution taxes out of fear that they would be reduced or eliminated over time. A related strategic reason for environmentalists' opposition of tax instruments is that a shift from command-and-control to tax-based environmental regulation would shift authority from environment committees in the Congress, frequently dominated by pro-environment legislators, to tax-writing committees, which are generally more conservative.[130]

Third, environmental organizations may object to decentralized instruments on technical grounds. Although market-based instruments are theoretically superior in terms of cost-effectiveness, problems may arise in translating theory into practice.[131] For example, an emission tax or tradeable permit scheme can lead to localized "hot spots" with relatively high levels of ambient pollution.[132] While this problem can be addressed in theory through the use of permits or charge systems that are denominated in units of environmental degradation, the design of such systems might be perceived as excessively cumbersome.[133]

C. Labor

Since unions generally seek to protect jobs, they might be expected to oppose instruments likely to lead to plant closings or other large industrial dislocations. Under a tradeable permit scheme, for example, firms might close their factories in heavily polluted areas, sell permits, and relocate to less polluted areas, where permits are less expensive.[134] In contrast, command-and-control standards have generally been tailored to protect aging plants. The threat of factory dislocation is a likely explanation of support from northern, urban members of Congress for the PSD policy in clean

---

[129]See 42 U.S.C. § 765b(f) (1994).

[130]See Kelman, supra note 104, at 139–42. Note that these strategic arguments refer, for the most part, to pollution taxes, not to market-based instruments in general. Indeed, one reason environmental groups such as EDF have endorsed the tradeable permits approach is that it promises the cost savings of taxes without the drawbacks that environmentalists associate with tax instruments.

[131]See Robert W. Hahn & Robert L. Axtell, "Reevaluating the Relationship Between Transferable Property Rights and Command-and-Control Regulation," 8 *J. Reg. Econ.* 125, 126–27 (1995).

[132]See Richard L. Revesz, "Federalism and Interstate Environmental Externalities," 144 *U. Pa. L. Rev.* 2341, 2412 (1996).

[133]See id. at 2412–14.

[134]See Hahn & Noll, supra note 105, at 358.

air regulation, which has discouraged movement of industry out of urban areas in the northeast into high-quality air sheds in the South and West.[135] Depending on the tradeoffs between job creation and preservation effects, labor might support stricter command-and-control standards for new sources.[136]

D. Consumers

To the extent that consumer groups have preferences among environmental policy instruments, one might expect them to favor those instruments that minimize any increases in the prices of consumer goods and services; this would seem to suggest cost-effective (hence, market-based) instruments over command-and-control.[137] In practice, however, these groups typically have not expressed strong demand for environmental policies. As mentioned above, free-riding and limited information are likely to present greater obstacles for consumer organizations than for environmental groups, especially on environmental issues. Thus demand from consumer groups for environmental policy instruments is likely to be muted. Moreover, environmental policy may lie outside the core concerns of consumer groups' constituents. Indeed, when consumer groups do get involved, it may be on "consumer health and safety" issues, where their interests are aligned with those of environmentalists. Calls for cost-effective policies might also be voiced by taxpayer organizations, but again, the minutiae of instrument choice lie outside the scope of these groups' primary concerns. Hence, environmental groups are unlikely to face significant opposition from other public interest organizations.

V. Supply of Environmental Policy Instruments

There are several plausible positive political economy explanations for the nature of the supply of environmental policy instruments. First, legislators and their staffs are thought to be predisposed by their predominantly le-

---

[135]See, e.g., Crandall, supra note 105, at 127–29 (1983); B. Peter Pashigan, "Environmental Regulation: Whose Self-Interests Are Being Protected?," 23 *Econ. Inquiry* 551, 552–53 (1985).

[136]There are other examples of labor concern over the choice of environmental policy instruments. In the 1977 debates over amendments to the Clean Air Act, eastern coal miners' unions fought to include a command-and-control standard that effectively required scrubbing, thereby seeking to ensure continued reliance on cheap, high-sulfur coal from the east, over cleaner western coal. See Ackerman & Hassler, supra note 117, at 31. Likewise, in the debates over the SO_2 allowance trading system in the 1990 amendments to the CAA, the United Mine Workers opposed the system because it would create incentives for the use of low-sulfur coal from largely non-unionized mines in Wyoming's Powder River Basin over high-sulfur coal from eastern, unionized mines. See "Clean Air Reauthorization: Hearing Before the Subcomm. on Energy and Power of the House Comm. on Energy and Commerce," 101st Cong. 455–56 (1989) (statement of Richard L. Trumka, President, United Mine Workers).

[137]It is also possible to distinguish among types of market-based instruments and types of command-and-control instruments, given that any environmental policy instrument that generates privately retained scarcity rents (such as new source performance standards, grandfathered tradeable permits, and others) also raises consumer prices, relative to a policy that does not generate such rents. See Fullerton & Metcalf, supra note 19, at 44.

gal training to favor command-and-control approaches to regulation.[138] Similarly, legislators may need to spend time learning about unfamiliar policy instruments before they can provide substantial support, thereby giving rise to a status quo bias in favor of the current regime of command-and-control regulation.[139] Both these effects may become weaker in the coming years, as a result of the increasing understanding of economics among lawyers as well as among legislators and their staffs.[140]

Second, ideology plays a significant role in instrument choice. A conservative lawmaker who generally supports the free market might be predisposed to support market-based instruments; a legislator with more faith in government and less faith in the private sector might, all else being equal, prefer a command-and-control approach. A 1981 survey of congressional staff members found that support and opposition to effluent charges was based largely on ideological grounds.[141] For example, Republicans who supported the concept of pollution charges offered assertions such as "I trust the marketplace more" or "less bureaucracy" is desirable, without any real awareness or understanding of the economic arguments for market-based programs.[142] Likewise, Democratic opposition was largely based upon analogously ideological factors, with little or no apparent understanding of the real advantages or disadvantages of the various instruments.[143]

Third, constituents react to their perceptions of the costs and benefits to themselves and others of a particular policy, regardless of the real costs

---

[138]See Allen V. Kneese & Charles L. Schulze, *Pollution, Prices, and Public Policy* 116–17 (1975).

[139]See id. at 114–15. This argument assumes that a legislator (or at least her staff) needs to understand an instrument in order to support it. Although such understanding might not be a precondition for voting in favor of the instrument, it is more important for other forms of support, such as insertion of a statement into the legislative history, efforts to get a bill through committee, or attempts to persuade other legislators. Moreover, a lack of understanding may hurt the legislator in her reelection campaign if the press or an opponent seeks to make it an issue. Thus, the greater the prominence of an issue, the more important it will be for a legislator to have a compelling rationale for her position. Responding to this need, interest groups may supply legislators with justifications for supporting given policies. See, e.g., Fenno, supra note 79, at 141–43; Kingdon, supra note 42, at 46–48.

[140]See Hahn & Stavins, supra note 104, at 31, 36. Thus, outreach efforts by economists and others may be thought to have both demand-side and supply-side effects. On the demand side, increased understanding of market-based instruments may have increased the demand for these instruments by various interest groups. On the supply side, increased understanding reduces learning costs for legislators. Since both effects translate into rightward shifts of the respective functions, the outcome is unambiguous in terms of increased degrees of support.

Economists have also played a sometimes significant role as advocates of market-based instruments on efficiency grounds, not only in aspects of environmental policy (such as the U.S. acid rain program) but also in other policy areas, such as the allocation of airport landing spots and the broadcast spectrum. Economists therefore might be seen as acting as "policy entrepreneurs" outside of the interest group-politician nexus (i.e., outside of the strict supply-and-demand framework posited here). See id. at 41.

[141]See Kelman, supra note 104, at 100.

[142]See id. at 100, 104.

[143]See id. at 100–01.

and benefits.[144] The more visible the benefits, the greater the demand for an instrument; the more visible the costs, the greater the opposition and thus the political costs to the legislator. The importance of perceived costs and benefits is a consequence of the limited information most voters have about the details of public policy.[145] Hence, politicians are likely to prefer command-and-control instruments because they tend to hide the cost of regulation in the price increases passed on to consumers.[146] In contrast, though they impose lower total costs, market-based instruments generally impose those costs directly, in the form of effluent or permit charges.[147] Grandfathered permits fare better on the visibility criterion than auctioned permits or taxes, because no money is exchanged at the time of the initial allocation.[148]

Fourth, voters' limited information may also lead politicians to engage in symbolic politics: the use of superficial slogans and symbols to attract constituent support, even when the policies actually implemented are either ineffectual or inconsistent with the symbols employed. Such symbolism offers the legislator political benefits at little opportunity cost. Command-and-control instruments are likely to be well suited to symbolic politics, because strict standards, as strong statements of support for environmental protection, can be readily combined with less visible exemptions.[149] Congress has on several occasions passed environmental laws with strict compliance standards, while simultaneously including lax or insufficient enforcement measures.[150] Tradeable permits and taxes do not offer

---

[144]See, e.g., Matthew D. McCubbins & Terry Sullivan, "Constituency Influences on Legislative Policy Choice," 18 *Quantity & Quality* 299, 301–02 (1984); Robert W. Hahn, "Jobs and Environmental Quality: Some Implications for Instrument Choice," 20 *Pol'y Sci.* 289, 299 (1987).

[145]A rational voter will choose to remain ignorant on most issues, because the costs of gathering information are likely to outweigh the nearly insignificant benefits from voting knowledgeably. See Anthony Downs, *An Economic Theory of Democracy* 212–13 (1957). In contrast, organized interest groups with large stakes in an issue are likely to be well-informed and thus overrepresented in the political process. These issues raised by asymmetric information are particularly relevant to instrument choice, because votes on instrument choice are often much more technical than votes on policy goals, and therefore attract even less attention from average voters. See generally James T. Hamilton, "Taxes, Torts, and the Toxics Release Inventory: Congressional Voting on Instruments to Control Pollution," 35 *Econ. Inquiry* 745 (1997).

[146]See McCubbins & Sullivan, supra note 144, at 306. The point that politicians prefer, all else being equal, regulatory instruments with "invisible" associated costs is related to the more general notion that legislators may seek to disguise transfers to special interests. See Stephen Coate & Stephen Morris, "On the Form of Transfers to Special Interests," 103 *J. Pol. Econ.* 1210, 1212 (1995).

[147]The potential government revenue offered by auctions and taxes is likely to be politically attractive. See Hahn & McGartland, supra note 19, at 608–09.

[148]One commentator emphasized the importance of observable costs and benefits in explaining why Wisconsin chose a largely state-funded pollution-credit program over an effluent charge. See Hahn, supra note 144, at 299. The instrument offered visible job creation, by favoring the construction of new facilities, at the expense of diffuse, less visible costs to widely distributed third parties. In contrast, the market-based alternative would have appeared to sacrifice jobs while its cost-saving benefits would have been less evident. See id. at 299–300.

[149]See Hahn & Noll, supra note 105, at 361. Of course, the reliance on voter ignorance may be countered by better informed interest groups.

[150]See id.

the powerful symbolic benefits of declaring strict standards. Moreover, it may be difficult to have market-based instruments which simultaneously "exempt" certain parties or which are "loosely" enforced.[151]

Fifth, if politicians are risk averse, they will prefer instruments involving more certain effects.[152] With respect to environmental policy instruments, uncertainty is likely to arise with respect to the distribution of costs and benefits among the affected actors and to the implementation of the legislative decision by the bureaucracy. The flexibility inherent in permits and taxes creates uncertainty about distributional effects and local levels of environmental quality.[153] Typically, legislators are more concerned with the distribution of costs and benefits than with a comparison of total benefits and costs.[154] For this reason, aggregate cost-effectiveness, perhaps the major advantage of market-based instruments, is likely to play a less significant role in the legislative calculus than whether a politician is getting the best deal possible for her constituents.[155] Moreover, politicians are likely to oppose instruments (such as tradeable permit schemes) that may induce firms to close business and relocate elsewhere, leading to localized unemployment.[156] Although there will be winners as well as losers from such relocation, potential losers are likely to be more certain of their status than potential gainers. This asymmetry creates a bias in favor of the status quo.[157]

---

[151]But see Joskow & Schmalensee, supra note 21 (examining Congressional attempts to confer benefits on particular firms within the context of the SO_2 allowance trading program).

[152]See Matthew D. McCubbins et al., "Structure and Process, Politics and Policy: Administrative Arrangements and the Political Control of Agencies," 75 *Va. L. Rev.* 431, 437 n.22 (1989) ("Legislators are likely to behave as if they are risk averse, even if they are personally risk neutral, if their constituents punish unpredictable policy choices or their reelection probability is nearly unity.")

[153]See Matthew D. McCubbins & Talbot Page, "The Congressional Foundations of Agency Performance," 51 *Pub. Choice* 173, 178 (1986).

[154]See Hahn & Stavins, supra note 104, at 38–41.

[155]See Kenneth A. Shepsle & Barry Weingast, "Political Solutions to Market Problems," 78 *Am. Pol. Sci. Rev.* 417, 418–20 (1984).

[156]See Hahn & Noll, supra note 105, at 358. Tradeable permits are more likely to be adopted in cases where the industry to be regulated is relatively dispersed and has relatively homogeneous abatement costs. See id. at 363–64. But such homogeneity also means that the gains from a market-based approach are more limited.

[157]The Clean Air Act Amendments of 1977 provide an example of legislation built upon such compromises. See id. at 361–62. Stringent standards for urban non-attainment areas were offset by industry-specific exemptions and by measures preventing relocation of urban factories to less polluted areas, the so-called PSD policy described above. See id. at 361. The winning coalition would likely not have held up under a tradeable permit scheme, which would have allowed rust belt firms to purchase pollution permits from firms in cleaner areas and thus to relocate. See id. On the other hand, a tradeable permit scheme that prevented interregional trading could presumably have protected northern factory jobs just as well.

For the same reason, grandfathering of tradeable permits is more widely to attract a winning coalition than auctions, since grandfathering allows leeway in rewarding firms and distributing the costs and benefits of regulation among jurisdictions. Several prominent researchers have examined the political process of allocating SO_2 emissions permits in the 1990 amendments to the Clean Air Act. See Joskow & Schmalensee, supra note 21. Their focus was on empirically measuring the role of interest group politics and rent-seeking in how those permits were allocated, but another point is made clear by their work: allocating permits by grandfathering can produce fairly clear "winners: and "losers" among firms and states. See id. An auction, on the other hand, would allow no such political maneuvering.

Sixth, command-and-control instruments offer Congress greater control with respect to the implementation of legislative outcomes by administrative agencies. To ensure that the interests of the winning coalition are protected in implementation, Congress may effectively prescribe administrative rules and procedures that favor one group over another.[158] In theory, such a practice protects intended beneficiaries of legislation by constraining the scope of subsequent executive intervention in implementation.[159] If stacking the deck is an important aspect of policymaking, it is more likely to be successful in the context of command-and-control legislation. Market-based instruments leave the allocation of costs and benefits up to the market, treating polluters identically.[160] Standards, on the other hand, open up possibilities for stacking the deck, by building protections in favor of particular constituencies.[161] For example, Congress might favor industry by placing the burden of proof in standard-setting on the administrative agencies, or alternatively help out environmental groups by including citizen-suit provisions allowing legal action to impel standards enforcement.

Seventh, bureaucrats are less likely to undermine the legislative decision if their preferences over policy instruments are accommodated. Administrative decisionmakers are likely to oppose decentralized instruments on several grounds: they are familiar with command-and-control approaches; market-based instruments may not require the same kinds of technical expertise that agencies have developed under command-and-control regulation; and market-based instruments imply a scaled-down role for the agency by shifting decisionmaking from the bureaucracy to private firms, undermining the agency's prestige and its staff's job security.[162]

VI. Conclusions

This Article has attempted to synthesize the seemingly diverse trends of the positive political economy literature by viewing them as relating to component parts of a political market framework. In this framework, interest groups have demands for particular instruments. Legislators, in turn, provide political support for such instruments. The demands of the various interest groups are aggregated, as are the supplies of support from individual legislators. The interaction of such aggregate demand and supply produce a legislature's equilibrium level of aggregate support, with each member simultaneously determining her effective support level. The effective support levels of the various legislators are combined, in an institutional context, to produce the legislature's choice of policy instrument.

---

[158]See McCubbins et al., supra note 152, at 244.
[159]See id. at 261–62.
[160]See Hahn & Noll, supra note 105, at 362.
[161]See id.
[162]See Hahn & Stavins, supra note 104, at 14, 21.

This framework is far from complete, since it focuses on the decisions of individual legislators, while leaving unanswered those questions of how individual (and continuous) legislator support translates into binary votes and how such support or votes are aggregated to the level of the legislature. For example, the model does not deal with the nature of competition among legislators, only briefly considers the role that congressional committees and other institutions play in structuring and influencing instrument choice, and does not explain how instrument choices are framed. Likewise, this is only a competitive legislative model as a first approximation; alternative approaches were discussed briefly. These issues represent promising avenues for extending this framework and building a workable model of instrument choice.

This Article takes a modest step toward a unified framework for positive analysis of policy instrument choice. This framework may permit greater understanding than approaches that focus almost exclusively on one component of the problem at a time. Thus, for example, if one considers only the benefits that a particular industry derives from a proposed regulatory program, one might conclude that a program will be forthcoming if the benefits are sufficiently high. Attention to questions of supply shows why this might not be the case. If the legislature prefers the status quo to the instrument demanded by the interest group, and if the legislature's aggregate supply function is sufficiently inelastic, there may be no equilibrium under which the legislature provides positive support for the demanded instrument. Indeed, the supply function of such a legislature might be above the industry demand function everywhere in the politically relevant domain. Similarly, whether a large shift in the demand for a particular instrument resulting from exogenous factors causes a comparable shift in the actual support provided by the legislature depends on the elasticity of supply. There will be relatively little change in equilibrium support if supply is inelastic, but a far larger change if supply is elastic.

This framework helps us to organize and synthesize available explorations of the four gaps which introduced the Article: three gaps between economic prescription and political reality and one gap between past and current political practices. With respect to the first—the predominance of command-and-control over market-based instruments despite the economic superiority of the latter—firms are likely to prefer command-and-control standards to auctioned permits and taxes. Standards produce rents, which can be sustainable if coupled with sufficiently more stringent requirements for new sources. In contrast, auctioned permits and taxes require firms to pay not only abatement costs to reduce pollution to a specified level, but also costs of polluting up to that level. Environmental interest groups are also likely to prefer command-and-control instruments, for philosophical, strategic, and technical reasons.

On the supply side, command-and-control standards are likely to be supplied more cheaply by legislators for several reasons: the training and experience of legislators may make them more comfortable with a direct standards approach than with market-based approaches; the time needed to learn about market-based instruments may represent significant opportunity costs; standards tend to hide the costs of pollution control while emphasizing the benefits; and standards may offer greater opportunities for symbolic politics. Finally, at the level of the legislature, command-and-control standards offer legislators a greater degree of control over the distributional effects of environmental regulation. This feature is likely to make majority coalitions easier to assemble, because legislative compromise is easier in the face of less uncertainty, and because the winning coalition can better guarantee that its interests will be served in the implementation of policy.

The second gap—that when command-and-control standards have been used, the standards for new sources have been far more stringent than those for existing sources, despite the potentially perverse incentives of this approach—can also be understood in the context of this market framework. Demand for new source standards comes from existing firms, which seek to erect entry barriers to restrict competition and protect the rents created by command-and-control standards. In turn, environmentalists often support strict standards for new sources because they represent environmental progress, at least symbolically. On the supply side, more stringent standards for new sources allow legislators to protect existing constituents and interests by placing the bulk of the pollution control burden on unbuilt factories.

Many of these same arguments can also be used to explain the third gap—the use of grandfathered tradeable permits as the exclusive market-based mechanism in the United States, despite the disadvantages of this allocation scheme. Like command-and-control standards, tradeable permits create rents; grandfathering distributes those rents to firms, while auctioning transfers the rents to government. Moreover, like stringent command-and-control standards for new sources, but unlike auctioned permits or taxes, grandfathered permits give rise to entry barriers. Thus, the rents conveyed to the private sector by grandfathered tradeable permits are, in effect, sustainable.

Moreover, grandfathered tradeable permits are likely to be less costly for legislators to supply. The costs imposed on industry are less visible and less burdensome for grandfathered permits than for auctioned permits or taxes. Also, grandfathered permits offer a greater degree of political control over the distributional effects of regulation, facilitating the formation of majority coalitions. In both these respects, grandfathered permits are somewhat analogous to command-and-control standards.

The fourth and final gap—between the recent rise of the use of market-based instruments and the lack of receptiveness such schemes had encountered in the past—can be credited to several factors. These include: the increased understanding of and familiarity with market-based instruments; niche-seeking by environmental groups interested in both environmental quality and organizational visibility; increased pollution control costs, which create greater demand for cost-effective instruments; attention to new, unregulated environmental problems without constituencies for a status quo approach; and a general shift of the political center toward a more favorable view of using the market to solve social problems. Overall, the image is one of both demand and supply functions for market-based instruments shifting rightward, leading to greater degrees of political support for these market-based instruments over time.[163]

Although some of the current preferences for command-and-control standards simply reflects a desire to maintain the regulatory status quo, the aggregate demand for a market-based instrument is likely to be greatest (and the opportunity costs of legislator support is likely to be least) when the environmental problem has not previously been regulated.[164] Hence, the prospects may be promising with respect to the introduction of such market-based instruments for new problems, such as global climate change, rather than for existing, regulated problems, such as abandoned hazardous waste sites.

Such a market framework can generate empirical work on the positive political economy of instrument choice for environmental regulation. So far, most of the academic work in this area has been theoretical; very few arguments have been subjected to empirical validation. Several of the existing empirical studies have addressed the question of why firms might support particular instruments, rather than whether firms actually provide such support. No empirical studies have constructed demand functions by determining how much firms actually are willing to pay (in the form of lobbying expenses and campaign contributions, for example) to secure particular outcomes. Similarly, no work has sought to determine the nature of demand by interest groups other than industry. In particular, the motives of environmental organizations merit more consideration. This Article discussed the possible self-interested motives of such organizations, and how their demands for particular policy instruments may be motivated by niche-seeking. Whether their expenditures in the political process comport with this theory remains essentially untested.

On the supply side, substantial impediments to empirical work remain. Existing studies have primarily attempted to determine the factors that affect legislative votes on particular programs.[165] In recent years, however, Congress has enacted a greater proportion of legislation by voice vote, rather than recorded vote. There has also been a shift from votes on comparatively narrow bills to votes on omnibus bills, which make it virtually impossible to determine a legislator's actual position with respect to specific components. Thus, the relative dearth of new data makes it difficult to perform studies of legislative voting behavior.

Legislative voting studies also share a substantial problem: distinguishing votes that reflect a legislator's true views about a bill from votes

---

[163]It is also possible that changes in some of the institutional features identified above have affected individual legislators' degrees of support. For example, changes may have occurred that led to particular legislators taking on important committee positions, thus changing their production functions, and hence their opportunity costs.

[164]See Hahn & Stavins, supra note 104, at 42.

[165]See generally Hamilton, supra note 145; see also Pashigan, supra note 135, at 551–54.

cast as part of an implicit or explicit logrolling trade, in which a legislator votes in favor of a program that she otherwise opposes in order to obtain a more valuable quid pro quo.[166] Moreover, as argued above, a vote constitutes only one component of the support that a legislator can extend to a bill. But the other components of support are less well suited to quantitative analysis.[167] Thus, in some cases, the best way to explore empirically the supply side of the equilibrium framework may be through detailed case studies of the legislative decisionmaking process.[168]

The market model will, in the end, be an imperfect and incomplete description of political behavior. But there are real advantages to considering instrument choice within this framework, and from developing more fully the details of the market model and its implications. The ultimate test of the usefulness of such a framework will be the extent to which it enables reliable predictions of the choices legislatures make, and the extent to which it facilitates the design of policy instruments that are both economically rational and politically successful.

---

[166]Compare Kau & Rubin, supra note 43, at 380–81 (attempting to measure the importance of logrolling with a conditional probability model that examined votes as a function of one another) with Jackson & Kingdon, supra note 44, at 807 (criticizing aspects of Kau and Rubin study).

[167]A pattern of votes on a series of amendments may be used as a proxy for a continuous underlying support variable, overcoming this problem. See Silberman & Durden, supra note 61, at 322–27. Such series of closely related votes, however, are rarely available, particularly in the case of instrument choice. A different approach has examined the relationship between campaign contributions and degrees of participation in committee activities. See Hall & Wayman, supra note 61, at 805–09.

[168]See generally Ackerman & Hassler, supra note 117.

30 Environmental Policy Since Earth Day I: What Have We Gained?*

A. Myrick Freeman III

A. Myrick Freeman III is William D. Shipman Research Professor of Economics, Emeritus, Bowdoin College, Brunswick, Maine.

Earth Day I, which occurred on April 22, 1970, is an appropriate starting point for an examination of the economic benefits and costs that have been realized through United States environmental policy. There were federal laws on the books dealing with air and water pollution prior to that date. But those laws placed primary responsibility for the implementation and enforcement of pollution control requirements on the states, and by 1970, they had not accomplished very much.

The first Earth Day reflected a major increase in public awareness of and concern about environmental problems. It was followed in relatively quick succession by the passage of the Clean Air Act of 1970, the formation of the Environmental Protection Agency (EPA) in December 1970, and the passage of the Federal Water Pollution Control Act of 1972, now known as the Clean Water Act. In these two acts, much more stringent pollution control objectives were established, and responsibility for establishing and enforcing pollution control requirements was shifted largely to the federal government.[1] The next ten years saw the enactment of the Safe Drinking Water Act (1974), the Toxic Substances Control Act (1976), the Resource Conservation and Recovery Act (1976), the Comprehensive Environmental Response, Compensation and Liability Act (known as Superfund) (1980) and major amendments to the Federal Insecticide, Fungicide and Rodenticide Act (1972).

Broadly speaking, the goals of environmental policy can be based either on a balancing of benefits and costs (economic efficiency) or on some other goal, such as safety, protection of human health, protection of ecosystems or

---

"Environmental Policy Since Earth Day I: What Have We Gained?" by A. Myrick Freeman III, *Journal of Economic Perspectives* 16(1):125–146 (Winter 2002).

*I am grateful to J. Clarence Davies, Lauren E. Freeman, Robert W. Hahn, DeWitt John, Paul R. Portney, V. Kerry Smith, Robert Stavins, David Vail and the editors of this journal for helpful comments and suggestions.

[1]For discussion of the context in which the Clean Air Act of 1970 and the Federal Water Pollution Control Act of 1972 were passed and the goals and aims of these acts, see Portney (2000) and Freeman (2000), respectively.

the achievement of technically feasible levels of emissions control. Economic efficiency in environmental policy requires that the marginal benefit of environmental improvement in each dimension be set equal to its marginal cost and that each environmental improvement be achieved at least cost.

In the first two major environmental laws of the early 1970s—the Clean Air Act and the Federal Water Pollution Control Act—Congress explicitly rejected the economic approach to goal setting. With regard to clean air, it emphasized protecting human health. With regard to clean water, it emphasized achieving fishable and swimmable water quality. However, more recently, Congress has written implicit or explicit economic efficiency criteria into three major environmental laws: the Toxic Substances Control Act of 1976, the Federal Insecticide, Fungicide and Rodenticide Act of 1976 and the Safe Drinking Water Act Amendments of 1996. Moreover, as a result of a series of executive orders by presidents of both parties stretching back to the Nixon administration, there has been an expanding set of requirements for federal agencies to perform economic assessments of all major proposed regulations, including an assessment of their benefits and costs (Smith, 1984; Morgenstern, 1997; Hahn, 1996, 1998, 2000). These assessments are commonly referred to as "regulatory impact assessments."

In this paper, I will review the available information on trends in the major indicators of performance of the clean air and water laws over the past three decades and what can be said about the roles of these laws in explaining these trends. My main focus will be on what these improvements are worth to people (their benefits) and what they have cost. In aggregate, federal environmental laws are imposing significant costs on the American society. The most recent comprehensive EPA survey of the annual costs of compliance with existing environmental laws, done in 1990, estimated costs in the year 1990 to be about $152 billion, rising to perhaps $225 billion in 2000 (U.S. Environmental Protection Agency, 1990).[2] (All dollar values presented in this paper are expressed in 2000 prices.) Are the benefits of these far-reaching environmental laws commensurate with their costs?

The Clean Air Act

The goals of the Clean Air Act of 1970 are expressed in two major sets of provisions. First, Congress specified that EPA should establish the maximum allowable concentrations in the air for the six major "conventional" air pollutants: sulfur dioxide, nitrogen oxides, particulate matter, carbon

---

[2]Unfortunately, the EPA has not updated its 1990 analysis, and I know of no other recent, comprehensive and credible estimate of total compliance costs for more recent years. Moreover, some analysts have substantial reservations about the methods used by the EPA to project compliance costs forward from 1990; they suspect that the costs for 2000 were substantially overestimated (Paul Portney, personal communication, July 26, 2001).

monoxide, ozone and lead. These air quality standards were to be set so as to "protect human health . . . allowing an adequate margin of safety. . . ." This language and the absence of any reference to cost have generally been interpreted as meaning that the cost of attaining the standard was not to be taken into account in setting the standard.

The second major provision regarding goals in the original Clean Air Act was the establishment of specific tailpipe emissions standards for new cars, to be met originally by 1975 and 1976. These standards entailed reductions of 84 percent to 90 percent in emissions per mile traveled from the then current uncontrolled levels. These reduction targets were based on a crude calculation of what would be required to reduce the concentrations of these pollutants to levels where no adverse health effects were expected (Seskin, 1978; Tietenberg, 2000, p. 427). In subsequent amendments to the Clean Air Act, these tailpipe emissions standards have been further tightened, but these revisions have not been based on any explicit consideration of human health or cost.

Emissions and Air Quality

To assess the effects of the Clean Air Act on emissions and air pollution levels, it is not enough to show downward trends in measures of pollution. It is necessary to compare what emissions and air quality would have been in the absence of the act with what has actually been observed. As part of a retrospective analysis of the benefits and costs of the Clean Air Act, EPA developed a model of the United States economy to generate estimates of emissions of five major air pollutants both with the act and what they would have been in the absence of the regulations promulgated under the act (U.S. Environmental Protection Agency, 1997a). Figure 1 shows the actual estimated emissions of total suspended particulate matter for the country as a whole from 1950 to 1990 (labeled "Trends") along with the predicted emissions under the "Control" (the law passed) and "No-control" (the law didn't pass) scenarios. It shows that emissions actually declined from 1950 to 1970 and that the decline accelerated during the first decade of the Clean Air Act. Also, during the 20 years covered by the act, actual and predicted emissions were approximately equal. Finally, it shows that an increasing trend in emissions was expected to occur from 1970 to 1990 in the absence of the controls imposed by the act. The two principal sources of the projected increases were electric utilities and motor vehicles.

Figure 2 shows similar estimates of actual, control and no-control emissions of nitrogen oxides from 1950 to 1990. Actual emissions were increasing over the period 1950 to 1980 and were approximately constant from 1980 to 1990. EPA projected that in the absence of the act, the rising trend of emissions would have continued throughout the period. EPA has generated similar figures for emissions trends for sulfur dioxide, volatile organic compounds and carbon monoxide (U.S. Environmental Protection Agency, 1997a). In all cases, the analysis shows that the act had a significant effect in reducing emissions. These data suggest that the observed

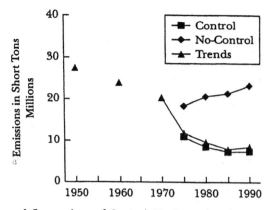

Figure 1 Comparison of Control, No-Control and Trends Total Suspended Particulates Emission Estimates

Source: U.S. Environmental Protection Agency (1997a).

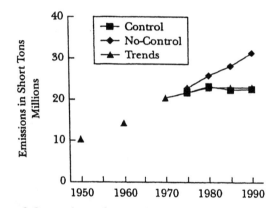

Figure 2 Comparison of Control, No-Control and Trends Nitrogen Oxides Emission Estimates

Source: U.S. Environmental Protection Agency (1997a).

decreases in the national average concentrations of these pollutants can reasonably be attributed to the Clean Air Act. For more discussion of emissions and air quality, see Portney (2000) or U.S. Environmental Protection Agency (1998).

A similar modeling exercise undertaken for the prospective analysis of the benefits and costs of the Clean Air Act Amendments of 1990 projected emissions of the major air pollutants both with and without the amendments for the years 2000 and 2010 (U.S. Environmental Protection Agency, 1999). These projections show substantial decreases in the predicted emissions of volatile organic chemicals, nitrogen oxides and sulfur dioxide.

Benefits and Costs

At the time that the original Clean Air Act was being considered by Congress in the late 1960s, no comprehensive assessments existed of the likely benefits and costs of the act—nor of any alternative changes in air pollution policy. In the ten years or so after its enactment, a number of studies were done of specific benefits from cleaner air, including health, reduced materials damage, public amenities and higher crop yields. In 1982, I published a review and synthesis of the available studies and compared my best estimate of the aggregate benefits realized as of 1978 with the costs as estimated by the Council on Environmental Quality (Freeman, 1982).[3] My estimate of benefits was based on the assumption that in the absence of the act, total emissions would have remained at the 1970 level. I considered costs and benefits separately for mobile sources—primarily motor vehicles—and for stationary sources—primarily industrial and power plants. I provided both best estimates and subjective uncertainty bounds, which were substantial.

As Table 1 shows, I found that the control of stationary sources was yielding substantial net benefits, but the emissions standards for automobiles were not. Almost 80 percent of the benefits were in the form of improvements to human health; and most of that category was due to reductions in premature mortality associated with airborne particulates. At that time, there was a great deal of controversy about the possible link between particulates and premature mortality. Now the evidence for such a link is substantially stronger, although controversy continues.

In Section 812 of the Clean Air Act Amendments of 1990, Congress expressed its concern over the economic consequences of the original Clean Air Act by directing EPA to undertake a "comprehensive analysis of the impact of this Act on the public health, economy, and the environment. . . ." This report is known as the "Retrospective Analysis." Congress also required that EPA publish an update of the original analysis and projections of future benefits and costs every two years thereafter. These reports are known as the "Prospective Analyses." Finally, Congress directed EPA to establish an independent panel of experts to review the methodologies, data and findings of the assessment.[4]

The EPA released its Retrospective Analysis (U.S. Environmental Protection Agency, 1997a) some six years after the deadline for publication. EPA modeled economic activity and the resulting emissions in the United States over the period 1970–1990 both with the Clean Air Act and under the assumption of no requirements other than those already in place in 1970. It estimated the monetary values of the reductions in the adverse effects of pollution brought about by the act. These effects included premature mortality, chronic bronchitis, other respiratory health effects, reductions in IQ associated with elevated blood lead levels in children, reductions in visibility, and damages to materials and crops.

---

[3]For further discussion of these estimates, see Portney (1990).

[4]In the interest of full disclosure, I served on this panel, which is known as the Advisory Council on Clean Air Compliance Analysis, from its inception in 1992 until 2000.

Table 1 Benefits and Costs of the Clean Air Act as of 1978
(in billions of 2000 dollars per year)

	Mobile Sources	*Stationary Sources*	*Total*
Benefits	$ 0.8	$56.5	$57.3
Costs	$20.1	$23.8	$43.8

Source: Freeman (1982).

Table 2 shows that in this analysis, the estimated benefits exceeded the costs by a ratio of about 28:1, 45:1 and 48:1 in the three years selected. The EPA also carried out Monte Carlo Analyses of benefits and reported sensitivity analyses of various categories of benefits under alternative assumptions. Even the 95 percent lower bound on benefits was an order of magnitude greater than the estimated costs. However, the EPA estimates understate the true uncertainty. The analysis of uncertainty in benefits considered only statistical uncertainties in the estimation of impacts and valuations. It did not include model uncertainties or uncertainties in estimates of emissions and changes in air quality. Also, there was no treatment of uncertainty in the cost estimates.

How plausible are these EPA figures? The EPA's estimates of average annual benefits are an order of magnitude higher than my estimates in 1982. Four factors account for most of this difference: the higher values used by EPA for the value of reducing the risk of premature mortality (based on more recent evidence); greater sensitivity of mortality to particulate matter exposures (again based on more recent evidence); different assumptions about air pollution levels in the absence of the act; and the inclusion of additional years with improved air quality.

The whole stream of benefits estimated by the EPA from 1970 to 1990 comes to $30 trillion (brought forward at 5 percent per year in 2000 dollars). Lutter and Belzer (2000) think that this amount is implausibly high, pointing out that this is "roughly the aggregate net worth of all U.S. households in 1990" (see also Portney, 2000, p. 110). But that comparison is somewhat misleading. A more accurate description would be to say that as of 1970 (the starting point of the Retrospective Analysis), the present value of the stream of future benefits from the Clean Air Act from 1971 to 1990 was about 20 percent of the present value of the future stream of personal income in the United States over that time. Many might feel that this amount is still too high. But I would argue that it is not wildly implausible that people would be willing to give up 20 percent of their income to avoid the increase in air pollution emissions that the EPA had projected for 1970 to 1990 and instead to experience the falling emissions and improving air quality associated with the act.

The EPA report does not provide separate estimates of the benefits of controlling mobile and stationary sources nor of the costs of elimi-

Table 2 Benefits and Costs of the Clean Air Act for Selected Years
(in billions of 2000 dollars per year)

	1975	1980	1990
Benefits[a]	$468	$1,225	$1,644
Costs			
Mobile Sources[b]	$7.2	$7.7	$8.8
Stationary Sources[b]	$8.1	$16.7	$23.5
Other[c]	$2.7	$2.9	$2.0
Total	$18.0	$27.4	$34.3

aTable I-5.
bTable A-9.
cTable A-9; monitoring, enforcement and R&D costs by governments.
Note: Column totals may not match due to rounding.
Source: U.S. Environmental Protection Agency (1997a).

nating lead in gasoline so that program-specific benefits and costs can be compared.[5] But some interesting lessons can still be learned. First, 75 percent of the total benefits claimed by EPA come from reducing premature mortality associated with fine particles,[6] and another 8 percent of the total benefits come from reduced incidence of chronic bronchitis from the same cause. Since fine particles come mostly from stationary sources, the analysis shows that the benefits of stationary source controls on the emissions of fine particles and their precursors (oxides of sulfur and nitrogen) very substantially outweigh the costs. Second, the benefits of eliminating lead in gasoline are about 8 percent of the total, and they accrue primarily after 1985. Even if all of the mobile source control costs were attributed to removing lead, the benefits of lead removal would substantially outweigh the costs, and probably no more than 10 percent of the mobile source control costs reported here are associated with the lead program (U.S. Environmental Protection Agency, 1985). Finally, even if all of the remaining

---

[5]This was one of the major criticisms of both the Retrospective and Prospective Reports by the Council. See the Council letters to the Administrator, U.S. Environmental Protection Agency, Science Advisory Board (1997, 1999) available at (http://www.epa.gov/sab/fisclrpt.htm). See also Lutter and Belzer (2000).

[6]Since reductions in mortality figure so importantly in the estimates of the benefits of environmental policies described in this paper, it is useful to say a few words about how the monetary value of these benefits is calculated. The typical approach is to translate individuals' willingness to pay for a small reduction in the risk of death into a value per statistical life protected. This number is the average individual's willingness to pay for a small risk reduction divided by the change in risk. For example, if the average person had a willingness to pay of $50 for a reduction in the risk of death of 0.00001, the value of a statistical life would be $5 million. For a population of 100,000, there would be on average one fewer death per year; and the sum of the individuals' willingness to pay for the risk reduction would be $5 million. For further discussions of the issues involved in the economics of valuation of lifesaving policies and reviews of recent estimates of this value, see Viscusi (1992) and U.S. Environmental Protection Agency (1999).

categories of benefits (primarily other respiratory health effects and crop damages) were attributed to controlling mobile source emissions other than lead, their costs would substantially exceed benefits.

The EPA has now published its first Prospective Analysis, which estimates the benefits and costs associated with the Clean Air Act Amendments of 1990 (U.S. Environmental Protection Agency, 1999). It also shows total benefits well in excess of costs. However, the only explicit comparison of benefits and costs for a specific program is for Title VI, which limits emissions of stratospheric ozone-depleting substances such as chlorofluorocarbons. For this title, annual benefits are estimated at $33 billion over the next 75 years compared to annual costs of only $1.8 billion. Even if one looks at only the lower end of the 95 percent confidence interval for benefits, benefits for this title would exceed costs by nearly a factor of four (Table 8-4).

The EPA's estimate of the benefits of Title VI might be biased upward for several reasons. Reducing fatalities from melanoma (a form of skin cancer) is a major component of the benefits of controlling ozone depleting substances, but there is substantial uncertainty about the relationship between ultraviolet radiation and melanoma (U.S. Environmental Protection Agency, Science Advisory Board, 1999). Also, the analysis assumes no changes in behavior to reduce exposure to ultraviolet radiation as a way of mitigating the effects of stratospheric ozone depletion. It further assumes no improvements in cure rates for melanoma due to expanded early detection programs or improved treatment. On the other hand, benefits are understated to the extent that there might be significant ecological impacts due to ultraviolet radiation that are difficult to predict and evaluate in economic terms.

For the remaining parts of the Clean Air Act Amendments of 1990, aggregate benefits exceed costs by 4 to 1. But the 95 percent lower bound on benefits is less than the estimated costs. Moreover, as in the case of the Retrospective Analysis study, the true uncertainties are understated.

Again, it is possible to get some sense of the relative costs and benefits of the stationary source and mobile source programs by digging into the numbers. Title II establishes the emissions standards for vehicles, the reformulated gasoline and clean vehicle requirements and the requirements for inspection and repair of vehicles. The annual costs of Title II in 2010 are predicted to be almost $12 billion (U.S. Environmental Protection Agency, 1999, Table 8-3). Of the estimated $145 billion in annual benefits for that year, about $139 billion are attributed to the health benefits of controlling particulate matter emissions (U.S. Environmental Protection Agency, 1999, Table H-5). Even if *all* of the remaining $6 billion in benefits could be attributed to reductions in ozone concentrations due to Title II (and they cannot be), the total cost of Title II would be twice its benefits.

But even this comparison is too crude to be of much help to policymakers, since it does not identify which components of this complex set of legislative mandates and regulations are to blame for the negative net benefits of the Title II program as a whole. What is needed is an analysis that breaks out both benefits and costs for the specific components of this program (U.S. Environmental Protection Agency, Science Advisory Board, 1999).

All of this discussion takes the numbers in these two reports at face value. But it should be no surprise that the numbers themselves are quite controversial. The most controversial feature of the analysis is the relationship between particulate matter and premature mortality used by the EPA in calculating benefits (Crandall, 1997; Lutter and Belzer, 2000; Portney, 2000). The EPA's analysis implies that about 10 percent of all mortality in the United States is associated with particulate air pollution, which, at a glance, looks high. However, the EPA predictions do have some reputable evidence behind them. They are based on a long-term cohort epidemiology study that tracked more than 500,000 subjects from 151 cities over an eight-year period (Pope et al., 1995); and an earlier, smaller study from six cities estimated an even stronger relationship between premature mortality and particulate matter (Dockery et al., 1993). More recently, the Health Effects Institute reanalyzed the data from both studies and confirmed the results (Krewski et al., 2000). The association between premature mortality and particulate matter is also consistent with a number of studies of the relationship between daily mortality rates and daily changes in air pollution. For further discussion of these issues, see U.S. Environmental Protection Agency (1997a, 1999).

Another point of controversy in these EPA studies is the value placed on reducing premature mortality. EPA used a value per life saved of $6.3 million, drawn from an analysis of a set of estimates based mostly on the wage-risk tradeoffs revealed in labor markets. The sample mean willingness to pay for a reduction in risk from the labor market studies is for a roughly 40 year-old healthy worker with a substantial remaining life expectancy. But a major fraction of the people at risk of death due to elevated particulate matter is much older, typically 70 and above. The life years to be saved are much fewer for the group experiencing the greatest reduction in the risk of premature mortality. It can be argued that the willingness to pay to reduce the risk of death for people in this group would be less than that of a typical 40-year-old.

Another issue involves the omission of indirect or general equilibrium effects in the estimate of costs. The EPA's cost estimate is the sum of annual direct expenditures on operation and maintenance and the amortized capital investments in pollution control equipment. Not included are the indirect costs that arise through general equilibrium effects in labor and capital markets that are already distorted by income and other taxes (Parry and Oates, 2000). These indirect costs could increase estimated costs by 25 percent to 35 percent (U.S. Environmental Protection Agency, Science Advisory Board, 1999).

While taking note of the issues raised here as well as of other matters, the panel that was established by Congress to review these studies characterized them as "serious, careful stud[ies] that, in general, employ[ed] sound methods and data" and produced conclusions that were "generally consistent with the weight of available evidence" (U.S. Environmental Protection Agency, Science Advisory Board, 1997, 1999).

Another way to assess the welfare implications of the Clean Air Act is to examine the regulatory impact assessments for specific regulations promulgated under the act. Hahn (2000) looked at 136 of these regulatory impact assessments carried out between 1981 and mid-1996 from eight different agencies, including those for 45 rules promulgated or proposed by EPA under the Clean Air Act. He put the regulatory impact assessments on a comparable footing by standardizing the discount rate (at 5 percent) and the valuation of reductions in premature mortality (at $5.6 million per statistical life). For the Clean Air Act, he found that in aggregate, the 35 final rules actually promulgated were estimated to produce net benefits of about $660 billion in present value terms. Almost two-thirds of this total is due to one regulation that substantially reduced the lead content of gasoline in 1985. Only 19 of the 35 rules had significant positive net benefits when evaluated separately. Similar results held for the proposed rules. Hahn argued that regulatory agencies in general are likely to overstate benefits and understate costs in these analyses, so that the true picture would be less favorable than his analysis shows.

The New Air Quality Standards for Particulate Matter and Ozone

The most significant recent policy choice made under the Clean Air Act is the revision to the air quality standards for particulate matter and ozone. The EPA is required to review the scientific evidence and consider revisions to each standard every five years. In 1996, the EPA proposed a significant tightening of these standards. In 1997, it released its regulatory impact assessment for the proposed standards. The proposal is interesting for both the legal and economic issues it raised.

The legal requirement that standards be set so as to protect human health with an adequate margin of safety can only be satisfied if the relationship between the concentration of the pollutant and the health effect has a threshold, as illustrated by function A in Figure 3. If there is no threshold, as with function B, reductions in concentrations all the way down to zero (or at least to the background environmental level) will increase the degree of protection against adverse health effects. For ozone and particulate matter, the scientific consensus is that there is no threshold (U.S. Environmental Protection Agency, Science Advisory Board, 1995; 1996). So how can the EPA comply with the mandate of the Clean Air Act?

The EPA promulgated revised standards for particulates and ozone that were above the zero or background level in July 1997. Affected groups, including the American Trucking Associations, appealed these standards to the U.S. Circuit Court. In *American Trucking Associations v. Browner* (No. 97-1441), the U.S. Circuit Court (1999) stated that "the only concentration for ozone and PM that is utterly risk free . . . is zero," "For EPA to pick

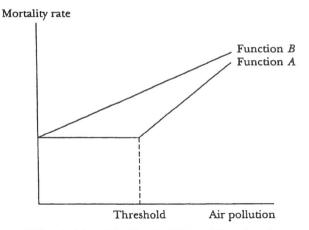

Figure 3 Threshold and No-Threshold Dose-Effect Functions

any non-zero level it must explain the degree of imperfection permitted," and "EPA . . . has failed to state intelligibly how much is too much." The court also ruled that since the Clean Air Act provided no clear basis for deciding how much air pollution to allow, it was an unconstitutional delegation of legislative power. At the same time, the appeals court rejected the plaintiffs' claim that the Clean Air Act allows the EPA to take costs into account in setting air quality standards. Both parties appealed this ruling to the Supreme Court.

Of course one intelligible way to say "how much is too much" is to take costs into account and to balance costs against benefits either formally or informally. In fact, the AEI-Brookings Joint Center for Regulatory Studies (2000) submitted a friend-of-the-court brief in the case signed by 39 prominent economists, including Kenneth Arrow, Milton Friedman and Robert Solow, arguing that point. However, in *Whitman v. American Trucking Associations* (No. 99-1257), the U.S. Supreme Court (2001) ruled that the Clean Air Act does preclude consideration of costs in setting air quality standards and that the limits on the EPA's discretion in setting standards are no more vague than in other statutes that have withstood judicial scrutiny. While this decision leaves the EPA's new standards for particulates and ozone intact, it also leaves the EPA with no guidance about how close to zero to set its pollution standards in future revisions. The U.S. Supreme Court decision has set up an awkward situation in which the EPA is required by the executive order to carry out what is, in effect, a benefit-cost analysis of alternative levels for the standards, but is bound by law to ignore the cost side of the analysis when making its decisions.

Despite this anomalous situation, the regulatory impact assessments done for the particulate and ozone standards are illuminating. The EPA reported estimates of benefits and costs of both partial attainment and full attainment of the proposed standards. This was because they could not identify control technologies that were capable of achieving the proposed standards in all parts of the country. The full attainment costs were based on the assumption that additional control technologies would become available at costs not to exceed about $10,000 per ton of emissions controlled. Although the EPA argued on the grounds of technological optimism that full attainment costs were likely overstated, it seems more likely that the costs are underestimated.

The EPA reported "low-end" and "high-end" estimates of costs and benefits, but did not report a best estimate or expected value. Neither did they incorporate uncertainties in the cost estimates. The results for partial attainment are shown in Table 3. The substantial net benefits for the proposed particulate matter standard come primarily in the form of reduced risk of premature mortality, and, as noted above, there is controversy over the magnitude of this relationship. However, if the EPA's numbers are taken at face value, there is the additional question of whether an even stricter standard might be justified on the basis of marginal benefits vs. marginal costs. The EPA did do an assessment of the benefits and costs of partial attainment of a more strict standard for particulates, but they only reported the high-end value for benefits. The high-end analysis showed positive marginal net benefits. However, the best estimate of marginal net benefits is not reported, leaving open the possibility that they might be negative.

According to the EPA numbers, the net benefits of the proposed ozone standard could be positive. But the high-end estimate of benefits is based on a recent study that shows an association between elevated ozone levels and premature mortality. This finding is even more controversial than the particulate mortality relationship and has not been found consistently in other studies. If ozone does not cause premature mortality, then the proposed ozone standard does not appear to pass a benefit-cost test. Many analysts believe that the EPA substantially underestimated the costs of partial attainment of the ozone standard (for example, Krupnick, 1997). Thus, even the high-end positive net benefits are in doubt.

The Clean Water Act

The original version of the Clean Water Act became law in 1972 and established national goals for water pollution policy: the attainment of fishable and swimmable waters by July 1, 1983, and the elimination of all discharges of pollutants into navigable waters by 1985. The means selected for achieving this goal were a system of technology-based standards to be established by the EPA and applied to discharges from all industrial and municipal (especially sewage treatment plant) sources. These standards were to define the maximum quantities of pollutants that each source would be allowed to discharge. The standards were to be based strictly on technological factors, such as what kind of pollution abatement equipment was

Table 3 The Annual Benefits and Costs of Partial Attainment of the Proposed Air Quality Standards by $PM_{2.5}$ and Ozone
(in 2000 dollars)

	Benefits	*Costs*	*Net Benefits*
$PM_{2.5}$	\$25 to \$137 billion	\$11.3 billion	\$13.7 to \$126 billion
Ozone	\$0.5 to \$2.8 billion	\$1.4 billion	−\$0.9 to \$1.4 billion

Note: $PM_{2.5}$ is fine particles less than 2.5 microns in diameter.
Source: U.S. Environmental Protection Agency (1997b).

available, rather than on water quality objectives. Under the act, regulators did not need to estimate the capacity of bodies of water to assimilate pollutants nor to consider the relationship between individual dischargers and water quality. The act called for the same effluent standards to be applied to all dischargers within classes and categories of industries, rather than a plant-by-plant determination of allowable discharges on the basis of water quality considerations.

Economics played only a minor role in this process, in the sense that the requirement to use the best feasible technology was accompanied by phrases such as "at reasonable cost." But the relationship between benefits and costs played no explicit role in determining what levels of pollution abatement would be required under the act.

Accomplishments of the Clean Water Act

Bingham et al. (1998) used a model of pollution discharges and water quality across the United States to predict how much the water quality of our rivers improved because of the Clean Water Act as of the mid-1990s, compared with a baseline that assumed no additional controls on discharges with the passage of the act. The improvement in the number of river miles meeting water quality standards for various uses is relatively small. The number of river miles meeting standards for swimming, fishing and boating increased by only 6.3 percent, 4.2 percent and 2.8 percent, respectively.

In a review of this and other evidence on accomplishments of the Clean Water Act 1972, Freeman (2000) suggests that average water quality was not too bad in 1972 and has improved only modestly since then. However, certain local areas that were quite bad in 1972 have been cleaned up dramatically. Although the Clean Water Act has done a good job on "point sources" of pollution from factories and sewage treatment plants, it has done little to address "nonpoint sources" of water pollution, like runoff from urban and agricultural areas, which seem to be increasing.

Benefits and Costs

At the time of the passage of the original version of the Clean Water Act in 1972, no assessment of the benefits and costs of its major provisions existed. During the next decade, a number of studies of various categories of benefits were carried out, especially for water-based recreation. None of these studies would meet modern standards of benefit-cost assessment. They did not, for the most part, model the relationship between reductions in discharges and improvements in water quality, nor did they establish scenarios for what water quality would have been in the absence of the provisions of the act. Nevertheless, in 1982, I reviewed a number of these studies, synthesized their results and compared them with the limited information available on the costs of water pollution control under the act (Freeman, 1982). I concluded that the total costs of meeting the 1983 and 1985 targets were very likely in excess of the benefits.

The Bingham et al. (1998) study described above also provided estimates of the benefits of the predicted water quality improvements attributable to the Clean Water Act. It used estimates of willingness to pay for various levels of improved water quality from a contingent valuation study by Carson and Mitchell (1993) to calculate the benefits of attaining water quality targets for each river.[7] Total willingness to pay for the United States urban population was about $9.9 billion per year. This figure counts only benefits of in-stream uses and the pleasure received from the control of conventional pollutants. It does not include benefits for improvements in water quality in lakes, ponds, estuaries, and marine waters, benefits from the control of toxic discharges, or benefits associated with diversionary uses of water, such as municipal water supply.

However, the EPA estimates that the annual costs of water pollution control in 1990 were about $59.7 billion per year (U.S. Environmental Protection Agency, 1990). This is not directly comparable to the estimate of willingness to pay, since the years are different and the willingness to pay covers only some of the benefits of cleaner water. However, the rough magnitude of these estimates tends to support the conclusion that the Clean Water Act does not appear to have achieved benefits commensurate with its costs.

The assessments of specific regulations promulgated under the Clean Water Act are consistent with this conclusion. Hahn's (2000) study of the regulatory impact assessments carried out between 1981 and 1996 shows that for the eight final rules analyzed, aggregate benefits were about 5 percent of aggregate costs. The same conclusion held for the four proposed rules that were analyzed. Earlier, Hahn (1996, p. 215) had reported that only one of the rules analyzed between 1990 and mid-1995 had positive net benefits.

---

[7]In a contingent valuation study, values of environmental protection are determined from responses to hypothetical survey questions about willingness to pay for specified improvements in environmental quality. For discussion of these methods, see Portney (1994) and the exchange between Diamond and Hausman (1994) and Hanemann (1994) in the *Journal of Economic Perspectives*.

The Federal Insecticide, Fungicide and Rodenticide Act, the Toxic Substances Control Act and "Unreasonable Risk"

In 1972, Congress amended the Federal Insecticide, Fungicide and Rodenticide Act to allow pesticides to be registered for use so long as the EPA found that they would not "cause unreasonable adverse effects on the environment," "taking into account the economic, social, and environmental costs and benefits" of use. The second phrase, which is part of the definition of "unreasonable adverse effects," is clearly a call to balance benefits against costs in making decisions. In 1976, Congress enacted the Toxic Substances Control Act, which included authorization to regulate the production and use of existing and new chemicals if the EPA finds that they pose an "unreasonable risk of injury to health or the environment." Because of its legislative history and the earlier language in the Federal Insecticide, Fungicide and Rodenticide Act, the Toxic Substances Control Act has also generally been interpreted as allowing a balancing of benefits and costs (Shapiro, 1990; Augustyniak, 1997).

The evidence on costs and benefits of the rules promulgated under these two acts is somewhat limited, but there are two main pieces of evidence. The first comes from Hahn's (2000) study of rules proposed or promulgated between 1981 and mid-1996. There were only six major rules promulgated during this time period under these acts. Their total present value of costs of almost $24 billion yielded only a little more than $0.3 billion in identified *and* monetized benefits. Hahn (2000, p. 44) reported that in most cases the EPA either identified benefits without quantifying them or did not identify any benefits.

The second piece of evidence is an analysis of EPA decision making under these two acts carried out by Van Houtven and Cropper (1996). This study looked at 245 decisions made between 1975 and 1989 about whether an existing pesticide could be reregistered for use. These decisions involved 19 active ingredients that are known or suspected carcinogens. The authors estimated a model to predict the probability that a specific use of an ingredient would be banned. Explanatory variables included expected numbers of cancer cases avoided for food consumers, those who apply the pesticide, and those who mix or load it, and the estimated costs of the ban. They found that the coefficients on cancer cases avoided for those who apply the pesticide and costs were both significant and of the expected sign, indicating that the EPA was considering both costs and benefits in its decisions. However, the average cost per cancer case avoided by banning uses was more than $70 million. Even if all pesticide-induced cancers were fatal, this cost is an order of magnitude larger than the value of statistical lifesaving typically used in analyses of benefits of regulation. This indicates that if a benefit-cost analysis of the whole package of decisions was done with a reasonable value of statistical life (say in the range of $3 million to $6 million), the program would fail unless other categories of benefits were quite large. However, it remains possible that certain individual decisions could pass a benefit-cost test.

Van Houtven and Cropper (1996) also conducted a similar analysis of EPA decisions under the Toxic Substances Control Act regarding banning the use of asbestos in a number of products. This analysis showed an even higher cost per cancer case avoided, suggesting that costs exceeded benefits here as well.

However, these studies give an incomplete picture of the impacts of these two laws. These laws, with their requirements for prior approval of new chemicals and pesticides, no doubt had a preventive effect that went beyond the specific approvals or denials of applications for uses. It is likely that some manufacturers chose not to develop some potential chemicals and apply for approvals on the expectation that the applications would be denied. To the extent that those potential chemicals would have had social costs that exceeded social benefits, the laws brought unmeasured economic benefits.[8] But it is also possible that these laws discouraged the development of some chemicals that would have been socially beneficial.

The Safe Drinking Water Act

The Safe Drinking Water Act was first enacted in 1974. It directed the EPA to establish safe standards for drinking water supplied by public water systems above a certain small size. These standards take the form of maximum allowable concentrations for chemical and microbial contaminants. In the first ten years after the passage of the act, the EPA promulgated only one maximum allowable concentration. Congress responded in 1986 by amending the act to include a listing of 83 contaminants and the requirement that maximum allowable concentrations be established for these contaminants within three years. While the EPA was not able to meet the three-year deadline, the task is now essentially complete.

For these water quality standards, are the benefits in the forms of improved human health and reduced risk of disease commensurate with costs of meeting these standards? The EPA was not required by law to address this question, and I know of no comprehensive assessment of this question. However, some revealing partial evidence is available.

A study of the results of the Safe Drinking Water Act done for the EPA by Raucher et al. (1993) sheds some light on the subject. Their analysis was limited to contaminants posing a risk of cancer. They first reported costs and cancer deaths avoided for the program as a whole. The result is a cost per cancer death avoided of about $4.7 million. This value compares favorably with the value of statistical life used by the EPA in several recent assessments ($6.3 million), which suggests that the benefits of the maximum allowable concentrations for carcinogens exceed the costs.

---

[8]I am indebted to J. Clarence Davies for suggesting this point.

The authors then reported costs and deaths avoided for the ten most cost-effective contaminants (primarily volatile organic compounds). The cost per death avoided for these contaminants was an even more favorable $2.9 million, well below the EPA's value of statistical life. However, from these data it is possible to estimate the cost per life saved associated with the maximum allowable concentrations for the remaining carcinogens (more than 60 substances). This amount is a very high $127 million per death avoided, suggesting that the costs for these maximum allowable concentrations substantially exceeded their benefits. However, this calculation does ignore any benefits associated with reducing health effects other than cancer for these substances and also ignores the benefits and costs of reducing exposures to those substances that do not cause cancer.

Hahn's (2000) analysis of regulatory impact assessments carried out between 1981 and 1996 includes five final rules and three proposed rules under the Safe Drinking Water Act. Both the proposed and final rules taken as a group show aggregate benefits exceeding costs. But almost all of the benefits of the final rules are attributable to only one rule—regarding lead in drinking water (see also Levin, 1997). Again, it is thus possible to infer that the benefits are less than the costs for the other rules.

Amendments to the Safe Drinking Water Act in 1996 directed EPA to undertake an economic analysis of future proposed maximum allowable concentrations to determine if the benefits justify the costs and to adjust the maximum allowable concentrations in light of this analysis as necessary. Thus, the Safe Drinking Water Act joined the Federal Insecticide, Fungicide and Rodenticide Act and Toxic Substances Control Act as the only environmental laws that explicitly call for consideration of benefits and costs. The EPA has now finalized a rule for a maximum allowable concentration for radon.[9] As Hahn and Burnett (2001) point out, the EPA's own data show a benefit-cost ratio of only about 0.3 for this rule, and deficiencies in the EPA's analysis likely result in an overestimate of the benefits of the rule.

The Comprehensive Environmental Response, Compensation and Liability Act: Superfund

The Comprehensive Environmental Response, Compensation and Liability Act, commonly known as Superfund, was enacted in 1980 to provide for the cleanup of hazardous waste sites already in existence. Thanks to the Superfund Amendments and Reauthorization Act of 1986, more stringent cleanup requirements are in place today. The primary focus of the cleanup requirements is the protection of human health. The EPA investigates

---

[9]In the closing days of the Clinton administration, the EPA established a new, more strict maximum allowable concentration for arsenic. But within weeks of taking office, the Bush administration withdrew the rule for further study and review of the scientific and economic bases for the standard.

contaminated sites, estimates risks to health, and for those sites deemed to pose a risk to health, establishes a remediation plan based on criteria set forth in the act. Remediation plans are not subjected to a benefit-cost analysis.

Hamilton and Viscusi (1999a, b) have carried out a comprehensive analysis of the risks, costs and cost-effectiveness of the remediation plans for a selected sample of 150 Superfund sites in 1991–1992. The best single indicator of the relationship between the benefits and costs of remediation at these sites is Hamilton and Viscusi's estimates of the cost per cancer case avoided by the selected remediation plan. They found that for the 145 sites for which data are available, the mean cost is about $3.5 million per case avoided. Making the assumption that all cancers are fatal, this implies that a benefit-cost analysis using a value of anything above $3.5 million per death avoided would show that the program was economically justified. However, this result occurs because the aggregate data are dominated by a relatively small number of sites with low costs per cancer case avoided. About 70 percent of the sites have estimated costs per case avoided that are greater than about $112 million, implying that unless there are significant benefits in such categories as avoiding noncancer health effects and ecological and natural resource effects, the majority of the remediation plans are not economically justified, at least not at their present scope and degree of cleanup.

Conclusions

We have looked at the available evidence concerning the benefits and costs of the six major environmental laws enacted or substantially amended since Earth Day I: the Clean Air Act, the Clean Water Act, the Federal Insecticide, Fungicide and Rodenticide Act, the Toxic Substances Control Act, the Safe Drinking Water Act and the Comprehensive Environmental Response, Compensation and Liability Act. It is not a particularly useful exercise to attempt to aggregate all of the benefit and cost data reviewed here to arrive at a total net benefit estimate to try to see whether environmental regulation as a whole has been positive or negative. There have been some winners and some losers. The important question is what changes can we make to the current set of policies to improve the net benefits.

Among the winners in terms of net economic benefits are the following: the removal of lead from gasoline; controlling particulate matter air pollution; reducing the concentration of lead in drinking water under the Safe Drinking Water Act; the setting of maximum allowable concentrations on some volatile organic compounds under the Safe Drinking Water Act; the cleanup of those hazardous waste sites with the lowest cost per cancer case avoided under Superfund; and probably also the control of emissions of chlorofluorocarbons. These winners share the common characteristics of involving threats to human health, especially mortality, and widespread exposures of people. Even in the case of lead, which is primarily known for its toxic effect on nervous systems, a major portion of the monetizable benefits of controlling lead comes from the reduction in hypertension and the associated risk of cardiovascular disease in adults.

The environmental rules that appear to be losers in terms of net economic benefits include the following: mobile source air pollution control; much of the control of discharges into the nation's waterways, with the exception of some lakes and rivers that were especially polluted; and many of the regulations, standards and cleanup decisions taken under the Federal Insecticide, Fungicide and Rodenticide Act, the Toxic Substances Control Act, the Safe Drinking Water Act and Superfund.

Before turning to the policy implications of these findings, we need to identify some qualifications and caveats. All benefit-cost analyses have uncertainties and omissions. For example, there may be important effects of pollutants on human health that have so far escaped detection. If this is the case, present estimates of the health benefits of environmental cleanup are biased downward. Also, omitted benefits could include the protection of ecological systems and their services, preservation of biodiversity and what are called "nonuse" or "existence" values, meaning the value that people place on a cleaner environment as a goal in itself. Many natural scientists argue that ecosystem and biodiversity values are not given sufficient attention by economists (for example, Daily, 1997). But there is very limited evidence concerning the effects of present-day environmental policy decisions on ecological systems and biodiversity and these values were not a principal focus of most of the environmental laws considered here.

On the cost side, it is sometimes argued that costs are systematically overestimated because of the inability to anticipate the technological improvements in pollution control, process change and input substitution that are stimulated by the requirements of the regulations themselves (for example, Porter, 1991; Porter and van der Linde, 1995). On the other hand, Hahn (1996) argues that agencies have systematic incentives to underestimate costs and to overestimate benefits. Harrington, Morgenstern and Nelson (2000) found a limited number of cases of underestimation of costs but for half of the rules they studied, they found overestimation of costs to be the case. Moreover, at least the most extreme versions of technological optimism regarding pollution control are not supported by the evidence (Palmer, Oates and Portney, 1995; Jaffe et al., 1995).

The first and perhaps most important policy implication of this analysis is to emphasize that virtually all environmental policies and programs could be improved by making them more cost-effective, that is, by finding ways to reduce the costs of attaining given targets.

One method to improve cost-effectiveness is to replace command and control policy instruments with market-based incentives, such as tradeable emissions permits, emission taxes and deposit-refund systems. The potential for effluent taxes, fuel taxes and tradeable permits to improve cost-effectiveness is especially relevant for water and mobile source air pollution control. For further discussion of the present potential of market-based environmental tools, see Stavins (2000), Portney (2000) and Freeman (2000). The cost-effectiveness of regulatory programs can also be improved by scaling back or eliminating specific regulations and standards where the costs per unit of measurable performance (for example, cost per cancer case avoided) are high and adopting more strict standards where costs per unit of performance are low. See, for example, Hahn (1996, 2000), Hamilton and Viscusi (1999b) and Raucher et al. (1993).

Another way to improve the economic performance of environmental policy is to give more weight to the comparison of benefits and costs, especially at the margin, in making environmental choices. As we have seen, some laws preclude balancing of costs and benefits in setting standards. But even where balancing is allowed or required—as in the Federal Insecticide, Fungicide and Rodenticide Act, the Toxic Substances Control Act and the Safe Drinking Water Act—the economic performance of environmental regulation has been spotty at best. Standards and regulations have been adopted even when realistic assessments show that the benefits are less than the costs. At a minimum, this result should make one skeptical of the argument that environmental regulatory agencies have been "captured" by polluting interests. Indeed, Hahn (1996) has argued that the substantial number of cases where environmental costs exceed benefits is evidence that regulatory agencies have been successful in increasing their power and expanding their budgets and roles in the American economy.

However, there are alternative explanations for what appears to be overregulation. One is that there may be benefits of regulation that economics has not been able to identify and quantify. It may be that these benefits are recognized by environmental decision makers and by the voters who apparently support these policies. Another way to put this is to argue that the American people, by their willingness to continue to support environmental programs that show measurable benefits that are less than costs, are revealing that they are willing to pay more for these environmental improvements than the amount captured by conventional measures of benefits.

Another possibility is that voters believe that at least for the policies they support, the costs are borne by others, the "black hat polluters." If this is the case, then the challenge for policymakers is to describe the opportunity costs of excess regulation to those who actually bear them and commit themselves to maintaining or improving standards in those areas where benefits demonstrably exceed costs. A public perception that the benefits of environmental protection can be realized while costs are borne by others will sooner or later collide with the reality that for the more intractable of our environmental problems—for example, the pollution and congestion externalities associated with private automobile transportation—we all will have to pay for any benefits we expect to receive.

It is difficult to know whether the American public would support a set of environmental policies that is economically rational by conventional measures. The challenge for policymakers may be to build credibility for cost-benefit analysis by making a public commitment to maintaining or improving environmental standards in those areas where benefits demonstrably exceed costs. By offering vocal support for environmental policies that do provide net benefits, and perhaps giving the benefit of the doubt to cases where the measureable net benefits are close to zero, policymakers may be able to build credibility when they need to argue that certain regulations have opportunity costs in excess of their benefits.

References

AEI-Brookings Joint Center for Regulatory Studies. 2000. "Brief *Amici Curiae* in American Trucking Associations, Inc., et al. v. Carol Browner." July 21. Available at http://www.aei.brookings.org/publications/briefs/brief_00_01.pdf.

Augustyniak, Christine M. 1997. "Asbestos," in *Economic Analysis at EPA: Assessing Regulatory Impact.* Richard D. Morgenstern, ed. Washington, D.C.: Resources for the Future, pp. 171–203.

Bingham, Tayler H. et al. 1998. *A Benefits Assessment of Water Pollution Control Programs Since 1972.* Revised draft report to the U.S. Environmental Protection Agency. Research Triangle Park, N.C.: Research Triangle Institute.

Carson, Richard T. and Robert Cameron Mitchell. 1993. "The Value of Clean Water: The Public's Willingness to Pay for Boatable, Fishable, and Swimmable Quality Water." *Water Resources Research.* 29:7, pp. 2445–54.

Crandall, Robert W. 1997. "The Costly Pursuit of the Impossible." *The Brookings Review.* Summer, 15:3, pp. 41–47.

Daily, Gretchen C., ed. 1997. *Nature's Services: Societal Dependence on Natural Ecosystems.* Washington, D.C.: Island Press.

Diamond, Peter A. and Jerry A. Hausman. 1994. "Contingent Valuation: Is Any Number Better than No Number?" *Journal of Economic Perspectives.* Fall, 8:4, pp. 45–64.

Dockery, D. W. et al. 1993. "An Association Between Air Pollution and Mortality in Six U.S. Cities." *New England Journal of Medicine.* 329:24, pp. 1753–59.

Freeman, A. Myrick III. 1982. *Air and Water Pollution Control: A Benefit-Cost Assessment.* New York: John Wiley.

Freeman, A. Myrick III. 2000. "Water Pollution Policy," in *Public Policies for Environmental Protection, Second Edition.* Paul R. Portney and Robert N. Stavins, eds. Washington, D.C.: Resources for the Future, pp. 97–149.

Hahn, Robert W. 1996. "Regulatory Reform: What Do the Government's Numbers Tell Us?" in *Risks, Costs, and Lives Saved: Getting Better Results from Regulation.* Robert Hahn, ed. New York: Oxford University Press, pp. 208–53.

Hahn, Robert W. 1998. "Policy Watch: Government Analysis of the Benefits and Costs of Regulation." *Journal of Economic Perspectives.* Fall, 12:4, pp. 201–10.

Hahn, Robert W. 2000. *Reviving Regulatory Reform: A Global Perspective.* Washington, D.C.: AEI-Brookings Joint Center for Regulatory Studies.

Hahn, Robert W. and Jason K. Burnett. 2001. "The EPA's Radon Rule: A Case Study in How Not to Regulate Risks." AEI-Brookings Joint Center for Regulatory Studies Regulatory Analysis 01-01. January.

Hamilton, James T. and W. Kip Viscusi. 1999a. "How Costly is 'Clean'? An Analysis of the Benefits and Costs of Superfund Remediations." *Journal of Policy Analysis and Management.* 18:1, pp. 2–27.

Hamilton, James T. and W. Kip Viscusi. 1999b. *Calculating Risks: The Spatial and Political Dimensions of Hazardous Waste Policy.* Cambridge, Mass.: MIT Press.

Hanemann, W. Michael. 1994. "Valuing Environment Through Contingent Valuation." *Journal of Economic Perspectives.* Fall, 8:4, pp. 19–43.

Harrington, Winston, Richard D. Morgenstern and Peter Nelson. 2000. "On the Accuracy of Regulatory Cost Estimates." *Journal of Policy Analysis and Management.* 19:2, pp. 297–322.

Jaffe, Adam B. et al. 1995. "Environmental Regulation and the Competitiveness of U.S. Manufacturing: What Does the Evidence Tell Us?" *Journal of Economic Literature.* 33:1, pp. 132–63.

Krewski, D. et al. 2000. *Reanalysis of the Harvard Six Cities Study and the American Cancer Society Study of Particulate Air Pollution and Mortality.* Cambridge, Mass.: Health Effects Institute.

Krupnick, Alan J. 1997. "The Proposed NAAQS for PM and Ozone." Testimony before the Subcommittee on Clean Air, Wetlands, Private Property and Nuclear Safety, Committee on Environment and Public Works, U.S. Senate, Washington, D.C.

Levin, Ronnie. 1997. "Lead in Drinking Water," in *Economic Analysis at EPA: Assessing Regulatory Impact.* Richard D. Morgenstern, ed. Washington, D.C.: Resources for the Future, pp. 205–32.

Lutter, Randall and Richard B. Belzer. 2000. "EPA Pats Itself on the Back." *Regulation.* 23:3, pp. 23–8.

Morgenstern, Richard D. 1997. *Economic Analysis at EPA: Assessing Regulatory Impact.* Washington, D.C.: Resources for the Future.

Palmer, Karen, Wallace E. Oates and Paul R. Portney. 1995. "Tightening Environmental Standards: The Benefit-Cost or the No-Cost Paradigm?" *Journal of Economic Perspectives.* Winter, 9:1, pp. 129–32.

Parry, Ian W.H. and Wallace E. Oates. 2000. "Policy Analysis on the Presence of Distorting Taxes." *Journal of Policy Analysis and Management.* 19:4, pp. 603–13.

Pope, C.A. et al. 1995. "Particulate Air Pollution as a Predictor of Mortality in a Prospective Study of U.S. Adults." *American Journal of Respiratory and Critical Care Medicine.* 151:3, pp. 669–74.

Porter, Michael E. 1991. "America's Green Strategy." *Scientific American.* 264:4, p. 168.

Porter, Michael E. and Claas van der Linde. 1995. "Toward a New Conception of the Environment-Competitiveness Relationship." *Journal of Economic Perspectives.* Fall, 9:4, pp. 97–118.

Portney, Paul R. 1990. "Air Pollution Policy," in *Public Policies for Environmental Protection.* Paul R. Portney, ed. Washington, D.C.: Resources for the Future, pp. 27–96.

Portney, Paul R. 1994. "The Contingent Valuation Debate: Why Economists Should Care." *Journal of Economic Perspectives.* Fall, 8:4, pp. 1–17.

Portney, Paul R. 2000. "Air Pollution Policy," in *Public Policies for Environmental Protection, Second Edition.* Paul R. Portney and Robert N. Stavins, eds. Washington, D.C.: Resources for the Future, chapter 4.

Portney, Paul R. 2001. Personal Communication. July 26.

Raucher, Robert S. et al. 1993. *An Evaluation of the Federal Drinking Water Program under the Safe Drinking Water Act as Amended in 1986.* Prepared for the American Water Works Association by RCG/Hagler, Bailly, Inc., Boulder, Colo.

Seskin, Eugene P. 1978. "Automobile Air Pollution Policy," in *Current Issues in U.S. Environmental Policy.* Paul R. Portney, ed. Baltimore, Md.: Johns Hopkins University Press, pp. 68–104.

Shapiro, Michael. 1990. "Toxic Substances Policy," in *Public Policies for Environmental Protection*. Paul R. Portney, ed. Washington, D.C.: Resources for the Future, pp. 195–241.

Smith, V. Kerry, ed. 1984. *Environmental Policy Under Reagan's Executive Order: The Role of Benefit-Cost Analysis*. Chapel Hill, N.C.: University of North Carolina Press.

Stavins, Robert N. 2000. "Market-Based Environmental Policies," in *Public Policies for Environmental Protection, Second Edition*. Paul R. Portney and Robert N. Stavins, eds. Washington, D.C.: Resources for the Future, chapter 3.

Tietenberg, Tom. 2000. *Environmental and Natural Resource Economics, Fifth Edition*. Reading, Mass.: Addison-Wesley.

U.S. Circuit Court of Appeals. 1999. *American Trucking Associations v. Browner*. No. 97-1441, May 26.

U.S. Environmental Protection Agency. 1985. *Costs and Benefits of Reducing Lead in Gasoline*. Washington, D.C.: Office of Policy Analysis.

U.S. Environmental Protection Agency. 1990. *Environmental Investments: The Cost of Clean Environment*. Washington, D.C.: Office of Policy Analysis.

U.S. Environmental Protection Agency. 1997a. *The Benefits and Cost of the Clean Air Act: 1970–1990*. Washington, D.C.: Office of Policy Analysis.

U.S. Environmental Protection Agency. 1997b. *Regulatory Import Assessment for Particulate Matter and Ozone NAAQS and Proposed Regional Haze Rule*. Washington, D.C.: Office of Policy Analysis.

U.S. Environmental Protection Agency. 1998. *National Air Quality and Emissions and Trends Report*. Research Triangle Park, N.C.: Office of Air Quality Planning and Standards.

U.S. Environmental Protection Agency. 1999. *The Benefits and Cost of the Clean Air Act: 1990–2010*. Washington, D.C.: Office of Policy Analysis.

U.S. Environmental Protection Agency, Science Advisory Board, Clean Air Science Advisory Committee. 1995. *Letter to Honorable Carol Browner, Administrator of U.S. EPA (EPA-SAB-CASAC-LTR-96-002)*. Washington, D.C.: U.S. Environmental Protection Agency.

U.S. Environmental Protection Agency, Science Advisory Board, Clean Air Science Advisory Committee. 1996. *Letter to Honorable Carol Browner, Administrator of U.S. EPA (EPA-SAB-CASAC-LTR-96-003)*. Washington, D.C.: U.S. Environmental Protection Agency.

U.S. Environmental Protection Agency, Science Advisory Board, Advisory Council on Clean Air Act Compliance Analysis. 1997. *Letter to Honorable Carol Browner, Administrator of U.S. EPA (EPA-SAB-COUNCIL-LTR-97-008)*. Washington, D.C.: U.S. Environmental Protection Agency.

U.S. Environmental Protection Agency, Science Advisory Board, Advisory Council on Clean Air Act Compliance Analysis. 1999. *Letter to Honorable Carol Browner, Administrator of U.S. EPA (EPA-SAB-COUNCIL-ADV-00-002)*. Washington, D.C.: U.S. Environmental Protection Agency.

U.S. Supreme Court. 2001. *Whitman v. American Trucking Associations*. No. 99-1257, February 27, 2001.

Van Houtven, George and Maureen L. Cropper. 1996. "When is a Life Too Costly to Save? The Evidence from U.S. Environmental Regulations." *Journal of Environmental Economics and Management*. 30:3, pp. 344–68.

Viscusi, W. Kip. 1992. "The Value of Risks to Life and Health." *Journal of Economic Literature*. 31:4, pp. 1912–46.

31 Environmental Regulation in the 1990s: A Retrospective Analysis*

Robert W. Hahn
Sheila M. Olmstead
Robert N. Stavins

Robert W. Hahn is Director, AEI-Brookings Joint Center for Regulatory Studies, and Resident Scholar, American Enterprise Institute. Sheila M. Olmstead is Assistant Professor of Environmental Economics, School of Forestry and Environmental Studies, Yale University. Robert M. Stavins is Albert Pratt Professor of Business and Government, John F. Kennedy School of Government, Harvard University, and University Fellow of Resources for the Future.

1. Introduction

This Article addresses the influence of economics on environmental and resource policy-making during the 1990s. We focus on the Clinton administration and highlight important trends and changes in the impacts of economic concepts such as efficiency, cost-effectiveness and distributional equity.[1]

"Environmental Regulation in the 1990s: A Retrospective Analysis," by Robert W. Hahn, Sheila M. Olmstead, and Robert N. Stavins, *Harvard Environmental Law Review*, 27:377–415 (2003).

*Helpful comments on a previous version of this Article were provided by: Arthur Fraas, George Frampton, Myrick Freeman, José Gómez-Ibáñez, Alan Krupnick, Randall Lutter, Albert McGartland, Richard Morgenstern, Paul Portney, Richard Schmalensee, Jason Shogren, and Murray Weidenbaum. Research assistance was provided by Simone Berkowitz, and financial support was provided by the Savitz Family Fund for Environment and Natural Resource Policy and the Ford Fund at Harvard University. The authors alone are responsible for any remaining errors. A longer, related paper by Sheila M. Cavanagh et al. includes comprehensive tables describing specific environmental and resource statutes and regulations. See SHEILA M. CAVANAGH (OLMSTEAD) ET AL. NATIONAL ENVIRONMENTAL POLICY DURING THE CLINTON YEARS (John F. Kennedy School of Government, Center for Business and Government, Regulatory Policy Program Working Paper RPP-2001-10, 2001). For surveys of environmental and resource policy in the 1980s, see PAUL R. PORTNEY, NATURAL RESOURCES AND THE ENVIRONMENT: THE REAGAN APPROACH (1984) and W. Kip Viscusi, *Health and Safety Regulation*, in AMERICAN ECONOMIC POLICY IN THE 1980s 453 (Mar.in Feldstein ed., 1994).

[1]We follow the standard definition of an "efficient" environmental policy as being one which involves a target—such as a fifty percent reduction in sulfur dioxide ("SO_2") emissions—that maximizes the difference between social benefits and social costs (i.e., a target level at which marginal benefits and marginal costs are equated). By "cost-effecti e" policies, we refer to those which take (possibly inefficient) targets as given by the political process, but achieve those targets with policy instruments—such as a tradeable permit system in the SO_2 case—that minimize aggregate costs. Assessments of the "distributional" implications of environmental policies include analyses of the distributions of costs and benefits.

The continuing controversy over the appropriate role for economics in environmental policy design makes this a particularly good time to analyze environmental policy during the 1990s from an economic perspective.

We note that the role of efficiency as a criterion for assessing environmental and natural resource rules and regulations was very controversial in the Clinton administration, while efficiency emerged as a central goal of the regulatory reform movement in Congress. Cost-effectiveness was embraced by both the administration and Congress in the 1990s as a criterion for adopting specific policy instruments. In addition, the decade witnessed an increasing role for equity concerns as a consideration in environmental policy-making.

The attention given to environmental and natural resource issues in the United States has grown over the past several decades, a period during which greater consideration has been given to economic analysis of laws and regulations intended to protect the environment or improve natural resource management. Although several of the major environmental statutes are ambivalent about the role of economic analysis, in some cases prescribing it, in others proscribing it, a series of presidential executive orders has called for a larger role for economic analysis.

Administrations can have substantial influence over the application of economics to environmental policy through a variety of mechanisms. The conventional wisdom in the United States is that Democratic administrations are predisposed toward more active environmental regulation and less inclined toward economic analysis of environmental policy than their Republican counterparts. The Clinton administration, for example, is widely perceived to have been predisposed to environmental quality and resource preservation and less supportive of economic analysis of such issues, in comparison with its Republican predecessor and successor (the administrations of George H. W. Bush and George W. Bush, respectively).

In fact, environmental and natural resource policy in the 1990s was characterized by continuity and by change. Two important trends that began in the 1970s continued through the 1990s—environmental quality improved, and environmental targets were made more stringent. In some cases, these improvements can be linked directly to federal policies and regulations; in others, such linkage has yet to be established.[2]

Trends in emissions of Clean Air Act criteria air pollutants are described in Table 1. Emissions of some of these pollutants decreased significantly during the decade.[3] Although a number of studies show continued improvements

---

[2]In order to attribute environmental quality improvements to specific policies, we must compare actual emissions to what they would have been in the absence of policies.

[3]*See* U.S. EPA PUB. No. 454/R-00-002, NATIONAL AIR POLLUTANT EMISSION TRENDS 1900–1998 (2000) [hereinafter EPA, 1900–1998 TRENDS REPORT]; U.S. EPA PUB. No. 454/R-00-003, NATIONAL AIR QUALITY AND EMISSION TRENDS REPORT, 1998 (2000). Real improvements in environmental quality would be measured by changes in exposure and resulting changes in human morbidity and mortality, ecosystem health, etc. Improvements in emissions are not, themselves, measures of environmental quality improvements, although they may be highly correlated with such improvements.

Table I U.S. Emissions of Seven Major Pollutants, 1970–1998

Year	SO_2	NO_x	VOCs	CO	Lead	PM_{10}	$PM_{2.5}$
1970	100	100	100	100	100	N/A	N/A
1980	83	117	85	91	34	N/A	N/A
1989	75	114	73	82	3	100	N/A
1990	76	115	68	76	2	54	100
1991	74	116	68	78	2	53	97
1992	73	118	67	75	2	53	96
1993	72	119	67	76	2	50	92
1994	70	121	70	79	2	56	100
1995	62	119	67	72	2	48	90
1996	61	118	60	74	2	61	103
1997	63	119	61	73	2	63	107
1998	63	117	58	69	2	64	105

Notes: Figures are indexed from EPA data, with 1970 aggregate U.S. emissions equal to 100 for all pollutants except PM_{10} (1989=100) and $PM_{2.5}$ (1990=100). Data for 1970 and 1980 are drawn from U.S. EPA, Pub. No. 454/R-00-002, NATIONAL AIR POLLUTANT EMISSION TRENDS 1900–1998 (2000). Data for 1989, 1991–1995, and 1997 are drawn from U.S. EPA, Pub. No. 454/R-00-003, NATIONAL AIR QUALITY AND EMISSIONS TRENDS REPORT, 1998 (2000). Data for 1990, 1996, and 1998 appear in both reports. (Data for PM_{10} differ between the two reports—for this pollutant, the 1998 report data were used exclusively.) Data for particulate matter ("PM") include only directly emitted PM. No figures are shown for PM_{10} and $PM_{2.5}$ in 1970 or 1980; while estimates exist, they do not include natural sources, agriculture, forestry, fugitive dust and other sources which together comprise almost ninety percent of directly emitted PM_{10} and almost seventy percent of directly emitted $PM_{2.5}$ in 1990.

in water quality during the 1990s,[4] following the pattern of thirty-year trends, improvements in water quality during the 1990s were both less dramatic and more difficult to measure than improvements in air quality.[5]

Emissions of many air and water pollutants declined dramatically from 1970 to 1990, when the "low-hanging fruit" among air and water quality problems were being addressed.[6] For example, air emissions of lead, which declined significantly due to the shift to unleaded gasoline (completed in

---

[4]*See* TAYLER H. BINGHAM ET AL., A BENEFITS ASSESSMENT OF WATER POLLUTION CONTROL PROGRAMS SINCE 1972 (U.S. EPA, revised draft report, 1998); Myrick A. Freeman, *Water Pollution Policy, in* PUBLIC POLICIES FOR ENVIRONMENTAL PROTECTION 169 (Paul R. Portney and Robert N. Stavins eds., 2000); Myrick A. Freeman, *Environmental Policy Since Earth Day I—What Have We Gained?*, 16 J. ECON. PERSP., Winter 2002, at 125.

[5]Improvements in water quality have been achieved largely through point source regulation. James Boyd, The New Face of the Clean Water Act: A Critical Review of the EPA's Proposed TMDL Rules 4 (Resources for the Future, Discussion Paper 00-12, Mar. 2000). Non-point source pollution in the form of runoff from cities and agricultural areas may actually have increased during the 1990s. Freeman, *supra* note 4, at 137.

[6]Important exceptions are emissions of toxic substances to air and water. Unlike conventional pollutants, decreases in air and water toxins emissions during the 1990s were likely greater than decreases in previous decades. The Toxics Release Inventory ("TRI") data show a decrease in toxic discharges to air of forty percent, and a decrease in toxic discharges to surface water of sixty-seven percent, between 1990 and 1994. Environmental Defense, *Toxics Release Inventory Data Summary, at* http://www.scorecard.org/env-releases/us.tcl#data_summary (last visited Apr. 25, 2003) (on file with the Harvard Environmental Law Review).

1987), saw little further improvement during the 1990s.[7] Pollutant emissions to water declined dramatically during the 1970s and 1980s due to expanded municipal sewage treatment, a shift that was largely completed before 1990.[8]

In addition to environmental quality, the stringency of environmental targets continued to increase during the 1990s. An important example was the Clinton administration's 1997 National Ambient Air Quality Standards ("NAAQS") for ambient ozone and particulate matter. The new NAAQS were far stricter than previous standards, carrying substantial potential benefits and costs.

Public policy affecting natural resource management during the Clinton years was heavily weighted toward environmental protection. The administration proposed initiatives to reduce subsidies for private resource extraction on public lands, but Congress was not receptive. The administration did, however, shift U.S. Forest Service ("USFS") priorities away from timber production to resource protection, placing some sixty million acres of federal forests off limits to road building. President Clinton also designated more than twenty new national monuments, thereby restricting the use of six million additional acres of federal lands.[9]

Our ability to offer sound judgments about the influence of Clinton-era policies on environmental quality improvements is restricted by two problems. First, the fact that quality improvements occurred contemporaneously with the term of a particular administration or legislature is not proof that policies promulgated during this term actually caused those quality improvements. With the exception of reduced emissions of criteria air pollutants in the 1990s, we find no studies that establish such a causal relationship between 1990s policies and environmental quality changes.[10]

Second, a fundamental issue that would confront any assessment of policy initiatives associated with a particular administration is the choice of an appropriate basis of comparison for evaluating policy initiatives—a counterfactual. It might appear reasonable to contrast first-term Clinton administration initiatives with what might have been anticipated from a hypothetical second-term administration of George H. W. Bush. But what would be the appropriate counterfactual for the second Clinton term?

For these reasons, establishing a causal relationship between improvements in environmental quality or resource management and the policies of any particular administration or Congress is difficult, if not impossible, and is not attempted here. Instead, we apply economic criteria for policy assessment—principally efficiency, cost-effectiveness and distributional equity.

The combined trends of more stringent standards for air and water quality and increased private land-use restrictions and protections for public

---

[7]*See* EPA, 1900–1998 Trends Report, *supra* note 3.

[8]Boyd, *supra* note 5, at 3. The percentage of the U.S. population connected to wastewater treatment systems increased from forty-two percent to seventy-four percent between 1970 and 1985.

[9]Reed McManus, *Six Million Sweet Acres*, Sierra, Sept.–Oct. 2001.

[10]Based on EPA modeling of trends in emissions within and without the Clean Air Act, the observed decreases in emissions of criteria air pollutants between 1990 and 2000 can be attributed to the Clean Air Act and its amendments. Freeman, *supra* note 4, at 127–28.

lands have brought both increased benefits and an increasing price tag. As a result, economic concepts like benefit-cost analysis and the selection of least-cost environmental and natural resource regulations have received more attention since the late 1980s than they did in the early years of U.S. federal environmental regulation.

We note in this Article that, rather than a simple split along party lines, politicians in the 1990s endorsed the use of the efficiency criterion where its results were likely to coincide with their own ideological agendas. For example, Congress during the 1990s supported improvements in the efficiency of pollution control standards, which would have lightened regulatory burdens on some industries, and did not support increased efficiency in natural resource management, where subsidy reduction would have hurt communities dependent on resource extraction in the conservative West. The administration, likewise, promoted the reduction of natural resource extraction subsidies, but was unsupportive of benefit-cost analysis of pollution control regulations; both viewpoints were consistent with those of supporters in the environmental community. We analyze these issues in light of the increased focus on the distribution of benefits and costs of environmental and natural resource regulation.

Our analysis is primarily qualitative, although in cases in which quantitative economic analyses of environmental policies have been produced, we discuss those results. The analysis is not exhaustive, but we do our best to consider the most important and most prominent intersections of economics and environmental regulation over the decade.

In section II, we highlight the ways in which the role of efficiency as a criterion for assessing environmental and natural resource rules and regulations was very controversial in the Clinton administration, while economic efficiency emerged as a central goal of the regulatory reform movement in Congress. In section III, we examine how cost-effectiveness was embraced by both the administration and Congress in the 1990s as a criterion for adopting specific policy instruments. In section IV, we examine how and why the decade witnessed an increasing role for equity concerns as a consideration in environmental policy-making. In section V, we conclude.

II. Efficiency as a Criterion for Assessing Rules and Regulations

The primary economic criterion for the analysis of environmental and natural resource regulation is efficiency. An efficient policy enacts a level of pollution control or rate of resource extraction that maximizes the difference between social benefits and social costs.[11] Assessing the efficiency of policies requires benefit-cost analysis.

---

[11]In a dynamic context, the efficient rate of resource extraction or pollution control maximizes the present value of net social benefits.

The Clinton administration established a framework for benefit-cost analysis of major regulations that was very similar to those of previous administrations, but the influence of economic thinking in analyzing environmental rules and regulations within EPA declined significantly during the 1990s. While economists in other parts of the administration strongly pressed for efficiency in natural resource management, a negligible portion of their initiatives became policy. Congress did not support the administration's proposals for efficiency in natural resource management, but did embrace efficiency as a criterion for environmental policy as part of its overarching regulatory reform agenda, and succeeded in making substantive, efficiency-related changes to a handful of existing environmental statutes.

A. Role and Acceptance of the Efficiency Criterion in the Clinton Administration

1. Executive Order on Regulatory Impact Analysis. The Clinton administration, like its two immediate predecessors, issued an executive order ("EO") requiring benefit-cost analysis of all federal regulations with expected annual costs greater than $100 million.[12] Throughout the Reagan and Bush administrations, these Regulatory Impact Analyses ("RIAs") were required under Reagan EOs 12,291 and 12,498.[13] President George H. W. Bush created a Council on Competitiveness, chaired by Vice President Dan Quayle, which reviewed the impact on industry of selected regulations.

Shortly after taking office in 1993, Clinton abolished the Council on Competitiveness and revoked both of the Reagan orders, replacing them with EO 12,866, "Regulatory Planning and Review."[14] The Clinton EO was substantively and administratively similar to the Reagan orders. It was qualitatively different in tone, however, signaling a less strict efficiency test.

---

[12]Exec. Order No. 12,866, 58 Fed. Reg. 51,735 (Sept. 30, 1993). The threshold is not indexed for inflation and has not been modified over time. Elsewhere in this Article, we refer to year 2000 dollars, unless we indicate otherwise.

[13]Exec. Order No. 12,291, 46 Fed. Reg. 13,193 (Feb. 17, 1981) required agencies to conduct a RIA for all proposed and final rules that were anticipated to have an effect on the national economy in excess of $100 million. EO 12,291 has been called the "foremost development in administrative law of the 1980s." *See* Richard D. Morgenstern, *The Legal and Institutional Setting for Economic Analysis at EPA, in* ECONOMIC ANALYSES AT EPA: ASSESSING REGULATORY IMPACT 5–23 (Richard D. Morgenstern ed., 1997). But, the Reagan EOs were not the first presidential effort at regulatory efficiency. Nixon required a "Quality of Life" review of selected regulations in 1971. Robert W. Hahn, *The Impact of Economics on Environmental Policy*, 39 J. ENVTL. ECON. & MGMT. 375, 385 (2000). Ford formalized this process in 1974 with Exec. Order 11,821, 39 Fed. Reg. 41,501 (November 29, 1974). Carter's EO 12,044 required analysis of proposed rules and centralized review by the Regulatory Analysis Review Group. Hahn, *supra*. The administration of President George W. Bush has continued to enforce the RIA requirements of Clinton's EO 12,866 rather than issuing a new EO. *See* John D. Graham, *Presidential Review of Agency Rule-making by OIRA*, Memorandum for the President's Management Council (2001), available at www.whitehouse.gov/omb/inforeg/oira_review-process.html, (last visited Apr. 25, 2003) (on file with the Harvard Environmental Law Review).

[14]Exec. Order 12,866, *supra* note 12.

While the Reagan orders required that benefits *outweigh* costs, the Clinton order required only that benefits *justify* costs. The Clinton EO allowed that: (1) not all regulatory benefits and costs can be monetized; and (2) non-monetary consequences should be influential in regulatory analysis.[15]

The requirements for RIA, however, have not necessarily improved the efficiency of individual federal environmental rules. In the first fifteen years of the review process, under both Republican and Democratic administrations, about two-thirds of the federal government's approved environmental quality regulations failed benefit-cost analyses using the government's own numbers.[16] A good example during the Clinton years is the 1997 NAAQS for ozone, for which EPA submitted a RIA that listed $2.0 to $11.2 billion in monetized benefits and $12.7 billion in costs through 2010, assuming full attainment.[17]

Regulatory impact analysis is required only for major rules,[18] a small fraction of all rules issued by EPA and other agencies. Rules that do not meet this threshold pass under the efficiency radar, as do EOs such as those Clinton used to designate twenty new national monuments comprising six million additional acres, restricting natural resource extraction and other commercial activities therein.

2. Diminished Role of Economic Analysis at EPA.[19] Given the increase in requirements for and attention to benefit-cost analysis by Congress during the 1990s, discussed below, EPA probably was required to do more applied economic analysis during the 1990s than at any other time in its thirty-year history. Perhaps in response to this workload, the share of EPA employees with graduate degrees in economics grew during the 1990s.[20]

---

[15]W. Kip Viscusi, *Regulating the Regulators*, 63 U. Chi. L. Rev. 1423, 1430 (1996).

[16]Hahn, *supra* note 13.

[17]U.S. Off. of Mgmt. & Budget, Report to Congress on the Costs and Benefits of Federal Regulations 55 (1998). In other cases, issuing agencies do not provide enough information to assess the benefits and costs of rules. During the Clinton administration, a good example is the RIA for the U.S. Forest Service's Roadless Areas proposal, which discusses benefits and costs in general and qualitative terms but does not offer the information necessary to make a direct, quantitative comparison of costs and benefits. *See* U.S. Forest Service, Regulatory Impact Analysis for the Roadless Area Conservation Rule (2001).

[18]Exec. Order 12,866, *supra* note 12.

[19]We discuss at length the use and acceptance of economics at the EPA, since rules promulgated by EPA comprise a substantial majority of total costs and benefits of all federal environmental regulation. Fifty-four percent of total annual regulatory benefits and fifty percent of total annual regulatory costs identified by the Office of Management and the Budget ("OMB") in 1997 were attributed to environmental regulations. Susan Dudley and Angela Antonelli, *Shining a Bright Light on Regulators: Tracking the Costs and Benefits of Federal Regulation*, in The Heritage Foundation Backgrounder (1997); Off. of Mgmt. & Budget, *supra* note 17. Discussion of similar issues at the Departments of Energy, Agriculture, the Interior and other agencies is beyond the scope of this study.

[20]Between 1996 and 2000, the percentage of EPA employees with graduate degrees who held either masters or doctoral degrees in economics increased by fifteen percent, compared to a 7.7 percent overall increase in EPA employees with graduate degrees. Richard D. Morgenstern, *Decision making at EPA: Economics, Incentives and Efficiency*, Draft conference paper, "EPA at Thirty: Evaluating and Improving the Environmental Protection Agency," Duke University, 36–38 (2000).

However, the influence of economists and the acceptance of economic analysis at EPA were almost certainly lowered during the Clinton years.[21]

The mixed record of political and administrative integration of economic analysis within EPA during the Clinton years reflects the ambivalence of the major environmental statutes with respect to the role of economic analysis.[22] EPA is not an economic agency. It has a mandate to protect human health and the environment through the administration of the major statutes.[23] Many of those statutes constrain economic analysis, and the representation of economists within most EPA offices is relatively thin, particularly at the level of the senior executive service.[24] However, there is a good deal of flexibility in the extent to which economic analysis influences EPA processes and decisions. As a result, the use and role of economic analysis at EPA has varied substantially from one administration to another.

a. *Organizational Location of Core Economics Staff.* During the Clinton administration, economics staff at the agency were marginalized. When Clinton took office in 1992, the core economics staff at EPA were located within the Office of Policy, Planning and Evaluation (OPPE), as they had been since before 1980. OPPE reviewed all draft regulations and provided the administrator with an independent economic perspective, which could be quite different from program office analyses. Within weeks of the Clinton inauguration, however, this role was eliminated.

The substantive role of economic analysis in the development and review of EPA regulations was abandoned by EPA in 1995, when the program offices, rather than the administrator, became the official recipients of these analyses.[25] In 1999, OPPE was eliminated, shifting the core economics staff to a new Office of Policy and Reinvention. The shifts in organizational location of the core economics staff at EPA are documented in Table 2.

Administrator Browner was openly dismissive of economics as an appropriate framework for environmental decisions. In her remarks in honor of the thirtieth anniversary of the first Earth Day, she commented on the establishment of EPA, and recalled that "the nation committed itself to the

---

[21]*See id.*

[22]U.S. environmental laws alternately "forbid, inhibit, tolerate, allow, invite, or require the use of economic analysis in environmental decision making." *Id.* at 20.

[23]The term "major environmental statutes" in this Article refers to the following federal laws (and all amendments thereto): the Clean Air Act ("CAA"); Federal Water Pollution Control Act (Clean Water Act, "CWA"); Toxic Substances Control Act ("TSCA"); Federal Insecticide, Fungicide and Rodenticide Act ("FIFRA"); Comprehensive Environmental Response, Compensation and Liability Act ("CERCLA"); Resource Conservation and Recovery Act ("RCRA"); and Safe Drinking Water Act ("SDWA").

[24]*See* Morgenstern, *supra* note 13, at 16. Of the 193 EPA senior executive service members with graduate degrees in 1996, only four (two percent) held graduate economics degrees; in contrast, almost one-third held law degrees, and one-fifth held graduate science degrees. Despite their minority status relative to lawyers, scientists and engineers, EPA probably employs more economists working on environmental issues than any other single institution. *Id.* at 14.

[25]Morgenstern, *supra* note 20, at 39.

Table 2 Shifts in Organizational Location of Economic Analysis at EPA

Years	Location of Core Economics Staff at EPA
1980–1983	Benefits Staff, Office of Policy Evaluation, Office of Policy and Resource Management
1983–1987	Benefits Branch, Office of Policy Analysis, Office of Policy, Planning and Evaluation
1987–1990	Economic Analysis Branch, Office of Policy Analysis, Office of Policy, Planning and Evaluation
1990–1996	Economic Analysis and Research Branch, Office of Policy Analysis, Office of Policy, Planning and Evaluation
1996–1999	Economy and Environment Division, Office of Economy and Environment, Office of Policy, Planning and Evaluation
1999–2000	Economic and Policy Analysis Division and Economy and Environment Division, Office of Economy and Environment, Office of Policy and Reinvention
2000–2001	National Center for Environmental Economics, Office of Policy, Economics and Innovation

Source: U.S. EPA, National Center for Environmental Economics World Wide Web site, *available at* http://www.yosemite.epa.gov/ee/epa/eed.nsf/pages/aboutncee#OrganizationalStructureandHistory (last visited Mar. 16, 2003) (on file with the Harvard Environmental Law Review).

task of eliminating pollution, to restoring our lands and waters to their uses, and to protecting public health without regard to cost. Let me repeat those last four words—without regard to cost."[26] The administrator referred to the introduction of benefit-cost analysis into EPA regulations intended to protect public health as "poison[ing] the well."[27] The reduction in acceptance of economic analysis at EPA was likely influenced by Vice President Al Gore, who was known to be skeptical about the application of benefit-cost analysis to environmental policy.[28]

 b. Role of the Environmental Economics Advisory Committee. Despite the reduced role of economics within EPA, policy advising by government economists outside of EPA occurred throughout the 1990s. Deputy Administrator Fred Hansen worked closely with the Environmental Economics Advisory Committee ("EEAC") within EPA's Science Advisory Board to develop an aggressive mission statement for EEAC that focused

---

[26]Carol M. Browner, Speech marking the thirtieth anniversary of Earth Day, John F. Kennedy School of Government, Harvard University (Apr. 17, 2000) (transcript available at http://www.epa.gov/history/topics/epa/30a.htm) (last visited Apr. 25, 2003) (on file with Harvard Environmental Law Review).

[27]*Id.* Although she referred to benefit-cost analysis, what Administrator Browner described was more like a strict benefit-cost test that would disallow rules unless quantified benefits outweighed costs.

[28]*See generally* AL GORE, EARTH IN THE BALANCE: ECOLOGY AND THE HUMAN SPIRIT (1992).

on giving expert advice on broad issues of importance to the agency, rather than simply carrying out end-of-pipe reviews of agency RIAs.[29] During the 1990s, the EEAC conducted the first comprehensive review and revision in fifteen years of EPA's Economic Analysis Guidelines.[30] They also thoroughly reviewed EPA's methodology for valuing reductions in cancer-induced mortality.[31] External economists also served on the Advisory Council on Clean Air Act Compliance, required under the 1990 CAA Amendments to provide technical and economic input on EPA's benefit-cost analyses of CAA impacts.[32] The council had a major impact on the identification of key research issues and the treatment of uncertainty in these analyses.[33]

3. Role of Other Executive Branch Economists in Natural Resource Policy. Having noted the diminished role of economics at EPA during the Clinton years, it is also important to recognize economists external to EPA. In particular within the Council of Economic Advisors ("CEA"), OMB, and the Treasury Department, economists did have some influence over the administration's policy proposals regarding efficiency in natural resource management.[34]

The most important artifact of the White House economic agencies' influence in emphasizing efficiency in environmental and natural resource policy is the Clinton administration's 1993 economic stimulus and deficit reduction proposal.[35] The administration proposed a variety of policies related to natural resource subsidy reduction. First, it proposed increasing the baseline federal grazing fee on public lands by almost two hundred percent. The baseline federal grazing fee had been calculated at only fifty-six to eighty-three percent of federal costs per animal unit month in 1990 and was a much smaller percentage (perhaps eighteen to forty percent) of private market rates.[36] In theory, below-market fees for grazing livestock on public lands cause (economic) over-grazing. In practice, low fees have been

---

[29]The EEAC was established by the Science Advisory Board in 1990.

[30]*See* U.S. EPA, GUIDELINES FOR PREPARING ECONOMIC ANALYSES, 240-R-00-003 (Sept. 2000); SCIENCE ADVISORY BOARD, U.S. EPA, AN SAB REPORT ON THE EPA GUIDELINES FOR PREPARING ECONOMIC ANALYSES, EPA-SAB-EEAC-99-020 (Sept. 1999).

[31]SCIENCE ADVISORY BOARD, U.S. EPA, AN SAB REPORT ON EPA'S WHITE PAPER "VALUING THE BENEFITS OF FATAL CANCER RISK REDUCTION," EPA-SAB-EEAC-00-013 (July 2000).

[32]42 U.S.C. § 7612 (2000).

[33]*See* Morgenstern, *supra* note 20.

[34]*See* Jonathan Orszag et al., *The Process of Economic Policy-Making During the Clinton Administration, in* AMERICAN ECONOMIC POLICY IN THE 1990s 983, 994 (Jeffrey A. Frankel & Peter R. Orszag eds., 2002).

[35]Richard L. Berke, *Clinton Backs Off From Policy Shift on Federal Lands*, N.Y. TIMES, Mar. 31, 1993, at A1; *Last Round Up for the Old West*, ECONOMIST, Mar. 6, 1993, at 23.

[36]Betsy A. Cody, *Grazing Fees: An Overview* (Congressional Research Service Report for Congress 96–450 ENR, 1996), *available at* http://www.ncseonline.org/NLE/CRSreports/Agriculture/ag-5.cfm (on file with the Harvard Environmental Law Review).

criticized from a budgetary perspective, since current fees do not cover the costs of federal public range management.[37]

Similarly, below-cost timber sales from federal lands theoretically lead to logging at faster-than-efficient rates, and where revenues do not cover costs, they also contribute to budget deficits. The administration's 1993 budget proposal sought to phase out below-cost timber sales. By USFS estimates, 77 of the 120 national forests showed net losses from timber sales over the period FY 1989–FY 1993, and sixty reported losses in every year over this period.[38]

Neither subsidy reduction proposal—the grazing fee increase nor the below-cost timber sales phase-out—became law, however. The grazing fee proposal led to a Senate filibuster on FY 1994 Interior Appropriations during the 103d Congress and was taken up again in the 104th Congress, resulting in a negligible price increase, leaving rates still many times lower than the average private market rate. The plan to reduce below-cost timber sales was eliminated from Clinton's final budget proposal, and a USFS draft plan to phase out below-cost sales on one-half of forest service lands over four years was not adopted by the administration.[39]

The administration's attempt to reduce natural resource subsidies in the 1993 budget proposal also included introduction of royalties for hardrock mining on public lands governed under the 1872 General Mining Law,[40] increased fees for recreational use of federal public lands, and a British thermal unit ("BTU") tax, which would have taxed essentially all fuels. The BTU tax proposal faced stiff opposition in the first session of the 103d Congress, narrowly passing the House of Representatives. Recognizing that the proposal did not have enough votes in the Senate, the administration removed the BTU tax from its budget proposal.[41]

During the 1990s, economists at the U.S. Department of Commerce ("DOC") began work on the issue of "green accounting." Incorporating natural resource depletion and other non-market activity within the National Income and Product Accounts ("NIPA") has been a longstanding recom-

---

[37]Id. The baseline grazing fee for federal lands in 1990 was $1.81 per animal unit month (AUM), while the various livestock grazing programs' cost to government ranged from $2.18 to $3.24 per AUM. The fair market value of grazing on federal land was last updated in 1986 and ranged from $4.68 to $10.26 per AUM for cattle and horses, varying by region. (These figures have not been converted to constant dollars.) The administration continued to lobby for fee increases, and the 104th Congress established a new fee formula that resulted in a small increase in the baseline fee, still many times lower than the average private market rate.

[38]See Ross W. Gorte, Below-Cost Timber Sales: Overview (Congressional Research Service Report for Congress 95-15 ENR, 1994).

[39]Id.

[40]30 U.S.C. § § 22–54 (2000).

[41]The Senate later passed a much more modest Transportation Fuels Tax in 1993, with revenues flowing to the General Fund. This was a retail tax on commercial gasoline sales of less than five cents per gallon. The BTU tax would have been imposed on coal, natural gas, liquid petroleum gases, nuclear electricity, hydroelectricity, and all imported electricity ($0.0257/million BTU); a higher tax ($0.599/million BTU) would have been imposed on refined petroleum products. See FEDERAL BUDGET ISSUE: DO WE NEED AN ENERGY TAX?, National Center for Policy Analysis Policy Backgrounder No. 127 (June 4, 1993).

mendation of economists.[42] In 1993 the Clinton administration ordered the Bureau of Economic Analysis ("BEA") at the DOC to begin working on this process.[43] The BEA produced the first official U.S. Integrated Environmental and Economic Satellite Accounts in 1994, accounting only for selected subsoil minerals. Shortly afterward, Congress suspended BEA's work on environmental accounting, pending external review by a blue-ribbon panel convened by the National Research Council's Committee on National Statistics. Though the panel's review, released in 1999, strongly supported BEA's efforts and endorsed further efforts to extend the NIPA,[44] Congress did not fund additional work on green accounting.

B. Role and Acceptance of the Efficiency Criterion in Congress

While Congress was unsupportive of efficiency as a criterion for natural resource management, benefit-cost analysis of environmental regulation emerged as a major goal of Congressional regulatory reform efforts of the 1990s. We examine general and specific regulatory reform proposals considered by the 103d through 106th Congresses, as well as changes to individual environmental statutes.[45]

1. Cross-Cutting Regulatory Reform Proposals. The 103d Congress (1993–1995), the Clinton administration's first legislative "partner," actively debated benefit-cost analysis and risk analysis as methods for informing environmental protection decisions.[46] Three of the lightning rods for regulatory relief interests were "takings" issues or private property rights, unfunded mandates, and risk analysis. With Democratic majorities in both houses, none of the Republican minority's initiatives were enacted into law during the 103d Congress, or even offered for presidential signature.

The regulatory reform movement gained momentum when members of the 104th Congress (1995–1997) took their seats after the 1994 mid-term

---

[42]*See e.g.*, ARTHUR C. PIGOU, THE ECONOMICS OF WELFARE (1920); Martin L. Weitzman, *On the Welfare Significance of National Product in a Dynamic Economy*, 90 Q. J. ECON. 156 (1976); Robert Solow, "An Almost Practical Step Toward Sustainability," Invited Lecture on the Occasion of the Fortieth Anniversary of Resources for the Future (October 1992); NATURE'S NUMBERS: EXPANDING THE NATIONAL ECONOMIC ACCOUNTS TO INCLUDE THE ENVIRONMENT (William D. Nordhaus & Edward C. Kokkelenberg eds., 1999).

[43]Nordhaus & Kokkelenberg, *supra* note 42, at 154.

[44]*Id.* at 155.

[45]A comprehensive summary of successful and unsuccessful regulatory reform initiatives of the Congresses of the 1990s that would have influenced the application of efficiency, risk analysis, or cost-effectiveness criteria to environmental regulation is found in Table 2 of SHEILA M. CAVANAGH (OLMSTEAD) ET AL., NATIONAL ENVIRONMENTAL POLICY DURING THE CLINTON YEARS (Regulatory Policy Program Working Paper RPP-2001-10, Center for Business and Government, John F. Kennedy School of Government, 2001).

[46]*See* John E. Blodgett, Environmental Policy and the Economy: Conflicts and Concordances (Congressional Research Service Report for Congress 95-147 ENR, 1995), *available at* http://www.ncseonline.org/NLE/CRS.../econ-1.cfm; Martin R. Lee, Environmental Protection: From the 103rd to the 104th Congress (Congressional Research Service Report for Congress 95-58 ENR, 1995).

election, in which Republicans gained control of both the Senate and the House of Representatives. Reform-oriented bills in 1995–1996 included mandates for benefit-cost analysis, maximum likelihood risk assessments (rather than upper bounds), and regulatory process reforms.[47]

a. General Regulatory Reform: The Contract with America. Most of the 104th Congress's general regulatory reform proposals either failed to pass both houses or were vetoed by President Clinton. Item 8 of the 1994 Contract with America, the "Job Creation and Wage Enhancement Act of 1995,"[48] did not reach the president's desk. It would have made Reagan's EO 12,291 statutory, superseding the Clinton EO—as well as the language in several other important statutes—and would have required that the benefits of regulations outweigh their costs.[49] Although this component of the Contract with America did not become law, it did lead to a prominent public debate over regulatory reform, in which benefit-cost analysis was a central issue.

b. Specific Regulatory Reform Proposals. The Small Business Regulatory Enforcement Fairness Act[50] ("SBREFA") amended the 1980 Regulatory Flexibility Act. As one of the affected agencies, EPA must prepare a regulatory flexibility analysis of all rules with "significant economic impact" on a "substantial number" of small entities (businesses, non-profits, and small government organizations).[51] Embedded within SBREFA, but for the most part unrelated to its other provisions, was the Congressional Review Act (CRA),[52] which established a process of Congressional review and possible rejection of agency rules on efficiency grounds.[53]

In late 1996, in another attempt to emphasize efficiency in regulation, the 104th Congress attached a benefit-cost requirement to Section 645(a) of

---

[47]*See* Viscusi, *supra* note 15.

[48]H.R. 9, 104th Cong. (1995).

[49]Item 8 also focused on the reduction of so-called "unfunded mandates," and on strengthening the Regulatory Flexibility Act of 1980, 5 U.S.C. §§ 601–612 (2000), resulting in the Small Business Regulatory Enforcement Fairness Act of 1996 (SBREFA), 5 U.S.C §§ 801–808 (2000) and the Unfunded Mandates Reform Act of 1995, 2 U.S.C. §§ 658, 1501–1571 (2000). There were many other unsuccessful attempts at regulatory reform legislation during the 104th Congress, including: "Risk Assessment and Cost-Benefit Act of 1995," H.R. 1022, 104th Cong. (1995); H.R.J. Res. 27 & 54, 104th Cong. (1995), proposing a Constitutional amendment to ban unfunded mandates; "Regulatory Relief and Reform Act," H.R. 47, 104th Cong. (1995); and H.R. 122, 104th Cong. (1995) to establish a Regulatory Sunset Commission. Detailed discussion of these is beyond the scope of this study. We mention them only to emphasize the scope and depth of the 104th Congress' focus on regulatory reform.

[50]5 U.S.C. §§ 801–808.

[51]*Id.* These analyses, which are reviewed by Congress, examine the type and number of small entities potentially subject to the rule, record-keeping and compliance requirements, and significant regulatory alternatives. The statute does not require formal benefit-cost analysis beyond that already required by environmental regulations and EO; rather, it requires that EPA submit to Congress "a complete copy of the benefit-cost analysis of the rule, if any," along with the regulatory flexibility analysis. *Id.* From an economic efficiency perspective, the focus on small entities makes little, if any sense.

[52]*Id.* at §§ 801–802.

[53]The CRA was the basis for the George W. Bush administration's overturning of the Occupational Safety and Health Administration's ergonomics rule in March 2001. Pub. L. 107-5, 115 Stat. 7 (2001). The CRA has not been used to overturn any environmental regulations.

the Treasury, Postal Services and General Government Appropriations Act of 1997.[54] To meet this requirement, the OMB is required to submit to Congress a report estimating the "total annual costs and benefits of federal regulatory programs, including quantitative and non-quantitative measures."[55] The legislation also requires OMB to estimate individually the benefits and costs of rules with annual costs to the economy of $100 million or more. Importantly, OMB also is required to recommend the reform or elimination of any regulation that appears to be inefficient. Under this requirement, reports were submitted yearly, 1997 through 2000.[56] The requirement has further centralized regulatory oversight in the hands of OMB, which already had been charged with reviewing the RIAs required by EOs since 1981.

Congressional regulatory reform efforts continued through the end of the Clinton administration. The 105th and 106th Congresses considered establishing further checks on agency regulation. The Regulatory Improvement Act of 1999 (also known as the Thompson-Levin bill) would have allowed courts to remand or invalidate rules formulated by an agency that fails to perform sufficient benefit-cost analyses.[57] While this bill never became law, the 106th Congress did pass a major piece of regulatory reform legislation, the Truth in Regulating Act ("TIRA"),[58] which was signed into law by President Clinton in October 2000. The TIRA established a three-year pilot project beginning in early 2001, which required the Government Accounting Office ("GAO") to review RIAs to evaluate agencies' benefit estimates, cost estimates, and analysis of alternative approaches, upon request by Congress. Because funding was never provided, TIRA was not implemented. If TIRA had been implemented, it likely would have increased the importance of economic analysis in regulatory decision making.

2. Successful Changes to Individual Statutes. In addition to these attempts at cross-cutting regulatory reform, the Congresses of the Clinton years pursued efficiency within environmental statutes themselves.[59] In

---

[54]Pub. L. No. 104-208, 110 Stat. 3009 (1997). This provision was typically referred to as "regulatory accounting."

[55]*See* U.S. OMB, *supra* note 17.

[56]The continuation of this provision was proposed by the Regulatory Right-to-Know Act of 1999, S. 59, 106th Cong. (1999). Introduced as H.R. 1074, 106th Cong. (1999) in the House, the bill would have required much more stringent analysis by OMB: an annual accounting statement of total costs and benefits of federal regulations, including direct and indirect impacts on federal, state, local and tribal government; the private sector; small business; wages; and economic growth.

[57]The Regulatory Improvement Act was first proposed as S. 981, 105th Cong. (1997) in 1997 and continued with the same title into 1998. It was introduced in various versions in both houses of Congress throughout 1997–1999, and took on the Thompson-Levin moniker in May 1999.

[58]Pub. L. No. 106-312, 114 Stat. 1248 (2000).

[59]During the 1990s, Congress also pursued reforms on non-environmental statutes that affected environmental regulation. For example, the Accountable Pipeline Safety and Partnership Act of 1996, 49 U.S.C. § 60102(b)(5) (2000), requires the Secretary of Transportation to issue pipeline safety regulations only upon justification that benefits exceed costs. *See* John E. Blodgett, *Environmental Reauthorizations and Regulatory Reform: From the 104th Congress to the 105th* (Congressional Research Service Report for Congress 96-949 ENR, 1998), *available at* http://www.ncseonline.org/NLE/CRSreports/legislative/leg-22.cfm (last visited Apr. 25 2003).

general, Congress was more successful during the 1990s at passing cross-cutting regulatory reform bills than it was at reforming individual environmental statutes, although important exceptions were the 1996 SDWA amendments[60] and the partial reform of pesticide permitting under the Federal Food, Drug and Cosmetic Act ("FFDCA").

a. SDWA Amendments of 1996. The 1996 SDWA amendments[61] include the most far-reaching requirements for benefit-cost analysis in any environmental statute. The amendments focus EPA regulatory efforts on contaminants that pose the greatest health risks by: (1) requiring benefit-cost analysis of new rules; (2) removing the mandate that EPA regulate twenty-five new contaminants every three years; (3) allowing EPA to use cost information to adjust its "feasibility standards" for water system reduction of contaminants; and (4) requiring the administrator to balance risks among contaminants to minimize the overall risk of adverse health effects.[62] While the amendments require EPA to determine whether the benefits of each new drinking water maximum contaminant level ("MCL") regulation justify the costs, they also allow the agency to adopt more stringent standards than those that maximize net benefits, explaining the reasons for not selecting the efficient standard.[63]

b. Food Quality Protection Act of 1996. The Food Quality Protection Act of 1996 ("FQPA")[64] amends both FIFRA[65] and FFDCA,[66] removing pesticide residues on processed food from the group of Delaney "zero-risk standard" substances. The Delaney standard has long been a target of economic criticism on the grounds that it specifies an often unachievable regulatory standard for the benefits of regulation, and hence leads to associated costs that may greatly exceed benefits. While the standard continues to apply to non-pesticide food additives, the FQPA eliminated the distinction between pesticide residues on raw foods (which had been regulated under FFDCA section 408)[67] and processed foods (which had been regulated under FFDCA section 409—the Delaney Clause).[68]

---

[60]42 U.S.C. § 300 (2000), *amended by* Pub. L. No. 104-182, 110 Stat. 1613 (1996).

[61]110 Stat. 1613.

[62]Mary Tiemann, *Safe Drinking Water Act Amendments of 1996: Overview of P.L. 104-182* (Congressional Research Service Report for Congress 96-722, 1999), *available at* http://www.ncseonline.org/nle//CRSreports/water/h2o-17.cfm (last visited Apr. 25 2003).

[63]*See* 42 U.S.C. § 300g-1(a). The amendments do not allow standards published before the SDWA to be subjected to an *ex-post* benefit-cost analysis.

[64]Pub. L. No. 104–170, 110 Stat. 1489 (1996).

[65]7 U.S.C. § 136 (2000).

[66]21 U.S.C. §§ 301–397 (2000).

[67]21 U.S.C. § 346a (1994).

[68]*Id.* at § 348. The FQPA also mandates that EPA coordinate pesticide regulation under FIFRA and FFDCA. For example, once a pesticide registration is canceled under FIFRA, the food-use tolerance under FFDCA must be revoked within 180 days, rather than the average six year time frame noted in a 1994 GAO report. *See* Linda Jo Schierow, *Pesticide Legislation: Food Quality Protection Act of 1996* (Congressional Research Service Report for Congress 96-759 ENR, 1996), *available at* http://www.ncseonline.org/nle/crsreports/pesticides/pest-8.cfm; U.S. Gen. Accounting Office, Pesticides: Reducing Exposure to Residues of Canceled Pesticides, GAO/RCED-95-23 (1994).

   c. *Failed Attempts at Changes to Individual Statutes.* Two of the environmental statutes most frequently criticized on efficiency grounds—CERCLA (Superfund)[69] and the CWA[70]—remained relatively untouched by Congress in the 1990s, despite its focus on regulatory reform. Superfund's critics have focused on the low benefits and high costs of achieving the statute's standards.[71] Reauthorization and reform were considered during the 105th Congress, but no legislation was passed. Rather than efficiency, liability issues and questions of how to finance Superfund were the major foci of legislative discussions. The taxes that support the Superfund trust fund (primarily excise taxes on petroleum and specified chemical feedstocks and a corporate environmental income tax) expired in 1995 and have not been reinstated.[72]

   The 104th Congress also pursued efficiency-oriented reform of the CWA through the reauthorization process, but the effort failed in the Senate. During the 104th Congress, the House passed a comprehensive CWA reauthorization[73] that would have been more flexible and less prescriptive than the current statute, but the Senate did not take up the bill.[74] No reauthorization legislation was considered in the 105th or 106th Congress.

C. Limited Effect of Regulatory Reform Legislation and Changes to Statutes

The cross-cutting legislative regulatory reform measures passed in the 1990s and the efficiency-related changes to specific environmental statutes had limited effects on regulation during the decade. This is in part due to differences between the administration and Congress in the acceptance of efficiency as an appropriate criterion for managing the environment and natural resources. An additional explanation is the existing statutory bias against benefit-cost analysis in some cases, particularly under the CAA. In such cases, substantial movement toward efficiency in regulation cannot be expected without substantial changes in the authorizing legislation.

   The SDWA Amendments of 1996 incorporated a strong benefit-cost criterion, in comparison to other environmental statutes. However, the

---

[69]42 U.S.C. §§ 9601–9675 (2000).

[70]33 U.S.C. §§ 1251–1387 (2000).

[71]*See, e.g.*, W. KIP VISCUSI, FATAL TRADEOFFS: PUBLIC AND PRIVATE RESPONSIBILITIES FOR RISK (1992); STEPHEN BREYER, BREAKING THE VICIOUS CIRCLE: TOWARD EFFECTIVE RISK REGULATION (1993); James T. Hamilton & Kip W. Viscusi, *How Costly Is Clean?: An Analysis of the Benefits and Costs of Superfund Site Remediations*, 18 J. POL'Y ANAL. & MGMT. 2 (1999).

[72]The revenue now flowing into the trust fund comes from so-called "potentially responsible parties," interest on the fund's investments, fines, and penalties. Then-chairman of the House Ways and Means Committee, Bill Archer (R-Tex.), made it known that no reinstatement of the Superfund taxes would be considered without major reform of the statute's liability provisions and other features. Mark Reisch, Superfund Reauthorization Issues in the 106th Congress (Congressional Research Service Issue Brief for Congress IB10011, 2000).

[73]H.R. 961, 104th Cong. (1995).

[74]The 103d Congress had considered similar legislation, H.R. 3948, S. 2093, 103d Cong. (1994). However, no floor action on CWA reauthorization was taken in either house.

decisions made on MCLs since the SDWA Amendments have not placed great weight on the results of required benefit-cost analyses. Two major rules proposed since the 1996 amendments were those regulating allowable levels of arsenic and radon in drinking water.[75] EPA's benefit-cost analyses for the radon and arsenic MCLs can be interpreted as indicating that monetized costs exceed monetized benefits for both rules (by more than $50 million annually for radon, and $30 million annually for arsenic). The agency maintained, however, that benefits of both rules justify their costs when unquantified benefits are included.[76]

Importantly, the regulatory reform initiatives passed by Congress in the 1990s apparently did not influence EPA's issuance of NAAQS for ozone and particulate matter in July 1997. Due to their high potential compliance costs, the revised standards were immediately controversial; both the decision to tighten the standards and the quality of the research used to support the new standards came under fire. EPA's cost estimates for the ozone standard were singled out for criticism; some analysts found them to be too low by a considerable margin.[77] On the other hand, the particulate standard exhibited expected benefits that could well exceed costs by a considerable margin. Table 3 provides EPA's estimated benefits and costs for both standards.

The regulated community challenged the new NAAQS in court, and the case reached the U.S. Supreme Court in October, 2000.[78] Under the CAA, EPA is required to set health-based standards for specified pollutants

---

[75]The arsenic rule was finalized on January 22, 2001, but implementation was delayed while the rule was taken under review by the George W. Bush Administration, citing concerns about the rule's costs and benefits. After an expedited review by the National Academy of Sciences, in October, 2001, EPA Administrator Christine Whitman announced the agency's intention to enforce the Clinton arsenic standard. *See* Press Release, EPA, EPA Announces Arsenic Standard for Drinking Water of 10 Parts per Billion (Oct. 31, 2001) (on file with Harvard Environmental Law Review). No final action has been taken on radon.

[76]*See* U.S. EPA, PROPOSED ARSENIC IN DRINKING WATER RULE: REGULATORY IMPACT ANALYSIS (2000), U.S. EPA, HEALTH RISK REDUCTION AND COST ANALYSIS FOR RADON IN DRINKING WATER (2000). EPA's cost and benefit figures for these rules were presented as annualized 1999 dollar values using a seven percent discount rate. The AEI-Brookings Joint Center for Regulatory Analysis performed its own benefit-cost analysis of the arsenic rule, and concluded that in all likely scenarios the cost per life saved by the rule would never be less than $6.6 million, and that in its "most likely" scenario, cost per life saved was approximately $67 million. *See* Jason K. Burnett & Robert W. Hahn, EPA's Arsenic Rule: The Benefits of the Standard Do Not Justify the Costs (AEI-Brookings Joint Center for Regulatory Studies, Regulatory Analysis 01-02, Jan. 2001). For a critical review of the EPA analysis and Burnett & Hahn, see Cass Sunstein, *The Arithmetic of Arsenic*, 90 GEO. L.J. 2255 (2002).

[77]*See* Jason F. Shogren, *A Political Economy in an Ecological Web*, 11 ENVTL. & RESOURCE ECON. 557; Randall Lutter, *Is EPA's Ozone Standard Feasible?*, (REGULATORY ANALYSIS 99-6, AEI-Brookings Joint Center for Regulatory Studies) (1999).

[78]*See* Whitman v. Am. Trucking Ass'ns, Inc., 531 U.S. 457 (2001). A group of forty economists filed a brief *amici curiae* in the Supreme Court, suggesting that benefit-cost analysis should be considered in the setting of ambient air quality standards. *See* AEI-Brookings Joint Center *et al.* Brief Amici Curiae in the Supreme Court of the United States, American Trucking Ass'ns v. Browner, 530 U.S. 1202 (2000) (NO. 99-1426).

Table 3 Benefits and Costs, Revised NAAQS for Ozone and Particulate Matter

NAAQS (1997)	Annual Monetized Benefits	Annual Monetized Costs
Ozone	$2.0 to $11.2 billion	$12.7 billion
Particulate Matter	$26.4 to $145 billion	$48.8 billion

Source: U.S. OMB, REPORT TO CONGRESS ON THE COSTS AND BENEFITS OF FEDERAL REGULATIONS (1998). EPA estimates were in constant 1990 dollars; those reported here are 2000 dollars. Cost and benefit estimates assume full attainment.

without consideration of costs. In February 2001, the Supreme Court ruled unanimously that the CAA does not allow EPA to consider costs in setting NAAQS for the criteria air pollutants, and that the statute's mandate that the NAAQS protect the public health with "an adequate margin of safety" allows an acceptable scope of discretion to EPA.[79]

Given that the ozone standard's estimated costs appear to outweigh its benefits by a significant margin, EPA has been under considerable pressure to revise the standard, despite the Supreme Court's decision.[80] The situation is very different, of course, for particulate matter, for which estimated benefits appear to outweigh estimated costs. If the courts continue to uphold the standards and if the statutes preventing cost considerations remain unchanged, the stricter NAAQS for ozone and particulate matter may be one of the Clinton administration's most enduring environmental legacies, in terms of both potential benefits and potential costs.[81]

The differences in opinion between Congress and the executive branch (especially EPA) on the usefulness of efficiency analysis resulted in an effective stalemate. Even where statutes were explicitly altered to require benefit-cost analysis, as was the case for the setting of MCLs under the SDWA, rules promulgated during the 1990s do not appear to be any more or less efficient than rules promulgated during earlier decades.

---

[79]See Am. Trucking Ass'ns, 531 U.S. at 457. The Supreme Court decision was greeted positively by EPA Administrator Whitman: " . . . Congress delegated to EPA the standard-setting function, and EPA carried it out appropriately." See Press Release, EPA, Supreme Court Upholds EPA Position on Smog, Particulate Rules (Feb. 27, 2001) (on file with Harvard Environmental Law Review). The Court acknowledged that EPA and the states could continue to take costs into account in implementing the standards, which may serve as an impetus for the adoption of cost-effective policy instruments.

[80]EPA has agreed to reconsider its analysis of ozone NAAQS benefits in at least one respect. The agency's initial analysis did not consider the possible damages associated with *decreases* in ground-level ozone, which leads to increases in some ultraviolet radiation ("UV-B") exposure. See Randall Lutter & Christopher Wolz, *UV-B Screening by Tropospheric Ozone: Implications for the National Ambient Air Quality Standard*, 31 ENVTL. SCI. & TECH. 142A (1997).

[81]It remains to be seen whether some urban areas will be able to comply with the new ozone standards. One analyst estimates the costs to Los Angeles of meeting the ozone standard in 2010 will be about $15 billion in constant 2000 dollars, assuming a five percent decrease in current abatement costs due to technological change. Lutter, *supra* note 77, at 7.

III. Cost-Effectiveness as a Criterion for Assessing Public Policies

Many or most environmental laws and regulations are not cost-effective, typically specifying technologies or uniform emissions limits, despite tremendous variation in abatement costs among sources.[82] While uniform standards may effectively limit emissions of pollutants, they typically exact relatively high costs in the process, by forcing some firms to resort to unduly expensive means of controlling pollution. For example, under current regulations, the marginal cost of abating lead emissions ranges from $13 per ton in the non-metal products sector to $56,000 per ton in the food sector.[83]

Market-based approaches to environmental protection can be used to achieve the least-cost allocation of pollution reduction, even if the aggregate target is not efficient. Thus, cost-effectiveness is a criterion quite separate and distinct from efficiency.[84] A cost-effective regulatory policy takes environmental quality or natural resource extraction targets as given by the political process, but achieves those targets at minimum aggregate cost. Since the 1970s, the advantages of market-based (or economic-incentive) approaches in reducing the costs of environmental regulation have received serious political attention, and there have been increasing numbers of applications in the United States and other countries.[85] Both the Clinton administration and Congress embraced cost-effectiveness as a criterion for adopting environmental and natural resource policies during the 1990s.

A. Support for the Cost-Effectiveness Criterion Within the Clinton Administration

The Clinton administration's support for the use of a cost-effectiveness criterion in choosing environmental policies was demonstrated in a variety of contexts. The administration included selection of cost-effective regulatory alternatives within Clinton EO 12,866, requiring regulatory impact analysis. And in the same Earth Day speech that was so critical of benefit-cost analysis, EPA Administrator Browner highlighted EPA's cost-effective regulatory measures and flexible approaches to pollution reduction.[86] During the Clinton years, EPA continued to emphasize cost-effective approaches to pollution control, including the use of information disclosure and voluntary programs, and the administration aggressively promoted international

---

[82]See Richard G. Newell & Robert N. Stavins (2003), *Cost Heterogeneity and the Potential Savings from Market-Based Policies*, 23 J. REG. ECON. 43 (2003); T.H. Tietenberg, *Economic Instruments for Environmental Regulation*, 6 OXFORD REV. ECON. POL'Y 17 (1990).

[83]See RAYMOND S. HARTMAN ET AL., THE COST OF AIR POLLUTION ABATEMENT (World Bank Policy Research Working Paper #1398, Dec. 1994); Morgenstern, *supra* note 20, at 17–18.

[84]William J. Baumol & Wallace E. Oates, *The Use of Standards and Prices for Protection of the Environment*, 73 SWED. J. ECON. 42 (1971).

[85]Robert N. Stavins, *Experience with Market-Based Environmental Policy Instruments*, *in* THE HANDBOOK OF ENVIRONMENTAL ECONOMICS (Karl-Göran Mäler & Jeffrey Vincent eds., forthcoming 2003).

[86]Browner, *supra* note 26.

market-based policy instruments for greenhouse gas emissions control (specifically, emissions trading).

1. Reinventing EPA. Administrator Browner announced the creation of EPA's Office of Reinvention in 1997, although it is fair to say that reform efforts at EPA had been underway since the mid-1980s. Vice President Gore's National Performance Review Report and the Government Performance and Results Act of 1993[87] brought increased attention to such efforts at EPA, and the agency launched the centerpiece of its "reinvention" program, the Common Sense Initiative ("CSI") in 1994.[88]

Although the CSI can be considered within the umbrella of policies intended to foster greater cost-effectiveness, it is unclear whether the CSI improved the cost-effectiveness of environmental regulation in the 1990s. The CSI engaged six major industries in dialogue with EPA with the purpose of reducing compliance costs, introducing flexibility by moving toward regulation by industry rather than by pollutant, and reducing costly litigation through stakeholder participation.[89] But in 1997, two GAO reports found that too many CSI resources had been spent on process and too few on substance and results. In addition, progress had been limited by the lack of consensus among industry workgroups on the most important issues, and the effort lacked results-oriented measures to assess progress.[90]

In 1995, Vice President Gore and Administrator Browner announced a set of twenty-five specific reinvention reforms at EPA, in addition to the CSI. One of these new programs was Project XL ("Excellence and Leadership"), which set a goal of fifty pilot projects allowing regulated firms to propose alternatives to existing command-and-control regulations that would attain higher levels of pollution control at lower cost.[91] The National Environmental Performance Partnership System sought to give states greater flexibility in achieving environmental goals by allowing them to convert some types of categorical federal grants into more flexible block grants.

---

[87]Pub. L 103-62, 107 Stat. 285 (1993).

[88]Other organizations and institutions may also have played a role in EPA's focus on reinvention. A 1995 National Academy of Public Administration report suggested reforms at EPA, including better use of risk and cost information to rank priorities. In 1996, the Center for Strategic and International Studies launched "Enterprise for the Environment," an effort to build consensus for systematic environmental management reform. And the regulatory reform focus of the 104th Congress may also have prompted EPA to attempt to carry out reform efforts, in part to forestall Congressionally mandated changes. *See* Claudia Copeland, *Reinventing the Environmental Protection Agency and EPA's Water Programs* (Congressional Research Service Report to Congress 96-283 ENR, Mar. 1996), *available at* http://www.nsceonline.org/NLE/CRSreports/water/h2o-20.cfm.

[89]The participating industries were auto manufacturing, computers and electronics, iron and steel, metal finishing, petroleum refining, and printing.

[90]*See* U.S. Gen. Accounting Office, GAO/RCED-97-155, Environmental Protection: Challenges Facing EPA's Efforts to Reinvent Environmental Regulation (1997); U.S. Gen. Accounting Office, GAO/RCED-97-164, Regulatory Reinvention: EPA's Common Sense Initiative Needs an Improved Operating Framework and Progress Measures (1997).

[91]Lisa C. Lund, *Project XL: Good for the Environment, Good for Business, Good for Communities*, 30 Envtl. L. Rep. (Envtl. L. Inst.) 10,140 (2000).

In its assessment of EPA's reinvention program, GAO noted that EPA's efforts could have only limited success in introducing cost-effective changes, because significant progress would require reform of the legislative framework for environmental protection, rather than process reforms within EPA.[92]

2. Information Disclosure and Voluntary Programs. In addition to its reinvention efforts, EPA significantly increased use of information disclosure regulations during the 1990s. TRI was initiated in 1988 under the Emergency Planning and Community Right-to-Know Act Section 313[93] and requires firms to report on use, storage and release of hazardous chemicals. A 1993 Clinton EO required TRI reporting by federal facilities.[94] In 1994, EPA added 286 new chemicals to the list requiring TRI reporting, an eighty percent increase in the number of listed chemicals.[95] Further, EPA lowered reporting thresholds in 1999 for many persistent bioaccumulative toxic chemicals and added more of these chemicals to the TRI list.[96] The Clinton administration announced another expansion of TRI on January 17, 2001, considerably lowering the threshold for reporting lead emissions.[97]

Releases reported under TRI declined by forty-five percent from 1988 to 1998, but no analysis has yet been able to attribute that reduction to the policy itself. Limited evidence exists that publicly available information about firms' TRI emissions (either in absolute terms or relative to some benchmarks) negatively affects stock prices.[98] Other possible avenues through which the TRI may influence emissions are green consumerism, redirection of firms' attention toward measures that increase environmental performance while saving costs, and community pressure, but there is little solid evidence that any of these forces are at work.[99]

---

[92]U.S. GAO, GAO/RCED-97-155, *supra* note 90.

[93]P.L. 99-499, Title III, § 313, 100 Stat. 1741 (1986) (codified as amended at 42 U.S.C. § 11023 (2000)).

[94]Exec. Order 12,856, 58 Fed. Reg. 41981 (August 6, 1993).

[95]Linda Jo Schierow, Toxics Release Inventory: Do Communities Have a Right to Know More?, (Congressional Research Service Report for Congress 97-970 ENR, 1997).

[96]The EPA under Clinton also continued the 33/50 program, started under the Bush administration, which engaged TRI-reporting industries in achieving voluntary accelerated emissions reduction targets in exchange for public "certification."

[97]40 C.F.R. § 372.28 (2000). The previous standard required reporting by facilities that manufacture or process more than 25,000 pounds of lead annually or that use more than 10,000 pounds annually. The newer standard required reporting by any facility that manufactures, processes, or uses more than 100 pounds annually. The Bush administration announced its intention to uphold the new threshold on April 17, 2001.

[98]See James T. Hamilton, *Pollution as News: Media and Stock Market Reactions to the Toxics Release Inventory Data*, 28 J. ENVTL. ECON. & MGMT. 98 (1995); Shameek Konar & Mark A. Cohen, *Information as Regulation: The Effect of Community Right to Know Laws on Toxic Emissions*, 32 J. ENVTL. ECON. & MGMT. 109 (1997); Madhu Khanna et al., *Toxics Release Information: A Policy Tool for Environmental Protection*, 36 J. ENVTL. ECON. & MGMT. 243 (1998).

[99]See Lori D. Snyder, Regulating Pollution Through Information Disclosure: Modeling Firm Response to the Toxics Release Inventory (Kennedy School of Government, Draft Working Paper, May 2001).

In addition to the TRI, EPA established new and expanded existing information programs during the 1990s. In 1997, EPA expanded the existing Energy Star Buildings program, consolidating it with the Green Lights program, both of which are information disclosure programs related to energy efficiency. In 1998, the agency began requiring public water systems to issue annual Drinking Water Consumer Confidence Reports.[100] In 2000, it posted automobile "pollution rankings" on the EPA Web site, ranking vehicles based on hydrocarbon and NO_x tailpipe emissions. While these programs could, in theory, provide cost-effective ways of reaching environmental objectives, there is no solid evidence of their actual effects.

3. Cost-Effectiveness and Climate Change Policy. In October 1993, the administration released its Climate Change Action Plan, which recommended fifty-two voluntary measures to meet greenhouse gas emissions goals.[101] The nature of the initiatives in the plan is not unlike those that might have been expected from a second-term Bush administration, with their emphasis on voluntary programs, government-industry cooperation, cost-effectiveness, use of market incentives, and minimal mandatory government intervention.[102] But, even if not different in substance, the Clinton administration's Climate Action Plan differed greatly in tone from what had been Bush administration policy. Whereas the Bush administration was moderate in its characterization of the climate change problem, the Clinton administration characterized the challenge in much more dramatic terms. Not surprisingly, this complex set of voluntary initiatives had relatively little effect. By 1995, the United States acknowledged that it would fall short of its goals by at least fifty percent.

A key component of the Clinton administration's climate change policy was its strong and unwavering support for cost-effective approaches, including market-based instruments, and in particular, tradeable permit mechanisms.[103] The administration's formal proposal released in preparation for the Third Conference of the Parties of the Framework Convention on Climate Change, held in Kyoto, Japan, in November 1997, called

---

[100]U.S. EPA, Pub. No. 240/R-01-001, THE UNITED STATES EXPERIENCE WITH ECONOMIC INCENTIVES FOR PROTECTING THE ENVIRONMENT 161 (2001).

[101]Climate Change Action Policy, *available at* http://gcrio.gcrio.org/USCCAP/toc.html (Oct. 1993) (last visited Apr. 25, 2003) (on file with the Harvard Environmental Law Review).

[102]In 1993, the administration also established the U.S. Initiative on Joint Implementation under the Climate Change Action Plan. Joint implementation arrangements allow firms or other entities in one country to meet part of their greenhouse gas reduction commitments by financing mitigation in another country. The U.S. Initiative through 1997 had approved twenty-two arrangements whereby U.S. firms agreed to finance projects in eleven other countries. WORLD BANK, ENVIRONMENTALLY SUSTAINABLE DEVELOPMENT STUDIES AND MONOGRAPHS SERIES NO. 18, FIVE YEARS AFTER RIO: INNOVATIONS IN ENVIRONMENTAL POLICY 40 (1997).

[103]The prior Bush administration had taken a similar though less aggressive position. *See, e.g.,* Richard B. Stewart & Jonathon B. Wiener, *The Comprehensive Approach to Global Climate Policy: Issues of Design and Practicality,* 9 ARIZ. J. INT'L. & COMP. L. 83 (1992).

for domestic and international emissions trading.[104] In fact, it was largely because of the efforts of the U.S. negotiating team that the Kyoto Protocol included significant provisions for international emissions trading among industrialized nations, as well as what came to be known as the Clean Development Mechanism for offsets in developing countries.

Subsequently the United States proposed rules for international emissions trading in 1998, at preparatory talks for the Fourth Conference of the parties. The U.S. proposal faced substantial opposition, most significantly from the European Union. No agreement was reached on emissions trading at the Fourth (1998), Fifth (1999), or Sixth (2000) Conferences of the parties. Indeed, at the Sixth Conference of the parties, which met in the Hague in November 2000, disagreements between the United States and the European Union over the role of carbon sequestration and emissions trading led to the ultimate breakdown of the talks.[105]

Economic considerations appear to have played a much more substantial role in the development of the administration's international negotiating position on climate change than they did in the development of domestic regulatory policies with substantial economic costs, such as the NAAQS for ozone and particulate matter. Within the White House, weekly (and even more frequent) meetings on climate change leading up to the Kyoto conference were chaired by the National Economic Council ("NEC"), the coordinating body for economic policy during the Clinton years.[106] In contrast, EPA was relatively disengaged on this issue.

The NEC was created by Clinton to coordinate the development and implementation of the administration's major domestic and international economic policies. During the Clinton years, the Council of Economic Advisers ("CEA") continued to provide economic analysis, forecasting, and advice on the topics of regulatory reform and the environment, as well its traditional areas of expertise. The NEC acted for the White House as a coordinating filter and organizer of information from agencies engaging in economic policy throughout the administration, including the CEA.[107]

CEA testimony on this and many other occasions emphasized the enormous cost savings that could be achieved through emissions trading and through participation by developing countries, possibly contributing to the passage of Senate Resolution 98.[108] In addition, in its 1998 report on the

---

[104]See Press Release, White House Office of the Press Secretary, President Clinton to Participate in White House Conference on Climate Change (Oct. 2, 1997) (on file with the Harvard Environmental Law Review).

[105]Andrew C. Revkin, *Old Culprits in Collapse of Climate Talks*, N.Y. TIMES, Nov. 28, 2000, at F1.

[106]The major role of the economic agencies in developing U.S. climate change policy began at least as early as July 1997, when then-chair of the CEA, Janet Yellen, testified before the House Commerce Committee, Subcommittee on Energy and Power. Statement Before the Senate Committee on Environment and Public Works (July 17, 1997), *available at* www.senate.gov/~epw/105th/yell7-17.htm (last visited Apr. 25, 2003) (on file with the Harvard Environmental Law Review).

[107]Orszag et al., *supra* note 34, at 995.

[108]S. Res. 98, 105th Cong. (1997). The "Byrd-Hagel resolution" stated that the United States should not approve any agreement at the Third Conference of the parties in Kyoto, that did not impose binding emission reduction targets on major developing countries as well as industrialized nations.

costs of complying with the Kyoto Protocol, the CEA resisted pressure to adopt overly optimistic assumptions about technological change and energy efficiency advanced by the so-called DOE Five Lab study and by the Interagency Analytical Team study on the economic effects of global climate change policies.

B. Support for the Cost-Effectiveness Criterion from Congress

In 1995, the 104th Congress enacted the Unfunded Mandates Reform Act.[109] The main purpose of the Act was to require quantitative assessment of benefits and comparison of benefits with costs for proposed and final rules with expected costs of $100 million or more to state, local, and tribal governments or to the private sector. The Act also mandated that agencies choose the least-cost regulatory alternative, or explain why they have not done so.[110]

C. Mixed Results on Cost-Effectiveness of Specific Policies

Integration of the cost-effectiveness criterion into environmental policy-making made more progress than the efficiency criterion in the 1990s. We consider implementation of the 1990 CAA Amendments during the decade as a case study.

1. Implementation of the 1990 CAA Amendments. While the judiciary in the 1990s upheld CAA provisions preventing EPA from taking costs into account when setting the NAAQS, the 1990 Amendments provided the basis for implementation of cost-effective regulation. Under Title IV of the amendments, Congress directed EPA not to mandate specific pollution control technologies for sulfur dioxide ("SO_2") emissions from power plants, but set up instead a permit trading system.[111] Not all regulations promulgated under the 1990 CAA Amendments were equally as cost-effective, however. The amendments explicitly required EPA to issue technology standards for 188 toxic air pollutants, perhaps one of the most expensive and least cost-effective components of the statute.[112]

a. Market-Based Instruments in CAA Amendment Implementation. EPA provided averaging, banking, and trading opportunities for most of the new standards promulgated under the 1990 CAA Amendments, including those aimed at mobile sources. EPA's implementation of the reformulated

---

[109]Pub. L. No. 104-4, 109 Stat. 48 (codified in scattered sections of 2 U.S.C.).

[110]2 U.S.C. § 1535 (2000).

[111]Paul R. Portney, *Air Pollution Policy, in* Public Policies for Environmental Protection 77, 89 (Paul R. Portney & Robert N. Stavins eds., 2000).

[112]Paul R. Portney, *Policy Watch: Economics and the Clean Air Act*, J. Econ. Persp., Fall 1990, at 173, 178.

gasoline provisions of Title II of the amendments allowed refinery-level trading of oxygen, aromatics, and benzene content.[113] Title II also authorized EPA to regulate particulate matter, NO_x, and other emissions from heavy-duty trucks. The resulting regulations were promulgated at the vehicle engine-manufacturing level, and allow averaging, banking, and trading.[114] The Tier 2 emissions standards for cars and light-duty trucks, issued in February 2000, allow vehicle manufacturers to average NO_x emissions throughout their fleets to meet the new national tailpipe standards. They also allow refiners and gasoline importers to average, bank, and trade gasoline sulfur content to meet new Tier 2 standards.[115]

With respect to stationary sources, the regional NO_x cap-and-trade program in the Northeast is another significant market-based policy instrument developed and implemented under the 1990 CAA Amendments. Although the SO_2 allowance trading program was created under the Bush administration, implementation of Phase I and Phase II occurred during the 1990s. These two programs are described below, as are two significant rulemakings that have been more heavily criticized from an economic perspective: the revised NAAQS for ozone and particulate matter; and new regulations on toxic air pollutants.

b. SO2 Allowance Trading. The tradeable permit system that regulates SO_2 emissions, the primary precursor of acid rain, was established under Title IV of the CAA Amendments of 1990. The statute is intended to reduce SO_2 and NO_x emissions from 1980 levels by ten million tons and two million tons, respectively.[116] The first phase of SO_2 emissions reductions was started in 1995, with a second phase of reduction initiated in the year 2000.[117]

A robust market of bilateral SO_2 permit trading emerged in the 1990s, resulting in cost savings on the order of $1 billion annually, compared with the costs under some command-and-control regulatory alternatives.[118]

---

[113]U.S. EPA, *supra* note 100, at 88. The initial guidance for the reformulated gasoline trading programs was issued in October 1992, during the Bush administration. Trading at the refinery level has been very active.

[114]*Id.* at 89. While a great deal of averaging and banking has taken place, only one trade was completed through 2000.

[115]*Id.* The average sulfur content cap drops annually between 2004 and 2006, and credits produced within that time frame have a limited life, while credits produced after the introduction of the strictest standard (2006) have unlimited life.

[116]*See* Brian L. Ferrall, *The Clean Air Act Amendments of 1990 and the Use of Market Forces to Control Sulfur Dioxide Emissions*, 28 HARV. J. ON LEGIS. 235, 241 (1991).

[117]In Phase I, individual emissions limits were assigned to 110 plants, located largely at coal-fired power plants east of the Mississippi River. Under Phase II of the program, beginning January 1, 2000, all electric power generating units greater than 25 MW burning fossil fuels were brought within the system. Dallas Burtraw, *The SO2 Emissions Trading Program: Cost Savings Without Allowance Trades*, 14 CONTEMP. ECON. POL'Y, at 79, 82 (1996).

[118]Curtis Carlson et al., *Sulfur Dioxide Control by Electric Utilities: What Are the Gains from Trade?*, 108 J. POL. ECON. 1292 (2000).

Although the program had low levels of trading in its early years,[119] trading levels increased significantly over time.[120]

c. *Regional NO$_x$ Budget Program.* Under EPA guidance, twelve northeastern states and the District of Columbia implemented a regional NO$_x$ cap-and-trade system in 1999 to reduce compliance costs associated with the Ozone Transport Commission ("OTC") regulations of the 1990 CAA Amendments.[121] Required reductions are based on targets established by the OTC and include emissions reductions by large stationary sources. The program is known as the Northeast Ozone Transport Region.[122]

EPA distributes NO$_x$ allowances to each state, and states then allocate allowances to sources in their jurisdictions. Each source receives allowances equal to its restricted percentage of 1990 emissions, and sources must turn in one allowance for each ton of NO$_x$ emitted over the ozone season. Sources may buy, sell, and bank allowances. Potential compliance cost savings of 40 percent to 47 percent have been estimated for the period 1999–2003, compared with a base case of continued command-and-control regulation without trading or banking.[123]

d. *Maximum Available Control Technology for Air Toxics.* The air toxics regulations necessitated by the 1990 CAA Amendments could be among the least cost-effective components of the CAA, depending on how they are implemented. The amendments mandated that EPA issues standards for 188 toxic air pollutants, substances that are less common than the criteria pollutants for which NAAQS are promulgated, but may pose threats to human health.

Unlike in the case of the NAAQS, however, the administrator of EPA is directed to require the maximum degree of emissions reduction achievable, taking costs into consideration. Despite the fact that EPA is allowed to take costs into account when determining standards for hazardous air pollutants, the type of regulation required by the CAA amendments is a technology standard—Maximum Achievable Control Technology—not a market-based approach. From 1992 through August 2000, EPA issued technology standards for forty-five of these substances, covering eighty-two categories of industrial sources.

---

[119]*See* Burtraw, *supra* note 117, at 82.

[120]*See* R. Schmalensee et al., *An Interim Evaluation of Sulfur Dioxide Emissions Trading*, J. ECON. PERSP., Summer 1998, at 53; Robert N. Stavins, *What Can We Learn from the Grand Policy Experiment? Lessons from SO$_2$ Allowance Trading*, J. ECON. PERSP., Summer 1998, at 69; Dallas Burtraw & Erin Mansur, *Environmental Effects of SO$_2$ Trading and Banking*, 33 Envtl. Sci. & Tech. 3489 (1999).

[121]42 U.S.C. § § 7401–7671 (1970), *amended by* Pub. L. No. 101-549 (1990). Seven OTC states have also implemented state-level NO$_x$ trading programs: New Jersey, Connecticut, Delaware, New York, Massachusetts, New Hampshire, and Maine. *See* Barry D. Solomon, *New Directions in Emissions Trading: The Potential Contribution of New Institutional Economics*, 30 ECOLOGICAL ECON. 371 (1999).

[122]*See* Alex Farrell et al., *The NO$_x$ Budget: Market-Based Control of Tropospheric Ozone in the Northeastern United States*, 21 RESOURCE & ENERGY ECON. 103 (1999).

[123]*Id.* at 117.

While there are no estimates of the total monetized costs and benefits of this new set of technology standards for hazardous air pollutants, one analyst in 1990 estimated that when fully implemented, compliance costs would range from $7.9 to $13.2 billion per year, and benefits would range from $0 to $5.3 billion per year.[124] The lower bound of zero on potential benefits is indicative of the considerable uncertainty over risks posed by these pollutants to human health. Some analysts have been particularly critical of EPA's very conservative estimates of risks to human health from air toxics in its promulgation of standards.[125]

The mix of market-based and command-and-control regulations within the 1990 CAA Amendments demonstrates that while cost-effectiveness was increasingly accepted by the administration and Congress, application to actual policies was inconsistent. In reality, market-based policy instruments are used to implement only a very small fraction of environmental regulation in the United States.

2. Cost-Effectiveness of Selected EPA Regulations. Most of the "stock" of regulations currently on the books were created without regard to choosing least-cost compliance alternatives, and the cost-effectiveness criterion influences only a small portion of the "flow" of regulations. To keep this fact firmly in mind, we provide the cost per statistical life saved of selected EPA rules from the 1980s and the 1990s in Table 4.

IV. Increasing Role of Distributional Equity

The increase in attention to efficiency and cost-effectiveness in environmental regulation is correlated with the substantial increase in the cost of such regulations to the U.S. economy from the 1970s through the 1990s.[126] There has also been an increase in the benefits of environmental regulation over the same period. The third theme in our analysis suggests that as both costs and benefits of environmental and natural resource regulation have increased, attention to the *distribution* of these costs and benefits has increased as well.

---

[124]*See* Portney, *supra* note 112, at 178–79. These figures were Portney's "educated guess" in 1990, based on the George H. W. Bush administration estimates and those of a 1990 consulting firm study. We have converted them to 2000 dollars, assuming that they were originally stated in 1990 dollars.

[125]*See* Richard L. Stroup, *Air Toxics Policy: Liabilities from Thin Air, in* CUTTING GREEN TAPE: TOXIC POLLUTANTS, ENVIRONMENTAL REGULATION AND THE LAW 59 (Richard L. Stroup & Roger E. Meiners eds., 2000); George M. Gray & John D. Graham, *Risk Assessment and Clean Air Policy*, 10 J. POL'Y ANAL. & MGMT. 286 (1991).

[126]*See* Paul R. Portney, *Counting the Cost: The Growing Role of Economics in Environmental Decisionmaking*, ENV'T, Mar. 1998 at 14; Adam B. Jaffe et al., *Environmental Regulation and the Competitiveness of U.S. Manufacturing: What Does the Evidence Tell Us?*, 33 J. ECON. LITERATURE 132 (1995).

Table 4 Cost of Selected EPA Regulations per Statistical Life Saved

Environmental Protection Agency Regulation	Year	Cost per Statistical Life Saved (millions of 2000 $)
Benzene fugitive emissions	1984	5
Radionuclides at uranium mines	1984	11
Asbestos prohibitions: manufacture, importation, processing and distribution in commerce (total)	1989	21
National primary and secondary water regulations—Phase II: MCLs for 38 contaminants	1991	28
Hazardous waste management system—wood preservatives	1990	57
Sewage sludge use and disposal regulations, 40 CFR Part 503	1993	215
Land disposal restrictions for third scheduled waste	1990	215
Hazardous waste management system: final solvents and dioxins land disposal restrictions rule	1986	226
Prohibition on land disposal of first third of scheduled wastes ("second sixth" proposal)	1988	452
Land disposal restrictions, Phase II: universal treatment standards and treatment standards for organic toxicity, characteristic wastes, and newly listed wastes	1994	1,030
Drinking water regulations, synthetic organic chemicals, Phase V	1992	10,800
Solid waste disposal facility criteria, 40 CFR Parts 257 and 258	1991	40,700

Source: ROBERT W. HAHN ET AL., DO FEDERAL REGULATIONS REDUCE MORTALITY? 16–17 (AEI-Brookings Joint Center for Regulatory Studies, Washington, D.C., 2000). "Cost per statistical life saved" refers to net costs (costs minus cost savings, but not taking into account benefits in terms of reduced mortality risk) of discounted lives saved. The estimates for the first two rules in the table (both 1984) are from W. Kip Viscusi, *Regulating the Regulators*, 63 U. CHI. L. REV. 1423 (1996), noting that all values are millions of 2000 dollars annually. These final rules are ranked in order of decreasing cost-effectiveness.

A. Environmental Justice and the Distribution of Environmental Benefits

In addition to requiring RIAs, Clinton's EO 12,866 instructed agencies to select regulatory approaches that would maximize net benefits, *including distributive impacts and equity,* unless a statute required otherwise.[127] This was the first time that distributional concerns had been included within the series of presidential EOs dealing with regulatory analysis.

Increased attention to equity concerns during the 1990s was frequently characterized under the rubric of "environmental justice." In 1994, EO 12,898 instructed federal agencies to identify and address "disproportionately high

---

[127]Exec. Order No. 12,866, 58 Fed. Reg. 51,735 (Sept. 30, 1993).

and adverse human health or environmental effects of its programs, policies, and activities on minority populations and low-income populations."[128]

In practice, agencies have responded to the two EOs by including a separate distributional impact analysis within RIAs. Subsequent to EO 12,898, environmental justice was mentioned in RIAs for rules in which agencies were required to address the issue, but only infrequently was quantitative analysis included.[129] In no case did the administration's explicit concern for equity clearly alter proposed policies.

B. Property Rights Movement and the Distribution of Regulatory Costs

Increased attention to the distribution of the costs of environmental and natural resource regulation in the 1990s was exemplified by the rise of the "property rights" movement, concerned with costs to private landowners, especially in western states, of laws such as the Endangered Species Act ("ESA")[130] and wetlands regulations under Section 404 of the CWA.[131] In addition, concern about the distribution of costs may partly underlie continued inefficient subsidization of natural resource extraction during the 1990s.

1. Endangered Species Act. The distributional implications of the ESA were the focus of much debate during the 1990s. Private landowners objected to restrictions they claimed amounted to de facto seizures of private property ("takings") under the Fifth Amendment to the U.S. Constitution. Such interpretation of regulatory restrictions on private land use under the ESA as "takings" has generally not been upheld by the courts, but from an economic perspective, the concern of private property owners that they bear the costs of public goods provision is a distributional issue.

Attempts to reauthorize the ESA in the 1990s failed, but the Clinton administration made substantive administrative changes, aimed at rationalizing the incentives for private landowners under the Act.

The administration implemented four provisions that had been included within many of the unsuccessful Congressional reauthorization attempts and had broad bipartisan support. First, the administration emphasized habitat conservation plans ("HCPs") as a tool to manage endangered and threatened species on non-federal lands. Under Section 10 of the ESA, private landowners applying for an "incidental take" permit must submit a HCP, in which they agree to restrict some uses in the interest of species and habitat protection in exchange for the permit.[132] More than 250 HCPs were completed between 1992 and 2000, compared to 14 between 1982 and 1992.[133] HCPs

---

[128]Exec. Order No. 12,898, 59 Fed. Reg. 7,629 (Feb. 11, 1994).

[129]In some cases, RIAs mention that distributional impact analysis was conducted, but the analysis is not presented.

[130]16 U.S.C. §§ 1531–1543 (2000).

[131]33 U.S.C. § 1344 (2000).

[132]16 U.S.C. § 1539(a) (2000).

[133]Timothy Beatley, *Habitat Conservation Plans: A New Tool to Resolve Land Use Conflicts*, Land Lines (Lincoln Inst. of Land Policy) Sept. 1995.

are considerably more flexible than direct enforcement of the Act. Second, voluntary "safe harbor" agreements guarantee that increases in species populations on private lands will not restrict future land use decisions.[134] Third, the "no surprises" rule guarantees that a landowner properly carrying out a habitat conservation plan will not experience further restrictions or costs without mutual consent. Fourth, "candidate conservation agreements" allow landowners to protect declining species that are not yet listed, in exchange for assurance that no additional measures will be required if species are listed.[135] The changes had broad bipartisan support in Congress.

2. Wetlands Regulation. The debate over land-use restrictions governed by wetlands regulation under Section 404 of the CWA in the 1990s was similar in nature to the ESA "takings" debate. Congress did not pass any major changes to federal wetlands regulation, although a series of actions by the Clinton administration during the decade exemplify conflicts over distributional concerns within the regulatory framework. In 1998, the Army Corps of Engineers greatly reduced the scope of nationwide permit 26, which authorizes discharges into non-tidal headwaters and isolated waters, a change that resulted in lawsuits by the development and commercial communities.[136] In addition, the Clinton administration endorsed the concept of wetlands mitigation banking in 1993. Mitigation banking would likely reduce the costs of wetlands regulation to private land owners and developers, but it has been opposed by environmental advocacy groups on the grounds that it does not adequately protect these ecologically valuable areas.

3. Natural Resource Extraction Subsidies. Within its first budget proposal to Congress, the Clinton administration proposed reducing a variety of natural resource extraction subsidies, including those for logging, mining, and grazing livestock on public lands. These efforts were opposed vigorously by advocates of the "property rights" movement. Congress opposed all of the natural resource initiatives in the Clinton proposal, with one exception: the 104th Congress established a framework for user fee demonstration projects within the National Park Service.[137]

---

[134]*See* EUGENE H. BUCK ET AL., ENDANGERED SPECIES: DIFFICULT CHOICES 13 (CRS Issue Brief for Congress IB10072, 2003).

[135]*Id.*

[136]*See* COPELAND, *supra* note 88. The so-called nationwide permits authorize landowners to proceed with specified categories of activities without obtaining individual permits, reducing regulatory burdens.

[137]Omnibus Consolidated Recissions and Appropriation Act of 1996, Pub. L. No. 104-134, 110 Stat. 1321 (1996). Congress also opposed, in one important case, the application of the cost-effectiveness criterion to natural resource management. The Sustainable Fisheries Act of 1996, 18 U.S.C. § 1853(d)(1) (2000), amended the Magnuson-Stevens Fishery Conservation and Management Act, 16 U.S.C. § 1881d(e) (2000), imposing a four-year moratorium on new individual transferrable quota programs among the nation's eight regional fishery management councils and repealing one such program that had been created in 1995. *See* Eugene H. Buck, *Magnuson Fishery Conservation and Management Act Reauthorization*, (Congressional Research Service Issue Brief for Congress IB95036, 1996), *available at* http://www.ncseonline.org/nle/crsreports/marine/mar-3.cfm (last visited Apr. 25, 2003). The Act did not, however, repeal the five other existing ITQ programs.

C. Efficiency and Equity as Issues of Political Convenience

The Clinton administration's focus on environmental justice in the 1990s could be seen as the desire of a Democratic administration to reach out to minority and low-income communities. The administration's many attempts to introduce a greater efficiency in natural resource management through subsidy reduction could be seen as an attempt to support efficiency where efficient policies were in close alignment with the preferences of the environmental community, a strong base of Democratic support.[138]

Similarly, Congressional opposition to natural resource subsidy reduction, when compared with its strong support for efficiency in environmental pollution control regulation, could be seen as the desire of a Republican legislature to forward the interests of supporters in the regulated community, typically conservative voters. Congressional support for extensive subsidies to grazing, timber extraction, mining, and other activities expanded the message of regulatory reform from the traditional industry association community to working-class, resource-based communities, particularly in the western United States. Congress in the 1990s appears to have supported efficiency when efficient policies were in close alignment with the preferences of its conservative base.

The notion of using benefit-cost analysis as a guide to regulation for environmental protection and natural resource management does not appeal to most interest groups or policy partisans, except where it is seen as a tool to achieve pre-determined goals. Politicians may thus endorse the use of the efficiency criterion only where its results are likely to be compatible with their own ideological agendas. The inconsistent application of efficiency analysis to environmental and natural resource regulation in the 1990s is part of a wider pattern of focus on the distribution of the costs and benefits of environmental and natural resource regulation in the United States.

D. Distribution Becomes More Salient as the Economic Impacts of Policies Increase

The tremendous increase in the aggregate costs and benefits of environmental and natural resource regulation over the past thirty years has focused substantial attention on the efficiency and cost-effectiveness of

---

[138]The views of economists on natural resource extraction and pricing are closely aligned with those of strict conservationists, while economists' views on pollution control often contradict those of strict conservationists. That is, current rates of natural resource extraction in many countries are likely greater than the efficient rates, due to substantial subsidies and unregulated negative externalities. Thus, the economist's call for efficiency in resource management often supports higher prices and slower extraction. In contrast, the economist's call for efficiency in environmental regulation may often support a decrease in existing pollution control standards, as most industrialized countries have experienced a period of increasing stringency of environmental pollution control regulation over the past thirty years, and some of this regulation may have costs that exceed associated benefits.

regulation. In addition, the presence of large costs and benefits from regulation has focused the attention of lawmakers and other participants in the policy process on the distribution of these costs and benefits.

Where pollution damages are highly localized, regulations that set aggregate standards for pollution emissions or concentrations can have differential distributional impacts that may be unappealing on equity grounds.[139] Policies that restrict natural resource management alternatives have inherently differential distributional impacts in the United States, where economic dependence upon resource extraction is highly localized. Even where it may be efficient to proscribe specific commercial activities or other resource uses from a national perspective, some local communities will experience substantial net losses from such policies.

An example may be the USFS Roadless Area Initiative ("Roadless Rule"). The USFS regulatory impact analysis for the rule did not quantify benefits and costs. Hence, no definitive efficiency conclusions can be drawn. But inventoried roadless areas comprise about two percent of the U.S. landmass, and thirty-one percent percent of the USFS's property. These areas are characterized by rugged terrain and low-value timber, and they may be ecologically sensitive. These characteristics may suggest relatively low costs to leaving them in their current state, and relatively high environmental benefits of preservation.[140] Nonetheless, any reduction in commercial timber harvest associated with the Roadless Rule negatively affects some communities.[141]

Given that natural resource management regulations will necessarily have uneven distributional impacts, Congressional opposition to increasing efficiency and cost-effectiveness in natural resource management during the 1990s is not surprising. When the "winners" from a natural resource management policy are American citizens as a whole and the "losers" are identifiable members of particular Congressional districts, members of Congress are reluctant to impose those losses on their own district or a colleague's

---

[139]Uneven distributional impacts can have implications for the efficiency of a regulation as well, if damages are nonlinear. If marginal damages increase at an increasing rate, total damages (hence total benefits of regulation) may increase when damages are concentrated in certain areas.

[140]Clinton Forest Service Chief Mike Dombeck pointed out that these areas were the 58.5 million acres of Forest Reserves created between 1891 and 2000, many of which had remained roadless through twenty presidencies. In addition, by USFS calculations, less than 0.3 percent of the U.S. timber harvest and less than 0.4 percent of U.S. oil and natural gas reserves will be affected by the Roadless Rule. Mike Dombeck, *Roadless Area Conservation: An Investment for Future Generations, at* http://roadless.fs.fed.us/documents/rule/dombeck_stmt.htm (last visited Apr. 25, 2003) (Jan. 5, 2001) (on file with the Harvard Environmental Law Review). Any benefit-cost calculation would also have to account for the costs of maintaining forest system roads. In 2000, USFS maintained a road system of more than 386,000 miles, with a maintenance backlog in excess of $8 billion. *Id.*

[141]The state of Idaho, the Kootenai Indian tribe, and logging groups challenged the Roadless Rule in federal court. In May 2001, a U.S. District Court judge in Idaho issued a preliminary injunction blocking the rule. Kootenai Tribe of Idaho v. Veneman, 142 F.Supp.2d 1231 (D. Idaho 2001). The Bush administration declined to appeal the ruling. In December 2002, the U.S. Court of Appeals for the Ninth Circuit overturned the District Court ruling, reinstating the Roadless Rule. Kootenai Tribe of Idaho v. Veneman, 313 F.3d 1094 (9th Cir. 2002).

district. Similarly, as the substantial gains from thirty years of environmental pollution control regulation have been seen to accrue disproportionately to some communities over others, the debate has shifted somewhat from efficiency to distributional equity.

The implications of the increased focus on distribution in environmental and natural resource policy are twofold from the perspective of economics. First, while economists can analyze the distribution of costs and benefits from a regulation, they have little to contribute to the debate over how costs and benefits *should* be distributed. Second, in some cases, attempts to meet distributional goals (whether they succeed or not) may interfere with attempts to satisfy criteria of efficiency and cost-effectiveness.

V. Conclusions

Three conclusions emerge from our review of the role of economic analysis in environmental and natural resource policy during the 1990s. First, the use of efficiency as a criterion for assessing environmental and natural resource rules and regulations was controversial in the Clinton administration, while economic efficiency emerged as a central goal of the regulatory reform movement in Congress. Second, cost-effectiveness as a criterion for adopting specific policy instruments was embraced by both the administration and Congress in the 1990s. Most interest groups in the environmental community and the regulated community could support cost-effectiveness because it reduced the burden of compliance on industry and made stringent environmental targets more affordable. But benefit-cost analysis raised the issue of goals or standards, as well as costs, and the process of setting goals was, and is, inherently more controversial than minimizing the costs of achieving them.

Third, during the 1990s, equity concerns played increasing roles in environmental and natural resource policy debates. Both the efficiency and the cost-effectiveness criteria may be hard to swallow when the distributional impacts of regulation are highly skewed. Examples continue to surface regularly in debates over the fairness of policies such as individual transferable quota systems for fisheries management, differential exposure to environmental hazards, and impacts on western farming communities of reduced availability of irrigation water to protect endangered species. The focus on equity in environmental policy debates is likely to intensify as the costs and benefits of regulation continue to rise.

32 *The Impact of Economics on Environmental Policy*

Robert W. Hahn[1]

Robert W. Hahn is Director of the AEI–Brookings Joint Center for Regulatory Studies, a Resident Scholar at AEI, and a Research Associate at Harvard University.

1. Introduction

Many scholars dream about having their ideas put into practice. Yet, when the dream becomes a reality, it frequently feels different—in large part because of the gulf between the ivory tower and the real world. Environmental economists have seen their ideas translated into the rough-and-tumble policy world for over two decades. They have played an important role in shaping some key aspects of policy. They have, for example, witnessed the application of economic instruments to several environmental issues, including preserving wetlands, lowering lead levels, and curbing acid rain. Despite a few notable successes, the influence of economists on environmental policy to date has been modest.

I will focus on two related, but distinct phenomena—the increasing interest in using incentive-based mechanisms, such as tradable permits, to achieve environmental goals, and the increasing interest in using analytical tools such as benefit–cost analysis in regulatory decision making.[2] For purposes of this essay, an economic instrument is defined as any instrument that is expected to increase economic efficiency relative to the status quo. This broad definition includes traditional incentive-based mechanisms,

"The Impact of Economics on Environmental Policy," by Robert W. Hahn, *Journal of Environmental Economics and Management,* 39:375–399 (2000).

[1]The views in this paper reflect those of the author and do not necessarily represent the views of the institutions with which he is affiliated. The helpful comments of Dallas Burtraw, Maureen Cropper, Henry Lee, Anne Sholtz, and Robert Stavins are gratefully acknowledged. Petrea Moyle and Fumie Yokota provided valuable research assistance.

[2]Other tools include cost-effectiveness analysis and risk–risk analysis. By risk–risk analysis, I mean an evaluation of potential increases in health risks that may arise from efforts to combat a targeted health risk. Such an evaluation can help decision makers compare policies [50]. Farmers, for example, may increase the use of an equally toxic alternative pesticide if use of the original pesticide is restricted or banned to prevent drinking water contamination. For a more detailed description of risk–risk analysis, see Graham and Wiener [34].

process reforms, and economic analysis that is used as a basis for designing more efficient policies.[3]

Economists can influence environmental policy in several ways. One is by advocating the use of particular tools for achieving better environmental outcomes through research, teaching, and outreach to policy makers. Another is by analyzing the benefits and costs of regulations and standards, which may demonstrate the inefficiencies of the goals themselves. A third way is by analyzing how decisions are made—by examining the political economy of environmental regulation.[4] Each of these approaches can eventually have an impact on the different branches of government.

My thesis is that economists and economic instruments are playing an increasingly important role in shaping environmental, health and safety regulation. Although the role of economics is becoming more prominent, it does not follow that environmental policy will become more efficient. This apparent inconsistency can be explained by the political economy of environmental policy. I argue that economists need to do more than simply develop good ideas to influence policy. They need to understand how the political process affects outcomes, and actively market the use of appropriate and feasible economic instruments for promoting more efficient environmental policy.

Section 2 provides background on U.S. laws and regulations. Section 3 highlights the use of economic instruments in environmental policy.[5] Section 4 examines critical factors leading to the increased prominence of economics in environmental policy and also explains why economic efficiency is rarely central in environmental decision making. Section 5 summarizes the main arguments and suggests ways to enhance the impact of economists on environmental policy.

2. Laws, Regulations, and the Need for Economic Instruments

Most environmental laws cover specific media, such as air, water, and land, and specific problems such as the control of toxic substances and the prevention of oil spills. They give rise to a staggering array of regulations requiring firms to obtain permits and meet specific requirements and guide-

---

[3]The narrow definition of economic instruments is typically restricted to incentive-based mechanisms, such as emission taxes, deposit-refund schemes, tradable permits, subsidies, and removal of subsidies. Such mechanisms have the potential to achieve environmental outcomes at a lower cost than direct regulation. For a broader perspective on economic instruments that highlights the importance of transaction costs, see Richards [73]. Note that the definition used here explicitly allows for command-and-control regulation to be an economic instrument in situations where it would lead to improvements in economic efficiency.

[4]See, for example, Metrick and Weitzman [55] for an analysis of choices related to biodiversity preservation.

[5]I focus on the United States because that is the country with which I am most familiar; however, I believe the theses advanced in the paper are generally applicable to a wide range of developed countries as well as some developing countries.

lines. In some cases, firms must gain permission from federal or state authorities before making changes to production processes that have little or no impact on environmental quality.

There are now at least 10 major U.S. federal laws that address environmental quality.[6] The largest in terms of estimated costs are the Clean Air Act (CAA), the Resource Conservation and Recovery Act (RCRA), and the Safe Drinking Water Act (SDWA).[7] According to the first comprehensive government report on the benefits and cost of federal regulation produced by the Office of Management and Budget, the direct cost of federally mandated environmental quality regulations in 1997 is approximately $147 billion (OMB, 1997).[8,9] This is more than half of total federal government spending on all domestic discretionary programs.[10] Estimates of direct and indirect costs using general equilibrium approaches suggest that the costs are substantially higher [40, 44].[11] The benefits from these laws are less certain than the costs. Some estimates suggest that aggregate benefits are in the neighborhood of costs [29, 63]; others suggest that they substantially exceed costs [91].[12]

The aggregate analysis of benefits and costs masks some important information on individual regulations, such as evidence that many environmental regulations would not pass a standard benefit–cost test. For example, more than two-thirds of the federal government's environmental quality regulations from 1982 to 1996 fail a strict benefit–cost test using the government's own numbers.[13] Indeed, if the government did not implement

---

[6]Consider the following laws that primarily the EPA administers: the Federal Insecticide, Fungicide, and Rodenticide Act, Clean Water Act, Clean Air Act, Resource Conservation and Recovery Act, Ocean Dumping Act, Safe Drinking Water Act, Toxic Substance Control Act, Comprehensive Environmental Response, Compensation, and Liability Act (Superfund), Emergency Planning and Community Right-to-Know Act, and Pollution Prevention Act. The list would be longer if it included laws not primarily under EPA's jurisdiction, such as the Endangered Species Act.

[7]According to the present value of compliance costs for final regulations published between 1982 and 1996, the CAA is the most burdensome with $192 billion, second is RCRA with $121.6 billion, and third is SDWA with $43.6 billion in 1995 dollars [35].

[8]Direct costs include the costs of capital equipment and labor needed to comply with a standard or regulation. Most of the cost estimates of individual regulations used by the OMB to calculate the aggregate costs only include direct costs, although a few also include indirect net changes in consumer and producer surplus. The OMB derives the aggregate cost estimate by using the EPA's estimate of the federally mandated compliance cost [89] as the baseline estimate for 1988 and adding the incremental costs from EPA's major regulations finalized between 1987 and 1996 [62].

[9]Unless otherwise stated, all dollar figures have been converted to 1997 dollars using the GDP implicit price deflator [19].

[10]The total outlays in 1997 for domestic discretionary programs were $258 billion [6]. This figure does not include expenditures related to national defense or international affairs.

[11]Hazilla and Kopp [40] find that although social costs were below EPA's compliance cost estimates in 1975, they exceeded compliance costs in the 1980's. This result is partially explained by people's substitution of leisure for direct consumption as a result of pollution control regulation, thereby decreasing output over time.

[12]The EPA estimates that the total benefits from the Clean Air Act between 1970 and 1990 are in the range of $5.6 to $49.4 trillion in 1990 dollars, while the direct compliance costs for the same period are $0.5 trillion in 1990 dollars [91]. For an insightful critique of the EPA's estimate, see Lutter [53].

[13]Of the 70 final EPA regulations analyzed, monetized benefits exceeded the costs for only 31% [35].

all major social regulations that failed a benefit–cost test during this period, net benefits would have increased by about $280 billion [35]. Moreover, there is ample room to reallocate expenditures to save more lives at lower cost [31, 57]. A reallocation of mandated expenditures toward the regulations with the highest payoff to society could save as many as 60,000 more lives a year at no additional cost [83].

For over two decades, economists have highlighted two significant problems with the current legal framework in U.S. environmental policy. The first is that the laws are overly prescriptive. Both laws and regulations frequently specify a preferred technology or set of technologies for achieving an outcome. For example, scrubbers were required for some power plants as part of a compromise reached under the 1977 Clean Air Act Amendments [1]. Economists have argued that a more flexible approach, such as an emissions tax, could achieve the same or similar environmental results at much lower cost (see e.g., [12, 86]). A second problem is that, while some statutes now require agencies to at least consider, if not balance, the benefits and costs of regulations, many laws prohibit such balancing [20, 70]. According to the courts interpretation of Section 109 of the Clean Air Act, for example, the Environmental Protection Agency cannot consider the costs of determining national ambient air quality standards for designated pollutants. The result has been that many environmental programs and regulations have been put in place that would not pass a strict benefit–cost test. Both observations suggest that economic instruments could play a critical role in designing more efficient policies.

3. An Overview of Economic Instruments

As noted above, an economic instrument is one that is expected to increase economic efficiency. That definition of economic instruments has the advantage that it includes a wide array of instruments. One drawback is that, unlike the conventional definition, an instrument is not necessarily an economic instrument just because it is incentive-based. For example, an emission fee need not be an economic instrument using my definition if it leads to a reduction in economic efficiency. The definition used here requires the ability to specify a counterfactual—what would have happened in the absence of the application of a particular economic instrument—to determine how the policy would affect efficiency. I offer this definition because it seems natural that we should want economic instruments to improve economic efficiency.

Economists rarely frame the instrument choice problem in such general terms. Instead, they tend to focus on particular mechanisms, such as fees and permits, which are known to have efficiency-enhancing properties in theory. Below I examine these instruments, but I also consider other instruments, including the increasing role of economic analysis in the formulation of environmental policy.

It is useful to consider two categories of economic instruments for framing policy choices: incentive based mechanisms and process reforms. The two categories are related in the sense that process reforms could help policy makers determine whether to use different types of incentive-based mechanisms. Incentive-based mechanisms include emission fees, tradable permits, deposit-refund schemes, direct subsidies, removal of subsidies with negative environmental impacts, reductions in market barriers, and performance standards.[14] The idea behind such instruments is that they create incentives for achieving particular goals that are welfare enhancing. Generally not included in this category are highly prescriptive technology-based standards. Process reforms include accountability mechanisms and analytical requirements. Accountability mechanisms include peer review, judicial review, sunset provisions, regulatory budgets, and requirements to provide better information to Congress. Analytical requirements include mandates to balance costs and benefits, consider risk–risk tradeoffs, and evaluate the cost-effectiveness of different regulatory alternatives.

The Increasing Use of Incentive-Based Mechanisms

A broad array of incentive-based mechanisms have been used in U.S. federal environmental policy. Table I highlights some of the more important federal applications of fees, subsidies, tradable permits, and the provision of information. These mechanisms have been used for all media in a variety of applications.[15] Perhaps best known in terms of their potential for achieving cost savings are tradable permits. As can be seen from the table, their use has steadily increased over time at the federal level. Moreover, there has been increasing interest in the potential application of economic instruments as well [90].

The table shows that the ideas of economists regarding economic instruments are being taken seriously. President Clinton's 1993 Executive Order 12866 for Regulatory Planning and Review provides a good example. The order directs agencies to identify and assess incentive-based mechanisms, such as user fees and tradable permits, as an alternative to traditional command-and-control regulation, which provides less flexibility in achieving environmental goals.

The use of incentive-based mechanisms at the state level is also growing. Table II shows that many states are exploring a diverse array of incentive-based approaches. There are also many programs at the regional level, such as Southern California's Regional Emissions Clean Air Incentives Market

---

[14]See Stavins [80] for a good overview of instrument types and their application. Kneese and Schultze [48] provide an early treatment of some of the practical issues to consider in shifting to effluent taxes.

[15]This section focuses on efforts to improve environmental quality through pollution control measures, and does not review incentive-based mechanisms used in natural resource management. There are, however, notable initiatives at the state and federal level such as wetlands mitigation banking programs.

Table I Examples of Federal Incentive-Based Programs

Fees/charges/taxes		
Air	1978–	Gas Guzzler Tax
	1990–	Air Emission Permit Fees
	1990–	Ozone Depleting Chemicals Fees
	2005–	Ozone Nonattainment Area Fees
Land	1980–1995	Crude Oil and Chemical Taxes (Superfund)
	NA	Public Land Grazing Fees
Water	NA	National Pollution Discharge Elimination Permit System Fees
Subsidies		
Air	NA	Clean Fuel and Low-Emission Vehicle Subsidies
	NA	Renewable Energy and Energy Conservation Subsidies
Land	1995–	Brownfield Pilot Project Grants
Water	1956–	Municipal Sewage Treatment Construction
Cross media	early 1980's–	Supplemental Environmental Projects for Non-Compliance Penalty Reduction
Tradeable permits		
Air	1974–	Emissions Trading Program
	1978–	Corporate Average Fuel Economy Standards
	1982–1987	Lead Credit Trading
	1988–	Ozone Depleting Chemicals Allowance Trading
	1990–	Heavy-Duty Truck Manufacturers Emissions Averaging
	1992–	Reformulated Gasoline Credit Trading Program
	1992–	Hazardous Air Pollutant Early Reduction Program
	1992–	Greenhouse Gas Emission Reduction Joint Implementation Program
	1994–	Synthetic Organic Chemical Manufacturing Emissions Averaging (NESHAPS)
	1995–	Acid Rain Allowance Trading for SO_2 and NO_x
	1995–	Petroleum Refining Emissions Averaging (NESHAPS)
	1995–	Marine Tank Vessel Loading Operations Emissions Averaging (NESHAPS)
	1998–	Open Market Trading Ozone
	pending	El Paso Region Cross Border Air Emission Trading
	NA	Clean Fuel Vehicle Credit Trading Program
Water	1983	Iron and Steel Industry Effluent "Bubble" Trading System
Other		
Cross media	1986	Emergency Planning and Community Right-To-Know Act

Note: NESHAPS = National Emissions Standards for Hazardous Air Pollutants.
Sources: Anderson and Lohof [3]; Stavins [80].

(RECLAIM), that allow polluters to trade emission allowances to achieve air pollution goals.

The interest in using incentive-based mechanisms is also growing in other countries. A survey by the Organization for Economic Co-operation and Development (OECD) showed that, in 1992, 21 OECD countries had various fees and charges for emissions, 20 had fees and charges for specific

Table II Examples of State/Regional Incentive-Based Programs

Deposit-refund schemes		
Land	1972–	Beverage Container Deposit Systems
	1985–	Maine Pesticide Container Deposit System
	1988–	Rhode Island Tire Deposit
	NA	Lead–Acid Battery Deposit Systems
	NA	Performance Bonds
Fees/charges/taxes		
Air	1989–	Texas Clean Fuel Incentive Charge
	1995–	Congestion Pricing Schemes
	NA	California "Hot Spots" Fees
Land	1993–1995	Advance Product Disposal Fees
	1995–	Minnesota Contaminated Property Tax
	NA	Variable Cost Pricing for Household Waste
	NA	Landfill Operator Taxes
	NA	Hazardous Waste Generation and Management Taxes
	NA	Tire Charges
	NA	Rhode Island "Hard-to-Dispose Materials" Tax
	NA	Fertilizer Charges
	NA	"Pay-as-you-throw" Garbage Disposal Fees
	NA	Wetlands Compensation Fees
	NA	Public Land Grazing Fees
	NA	Wetlands Mitigation Banking
Water	NA	California Bay Protection and Toxic Cleanup Fees
	NA	Stormwater Runoff Fees
Subsidies		
Air	NA	Polluting Vehicle Scrappage Programs
	NA	Clean Fuel and Low-Emission Vehicle Subsidies
Land	1990–	New Jersey Illegal Dumping Information Awards Program
	NA	Recycling Loans and Grants
	NA	Recycling Tax Incentives
	NA	Brownfield Tax Incentives and Loans
Cross media	1990–1992	Louisiana Environmental Scorecard
	NA	Tax Benefits for Pollution Control Equipment
	NA	Loans and Tax-Exempt Bonds for Pollution Control Projects
Treadeable permits		
Air	1987–	Colorado Wood Stove and Fireplace Permit Trading
	1990–	Spokane Grass Burning Permit Trading
	1993–	Texas Emission Credit Reduction Bank and Trading Program
	1994–	Los Angeles Regional Clean Air Incentives Market
	1995–	Massachusetts Emissions Trading for VOC, NO_x, and CO
	1996–	Delaware Emissions Trading for VOCs and NO_x
	1996–	Michigan Emissions Trading for VOCs and Criteria Pollutants
	1996–	Wisconsin Emissions Trading for VOCs and NO_x
	1997–	Illinois Clean Air Market for VOCs
	1999–	OTC/OTAG Regional NO_x Reduction Program
	pending	New Jersey Emissions Trading
Water	1981–	Wisconsin Fox River Point-to-Point Source Effluent Trading
	1984–	Point-to-Nonpoint Source Effluent Trading

Note: If a state is not specified, multiple states have implemented similar programs.
Source: Anderson and Lohof [3].

high pollution products, 16 countries had deposit-refund programs, and 5 countries had a tradable permit program [65]. Although the United States has predominantly used the tradable permits scheme at the federal level, European countries have more often used fees to help achieve their environmental goals. These fees typically have not had a direct effect on pollution because they have not been set at a level that directly affects behavior.[16]

In principle, the use of these mechanisms has the potential to achieve environmental objectives at the lowest cost. Many economic studies have projected cost savings from replacing the traditional command-and-control regulations with more flexible incentive-based regulations. A review of *ex ante* empirical studies on cost savings from achieving least-cost air pollution control pattern shows significant potential gains from incentive-based policies [87]. The ratio of costs from a traditional command-and-control approach to the least-cost policy for the 11 studies reviewed ranged from 1.07 to 22.00, with an average of 6.13. These studies generally assume that a market-based approach will operate with maximum efficiency to achieve the same level of environmental quality at lower cost. In the real world, the counterfactual is less clear. It would be more realistic to compare actual command-and-control policies with actual market-based approaches [37].

An aggregate savings estimate from all current incentive-based mechanisms for air, water, and land pollution control in the United States was developed by Anderson and Lohof [3] using published estimates of potential savings and rough estimates where no studies were available. The authors estimate that in 1992, existing incentive-based programs saved $11 billion over command-and-control approaches, and that they will save over $16 billion by the year 2000. This estimate includes significant state programs in addition to federal initiatives.

Although such an estimate provides a rough picture of the magnitude of potential cost savings, it does not provide an assessment of the actual cost savings. Many of the studies used to compile the estimate are based on *ex ante* simulations that assume incentive-based mechanisms achieve the optimal result. This is rarely the case in practice. Political obstacles frequently lead to markets that have high transaction costs and institutional barriers that reduce the potential for cost savings. Another problem with the estimation of savings is that it is difficult to assess what would have happened in the absence of a particular program. Even where cost savings are measured based on actual market data, it is not always clear if the program in question can be solely credited with the savings.[17]

There are three general categories of cost savings estimates for incentive-based mechanisms. The first is *ex ante* savings estimates that generally rely on simulations that assume the least cost abatement pattern is achieved.

---

[16]Revenues from these fees, however, are often used to invest in improvements in environmental quality.

[17]For example, railroad deregulation led to lower than expected prices for sulfur dioxide allowances by reducing the premium for low-sulfur coal [16].

The second is *ex post* savings estimates that rely on market simulations similar to the *ex ante* estimates. The third is *ex post* savings estimates that use actual data from trades. Although there are a number of *ex ante* simulation studies of potential cost savings from achieving the least-cost pollution abatement scheme for various pollutants, there are relatively few *ex post* assessments of actual incentive-based programs and even fewer *ex post* assessments of actual cost savings. Table III highlights some of the problems with current knowledge of cost savings. The table shows *ex ante* and/or *ex post* estimates of cost savings for five tradable permit programs for air pollution control. I chose these programs since they represent programs where the most information is available; however, as the table shows, there are relatively few assessments of the actual impact of programs.

I was not able to find any *ex ante* assessments of the potential savings from the various parts of the Emissions Trading Program designed to reduce the cost of meeting air pollution regulation.[18] Hahn and Hester [36] produced the only comprehensive study of cost savings based on actual trades. They estimated that the program achieved savings on the order of $1.4 to $19 billion over the first 14 years. These savings, however, do not represent the full extent of potential cost savings. The program generally failed to create an active market for emission reduction credits, but it did allow for the environmental goals to be met at a lower cost [36].

Lead trading, on the other hand, comes much closer to the economist's ideal for a smoothly functioning market. The EPA originally projected cost savings of $310 million to refiners from the banking provision of the program between 1985 and 1987 [88]. The actual cost savings may be much higher than anticipated since the level of banking was higher than EPA's expectations. There are no *ex post* estimates of cost savings based on actual trading.

There was at least one *ex ante* study of cost savings using an incentive-based approach to curb the use of ozone-depleting chemicals. Palmer *et al.* estimated that between 1980 and 1990, a price-based incentive policy would save a total of $143 million over a command-and-control approach [30]. The EPA implemented an allowance trading program, and a tax on the ozone depleting chemicals was later added. Although the primary intent of the tax was to raise revenue, it may have been set high enough to have a significant incentive effect. The actual cost savings from the two approaches are unclear since there are no comprehensive *ex post* studies.

There have been some *ex ante* and *ex post* studies of the sulfur dioxide allowance trading program to reduce acid rain. *Ex ante* studies projected savings on the order of $1 billion per year [42]. The magnitude of actual cost savings achieved is estimated to be significantly less.[19]

---

[18]For examples of early assessments of cost savings from using market-based approaches to achieve particular air pollution goals, see General Accounting Office [30] and Tietenberg [86].

[19]This discussion draws from Stavins [81].

Table III Estimates of Cost Savings over Command-and-Control Approach

Emission Trading Program (1974–)
ex ante   No comprehensive studies on compliance cost savings.
ex post   Total cost savings between 1974 and 1989 were   Hahn and
          between $960 million and $13 billion. "Netting"   Hester [36]
          portion of the program was estimated to have saved
          $25 million to $300 million in permitting costs and
          $500 million to $12 billion in emission control costs.
          "Bubbles" provision of the program was estimated to
          have saved $300 million from federally approved
          trades and $135 million from state approved trades
          (1984 collars).

Lead Credit Trading (1982–1987)
ex ante   Refiners were expected to save approximately $200   EPA [88]
          million over the period 1985 to 1987 (1983 dollars).
ex post   None of 1998.

Ozone Depleting Chemicals Allowance Trading (1988–)
ex ante   The total compliance cost would be $77 million, or   Palmer *et al.* as
          roughly 40% less than a command-and-control   reported in
          approach, between 1980 and 1990 (1980 dollars).   GAO [30]
ex post   None as of 1998.

Sulfur Dioxide Allowance Trading (1995–)
ex ante $689 million to $973 million per year between 1993   ICF[42]
          and 2010 or 39 to 44% less than the costs without
          allowance cost trading (1990 dollars).
          Annual savings in 2002 is $1.9 billion with internal   GAO [31]
          trading, $3.1 billion with interutility trading or 42 and
          68% less than the cost absent trading (1992 dollars).
ex post   Total annual compliance cost savings in 2010 under   Carlson *et al.* [17]
          the least cost approach is $600 million or 35% less
          than the command and control approach (1995
          dollars).
          $225 to $375 million dollars or 25 to 35% of   Schmalensee
          compliance costs absent trading (1995 dollars).   *et al.* [75]

RECLAIM (1994–)
ex ante   The RECLAIM program is expected to reduce   Johnson and
          compliance costs by $38.2 million in 1994, $97.8   Pekelney [43]
          million in 1995, $46.6 million in 1996, $32.9 million in
          1997, $67.7 million in 1998, and $64.0 million in 1999
          (1987 dollars). In the early years, the compliance costs
          are approximately 80% less than under a command-
          and-control approach, and close to 30% less in the
          later years.
ex post   None as of 1998.

The pattern of prices provides one indicator of cost savings, assuming that the marginal cost of abatement equals the price and total costs increase as marginal costs increase. In 1990, predictions of SO_2 permit prices were $400 to $1,000 per ton. The estimates from the beginning of the current phase of the program were significantly lower—between $250 and $400 per ton. Today actual SO_2 permit prices are about \$90 to \$110 per ton.[20] The discrepancy arises for a couple of reasons. First, early analyses did not include all provisions of the final bill such as the distribution of 3.5 million extra bonus allowances. The one estimate that included the extra allowances predicted prices of \$170 to \$200 per ton. Second, much of the remaining difference between predicted and actual permit prices is due to railroad deregulation, the resulting fall in the price of low-sulfur coal, and the decision to scrub [18, 75].

Although the absolute savings that were projected have not materialized, relative savings are in the range predicted by *ex ante* studies— approximately 25 to 35% of costs absent trading [17]. Interestingly, Burtraw [16] has found that the primary source of cost savings was not directly from trading across utilities, but rather from the flexibility in choosing abatement strategies within utilities, which is consistent with earlier predictions. Therefore, improving the trading program may allow utilities to achieve further cost savings.[21]

The **RECLAIM** program in Southern California has received much attention over the past few years. The program was expected to produce significant cost savings. The South Coast Air Quality Management District (SCAQMD) had estimated that the program would yield cost savings of \$52 million in 1994 [43]. Although the potential savings are sizable and a review of the trading activity to date suggests significant cost savings have been achieved, there are no comprehensive studies that have assessed the actual savings.

As these examples show, the use of these mechanisms has increased and the potential savings are substantial; however, a more detailed review of these applications suggests that their performance has varied widely [36]. The variation in performance of these programs can be explained, in part, by differences in the underlying politics governing the choice and design of these programs. These political forces have led to policies that deviate from the economist's ideal.

Although the tradable permit schemes reviewed here did not exhaust cost savings, the programs generally improved environmental quality at a lower cost than alternatives under consideration. In contrast, the purpose of many environmental taxes and fees in the U.S. has been to raise revenue rather than reduce pollution. For example, the Superfund tax levied on crude oil, chemicals, and gross business profits is used to help finance cleanup. When fees have been levied directly on pollution, they have not

---

[20]Actual incremental SO_2 abatement costs may be on the order of \$200 per ton. Permit prices are lower than abatement costs for three reasons. First, in the 1990 CAA Amendments, allowances are "not property rights," which means that the allowance would have a lower value than if they were a secure property right. Second, public utility commissions place restrictions on some utilities' ability to purchase permits, thus raising their abatement costs. Third, utilities may have believed early high price predictions, and so overinvested in scrubbers.

[21]However, these savings are likely to be less than the savings that accrue from intrautility trading [41].

been large enough to have significant impacts on behavior. Absent adequate incentives from fees, regulators have relied on command-and-control approaches to achieve desired levels of environmental protection. Thus, most environmental fees in the U.S. would not be economic instruments using the definition in this paper.[22]

The incentive-based mechanisms considered above are primarily concerned with issues of cost effectiveness—that is, achieving a given goal at low cost. In contrast, the regulatory analysis considered below addresses the choice of goals.

Moves Toward Analyzing the Benefits and Costs of Environmental Regulation

To address the dramatic increase in regulatory activity beginning in the late 1960s, the past five Presidents have introduced mechanisms for overseeing regulations with varying degrees of success. A central component of later oversight mechanisms was formal economic analysis, which included benefit–cost analysis and cost-effectiveness analysis.

As a result of concerns that some environmental regulations were ineffective or too costly, President Nixon established a "Quality of Life" review of selected regulations in 1971. The review process, administered by OMB, required agencies issuing regulations affecting the environment, health, and safety to coordinate their activities. In 1974, President Ford formalized and broadened this review process in Executive Order 11281. Agencies were required to prepare inflationary impact statements of major rules. President Carter further strengthened regulatory oversight in 1978 by issuing Executive Order 12044, which required detailed regulatory analyses of proposed rules and centralized review by the Regulatory Analysis Review Group. This group consisted of representatives from the Executive Office of the President, including the Council of Economic Advisers, and regulatory agencies. A major focus of this review group was on environmental regulations such as the ozone standard, diesel particulate emissions, and heavy-duty truck emissions [92].

Since 1981, Presidents have required agencies to complete a regulatory impact analysis (RIA) for every major regulation. President Reagan's Executive Order 12291 required an RIA for each "major" rule whose annual impact on the economy was estimated to exceed $100 million [77].[23] The aim of this Executive Order was to develop more effective and less costly regulation. President Bush used the same Executive Order. President Clinton issued Executive Order 12866, which is similar to Reagan's order in terms of

---

[22]Some fees in Europe, such as Sweden's charge on nitrogen oxides from stationary sources, would be economic instruments [78].

[23]While the definition of "major" has changed somewhat over time, it is currently defined as a regulation that has "an annual effect on the economy of $100 million or more, or adversely affects, in a material way, a sector of the economy, productivity, competition, jobs, the environment, public health or safety, or state, local, or tribal government or communities" (3(f)(1)(EO 12866)).

its analytical requirements but adds and changes some requirements. Generally, Clinton's Executive Order directs agencies to choose the most cost-effective design of a regulation to achieve the regulatory objective, and to adopt a regulation only after balancing the costs and benefits. Clinton's order requires agencies to promulgate regulations if the benefits "justify" the costs. This language is generally perceived as more flexible than Reagan's order, which required the benefits to "outweigh" the costs. Clinton's order also places greater emphasis on distributional concerns.[24] Clinton's order requires a benefit–cost analysis for major regulations as well as an assessment of reasonably feasible alternatives to the planned regulation and a statement of why the planned regulation was chosen instead of the alternatives. Most of the major federal environmental, health, and safety regulations that have been reviewed to date are promulgated by the EPA because those regulations tend to be the most expensive.

The Congress has been slower to support efforts to require the balancing of benefits and costs of major environmental regulations. In 1982 the Senate unanimously passed such a law, but it was defeated in the House of Representatives. The two primary environmental statutes that allowed the balancing of benefits and costs prior to the mid-1990s are the Toxic Substances Control Act and the Federal Insecticide, Fungicide, and Rodenticide Act [27]. Recently, Congress has shown greater interest in emphasizing the balancing of benefits and costs. Table IV reviews recent regulatory reform initiatives, which could help improve environmental regulation and legislation. The table suggests that Congress now shares the concern of the Executive Branch that the regulatory system is in need of repair and could benefit from economic analysis [20]. All reforms highlighted in the table emphasize a trend towards considering the benefits and costs of regulation, although the effectiveness of the provisions is as of yet unclear. Perhaps owing to the politicized nature of the debate over regulatory reform, these reform efforts have come about in a piecemeal fashion, and there is some overlap in the requirements for analysis.[25] These incremental efforts fall into the two categories of process reforms described earlier in the paper: accountability mechanisms and analytical requirements.

Examples of accountability mechanisms include the provision in the Small Business Regulatory Enforcement Fairness Act of 1996 that requires agencies to submit final regulations to Congress for review. The Telecommunications Act of 1996 requires the Federal Communications Commission to conduct a biennial review of all regulations promulgated under the Act.

---

[24]For instance, Clinton's Principles of Regulation instructs that ". . . each agency shall consider . . . distributive impacts, and equity. On the other hand, Reagan's Executive order instructs agencies merely to identify the parties most likely to receive benefits and pay costs.

[25]There has been some recent interest in Congress in reducing this overlap by establishing a single congressional agency that would have the responsibility for assessing the government regulation. This agency would be similar to the Congressional Budget Office but have responsibility for regulation. It could help stimulate better analysis and review of agency rules by providing an additional source of information.

Table IV Recent Regulatory Reform Regulation

Legislation	Description
Unfunded Mandates Reform Act of 1995	Requires the Congressional Budget Office to estimate the direct costs of unfunded federal mandates with significant economic impacts. Direct agencies to describe the costs and benefits of the majority of such mandates. Requires agencies to identify alternatives to the proposed mandate and select the "least costly, most cost-effective, or least burdensome alternative" that achieves the desired social objective.
Small Business Regulatory Enforcement Fairness Act of 1996	Requires agencies to submit each final regulation with supporting analyses to Congress. Congress has 60 days to review major regulations, and can enact a joint resolution of disapproval to void the regulation if the resolution is passed and signed by the President. Strengthens judicial review provisions to hold agencies more accountable for the impacts of regulation on small entities.
Food Quality Protection Act of 1996	Eliminates the Delancy Clause of the Food, Drug, and Cosmetic Act, which set a zero-tolerance standard for pesticide residues on processed food. Establishes a "safe" tolerance level, defined as "a reasonable certainty of no harm." Allows the Administrator of the Environmental Protection Agency to modify the tolerance level if use of the pesticide protects consumers from health risks greater than the dietary risk from the residue, or if use is necessary to avoid a "significant disruption" of the food supply. Amends the Federal Insecticide, Fungicide, and Rodenticide Act by requiring a reevaluation of the safe tolerance level after the Administrator determines during the reregistration process whether a pesticide will present an "unreasonable risk to man or the environment, taking into account the economic, social, and environmental costs and benefits of the use of any pesticide."
Safe Drinking Water Act Amendments of 1996	Amends the procedure to set maximum contaminant levels for contaminants in public water supplies. Adds requirement to determine whether the benefits of the level justify the costs. Maintains feasibility standard for contaminant levels, unless feasible level would result in an increase in the concentration of other contaminants, or would interfere with the efficacy of treatment techniques used to comply with other national drinking water regulations. Requires the Administrator to set contaminant levels to minimize the overall risk of adverse health effects by balancing the risk from the contaminant and the risk from other contaminants in such cases.
Regulatory Accountability Provision of 1996, 1997, and 1998	In separate appropriations legislation in 1996, 1997, and 1998, Congress required the Office of Management and Budget to submit an assessment of the annual benefits and costs of all existing federal regulatory programs to Congress for 1997, 1998, and 2000, respectively. The Office of Management and Budget already must review and approve analyses submitted by agencies estimating the costs and benefits of major proposed rules. The annual report provisions build on this review process.

Source: Hahn [35].

Congress added regulatory accountability provisions to senate appropriations legislation in 1996, 1997, and 1998 that require the Office of Management and Budget to assess the benefits and costs of existing federal regulatory programs and present the results in a public report. The OMB must also recommend programs or specific regulations to reform or eliminate. The reports represent the most significant recent step towards strengthening the use of economic analysis in the regulatory process.[26]

The addition of analytical requirements has generally received more attention than the addition of accountability mechanisms, partly because of their prominence in the Reagan and Clinton executive orders and partly because of controversy regarding their impact. The variation of the language and the choice of analytical requirement for each of the statutes listed in Table IV reflect the results of the ongoing controversy regarding analytical requirements, which takes place every time Congress debates using them. Some statutes require only cost-effectiveness analysis, some require full-fledged benefit–cost analysis, and some combine some form of benefit–cost analysis with risk–risk analysis.

The Unfunded Mandates Reform Act of 1995 requires agencies to choose the "most cost-effective" alternative and to describe the costs and benefits of any unfunded mandate, but does not require the benefits of the mandate to justify the costs. The Safe Drinking Water Amendments of 1996 require the Administrator of the Environmental Protection Agency to determine whether the benefits justify the costs of a drinking water standard, but the Administrator does not have to set a new standard if the benefits do not justify the costs.[27] Amendments in 1996 to the process through which the Secretary of Transportation sets gas pipeline safety standards, on the other hand, require the Secretary to propose a standard for pipeline safety *only* if the benefits justify the costs. Other statutes simply require the agency to only consider costs and benefits. The Food Quality Protection Act of 1996 is even more vague. The Act eliminates the Delaney Clause in the Food, Drug, and Cosmetic Act, the zero-tolerance standard for carcinogenic pesticide residues on processed food. Instead, the Administrator of the Environmental Protection Agency must set a tolerance level that is "safe," defined as "reasonable certainty of no harm." While the Food Quality Protection Act does not explicitly require the Administrator to consider benefits and costs when determining safe tolerance

---

[26]Other examples in the policy category include the Paperwork Reduction Act, which sets measurable goals to reduce the regulatory burden, and the Government Performance and Results Act, which establishes requirements for agencies to develop mission statements, performance goals, and measures of performance.

[27]The Amendments also require some form of risk–risk analysis. They require the Administrator of the Environmental Protection Agency to set maximum levels for contaminants in drinking water at a "feasible" level, defined as feasible with the use of the best technology and treatment techniques available, while "taking cost into consideration." The Administrator must ignore the feasibility constraint if the feasible level would result in an increase in the concentration of other contaminants in drinking water or would interfere with the efficacy of treatment techniques used to comply with other national primary drinking water regulations. If the feasibility constraint does not apply, the Administrator must set the maximum level to minimize "the overall risk of adverse health effects by balancing the risk from the contaminant and the risk from other contaminants."

levels, the new language suggests increased balancing of costs and benefits relative to the original requirement. While the addition of such language to statutes represents an improvement over the status quo, it is clear that the major aims of the efforts to date have been to require more information on the benefits and costs of regulations and to increase oversight of regulatory activities and agency performance. Ensuring that regulations pass some form of a benefit–cost test has not been a priority.

There is evidence that states are also moving toward the systematic analysis of significant regulatory actions. According to a survey by the National Association on Administrative Rules Review (NAARR) in 1996, administrative law review officials in 27 states noted that their state statutes require an economic impact analysis for all proposed rules, and 10 states require benefit–cost analysis for all proposed rules.[28] Table V highlights efforts in six states. The first section describes efforts to review existing rules and procedures including any measures of success, and the second section describes the analysis requirements for new activities. While the efforts vary in their authority, coverage of activities, and amount of resources, they all place greater emphasis on economic analysis and the review of existing regulations and procedures. In addition, some states have begun to document the success of their efforts; however, the measures have generally been limited to the number of rules reviewed or eliminated. No estimates of actual welfare gains are available.

The use of economic analysis is also increasing in other countries. Although the requirements for analysis and the structure of oversight vary from country to country, there are 18 OECD countries, including the United States, that require some assessment of the impacts of their regulations [66]. Although there is some anecdotal evidence of significant impacts RIAs have had on policy, the OECD study concluded that RIAs generally only have a "marginal influence" on decision making. Just as the review of U.S. federal experience with RIAs in Hahn [35] showed inconsistencies in the quality of the analysis, the same pattern appears to exist in other countries.

The preceding discussion suggests that both incentive-based mechanisms and process reforms are playing a more important role in environmental policy. One key challenge is to better understand the ways in which economics can influence the environmental policy debate.

4. Understanding the Role of Economics and Economists in Shaping the Reforms

This section addresses the avenues through which economists have affected environmental policy, the limited influence of economics on policy, and the likely impact economists will have on future policy.

---

[28]All 50 states, except for Rhode Island, responded to a questionnaire sent by the NAARR [58]. Unfortunately, little is known about the level of compliance with these requirements, the quality of the analysis, and the influence it has on decision making.

Table V State Efforts to Assess the Economic Impacts of Regulation

	Review of existing rules			Analysis of new rules		
	Initiated	Coverage	Examples of results	Key revisions[a]	Required analysis	Requirement that benefits exceed costs
Arizona	1986	Continuous (S)	49% of 1,392 rules reviewed in FY 1996 were identified for modification.	1993	Economic impact (S)	All rules (S)
California	1995	One-time (E)	3,900 regulations were identified for repeal; 1,700 were recommended for modification.	1991–1993, 1997	Economic impact (S, E)	Selected rules (S, E)
Massachusetts	1996	One-time (E)	Of the 1,595 regulations reviewed, 19% were identified for repeal and 44% were identified for modification.	1996	Economic impact (E)	All rules (E)
New York	1995	One-time (E)	In progress.	1995	Economic impact (S, E); Benefit–cost for selected rules (E)	All rules (E)
Pennsylvania	1996	One-time (E)	The Department of Environmental Protection identified 1,716 sections of regulations to be eliminated.	1996	Economic impact for selected rules (S); Benefit–cost for selected rules (E)	All rules (E)
Virginia	1994	Continuous (E)	Of the rules reviewed, 27% were identified for repeal and 40% for modification.	1994	Economic impact (S, E)	None

Note: Authority: E = Executive Order, S = Statute.
Source: Hahn [35].

[a] Many of these states previously had some very limited requirements for analysis of new rules. Important revisions were made through new executive orders and statutory changes to clarify and expand requirements and establish oversight.

Avenues of Impact

There are three ways in which economists have influenced the debate over environmental policy—through research, teaching, and outreach.

The literature on economic instruments is voluminous and growing. There are three key ideas in the literature that have had an important impact on environmental policymaking: first, incentive-based instruments can help achieve goals at a lower cost than other instruments; second, benefit–cost analysis can provide a useful framework for decision making; and third, all policies and regulations have opportunity costs. Those ideas may seem obvious to economists, but they have not always been heeded in policy debates.

Economists have provided a normative framework for evaluating environmental policy and public goods (see, e.g., [9, 74]).[29] The literature on using incentive-based instruments to internalize externalities dates back to Pigou [69], and for tradable permits to Crocker [21] and Dales [24]. The application of benefit–cost analysis to public projects begins with Eckstein [25]. Economists have also been helpful in comparing benefit–cost analysis with other frameworks for assessing the impacts of policies (see, e.g., [50, 67]).

Studies of incentive-based instruments have revealed that there are large potential cost savings from applying those instruments [86]. Moreover, economists have now marshaled some evidence of the potential cost savings of such systems in practice, as shown in Table III.

The second way in which economists have translated their ideas into policy is by educating students who subsequently enter the world of policy and business. Many of those students embrace aspects of the economist's paradigm, in this case, as it applies to environmental policy. Thus, for example, as more students in policy schools, business schools, and law schools are exposed to the idea of pollution taxes and tradable permits, it is more likely that they will consider applying economic ideas to particular problems, such as curbing acid rain and limiting greenhouse gas emissions.

Formal education is part of the process of diffusion from the ivory tower to the policy world. Most major environmental groups, businesses, and agencies involved in environmental policy now have staff members with at least some graduate training in economics. Environmental advocates are more likely to support policies that embrace incentive-based mechanisms, and their advocacy is more likely to be couched in the language of economics. A comparison of today's debate over policy instruments for climate change with earlier debates on emission fees is revealing. In the seventies, emission fees and tradable permits were more likely to be viewed as "licenses to pollute." Today, most policy discussions on climate change identify the need for using incentive-based instruments to achieve goals in a cost-effective manner. The sea change in attitude toward the use of incentive-based instruments represents one of the major accomplishments of environmental economics over the last three decades.

---

[29]An excellent survey of the academic literature is provided by Cropper and Oates [22].

A third, more direct way that economists have translated their ideas into policy is through policy outreach and advocacy. They have become increasingly effective "lobbyists for efficiency" [47].[30] For example, my colleague, Robert Stavins, developed a very influential policy document that helped affect the course of the debate on acid rain by highlighting the potential for using incentive-based mechanisms [79]. Another example is the letter on climate change policy signed by over 2,500 economists [6]. I have personally been involved in several efforts that developed a consensus among academics to help inform the broader policy community [5, 20]. The impact of such consensus documents, while difficult to measure, should not be underestimated.

To increase their influence on policy, economists may wish to think carefully about how they allocate their time among the activities discussed above. In terms of getting policies implemented effectively, it is generally not sufficient simply to develop a good idea. Some kind of marketing is necessary before the seedling can grow into a tree.

Limitations of Impact: Economics in the Broader Policy Process

Economists, of course, are only one part of the environmental policymaking puzzle. Politics affects the process in many ways that can block outcomes that would result in higher levels of economic welfare. Indeed, one of the primary lessons of the political economy of regulation is that economic efficiency is not likely to be a key objective in the design of policy [10, 59].

Policy ideas can affect interest group positions directly, which can then affect the positions of key decision makers (such as elected officials and civil servants), who then structure policies through the passage of laws and regulations that meet their political objectives. Alternatively, ideas may influence decision makers directly.[31]

Policy proposals can help shape outcomes by expanding the production possibility frontier; however, the precise position on the frontier is determined by several factors. Take, for example, the design of incentive-based instruments for environmental protection (see, e.g., [18, 28, 38]). Several scholars have argued that the actual design of economic instruments typically departs dramatically for political reasons from the "efficient" design of such instruments (see, e.g., [7, 15, 36, 46, 54]). Frequently, taxes have been used to raise revenues rather than to reflect optimal damages [7]. Standards have been made more stringent on new sources than old sources as a way of inhibiting growth in selected regions [1]; and agricultural interests have fought hard against the idea of transferable water rights because of

---

[30]There are also a growing number of economic consultants and part-time consultants that may serve to impede the cause of efficiency [59].

[31]In this discussion, the institutional environment (e.g., the three branches of government and the rules governing each branch) is taken as a given. Obviously, other ideas can affect the structure of those institutions.

concerns over losing a valuable entitlement. In some cases, the government has argued for a command-and-control approach when affected parties were ready to endorse a more flexible market-oriented approach. This was the case, for example, in the debate over restoring the Everglades [68]. In short, rent-seeking and interest group politics have been shown to have a very important impact on the design of actual policy [93].[32]

Political concerns affect not only the design of incentive-based instruments, but also the use and abuse of economic analysis in the political process. Notwithstanding such concerns, some scholars have argued that economic analysis has had a constructive impact on the policy process [27, 56, 71]. In certain instances, research suggests that such optimism is justified; however, one must be careful about generalizing from a small sample. In many situations, analysis tends to get ignored or manipulated to achieve political ends. This is particularly true for environmental issues that have political saliency.[33] At the same time, by exposing such analysis to sunshine and serious reanalysis, there is a hope that politicians may be encouraged to pursue more efficient policies in some instances. My own experience suggests that analysis can help shape the debate in selected instances by making tradeoffs clearer to decision makers.[34]

The key point is that environmental economists should not be too optimistic about implementing some of their most fervently held professional beliefs in the real world. By improving their understanding of the constraints imposed by the political system, economists can help design more efficient policies that have a higher probability of being implemented.[35]

Likely Impact in the Future

To understand the likely impact of economics on environmental policy in the future, it is helpful to understand the reasons for its importance in the past. A simple story is that federal environmental policy was initially designed without much regard to cost in the wake of Earth Day in 1970, which marked the beginning of an acute national awareness of environmental issues. As the costs increased and became more visible, and the goals became more ambitious, the constituencies opposing such regulation on economic grounds grew. Currently, the political (as opposed to economic) demands for environmental quality are high, but the costs are also high in

---

[32]In addition, examination of particular rule-making proceedings has shown the relative influence of particular factors in shaping environmental decisions (see, e.g., [23, 53a]).

[33]See, for example, the optimistic account of the cost to the U.S. of reducing greenhouse gases provided by the Council of Economic Advisers [95].

[34]The impact of analysis on policy outcomes is not well understood; however, participants in the process can usually point to special cases where analysis was important. For example, in the clean air debate over alternative fuels, analysis of the cost and benefits of requiring companies to sell a large fraction of methanol-powered vehicles made this option look very unattractive.

[35]For example, in the debate over acid rain, it was clear there would be some implicit or explicit compensation to high sulfur coal interests. The challenge was to develop approaches that would maximize cost savings subject to that constraint.

many instances. This is an obvious situation in which economists can help by building more cost-effective mechanisms for achieving goals.

So far, environmental economists have enjoyed limited success in seeing their ideas translated into practice. That success is likely to continue in the future. In particular, there are likely to be more incentive-based mechanisms, greater use of benefit–cost analysis, and more careful consideration of the opportunity costs of such policies. But that does not mean that the overall net benefits of environmental policy will necessarily increase because the political forces that lead to less efficient environmental policy will be strong.[36]

For those who believe benefit–cost analysis should play a more prominent role in decision making—in particular, the setting of goals—it will be a long, uphill struggle. The recent fight over the Regulatory Improvement Act of 1998 sponsored by Senators Levin and Thompson provides a good example. This bill essentially codifies the Executive Orders calling for benefit–cost analysis of major rules; yet many within the environmental community are strongly opposed, arguing that it could lead to an analytical quagmire [39, 76]. There are at least three reasons such opponents would take this stand: first, because making such claims is good for mobilizing financial support;[37] second, because of concerns that such legislation could help lead to more serious consideration of economics in environmental decision making; third, because opponents are concerned that agencies will misuse cost–benefit analysis and related analytical tools. In particular, there is concern with what will happen if politicians decide that cost is no longer a "four-letter" word— so that benefits and costs can be compared explicitly! Given the limited scope of this bill and the level of resistance encountered thus far, it is clear that the potential for change in the short term is limited.

The problem facing economists who want benefit–cost analysis to play a greater role in decision making is that it is difficult for politicians to oppose environmental laws and regulations simply because they may fail a benefit–cost test. After all, who could be against an environmental policy if it has some demonstrable benefits for some worthy constituency? It is hard to make arguments opposing such regulation in a 10-second soundbite on television.

But economists will continue to make slow progress in the area of balancing benefits and costs. In the short term, they will do so by making arguments about the potential for reallocating regulatory expenditures in ways that can save more lives or trees. Over the longer term, they will build a better information base that clearly shows that many environmental policies will pass a benefit–cost test if they are designed judiciously, but many also will not.

---

[36]Environmentalists have been successful in framing the debate as being either "for" or "against" the environment, making it difficult to introduce the notion of explicit tradeoffs. Their success is likely to continue for the foreseeable future.

[37]The 1994 Republican plan to repeal regulations, for example, breathed new life into the green movement. The highly publicized plan resulted in a dramatic increase in memberships to environmental groups and an increase in donations by active members [85]. To the extent that benefit–costs analysis is perceived as a means to repeal regulations, opposing the use of such tools may have a similar revenue-enhancing effect.

5. Concluding Thoughts

This paper has made a preliminary attempt to assess the impact of economics on environmental policy. There are at least three key points to be made about the nature of this impact. First, the impact often occurs with considerable time lags. Second, the introduction of economic instruments occurs in a political environment, which frequently has dramatic effects on the form and content of policy. Third, economists are not very close to a public policy heaven in which benefit–cost analysis plays a major role in shaping environmental policy decisions that governments view within their domain.

The latter topic concerning the appropriate domain for environmental policy may be one on which the profession contributes a great deal in the future. In particular, it is difficult to determine when it is "appropriate" for a particular level of government to intervene in the development of environmental policy [61, 72]. This is a subject on which there is a great deal of legitimate intellectual and political ferment. At one extreme, free market environmentalists wish to leave most, if not all, choices about such policy to the market [2, 49]. At the other extreme, some analysts believe there is a need for many levels of government intervention, including the design of a global environmental institution (see, e.g., [26]). Achieving some degree of consensus on that issue is likely to be difficult, but not impossible. For example, most economists agree that for global environmental problems, it is difficult to address them effectively without having some kind of international agency or agreement. At the same time, many economists recognize that the arguments suggesting competitive jurisdictions will under-provide environmental amenities is somewhat weaker than was suggested two decades ago (see, e.g., [82]).

Environmental economists will have many opportunities to shape the policy debate in new areas. Examples include international trade and the environment and the development of new taxation systems [11, 33, 45, 84]. One of the critical factors that will affect the rate of diffusion of ideas from environmental economists to the policy world is the *perception* of their success. If, for example, markets for environmental quality are viewed as a successful mechanism for achieving goals by both business and environmentalists, their future in the policymakers' tool chest looks brighter. The same can be said of benefit–cost analysis.

There are many challenges that lie ahead for the environmental economics community. The most important one is becoming more policy-relevant.[38] To achieve that end, economists need to become more problem-driven rather that tool-driven. There seems to be a move in this direction,

---

[38]It is possible that the influence of economics on environmental policy in developing countries may be greater because these countries have fewer resources to waste. That is, governments in developing countries may more likely use the tools advocated by economists to develop policies. While there are certainly many applications of economics in environmental policy in developing countries, the general thesis has yet to be demonstrated (see, e.g., [94]). Moreover, judging by the levels of inefficiency of other policies in developing countries, it is unclear why environmental policies may be designed more efficiently (see e.g., [87]).

but there are also incentives in the profession that still push it in the opposite direction—most notable publish or perish.

Another challenge for the economics community is to determine how far it is willing to push the paradigm. Some would like government regulations, including environmental regulations, to a least pass a broadly defined benefit–cost test [20]. Others more skeptical about the tool and less skeptical about the outcomes of certain kinds of government intervention think economists and policymakers should not ask benefit–cost analysis to bear too much weight (see, e.g., [14, 50]).

Finally, economists need to get more comfortable with the idea of being lobbyists for efficiency or advocates for policies in which they believe. This comfort level is increasing slowly. Moreover, economists are finding ways to institutionalize their power in certain policy settings. A good example is the Environmental Economics Advisory Committee within the Science Advisory Board at the Environmental Protection Agency. The primary function of that group is to help provide economic guidance to the agency on important regulatory issues. Now economists have a voice.

In sum, the impact of economists on environmental policy to date has been modest. Economists can claim credit for having helped changed the terms of the debate to include economic instruments—no small feat. They can also claim some credit for legislation that promotes greater balancing of costs and benefits. But specific victories of consequence are few and far between. Most of the day-to-day policy that real folks must address involves the activities associated with complying with standards, permits, guidelines and regulations. While economists have said a few intelligent things about such matters, their attention has largely been focused on those parts of environmental policy that they enjoy talking about—areas where theoretical economics can offer relatively clean insights. Perhaps if we expand our domain of inquiry judiciously and continue to teach tomorrow's decision-makers, we can also expand our influence. Hope springs eternal.

References

1. B. A. Ackerman and W. T. Hassler, "Clean Coal/Dirty Air: Or How the Clean Air Act Became a Multibillion-Dollar Bail-out for High-Sulfur Coal Producers and What Should Be Done About It," Yale Univ. Press, New Haven, CT (1981).
2. T. L. Anderson and D. R. Leal, "Free Market Environmentalism," Pacific Research Institute for Public Policy, San Francisco (1991).
3. R. C. Anderson and A. Q. Lohof, "United States Experience with Economic Incentives in Environmental Pollution Control Policy," Environmental Law Institute, Washington DC (1997).
4. R. C. Anderson, A. Carlin, A. McGartland, and J. Weinberger, Cost savings from the use of market incentives for pollution control, in "Market-Based Approaches to Environmental Policy" (R. Kosobud and J. Zimmerman, Eds.), Van Nostrand Reinhold, New York (1997).

5. K. J. Arrow, M. L. Cropper, G. C. Eads, R. W. Hahn, L. B. Lave, R. G. Noll, P. R. Portney, M. Russell, R. Schmalensee, V. K. Smith, and R. N. Stavins, "Benefit-Cost Analysis in Environmental, Health, and Safety Regulation: A Statement of Principles," AEI Press, Washington, DC (1996).

6. K. J. Arrow, D. Jorgenson, P. Krugman, W. Nordhaus, and R. Solow, "The Economist's Statement on Climate Change," Redefining Progress, San Francisco, CA (1997).

7. T. A. Barthold, Issues in the design of environmental excise taxes, *J. Econom. Perspect.* 8, 133–151 (1994).

8. R. H. Bates, "Markets and States in Tropical Africa: The Political Basis of Agricultural Policies," Univ. of California Press, Berkeley, CA (1981).

9. W. Baumol and W. Oates, "The Theory of Environmental Policy," 2nd ed., Prentice-Hall, Englewood Cliffs, NJ (1988).

10. G. Becker, A theory of competition among pressure groups for political influence, *Quart. J. Econom.* 97, 371–400 (1983).

11. J. Bhagwati and T. N. Srinivasan, Trade and the environment: Does environmental diversity detract from the case for free trade?, *in* "Fair Trade and Harmonization: Prerequisites for Free Trade?" (J. Bhagwati and R. Hudec, Eds.), MIT Press, Cambridge, MA (1996).

12. P. Bohn and R. S. Clifford, Comparative analysis of alternative policy instruments, *in* "Handbook of Natural Resource and Energy Economics, Volume I" (A. V. Kneese and J. L. Sweeney, Eds.), pp. 395–460, North-Holland, Amsterdam (1985).

13. A. Bovenberg and L. H. Goulder, Optimal environmental taxation in the presence of other taxes: General equilibrium analysis, *Amer. Econom. Rev.* 86, 985–1000 (1996).

14. D. W. Bromley, The ideology of efficiency: Searching for a theory of policy analysis, *J. Environ. Econom. Management* 19, 86–107 (1990).

15. J. M. Buchanan and G. Tullock, Polluters' profits and political response: Direct controls versus taxes, *Amer. Econom. Rev.* 65, 139–147 (1975).

16. D. Burtraw, "Cost Savings Sans Allowance Trades? Evaluating the SO_2 Emission Trading Program to Date," Discussion Paper 95-30-REV, Resources for the Future, Washington, DC (1996).

17. C. Carlson, D. Burtraw, M. Cropper, and K. L. Palmer, "SO_2 Control by Electric Utilities: What Are the Gains from Trade?" Discussion Paper, Resources for the Future, Washington, DC, forthcoming (1998).

18. T. N. Cason, Seller incentive properties of EPA's emission trading auction, *J. Environ. Econom. Management* 25, 177–195 (1993).

19. Council of Economic Advisers, "Economic Report of the President," U.S. Government Printing Office, Washington, DC (1998).

20. R. W. Crandall, C. DeMuth, R. W. Hahn, R. E. Litan, P. S. Nivola, And P. R. Portney, "An Agenda for Reforming Federal Regulation," AEI Press and Brookings Institution Press, Washington, DC (1997).

21. T. Crocker, The structuring of atmospheric pollution control systems, *in* "The Economics of Air Pollution" (H. Wolozin, Ed.), pp. 61–86, Norton, New York (1966).

22. M. L. Cropper and W. E. Oates, Environmental economics: A survey, *J. Econom. Lit.* 30, 675–740 (1992).

23. M. L. Cropper *et al.*, The determinants of pesticide regulation: A statistical analysis of EPA decision making, *J. Pol. Econom.* 100, 175–197 (1992).

24. J. H. Dales, "Pollution, Property and Prices," University Press, Toronto (1968).

25. O. Eckstein, "Water-Resource Development: The Economics of Project Evaluation," Harvard Univ. Press, Cambrigde, MA (1958).
26. D. C. Esty, "Greening the GATT: Trade, Environment, and the Future," Institute for International Economics, Washington, DC (1994).
27. A. G. Fraas, The role of economic analysis in shaping environmental policy, *Law Contemp. Problems 54*, 113–125 (1991),
28. R. Franciosi, R. M. Isaac, D. E. Pingry, and S. S. Reynolds, An experimental investigation of the Hahn–Noll revenue neutral auction for emissions licenses, *J. Environ. Econom. Management 24*, 1–24 (1993).
29. A. M. Freeman, Water Pollution Policy, *in* "Public Policies for Environmental Protection" (P. R. Portney, Ed.), Resources for the Future, Washington, DC (1990).
30. General Accounting Office, "A Market Approach to Air Pollution Control Could Reduce Compliance Costs without Jeopardizing Clean Air Goals," PAD-82-15, General Accounting Office, Washington, DC (1982).
31. General Accounting Office, "Air Pollution: Allowance Trading Offers an Opportunity to Reduce Emissions at Less Costs," GAO/RCED-95-30, Resources, Community, and Economic Development Division, General Accounting Office, Washington, DC (1994).
32. I. Goklany, Rationing health care while writing blank checks for environmental hazards, *Regulation*, 14–15, (1992).
33. L. Goulder, Environmental taxation and the "double dividend:" A reader's guide. *Int. Tax Public Finance 2*(2), 157–184 (1995).
34. J. D. Graham and J. B. Wiener (Eds.), "Risk vs. Risk: Tradeoffs in Protecting Health and the Environment," Harvard Univ. Press, Cambridge, MA (1995).
35. R. W. Hahn, "Reviving Regulatory Reform: A Global Perspective," AEI Press and Brookings Institution, New York, NY, forthcoming (2000).
36. R. W. Hahn and G. L. Hester, Marketable permits: Lessons for theory and practice, *Ecology Law Quart, 16*, 361–406 (1989).
37. R. W. Hahn and R. N. Stavins, Economic incentives for environmental protection: Integrating theory and practice, *Amer. Econom. Rev. 82*, 464–468 (1992).
38. K. Hausker, The politics and economics of auction design in the market for sulfur dioxide pollution, *J. Policy Anal. Management 11*, 553–572 (1992).
39. D. Hawkins and G. Wetstone, Regulatory obstacle course, *Washington Post*, A18, March 9 (1998).
40. M. Hazilla and R. J. Kopp, The social cost of environmental quality regulations: A general equilibrium analysis, *J. Polit. Econom. 98*, 853–873 (1990).
41. ICF Resources, Inc., "Economic Environmental, and Coal Market Impacts of SO_2 Emissions Trading under Alternative Acid Rain Control Proposals," prepared for the U.S. Environmental Protection Agency, OPPE, Fairfax, VA (1989).
42. ICF Resources, Inc., "Regulatory Impact Analysis of the Final Acid Rain Implementation Regulations," prepared for the Office of Atmospheric and Indoor Air Programs, Acid Rain Division, U.S. Environmental Protection Agency, Washington, DC, October 19 (1992).
43. S. L. Johnson and D. M. Pekelney, Economic assessment of the regional clean air incentives market: A new emissions trading program for Los Angeles, *Land Econom. 72*, 277–297 (1996).
44. D. W. Jorgenson and P. J. Wilcoxen, Environmental regulation and U.S. economic growth, *Rand J. Econom. 21*, 314–340 (1990).
45. J. P. Kalt, Exhaustible resource price policy, international trade, and intertemporal welfare, *J. Environ. Econom. Management, 17* (1989).

46. N. Keohane, R. Revesz, and R. N. Stavins, The positive political economy of instrument choice in environmental policy, *in* "Environmental Economics and Public Policy: Essays in Honor of Wallace Oates" (Arvind Panagariya, P. Portney and R. Schwab, Eds.), Edward Elgar, London, 1999, pp. 89–125.

47. S. Kelman, "What Price Incentives? Economists and the Environment," Auburn House, Boston (1981).

48. A. V. Kneese And C. L. Schultze, "Pollution, Prices, and Public Policy," Brookings Institution, Washington, DC (1975).

49. J. E. Krier, The tragedy of the commons, part two, *Harvard J. Law Pub. Policy* *15*, 325–347 (1992).

50. L. B. Lave, "The Strategy of Social Regulation," Brookings Institution, Washington, DC (1981).

51. L. B. Lave, Benefit-cost analysis: Do the benefits exceed the costs? *in* "Risks, Costs, and Lives Saved: Getting Better Results from Regulation" (R. W. Hahn, Ed.), Oxford Univ. Press/AEI Press, New York (1996).

52. R. E. Litan and W. D. Nordhaus, "Reforming Federal Regulation," Yale Univ. Press, New Haven, CT (1983).

53. R. Lutter, "An Analysis of the Use of EPA's Clean Air Benefit Estimates in OMB's Draft Report on the Costs and Benefits of Regulation," Regulatory Analysis 98-2, AEI–Brookings Joint Center for Regulatory Studies, Washington, DC (1998).

53a. W. Magat, A. Krupnick, and W. Harrington, "Rules in the Making: A Statistical Analysis of Regulatory Agency Behavior," Resources for the Future, Washington, DC (1986).

54. M. Maloney and R. E. McCormick, A positive theory of environmental quality regulation, *J. Law Econom. 25*, 99–123 (1982).

55. A. Metrick and M. L. Weitzman, Conflicts and choices in biodiversity preservation, *J. Econom. Perspectives 12*(3), 21–34 (1998).

56. R. D. Morgenstern (Ed.), "Economic Analysis at EPA: Assessing Regulatory Impact," Resources for the Future, Washington, DC (1997).

57. J. F. Morrall, A review of the record, *Regulation 10*, 25–34 (1986).

58. National Association of Administrative Rules Review, "The National Association on Administrative Rules Review 1996–97 Administrative Rules Review Directory and Survey," The Council of State Governments, Midwest Office, Lexington, KY (1996).

59. R. G. Noll, The economics and politics of the slowdown *in* regulatory reform, in "Reviving Regulatory Reform: A Global Perspective" (R. W. Hahn, Ed.), Cambridge Univ. Press/AEI Press, New York, forthcoming (1998).

60. R. G. Noll, Economic perspectives on the politics of regulation, in "Handbook of Industrial Organization" (R. Schmalensee and R. Willig, Eds.), North-Holland, Amsterdam (1989).

61. W. E. Oates and R. M. Schwab, Economic competition among jurisdictions: Efficiency enhancing or distortion inducing? *J. Public Econom. 35*, 333–354 (1988).

62. Office of Management and Budget, "More Benefits, Fewer Burdens" Creating A Regulatory System that Works for the American People," a Report to the President on the Third Anniversary of Executive Order 12866, Office of Management and Budget, Office of Information and Regulatory Affairs, Washington, DC (1996).

63. Office of Management and Budget, "Report to Congress on the Costs and Benefits of Federal Regulations," Office of Management and Budget, Office of Information and Regulatory Affairs, Washington, DC (1997).

64. Office of Management and Budget, "Budget of the United States Government, Fiscal Year 1999: Historical Tables," Executive Office of the President, Office of Management and Budget, Washington, DC (1998).

65. J. B. Opschoor, A. F. de Savornin Lohman, and H. B. Vos, "Managing the Environment: Role of Economic Instruments," Organisation for Economic Co-operation and Development, Paris, France (1994).

66. Organisation for Economic Co-operation and Development, "Regulatory Impact analysis: Best Practices in OECD Countries," Organisation for Economic Co-operation and Development, Paris, France (1997).

67. T. Page, "Conservation and Economic Efficiency: An Approach to Materials Policy," published for Resources for the Future, Johns Hopkins University Press, Baltimore, MD (1977).

68. P. Passell, A free-enterprise plan for an Everglades cleanup, New York Times, May 1 (1992).

69. A. C. Pigou, "The Economics of Welfare," Macmillan & Co., London, (1932); 4th ed. (1952).

70. P. R. Portney (Ed.), "Public Policies for Environmental Protection," Resources for the Future, Washington, DC (1990).

71. P. R. Portney, Counting the cost: The growing role of economics in environmental decisionmaking, Environment 40, 14–21 (1998).

72. R. L. Revesz, Rehabilitating interstate competition: Rethinking the 'race-to-the-bottom' rationale for federal environmental regulation, New York Univ. Law Rev. 67, 1210–1254 (1992).

73. K. R. Richards, "Framing Environmental Policy Instrument Choice, Working Paper, School of Public and Environmental Affairs, Indiana University, Bloomington, Indiana (1998).

74. P. A. Samuelson, The pure theory of public expenditure, Rev. Econom. Stat. 36, 387–389 (1954).

75. R. Schmalensee, P. L. Joskow, A. D. Ellerman, J. P. Montero, and E. M. Bailey, An interim evaluation of sulfur dioxide emissions trading, J. Econom. Perspect., 12(3) 53–68 (1998).

76. C. Skrzycki, A bipartisan bill runs into a Lott of opposition, Washington Post, F01, March 20 (1998).

77. V. K. Smith (Ed.), "Environmental Policy under Reagan's Executive Order: The Role of Cost–Benefit Analysis." Univ. North Carolina Press, Chapel Hill, NC (1984).

78. S. Smith and H. B. Vos, "Evaluating Economic Instruments for Environmental Policy," Organisation for Economic Co-operation and Development, Paris, France (1997).

79. R. N. Stavins (Ed.), "Project 88: Harnessing Market Forces to Protect Our Environment—Initiatives for the New President," Public Policy Study sponsored by Senator Timothy E. Wirth and Senator John Heinz, Washington, DC (1998).

80. R. N. Stavins, "Market Based Environmental Policies," Discussion Paper 98-26, Resources for the Future, Washington, DC (1998).

81. R. N. Stavins, What can we learn from the grand policy experiment: Positive and normative lessons from the SO_2 allowance trading, J. Econom. Perspect. 12(3), 69–88 (1998).

82. R. B. Stewart, Pyramids of sacrifice? Problems of federalism in mandating state implementation of national environmental policy, Yale Law J. 86, 1196–1272 (1977).

83. T. O. Tengs and J. Graham, The opportunity cost of haphazard social regulation, *in* "Risks, Costs and Lives Saved: Getting Better Results from Regulation" (R. W. Hahn, Ed.), Oxford Univ. Press/AEI Press, Washington, DC (1996).

84. D. Terkla, The efficiency value of effluent tax revenues, *J. Environ. Econom. Management 11*, 107–123 (1984).

85. The *Economist*, The defense of nature (2): Sprouting again, The Economist Newspaper Limited, April 12 (1997).

86. T. Tietenberg, "Emissions Trading: An Exercise in Reforming Pollution Policy," Resources for the Future, Washington, DC (1985).

87. T. Tietenberg, Economic instruments for environmental regulation, *Oxford Rev. Econom. Policy 6*, 17–33 (1990).

88. U.S. Environmental Protection Agency, "Costs and Benefits of Reducing Lead in Gasoline," Final Regulatory Impact Analysis III-2, U.S. Environmental Protection Agency, Office of Policy Analysis, Washington, DC (1985).

89. U.S. Environmental Protection Agency, "Environmental Investments: The Cost of a Clean Environment," U.S. Environmental Protection Agency, Office of Policy, Planning and Evaluation, Washington, DC (1990).

90. U.S. Environmental Protection Agency, "Economic Incentives: Options for Environmental Protection," U.S. Environmental Protection Agency, Policy, Planning and Evaluation, Washington, DC (1991).

91. U.S. Environmental Protection Agency, "The Benefits and Costs of the Clean Air Act: 1970 to 1990," U.S. Environmental Protection Agency, Office of Air and Radiation, Washington, DC (1997).

92. L. J. White, "Reforming Regulation: Processes and Problems," Prentice-Hall, Englewood Cliffs, NJ (1981).

93. B. Yandle, Bootleggers and Baptists in the market for regulation, *in* "The Political Economy of Government Regulation" (J. F. Shogren, Ed.), Topics in Regulatory Economics and Policy Series, Kluwer, Dordrecht/London, Norwell, MA (1989).

94. D. Wheeler, "Pollution Charge Systems in Developing Countries," World Bank, mimeo, Washington, DC (1998).

95. J. Yellen, statement of Janet Yellen, Chair, White House Council of Economic Advisers, before the U.S. Senate Committee on Agriculture, Nutrition, and Forestry on the Economics of the Kyoto Protocol, Washington, DC March 5 (1998).